VOICES
FROM THE
HARLEM
RENAISSANCE

VOICES FROM THE HARLEM RENAISSANCE

Edited by
NATHAN IRVIN HUGGINS

OXFORD UNIVERSITY PRESS
New York   Oxford

Oxford University Press

Oxford   New York
Athens   Auckland   Bangkok   Bombay
Calcutta   Cape Town   Dar es Salaam   Delhi
Florence   Hong Kong   Istanbul   Karachi
Kuala Lumpur   Madras   Madrid   Melbourne
Mexico City   Nairobi   Paris   Singapore
Taipei   Tokyo   Toronto

and associated companies in
Berlin   Ibadan

Copyright 1995 by Brenda Smith Huggins

First published in 1976 by Oxford University Press, Inc.,
198 Madison Avenue, New York, New York 10016

Oxford is a registed trademark of Oxford University Press

Library of Congress Cataloging-in-Publication Data
Voices from the Harlem Renaissance / edited by Nathan Irvin Huggins.
p.   cm.
ISBN 978-0-19-509360-5
1. American literature—Afro-American authors.   2. Harlem (New
York, N.Y.)—Intellectual life.   3. Afro-Americans—Politics and
government.   4. Afro-Americans—Literary collections.   5. American
literature—New York (N.Y.)   6. Afro-American arts—New York (N.Y.)
7. American literature—20th century.   8. Harlem Renaissance.
I. Huggins, Nathan Irvin, 1927–
PS509.N4V6   1994
810.8'0896073—dc20   94-33190

9
Printed in the United States of America

For Howard Thurman

TABLE OF CONTENTS

CHRISTIANITY: ALIEN GOSPEL OR SOURCE OF INSPIRATION? 341

ALIENATION, ANGER, RAGE, 351

3. REFLECTIONS ON THE RENAISSANCE AND ART FOR A NEW DAY, 367

VOICES FROM THE HARLEM RENAISSANCE

INTRODUCTION

We risk distortion and inaccuracy when we pick out one moment in time, whether a century or a decade, as a crucial point of change. We are, nevertheless, tempted to do it because it is a convenient way to give focus to a process. We like to conceive of a line; on one side we see the old way, and on the other side we see the old transformed into something new. So it has been with the Harlem Renaissance, both for those who were a part of it as well as for us who look to it as the point of change in Afro-American culture. For it appears that in the decade of the 1920s, the Afro-American came of age; he became self-assertive and racially conscious as if for the first time. He proclaimed himself to be a man and deserving of respect, not a ward of society, nor a creature to be helped, pitied, or explained away.

Those Afro-Americans who were part of that decade of change—roughly between World War I and the Great Depression—saw themselves as principals in that moment of transformation from the old to the new. Thus, for them, the expression "New Negro" told the world of their self-concept. They characterized this "New Negro," this new man, as having shed the costume of the shuffling darky, the uncle and aunty, the subservient and docile retainer, the clown. He was, rather, a man and a citizen in his own right—intelligent, articulate, self-assured. The "New Negro" was telling all Americans that it was a new ballgame, and that he was a revived and inspired competitor. No longer could he be dismissed by contempt, pity, or terror. He would insist upon his rights and, if necessary, return violence, blow for blow. It was all suggestive of the shift in sentiment from the leadership of Booker T. Washington to that of W. E. B. DuBois.

From their point of view, from the place where they stood looking into the future, the Afro-American was to be on the stage in a different guise—true to himself and his manhood—no longer to be confused with the minstrelman who wore the mask of stereotype demanded by his white audience. The "New Negro" intended to define himself in new terms, outside the convenient stereotype. The audience, black and white, could take it or leave it.

Looking back to the 1920s, we have tended to accept this view of the period and of the black intellectuals. We know, somehow, that the state of mind of black Americans was different following World War I and the 1920s from what it had been before. We tend to accept the notion that the "New Negro" was born in the decade after the war. We tend to associate that new mood with the shift of black leadership from Tuskegee to New York and, for some, even to the African nationalism of Marcus Garvey. Whatever the emphasis, we have accepted the assumption of *newness*.

For us, looking back, as for those who took part, the clearest expression of that moment of change is to be found in the remarkable outpouring of literature, art, and music. Thus, the Harlem Renaissance has become a phenomenon marking something more than the fact that Afro-Americans wrote poems and stories, painted and sculpted, and infused new life into the American theater. Rather, it symbolizes black liberation and sophistication—the final shaking off of the residuals of slavery, in the mind, spirit, and character. The Emancipation Proclamation had been a grudging pronouncement by President Lincoln, subsequently denied in effect. The proclamation of the "New Negro" was a statement by black intellectuals that actual emancipation could no longer be denied. This time, being the proclamation of the spirits of black people themselves, it could not be ignored by anyone.

Symbolically, then, the Harlem Renaissance stands for something more than the actual works of art it produced. Like all symbols, its primary significance is the deep emotional force it embodies, both for those whose experience it was and for those of us who find in it an important moment in our past. It is for us a principal emotional source, verifying our manliness and womanliness. Through the impact of it, we re-experience the triumph of that time and emerge as sensitive, sophisticated, complicated, and resourceful human beings who are capable of tolerance, co-operation, and love but who also have ample capacity for anger, hatred, resentment, and retaliation. The experience of the Harlem Renaissance tells us that we are to be taken seriously—by ourselves as well as by others.

For these reasons, literary or historical analysis, with its academic distance, provokes profound uneasiness. Attempting to draw generalizations about the Harlem Renaissance from a critical analysis of its art is different from doing the same for other schools, periods, or artists whose work does not embody such living emotional and symbolic significance. While there will be those who will find importance in the stories of Hamlin Garland, George Washington Cable, and Bret Harte, and there will be those who will defend the poetry of Edgar Allan Poe, James Russell Lowell, or James Whitcomb Riley, just to grab a random handful, few would find their works to be symbols of racial or ethnic achievement and experience, confirming a people's culture and underwriting their identity and self-respect. Claude McKay's "If We Must Die," on the other hand, is more than a fourteen-line sonnet in iambic pentameter. And Langston Hughes's "The Negro Speaks of Rivers" has a meaning which defies close-reading exercises. The experience out of which they were written by black men, their publication in that time, the fact that the poems—whatever critics may say of their "art"—provide the "shock of recognition" of our own experiences as well as exemplify qualities of character and spirit that we know as our own, all make these poems essential to us. So it is that academic criticism of the works of the Harlem Renaissance seem always to miss the point and, indeed, to challenge something within us that we know to be true.

In this way, the Harlem Renaissance *lives* as an important moment in the Afro-American experience, having nothing much to do with the quality of the art that came from it. That is why one might be more likely to find a critical review of Gwendolyn Brooks, Melvin Tolson, Ralph Ellison, or Ishmael Reed than of Countee Cullen, Langston Hughes, or Claude McKay. We feel that the latter are a part of the race's coming of age, whereas the more recent black writers—a sturdier and more resilient group—have not come to symbolize our humanity and self-respect. Wallace Thurman, sensing the fragile nature of the art of his fellow Harlemites, entitled his novel about them *Infants of the Spring*. The fragility and precariousness of those early buds have made us protective of them. But to the credit of the Harlem Renaissance, the black artists and writers of the 1920s, in claiming a place for themselves, did their work so well that we have not felt the need to defend the legitimacy of the Afro-American art that has followed them.

While it is important to recognize this emotive and symbolic character of the Harlem Renaissance, it is equally important to treat it as a historical and cultural phenomenon that must be defined and explained if we are to have more than an impressionistic and hortatory sense of Afro-American history and culture. Examining the Harlem Renaissance in its historical context and analyzing the character of its art make us reach for the substance, rather than the symbols, to discover the historical process of which it was a part. Undoubtedly, some of the symbolic and emotional power is lost. But it is traded for what should be a richer and deeper understanding of what the Afro-American experience really was and how it matured. For some purposes, that is worth far more than a feeling of what it stood for.

Of course, like other historical "watersheds," the Harlem Renaissance is merely a convenient fiction. There is no actual year or decade forming a line which divides the old from the new. Those qualities and characteristics which seemed to mature in the 1920s actually can be found earlier. Also, those features of the "Old Negro" presumed to have been buried with World War I surely persisted long afterward. Certainly, Harlem intellectuals and writers in the 1920s were no more the creators of black self-respect than were their grandchildren in the 1960s the discoverers that black was beautiful. Nevertheless, something did happen, suggesting a dramatic change, having its focal point in Harlem at that moment in time.

There was a confluence of forces that created the atmosphere in which the Harlem Renaissance developed. The urbanization of American society created the fact of Harlem, and brought changes in assumptions and habits of life that transformed both white and black Americans into new people.

The most striking thing about the "New" as opposed to the "Old" Negro was that he was urban rather than rural. Even if blacks were still to be exploited in the cities, it would be a different kind of exploitation, permitting the illusion of independence. The traditional "place" of blacks was in the South, where sharecropping and tenant-farming locked them into the peonage of the post-Reconstruction era. But hard times and violence had pushed them from the South; and the European war, which caused industrial expansion in the North, had cut off traditional sources of immigrant labor. Thus, industrial demands pulled blacks into the North. They were helped along by travel subsidies from industries in dire need of manpower. They gathered in industrial towns like East St. Louis, Illinois, as well as in the larger cities: Chicago, Philadelphia, New York.

Not any city would have done for a Renaissance. New York had it all. There was a large and growing black population, a relatively long history of black performance in the arts, and an exciting community—Harlem—which had just been opened to black residents. New York was also the center of American publishing, art, music, and drama. It was America's cultural capital, open to cross-currents from around the world. Blacks were coming to the city not only from the South but also from the French and British West Indies and Africa. In New York, then, there was to be a cross-fertilization of black intelligence and culture as in no other place in the world. At the same moment, blacks from the British empire were using London as their stage for promoting their futures. And others from Martinique, Haiti, and Senegal were delivering manifestoes from Paris. It would seem that the entire world of colored people was in ferment.

World War I was all-important to the consciousness of the "New Negro." Afro-American promoters in the North, the *Chicago Defender* for instance, were quick to see the migration of blacks as proof of a spirit which would defy a system of perpetual peonage. Their very movement was a defiance of a system of white supremacy, Jim Crow, terror, and the Ku Klux Klan. Southern blacks had been disfranchised, but in the years before America's entry into World War I they voted with their feet against tyranny and for their future as self-reliant citizens. They stood as proof, to those who chose to see, that blacks were not content and docile in what had been designated as their "place." And in the North, where there were no voting restrictions, they would, in time, weigh in the political balance.

The War dislodged blacks throughout the world—blacks from the various imperial systems were called to serve the war effort. They were, thus, pulled out of their various traditional contexts and introduced to a world-view that had been previously available to only a few of them. They became conscious of one another—colonials with similar experiences under English-, French-, Portuguese-, or German-speaking masters. They found in each other the promise and the dream of worldwide black unity. And they built out of those dreams organizations through which Pan Africanism might become a countervailing force against the apparently crumbling Western European colonial empires. Paris, London, and New York became the stages from which this new black consciousness was amplified.

World War I seemed to quicken the onset of the disintegration of a world-system based on nineteenth-century European values and a world hegemony of Western European tutelage and power. To the extent that this was so, it also heralded the great possibility for the colored peoples of the world to come into their own. So, when Afro-Americans proclaimed the era of the "New Negro," they were, perhaps unconsciously, resonating a worldwide voice of emerging black self-assertion.

The same ethnocentrism that had engulfed Europe in war made self-determination one of the major war objectives. This principle, which was to justify nationhood for Irish, Magyars, and Czechs, would have implications for Africans as well. The high idealism of the Allies' war aims, the charges of barbarism leveled against the "Huns," could equally condemn the Belgians for their atrocities in the Congo. In short, the war exposed Europe to the eyes of the colored world and invited judgment in terms of its own criterion of "civilization." The "civilized" European, the justification for the "white man's burden," seemed a macabre joke in the gas and gore of trench warfare.

The War thus undermined the faith of whites and non-whites alike in the standards and proprieties of Western Europe. Joining the new insights of Freudian psychology with a traditional fascination with the exotic, Americans and Europeans were persuaded to indulge in romantic fantasies about the more open and healthy psychic natures of "primitive" peoples who were untroubled by the arbitrary restraints of the super-ego. "Native" peoples, always viewed as children by some, were seen to suggest through their openness and honesty and the directness of their emotional lives a salvation for whites, whose subconscious had been knotted by the constraints of the Puritan ethic.

Echoing this romanticism, Africans and Afro-Americans found positive value in the very stereotypes that had formerly marked them as limited. The Puritan compulsions to order, frugality, temperance, decorum, etc. had always served to distinguish "civilized" whites from the darker peoples they colonized; the subject-peoples were rightly to be tutored because they embodied just the opposite of these characteristics. Their lack of control over the "inner man" supposedly made for chaos, and their enslavement to appetites made them incompetent without European discipline. But African intellectuals like Léopold Senghor of Senegal promoted this stereotype as positive, celebrating the soulful and artistic qualities of "native" peoples, which they called Negritude. Afro-Americans, too, like Claude McKay, created fictional characters who were heroes because they were primitives, free from the compulsions of the Puritan ethic.

Such romanticism bred a new appreciation of Africa in the West. African sculpture and design had already breathed new life into European Post-Impressionism. The fresh conceptions of Georges Bracque, Pablo Picasso, Henri Matisse, and others owed much to the abstract, analytical power of African forms. For black intellectuals, this influence on European art seemed to give a legitimacy to African culture, supported by the new works of anthropology that were discovering African societies to be sophisticated, cultivated, and highly complex cultures. Similar legitimacy came, especially for Afro-Americans, from the adoption of jazz idioms by European composers such as Igor Stravinsky and Darius Milhaud. It seemed that the black man was being "discovered" through his music and art, and it seemed to be his spirit which symbolized the Jazz Age.

It had been characteristic of Afro-Americans to refer to Africans as benighted, pagan, enthralled by sensuality. These qualities, it was assumed, determined African limitations in an industrializing world. They seemed even to justify colonization. They placed the onus on the Westernized black to enlighten the dark continent. To blacks with such a view, Africa was an embarrassment, and the African a proper subject for uplifting. But World War I, the apparent end-product of the industrializing and commercial West, awakened among blacks a new appreciation of what was seen to be the "natural," non-mechanized, non-commercial qualities of the African spirit. To be unable to punch a time-card, to be one with nature, to be open to life, all seemed admirable virtues when the Great War was the ultimate achievement of "civilization," and psychosis the consequence of compulsive restraints. The African could thus be viewed with a new appreciation, and the Afro-Americans could look to their roots with less ambivalence, feeling freer to assert their own tastes and character as positive, rather than as qualities to be disguised or converted into standard proprieties. The self-assertiveness and pride of the "New Negro" was a consequence of this new self-concept.

The Harlem Renaissance was thus not isolated but part of a worldwide phenomenon. It was also a part of a process that had been well under way by the opening of the 1920s. The cultural and artistic activity generally associated with the Harlem Renaissance reached its height in the last years of that decade; though the "New Negro" as a concept had been around since before America's entry into the war.

The "New Negro" was actually a creature of the pre-war years. If anything, his radicalism was more sharply political in the early years of the war than it was to be in the 1920s. It was from 1917 to 1920 that black spokesmen, through magazines such as *The Messenger* and *Crisis,* began to call the nation to account for its idealistic pretensions. A world made safe for democracy should liberate Afro-Americans. Self-determination should mean self-rule for Africans. Systems of exploitation were attacked, both the old system of empire and capitalism itself. Socialism was the answer to some, while some radicals combined Marxian analysis and race consciousness to suggest fresh approaches to Afro-American nationalism. At the same time, black spokesmen demanded an end to mob violence against blacks. The government, they said, should protect blacks from lynch mobs, or blacks should retaliate, meeting violence with violence. Black radicals also called for Afro-American identity with Africa and for some form of Pan African unity. Whether in the studied language of W. E. B. DuBois or in the more flamboyant rhetoric of Marcus Garvey, they were announcing a strikingly new independence for black Americans.

Political radicalism was beyond its zenith by the time of the armistice. Indeed, the 1920s was a period of its decline. The dénouement of the Garvey movement, his arrest and conviction and deportation for fraud, came in the early 1920s. Optimism over the future possibilities of Pan Africanism fell, one of the many casualties of Versailles. Black socialists and other political radicals became victims of the repression of the Left by Attorney General Mitchell Palmer in the early years of the decade. Indeed, *The Messenger,* which had called itself "the only radical Negro magazine," had by 1924 become a mere cultural organ, with surprising interest in bourgeois social life. This may well have been all of a piece with the general political repression that afflicted American society during the first "Red Scare."

However, though black political radicalism subsided, the "New Negro" lived on. What we have come to think of as the Harlem Renaissance seems to have been a channeling of energy from political and social criticism into poetry, fiction, music, and art. These were safer ground than politics. In an atmosphere of political repression, the aggressive, optimistic, self-assertive "New Negro" could best thrive as a cultural being, not as a political force. White American intellectuals—the Lost Generation—rejecting the philistines and Babbitts of America, tried to escape to Europe and their art. Blacks could not yet reject the "promise of America," for belief in that future was part of what the "New Negro" was about. So their art reflects their continued faith. Certainly, there was pain, pathos, and anger in it. But underneath was the expectation that all would be right, and that art itself—the poems, stories, and music—was to be an instrument in the transformation of American life into the ideal. Especially in black music and theater was there an openness, exuberance, freshness, and *joie de vivre* which no other American expression of the time had. It was infectious, especially in the post-war decade, and so Harlem became a generative force for all of New York, and all of the nation for that matter.

The art of the Harlem Renaissance necessarily reflects its origins and contexts. Beneath its innocence are to be found the standard Afro-American preoccupations. It took its excitement from the city. It emphasized the urbanity of the "New Negro" and reflected the joy of blacks discovering the variety in themselves, yet their oneness. It struggled to find a definition of the "New Negro" in some past. Identity was central. What did Africa mean? What did the slave and peasant past mean? What could a folk tradition mean to the "New Negro"? What was color, itself? Blackness, clearly, was not only a color, it was a state of mind. So, what of the mulatto, and what of "passing"? This art also had a consciousness of itself as art. Could it be a contrived instrument of protest and social statement without losing the name of art? Could the black artist express himself honestly without being a "propagandist"? Could the art of Afro-Americans be great art and keep its integrity—not succumb to mimicry and European forms? Could those forces which had sustained Afro-American culture—notably the Christian Church—be relied on as a continuing inspiration for the "New Negro"? Could the black experience take the form of art if the product of that experience is anger and rage? Most of the artistic work of the Harlem Renaissance resonates these themes and questions. Although these same themes have since found various resolutions, they have remained crucial for Afro-American artists and intellectuals. It is the mere fact of their persistence that makes the work of the Harlem Renaissance artists of continuing importance to all of us.

We generally consider the Harlem Renaissance to have ended with the Depression of the 1930s. Surely, much changed. The end of Prohibition transformed Harlem night-life. That, together with the despair and poverty of the time, the dismal and dreary aspects of ghetto life, seemed more to define the district. There had always been poverty, unemployment, and futility in Harlem. But the gaiety and optimism of the 1920s brightened the picture of such realities. For instance, black and white writers of the 1920s viewed with amusement the fact that Harlemites, unable to pay their rent, popularized the custom of "rent parties," where guests were charged for admission and food and drink. In the 1930s, however, such desperation was no longer quaint. The Depression made the Harlem Renaissance, with its spirit of play and optimism, seem strange and naïve. So even those who had been a part of it looked back on it as if it were an innocent period and a failure in the rejuvenation of the black American. Then, with the riots in Harlem in 1935, it was impossible even for Alain Locke—the foremost champion of the Harlem Renaissance—to be indifferent to the fact that, with few exceptions, the artists of the 1920s had been unconscious of the realities of black life around them. The romanticized "natural" man, furthest down, had turned bitter when starvation became his lot.

The art of the 1930s had a new charge of political and social realism. Thus, decadence and art for art's sake—which had affected the 1920s—were indulgences that could not be tolerated. Social realism became the key, and the naturalism of Richard Wright seemed to obliterate the soft complaints of the writers a decade earlier. Now, ideology and politics— Socialism and Communism—had to be addressed, and most black writers and artists had to come to some terms with the Communist Party.

Of course, one might say that each generation has self-deceptions that it must indulge and grow out of. The 1920s had some, the 1930s others. Doubtless, our own generation has its as well. But the 1920s did bring into focus, with sharper intensity than ever before, the consciousness and reality of the Afro-American struggle for self-realization. It was a beginning and not an answer. And we have worked from that moment ever since. Yet it is because the Harlem Renaissance seems so seminal and symbolic of the Afro-American coming of age that it will always awaken in Afro-Americans a sense of personal trial and achievement.

This anthology has been compiled and organized both to establish the context in which the art of the Harlem Renaissance occurred and to provide the reader with a broad range of the work characteristic of the period. The selection has been made with an eye to historical and social significance as well as artistic merit. Hopefully, each selection will say something about itself, as a work of imagination, and about the movement of which it is a part.

Part I brings together samples of radical political writings of the years during and following World War I. It is mainly journalism, characterized by self-conscious social and economic radicalism. It is in this literature that the "New Negro" finds his definition.

Writings from the Harlem Renaissance itself are brought together according to themes that characterized the movement and which persist in Afro-American expression:

Harlem and the urban setting was a primary point of fascination. For a variety of reasons, the city experience was what the "New Negro" was all about. Much of the literature and art of the period proclaimed Harlem to be an international capital of the black man.

Afro-American identity was then, as it is now, a major preoccupation with black artists and writers. To be black in a white society, African in the "Western world," raised perplexing problems. The question, "who am I, this Afro-American, this new man," is a black version of a general American question.

A part of that search for self-definition was manifest in an exploration of history and the folk tradition. Legitimacy as a people and a culture required a heritage.

Art was the principal concern of the Harlem Renaissance, but there remained serious questions as to what was to be the role of Afro-American art. It was natural enough for blacks to protest against conditions and history, but was such protest merely propaganda? What standards should the Afro-American artist use? Was his ultimate object to produce a "European" art of "high culture"? If so, what was to be the measure of racial integrity?

Finally, much of the art of the Harlem Renaissance was a response to the oppression of blacks in America. As such, it had the voice of alienation, anger, and rage.

Most people concede that the Harlem Renaissance ended with the Depression. That, too, was the view of contemporaries. Part III of this collection contains reflections on the Renaissance by those who were a part of it and those who were artists in the 1930s and the years to follow. From the new perspective, the Harlem Renaissance seemed innocent and not very radical. The Depression brought a revival of political radicalism and forced many to look at art through the eyes of social realism.

If readers discover that there are themes in Afro-American expression which tie the present generation with the past, yet are able to discern the significant differences in style, rhetoric, and concept, then this anthology will have been successful in what it set out to do.

"NEW NEGRO" RADICALISM

1

World War I shifted Afro-Americans from southern farms to northern cities, Africans from villages to European battlefields, blacks from the West Indies to New York, London, and Paris. The idealism of the war—democracy for all, self-determination, etc.—along with the revolution in Russia raised expectations of blacks throughout the world. "New Negro" radicalism was an American expression of that new consciousness. A. Philip Randolph and Chandler Owen began the publication of The Messenger, *"the only radical Negro magazine," in 1917. W. E. B. DuBois had been editor of the NAACP's* Crisis *since its birth in 1910. Along with other Harlem radicals, these men considered themselves Marxists who were calling for a radical transformation of the American economic and social order so as to make a fair world for black men and women.*

It was out of such radicalism that the "New Negro" was defined. The assertion was far-reaching: demands for new social order, demands that blacks fight back against terror and violence, demands that blacks reconsider their notions of beauty, demands that Africa be freed from the bonds of imperialism. Only a small selection of this journalism can be included here to give a sense of its flavor and quality.

The war brought Africa to the center of attention of blacks throughout the world. All of the "New Negro" radicals would have supported some form of Pan Africanism. Few, however, were prepared for the flamboyance and mass appeal of Marcus Garvey. To Garvey, DuBois and the others appeared white-minded sycophants of Western Europe. To the others, Garvey's rhetoric made him seem a charlatan and fool, and they made themselves instruments in his ultimate conviction for fraud and deportation from the United States.

The form of political radicalism reflected in this journalism became muted in the mid-1920s. It fell victim to the repression of the Left during the "Red Scare" and the raids of Attorney General Mitchell Palmer. After years of trial and controversy, Marcus Garvey was deported in 1927, but his movement had been in decline for much of the decade.

THE NEGRO—A MENACE TO RADICALISM
EDITORS OF THE MESSENGER

There is much opposition nowadays to the very word—radicalism. The radicals are hunted, outlawed and jailed for propagating, as it were, "dangerous thoughts." Whoever seeks to find out the root-cause of social diseases is a radical. Hence socialism and industrial unionism and agnosticism are radical. They search for the forces which determine human actions and human institutions, in order to ascertain which methods to adopt either to destroy or to develop the institutions and to direct human actions to socially constructive ends. In short, all radicals are opposed to the status quo; they desire change; not mere change, but progressive change.

This is the crux of the opposition of the propertied class to all radical propaganda. Those who hold vested property interests and privileges under a given social system will resist with desperate determination any assault upon that system by the advocates of a new, a different social doctrine. Moreover, the beneficiaries of a social order strive through force or deception to secure the acquiescence and support of the victims of the social order. This is being done with respect to Negroes and the radical movements.

For instance, the leading capitalists of the country—the chief artfully and persistently prosecuting an insidious campaign of propaganda among Negroes, through the press, pulpit and school, with a view to making them fireproof to all liberal and democratic opinions. The jim-crow Negro censorship either withholds from or misrepresents the radical movements throughout the world, to the Negro. When one is uninformed of the nature of a movement he is disinclined to entertain it, and when one is misinformed concerning the objects and aims of a movement, he is inclined to oppose it. Hence, through ignorance or error the opposition of the Negro to the very movements which are calculated to achieve his economic, political emancipation, is being effected by big, hand-picked Negro leaders—and the plutocratic interests of this country. Witness a Negro minister of reputed light and leading in the city of Savanah stating in an address before a large convention that:

"Bolshevism was begotten in Germany, or that it is of German parentage, or that it was born in Russia, it took its name from a man named Bolsheviki, an insurrectionist or rioter, who raised an army to overthrow the recognized government of Russia. At that time the Government was tottering under the great blows of the German army. Bolsheviki thought that the time was ripe to establish new ideas and a new government that was somewhat after the idea of the Socialist. The definition or meaning of Bolshevism, as may be determined by research, is analogous to anarchy, the state of society where there is no law or supreme power, a state of lawlessness and general disor-

From *The Messenger,* Vol. II (May–June 1919).

der. A condition where human life and property, human rights and justice, all that is noble and great, trampled under the feet of human beasts."

(Taken from the Savanah Journal, of Saturday, March 22, 1919, a Negro weekly.)

This is a mild sample of the intellectual pabulum served up to Negroes on problems of world moment.

This is why, unless the Negro worker is unionized and the Negro public educated as to the nature and aims of radical movements, the Negro constitutes a definite menace to radicalism in America.

In the first place, the organized labor movement—the American Federation of Labor has either ignored or opposed Negro workers. Hence, the labor movement is not in their confidence. Secondly, no systematic effort has been made to arouse the interest and enlist the support of the Negro by radical labor and political organizations, with the exception, only recently, of the Socialist Party in New York.

Thirdly, capitalists through contributions to Negro schools, churches and charitable institutions, are impressing him with the idea that they are his real benefactors and friends. He (the Negro) sees workingmen forming the mobs of the South and opposes unions on the grounds that workingmen lynch him. Thus, the Negro is inclined always to choose the side of capital. Herein lies the menace of the Negro to the movement toward industrial democracy.

And this much the white radicals must learn that, ten million Negro soldiers and scabs will break the backbone of any radical movement. To maintain that the Negro is not ripe is not only fallacious but suicidal folly. Labor cannot afford to ignore any factor which capital does not ignore. Unhappily, the Negro is the most backward part of the working-class in America and the radical Negroes fear, lest he be used savagely to beat down the more radical wing of the working class. Negro soldiers, if ordered, will shoot down Negro workingmen as quickly as they will white workingmen; just as, for instance, white soldiers shot down white workingmen and women at Ludlow, Colorado, or just as white policemen beat up the heads of white girls striking for a living wage. Add to the Negro's obedience to order the factor of race feeling, and one can conceive of a saturnalia of blood that makes one sick at heart.

Hence, the Negro radical's task is doubly huge and difficult. They must educate the radicals to the realization of the fact that capital is ever weaving a network of lies around Negroes, and, to educate Negroes so that they may understand their class interests. Negroes must learn to differentiate between white capitalists and white workers, as yet they only see white men against black men. This makes the Negro both a menace to the radicals and the capitalists. For inasmuch as he thinks that all white men are his enemies, he is inclined to direct his hate at white employers as he is to direct it at white workers.

Hence the editors of the Messenger sound this note of warning to the white ruling and working-class in America of a gathering race storm which can only be averted by more sober, enlightened and dispassionate studying of the problem, with the purpose of removing the cause of an impending explosion.

Organized labor must harness the discontent of Negroes and direct it into working-class channels for working-class emancipation.

A NEW CROWD—A NEW NEGRO
A. PHILIP RANDOLPH

Throughout the world among all peoples and classes, the clock of social progress is striking the high noon of the Old Crowd. And why?

The reason lies in the inability of the old crowd to adapt itself to the changed conditions, to recognize and accept the consequences of the sudden, rapid and violent social changes that are shaking the world. In wild desperation, consternation and despair, the proud scions of regal pomp and authority, the prophets and high-priests of the old order, view the steady and menacing rise of the great workingclass. Yes, the Old Crowd is passing, and with it, its false, corrupt and wicked institutions of oppression and cruelty; its ancient prejudices and beliefs and its pious, hypocritical and venerated idols.

Its all like a dream! In Russia, one-hundred and eighty million of peasants and workmen—disinherited, writhing under the ruthless heel of the Czar, for over three hundred years, awoke and revolted and drove their hateful oppressors from power. Here a New Crowd arose—the Bolsheviki, and expropriated their expropriators. They fashioned and established a new social machinery—the soviet—to express the growing class consciousness of teaming millions, disillusioned and disenchanted. They also chose new leaders—Lenin and Trotsky to invent and adopt scientific methods of social control; to marshal, organize and direct the revolutionary forces in constructive channels to build a New Russia.

The "iron battalions of the proletariat" are shaking age-long and historic thrones of Europe. The Hohenzollerns of Europe no longer hold mastery over the destinies of the German people. The Kaiser, once proud, irresponsible and powerful; wielding his sceptre in the name of the "divine right of kings," has fallen, his throne has crumbled and he now sulks in ignominy and shame—expelled from his native land, a man without a country. And Nietzsche, Treitschke, Bismarck, and Bernhardi, his philosophic mentors are scrapped, discredited and discarded, while the shadow of Marx looms in the distance. The revolution in Germany is still unfinished. The Eberts and Scheidermanns rule for the nonce; but a New Crowd is rising. The hand of the Sparticans must raise a New Germany out of the ashes of the old.

Already, Karolyi of the old regime of Hungary, abdicates to Bela Kun, who

From *The Messenger,* Vol. II (May–June 1919).

wirelessed greetings to the Russian Federated Socialist Soviet Republic. Meanwhile the triple alliance consisting of the National Union of Railwaymen, the National Transport Workers' Federation and the Miners' Federation, threaten to paralyze England with a general strike. The imminence of industrial disaster hangs like a pall over the Lloyd George government. The shop stewards' committee or the rank and file in the works, challenge the sincerity and methods of the old pure and simple unions leaders. British labor would build a New England. The Seine Feiners are the New Crowd in Ireland fighting for self-determination. France and Italy, too, bid soon to pass from the control of scheming and intriguing diplomats into the hands of a New Crowd. Even Egypt, raped for decades, prostrate under the juggernaut of financial imperialism, rises in revolution to expel a foreign foe.

And the natural question arises: What does it all mean to the Negro?

First it means that he, too, must scrap the Old Crowd. For not only is the Old Crowd useless, but like the vermiform appendix, it is decidedly injurious, it prevents all real progress.

Before it is possible for the Negro to prosecute successfully a formidable offensive for justice and fair play, he must tear down his false leaders, just as the people of Europe are tearing down their false leaders. Of course, some of the Old Crowd mean well. But what matter it though poison be administered to the sick intentionally or out of ignorance. The result is the same—death. And our indictment of the Old Crowd is that: it lacks the knowledge of methods for the attainment of ends which it desires to achieve. For instance the Old Crowd never counsels the Negro to organize and strike against low wages and long hours. It cannot see the advisability of the Negro, who is the most exploited of the American workers, supporting a workingman's political party.

The Old Crowd enjoins the Negro to be conservative, when he has nothing to conserve. Neither his life nor his property receives the protection of the government which conscripts his life to "make the world safe for democracy." The conservative in all lands are the wealthy and the ruling class. The Negro is in dire poverty and he is no part of the ruling class.

But the question naturally arises: who is the Old Crowd?

In the Negro schools and colleges the most typical reactionaries are Kelly, Miller, Moton and William Pickens. In the press Du Bois, James Weldon Johnson, Fred R. Moore, T. Thomas Fortune, Roscoe Conkling Simmons and George Harris are compromising the case of the Negro. In politics Chas. W. Anderson, W. H. Lewis, Ralph Tyler, Emmet Scott, George E. Haynes and the entire old line palliating, me-to-boss gang of Negro Republican politicians, are hopelessly ignorant and distressingly unwitting of their way.

In the church the old crowd still preaches that "the meek will inherit the earth," "if the enemy strikes you on one side of the face, turn the other," and "you may take all this world but give me Jesus." "Dry Bones," "The Three Hebrew Children in the Firy Furnace" and "Jonah in the Belly of the Whale," constitute the subjects of the Old Crowd, for black men and women who are over-worked and under-paid, lynched, jim-crowed and disfranchised—a people who are yet languishing in the dungeons of ignorance and superstition. Such then is the Old Crowd. And this is not strange to the student of history, economics, and sociology.

A man will not oppose his benefactor. The Old Crowd of Negro leaders has been and is subsidized by the Old Crowd of White Americans—a group which viciously opposes every demand made by organized labor for an opportunity to live a better life. Now, if the Old Crowd of white people opposes every demand of white labor for economic justice, how can the Negro expect to get that which is denied the white working class? And it is well nigh beyond the realm of controversy that economic justice is at the basis of social and political equality.

For instance, there is no organization of national prominence which ostensibly is working in the interest of the Negro which is not dominated by the Old Crowd of white people. And they are controlled by the white people because they receive their funds—their revenue from them. It is, of course, a matter of common knowledge that Du Bois does not determine the policy of the National Association for the Advancement of Colored People; nor does Kinckle Jones or George E. Haynes control the National Urban League. The organizations are not responsible to Negroes because Negroes do not maintain them.

This brings us to the question as to who shall assume the reins of leadership when the Old Crowd falls.

As among all other peoples, the New Crowd must be composed of young men who are educated, radical and fearless. Young Negro radicals must control the press, church, schools, politics and labor. The condition for joining the New Crowd are: ability, radicalism and sincerity. The New Crowd views with much expectancy the revolutions ushering in a New World. The New Crowd is uncompromising. Its tactics are not defensive but offensive. It would not send notes after a Negro is lynched. It would not appeal to white leaders. It would appeal to the plain working people everywhere. The New Crowd sees that the war came, that the Negro fought, bled and died; that the war has ended, and he is not yet free.

The New Crowd would have no armistice with lynch-law; no truce with jim crowism and disfranchisement; no peace until the Negro receives complete social, economic and political justice. To this end the New Crowd would form an alliance with white radicals such as the I.W.W., the Socialists and the Non-Partisan League, to mold a new society, a society of equals, without class, race, caste or religious distinctions.

"IF WE MUST DIE"
W. A. DOMINGO

America won the war that was alleged to be fought for the purpose of making the world safe for democracy, but in the light of recent happenings in Washington, the Capital city, and Chicago, it would seem as though the United States is not a part of the world. In order to win the war President Wilson employed "force, unstinted force," and those who expect to bring any similar desirable termination to a just cause can do no less than follow the splendid example set them by the reputed spokesman of humanity. That the lesson did not take long to penetrate the minds of Negroes is demonstrated by the change that has taken place in their demeanor and tactics. No longer are Negroes willing to be shot down or hunted from place to place like wild beasts; no longer will they flee from their homes and leave their property to the tender mercies of the howling and cowardly mob. They have changed, and now they intend to give men's account of themselves. If death is to be their portion, New Negroes are determined to make their dying a costly investment for all concerned. If they must die they are determined that they shall not travel through the valley of the shadow of death alone, but that some of their oppressors shall be their companions.

This new spirit is but a reflex of the great war, and it is largely due to the insistent and vigorous agitation carried on by younger men of the race. The demand is uncompromisingly made for either liberty or death, and since death is likely to be a two-edged sword it will be to the advantage of those in a position to do so to give the race its long-denied liberty.

The new spirit animating Negroes is not confined to the United States, where it is most acutely manifested, but is simmering beneath the surface in every country where the race is oppressed. The Washington and Chicago outbreaks should be regarded as symptoms of a great pandemic, and the Negroes as courageous surgeons who performed the necessary though painful operation. That the remedy is efficacious is beyond question. It has brought results, for as a consequence the eyes of the entire world are focused upon the racial situation in the United States. The world knows now that the New Negroes are determined to observe the primal law of self-preservation whenever civil laws break down; to assist the authorities to preserve order and prevent themselves and families from being murdered in cold blood. Surely, no one can sincerely object to this new and laudable determination. Justification for this course is not lacking, for it is the white man's own Bible that says "Those who live by the sword shall perish by the sword," and since white men believe in force, Negroes who have mimicked them for nearly three centuries must copy them in that respect. Since fire must be fought with hell fire, and diamond alone can cut diamond, Negroes realize that force alone is an effective medium to counteract force. Counter

From *The Messenger,* Vol. II (September 1919).

irritants are useful in curing diseases, and Negroes are being driven by their white fellow citizens to investigate the curative values inherent in mass action, revolvers and other lethal devices when applied to social diseases.

The New Negro has arrived with stiffened back bone, dauntless manhood, defiant eye, steady hand and a will of iron. His creed is admirably summed up in the poem of Claude McKay, the black Jamaican poet, who is carving out for himself a niche in the Hall of Fame: *

DEFENSE OF NEGRO RIOTERS
EDITORS OF THE MESSENGER

The Messenger appeals to all citizens who believe in fair play and justice to address their attention now to the defense of the Negroes who participated in the rioting or who were arrested as alleged participators therein. Committees should be formed immediately in which practically all Negro organizations might participate for the collection of funds, the giving out of publicity, the ascertainment of facts, bailing and bonding, and giving aid and comfort and succor to the men who are in prison. In Chicago, we are informed, by the National Association for the Advancement of Colored People, that in connection with the Urban League and other organizations, a committee has been formed to look after work suggested along this line. We urge that that committee be extended in size and that its work begin to proceed with acceleration. The fraternal societies like the Pythians, Odd Fellows, Masons, Elks, Shriners, St. Luke's, etc., should lend their assistance. These organizations should not only appeal to their membership to support the cause of the defense of these men, but they would do credit to themselves to vote large sums of money, ranging from $500 to $10,000, directly out of their treasuries. Every Negro newspaper should also join in pushing the drive through; all Negroes whether working men or business people should join in the movement.

For defense, no special opportunity should be given to some aspiring young lawyer who wants to make a reputation by experimenting with these cases. The ablest lawyers in the country should be put at the defense of these men. Samuel Untermeyer, Clarence Darrow, George Gordon Battle, Louis Marshall, John B. Stanchfield, William D. Guthrie, Bourke Cochran— men of this type—should be the chief counsel for defense. What does it matter if the lawyers alone cost $25,000? Have not these Negroes taken the first line trenches for all of us? Were they not acting in self-defense? Not only in defense of themselves, but of the whole race?

We wish to call attention to the necessity of quick work too. There is no time for delay. The lawyers need to be on the job at this very moment, studying the evidence, getting in touch with witnesses, ferreting out contributory

* See page 353 for Claude McKay's poem.
From *The Messenger,* Vol. II (September 1919).

causes, interviewing different people. *Money and lawyers are the most important factors* just now. These are the immediate demands. Money must be collected and dispensed by persons whose honesty and efficiency are above reproach. Publicity must be given to all monies collected and all monies spent. Someone will have to be hired to do this work. Clerks, stenographers, managers and organizers, postage and literature, general publicity, will cost money. Don't let anyone make a foolish demand for voluntary service in the detailed and technical work. In order to place responsibility, someone must be paid.

On with the defense! Let every Negro become a part of the Defense Committee.

THE NEW NEGRO—WHAT IS HE?
EDITORS OF THE MESSENGER

Our title was the subject of an editorial in the New York *Age* which formed the basis of an extensive symposium. Most of the replies, however, have been vague and nebulous. *The Messenger,* therefore, undertakes to supply the New York Age and the general public with a definite and clear portrayal of the New Negro.

It is well nigh axiomatic that the most accurate test of what a man or institution or a movement is, is first, what its aims are; second, what its methods are, or how it expects to achieve its aims; and third, its general relations to current movements.

Now, what are the aims of the New Negro? The answer to this question will fall under three general heads, namely, political, economic, and social.

In politics, the New Negro, unlike the Old Negro, cannot be lulled into a false sense of security with political spoils and patronage. A job is not the price of his vote. He will not continue to accept political promisory notes from a political debtor, who has already had the power, but who has refused to satisfy his political obligations. The New Negro demands political equality. He recognizes the necessity of selective as well as elective representation. He realizes that so long as the Negro votes for the Republican or Democratic party, he will have only the right and privilege to elect but not to select his representatives. And he who selects the representatives controls the representative. The New Negro stands for universal suffrage.

A word about the economic aims of the New Negro. Here, as a worker, he demands the full product of his toil. His immediate aim is more wages, shorter hours and better working conditions. As a consumer, he seeks to buy in the market, commodities at the lowest possible price.

The social aims of the New Negro are decidedly different from those of the Old Negro. Here he stands for absolute and unequivocal *"social equality."* He realizes that there cannot be any qualified equality. He insists that a

From *The Messenger,* Vol. II (August 1920).

society which is based upon justice can only be a society composed of *social equals*. He insists upon identity of social treatment. With respect to intermarriage, he maintains that it is the only logical, sound and correct aim for the Negro to entertain. He realizes that the acceptance of laws against intermarriage is tantamount to the acceptance of the stigma of inferiority. Besides, laws against intermarriage expose Negro women to sexual exploitation, and deprive their offspring, by white men, of the right to inherit the property of their father. Statistics show that there are nearly four million mulattoes in America as a result of miscegenation.

So much then for the aims of the New Negro. A word now about his methods. It is with respect to methods that the essential difference between the New and the Old Negro relates.

First, the methods by which the New Negro expects to realize his political aims are radical. He would repudiate and discard both of the old parties—Republican and Democratic. His knowledge of political science enables him to see that a political organization must have an economic foundation. A party whose money comes from working people, must and will represent working people. Now, everybody concedes that the Negro is essentially a worker. There are no big capitalists among them. There are a few petit bourgeoisie, but the process of money concentration is destined to weed them out and drop them down into the ranks of the working class. In fact, the interests of all Negroes are tied up with the workers. Therefore, the Negro should support a working class political party. He is a fool or insane, who opposes his best interests by supporting his enemy. As workers, Negroes have nothing in common with their employers. The Negro wants high wages; the employer wants to pay low wages. The Negro wants to work short hours; the employer wants to work him long hours. Since this is true, it follows as a logical corollary that the Negro should not support the party of the employing class. Now, it is a question of fact that the Republican and Democratic Parties are parties of the employing or capitalist class.

On the economic field, the New Negro advocates that the Negro join the labor unions. Wherever white unions discriminate against the Negro worker, then the only sensible thing to do is to form independent unions to fight both the white capitalists for more wages and shorter hours, on the one hand, and white labor unions for justice, on the other. It is folly for the Negro to fight labor organization because some white unions ignorantly ignore or oppose him. It is about as logical and wise as to repudiate and condemn writing on the ground that it is used by some crooks for forgery. As a consumer, he would organize cooperative societies to reduce the high cost of living.

The social methods are: education and physical action in self defense. That education must constitute the basis of all action, is beyond the realm of question. And to fight back in self defense, should be accepted as a matter of course. No one who will not fight to protect his life is fit to live. Self defense is recognized as a legitimate weapon in all civilized countries. Yet the Old Crowd Negroes have counseled the doctrine of non-resistance.

24

As to current movements, the Negro would accept, praise and support that which his enemies reject, condemn and oppose. He is tolerant. He would restore free speech, a free press and freedom of assemblage. He would release Debs. He would recognize the right of Russia to self determination. He is opposed to the Treaty and the League of Nations. Yet, he rejects Lodge's reservations. He knows that neither will help the people. As to Negro leaders, his object is to destroy them all and build up new ones.

Finally, the New Negro arrived upon the scene at the time of all other forward, progressive groups and movements—after the great world war. He is the product of the same world-wide forces that have brought into being the great liberal and radical movements that are now seizing the reins of political, economic and social power in all of the civilized countries of the world.

His presence is inevitable in these times of economic chaos, political upheaval and social distress. Yes, there is a New Negro. And it is he who will pilot the Negro through this terrible hour of storm and stress.

AFRICA FOR THE AFRICANS

Certain elements of American Negroes, as well as similar elements of West Indians in their native islands, in Central America and in the principal cities on the Atlantic seaboard of the United States, are enthused over the idea of ousting all non-Negroes from Africa. The plan is variously and euphemistically described as "redeeming Africa" "back to Africa" and "getting a place in the sun." The *modus operandi* for the attainment of this end is extremely simple—transparently so. It involves neither politics nor cooperation with the native races of Africa. All that is necessary is unity—magic word!

Viewed seriously this state of mind must be regarded as being indicative of two things: A desire to end the oppression of the black race by Caucasians and a lack of understanding of the basic causes of that oppression.

In the first place the Negro is not the only race that is now being oppressed. Brown Hindu, Yellow Chinese and White Irishmen are equally, and in some instances, more oppressed than Negroes. The oppressors are not all Caucasians. Among the worst oppressors are found the Japanese, a yellow nation. In the dim past Negroes were among the greatest oppressors in the world. The Egyptians who, according to the Bible, enslaved the Jews were a dark people of admitted Negro blood.

Further, Negroes have been some of the most effective instruments for the oppression of members of their own race as well as of other races. Negroes were used by British-Peruvian Capitalists to exploit, murder and mutilate peaceable South Americans. Brown Sikhs and black troops have been used by white Britishers to conquer East Africa and Persia and are now being used for a similar purpose in Mesopotamia.

What does the foregone recital of facts disclose? This: that oppression is

From *The Messenger,* Vol. II (September 1920).

not racial; and that no particular race has absolutely clean hands. There may be degrees in suffering and oppression but none is absolutely "without sin."

Why do nations, races, classes and individuals oppress other human beings? Because they hate? No; but because they profit from such oppression. Nowhere do we find any intention on the part of a modern oppressor to exterminate weak peoples; but everywhere we see an intention to reduce them to political impotency and physical helplessness while their lands and labor are being exploited. The Egyptians did not slaughter all the Jews, the Japanese all the Koreans, the British all the Hindus, Ashantees, Irish and modern Egyptians. Each oppressing nation slaughtered only sufficient of the weaker race as is sufficient to cow the remainder into subjection. Wholesale slaughter is only resorted to when a people choose annihilation rather than economic serfdom, as in the case of the American Indian and the Australian Native. And usually the territory of the exterminated race must be climatically suitable for occupation by the "superior" race.

There is no race problem where a people are willing to toil in the interests of their military superiors. But do all of the stronger group benefit from the subjection of weaker peoples? Does the ignorant, deluded and patriotic dirt-eating cracker of Georgia benefit from the presence of American Marines in Haiti? Does the proud imperial Englishman who flounders in the filth of White Chapel benefit from the enslavement of the despoiled Zulu? Those who benefit are not the majority of England, America or Japan: they are the small group of financiers who have investments in Haiti, South Africa and Korea.

It is Alfred Beit and the Duke of Fife, brother-in-law of King George, and the directors of the National City Bank of New York City who profit from the robbery of native lands and the serfdom of their rightful owners. And these men form the powerful and respectable of England and America. They are dignified statesmen, liberal philanthropists, devout Churchmen and prominent social and political leaders.

The freedom of Africa from alien exploitation, if that is what is meant by redeeming Africa, must comprehend a defeat of these men and all the moral and physical resources they control.

It is safe to say that a people are weakest when they are most oppressed, and if South and East African Negroes are more oppressed than West Indian and American Negroes, it is because they (the Africans) are actually weaker. How then can the relatively stronger group help the weaker group? By sensational gestures? No. But by doing everything possible to weaken those who profit from oppression.

For instance, a boycott against all British goods by Negroes in America would be more effective than all the mass meetings and parades they may organize. England is the principal oppressor of Negroes, and the oppression brings profits to English bankers, manufacturers and merchants who dominate the British Empire, so in order to aid those who are injured it is good tactics to attack those who profit from the injury.

To free Africa the wishes of the natives should be consulted, methods secretly discussed and only such methods as are calculated to be successfully adopted. Emotion, ignorance, ambition, are poor material with which to expel the British Capitalists from Africa who have battleships, factories, airplanes, machine guns, poison gas, liquid fire and lying newspapers, ministers and other media of propaganda at their beck and call.

GARVEYISM
A. PHILIP RANDOLPH

Garveyism is an upshot of the Great World War. It sprang forth amidst the wild currents of national, racial and class hatreds and prejudices stirred and unleashed by the furious flames of battle. Under the strains and stresses of conflict, the state power and institutions of the ruling peoples were mobilized. The intelligentsia of the Central Powers apotheosized "Mittel Europa," Kultur, the Bagdad Railroad, and hurled imprecations upon the heads of the ungodly Entente. So, in turn, the high priests of morals and propaganda of the holy Allies sang a hymn of hate to the tune of the "Hun."

"Britannia, Britannia rules the waves. Britons will ne'r be slaves," "self determination of smaller nationalities," "revanche, Italia irridenta," "100 per cent Americanism," "we are fighting to make the world safe for democracy," "Deutschland Über Alles," "Pan-Slavism," etc., were the psychological armor and spear of Armageddon. Add to this psychic complex of blatant, arrogant and hypocritic alchauvinism the revolutionary, proletarian internationalism of the Russian Revolution: "no annexations, no punitive indemnities and self-determination for smaller nationalities," and it is at once apparent how nationalisms, racialisms and classisms, strangled and repressed in the cruel and brutal grip of imperialism, under the magic and galvanic stimulant of such moving slogans, would struggle to become more articulate, more defiant, more revolutionary.

The Easter Rebellion of Seinn Feinism, in 1916; Mahatma Gandhi non-co-operative philosophy of outraged India; Mustafa Kemal Pasha's adamant stand at Angora in the Levant, battling for a conquering, militant Pan Islamism; the erratic vagaries of d'Annunzio for a re-united Italy; together with the rumblings of unrest in Egypt and among other oppressed peoples, attest to the manner in which the war quickened the vison of hitherto adjudged backward peoples, and set free forces making for the overthrow of the institutions and the abolition of the conditions that gave it (the war) birth. Indeed, the war was fruitful of paradoxes. Movements grew both for and against the interest of society. Imperialism and revolution faced each other. The Kremlin and the Quai d'Orsay of the worker and capitalist, respectively, seemed to grow in power. Movements grotesque and sound, appear to flourish and decay for the nonce.

From *The Messenger*, Vol. III (September 1921).

All of these varied and variegated associated efforts have their rooting in the sub-soil of oppression and fear. The oppressed struggle to be freed; the oppressors fear their struggles. Hence, movements for liberation, whether they function through a sound methodology or not, are reactions to age-long injustices; they are reflexes of the universal urge for human freedom.

In the light of these principles, it is clear to anyone that Garveyism is a natural and logical reaction of black men to the overweening and supercilious conduct of white imperialists. Garveyism proclaims the doctrine of "similarity."

To the fallacy of "white man first" Garveyism would counter with a similar fallacy of "Negro first." If there be a "White House" in the Capitol of the nation, why not a Black House also; if there be a Red Cross and an American Legion, why not a Black Cross and a Black or Negro Legion, says the movement. And at the summit of this doctrine of "similarity" stands the African Empire as a counter-irritant to the white empires, monarchies and republics of the world. Out of this doctrine it is, indeed, not strange that transportation should partake of the magic romanticism of color. Why do persons ask, then, why a Black Star Line? And this is not said in a vein of levity, for whatever might be said of the Garvey Movement, it, at least, strives for consistency.

A word, now, concerning the doctrine of "similarity." Upon its face, it would appear to commend itself as a sound and logical course of action. Upon closer examination, however, one is largely disillusioned. It is hardly scientific, too, to make a sweeping condemnation of this doctrine on the grounds of its absolute inapplicability to the highly complex problems of the Negro. The stock argument raised by its proponents is that: "if a given thing is good for a white man, that very same thing is also good for the Negro. By this token of argument the conquest of Africa with a view to establishing an African empire, a Black Star Line, etc, is justified.

The fallacy of this logic consists in its total disregard of the relative value of the thing proposed to those for whom it is proposed. To illustrate: it does not follow that because there are subways in New York City owned and operated by white people that there should also be a subway in New York City owned and operated by Negroes. For in the first place it couldn't be done (the enthusiasts who proclaim the patent inanity that there is no such thing as "can't," to the contrary notwithstanding) and, in the second place, even if it could be done, it would be an economic injury instead of a benefit. The reasons for this are clear. The subways, elevated trains and surface lines are owned and controlled by the same financial interests. They are of the nature of a monopoly. These interests exercise great influence upon the City Administration which grants franchises to public utilities. Hence, a competing public carrier could not secure the necessary privilege; nor would the Money Trust extend the requisite capital, recognizing the inability of such a competitor to secure the same through the tedious and protracted method of small stock sales to an innocent public. Granting, however, that the necessary capital could be raised, a subway so established would immediately be thrown into bankruptcy through the rate cutting of fares by the older concern. The history of American business is replete with the failures of enterprises that have attempted to buck the big monopolies and trusts. The process has been that either a small competitor is absorbed or driven out of the field by the big syndicates. And when a small business is permitted to exist, it is decidedly against the interests of the public, because being unable to do large scale buying, to engage in extensive advertising, to employ the most highly skilled technicians of hand and brain, and to institute the most modern and scientific methods of economy, it is forced to sell its services or goods to the public at the highest price obtainable. In other words, a business which sells to 1,000 persons a day can sell at a lower price than the one which sells to only 100, because it buys more at a lower price. Such is the great advantage of the monopoly or trust over the small business. Of course, the trusts are robbing the people because they have the ability to raise prices at will. But they are the most efficient institution for producing and marketing goods and services yet devised.

What is true of transportation within cities is also true of transportation between cities. No sane business promoter would think of advising anyone to invest in an enterprise to construct a railroad to compete with the great Pennsylvania, or Grand Central railway systems. Such a venture by people of color for people of color, in the circles of experienced and intelligent business men, would only be regarded as a joke. Obviously, from a business point of view, such aforenamed undertakings are unsound. If they are unsound business enterprises, by what stretch of the imagination and race patriotism could they be justified as a phase of the solution of the Negro problem? Certainly, an intelligent person would not advocate an admittedly unscientific and inefficient plan of action in industry, business or finance, on the highly questionable grounds that Negroes should have such an enterprise of their own and for their own. *For, palpably, no benefits can flow to a people from the adoption of a program which the collective intelligence of society has discarded.* Again, while it is sometimes true that one profits from failures, it is also true that one may be destroyed by failures. Nor is it sufficient to counter with the argument that one must go through certain experiences in order to learn. *There is abundant evidence to show that experience is the most expensive and inconvenient method of acquiring knowledge.* No one will contend that it is necessary to take bichloride of mercury in order to ascertain whether it will really cause death or not. The purpose of scientific research is to place, at the convenience of society, a body of knowledge which will make it unnecessary for every one to go through the same painful and protracted process of discovering and organizing the same.

The accumulated knowledge of business economics, if consulted, would convince anyone of the folly today, of trying to build a new business with limited capital and limited brains, in a highly trustified field such as the railroad and shipping industries.

In the "Annalist" of August 15th, 1921, S. G. Riggs, writing on the subject

"Past Experience Gives Shipping a Gloomy Outlook," says, "that only one-fourth of the Government's ships are in operation, and there is about 33 per cent of the tonnage tied up in the world." He further makes this significant statement: "On June 30, 1914, there were 45.4 million gross tons of steamers in the world; today there are close to 54.8 million tons, a 20 per cent increase. On the other hand, the quantity of cargo moving is one-fourth less than in 1913, as has been proved by a compilation of imports and exports of twenty leading countries. A number of fine craft are being laid up and many more will have to follow, for at the figures at present ruling many voyages do not pay actual outgoing expenses, leaving nothing for interest and depreciation. [A citation of editorials during the years from 1897 to 1900 which he uses as typical of editorials of the shipping journals today."]

In conclusion, he says, "that shipping is facing a long, severe depression with little chance of an upward movement for years."

Such is the sober opinion of an expert of the shipping business.

In other words, today great shipping interests backed up with unlimited capital, with fleets of ships, (not makeshifts nor apologies) are hard put to it to make ends meet, on account of the supply of ships being greater than the demand. It is safe to say that no expert in the shipping business would advise even one with unlimited capital and skilled operators, to begin a brand new shipping business today, or to continue one if it is possible to stop without incurring a greater loss than by continuing.

In view of the foregoing facts, it is difficult to understand how any group of alleged intelligent and honest Negroes can continue to hold out the hope to well-meaning but misguided Negroes that they will build a great fleet of ships, plying between America, the West Indies and Africa, carrying Negroes and their Cargo.

The shipping business is controlled by a Shipping Trust.

It is about as possible and necessary to maintain a fleet of ships for *Negroes only,* as it is to build and maintain a railroad alongside that of the Pennsylvania railroad for *Negroes only.*

This is the excuse for the Black Star Line according to Mr. Garvey, as reported in the *Negro World* of Aug. 20, 1920:

"You know of the insults heaped upon Negro passengers on the steamships of other lines when those Negroes were able to secure passage on them. You know of the weeks and months they have been compelled to wait to secure passages from one place to another. The Black Star Line aims to remedy all this, but we must have ships, more and bigger ships."

It might not be unkind to ask how many Negroes do or can make use of ocean travel?

Now as to the matter of empire.

First, what is the status of Africa today?

According to the International Relations Series, edited by G. Lowes Dickinson, the area of Africa is about 11,500,000 square miles, and its population about 170 millions. "By 1914 the whole continent, with the exception of Abyssinia (350,000 square miles and eight millions population) and Liberia (area 40,000 square miles, population two millions), had been subjected to the control and government of European states," writes Dickinson. The following figures show what shares the various States took in this partition:

	Area	Population
France	4,200,000	25,000,000
Britain	3,300,000	35,000,000
Germany *	1,100,000	12,000,000
Belgium	900,000	7,000,000
Portugal	800,000	8,000,000
Italy	600,000	1,000,000
Spain	750,000	200,000

* (Now in the hands of Great Britain)

The foregoing figures will indicate just how much vacant, available territory exists in Africa today.

Since, then, there is no unclaimed land in Africa, the logical question to ask is: how does one expect to build an empire there?

Here again, we will let the chief spokesman of Garveyism speak. Says he, on August 20, 1921, according to the *Negro World,* its official organ:

"It falls to your lot to tear off the shackles that bind Mother Africa. Can you do it? (Cries of 'Yes! Yes!') You did it in the Revolutionary War; you did it in the Civil War; you did it in the Battle of the Marne; you did it at Verdun; you did it in Mesopotamia; you did it in Togoland, in German East Africa, and you can do it marching up the battle heights of Africa."

At this point it will be logical and sane to examine the relative power of the forces that control Africa and of those that propose conquering it, in order to ascertain the folly or wisdom of the enterprise.

The aforementioned powers are equipped with big dreadnoughts, submarines, aeroplanes and great armies. In modern warfare Lewisite Gas is said to be capable of destroying entire cities. Aeroplanes have been built that can carry a half-ton gas bomb. Modern artillery was instrumental in producing a deathlist in the great world war of nearly 10,000,000, together with nearly 30,000,000 wounded. The imperialists nation in Africa control all of the deathdealing engines of power.

The very fact that the great European powers have fought to conquer Africa, is pretty good evidence that they don't intend surrendering it to the cry of "Africa for the Africans." Thus, it means war to the death against the formidable armies and navies of the great powers in Africa. The Garvey forces haven't a single fighting craft. They have no military organization; no military or naval leadership. How, then, can Negroes conquer Africa? Someone says, "We will take the arms from the white man." This, I submit, is not the most reassuring and delightful task.

But, it is apparently understood that the Negroes' conquering Africa is a mere dream. For proclaims the leader:

"All of us might not live to see the higher accomplishment of an African

empire so strong and powerful, as to compel the respect of all mankind, but we in our lifetime can so work and so act, as to make the dream a possibility within another generation."

Loss of hope appears in the distance.

A word about the value of Garveyism to Negroes today. It has done some splendid things. It has inculcated into the minds of Negroes the need and value of organization. It has also demonstrated the ability of Negroes to come together in large masses under Negro leadership. Of course, the A. M. E. Church has done as much; so have the Negro Secret Orders. Garveyism, also, has conducted wholesome, vital, necessary and effective criticism on Negro leadership. It has stimulated the pride of Negroes in Negro history and traditions, thereby helping to break down the slave psychology which throttles and strangles Negro initiative, self-assertiveness, ambition, courage, independence, etc. It has further stiffened the Negro's backbone to resist the encroachments and insults of white people. Again, it has emphasized the international character of the Negro problem. As a propaganda organization, at one period of its history, it was highly useful in awakening Negro consciousness to the demand of the times.

But its business operations, as exposed by Dr. Du Bois, to which I have not as yet seen a convincing reply, have not been conceived altogether in harmony with approved, modern business economics. That Negroes should develop business enterprises is correct. To this there can be no intelligent objection. But the kind, at certain times, seems to me to be highly material. Also, that Garveyism has stimulated Negro business initiative, no fair-minded person will gainsay.

But the crux of Garveyism is the redemption of Africa, the building of an African Empire. This can not be defended as an immediate program of the Negro, in the light of modern world politics. The slogan "Africa for the Africans" no Negro, or for that matter liberal white man, will oppose; but "back to Africa" for the conquest of Africa is a different song.

The white mobocratic South, with its Tom Watsons, Cole Bleases, and John Williamses could not wish for a better ally than Garveyism, at this time. How is that, you ask?

It has been a recognized form of strategy of the ruling class in every country that whenever the discontent of the working people became a menace to them (the ruling class) that they (the ruling class) either started a war of aggression or invited a war of invasion. This was done to divert the attention of the masses from the causes of their poverty and misery at home to some imagainary foreign enemy. Witness the old Nobility of Russia today urging an invasion of their own country by foreign powers. During the Revolution in France 1789 to 1793, the old Feudal aristocracy invited the invasion of France by foreign nations.

In America, the problem of the Negro is a labor problem. Negroes constitute a laboring element. Unrest is widespread among them, even in the South. Radical white labor groups are reported to be calling to them. Washington, Chicago, Arkansas and Tulsa race riots show that Negroes are discontented and are ready to strike back. The increasing demand of Negroes for the abolition of the jim-crow car, disfranchisement, lynching; the insistence of a small minority for every right, even social equality; the trend of Negroes into labor unions; the activities of Negroes in the Socialist movement—all indicate the birth of a new consciousness.

Now to divert the Negroes' mind away from these fundamental problems is to weaken them and strengthen the Bourbon forces of the Negro-hating South and the exploiting capitalists of America.

This is why there is no opposition to the demonstrations of Garveyism, either in parades or public mass meetings in the Armory or Madison Square Garden.

Negro Socialists, on the other hand, are thwarted in their every attempt to conduct public educational meetings, and parades would be out of the question. The cry would go up: Anarchists, they want to overthrow the government by violence! Such is the smoke screen used to suffocate real radicalism.

The whites in America don't take Garveyism seriously. They dub Garvey a "Moses of the Negro" in order to get Negroes to follow him, which will wean them away from any truly radical economic program. They know that the achievement of his program, the redemption of Africa is unattainable, but it serves the purpose of engaging the Negroes' brains, energy and funds in a highly nebulous, futile and doubtful movement so far as beneficial results to Negroes are concerned.

Think of the solution of Garveyism for the present wave of unemployment!

Says Mr. Garvey in a recent speech, according to the *Negro World:*

"If you are employed by white men and they choose to dismiss you because of color tell him, "Brother, you remember the last war; all right, another one may come.' That is your trump card. You are not begging for jobs; you demand jobs because you made it possible for them to live in peace (Cheers), otherwise the Germans would have been at their door. You have a fair exchange for the money that is given to you. Let them know this: that your future service depends upon their present good treatment."

This is doubtless a rejoinder to the charge brought against the movement, viz., that when Negroes applied at certain business, or industrial plants for work, they were told to go to Mr. Garvey, the Negro King.

While it is absurd to charge Garvey with the plight of the Negro in the country today; yet what individual with the slightest conception of industrial problems, would accept the aforegoing statement of Mr. Garvey as a remedy for the Negroes' unemployment? It is not only childish, but it accentuates, and complicates the Negroes' difficulties by making the question of unemployment an issue as between white and black men, when, in fact, it is a product of the capitalist system which brings about overproduction at certain cycles, and consequent unemployment of workers regardless of race, creed, nationality or color. *In very truth, a strikingly anti-white man doctrine is both unsound and dangerous. For it is false to assume that all white men are agreed upon a program of opposition to Negroes.* The dominant groups in America, as in other parts of the world, are class groups. All white men are not in harmony with respect to human action and human institutions. The Great World War demonstrated that. Debs in jail is also proof as strong as "holy writ." Strikes and lockouts on the industrial field indicate a difference of class interests within the same race. Also the fights between Negro tenants and Negro landlords show that even Negroes may have different interests. In fact, the interests of a Negro tenant and white tenant are more in common than the interests between white tenants and white landlords or Negro tenants and Negro landlords.

Thus, Garveyism broadens the chasm between the black and white workers, and can only result in the creation of more race hatred which will periodically flare up into race riots.

However, with the elimination of the African program, the "Negro First" doctrine, the Black Star Line, the existing organization of Garveyism may be directed into some useful channel.

The Negro public is facing so serious a period that it should demand that the different schools of Negro thought come before it and present their programs. The programs should be examined and criticized by the Negro public so that it might accept or reject according to the merits or demerits of the different schools.

It was, indeed, astounding to read the following part of a resolution adopted on the Pan-African Congress meeting in Paris, at a public meeting of the U.N.I.A.:

"That we believe the motives of the congress are to undermine the true feeling and sentiment of the Negro race for complete freedom in their own spheres and for a higher social order among themselves, as against a desire among a certain class of Negroes for social contact, comradeship and companionship with the white race.

"We further repudiate the congress because we sincerely feel that the white race, like the black and yellow races, should maintain the purity of self, and that the congress is nothing more than an effort to encourage race suicide by the admixture of two opposite races.

"That the said W. E. B. DuBois and his associates, who called the congress, are making an issue of social equality with the white race for their own selfish purposes and not for the advancement of the Negro race."

Now, certainly, no one will accuse the MESSENGER of any bias in favor of Dr. DuBois. But here the Negro is faced with the rejection of a principle which has been the ardent hope of the South since Reconstruction—the principle of social equality. Can Negroes accept the stigma of inferiority upon the pretext of keeping the stock pure? By the way, no anthropologist, worthy of the name, would advocate the purity of ethnic groups by preventing miscegenation.

Further, to reject and condemn a principle on the ground that some one is using it to selfish ends, is as sensible as it would be to oppose the teaching of writing to Negro youth, because it has been used for forgery or that those who lynch Negroes use it. The issue is the value of an instrument for the achievement of certain ends. To reject social equality is to accept the jim-crow car, disfrancisement, lynching, etc. Without social equality the Negro will ever remain a political and economic serf.

Garveyism is spiritual; the need now, however, is a Negro renaissance in scientific thought.

AFRICA FOR THE AFRICANS
MARCUS A. GARVEY

For five years the Universal Negro Improvement Association has been advocating the cause of Africa for the Africans—that is, that the Negro peoples of the world should concentrate upon the object of building up for themselves a great nation in Africa.

When we started our propaganda toward this end several of the so-called intellectual Negroes who have been bamboozling the race for over half a century said that we were crazy, that the Negro peoples of the western world were not interested in Africa and could not live in Africa. One editor and leader went so far as to say at his so-called Pan-African Congress that American Negroes could not live in Africa, because the climate was too hot. All kinds of arguments have been adduced by these Negro intellectuals against the colonization of Africa by the black race. Some said that the black man would ultimately work out his existence alongside of the white man in countries founded and established by the latter. Therefore, it was not necessary for Negroes to seek an independent nationality of their own. The old time stories of "African fever," "African bad climate," "African mosquitos," "African savages," have been repeated by these "brainless intellectuals" of ours as a scare against our people in America and the West Indies taking a kindly interest in the new program of building a racial empire of our own in our Motherland. Now that years have rolled by and the Universal Negro Improvement Association has made the circuit of the world with its propaganda, we find eminent statesmen and leaders of the white race coming out boldly advocating the cause of colonizing Africa with the Negroes of the western world. A year ago Senator MacCullum of the Mississippi Legislature introduced a resolution in the House for the purpose of petitioning the Congress of the United States of America and the President to use their good influence in securing from the Allies sufficient territory in Africa in liquidation of the war debt, which territory should be used for the establishing of an independent nation for American Negroes. About the same time Senator France of Maryland gave expression to a similar desire in the Senate of the United States. During a speech on the "Soldiers' Bonus." He said: "We owe a big debt to Africa and one which we have too long ignored. I need not enlarge upon our peculiar interest in the obligation to the people of Africa. Thousands of Americans have for years been contributing to the missionary work which has been carried out by the noble men and women who have been sent out in that field by the churches of America."

Germany to the Front

This reveals a real change on the part of prominent statesmen in their attitude on the African question. Then comes another suggestion from Germany, for which Dr. Heinrich Schnee, a former Governor of German East Africa, is author. This German statesman suggests in an interview given out in Berlin, and published in New York, that America takes over the mandatories of Great Britain and France in Africa for the colonization of American Negros. Speaking on the matter, he says, "As regards the attempt to colonize Africa with the surplus American colored population, this would in a long way settle the vexed problem, and under the plan such as Senator France has outlined, might enable France and Great Britain to discharge their duties to the United States, and simultaneously ease the burden of German reparations which is paralyzing economic life."

With expressions as above quoted from prominent world statesmen, and from the demands made by such men as Senators France and McCullum, it is clear that the question of African nationality is not a far-fetched one, but is as reasonable and feasible as was the idea of an American nationality.

A "Program" at Last

I trust that the Negro peoples of the world are now convinced that the work of the Universal Negro Improvement Association is not a visionary one, but very practical, and that it is not so far fetched, but can be realized in a short while if the entire race will only co-operate and work toward the desired end. Now that the work of our organization has started to bear fruit we find that some of these "doubting Thomases" of three and four years ago are endeavoring to mix themselves up with the popular idea of rehabilitating Africa in the interest of the Negro. They are now advancing spurious "programs" and in a short while will endeavor to force themselves upon the public as advocates and leaders of the African idea.

It is felt that those who have followed the career of the Universal Negro Improvement Association will not allow themselves to be deceived by these Negro opportunists who have always sought to live off the ideas of other people.

The Dream of a Negro Empire

It is only a question of a few more years when Africa will be completely colonized by Negroes, as Europe is by the white race. What we want is an independent African nationality, and if America is to help the Negro peoples of the world establish such a nationality, then we welcome the assistance.

It is hoped that when the time comes for American and West Indian Negroes to settle in Africa, they will realize their responsibility and their duty. It will not be to go to Africa for the purpose of exercising an over-lordship over the natives, but it shall be the purpose of the Universal Negro Improvement Association to have established in Africa that brotherly co-operation which will make the interests of the African native and the American and West Indian Negro one and the same, that is to say, we shall enter into a common partnership to build up Africa in the interests of our race.

Oneness of Interests

Everybody knows that there is absolutely no difference between the native African and the American and West Indian Negroes, in that we are descendants from one common family stock. It is only a matter of accident that we have been divided and kept apart for over three hundred years, but it is felt that when the time has come for us to get back together, we shall do so in the spirit of brotherly love, and any Negro who expects that he will be assisted here, there or anywhere by the Universal Negro Improvement Association to exercise a haughty superiority over the fellows of his own race, makes a tremendous mistake. Such men had better remain where they are and not attempt to become in any way interested in the higher development of Africa.

The Negro has had enough of the vaunted practice of race superiority as inflicted upon him by others, therefore he is not prepared to tolerate a similar assumption on the part of his own people. In America and the West Indies, we have Negroes who believe themselves so much above their fellows as to cause them to think that any readjustment in the affairs of the race should be placed in their hands for them to exercise a kind of an autocratic and despotic control as others have done to us for centuries. Again I say, it would be advisable for such Negroes to take their hands and minds off the now popular idea of colonizing Africa in the interest of the Negro race, because their being identified with this new program will not in any way help us because of the existing feeling among Negroes everywhere not to tolerate the infliction of race or class superiority upon them, as is the desire of the self-appointed and self-created race leadership that we have been having for the last fifty years.

The Basis of an African Aristocracy

The masses of Negroes in America, the West Indies, South and Central America are in sympathetic accord with the aspirations of the native Africans. We desire to help them build up Africa as a Negro Empire, where every black man, whether he was born in Africa or in the Western world, will have the opportunity to develop on his own lines under the protection of the most favorable democratic institutions.

It will be useless, as before stated, for bombastic Negroes to leave America and the West Indies to go to Africa, thinking that they will have privileged positions to inflict upon the race that bastard aristocracy that they have tried to maintain in this Western world at the expense of the masses. Africa shall develop an aristocracy of its own, but it shall be based upon service and loyalty to race. Let all Negroes work toward that end. I feel that it is only a question of a few more years before our program will be accepted not only by the few statesmen of America who are now interested in it, but by the strong statesmen of the world, as the only solution to the great race problem. There is no other way to avoid the threatening war of the races that is bound to engulf all mankind, which has been prophesied by the world's greatest thinkers; there is no better method than by apportioning every race to its own habitat.

The time has really come for the Asiatics to govern themselves in Asia, as the Europeans are in Europe and the Western world, so also is it wise for the Africans to govern themselves at home, and thereby bring peace and satisfaction to the entire human family.

THE FUTURE AS I SEE IT

It comes to the individual, the race, the nation, once in a life-time to decide upon the course to be pursued as a career. The hour has now struck for the individual Negro as well as the entire race to decide the course that will be pursued in the interest of our own liberty.

We who make up the Universal Negro Improvement Association have decided that we shall go forward, upward and onward toward the great goal of human liberty. We have determined among ourselves that all barriers placed in the way of our progress must be removed, must be cleared away for we desire to see the light of a brighter day.

The Negro Is Ready

The Universal Negro Improvement Association for five years has been proclaiming to the world the readiness of the Negro to carve out a pathway for himself in the course of life. Men of other races and nations have become alarmed at this attitude of the Negro in his desire to do things for himself and by himself. This alarm has become so universal that organizations have been brought into being here, there and everywhere for the purpose of deterring and obstructing this forward move of our race. Propaganda has been waged here, there and everywhere for the purpose of misinterpreting the intention of this organization; some have said that this organization seeks to create discord and discontent among the races; some say we are organized for the purpose of hating other people. Every sensible, sane and honest-minded person knows that the Universal Negro Improvement Association has no such intention. We are organized for the absolute purpose of bettering our condition, industrially, commercially, socially, religiously and politically. We are organized not to hate other men, but to lift ourselves, and to demand respect of all humanity. We have a program that we believe to be righteous; we believe it to be just, and we have made up our minds to lay down ourselves on the altar of sacrifice for the realization of this great hope of ours, based upon the foundation of righteousness. We declare to the world that Africa must be free, that the entire Negro race must be emancipated from industrial bondage, peonage and serfdom; we make no compromise, we make no apology in this our declaration. We do not desire to create offense on the part of other races, but we are determined that we shall be heard, that we shall be given the rights to which we are entitled.

The Propaganda of Our Enemies

For the purpose of creating doubts about the work of the Universal Negro Improvement Association, many attempts have been made to cast shadow and gloom over our work. They have even written the most uncharitable things about our organization; they have spoken so unkindly of our effort, but what do we care? They spoke unkindly and uncharitably about all the reform movements that have helped in the betterment of humanity. They maligned the great movement of the Christian religion; they maligned the great liberation movements of America, of France, of England, of Russia; can we expect, then, to escape being maligned in this, our desire for the liberation of Africa and the freedom of four hundred million Negroes of the world?

We have unscrupulous men and organizations working in opposition to us. Some trying to capitalize the new spirit that has come to the Negro to make profit out of it to their own selfish benefit; some are trying to set back the Negro from seeing the hope of his own liberty, and thereby poisoning our people's mind against the motives of our organization; but every sensible far-seeing Negro in this enlightened age knows what propaganda means. It is the medium of discrediting that which you are opposed to, so that the propaganda of our enemies will be of little avail as soon as we are rendered able to carry to our peoples scattered throughout the world the true message of our great organization.

"Crocodiles" as Friends

Men of the Negro race, let me say to you that a greater future is in store for us; we have no cause to lose hope, to become faint-hearted. We must realize that upon ourselves depend our destiny, our future; we must carve out that future, that destiny, and we who make up the Universal Negro Improvement Association have pledged ourselves that nothing in the world shall stand in our way, nothing in the world shall discourage us, but opposition shall make us work harder, shall bring us closer together so that as one man the millions of us will march on toward that goal that we have set for ourselves. The new Negro shall not be deceived. The new Negro refuses to take advice from anyone who has not felt with him, and suffered with him. We have suffered for three hundred years, therefore we feel that the time has come when only those who have suffered with us can interpret our feelings and our spirit. It takes the slave to interpret the feelings of the slave; it takes the unfortunate man to interpret the spirit of his unfortunate brother;

and so it takes the suffering Negro to interpret the spirit of his comrade. It is strange that so many people are interested in the Negro now, willing to advise him how to act, and what organizations he should join, yet nobody was interested in the Negro to the extent of not making him a slave for two hundred and fifty years, reducing him to industrial peonage and serfdom after he was freed; it is strange that the same people can be so interested in the Negro now, as to tell him what organization he should follow and what leader he should support.

Whilst we are bordering on a future of brighter things, we are also at our danger period, when we must either accept the right philosophy, or go down by following deceptive propaganda which has hemmed us in for many centuries.

Deceiving the People

There is many a leader of our race who tells us that everything is well, and that all things will work out themselves and that a better day is coming. Yes, all of us know that a better day is coming; we all know that one day we will go home to Paradise, but whilst we are hoping by our Christian virtues to have an entry into Paradise we also realize that we are living on earth, and that the things that are practiced in Paradise are not practiced here. You have to treat this world as the world treats you; we are living in a temporal, material age, an age of activity, an age of racial, national selfishness. What else can you expect but to give back to the world what the world gives to you, and we are calling upon the four hundred million Negroes of the world to take a decided stand, a determined stand, that we shall occupy a firm position; that position shall be an emancipated race and a free nation of our own. We are determined that we shall have a free country; we are determined that we shall have a flag; we are determined that we shall have a government second to none in the world.

An Eye for an Eye

Men may spurn the idea, they may scoff at it; the metropolitan press of this country may deride us; yes, white men may laugh at the idea of Negroes talking about government; but let me tell you there is going to be a government, and let me say to you also that whatsoever you give, in like measure it shall be returned to you. The world is sinful, and therefore man believes in the doctrine of an eye for an eye, a tooth for a tooth. Everybody believes that revenge is God's, but at the same time we are men, and revenge sometimes springs up, even in the most Christian heart.

Why should man write down a history that will react against him? Why should man perpetrate deeds of wickedness upon his brother which will return to him in like measure? Yes, the Germans maltreated the French in the Franco-Prussian war of 1870, but the French got even with the Germans in 1918. It is history, and history will repeat itself. Beat the Negro, brutalize the Negro, kill the Negro, burn the Negro, imprison the Negro, scoff at the

Negro, deride the Negro, it may come back to you one of these fine days, because the supreme destiny of man is in the hands of God. God is no respecter of persons, whether that person be white, yellow or black. Today the one race is up, tomorrow it has fallen; today the Negro seems to be the footstool of the other races and nations of the world; tomorrow the Negro may occupy the highest rung of the great human ladder.

But, when we come to consider the history of man, was not the Negro a power, was he not great once? Yes, honest students of history can recall the day when Egypt, Ethiopia and Timbuctoo towered in their civilizations, towered above Europe, towered above Asia. When Europe was inhabited by a race of cannibals, a race of savages, naked men, heathens and pagans, Africa was peopled with a race of cultured black men, who were masters in art, science and literature; men who were cultured and refined; men who, it was said, were like the gods. Even the great poets of old sang in beautiful sonnets of the delight it afforded the gods to be in companionship with the Ethiopians. Why, then, should we lose hope? Black men, you were once great; you shall be great again. Lose not courage, lose not faith, go forward. The thing to do is to get organized; keep separated and you will be exploited, you will be robbed, you will be killed. Get organized, and you will compel the world to respect you. If the world fails to give you consideration, because you are black men, because you are Negroes, four hundred millions of you shall, through organization, shake the pillars of the universe and bring down creation, even as Samson brought down the temple upon his head and upon the heads of the Philistines.

An Inspiring Vision

So Negroes, I say, through the Universal Negro Improvement Association, that there is much to live for. I have a vision of the future, and I see before me a picture of a redeemed Africa, with her dotted cities, with her beautiful civilization, with her millions of happy children, going to and fro. Why should I lose hope, why should I give up and take a back place in this age of progress? Remember that you are men, that God created you Lords of this creation. Lift up yourselves, men, take yourselves out of the mire and hitch your hopes to the stars; yes, rise as high as the very stars themselves. Let no man pull you down, let no man destroy your ambition, because man is but your companion, your equal; man is your brother; he is not your lord; he is not your sovereign master.

We of the Universal Negro Improvement Association feel happy; we are cheerful. Let them connive to destroy us; let them organize to destroy us; we shall fight the more. Ask me personally the cause of my success, and I say opposition; oppose me, and I fight the more, and if you want to find out the sterling worth of the Negro, oppose him, and under the leadership of the Universal Negro Improvement Association he shall fight his way to victory, and in the days to come, and I believe not far distant, Africa shall reflect a splendid demonstration of the worth of the Negro, of the determination of the Negro, to set himself free and to establish a government of his own.

RACE PRIDE
W. E. B. DuBOIS

Our friends are hard—very hard—to please. Only yesterday they were preaching "Race Pride."

"Go to!" they said, "and be PROUD of your race."

If we hesitated or sought to explain—"Away," they yelled; "Ashamed-of-Yourself and Want-to-be-White!"

Of course, the Amazing Major is still at it, but do you notice that others say less—because they see that bull-headed worship of any "race," as such, may lead and does lead to curious complications?

For instance: Today Negroes, Indians, Chinese, and other groups, are gaining new faith in themselves; they are beginning to "like" themselves; they are discovering that the current theories and stories of "backward" peoples are largely lies and assumptions; that human genius and possibility are not limited by color, race, or blood. What is this new self-consciousness leading to? Inevitably and directly to distrust and hatred of whites; to demands for self-government, separation, driving out of foreigners: "Asia for the Asiatics," "Africa for the Africans," and "Negro officers for Negro troops!"

No sooner do whites see this unawaited development than they point out in dismay the inevitable consequences: "You lose our tutelage," "You spurn our knowledge," "You need our wealth and technique." They point out how fine is the world rôle of Elder Brother.

Very well. Some of the darker brethren are convinced. They draw near in friendship; they seek to enter schools and churches; they would mingle in industry—when lo! "Get out," yells the White World—"You're not our brothers and never will be"—"Go away, herd by yourselves"—"Eternal Segregation in the Lord!"

Can you wonder, Sirs, that we are a bit puzzled by all this and that we are asking gently, but more and more insistently, Choose one or the other horn of the dilemma:

1. Leave the black and yellow world alone. Get out of Asia, Africa, and the Isles. Give us our states and towns and sections and let us rule them undisturbed. Absolutely segregate the races and sections of the world

Or—

2. Let the world meet as men with men. Give utter Justice to all. Extend Democracy to all and treat all men according to their individual desert. Let it be possible for whites to rise to the highest positions in China and Uganda and blacks to the highest honors in England and Texas.

Here is the choice. Which will you have, my masters?

From *Crisis,* Vol. XIX (1920).

HARLEM RENAISSANCE: THE URBAN SETTING

2

Harlem became a black section of New York in the early years of the 1914–18 war. To most Afro-Americans Harlem came to symbolize a new age of urbanity and sophistication for blacks in America. Of course, blacks produced works of art elsewhere in the United States, but Harlem put its stamp on the movement because it seemed to represent all that was most advanced in thought and culture. Naturally, the writings of the Renaissance had a strong urban flavor.

In 1925 Alain Locke, a professor of philosophy at Howard University, brought out a collection of essays, stories, and poetry called The New Negro. His introductory essay served to redefine the "New Negro" in cultural terms, almost ignoring the political emphasis of a decade earlier. It is fair to say that the Harlem Renaissance began with the publication of this volume.

James Weldon Johnson actually witnessed the transformation of Harlem from a white to a black section of Manhattan. His description of blacks in New York City in the years around World War I remains the most lucid, and his Black Manhattan suggests the optimism one could feel about Harlem as late as 1930.

The autobiographical writings, as well as poetry and stories, of such men as Langston Hughes and Claude McKay are as much about the impact of Harlem and New York City on them as they are about any other theme. We have included selections from these men's autobiographies to depict the city, of course, but also the youthfulness and exuberance of the period.

City themes provoked realism in the writings of many. Rudolph Fisher, novelist and medical doctor, illustrates city-wise realism in his story "Blades of Steel." Eric Walrond, the West Indian writer, suggests the citified artificiality in an act so natural as love-making. Richard Bruce's story fragment "Smoke, Lilies, and Jade" appeared in the only issue of the little magazine Fire. In his writing, realism had become decadence. All of these writers show a willingness to explore themes that were not normally treated in American literature.

Harlem became as important to whites as to blacks. Rudolph Fisher's article on white people invading Harlem reflects the amusement that most blacks felt about the phenomenon. Nancy Cunard, a daughter of British nobility, gives another perspective in "Harlem Revisited." It is worth considering what was so important about blacks and Harlem for white people.

HARLEM DIRECTORY
WHERE TO GO AND WHAT TO DO
WHEN IN HARLEM

There are four main attractions in Harlem: the churches, the gin mills, the restaurants, and the night clubs. It is not necessary here to define what churches are, so we will proceed to give a list of those which attract the largest congregations:

St. Mark's A.M.E.,
138th Street and St. Nicholas Avenue.
St. Philip's Episcopal,
133rd Street, between 7th and 8th Avenue.
Abyssinian Baptist,
138th Street, between Lenox and 7th.
Mother Zion,
136th Street, between Lenox and 7th.
Salem M.E.,
129th Street and 7th Avenue.
Metropolitan Baptist,
128th Street and 7th Avenue.
St. Mark's Catholic,
138th Street and Lenox Avenue.
Mt. Olivet Baptist,
120th Street and Lenox Avenue.
Grace Congregational,
139th Street, between 8th Avenue and Edgecombe Avenue.

And there are innumerable smaller churches and missions, countless spiritualists' rooms, a synagogue, a mosque, and a great number of Holy Roller refuges, the most interesting of which is at 1 West 137th Street.

Gin mills are establishments which have bars, family entrances, and other pre-Volstead luxuries. For reasons best known to ourselves and the owners of these places we will not give the addresses and even were these reasons not personal, there are far too many gin mills to list here. As a clue to those of our readers who might be interested we will tell them to notice what stands on every corner on 7th, Lenox, and 8th Avenues. There are also many such comfort stations in the middle of the blocks.

The best restaurants to go to in Harlem are Tabb's, located at 140th Street and Lenox Avenue, where you can get a good chicken dinner in the Grill Room and have ragtime music while you eat. The Marguerite, on 132nd Street between Lenox and Seventh Avenues, guarantees you a full stomach. Johnny Jackson's at 135th Street and Seventh Avenue. St. Luke's on 130th Street, between Lenox and Seventh. The Venetian Tea Room on 135th Street, between Seventh and Eighth Avenues, and the Blue Grass at 130th Street and Seventh Avenue, are also good bets. If you are broke and want

From *Harlem,* Vol. I (November 1928).

only coffee and rolls or a piece of pie, there are Coffee Pots next to every gin mill or if you should wish vino with your dinner there is the La Rosa on Seventh Avenue near 139th Street.

Among the best known Harlem night clubs are the Cotton Club at 142nd Street and Lenox Avenue; the Lenox Avenue Club on Lenox Avenue, between 142nd and 143rd Streets; Cairo's on 125th Street, between Lenox and Fifth Avenues; the Sugar Cane at 135th Street and 5th Avenue; Small's at 135th Street and 7th Avenue; Barron's at 134th Street and 7th Avenue; Connie's Inn at 131st Street and 7th Avenue; Club Harlem at 129th Street and Lenox Avenue, and the Bamboo Inn at 139th Street and 7th Avenue. Most of these places with the exception of The Cotton Club and Connie's Inn are fairly reasonable and are generally packed, but if you really desire a good time, make friends with some member on the staff of HARLEM and have him take you to Mexico's or to Pod and Jerry's or to the Paper Mill. We warn you that only the elect and the pure in heart are admitted to these places.

THE NEW NEGRO
ALAIN LOCKE

In the last decade something beyond the watch and guard of statistics has happened in the life of the American Negro and the three norns who have traditionally presided over the Negro problem have a changeling in their laps. The Sociologist, the Philanthropist, the Race-leader are not unaware of the New Negro, but they are at a loss to account for him. He simply cannot be swathed in their formulae. For the younger generation is vibrant with a new psychology; the new spirit is awake in the masses, and under the very eyes of the professional observers is transforming what has been a perennial problem into the progressive phases of contemporary Negro life.

Could such a metamorphosis have taken place as suddenly as it has appeared to? The answer is no; not because the New Negro is not here, but because the Old Negro had long become more of a myth than a man. The Old Negro, we must remember, was a creature of moral debate and historical controversy. His has been a stock figure perpetuated as an historical fiction partly in innocent sentimentalism, partly in deliberate reactionism. The Negro himself has contributed his share to this through a sort of protective social mimicry forced upon him by the adverse circumstances of dependence. So for generations in the mind of America, the Negro has been more of a formula than a human being—a something to be argued about, condemned or defended, to be "kept down," or "in his place," or "helped up," to be worried with or worried over, harassed or patronized, a social bogey or a social burden. The thinking Negro even has been induced to share this same general attitude, to focus his attention on controversial issues, to see himself in the distorted perspective of a social problem. His shadow, so to speak, has been more real to him than his personality. Through having had to appeal from the unjust stereotypes of his oppressors and traducers to those of his liberators, friends and benefactors he has had to subscribe to the traditional positions from which his case has been viewed. Little true social or self-understanding has or could come from such a situation.

But while the minds of most of us, black and white, have thus burrowed in the trenches of the Civil War and Reconstruction, the actual march of development has simply flanked these positions, necessitating a sudden reorientation of view. We have not been watching in the right direction; set North and South on a sectional axis, we have not noticed the East till the sun has us blinking.

Recall how suddenly the Negro spirituals revealed themselves; suppressed for generations under the stereotypes of Wesleyan hymn harmony, secretive, half-ashamed, until the courage of being natural brought them out—and behold, there was folk-music. Similarly the mind of the Negro seems suddenly to have slipped from under the tyranny of social intimidation and to be shaking off the psychology of imitation and implied inferiority. By shedding the old chrysalis of the Negro problem we are achieving something like a spiritual emancipation. Until recently, lacking self-understanding, we have been almost as much of a problem to ourselves as we still are to others. But the decade that found us with a problem has left us with only a task. The multitude perhaps feels as yet only a strange relief and a new vague urge, but the thinking few know that in the reaction the vital inner grip of prejudice has been broken.

With this renewed self-respect and self-dependence, the life of the Negro community is bound to enter a new dynamic phase, the buoyancy from within compensating for whatever pressure there may be of conditions from without. The migrant masses, shifting from countryside to city, hurdle several generations of experience at a leap, but more important, the same thing happens spiritually in the life-attitudes and self-expression of the Young Negro, in his poetry, his art, his education and his new outlook, with the additional advantage, of course, of the poise and greater certainty of knowing what it is all about. From this comes the promise and warrant of a new leadership. As one of them has discerningly put it:

> We have tomorrow
> Bright before us
> Like a flame.
>
> Yesterday, a night-gone thing
> A sun-down name.
>
> And Dawn today
> Broad arch above the road we came.
> We march!

This is what, even more than any "most creditable record of fifty years of freedom," requires that the Negro of to-day be seen through other than the dusty spectacles of past controversy. The day of "aunties," "uncles" and "mammies" is equally gone. Uncle Tom and Sambo have passed on, and even the "Colonel" and "George" play barnstorm rôles from which they escape with relief when the public spotlight is off. The popular melodrama has about played itself out, and it is time to scrap the fictions, garret the bogeys and settle down to a realistic facing of facts.

First we must observe some of the changes which since the traditional lines of opinion were drawn have rendered these quite obsolete. A main change has been, of course, that shifting of the Negro population which has made the Negro problem no longer exclusively or even predominantly Southern. Why should our minds remain sectionalized, when the problem itself no longer is? Then the trend of migration has not only been toward the North and the Central Midwest, but city-ward and to the great centers of industry—the problems of adjustment are new, practical, local and not peculiarly racial. Rather they are an integral part of the large industrial and social problems of our present-day democracy. And finally, with the Negro rapidly in process of class differentiation, if it ever was warrantable to regard and treat the Negro *en masse* it is becoming with every day less possible, more unjust and more ridiculous.

In the very process of being transplanted, the Negro is becoming transformed.

The tide of Negro migration, northward and city-ward, is not to be fully explained as a blind flood started by the demands of war industry coupled with the shutting off of foreign migration, or by the pressure of poor crops coupled with increased social terrorism in certain sections of the South and Southwest. Neither labor demand, the boll weevil nor the Ku Klux Klan is a basic factor, however contributory any or all of them may have been. The wash and rush of this human tide on the beach line of the northern city centers is to be explained primarily in terms of a new vision of opportunity, of social and economic freedom, of a spirit to seize, even in the face of an extortionate and heavy toll, a chance for the improvement of conditions. With each successive wave of it, the movement of the Negro becomes more and more a mass movement toward the larger and the more democratic chance—in the Negro's case a deliberate flight not only from countryside to city, but from medieval America to modern.

Take Harlem as an instance of this. Here in Manhattan is not merely the largest Negro community in the world, but the first concentration in history of so many diverse elements of Negro life. It has attracted the African, the West Indian, the Negro American; has brought together the Negro of the North and the Negro of the South; the man from the city and the man from the town and village; the peasant, the student, the business man, the professional man, artist, poet, musician, adventurer and worker, preacher and criminal, exploiter and social outcast. Each group has come with its own separate motives and for its own special ends, but their greatest experience has been the finding of one another. Proscription and prejudice have thrown these dissimilar elements into a common area of contact and interaction. Within this area, race sympathy and unity have determined a further fusing of sentiment and experience. So what began in terms of segregation becomes more and more, as its elements mix and react, the laboratory of a great race-welding. Hitherto, it must be admitted that American Negroes have been a race more in name than in fact, or to be exact, more in sentiment than in experience. The chief bond between them has been that of a common condition rather than a common consciousness; a problem in common rather than a life in common. In Harlem, Negro life is seizing upon its first chances for group expression and self-determination. It is—or promises at least to be—a race capital. That is why our comparison is taken with those nascent centers of folk-expression and self-determination which are playing a creative part in the world to-day. Without pretense to their political significance, Harlem has the same rôle to play for the New Negro as Dublin has had for the New Ireland or Prague for the New Czechoslovakia.

Harlem, I grant you, isn't typical—but it is significant, it is prophetic. No sane observer, however sympathetic to the new trend, would contend that the great masses are articulate as yet, but they stir, they move, they are more than physically restless. The challenge of the new intellectuals among them is clear enough—the "race radicals" and realists who have broken with the old epoch of philanthropic guidance, sentimental appeal and protest. But are we after all only reading into the stirrings of a sleeping giant the dreams of an agitator? The answer is in the migrating peasant. It is the "man farthest down" who is most active in getting up. One of the most characteristic symptoms of this is the professional man himself migrating to recapture his constituency after a vain effort to maintain in some Southern corner what for years back seemed an established living and clientele. The clergyman following his errant flock, the physician or lawyer trailing his clients, supply the true clues. In a real sense it is the rank and file who are leading, and the leaders who are following. A transformed and transforming psychology permeates the masses.

When the racial leaders of twenty years ago spoke of developing race-pride and stimulating race-consciousness, and of the desirability of race solidarity, they could not in any accurate degree have anticipated the abrupt feeling that has surged up and now pervades the awakened centers. Some of the recognized Negro leaders and a powerful section of white opinion identified with "race work" of the older order have indeed attempted to discount this feeling as a "passing phase," an attack of "race nerves" so to speak, an "aftermath of the war," and the like. It has not abated, however, if we are to gauge by the present tone and temper of the Negro press, or by the shift in popular support from the officially recognized and orthodox spokesmen to those of the independent, popular, and often radical type who are unmistakable symptoms of a new order. It is a social disservice to blunt the fact that the Negro of the Northern centers has reached a stage where tutelage, even of the most interested and well-intentioned sort, must give place to new relationships, where positive self-direction must be reckoned with in ever increasing measure. The American mind must reckon with a fundamentally changed Negro.

The Negro too, for his part, has idols of the tribe to smash. If on the one hand the white man has erred in making the Negro appear to be that which would excuse or extenuate his treatment of him, the Negro, in turn, has too often unnecessarily excused himself because of the way he has been treated. The intelligent Negro of to-day is resolved not to make discrimination an extenuation for his shortcomings in performance, individual or collective; he is trying to hold himself at par, neither inflated by sentimental allowances nor depreciated by current social discounts. For this he must know himself and be known for precisely what he is, and for that reason he welcomes the new scientific rather than the old sentimental interest. Sentimental interest in the Negro has ebbed. We used to lament this as the falling off of our friends; now we rejoice and pray to be delivered both from self-pity and condescension. The mind of each racial group has had a bitter weaning, apathy or hatred on one side matching disillusionment or resentment on the other; but they face each other to-day with the possibility at least of entirely new mutual attitudes.

It does not follow that if the Negro were better known, he would be better liked or better treated. But mutual understanding is basic for any subsequent coöperation and adjustment. The effort toward this will at least have the effect of remedying in large part what has been the most unsatisfactory feature of our present stage of race relationships in America, namely the fact that the more intelligent and representative elements of the two race groups have at so many points got quite out of vital touch with one another.

The fiction is that the life of the races is separate, and increasingly so. The fact is that they have touched too closely at the unfavorable and too lightly at the favorable levels.

While inter-racial councils have sprung up in the South, drawing on forward elements of both races, in the Northern cities manual laborers may brush elbows in their everyday work, but the community and business leaders have experienced no such interplay or far too little of it. These segments must achieve contact or the race situation in America becomes desperate. Fortunately this is happening. There is a growing realization that in social effort the co-operative basis must supplant long-distance philanthropy, and that the only safeguard for mass relations in the future must be provided in the carefully maintained contacts of the enlightened minorities of both race groups. In the intellectual realm a renewed and keen curiosity is replacing the recent apathy; the Negro is being carefully studied, not just talked about and discussed. In art and letters, instead of being wholly caricatured, he is being seriously portrayed and painted.

To all of this the New Negro is keenly responsive as an augury of a new democracy in American culture. He is contributing his share to the new social understanding. But the desire to be understood would never in itself have been sufficient to have opened so completely the protectively closed portals of the thinking Negro's mind. There is still too much possibility of being snubbed or patronized for that. It was rather the necessity for fuller, truer self-expression, the realization of the unwisdom of allowing social discrimination to segregate him mentally, and a counter-attitude to cramp and fetter his own living—and so the "spite-wall" that the intellectuals built over the "color-line" has happily been taken down. Much of this reopening of intellectual contacts has centered in New York and has been richly fruitful not merely in the enlarging of personal experience, but in the definite enrichment of American art and letters and in the clarifying of our common vision of the social tasks ahead.

The particular significance in the re-establishment of contact between the more advanced and representative classes is that it promises to offset some of the unfavorable reactions of the past, or at least to re-surface race contacts somewhat for the future. Subtly the conditions that are molding a New Negro are molding a new American attitude.

However, this new phase of things is delicate; it will call for less charity but more justice; less help, but infinitely closer understanding. This is indeed a critical stage of race relationships because of the likelihood, if the new temper is not understood, of engendering sharp group antagonism and a second crop of more calculated prejudice. In some quarters, it has already done so. Having weaned the Negro, public opinion cannot continue to paternalize. The Negro to-day is inevitably moving forward under the control largely of his own objectives. What are these objectives? Those of his outer life are happily already well and finally formulated, for they are none other than the ideals of American institutions and democracy. Those of his inner life are yet in process of formation, for the new psychology at present is more of a consensus of feeling than of opinion, of attitude rather than of program. Still some points seem to have crystallized.

Up to the present one may adequately describe the Negro's "inner objectives" as an attempt to repair a damaged group psychology and reshape a warped social perspective. Their realization has required a new mentality for the American Negro. And as it matures we begin to see its effects; at first, negative, iconoclastic, and then positive and constructive. In this new group psychology we note the lapse of sentimental appeal, then the development of a more positive self-respect and self-reliance; the repudiation of social dependence, and then the gradual recovery from hyper-sensitiveness and "touchy" nerves, the repudiation of the double standard of judgment with its special philanthropic allowances and then the sturdier desire for objective and scientific appraisal; and finally the rise from social disillusionment to race pride, from the sense of social debt to the responsibilities of social contribution, and offsetting the necessary working and commonsense acceptance of restricted conditions, the belief in ultimate esteem and recognition. Therefore the Negro to-day wishes to be known for what he is, even in his faults and shortcomings, and scorns a craven and precarious survival at the price of seeming to be what he is not. He resents being spoken of as a social ward or minor, even by his own, and to being regarded a chronic patient for the sociological clinic, the sick man of American Democracy. For the same reasons, he himself is through with those social nostrums and panaceas, the so-called "solutions" of his "problem," with which he and the country have been so liberally dosed in the past. Religion, freedom, education, money—in turn, he has ardently hoped for and peculiarly trusted these things; he still believes in them, but not in blind trust that they alone will solve his life-problem.

Each generation, however, will have its creed, and that of the present is the belief in the efficacy of collective effort, in race co-operation. This deep feeling of race is at present the mainspring of Negro life. It seems to be the outcome of the reaction to proscription and prejudice; an attempt, fairly successful on the whole, to convert a defensive into an offensive position, a handicap into an incentive. It is radical in tone, but not in purpose and only the most stupid forms of opposition, misunderstanding or persecution could make it otherwise. Of course, the thinking Negro has shifted a little toward the left with the world-trend, and there is an increasing group who affiliate with radical and liberal movements. But fundamentally for the present the Negro is radical on race matters, conservative on others, in other words, a "forced radical," a social protestant rather than a genuine radical. Yet under further pressure and injustice iconoclastic thought and motives will inevitably increase. Harlem's quixotic radicalisms call for their ounce of democracy to-day lest to-morrow they be beyond cure.

The Negro mind reaches out as yet to nothing but American wants, American ideas. But this forced attempt to build his Americanism on race values is a unique social experiment, and its ultimate success is impossible except through the fullest sharing of American culture and institutions. There should be no delusion about this. American nerves in sections unstrung with race hysteria are often fed the opiate that the trend of Negro advance is wholly separatist, and that the effect of its operation will be to encyst the Negro as a benign foreign body in the body politic. This cannot be—even if it were desirable. The racialism of the Negro is no limitation or reservation with respect to American life; it is only a constructive effort to build the obstructions in the stream of his progress into an efficient dam of social energy and power. Democracy itself is obstructed and stagnated to the extent that any of its channels are closed. Indeed they cannot be selectively closed. So the choice is not between one way for the Negro and another way for the rest, but between American institutions frustrated on the one hand and American ideals progressively fulfilled and realized on the other.

There is, of course, a warrantably comfortable feeling in being on the right side of the country's professed ideals. We realize that we cannot be undone without America's undoing. It is within the gamut of this attitude that the thinking Negro faces America, but with variations of mood that are if anything more significant than the attitude itself. Sometimes we have it taken with the defiant ironic challenge of McKay:

> Mine is the future grinding down to-day
> Like a great landslip moving to the sea,
> Bearing its freight of debris far away

> Where the green hungry waters restlessly
> Heave mammoth pyramids, and break and roar
> Their eerie challenge to the crumbling shore.

Sometimes, perhaps more frequently as yet, it is taken in the fervent and almost filial appeal and counsel of Weldon Johnson's:

> O Southland, dear Southland!
> Then why do you still cling
> To an idle age and a musty page,
> To a dead and useless thing?

But between defiance and appeal, midway almost between cynicism and hope, the prevailing mind stands in the mood of the same author's *To America,* an attitude of sober query and stoical challenge:

> How would you have us, as we are?
>   Or sinking 'neath the load we bear,
> Our eyes fixed forward on a star,
>   Or gazing empty at despair?
>
> Rising or falling? Men or things?
>   With dragging pace or footsteps fleet?
> Strong, willing sinews in your wings,
>   Or tightening chains about your feet?

More and more, however, an intelligent realization of the great discrepancy between the American social creed and the American social practice forces upon the Negro the taking of the moral advantage that is his. Only the steadying and sobering effect of a truly characteristic gentleness of spirit prevents the rapid rise of a definite cynicism and counter-hate and a defiant superiority feeling. Human as this reaction would be, the majority still deprecate its advent, and would gladly see it forestalled by the speedy amelioration of its causes. We wish our race pride to be a healthier, more positive achievement than a feeling based upon a realization of the short-comings of others. But all paths toward the attainment of a sound social attitude have been difficult; only a relatively few enlightened minds have been able as the phrase puts it "to rise above" prejudice. The ordinary man has had until recently only a hard choice between the alternatives of supine and humiliating submission and stimulating but hurtful counter-prejudice. Fortunately from some inner, desperate resourcefulness has recently sprung up the simple expedient of fighting prejudice by mental passive resistance, in other words by trying to ignore it. For the few, this manna may perhaps be effective, but the masses cannot thrive upon it.

Fortunately there are constructive channels opening out into which the balked social feelings of the American Negro can flow freely.

Without them there would be much more pressure and danger than there is. These compensating interests are racial but in a new and enlarged way. One is the consciousness of acting as the advance-guard of the African peoples in their contact with Twentieth Century civilization; the other, the sense of a mission of rehabilitating the race in world esteem from that loss of prestige for which the fate and conditions of slavery have so largely been responsible. Harlem, as we shall see, is the center of both these movements; she is the home of the Negro's "Zionism." The pulse of the Negro world has begun to beat in Harlem. A Negro newspaper carrying news material in English, French and Spanish, gathered from all quarters of America, the West Indies and Africa has maintained itself in Harlem for over five years. Two important magazines, both edited from New York, maintain their news and circulation consistently on a cosmopolitan scale. Under American auspices and backing, three pan-African congresses have been held abroad for the discussion of common interests, colonial questions and the future cooperative development of Africa. In terms of the race question as a world problem, the Negro mind has leapt, so to speak, upon the parapets of prejudice and extended its cramped horizons. In so doing it has linked up with the growing group consciousness of the dark-peoples and is gradually learning their common interests. As one of our writers has recently put it: "It is imperative that we understand the white world in its relations to the non-white world." As with the Jew, persecution is making the Negro international.

As a world phenomenon this wider race consciousness is a different thing from the much asserted rising tide of color. Its inevitable causes are not of our making. The consequences are not necessarily damaging to the best interests of civilization. Whether it actually brings into being new Armadas of conflict or argosies of cultural exchange and enlightenment can only be decided by the attitude of the dominant races in an era of critical change. With the American Negro, his new internationalism is primarily an effort to recapture contact with the scattered peoples of African derivation. Garveyism may be a transient, if spectacular, phenomenon, but the possible role of the American Negro in the future development of Africa is one of the most constructive and universally helpful missions that any modern people can lay claim to.

Constructive participation in such causes cannot help giving the Negro valuable group incentives, as well as increased prestigé at home and abroad. Our greatest rehabilitation may possibly come through such channels, but for the present, more immediate hope rests in the revaluation by white and black alike of the Negro in terms of his artistic endowments and cultural contributions, past and prospective. It must be increasingly recognized that the Negro has already made very substantial contributions, not only in his folk-art, music especially, which has always found appreciation, but in larger, though humbler and less acknowledged ways. For generations the Negro has been the peasant matrix of that section of America which has most undervalued him, and here he has contributed not only materially in labor and in social patience, but spiritually as well. The South has unconsciously absorbed the gift of his folk-temperament. In less than half a generation it will be easier to recognize this, but the fact remains that a leaven of humor, sentiment, imagination and tropic nonchalance has gone into the making of the South from a humble, unacknowledged source. A second crop of the Negro's gifts promises still more largely. He now becomes a conscious contributor and lays aside the status of a beneficiary and ward for that of a collaborator and participant in American civilization. The great social gain in this is the releasing of our talented group from the arid fields of controversy and debate to the productive fields of creative expression. The especially cultural recognition they win should in turn prove the key to that revaluation of the Negro which must precede or accompany any considerable further betterment of race relationships. But whatever the general effect, the present generation will have added the motives of self-expression and spiritual development to the old and still unfinished task of making material headway and progress. No one who understandingly faces the situation with its substantial accomplishment or views the new scene with its still more abundant promise can be entirely without hope. And certainly, if in our lifetime the Negro should not be able to celebrate his full initiation into American democracy, he can at least, on the warrant of these things, celebrate the attainment of a significant and satisfying new phase of group development, and with it a spiritual Coming of Age.

FROM
BLACK MANHATTAN
JAMES WELDON JOHNSON

XII

The year 1900 marked another epoch for the Negro in New York. On the night of August 12, a coloured man named Arthur Harris left his wife on the corner of Eighth Avenue and Forty-first Street for a moment to buy a cigar. When he returned he found her struggling in the grasp of a white man. Harris engaged with the man and was struck by him over the head with a club. He retaliated with a pocket-knife and inflicted a wound which proved fatal. He thereupon ran away. The white man was Robert J. Thorpe, a police officer in plain clothes, who claimed that he had arrested the woman for "soliciting." Thorpe was very popular with his brother officers, and his funeral was attended by a large contingent of the police force, in addition to a great throng of friends, sympathizers, and those drawn by morbid curiosity. Harris had disappeared; and during the day of the funeral the temper of the crowd to wreak vengeance upon some vicarious victim grew strong. As the day closed, rumours that there was going to be trouble flew faster and faster.

Early in the evening of August 15 the fourth great New York race riot burst in full fury. A mob of several thousands raged up and down Eighth Avenue and through the side streets from Twenty-seventh to Forty-second. Negroes were seized wherever they were found, and brutally beaten. Men and women were dragged from street-cars and assaulted. When Negroes ran to policemen for protection, even begging to be locked up for safety, they were thrown back to the mob. The police themselves beat many Negroes as cruelly as did the mob. An intimate friend of mine was one of those who ran to the police for protection; he received such a clubbing at their hands that he had to be taken to the hospital to have his scalp stitched in several places. It was a beating from which he never fully recovered.

During the height of the riot the cry went out to "get Ernest Hogan and Williams and Walker and Cole and Johnson." These seemed to be the only individual names the crowd was familiar with. Ernest Hogan was at the time playing at the New York Winter Garden, in Times Square; for safety he was kept in the theatre all night. George Walker had a narrow escape. The riot of 1900 was a brutish orgy, which, if it was not incited by the police, was, to say the least, abetted by them.

But this fourth of the great New York riots involving the Negro was really symptomatic of a national condition. The status of the Negro as a citizen had been steadily declining for twenty-five years; and at the opening of the twentieth century his civil state was, in some respects, worse than at the close of the Civil War. At the opening of the twentieth century the War Amendments passed in the Negro's behalf had been completely nullified or evaded in the Southern states; and he was disfranchised, "Jim Crowed," outraged, and denied the equal protection of the laws. In the decade ending in 1899, according to the records printed in the daily press, 1,665 Negroes were lynched, many of them with sadistic savagery, even by mutilation and by burning alive at the stake in the presence of great crowds. And these debauches in bestiality aroused no action on the part of the country nor any general protest. The outlook was dark and discouraging. The Negro himself had in a large measure lost heart. The movement that Frederick Douglass had so valiantly carried forward had all but subsided. The general spirit of the race was one of hopelessness or acquiescence. The only way to survival seemed along the road of sheer opportunism and of conformity to the triumphant materialism of the age. Idealism linked with courage was scarcely discernible. Nor did these conditions pertain solely to the South. The South lost the Civil War in 1865, but by 1900, in the fight waged on the Negro battle front, it had conquered the North; and all through the old free states there was a tendency to concede that the grand experiment was a failure.

Nowhere in the country was this decline in the spirit of self-assertion of rights more marked than in New York. A comparison between the times of Douglass, Garnett, and Crummell and the opening of the new century was like a comparison between the light of a tropic noon and a winter twilight. But the riot of 1900 woke Negro New York and stirred the old fighting spirit.

The answer to demands for an investigation of the riot was a series of excuses and delays on the part of the municipality and the police authorities; then the coloured citizens took steps to force action. A meeting was called at St. Mark's Church in West Fifty-third Street, and the Citizens Protective League was organized. The Rev. William H. Brooks, the pastor of the church, was made president; James E. Garner, a successful business man, was made treasurer; and T. Thomas Fortune was elected chairman of the executive committee. Mr. Fortune was editor of the New York *Age,* the oldest Negro newspaper in New York, and a writer of marked ability. For many years he was the acknowledged leader in the Negro newspaper world; and for a while he contributed a regular column to the New York *Sun.* In ability and courage he was a direct descendant of the leaders of twenty-five years before. The Citizens Protective League held a mass meeting in Carnegie Hall on September 12, and funds were raised. The organization retained a lawyer to prosecute police officers; and its membership grew to about five thousand. The league in a letter to Mayor Van Wyck demanded the conviction and removal from the force of those officers they were able to prove guilty of malfeasance or nonfeasance. The Mayor replied that the whole matter was in the hands of the Police Board. Finally an investigation was held in which coloured citizens who testified to having been beaten by the police were themselves treated as persons accused of crime, and the testimony of each was simply rebutted by policemen who were called to testify. The investigation turned out to be a sham and a whitewash; nevertheless, the Negroes of New York, moved by this sudden realization of their danger, had taken a step towards making that city anew the chief radiating centre of the forces contending for equal rights.

A promising move in this same direction had been made in 1889, when T. Thomas Fortune issued a call for the formation of the thinking and progressive coloured people of the country into a national organization to protest against the increasing disabilities and injustices to which the race was being subjected. The call was answered by one hundred and forty-one delegates from twenty-one states, who met in Chicago, January 15, 1890, and organized the Afro-American Council. J. C. Price, the head of Livingstone College in North Carolina, a man who had achieved considerable prestige as a leader, was chosen president, and T. Thomas Fortune, secretary. The following year the council met at Knoxville, Tennessee, and Mr. Fortune succeeded Mr. Price as president. The organization then lay dormant until 1898, when Bishop Alexander Walters, of New York, stirred by fresh outrages against Negroes, issued a call to Mr. Fortune to reassemble the council. The result was a meeting on September 15 of the same year at Rochester, New York, with one hundred and fifty delegates present, at the time when the monument to Frederick Douglass was being unveiled in that city. Another meeting was held at Washington in December to finish the business of the Rochester meeting. But the Afro-American Council did not realize its aim; it found it impossible to arouse the sort of spirit and response on the part of the coloured people of the country necessary for the real growth of the organization; nor was it able to raise sufficient funds to create a permanent and efficient machine; so after a somewhat languishing existence of several years longer, it died. But it had accomplished something; it had pointed the way—not a new one but the old one—and it was to be followed by a similar effort made in what was more nearly the fullness of time.

In 1895 Booker T. Washington made his epochal Atlanta speech. He had for ten years prior to that occasion been a rising figure, but after it his increase in power and prestige was so rapid that almost immediately he found himself the recognized leader of the Negro race. By his Atlanta speech he had at a stroke gained the sanction and support of both the South and the North—the South, in general, construing the speech to imply the Negro's abdication of his claim to full and equal citizenship rights, and his acceptance of the status of a contented and industrious peasantry; the North feeling that the opportunity had arisen to rid its conscience of a disturbing question and shift it over to the South. The great body of the Negroes, discouraged, bewildered, and leaderless, hailed Mr. Washington as a Moses. This was, indeed, a remarkable feat—his holding the South in one hand, the North in the other, and at the same time carrying the major portion of his race along with him. The feat of uniting these three factions in the attempt to benefit the third had been tried before, but never achieved; and the founder of Tuskegee was the first to approach an accomplishment of it. The fact that he succeeded so far as he did, notwithstanding the popular conception of him as only an earnest educator and an energetic builder, stamps him as one of the world's ablest diplomats. At the height of his career Booker T. Washington was by long odds the most distinguished man the South had produced after the era following that of the Civil War heroes. There can hardly be an intelligent American who would not be thrilled by the sheer romance of his life's story. Born a slave amidst a squalor and poverty difficult to describe; as a child sleeping "in and on a bundle of filthy rags laid upon the dirt floor"; [1] knowing nothing of his father, and set free at emancipation a ragged, illiterate, penniless bit of humanity, not possessing even a name beyond Booker; he rose to make the name of his own taking known throughout the world and to acquire a degree of power and influence second to that of no private individual in the country. Born in a log cabin where there was no such thing as a table, but where the children were handed a piece of bread here and a scrap of meat there, he lived to sit at table with the President of the United States, and to sip tea with the Queen of England. There is no more magical page in the *Arabian Nights.*

Dr. Washington encountered criticism from men of his own race. His critics felt that he was yielding more than what would be the ultimate worth of what he gained. The criticism grew louder, but it was not formulated, and the dissenters were without an authoritative voice. There was criticism of the fact that the doctrine of industrial education had been interpreted as meaning that it was the only education the Negro race would need to fit it for the place it was to occupy. There was also criticism of the minifying of political and civil rights. Over against these criticisms stood the great, concrete demonstration, Tuskegee; endorsed by the South, supported by the North, and not only doing a tremendous work for the Negroes of the South,

1. Booker T. Washington: *Up from Slavery.* New York, Doubleday, Page and Company.

but wielding an increasing influence on educational ideas with regard to the white youth of the country. In the face of these solid achievements the criticisms took on a doctrinaire aspect, an aspect of bickering and faultfinding.

In 1903 a book came out of Atlanta, written by a professor at Atlanta University. The book was *The Souls of Black Folk,* and the author was W. E. Burghardt Du Bois. The author of *The Souls of Black Folk,* like the author of *Up from Slavery,* was a Negro, but, aside from that, their antecedents were quite different. Du Bois was born two years after the close of the Civil War in a beautiful, cultured New England Town, Great Barrington, Massachusetts. He was educated in the grammar and high schools of his native town; then at Fisk University; then at Harvard; and then at the University of Berlin. He experienced the pride of knowing his ancestry; three generations of his forebears lay in the Great Barrington cemetery. When he began active life, it was with greater intellectual preparation than any American Negro had yet acquired. This book of his was at once hailed as a great book. It was a collection of essays, one of which was headed "Of Mr. Washington and Others" and contained an estimate of Booker T. Washington and a statement of the points on which the author differed with him. Because of the criticism it voiced, this chapter in the book immediately became the subject of a nation-wide controversy, especially sharp in the South; and the guns of criticism were turned upon Du Bois. But the chief significance of this essay lies in the effect wrought by it within the race. It brought about a coalescence of the more radical elements and made them articulate, thereby creating a split of the race into two contending camps, between which there has been a *rapprochement* only within the past ten years—a *rapprochement* achieved mostly through the moving over of the conservative group. And so, with the issuance of a book from Atlanta, a new leader stepped forth; and Du Bois found himself at the head of the scattered and almost silent remnants of the old militant Negro element.

Dr. Du Bois planned to bring the Negro militants together, and in answer to a call sent out by him, a conference was held, July 11–13, 1905, at Buffalo, New York. Twenty-nine coloured men were present from thirteen states and the District of Columbia. Three states of the old South—Georgia, Tennessee, and Virginia—were represented. A national organization was formed and called "the Niagara Movement." In the constitution that was adopted the following objects were stated: (a) freedom of speech and criticism; (b) an unfettered and unsubsidized press; (c) manhood suffrage; (d) the abolition of all caste distinctions based simply on race and colour; (e) the recognition of the principles of human brotherhood as a practical present creed; (f) the recognition of the highest and best human training as the monopoly of no class or race; (g) a belief in the dignity of labour; (h) united effort to realize these ideals under wise and courageous leadership.

The following year, in August, the Niagara Movement met at Harper's Ferry, the scene of John Brown's martyrdom, and adopted and sent out *An Address to the Country,* which, in part, read:

The men of the Niagara Movement coming from the toil of the year's hard work and pausing for a moment from the earning of their daily bread turn toward the nation and again ask in the name of ten million the privilege of a hearing. In the past year the work of the Negro hater has flourished in the land. Step by step the defenders of the rights of American citizens have retreated. The work of stealing the black man's ballot has progressed and the fifty and more representatives of stolen votes still sit in the nation's capital. Discrimination in travel and public accommodation has so spread that some of our weaker brethren are actually afraid to thunder against color discrimination as such and are simply whispering for ordinary decencies.

Against this the Niagara Movement eternally protests. We will not be satisfied to take one jot or tittle less than our full manhood rights. We claim for ourselves every single right that belongs to a freeborn American, political, civil and social; and until we get these rights we will never cease to protest and assail the ears of America. The battle we wage is not for ourselves alone but for all true Americans. It is a fight for ideals, lest this, our common fatherland, false to its founding, become in truth the land of the thief and the home of the Slave—a by-word and a hissing among the nations for its sounding pretensions and pitiful accomplishment.

Never before in the modern age has a great and civilized folk threatened to adopt so cowardly a creed in the treatment of its fellow-citizens born and bred on its soil. Stripped of verbiage and subterfuge and in its naked nastiness the new American creed says: Fear to let black men even try to rise lest they become the equals of the white. And this is the land that professes to follow Jesus Christ. The blasphemy of such a course is only matched by its cowardice.

In detail our demands are clear and unequivocal. First, we would vote; with the right to vote goes everything: Freedom, manhood, the honor of your wives, the chastity of your daughters, the right to work, and the chance to rise, and let no man listen to those who deny this.

We want full manhood suffrage, and we want it now, henceforth and forever.

Second. We want discrimination in public accommodation to cease. Separation in railway and street cars, based simply on race and color, is un-American, undemocratic, and silly. We protest against all such discrimination.

Third. We claim the right of freemen to walk, talk, and be with them that wish to be with us. No man has a right to choose another man's friends, and to attempt to do so is an impudent interference with the most fundamental human privilege.

Fourth. We want the laws enforced against rich as well as poor; against Capitalist as well as Laborer; against white as well as black. We are not more lawless than the white race, we are more often arrested, convicted, and mobbed. We want justice even for criminals and outlaws. We want the Constitution of the country enforced. We want Congress to take charge of Congressional elections. We want the Fourteenth Amendment carried out to the letter and every State disfranchised in Congress which attempts to disfranchise its rightful voters. We want the Fifteenth Amendment enforced and No State allowed to base its franchise simply on color.

The failure of the Republican Party in Congress at the session just closed to redeem its pledge of 1904 with reference to suffrage conditions at the South seems a plain, deliberate, and premeditated breach of promise, and stamps that party as guilty of obtaining votes under false pretenses.

Fifth. We want our children educated. The school system in the country districts of the South is a disgrace and in few towns and cities are the Negro schools what they ought to be. We want the national government to step in and wipe out illiteracy in the South. Either the United States will destroy ignorance or ignorance will destroy the United States.

And when we call for education we mean real education. We believe in work. We ourselves are workers, but work is not necessarily education. Education is the development of power and ideal. We want our children trained as intelligent human beings should be, and we will fight for all time against any proposal to educate black boys and girls simply as servants and underlings, or simply for the use of other people. They have a right to know, to think, to aspire.

These are some of the chief things which we want. How shall we get them? By voting where we may vote, by persistent, unceasing agitation; by hammering at the truth, by sacrifice and work.

Reading today the chapter from *The Souls of Black Folk,* "Of Mr. Washington and Others," it is, perhaps, impossible for those unfamiliar with the period to understand the extent of the reaction it caused and the bitterness of the animosities it aroused. The latter, at any rate, was due to causes not specifically contained in what Dr. Du Bois had written, but outside of it. The essay was not an attack. It contained no word of denunciation. Neither was there in it invective or irony, two of the author's favourite and most effective weapons. It was, in fact, a temperate analysis of Dr. Washington's position and policy and a rationally stated difference on certain points. The spirit of the whole essay can be fairly illustrated by two quotations, one near the beginning and the other near the end:

To gain the sympathy and cooperation of the various elements comprising the white South was Mr. Washington's first task; and this, at the time Tuskegee was founded, seemed, for a black man impossible. And yet ten years later it was done in the word spoken at Atlanta: "In all things purely social we can be as separate as the five fingers, and yet one as the hand in all things essential to material progress." This "Atlanta Compromise" is by all odds the most notable thing in Mr. Washington's career. The South interpreted it in different ways: the radicals received it as a complete surrender of the demand for civil and political equality; the conservatives as a generously conceived working basis for mutual understanding. So both approved it, and today its author is certainly the most distinguished Southerner since Jefferson Davis, and the one with the greatest personal following. . . .

The black men of America have a duty to perform, a duty stern and delicate,—a forward movement to oppose a part of the work of their greatest leader. So far as Mr. Washington preaches Thrift, Patience and Industrial Training for the masses, we must hold up his hands and strive with him, rejoicing in his honours and glorying in the strength of this Joshua called of God and of man to lead the headless host. But so far as Mr. Washington apologizes for injustice, North or South, does not rightly value the privilege and duty of voting, belittles the emasculating effects of caste distinctions, and opposes the higher training and ambition of our brightest minds,—so far as he, the South, or the nation, does this,—we must increasingly and firmly oppose them.

Much has happened and many changes have occurred in the North and in the South since those words were written. Last year the present head of Tuskegee, Dr. R. R. Moton, wrote a book, *What the Negro Thinks,*[1] which was in substance a restatement of the objects set forth by the Niagara Movement; and in answer he received words of approbation from the Southern press. The two groups once so sharply divided are today practically one, with regard to the fundamental aims of the American Negro. Dr. Moton says in his book: "In truth, they are working for the same thing in different spheres and by a different approach." In truth they have learned that a co-ordinated plan of battle calls for the militants to act as shock troops and for the conservatives to advance rapidly and hold the ground.

One of the visitors at the Harper's Ferry meeting of the Niagara Movement was Miss Mary White Ovington of New York, one of the few remaining inheritors of the abolition spirit, who had for several years been studying the condition of the Negro in the North and in the South. She went to report the conference for the New York *Evening Post.* In the fall of 1908, William English Walling had an article in the *Independent* on the race riots which had recently taken place in Springfield, Illinois, Abraham Lincoln's old home, in which Negroes had been beaten and killed in the streets of that city. After describing the brutalities committed upon coloured people in that outbreak, Mr. Walling declared: "Either the spirit of the abolitionists, of Lincoln and of Lovejoy, must be revived and we must come to treat the Negro on a plane of absolute political and social equality or Vardaman and Tillman will soon have transferred the Race War to the North." Miss Ovington wrote to Mr. Walling and later talked with him over the matter, together with Dr. Henry Moskowitz, early in January 1909. Plans were discussed for making a demonstration on February 12, the one hundredth anniversary of Abraham Lincoln's birth. Oswald Garrison Villard joined with the movement, and on Lincoln's birthday a call for a conference, drafted by Mr. Villard, was issued. Among the liberal whites who signed the call were Charles Edward Russell, Jane Addams, Samuel Bowles, John Dewey, Mary E. McDowell, John Haynes Holmes, Florence Kelley, Lillian D. Wald, John E. Milholland, Rabbi Stephen S. Wise, and William Dean Howells. Among the Negro liberals who joined in were Dr. W. E. Burghardt Du Bois, Bishop Alexander Walters, Ida Wells Barnett, and the Rev. Francis J. Grimké.

Charles Edward Russell, who had also talked with Mr. Walling following the appearance of the *Independent* article, was the presiding genius at the more or less stormy closing sessions of this first conference, when a temporary organization was formed. In May 1910 a second conference was held, in New York, at which there was consummated a merger of the forces of the Negro liberals of the Niagara Movement, and the white liberals of abolition traditions, thus forming the National Association for the Advancement of Colored People. The platform adopted was practically the same as that of

1. Robert Russa Moton: *What the Negro Thinks.* Garden City, Doubleday, Doran and Company, 1929.

the Niagara Movement. It was commented upon at the time as being extremely radical. In this same year the association called Dr. Du Bois to come as its Director of Publicity and Research. He resigned his professorship at Atlanta University and came to New York; and the publication of the *Crisis,* a monthly magazine, the organ of the association, with Dr. Du Bois as editor, was begun. The *Crisis* has now been doing pioneer work for twenty years; and Dr. Du Bois, more than any other one man, paved the way for the "New Negro." At about this time two other strong friends became allied with the movement, J. E. Spingarn and Arthur B. Spingarn.

The association has grown to be a powerful and effective organization. It has national headquarters in New York City and more than three hundred branches in forty-four states. Its record of accomplishment in the past twenty years is extraordinary. Besides its work in legal defence and its fight against lynching and against discriminations in the administration of the law, in facilities for education, and in the use of common carriers and places of public accommodation, it has carried to the United States Supreme Court and won four important and far-reaching decisions affecting the constitutional and citizenship rights of the American Negro. These were decisions in: the Louisville segregation case, the Arkansas peonage cases, the Texas white primary case, and the New Orleans segregation case. In addition it had a hand in winning the "grandfather clause" case.[1] One of the reasons for this degree of success in prosecuting the Negro's cause through the courts has been the fact that the association had the voluntary services of such lawyers as Moorfield Storey, Louis Marshall, Clarence Darrow, James A. Cobb, Charles H. Studin, and Arthur B. Spingarn as members of its legal committee.

The National Association for the Advancement of Colored People was the first and is still the only organization since the Anti-Slavery Society providing a common medium for the co-operation of blacks and whites in the work of securing and safeguarding the common citizenship rights of the Negro. With the founding of this association New York became again the centre of the organized forces of self-assertion of equal rights and of insistence upon the impartial application of the fundamental principles of the Republic, without regard to race, creed, or colour.

Shortly following the formation of the Advancement Association steps were taken which led to the establishment of another important national organization to work for the Negro, with headquarters in New York, the National League on Urban Conditions among Negroes. Among those who took part in the founding of the organization were: Mrs. Ruth Standish Baldwin, Edwin R. A. Seligman, Fred R. Moore, Miss Elizabeth Walton, L. Hollings-

---

1. "Grandfather clauses" began to be adopted in the constitutions of Southern states in 1898. They were disfranchising devices, in that they laid down as necessary to the right of suffrage a list of property, literacy, and character qualifications; and then provided that none of these qualifications need be met by any person who had the right to vote or had an ancestor who had the right to vote at the time of the close of the Civil War. The Supreme Court declared these clauses unconstitutional in 1915.

worth Wood, George E. Haynes, and Eugene Kinckle Jones. The main purpose for which this organization was formed was to work for the industrial, social, and health betterment of the coloured people, especially those living in urban centres. In addition to working for these ends, the Urban League has carried on research work and collected a great deal of valuable data and statistics on industrial, social, and health conditions among Negroes. It has grown rapidly and now has affiliated branches in the principal cities in all sections of the country. Each of these branch offices is manned by a trained secretary and social workers. The Urban League, like the Advancement Association, is an organization in which both races co-operate.

Ten years after the forming of these two bodies another organization destined to make Negro history in New York was in full swing—the Garvey movement.

The Negro population in 1910 of all the boroughs of the city was 91,709; and of Manhattan alone, 60,534.

XIII

If you ride northward the length of Manhattan Island, going through Central Park and coming out on Seventh Avenue or Lenox Avenue at One Hundred and Tenth Street, you cannot escape being struck by the sudden change in the character of the people you see. In the middle and lower parts of the city you have, perhaps, noted Negro faces here and there; but when you emerge from the Park, you see them everywhere, and as you go up either of these two great arteries leading out from the city to the north, you see more and more Negroes, walking in the streets, looking from the windows, trading in the shops, eating in the restaurants, going in and coming out of the theatres, until, nearing One Hundred and Thirty-fifth Street, ninety per cent of the people you see, including the traffic officers, are Negroes. And it is not until you cross the Harlem River that the population whitens again, which it does as suddenly as it began to darken at One Hundred and Tenth Street. You have been having an outside glimpse of Harlem, the Negro metropolis.

In nearly every city in the country the Negro section is a nest or several nests situated somewhere on the borders; it is a section one must "go out to." In New York it is entirely different. Negro Harlem is situated in the heart of Manhattan and covers one of the most beautiful and healthful sites in the whole city. It is not a fringe, it is not a slum, nor is it a "quarter" consisting of dilapidated tenements. It is a section of new-law apartment houses and handsome dwellings, with streets as well paved, as well lighted, and as well kept as in any other part of the city. Three main highways lead into and out from upper Manhattan, and two of them run straight through Harlem. So Harlem is not a section that one "goes out to," but a section that one goes through.

Roughly drawn, the boundaries of Harlem are: One Hundred and Tenth Street on the south; on the east, Lenox Avenue to One Hundred and Twenty-sixth Street, then Lexington Avenue to the Harlem River, and the

Harlem River on the east and north to a point where it passes the Polo Grounds, just above One Hundred and Fifty-fifth Street; on the west, Eighth Avenue to One Hundred and Sixteenth Street, then St. Nicholas Avenue up to a juncture with the Harlem River at the Polo Grounds. To the east of the Lenox Avenue boundary there are a score of blocks of mixed coloured and white population; and to the west of the Eighth Avenue boundary there is a solid Negro border, two blocks wide, from One Hundred and Sixteenth Street to One Hundred and Twenty-fifth Street. The heights north from One Hundred and Forty-fifth Street, known as Coogan's Bluff, are solidly black. Within this area of less than two square miles live more than two hundred thousand Negroes, more to the square acre than in any other place on earth.

This city within a city, in these larger proportions, is actually a development of the last fifteen years. The trek to Harlem began when the West Fifty-third Street centre had reached its utmost development; that is, early in the decade 1900–10. The move to West Fifty-third Street had been the result of the opportunity to get into better houses; and the move to Harlem was due to the same urge. In fact, Harlem offered the coloured people the first chance in their entire history in New York to live in modern apartment houses. West Fifty-third Street was superior to anything they had ever enjoyed; and there they were, for the most part, making private dwellings serve the purpose of apartments, housing several families in each house. The move to Harlem, in the beginning and for a long time, was fathered and engineered by Philip A. Payton, a coloured man in the real-estate business. But this was more than a matter of mere business with Mr. Payton; the matter of better and still better housing for coloured people in New York became the dominating idea of his life, and he worked on it as long as he lived. When Negro New Yorkers evaluate their benefactors in their own race, they must find that not many have done more than Phil Payton; for much of what has made Harlem the intellectual and artistic capital of the Negro world is in good part due to this fundamental advantage: Harlem has provided New York Negroes with better, cleaner, more modern, more airy, more sunny houses than they ever lived in before. And this is due to the efforts made first by Mr. Payton.

Harlem had been overbuilt with new apartment houses. It was far uptown, and the only rapid transporation was the elevated running up Eighth Avenue—the Lenox Avenue Subway had not yet been built. This left the people on Lenox Avenue and to the east with only the electric street-cars convenient. So landlords were finding it hard to fill their houses on that side of the section. Mr. Payton approached several of these landlords with the proposal to fill their empty houses with coloured tenants and keep them filled. Economic necessity usually discounts race prejudice—or any other kind of prejudice—as much as ninety per cent, sometimes a hundred; so the landlords with empty houses whom Mr. Payton approached accepted his proposal, and one or two houses on One Hundred and Thirty-fourth Street were taken over and filled with coloured tenants. Gradually other houses were filled. The white residents of the section showed very little concern about the movement until it began to spread to the west and across Lenox Avenue; then they took steps to check it. They organized, and formed plans to purchase through the Hudson Realty Company, a financial concern, all properties occupied by coloured people and evict the tenants. Payton countered by forming the Afro-American Realty Company, a Negro corporation organized for the purpose of buying and leasing houses to be let to coloured tenants. This counterstroke held the opposition in check for several years and enabled the Negroes to hold their own.

But the steady and increasing pressure of Negroes across the Lenox Avenue dead-line caused the opposition to break out anew; and this time the plans were more deeply laid and more difficult for the Negroes to defeat. These plans, formulated by several leading spirits, involved what was actually a conspiracy—the organization of whites to bring pressure on financial institutions to lend no money and renew no mortgages on properties occupied by coloured people. These plans had considerable success and reached beyond the situation they were formed to deal with. They still furnish one of the hardest and most unjustifiable handicaps the Negro property-owner in Harlem has to contend with.

The Afro-American Realty Company, for lack of the large amount of capital essential, was now defunct; but several individual coloured men carried on. Philip A. Payton and J. C. Thomas bought two five-story apartments, dispossessed the white tenants, and put in coloured ones. John B. Nail bought a row of five apartments and did the same. St. Philip's Episcopal Church, one of the oldest and richest coloured congregations in New York, bought a row of thirteen apartments on One Hundred and Thirty-fifth Street between Lenox and Seventh Avenues and rented them to coloured tenants. The situation now resolved itself into an actual contest. But the Negro pressure continued constant. Coloured people not only continued to move into apartments outside the zone east of Lenox Avenue, but began to purchase the fine private houses between Lenox and Seventh. Then, in the eyes of the whites who were antagonistic, the whole movement took on the aspect of an "invasion"—an invasion of both their economic and their social rights. They felt that Negroes as neighbours not only lowered the values of their property, but also lowered their social status. Seeing that they could not stop the movement, they began to flee. They took fright, they became panic-stricken, they ran amuck. Their conduct could be compared to that of a community in the Middle Ages fleeing before an epidemic of the black plague, except for the fact that here the reasons were not so sound. But these people did not stop to reason, they did not stop to ask why they did what they were doing, or what would happen if they didn't do it. The presence of a single coloured family in a block, regardless of the fact that they might be well-bred people, with sufficient means to buy their new home, was a signal for precipitate flight. The stampeded whites actually deserted house after house and block after block. Then prices dropped; they dropped lower than the bottom, and such coloured people as were able took advantage of these prices and bought. Some of the banks and lending companies that were compelled to take over deserted houses for the mortgages they held refused for a time to either sell or rent them to Negroes. Instead, they proposed themselves to bear the carrying charges and hold them vacant for what they evidently hoped would be a temporary period. Prices continued to drop. And this was the property situation in Harlem at the outbreak of the World War in Europe.

With the outbreak of the war there came a sudden change. One of the first effects of the war was to draw thousands of aliens out of this country back to their native lands to join the colours. Naturally, there was also an almost total cessation of immigration. Moreover, the United States was almost immediately called upon to furnish munitions and supplies of all kinds to the warring countries. The result of these converging causes was an unprecedented shortage of labour and a demand that was imperative. From whence could the necessary supply be drawn? There was only one source, and that was the reservoir of black labour in the South. And it was at once drawn on to fill the existing vacuum in the great industries of the North. Every available method was used to get these black hands, the most effective being the sending of labour agents into the South, who dealt directly with the Negroes, arranged for their transportation, and shipped them north, often in single consignments running high up into the hundreds. I witnessed the sending north from a Southern city in one day a crowd estimated at twenty-five hundred. They were shipped on a train run in three sections, packed in day coaches, with all their baggage and other impedimenta. The exodus was on, and migrants came north in thousands, tens of thousands, hundreds of thousands—from the docks of Norfolk, Savannah, Jacksonville, Tampa, Mobile, New Orleans, and Galveston; from the cotton-fields of Mississippi, and the coal-mines and steel-mills of Alabama and Tennessee; from workshops and wash-tubs and brick-yards and kitchens they came, until the number, by conservative estimate, went well over the million and a half mark. For the Negroes of the South this was the happy blending of desire with opportunity.

It could not be otherwise in such a wholesale migration than that many who came were ignorant, inefficient, and worthless, and that there was also a proportion of downright criminals. But industry was in no position to be fastidious; it was glad to take what it could get. It was not until the return of more normal conditions that the process of elimination of the incapable and the unfit set in. Meanwhile, in these new fields, the Negro was acquiring all sorts of divergent reputations for capability. In some places he was rated A 1 and in others N.G., and in varying degrees between these two extremes. The explanation, of course, is that different places had secured different kinds of Negroes. On the whole, New York was more fortunate in the migrants she got than were some of the large cities. Most of the industries in the manufacturing cities of the Middle West—except the steel-mills, which drew largely on the skilled and semi-skilled labour from the mills of Alabama and Tennessee—received migrants from the cotton-raising regions of the lower Mississippi Valley, from the rural, even the backwoods, districts, Negroes who were unused to city life or anything bearing a resemblance to modern industry. On the other hand, New York drew most of her migrants from cities and towns of the Atlantic seaboard states, Negroes who were far better prepared to adapt themselves to life and industry in a great city. Nor did all of New York's Negro migrants come from the South. The opportunity for Negro labour exerted a pull that reached down to the Negroes of the West Indies, and many of them came, most of them directly to New York. Those from the British West Indies average high in intelligence and efficiency. There is practically no illiteracy among them, and many have a sound English common school education. They are characteristically sober-minded and have something of a genius for business, differing almost totally, in these respects, from the average rural Negro of the South. Those from the British possessions constitute the great majority of the West Indians in New York; but there is also a large number who are Spanish-speaking and a considerable, though smaller, number who are French-speaking. The total West Indian population of Harlem is approximately fifty thousand.

With thousands of Negroes pouring into Harlem month by month, two things happened: first, a sheer physical pressure for room was set up that was irresistible; second, old residents and new-comers got work as fast as they could take it, at wages never dreamed of, so there was now plenty of money for renting and buying. And the Negro in Harlem did, contrary to all the burlesque notions about what Negroes do when they get hold of money, take advantage of the low prices of property and begin to buy. Buying property became a contagious fever. It became a part of the gospel preached in the churches. It seems that generations of the experience of an extremely precarious foothold on the land of Manhattan Island flared up into a conscious determination never to let that condition return. So they turned the money from their new-found prosperity into property. All classes bought. It was not an unknown thing for a coloured washerwoman to walk into a real-estate office and lay down several thousand dollars on a house. There was Mrs. Mary Dean, known as "Pig Foot Mary" because of her high reputation in the business of preparing and selling that particular delicacy, so popular in Harlem. She paid $42,000 for a five-story apartment house at the corner of Seventh Avenue and One Hundred and Thirty-seventh Street, which was sold later to a coloured undertaker for $72,000. The Equitable Life Assurance Company held vacant for quite a while a block of 106 model private houses, designed by Stanford White, which the company had been obliged to take over following the hegira of the whites from Harlem. When they were put on the market, they were promptly bought by Negroes at an aggregate price of about two million dollars. John E. Nail, a leading coloured real-estate dealer of Harlem and an appraisal authority, states that Negroes now own and control Harlem real property worth, at a conservative estimate, between fifty and sixty million dollars. Relatively, these figures are amazing. Twenty years ago barely a half-dozen coloured individuals owned land on Manhattan. Down to fifteen years ago the amount that Negroes had acquired in Harlem was by comparison negligible. Today a very large part of the property in Harlem occupied by Negroes is owned by Negroes.

It should be noted that Harlem was taken over without violence. In some of the large Northern cities where the same sort of expansion of the Negro population was going on, there was not only strong antagonism on the part of whites, but physical expression of it. In Chicago, Cleveland, and other cities houses bought and moved into by Negroes were bombed. In Chicago a church bought by a coloured congregation was badly damaged by bombs. In other cities several formerly white churches which had been taken over by a coloured congregation were badly damaged by bombs. In Detroit, mobs undertook to evict Negroes from houses bought by them in white neighbourhoods. The mob drove vans up to one house just purchased and moved into by a coloured physician, ordered him out, loaded all his goods into the vans, and carted them back to his old residence. These arrogated functions of the mob reached a climax in the celebrated Sweet case. A mob gathered in the evening round a house in a white neighbourhood which Dr. O. H. Sweet, a coloured physician, had bought and moved into the day before. When the situation reached a critical point, shots fired from within the house killed one person in the crowd and seriously wounded another. Dr. Sweet, his wife, and eight others, relatives and friends, who were in the house at the time, were indicted and tried for murder in the first degree. They were defended in two long trials by the National Association for the Advancement of Colored People, through Clarence Darrow and Arthur Garfield Hays, assisted by several local attorneys, and were acquitted. This was the tragic end of eviction by mob in Detroit.

Although there was bitter feeling in Harlem during the fifteen years of struggle the Negro went through in getting a foothold on the land, there was never any demonstration of violence that could be called serious. Not since the riot of 1900 has New York witnessed, except for minor incidents, any inter-racial disturbances. Not even in the memorable summer of 1919—that summer when the stoutest-hearted Negroes felt terror and dismay; when the race got the worst backwash of the war, and the Ku Klux Klan was in the ascendant; when almost simultaneously there were riots in Chicago and in Longview, Texas; in Omaha and in Phillips County, Arkansas; and hundreds of Negroes, chased through the streets or hunted down through the swamps, were beaten and killed; when in the national capital an anti-Negro mob held sway for three days, in which time six persons were killed and scores severely beaten—not even during this period of massacre did New York, with more than a hundred thousand Negroes grouped together in Harlem, lose its equanimity.

It is apparent that race friction, as it affects Harlem as a community, has grown less and less each year for the past ten years; and the signs are that there will not be a recrudescence. The signs are confirmed by certain basic conditions. Although Harlem is a Negro community, the newest comers do not long remain merely "Harlem Negroes"; astonishingly soon they become New Yorkers. One reason for this is that, by comparison with Chicago, Detroit, Pittsburgh, or Cleveland, there is no gang labour among Negroes in New York. The longshoremen are an exception, but the Negro longshoremen are highly unionized and stand on an equal footing with their white fellow-workers. Employment of Negroes in New York is diversified; they are employed more as individuals than as non-integral parts of a gang. This gives them the opportunity for more intimate contacts with the life and spirit of the city as a whole. A thousand Negroes from Mississippi brought up and put to work in a Pittsburgh plant will for a long time remain a thousand Negroes from Mississippi. Under the conditions that prevail in New York, they would all, inside of six months, be pretty good New Yorkers. One of the chief factors in the Chicago race riot in 1919 was the fact that at the time more than twelve thousand Negroes were employed at the stockyards. Moreover, there is the psychology of New York, the natural psychology of a truly cosmopolitan city, in which there is always the tendency to minimize rather than magnify distinctions of this sort, in which such distinctions tend to die out, unless kept alive by some intentional agency. New York, more than any other American city, maintains a matter-of-fact, a taken-for-granted attitude towards her Negro citizens. Less there than anywhere else in the country are Negroes regarded as occupying a position of wardship; more nearly do they stand upon the footing of common and equal citizenship. It may be that one of the causes of New York's attitude lies in the fact that the Negro there has achieved a large degree of political independence; that he has broken away from a political creed based merely upon traditional and sentimental grounds. Yet, on the other hand, this itself may be a result of New York's attitude.

At any rate, there is no longer any apparent feeling against the occupancy of Harlem by Negroes. Within the past five years the colony has expanded to the south, the north, and the west. It has gone down Seventh Avenue from One Hundred and Twenty-seventh Street to Central Park at One Hundred and Tenth Street. It has climbed upwards between Eighth Avenue and the Harlem River from One Hundred and Forty-fifth Street to One Hundred and Fifty-fifth. It has spread to the west and occupies the heights of Coogan's Bluff, overlooking Colonial Park. And to the east and west of this solid Negro area, there is a fringe where the population is mixed, white and coloured. This expansion of the past five years has taken place without any physical opposition, or even any considerable outbreak of antagonistic public sentiment.

The question inevitably arises: Will the Negroes of Harlem be able to hold it? Will they not be driven still father northward? Residents of Manhattan, regardless of race, have been driven out when they lay in the path of business and greatly increased land values. Harlem lies in the direction that path must take; so there is little probability that Negroes will always hold it as a residential section. But this is to be considered: the Negro's situation in Harlem is without precedent in all his history in New York; never before has he been so securely anchored, never before has he owned the land, never before has he had so well established a community life. It is probable that land through the heart of Harlem will some day so increase in value that Negroes may not be able to hold it—although it is quite as probable that there will be some Negroes able to take full advantage of the increased values—and will be forced to make a move. But the next move, when it comes, will be unlike the others. It will not be a move made solely at the behest of someone else; it will be more in the nature of a bargain. Nor will it be a move in which the Negro will carry with him only his household goods and utensils; he will move at a financial profit to himself. But at the present time such a move is nowhere in sight.

MY CITY
JAMES WELDON JOHNSON

When I come down to sleep death's endless night,
The threshold of the unknown dark to cross,
What to me then will be the keenest loss,
When this bright world blurs on my fading sight?
Will it be that no more I shall see the trees
Or smell the flowers or hear the singing birds
Or watch the flashing streams or patient herds?
No, I am sure it will be none of these.

But, ah! Manhattan's sights and sounds, her smells,
Her crowds, her throbbing force, the thrill that comes
From being of her a part, her subtle spells,
Her shining towers, her avenues, her slums—
O God! the stark, unutterable pity,
To be dead, and never again behold my city!

EDITORIAL
WALLACE THURMAN

In the past there have been only a few sporadic and inevitably unsuccessful attempts to provide the Negro with an independent magazine of literature and thought. Those magazines which have lived throughout a period of years have been organs of some philanthropic organization whose purpose was to fight the more virulent manifestations of race prejudice. The magazines themselves have been pulpits for alarmed and angry Jeremiahs spouting fire and venom or else weeping and moaning as if they were either predestined or else unable to do anything else. For a while this seemed to be the only feasible course for Negro journalists to take. To the Negro then the most important and most tragic thing in the world was his own problem here in America. He was interested only in making white people realize what

From *Harlem,* Vol. I (November, 1928).

dastards they were in denying him equal economic opportunities or in lynching him upon the slightest provocation. This, as has been said, was all right for a certain period, and the journalists of that period are not to be censored for the truly daring and important work they did do. Rather, they are to be blamed for not changing their journalistic methods when time and conditions warranted such a change, and for doing nothing else but preaching and moaning until they completely lost their emotional balance and their sense of true values. Every chord on their publicist instrument had been broken save one, and they continued raucously to twang this, unaware that they were ludicrously out of tune with the other instruments in their environment.

Then came the so-called renaissance and the emergence of the so-called new (in this case meaning widely advertised) Negro. As James Weldon Johnson says in the current issue of *Harper's* magazine: "The Negro has done a great deal thru his folk art creations to change the national attitudes toward him; and now the efforts of the race have been reinforced and magnified by the individual Negro artist, the conscious artist. . . . Overnight, as it were, America became aware that there were Negro artists and that they had something worthwhile to say. This awareness first manifested itself in black America, for, strange as it may seem, Negroes themselves, as a mass, had had little or no consciousness of their own individual artists."

Naturally these new voices had to be given a place in Negro magazines and they were given space that hitherto had been devoted only to propaganda. But the artist was not satisfied to be squeezed between jeremiads or have his work thrown haphazardly upon a page where there was no effort to make it look beautiful as well as sound beautiful. He revolted against shoddy and sloppy publication methods, revolted against the patronizing attitudes his elders assumed toward him, revolted against their editorial astigmatism and their intolerance of new points of view. But revolting left him without a journalistic asylum. True, he could, and did, contribute to the white magazines, but in doing this almost exclusively he felt that he was losing touch with his own group, for he knew just how few Negroes would continually buy white magazines in order to read articles and stories by Negro authors, and he also knew that from a sense of race pride, if nothing more, there were many Negroes who would buy a Negro magazine.

The next step then was for the artist himself to produce this new type of journal. With little money but a plethora of ideas and ambition he proceeded to produce independent art magazines of his own. In New York, *Fire* was the pioneer of the movement. It flamed for one issue and caused a sensation the like of which had never been known in Negro journalism before. Next came *Black Opals* in Philadelphia, a more conservative yet extremely worthwhile venture. Then came *The Quill* in Boston which was to be published whenever its sponsors felt the urge to bring forth a publication of their own works for the benefit of themselves and their friends. And there were other groups of younger Negroes in Chicago, Kansas City and Los Angeles who formed groups to bring out independent magazines which never became actualities.

This last development should have made someone realize that a new type of publication was in order. The old propagandistic journals had served their day and their generation well, but they were emotionally unprepared to serve a new day and a new generation. The art magazines, unsoundly financed as they were, could not last. It was time for someone with vision to found a wholly new type of magazine, one which would give expression to all groups, one which would take into consideration the fact that this was a new day in the history of the American Negro, that this was a new day in the history of the world and that new points of views and new approaches to old problems were necessary and inescapable.

Harlem hopes to fill this new need. It enters the field without any preconceived editorial prejudices, without intolerance, without a reformer's cudgel. It wants merely to be a forum in which all people's opinions may be presented intelligently and from which the Negro can gain some universal idea of what is going on in the world of thought and art. It wants to impress upon the literate members of the thirteen million Negroes in the United States the necessity of becoming "book conscious," the necessity of reading the newer Negro authors, the necessity of realizing that the Negro is not the only, nor the worst mistreated minority group in the world, the necessity of sublimating their inferiority complex and their extreme race sensitiveness and putting the energy, which they have hitherto used in moaning and groaning, into more concrete fields of action.

To this end *Harlem* will solicit articles on current events, essays of the more intimate kind, short stories and poetry from both black and white writers; the only qualification being that they have sufficient literary merit to warrant publication. *Harlem* will also promote debates on both racial and non-racial issues, giving voice to as many sides as there seem to be to the question involved. It will also be a clearing house for the newer Negro literature, striving to aid the younger writers, giving them a medium of expression and intelligent criticism. It also hopes to impress the Negro reading public with the necessity for a more concerted and well-balanced economic and political program. It believes that the commercial and political elements within the race are just as in need of clarification as the literary element and will expend just as much energy and time in the latter fields as in the former.

This is *Harlem's* program, its excuse for existence. It now remains to be seen whether the Negro public is as ready for such a publication as the editors and publishers of *Harlem* believe it to be.

THE CAUCASIAN STORMS HARLEM
RUDOLPH FISHER

It might not have been such a jolt had my five years' absence from Harlem been spent otherwise. But the study of medicine includes no courses in cabareting; and, anyway, the Negro cabarets in Washington, where I studied, are all uncompromisingly black. Accordingly I was entirely unprepared for what I found when I returned to Harlem recently.

I remembered one place especially where my own crowd used to hold forth; and, hoping to find some old-timers there still, I sought it out one midnight. The old, familiar plunkety-plunk welcomed me from below as I entered. I descended the same old narrow stairs, came into the same smoke-misty basement, and found myself a chair at one of the ancient white-porcelain, mirror-smooth tables. I drew a deep breath and looked about, seeking familiar faces. "What a lot of 'fays!" I thought, as I noticed the number of white guests. Presently I grew puzzled and began to stare, then I gaped—and gasped. I found myself wondering if this was the right place—if, indeed, this was Harlem at all. I suddenly became aware that, except for the waiters and members of the orchestra, I was the only Negro in the place.

After a while I left it and wandered about in a daze from night-club to night-club. I tried the Nest, Small's, Connie's Inn, the Capitol, Happy's, the Cotton Club. There was no mistake; my discovery was real and was repeatedly confirmed. No wonder my old crowd was not to be found in any of them. The best of Harlem's black cabarets have changed their names and turned white.

Such a discovery renders a moment's recollection irresistible. As irresistible as were the cabarets themselves to me seven or eight years ago. Just out of college in a town where cabarets were something only read about. A year of graduate work ahead. A Summer of rest at hand. Cabarets. Cabarets night after night, and one after another. There was no cover-charge then, and a fifteen-cent bottle of Whistle lasted an hour. It was just after the war—the heroes were home—cabarets were the thing.

How the Lybia prospered in those happy days! It was the gathering place of the swellest Harlem set: if you didn't go to the Lybia, why, my dear, you just didn't belong. The people you saw at church in the morning you met at the Lybia at night. What romance in those war-tinged days and nights! Officers from Camp Upton, with pretty maids from Brooklyn! Gay lieutenants, handsome captains—all whirling the lively onestep. Poor non-coms completely ignored; what sensible girl wanted a corporal or even a sergeant? That white, old-fashioned house, standing alone in 138th street, near the corner of Seventh avenue—doomed to be torn down a few months thence—how it shook with the dancing and laughter of the dark merry crowds!

But the first place really popular with my friends was a Chinese restaurant in 136th street, which had been known as Hayne's Café and then became the Oriental. It occupied an entire house of three stories, and had carpeted floors and a quiet, superior air. There was excellent food and incredibly good tea and two unusual entertainers: a Cuban girl, who could so vary popular airs that they sounded like real music, and a slender little "brown" with a voice of silver and a way of singing a song that made you forget your food. One could dance in the Oriental if one liked, but one danced to a piano only, and wound one's way between linen-clad tables over velvety, noiseless floors.

Here we gathered: Fritz Pollard, All-American halfback, selling Negro stock to prosperous Negro physicians; Henry Creamer and Turner Layton, who had written "After You've Gone" and a dozen more songs, and were going to write "Strut, Miss Lizzie;" Paul Robeson, All-American end, on the point of tackling law, quite unaware that the stage would intervene; Preacher Harry Bragg, Harvard Jimmie MacLendon and half a dozen others. Here at a little table, just inside the door, Bert Williams had supper every night, and afterward sometimes joined us upstairs and sang songs with us and lampooned the Actors' Equity Association, which had barred him because of his color. Never did white guests come to the Oriental except as guests of Negroes. But the manager soon was stricken with a psychosis of some sort, became a black Jew, grew himself a bushy, square-cut beard, donned a skull-cap and abandoned the Oriental. And so we were robbed of our favorite resort, and thereafter became mere rounders.

II

Such places, those real Negro cabarets that we met in the course of our rounds! There was Edmonds' in Fifth avenue at 130th street. It was a sure-enough honky-tonk, occupying the cellar of a saloon. It was the social center of what was then, and still is, Negro Harlem's kitchen. Here a tall brown-skin girl, unmistakably the one guaranteed in the song to make a preacher lay his Bible down, used to sing and dance her own peculiar numbers, vesting them with her own originality. She was known simply as Ethel, and was a genuine drawing-card. She knew her importance, too. Other girls wore themselves ragged trying to rise above the inattentive din of conversation, and soon, literally, yelled themselves hoarse; eventually they lost whatever music there was in their voices and acquired that familiar throaty roughness which is so frequent among blues singers, and which, though admired as characteristically African, is as a matter of fact nothing but a form of chronic laryngitis. Other girls did these things, but not Ethel. She took it easy. She would stride with great leisure and self-assurance to the center of the floor, stand there with a half-contemptuous nonchalance, and wait. All would become silent at once. Then she'd begin her song, genuine blues, which, for all their humorous lines, emanated tragedy and heartbreak:

> Woke up this mawnin'
> The day was dawnin'
> And I was sad and blue, so blue, Lord—
> Didn' have nobody
> To tell my troubles to—

It was Ethel who first made popular the song, "Tryin' to Teach My Good Man Right from Wrong," in the slow, meditative measures in which she complained:

76

I'm gettin' sick and tired of my railroad man
I'm gettin' sick and tired of my railroad man—
Can't get him when I want him—
I get him when I can.

It wasn't long before this song-bird escaped her dingy cage. Her name is a vaudeville attraction now, and she uses it all—Ethel Waters. Is there anyone who hasn't heard her sing "Shake That Thing!"?

A second place was Connor's in 135th street near Lenox avenue. It was livelier, less languidly sensuous, and easier to breathe in that Edmonds'. Like the latter, it was in a basement, reached by the typical narrow, headlong stairway. One of the girls there specialized in the Jelly-Roll song, and mad habitués used to fling petitions of greenbacks at her feet—pretty nimble feet they were, too—when she sang that she loved 'em but she had to turn 'em down. Over in a corner a group of 'fays would huddle and grin and think they were having a wild time. Slumming. But they were still very few in those days.

And there was the Oriental, which borrowed the name that the former Hayne's Café had abandoned. This was beyond Lenox avenue on the south side of 135th street. An upstairs place, it was nevertheless as dingy as any of the cellars, and the music fairly fought its way through the babble and smoke to one's ears, suffering in transit weird and incredible distortion. The prize pet here was a slim, little lad, unbelievably black beneath his high-brown powder, wearing a Mexican bandit costume with a bright-colored head-dress and sash. I see him now, poor kid, in all his glory, shimmying for enraptured women, who marveled at the perfect control of his voluntary abdominal tremors. He used to let the women reach out and put their hands on his sash to palpate those tremors—for a quarter.

Finally, there was the Garden of Joy, an open-air cabaret between 138th and 139th streets in Seventh avenue, occupying a plateau high above the sidewalk—a large, well-laid, smooth wooden floor with tables and chairs and a tinny orchestra, all covered by a propped-up roof, that resembled an enormous lampshade, directing bright light downward and outward. Not far away the Abyssinian Church used to hold its Summer camp-meetings in a great round circus-tent. Night after night there would arise the mingled strains of blues and spirituals, those peculiarly Negro forms of song, the one secular and the other religious, but both born of wretchedness in travail, both with their soarings of exultation and sinkings of despair. I used to wonder if God, hearing them both, found any real distinction.

There were the Lybia, then, and Hayne's, Connor's, the Oriental, Edmonds' and the Garden of Joy, each distinctive, standing for a type, some living up to their names, others living down to them, but all predominantly black. Regularly I made the rounds among these places and saw only incidental white people. I have seen them occasionally in numbers, but such parties were out on a lark. They weren't in their natural habitat and they often weren't any too comfortable.

But what of Barron's, you say? Certainly they were at home there. Yes, I know about Barron's. I have been turned away from Barron's because I was too dark to be welcome. I have been a member of a group that was told, "No more room," when we could see plenty of room. Negroes were never actually wanted in Barron's save to work. Dark skins were always discouraged or barred. In short, the fact about Barron's was this: it simply wasn't a Negro cabaret; it was a cabaret run by Negroes for whites. It wasn't even on the lists of those who lived in Harlem—they'd no more think of going there than of going to the Winter Garden Roof. But these other places were Negro through and through. Negroes supported them, not merely in now-and-then parties, but steadily, night after night.

III

Now, however, the situation is reversed. It is I who go occasionally and white people who go night after night. Time and again, since I've returned to live in Harlem, I've been one of a party of four Negroes who went to this or that Harlem cabaret, and on each occasion we've been the only Negro guests in the place. The managers don't hesitate to say that it is upon these predominant white patrons that they depend for success. These places therefore are no longer mine but theirs. Not that I'm barred, any more than they were seven or eight years ago. Once known, I'm even welcome, just as some of them used to be. But the complexion of the place is theirs, not mine. I? Why, I am actually stared at, I frequently feel uncomfortable and out of place, and when I go out on the floor to dance I am lost in a sea of white faces. As another observer has put it to me since, time was when white people went to Negro cabarets to see how Negroes acted; now Negroes go to these same cabarets to see how white people act. Negro clubs have recently taken to hiring a place outright for a presumably Negro party; and even then a goodly percentage of the invited guests are white.

One hurries to account for this change of complexion as a reaction to the Negro invasion of Broadway not long since. One remembers "Shuffle Along" of four years ago, the first Negro piece in the downtown district for many a moon. One says, "Oh yes, Negroes took their stuff to the whites and won attention and praise, and now the whites are seeking this stuff out on its native soil." Maybe. So I myself thought at first. But one looks for something of oppositeness in a genuine reaction. One would rather expect the reaction to the Negro invasion of Broadway to be apathy. One would expect that the same thing repeated under different names or in imitative fragments would meet with colder and colder reception, and finally with none at all.

A little recollection will show that just what one would expect was what happened. Remember "Shuffle Along's" successors: "Put and Take," "Liza," "Strut Miss Lizzie," "Runnin' Wild," and the others? True, none was so good as "Shuffle Along," but surely they didn't deserve all the roasting they got. "Liza" flared but briefly, during a holiday season. "Put and Take" was a loss, "Strut Miss Lizzie" strutted about two weeks, and the humor of

"Runnin' Wild" was derided as Neo-Pleistocene. Here was reaction for—wholesale withdrawal of favor. One can hardly conclude that such withdrawal culminated in the present swamping of Negro cabarets. People so sick of a thing would hardly go out of their way to find it.

And they *are* sick of it—in quantity at least. Only one Negro entertainment has survived this reaction of apathy in any permanent fashion. This is the series of revues built around the personality of Florence Mills. Without that bright live personality the Broadway district would have been swept clean last season of all-Negro bills. Here is a girl who has triumphed over a hundred obstacles. Month after month she played obscure, unnoticed rôles with obscure, unknown dark companies. She was playing such a minor part in "Shuffle Along" when the departure of Gertrude Saunders, the craziest blues-singer on earth, unexpectedly gave her the spotlight. Florence Mills cleaned up. She cleaned up so thoroughly that the same public which grew weary of "Shuffle Along" and sick of its successors still had an eager ear for her. They have yet, and she neither wearies nor disappoints them. An impatient Broadway audience awaits her return from Paris, where she and the inimitable Josephine Baker have been vying with each other as sensations. She is now in London on the way home, but London won't release her; the enthusiasm over her exceeds anything in the memory of the oldest reviewers.

Florence Mills, moreover, is admired by her own people too, because, far from going to her head, her success has not made her forgetful. Not long ago, the rumor goes, she made a fabulous amount of money in the Florida real-estate boom, and what do you suppose she plans to do with it? Build herself an Italian villa somewhere up the Hudson? Not at all. She plans to build a first-rate Negro theatre in Harlem.

But that's Florence Mills. Others have encountered indifference. In vain has Eddie Hunter, for instance, tried for a first-class Broadway showing, despite the fact that he himself has a new kind of Negro-comedian character to portray—the wise darkey, the "bizthniss man," the "fly" rascal who gets away with murder, a character who amuses by making a goat of others instead of by making a goat of himself. They say that some dozen Negro shows have met with similar denials. Yet the same people, presumably, whose spokesmen render these decisions flood Harlem night after night and literally crowd me off the dancing-floor. If this is a reaction, it is a reaction to a reaction, a swinging back of the pendulum from apathy toward interest. Maybe so. The cabarets may present only those special Negro features which have a particular and peculiar appeal, leaving out the high-yaller display that is merely feebly imitative. But a reaction to a reaction—that's differential calculus.

IV

Some think it's just a fad. White people have always more or less sought Negro entertainment as diversion. The old shows of the early nineteen hundreds, Williams and Walker and Cole and Johnson, are brought to mind as examples. The howling success—literally that—of J. Leubrie Hill around 1913 is another; on the road his "Darktown Follies" played in numerous white theatres. In Harlem it played at the black Lafayette and, behold, the Lafayette temporarily became white. And so now, it is held, we are observing merely one aspect of a meteoric phenomenon, which simply presents itself differently in different circumstances: Roland Hayes and Paul Robeson, Jean Toomer and Walter White, Charles Gilpin and Florence Mills—"Green Thursday," "Porgy," "In Abraham's Bosom"—Negro spirituals—the startling new African groups proposed for the Metropolitan Museum of Art. Negro stock is going up, and everybody's buying.

This doesn't sound unreasonable when it refers to certain things. Interest in the shows certainly presents many features of a fad. As in some epidemic fevers, there are sudden onset, swift contagion, brief duration, and a marked tendency to recur. Consider "Shuffle Along," for example, as a fad. Interest waned, as it will with fads. Disruption was hastened by internal dissension in the company: Sissle and Blake had written the songs and insisted on keeping the royalties therefrom, and Miller and Lyles had helped make the songs famous and contended that they too deserved a share of the proceeds. There was a deadlock and a split. "In Bamville" went one way and "Runnin' Wild" another, but neither went the prosperous way of the parent fad, "Shuffle Along."

Meanwhile, Creamer and Layton, among others, had found that the fad no longer infected. But if America was barren ground was not Europe virgin soil?

So, while Creamer remained to run the Cotton Club, Layton packed off to England, where already Hayes had done admirably in recital and Robeson was becoming well known on the stage. Layton and his new partner, Tandy Johnstone, were amazed at their success in England, and there they are at this writing. They earn more in a week there than they used to in many months over here. They have transplanted their fad into other susceptible communities—communities likely to become immune less swiftly. They are London vaudeville headliners, and their jazz has captivated the British. These entertainers will probably not soon lose that peculiar knack of striking a popular response. Turner Layton's father was for many years assistant director of music in the Washington public schools, and it is said that this imposing gentleman could get music out of a hall full of empty chairs. There may be something hereditary therefore in the way in which the most lifeless instrument responds to Turner's touch.

Followed Sissle and Blake to England, whence they have recently returned successful. Noble Sissle was the friend and companion of Jim Europe, who organized the New York Clef Club and was the most popular Negro musician of his day. After Europe's unfortunate death, Sissle and Eubie Blake became an extremely popular vaudeville team. Earlier, Blake used to play the piano for house-parties and dances around Baltimore, and later played in cabarets. Certain of his Baltimore friends point to him proudly now, and well they may: the accuracy and agility with which his fingers scamper over the keyboard is always a breath-taking wonder. Sissle and Blake, too, have learned the lessons taught by struggle and disaster. Time was when the "Shuffle Along" company, coming to Washington from New York for a Sunday afternoon engagement at the world's best Negro theatre, the Lincoln, entered the town with all the triumphal glamor of a circus. Almost every principal in the show had his or her own automobile, and they weren't designed or painted with an eye for modest retirement. The principals drove down from New York in their cars, if you please; which was entirely their own business, of course. The point is that they *could*. Sissle and Blake, it appears, still can. Such is the profitable contagion of a fad.

Pending a contemplated reunion of these unusual teams, Miller and Lyles have been playing with various Broadway revues. These comical fellows are both college graduates, and eminently respectable and conservative in private life. It is, by the way, a noteworthy thing about all of these men, Creamer, Johnstone, Layton, Sissle, Blake, Miller, and Lyles, that one never hears the slightest murmur of social criticism about any one of them. They have managed to conduct themselves off stage entirely above reproach. It is no accident that the private lives of these dark-skinned stars are so circumspect. It is part of the explanation of their success.

V

It is only a part, however; and the fad-like characteristics of their experience may be another part. It may be a season's whim, then, this sudden, contagious interest in everything Negro. If so, when I go into a familiar cabaret, or the place where a familiar cabaret used to be, and find it transformed and relatively colorless, I may be observing just one form that the season's whim has taken.

But suppose it is a fad—to say that explains nothing. How came the fad? What occasions the focusing of attention on this particular thing—rounds up and gathers these seasonal whims, and centers them about the Negro? Cabarets are peculiar, mind you. They're not like theatres and concert halls. You don't just go to a cabaret and sit back and wait to be entertained. You get out on the floor and join the pow-wow and help entertain yourself. Granted that white people have long enjoyed the Negro entertainment as a diversion, is it not something different, something more, when they bodily throw themselves into Negro entertainment in cabarets? "Now Negroes go to their own cabarets to see how white people act."

And what do we see? Why, we see them actually playing Negro games. I watch them in that epidemic Negroism, the Charleston. I look on and envy them. They camel and fish-tail and turkey, they geche and black-bottom and scronch, they skate and buzzard and mess-around—and they do them all better than I! This interest in the Negro is an active and participating interest. It is almost as if a traveler from the North stood watching an African tribe-dance, then suddenly found himself swept wildly into it, caught in its tidal rhythm.

Willingly would I be an outsider in this if I could know that I read it aright—that out of this change in the old familiar ways some finer thing may come. Is this interest akin to that of the Virginians on the veranda of a plantation's big-house—sitting genuinely spellbound as they hear the lugubrious strains floating up from the Negro quarters? Is it akin to that of the African explorer, Stanley, leaving a village far behind, but halting in spite of himself to catch the boom of its distant drum? Is it significant of basic human responses, the effect of which, once admitted, will extend far beyond cabarets? Maybe these Nordics at last have tuned in on our wavelength. Maybe they are at last learning to speak our language.

FROM
A LONG WAY FROM HOME
CLAUDE MCKAY

IX

Back in Harlem

Like fixed massed sentinels guarding the approaches to the great metropolis, again the pyramids of New York in their Egyptian majesty dazzled my sight like a miracle of might and took my breath like the banging music of Wagner assaulting one's spirit and rushing it skyward with the pride and power of an eagle.

The feeling of the dirty steerage passage across the Atlantic was swept away in the immense wonder of clean, vertical heaven-challenging lines, a glory to the grandeur of space.

Oh, I wished that it were possible to know New York in that way only—as a masterpiece wrought for the illumination of the sight, a splendor lifting aloft and shedding its radiance like a searchlight, making one big and great with feeling. Oh, that I should never draw nearer to descend into its precipitous gorges, where visions are broken and shattered and one becomes one of a million, average, ordinary, insignificant.

At last the ship was moored and I came down to the pavement. Ellis Island: doctors peered in my eyes, officials scrutinized my passport, and the gates were thrown open.

The elevated swung me up to Harlem. At first I felt a little fear and trembling, like a stray hound scenting out new territory. But soon I was stirred by familiar voices and the shapes of houses and saloons, and I was inflated with confidence. A wave of thrills flooded the arteries of my being, and I felt as if I had undergone initiation as a member of my tribe. And I was happy. Yes, it was a rare sensation again to be just one black among many. It was good to be lost in the shadows of Harlem again. It was an adventure to loiter down Fifth and Lenox avenues and promenade along Seventh Avenue.

Spareribs and corn pone, fried chicken and corn fritters and sweet potatoes were like honey to my palate.

There was a room for me in the old house on One Hundred Thirty-first Street, but there was no trace of Manda. I could locate none of my close railroad friends. But I found Sanina. Sanina was an attractive quadroon from Jamaica who could pass as white. Before prohibition she presided over a buffet flat. Now she animated a cosy speakeasy. Her rendezvous on upper Seventh Avenue, with its pink curtains and spreads, created an artificial rose-garden effect. It was always humming like a beehive with brown butterflies and flames of all ages from the West Indies and from the South.

Sanina infatuated them all. She possessed the cunning and fascination of a serpent, and more charm than beauty. Her clients idolized her with a loyalty and respect that were rare. I was never quite sure what was the secret of her success. For although she was charming, she was ruthless in her affairs. I felt a congeniality and sweet nostalgia in her company, for we had grown up together from kindergarten. Underneath all of her shrewd New York getting-byness there was discernible the green bloom of West Indian naïveté. Yet her poise was a marvel and kept her there floating like an imperishable block of butter on the crest of the dark heaving wave of Harlem. Sanina always stirred me to remember her dominating octoroon grandmother (who was also my godmother) who beat her hard white father in a duel they fought over the disposal of her body. But that is a West Indian tale. . . . I think that some of Sanina's success came from her selectiveness. Although there were many lovers mixing up their loving around her, she kept herself exclusively for the lover of her choice.

I passed ten days of purely voluptuous relaxation. My fifty dollars were spent and Sanina was feeding me. I was uncomfortable. I began feeling intellectual again. I wrote to my friend, Max Eastman, that I had returned to New York. My letter arrived at precisely the right moment. The continuation of *The Liberator* had become a problem. Max Eastman had recently resigned the editorship in order to devote more time to creative writing. Crystal Eastman also was retiring from the management to rest and write a book on feminism. Floyd Dell had just published his successful novel *Moon Calf,* and was occupied with the writing of another book.

THE TROPICS IN NEW YORK
CLAUDE MCKAY

Bananas ripe and green, and ginger-root,
  Cocoa in pods and alligator pears,
And tangerines and mangoes and grape fruit,
  Fit for the highest prize at parish fairs,

Set in the window, bringing memories
  Of fruit-trees laden by low-singing rills,

And dewy dawns, and mystical blue skies
   In benediction over nun-like hills.

My eyes grew dim, and I could no more gaze;
   A wave of longing through my body swept,
And, hungry for the old, familiar ways,
   I turned aside and bowed my head and wept.

HARLEM SHADOWS
CLAUDE MCKAY

I hear the halting footsteps of a lass
   In Negro Harlem when the night lets fall
Its veil. I see the shapes of girls who pass
   To bend and barter at desire's call.
Ah, little dark girls who in slippered feet
Go prowling through the night from street to
      street!

Through the long night until the silver break
   Of day the little gray feet know no rest;
Through the lone night until the last snow-flake
   Has dropped from heaven upon the earth's
      white breast,
The Dusky, half-clad girls of tired feet
Are trudging, thinly shod, from street to street.

Ah, stern harsh world, that in the wretched way
   Of poverty, dishonor and disgrace,
Has pushed the timid little feet of clay,
   The sacred brown feet of my fallen race!
Ah, heart of me, the weary, weary feet
In Harlem wandering from street to street.

CITY LOVE
ERIC WALROND

From a gulf in the dark low sea of rooftops there came mounting skyward
the fiery reflexes of some gaudy Convention Night on Lenox Avenue. With
the fate of a sinning angel the eye went *carombolling* 'cross the fizzing of a
street lamp, caught the rickety vision of a bus, topheavy with a lot of fat,
fanning Jews, tottering by on the cloudy August asphalt; flitted from the
moon-shingled edges of elm and oak, onward, finally settling on the dark
murmuring folk enlivening the park's green dusk rim.

"Quit that, honey!" warned the girl, softly. "I's skeert o' dirt, baby, don't you do that." She steered the lad's menacing hand out the way.

"No tellin' wheh some o' dat grabble might go," continued Nicey, making a pirate's cross bones of her legs.

A silence, dramatic to St. Louis, ensued. He was hurt, put out, ashamed of himself at Nicey's gently unanswerable rebuke.

He risked a pair of greedy, sun-red eyes round at her, and his courage took fresh impetus. "I know a place," he bristled suddenly with conviction, and Nicey's head turned involuntarily. "An' here Ah wuz—" he chuckled self-condemningly. "Come on, le's chance it."

"A nice place?" Nicey asked, quietly, not wishing to seem eager.

"Ah mean!" breathed Primus with deep-felt ardor.

"Yo' talk like yo' know it, like yo' done bin they orready," was what she was on the verge of saying, but large immediate interests possessed her, and she said instead, half-coyly, "No kiddin' now!"

"Honest," he said, getting up, "I ain't foolin'. I ain't green as I look. I bin there—"

"Oh yeah?" risked Nicey with surgical placidity.

"I mean," he stammered, admitting the error, but she checked the ripening flow of advances, and stood up. "That'll do," she said sagely, and walked, hips swinging, on down the hill in front of him.

He kept a little ways behind, feeling insecure and moody at his silly measure of self-puffing.

A flower coursed by, and she caught it, pressing the white dewy petals to her mouth. Dissatisfied, she flung it in a curdle of nettles. "Ah likes flowers dat got pa'fune," she said, "dis one ain't got a bit o' smell."

As they sped out on the flaky stone flight of steps leading toward St. Nicholas, clots of lovers, in twos and more than twos, leaned against the bowing foliage, forcing the dicks, bronze and pale-faced ones, to take refuge upon their fobs and palms behind the dark viny hedge.

A big muddy touring car filled with a lot of drinking Bolita Negroes skidded recklessly by into the gulch to One Hundred Thirty-Fifth Street. Pebbly dust bombarded the lids of Nicey's and Primus' eyes.

". . . fur to go, baby?"

"Thutty fo'th . . . not fur . . . come . . . look out . . . you'll get run ovah, too."

A shanty, lodged beside an aerial railway track, with switches and cross ties, hovered dark and low above the street. A mob of Negroes passing underneath it hurried on as the trains rushed by, the lusty pressure chipping dust and rust off the girders.

Cars lurched in and out of side streets, assuming and unloading cargoes of vari-hued browns and blacks of conflicting shades of ebony splendor.

"How much furrer we got to go, honey," cried Nicey, dusty, eager, ill-at-ease.

They stopt before a brownstone dwelling. In the thickening night-light they glimpsed a fat butter-yellow Negress lolling in a rocker on the stoop and fanning herself with the long end of her apron.

There they stood, naked of pleats and tucks, frills and laces . . . orphans.

"Go on down t' the basement," the woman directed, with a wave of her heavy hand.

"You'd better wait here, Nicey," Primus said, with a show of manly vigor. Skipping to the basement the smells of a Negro cook shop came somersaulting at him. His senses were placid beside the sickening essences of corn and pork and candied yams.

The man who shared in this riotous obscenity was spotted by a kerosene torch swaying from a hook nailed in the wall. He was bald and tall and huge and spade black. He wore a shirt and flabby blue jeans and braces. Under such a low ceiling his fading oak skull threatened to violate the plumbing. In such a tiny passageway he seemed with his thick rotund figure to be as squat as an inflated bull frog.

He turned, at the shadow absorbing a length of the trembling light, and there was hair on both sides of his broad black face. He looked into Primus' eyes and a mist of mutuality sprang between them.

"Wha' yo' wife at?" he muttered in a whining Southern voice.

"I'll call 'er—"

"No, yo' don't hav' to call her," he assured him. "She outside?"

"Yeah."

"That's orright."

"Any bags?" he plied further, eyeing St. Louis closely. "Wha' yo' bags at? Outside, too? Don't le' 'em stay dere. Bring 'em on down in yah."

"Bags?" cried Primus, quickly, "I ain't got no bags. Wha' kind o' bags?" He hung on eagerly for the rest.

"Ain't yo' know," the man said, with that faculty for understatement which seems to be the pride of Negroes of the late plantation class, "that yo can't register at no hotel without bags? Go git yo'self a armful o' bags!"

He fled, breathless, to the girl on the pavement.

"Well!" Nicey said, both hands on her spreading hips. He was excited and hurt, and he stuttered. "They—he—won't take us like this. I mean—we got to git weself some bags—bags—bags—"

Nicey sighed, a plaintive sight of relief—a sigh that was a monumental perplexity to him. "Don't look at me like that!" he swore, angry at his ineffectuality. "I did my darndest to git 'im to take us, but he won't do it. Says it's 'gainst the law."

"What yo' gwine do now?" she cut in, distrustful of self-defenses.

"Git me a bag, that's all! Ain't nothin' else to do. C'm awn!"

2

In the resistless languor of the summer evening the Negroes wandered restively over the tar-daubed roofs, squatted negligeed on shelterless window sills, carried on connubial pantomimic chatter across the circumscribed courts, swarmed, six to a square inch, upon curb and step, blasphemously jesting.

"I'll run up," he said, pausing before the portals of a greasy tower of flats. "You wait here, baby, I ain' gwine b' long."

And he cut a slanting passage through the mob, leaped up half a dozen crumbling steps, through a long narrow corridor, ending, blowing, before a knob on the sixth floor.

He rattled a key in the lock, and entered. A strip of oilcloth, dimly silvery in the shadowy interior, flashed at him. He put the strip behind him, flicked on the lights, and stared in Son Son's big starry eyes. The child was the browning purple of star apple and was gorgeously animated. He was strapped in a ram-upholstered chair cocked against the window opening out upon a canyon of street. He jiggled at Primus a plumed African Knight of a doll.

The doll, profuse with bells and spangled half-discs, tinkled annoyingly. "Less noise, sah!" shouted Primus, descending on all fours and industriously examining the debris piled under the davenport which separated the cluttered room in two. Dimples of satanic delight brightened the child's face. He jiggled his toy, wagged his legs, carolling. He puffed his cheeks and booed, scattering mouth-mist about.

"Ain't I tell you to less noise, yo' lil' water mout' imp yo'," cried St. Louis, flying up, seizing and confiscating the tasseled ebony knight and slapping the kid's dusk-down wrists. "Ain't I tell yo' not to botha' yo' pappy when 'e come 'ome, to less yo' noise?" The youngster's sudden recourse to imperturbability annoyed him. "Yo' ain't gwine cry no? Well, tek dat, an' dat, an' dat! Cry, Uh say, Cry! Yo' won't open yo' mout', no, yo' won't buss loose, yo'—"

A pair of claws fell viciously on Primus' back, and, combined with the soaring quality of Tiny's voice, served to wheel him aboutface with a swift downing jolt.

He had forgotten, alas! to push the bath room door when he came in.

"Look yah, man, wha' de hell yo' tink yo' his, hennyhow? Yo' tink yo' dey down in de Back Swamp whey yo' come from, wha' dem don' know nutton but fi' beat up people? Hey, dis yah sinting yo' Ah see 'tan' up yah, 'im tink 'im his back in Lucy a prog bout fi' yampies an' hunions in de picknee head. Come tumpin' de po' picknee roun' like him hone him!"

A fit of conquering rage narrowed and hardened and glistened Tiny's small, tight, mole-flecked face.

From the piano she flew to Son Son's side. The child was bashful, and in a dazed, defensive mood, "Hit dis yah picknee a next time 'n see if me don' cahl a policeman fi' yo' hay. Hey, yo' na'h ashame' o' yo'self, no, fi' come down pon' a puny liggle picknee like dis 'n a show arf yo' strengt'? Why yo' didn't knock de man de oddah day when 'im bruk 'im wheel barrow 'cross yo' neck back 'pon de wharf? Why yo' didn't ram yo' hook in 'im gizzard, yo' dutty old cowrd yo', yo' can't fight yo' match, but yo' must wait till yo' get 'ome an' tek it out pon' me po' boy picknee."

He was on his knees, ransacking the amassing litter.

"Yo' a prowl 'bout now," Tiny went on, hugging Son Son to her bosom, "like a cock sparrow, but go 'long. Me na'h say nutton to yo', me jes' ah wait till de cole weddah come roun' again. An', boy, me will see yo' faht blue hice fuss befor' yo' get anyt'ing from me to shub in yo' stinkin' guts! The day yo' say yo' got de back ache, an' de foot ache, an' de turrah ache, don't le' me hear yo' wit' me name 'pon yo' mout', yo' hear? Fo' if yo' tink yo' gwine get me fo' go out fi' scrub me finger nail dem white fi' cram bittle down a neygah man troat like yo', yo' is lie! Yo' bes' mek up yo' mine now it warm 'n get yo'self a helevator job fo' when de winter come. Fo' so 'elp me Gawd me will see yo' in holy hell fuss befo' yo' a see me trudge hup an' down dem yah stair' like I is any whore fi' do as yo' dam well please.''

"Oh, woman," he chuckled, unconcernedly, "tun yo'self out o' me way, yo' smell bad." He banged the door after him, a frayed straw valise under his arm.

3

He espied her, not leaning toward the frog-ringed moon rising out the river, against the red-spotted rods barricading the way to the cellar, where he had left her; but standing facing him, a speck in the dusk, on the opposing piazza, in an arrow of shadow in the court. He crossed the street, and was inside the marbled sink.

Nicey detached herself from the wall and waved a red, exacting mouth before his tense, sweating face. "Got any idea o' de time," she asked, impatiently.

He had taken a virgin pride in the valise, and was wrestling with it. "Le' me see—" He yanked out the coruscant disc, and Nicey's calm was star-cut. "Ten nine," he said, looking full and composed at her. It broke him up to be there facing her with the lamplight, stealing past her clouded face, giving an added lustre to the curves and brackets of her body.

"Well," she cried, aroused, "I'll be jail housed! You mean to tell me you had me waitin' down here fo' you fo' nearly a hour, yo' lanky suck egg son of a bitch!" She swung herself free of his grovelling embraces.

"Oh, Nicey," he begged, running after her, "don't go, sweet, I got de bag—"

"An' now yo' got it," she turned, interrogatively, "Wha' yo' expect to do with it?"

"Tek it on back there!" he avowed in one of his recurrent moments of self-assertiveness.

"Like hell we do!" she swore, "I'm gwine home."

"Oh, don't go, Nicey," he cried, swinishly, "I know a place. Don't let's go home after all the trouble we bin to."

"Aw, hell, boy, yo' give me a pain in the hip. Yo' know a place me eye! Where is this place at?"

"Come awn, I'll show yah! Don't be skeert, I know what I'm talkin' 'bout—"

"Like hell you do."

". . . it ain't the same one we bin to orready."

"Fur?" she perked up, with returning curiosity.

"Oh, no, jes' roun' de corner, I'll show yo'. Yo' tink it's fur? It ain't fur." His lurid efforts at self-assertion were taking a strange weight with her.

And so they peddled on. The dust, the city's dissoluteness, the sensory pursuits, gave a rigorous continuity to themselves, and to their needs, sent them burning against the sinister sovereignty of Upper Fifth Avenue.

Here there was a cluster of figures aloft. "Come on up," cried the man, "look out, lady, fo' dat ole runnin' hoss. Little Bits, ain't I tell you not to leave yo' things knockin' 'bout like dat? Come 'n tek 'em in miss . . . look out, mistah, get up there, Mignon, an' let the gemman pass."

As a sort of imposed ritual the woman remarked, with a friendly frown suggestive of a discovery of startling import, "Ain't it hot tonight?"

"Ain't it though?" returned Nicey, flopping grandly by.

"This way, folks," cried the man, showing them to the parlor.

Passing the opulent hangings, sinking ankle deep in the rugs, Nicey was moved to observe, "Gee, I'd like to sleep in a swell place like this." As the female of the occasion she was led to the reddest plush couch in the room. Outside by the coat rack the two men stopt.

Primus' head bared, he was dabbing for the sweat sizzling in the rim of his hat. He put the valise down and went through his pockets for the money.

A princely urbanity governed the man. He edged the light behind him and scanned the most vagrant impulses lurking in Primus' eyes.

"Why don't you people come right?" he scolded in fatherly fashion. "Yo' don't come right," he insisted, trusting to the fleetness of the young man's mind.

Of the two listening there was no doubt that Nicey's ears were cocked nearer the big man's voice.

"Now take the lady," he went on, with disarming felicity, "Why—why don't she wear a hat?"

With the feet of a deer, the girl shot out the parlor, sped past St. Louis, through the vestibule and out into the Harlem night.

"I keep on tellin' 'em they won't come right," he said, as Primus trotted, valise in hand, down the stairs. "Don't they know that folks don't travel that-a-way?"

As she was about to merge in with the dusk saturating Lenox Avenue, he caught up with her.

"Jee, you're an unlucky bastard!"

"I'm sorry, Nicey."

"I never heard o' anybody with your kind o' luck. Yo' must o' spit on a hot brick or somethin'."

"I'd give anything to prove to you, Nicey, that I ain't nobody's simp."

"You're a long time provin' it, big boy."

"Oh, honey, giv' me time!"

"Say, big fellah, go to the judge, don't come to me. I can't giv' yo' any mo' time."

"I'd do anything—"

"Go stick yo' head in a sewer then."

"Let's go back, sweet, come, let's."

"Go back where?"

"I mean—with a hat. I'll go git yo' a hat."

"Christ, what next, buyin' me a hat. All I got to do is stick roun' you long enough an' you'll be buyin' me a teddy aftah awhile."

At a Hebrew hat shop on the Avenue they stopt and when they came out again Nicey was none the worse for a prim little bonnet with bluebells galloping wildly over it.

Crowds of high-hitting Negroes, stevedores from the North River docks— Cubans prattling in sugar lofts on the Brooklyn water front—discarding overalls and gas masks and cargo hooks—revelling in canes and stickpins and cravats—strutting light browns and high blacks—overswept the Avenue. And the emotion of being part of one vast questing whole quickened the hunger in Nicey's and Primus' breasts.

Waddling down the long moldy corridor, he let the girl go on ahead of him. The man was behind him, carrying the candle and jingling keys, ready to exact the casuallest ounce of tribute. "Don't forget," he said, "that if you want hot water in the morning, it'll be fifty cents extra."

FROM
THE BIG SEA
LANGSTON HUGHES

Dormitory

Like the bullfights, I can never put on paper the thrill of that underground ride to Harlem. I had never been in a subway before and it fascinated me—the noise, the speed, the green lights ahead. At every station I kept watching for the sign: 135TH STREET. When I saw it, I held my breath. I came out onto the platform with two heavy bags and looked around. It was still early morning and people were going to work. Hundreds of colored people! I wanted to shake hands with them, speak to them. I hadn't seen any colored people for so long—that is, any Negro colored people.

I went up the steps and out into the bright September sunlight. Harlem! I stood there, dropped my bags, took a deep breath and felt happy again. I registered at the Y.

When college opened, I did not want to move into the dormitory at Columbia. I really did not want to go to college at all. I didn't want to do anything but live in Harlem, get a job and work there. But I had passed the entrance examinations and my father had paid my tuition by draft, so I had to go to college. When I went to get my room in the Hartley Hall dormitory on the campus, the lady at the office looked slightly startled and said: "Oh, there must be some mistake! All the rooms were gone long ago."

I said: "But I reserved mine *long ago,* and paid the required deposit by mail."

She said: "You did? Then let me see."

Of course, she found my reservation, made from Toluca, but she kept looking at me in a puzzled and not very friendly fashion. Then she asked if I were a Mexican. When she discovered I wasn't, she consulted with several other people, papers fluttered, a telephone call was made, but finally they gave me the admittance slip to the dormitory. Having made my reservation early, I had one of the most convenient rooms in Hartley Hall, on the first floor just off the lobby. But they certainly didn't seem any too anxious to give it to me because (no doubt) they realized I was colored.

Of course, later I was to run into much of that sort of thing in my grown-up travels in America, that strange astonishment on the part of so many whites that a Negro should expect any of the common courtesies and conveniences that other Americans enjoy.

Columbia

I didn't like Columbia. It was too big. It was not fun, like being in high school. You didn't get to know anybody, hardly. The buildings looked like factories.

By the end of my first term I got to know Chun, a Chinese boy, pretty well. And a boy named Best, whose father made pencils and who lived on Riverside Drive. And a very rich boy named Craig in my dormitory, who always asked me to help him do his French or write his English themes. The rich boy used to know lots of chorus girls and sometimes, after the Broadway shows were over, he would drive up to the Hartley Hall windows on the Amsterdam Avenue side with a taxi-full of girls, call some of his pals and they would all go out for a ride. He would never call me, of course, but if he saw a light in my window, he might yell in: "See you tomorrow, Lang, third hour, and we'll get on them French verbs. I don't need no verbs tonight."

Like me, Chun, the Chinese boy, didn't like the big University, either. He said white people were much nicer in the missionary school in China from which he came. Here nobody paid any attention to him, and the girls wouldn't dance with him at dances. (I didn't expect them to dance with me, but he did, not being used to American ways.)

Nobody asked him to join a frat and nobody asked me, but I didn't expect anyone to. When I tried out for the *Spectator,* they assigned me to gather frat house and society news, an assignment impossible for a colored boy to fill, as they knew. I remember Corey Ford was on the editorial board. And there was a pleasant young man around named Charles A. Wagner, a poet, who later became Book Editor of the *New York Mirror.* But they were upper classmen and, I suppose, not particularly interested in the relationship of Chinese and Negroes to the rest of the student body, anyhow. It was all a little like my senior year in high school—except more so—when one noticed that the kids began to get a bit grown and girl-conscious and stand-offish and anti-Negro in the American way, that increases when kids take on the accepted social habits.

As for the instructors at Columbia whom I knew, the only one who interested me much was a Mr. Wasson, who read Mencken aloud all the time. In physics, I never understood a thing. And the instructor would never explain. He always said you had to work it out for yourself—which isn't so easy if you haven't got that kind of a mind or anybody to help you. Higher mathematics were like a Chinese puzzle. And French was taught to an enormous class, with the instructor having each one recite by going down the roll with the speed of an express train—evidently so he could get some sort of mark down for everybody before the bell rang.

Living in New York was higher than my father had anticipated, and he asked every month for an accounting of my expenses, penny by penny. Since I had always spent it all, "All gone" seemed to me a sufficient accounting to give, simple and clear. But it did not please my father.

About that time, my mother and step-father had parted again. My mother came to New York to live, so I had to use my allowance to help her until she found a job. My father kept on wondering why I ran out of money so quickly. But I didn't have enough for college, my mother, and me, too.

What an unpleasant winter! I didn't like Columbia, nor the students, nor anything I was studying! So I didn't study. I went to shows, read books, attended lectures at the Rand School under Ludwig Lewisohn and Heywood Broun, missed an important exam in the spring to go to Bert Williams's funeral, sat up in the gallery night after night at *Shuffle Along,* adored Florence Mills, and went to Chinatown with Chun. I even acquired a small Mandarin vocabulary.

Of course, I finished the year without honors. I had no intention of going further at Columbia, anyhow. I felt that I would never turn out to be what my father expected me to be in return for the amount he invested. So I wrote him and told him I was going to quit college and go to work on my own, and that he needn't send me any more money.

He didn't. He didn't even write again.

On My Own

After the finals, I moved out of Hartley Hall at Columbia and down into Harlem, where I began life on my own. I was twenty.

Before June my mother had gone back to Cleveland. So I took a room alone and started to look for work. In those days there was no depression—at least, not much of a one—so there were lots of ads in the morning papers. I bought the papers and began to answer ads regarding jobs I thought I could handle—office boy, clerk, waiter, bus boy, and other simple occupations. Nine times out of ten—*ten* times out of ten, to be truthful—the employer would look at me, shake his head and say, with an air of amazement: "But I didn't advertise for a colored boy."

It was the same in the employment offices. Unless a job was definitely marked COLORED on the board outside, there was no use applying, I discovered. And only one job in a thousand would be marked COLORED. I found it very hard to get work in New York. Experience was proving my father right. On many sides, the color line barred your way to making a living in America.

I finally got work on a truck-garden farm on Staten Island. The farm belonged to some Greeks, who didn't care what nationality you were just so you got up at five in the morning and worked all day until it was too dark to see the rows in the field. They paid you fifty dollars a month, with bed and board. The bed was a pile of hay in the loft of the barn—but it was summer, and the hay was pleasant. They had two Greek hired hands, a couple of Italians, a Jewish boy from Brownsville, and me. These were good-natured people to work with, and the Greek owners, two brothers and their wives, worked hardest of all. They woke us up at daybreak, and worked along with us, or ahead of us, in the fields all day.

We had a breakfast of goat's cheese and coffee. At midday, a big dinner, at four o'clock more cheese and coffee in the open field. And a late supper after dark, of sandwiches and tea. Healthy food. Plenty of watermelons, onions, cheese, and tomatoes. We worked hard, ploughing, hoeing, spreading manure, picking weeds, washing lettuce, beets, carrots, onions, tying them and packing them for market, loading the wagons, and standing by lantern light to watch one of the indefatigable little Greek brothers drive off in the night to the New York market.

The food we had grown went off to market to feed a big city. There was something about such work that made you feel useful and important—sending off onions that *you* had planted and seen grow from a mere speck of green, that *you* had tended and weeded, had pulled up and washed and even loaded on the wagon—seeing them go off to feed the great city of New York. *Your* onions!

It was a pretty good job, and I liked it—that is, all but the mosquitoes in the dawn, that bit your ears off before the sun came out, blazing and strong.

We even worked Sunday mornings. Sunday afternoons we had off. Usually we slept then, dead-tired, among the flies in the heat of the barn, or else lay out under the shade of a lone tree, the only one on the whole farm. Sometimes some of the fellows went into Port Richmond to find girls and wine. Or occasionally to New York, but not often, for most of them were saving money to send back to the old country.

The Brownsville boy and I were the only two native Americans. The Brownsville boy confided to me that he wanted to stay away from Brooklyn until the police forgot about something he did not want to face.

Only once during the whole summer did I go to New York, and that was to see Rudolph Valentino in *Blood and Sand,* because I liked bullfights and I wanted to see if they had a real one in the picture. They didn't have much of a one. I guess the censors cut it out.

After a visit to Harlem, I got back to the farm after midnight. The other men had taken all the loose hay in the loft and were asleep on it, so I had to roll down an unopened bale for my bedding. The heavy bales were packed compactly one on top of another, so I had to climb to the top of the block-like heap and roll down a bale from there, eight or ten feet up. Unfortunately, however, not one but several bales came rolling down, shaking the whole barn, and making a great racket.

The next thing I knew, I was alone in the big loft and all the Greeks and Italians were running for dear life through the barnyard.

Astonished, I went to an opening in the loft and called out: "Hey! What's the matter?"

"*Terremotor!*" they yelled. "*Terremoto!* Come down quick! Come out!"

I began to shake with laughter. They thought it was an earthquake!

When the truck-farming season was over, I went back to New York with enough cash to buy an overcoat and pay a few weeks' rent in advance. I took a room with a kind woman in Harlem named Mrs. Dorsey, who had a son and a daughter about my own age. I wrote a few poems and sent them to the *Crisis*. Then shortly, I found a job delivering flowers for Thorley, but I didn't like the job.

The flowers were terrifically expensive and they usually went to very *comme il faut* people—the Baroness d'Erlanger at the Ritz, Marion Davies on a yacht, the Roosevelts at Oyster Bay, Vivienne Segal at the Empire. Each box I delivered was billed, as a rule, for more than my month's rent—more money for a box of flowers than I could earn in ten days—and those receiving the flowers seldom gave you a tip for bringing them! Butlers and maids usually took the boxes, so you didn't even see the celebrity whose flowers you carried. Sometimes you would catch a glimpse of the great one, though, and then you would feel a little more cheerful, having laid eyes on some famous and successful person. But when you got back to the shop, the boss would always ask why in the hell you took so long to make a delivery.

"Hurry up and get the next order out," would be his command. "Quick now! Hurry!"

My father would have loved his efficiency. He and Mr. Thorley could have been good friends.

On the day following those nights when you worked until nine o'clock, or more, you were entitled to come an hour late the following morning. One night I worked until almost midnight, making a delivery on Long Island. The next morning I came at ten. Mr. Thorley himself happened to be standing at the door, looking down Fifth Avenue. He said: "Don't you know better than to be showing up here at such an hour?"

I started to explain that the night before had been my late night, and that I had worked four or five hours overtime, but he cut me off to order me brusquely to take the whole morning off—because he would take a morning out of my pay, anyhow! He told me to come back after lunch.

I never went back again. But finding another job that fall was not easy. Want ads, employment offices, the Y, the railroad stations, the big hotels, the shoe shine stands. No luck.

But all those months in New York I'd kept remembering the smell of the sea on my first night in Vera Cruz. And it seemed to me now that if I had to work for low wages at dull jobs, I might just as well see the world, so I began to look for work on a ship.

. . .

Parties

In those days of the late 1920's, there were a great many parties, in Harlem and out, to which various members of the New Negro group were invited. These parties, when given by important Harlemites (or Carl Van Vechten) were reported in full in the society pages of the Harlem press, but best in the sparkling Harlemese of Geraldyn Dismond who wrote for the *Interstate Tattler.* On one of Taylor Gordon's fiestas she reports as follows:

> What a crowd! All classes and colors met face to face, ultra aristocrats, Bourgeois, Communists, Park Avenuers galore, bookers, publishers, Broadway celebs, and Harlemites giving each other the once over. The social revolution was on. And yes, Lady Nancy Cunard was there all in black (she would) with 12 of her grand bracelets. . . . And was the entertainment on the up and up! Into swell dance music was injected African drums that played havoc with blood pressure. Jimmy Daniels sang his gigolo hits. Gus Simons, the Harlem crooner, made the River Stay Away From His Door and Taylor himself brought out everything from "Hot Dog" to "Bravo" when he made high C.

A'Lelia Walker was the then great Harlem party giver, although Mrs. Bernia Austin fell but little behind. And at the Seventh Avenue apartment of Jessie Fauset, literary soirées with much poetry and but little to drink were the order of the day. The same was true of Lillian Alexander's, where the older intellectuals gathered.

A'Lelia Walker, however, big-hearted, night-dark, hair-straightening heiress, made no pretense at being intellectual or exclusive. At her "at homes" Negro poets and Negro number bankers mingled with downtown poets and seat-on-the-stock-exchange racketeers. Countee Cullen would be there and Witter Bynner, Muriel Draper and Nora Holt, Andy Razaf and Taylor Gordon. And a good time was had by all.

A'Lelia Walker had an apartment that held perhaps a hundred people. She would usually issue several hundred invitations to each party. Unless you went early there was no possible way of getting in. Her parties were as crowded as the New York subway at the rush hour—entrance, lobby, steps, hallway, and apartment a milling crush of guests, with everybody seeming to enjoy the crowding. Once, some royal personage arrived, a Scandinavian prince, I believe, but his equerry saw no way of getting him through the crowded entrance hall and into the party, so word was sent in to A'Lelia Walker that His Highness, the Prince, was waiting without. A'Lelia sent word back that she saw no way of getting His Highness in, either, nor could she herself get out through the crowd to greet him. But she offered to send refreshments downstairs to the Prince's car.

A'Lelia Walker was a gorgeous dark Amazon, in a silver turban. She had a town house in New York (also an apartment where she preferred to live) and a country mansion at Irvington-on-the-Hudson, with pipe organ programs each morning to awaken her guests gently. Her mother made a great fortune from the Madame Walker Hair Straightening Process, which had worked wonders on unruly Negro hair in the early nineteen hundreds—and which continues to work wonders today. The daughter used much of that money for fun. A'Lelia Walker was the joy-goddess of Harlem's 1920's.

She had been very much in love with her first husband, from whom she was divorced. Once at one of her parties she began to cry about him. She retired to her boudoir and wept. Some of her friends went in to comfort her, and found her clutching a memento of their broken romance.

"The only thing I have left that he gave me," she sobbed, "it's all I have left of him!"

It was a gold shoehorn.

When A'Lelia Walker died in 1931, she had a grand funeral. It was by invitation only. But, just as for her parties, a great many more invitations had been issued than the small but exclusive Seventh Avenue funeral parlor could provide for. Hours before the funeral, the street in front of the undertaker's chapel was crowded. The doors were not opened until the cortège arrived—and the cortège was late. When it came, there were almost enough family mourners, attendants, and honorary pallbearers in the procession to fill the room; as well as the representatives of the various Walker beauty parlors throughout the country. And there were still hundreds of friends outside, waving their white, engraved invitations aloft in the vain hope of entering.

Once the last honorary pallbearers had marched in, there was a great crush at the doors. Muriel Draper, Rita Romilly, Mrs. Roy Sheldon, and I were among the fortunate few who achieved an entrance.

We were startled to find De Lawd standing over A'Lelia's casket. It was a truly amazing illusion. At that time *The Green Pastures* was at the height of its fame, and there stood De Lawd in the person of Rev. A. Clayton Powell, a Harlem minister, who looked exactly like Richard B. Harrison in the famous role in the play. He had the same white hair and kind face, and was later offered the part of De Lawd in the film version of the drama. Now, he stood there motionless in the dim light behind the silver casket of A'Lelia Walker.

Soft music played and it was very solemn. When we were seated and the chapel became dead silent, De Lawd said: "The Four Bon Bons will now sing."

A night club quartette that had often performed at A'Lelia's parties arose and sang for her. They sang Noel Coward's "I'll See You Again," and they swung it slightly, as she might have liked it. It was a grand funeral and very much like a party. Mrs. Mary McCleod Bethune spoke in that great deep voice of hers, as only she can speak. She recalled the poor mother of A'Lelia Walker in old clothes, who had labored to bring the gift of beauty to Negro womanhood, and had taught them the care of their skin and their hair, and had built up a great business and a great fortune to the pride and glory of the Negro race—and then had given it all to her daughter, A'Lelia.

Then a poem of mine was read by Edward Perry, "To A'Lelia." And after that the girls from the various Walker beauty shops throughout America brought their flowers and laid them on the bier.

That was really the end of the gay times of the New Negro era in Harlem, the period that had begun to reach its end when the crash came in 1929 and the white people had much less money to spend on themselves, and practically none to spend on Negroes, for the depression brought everybody down a peg or two. And the Negroes had but few pegs to fall.

But in those pre-crash days there were parties and parties. At the novelist, Jessie Fauset's, parties there was always quite a different atmosphere from that at most other Harlem good-time gatherings. At Miss Fauset's, a good time was shared by talking literature and reading poetry aloud and perhaps enjoying some conversation in French. White people were seldom present there unless they were very distinguished white people because Jessie Fauset did not feel like opening her home to mere sightseers, or faddists momentarily in love with Negro life. At her house one would usually meet editors and students, writers and social workers, and serious people who liked books and the British Museum, and had perhaps been to Florence. (Italy, not Alabama.)

I remember, one night at her home there was a gathering in honor of Salvador de Madariaga, the Spanish diplomat and savant, which somehow became a rather self-conscious gathering, with all the Harlem writers called upon to recite their poems and speak their pieces. But afterwards, Charles S. Johnson and I invited Mr. Madariaga to Small's Paradise where we had a "ball" until the dawn came up and forced us from the club.

In those days, 409 Edgecombe, Harlem's tallest and most exclusive apartment house, was quite a party center. The Walter Whites and the Aaron Douglases, among others, lived and entertained there. Walter White was a jovial and cultured host, with a sprightly mind, and an apartment overlooking the Hudson. He had the most beautiful wife in Harlem, and they were always hospitable to hungry literati like me.

At the Aaron Douglases', although he was a painter, more young writers were found than painters. Usually everybody would chip in and go dutch on the refreshments, calling down to the nearest bootlegger for a bottle of whatever it was that was drunk in those days, when labels made no difference at all in the liquid content—Scotch, bourbon, rye, and gin being the same except for coloring matter.

Arna Bontemps, poet and coming novelist, quiet and scholarly, looking like a young edition of Dr. DuBois, was the mysterious member of the Harlem literati, in that we knew he had recently married, but none of us had ever seen his wife. All the writers wondered who she was and what she looked like. He never brought her with him to any of the parties, so she remained the mystery of the New Negro Renaissance. But I went with him once to his apartment to meet her, and found her a shy and charming girl, holding a golden baby on her lap. A year or two later there was another golden baby. And every time I went away to Haiti or Mexico or Europe and came back, there would be a new golden baby, each prettier than the last—so that was why the literati never saw Mrs. Bontemps.

Toward the end of the New Negro era, E. Simms Campbell came to Harlem from St. Louis, and began to try to sell cartoons to the *New Yorker*. My first memory of him is at a party at Gwendolyn Bennett's on Long Island. In the midst of the party, the young lady Mr. Campbell had brought, Constance Willis, whom he later married, began to put on her hat and coat and gloves. The hostess asked her if she was going home. She said: "No, only taking Elmer outside to straighten him out." What indiscretion he had committed at the party I never knew, perhaps flirting with some other girl, or taking a drink too many. But when we looked out, there was Constance giving Elmer an all-around talking-to on the sidewalk. And she must have straightened him out, because he was a very nice young man at parties ever after.

At the James Weldon Johnson parties and gumbo suppers, one met solid people like Clarence and Mrs. Darrow. At the Dr. Alexander's, you met the upper crust Negro intellectuals like Dr. DuBois. At Wallace Thurman's, you met the bohemians of both Harlem and the Village. And in the gin mills and speakeasies and night clubs between 125th and 145th, Eighth Avenue and Lenox, you met everybody from Buddy de Silva to Theodore Dreiser, Ann Pennington to the first Mrs. Eugene O'Neill. In the days when Harlem was in vogue, Amanda Randolph was at the Alhambra, Jimmy Walker was mayor of New York, and Louise sang at the old New World.

ESTHETE IN HARLEM
LANGSTON HUGHES

Strange,
That in this nigger place
I should meet life face to face;
When, for years, I had been seeking
Life in places gentler-speaking,
Until I came to this vile street
And found Life stepping on my feet!

RAILROAD AVENUE
LANGSTON HUGHES

Dusk dark
On Railroad Avenue.
Lights in the fish joints,
Lights in the pool rooms.
A box car some train
Has forgotten
In the middle of the block.

A player piano,
A victrola.
942
Was the number.
A boy
Lounging on the corner.
A passing girl
With purple powdered skin.
Laughter
Suddenly
Like a taut drum.
Laughter
Suddenly
Neither truth nor lie.
Laughter
Hardening the dusk dark evening.
Laughter
Shaking the lights in the fish joints,
Rolling white balls in the pool rooms,
And leaving untouched the box car
Some train has forgotten.

SMOKE, LILIES AND JADE
RICHARD BRUCE

He wanted to do something . . . to write or draw . . . or something . . . but it was so comfortable just to lay there on the bed . . . . . . his shoes off . . . and think . . . think of everything . . . short disconnected thoughts—to wonder . . . to remember . . . to think and smoke . . . why wasn't he worried that he had no money . . . he *had* had five cents . . . but he had been hungry . . . he *was* hungry and still . . . all he wanted to do was . . . lay there comfortably smoking . . . think . . . wishing he were writing . . . or drawing . . . or something . . . something about the things he felt and thought . . . but what did he think . . . he remembered how his mother had awakened him one night . . . ages ago . . . six years ago . . . Alex . . . he had always wondered at the strangeness of it . . . she had seemed so . . . so . . . so just the same . . . Alex . . . I think your father is dead . . . and it hadn't seemed so strange . . . yet . . . one's mother didn't say that . . . didn't wake one at midnight every night to say . . . feel him . . . put your hand on his head . . . then whisper with a catch in her voice . . . I'm afraid . . . sh don't wake Lam . . . yet it hadn't seemed as it should have seemed . . . even when he had felt his father's cool wet forehead . . . it hadn't been tragic . . . the light had been turned very low . . . and flickered . . . yet it hadn't been tragic . . . or weird . . . not at all as one should feel when one's father died . . . even his reply of . . . yes he is dead . . . had been commonplace . . . hadn't been dramatic . . . there had been no tears . . . no sobs . . . not even a sorrow . . . and yet he must have realized that one's father couldn't smile . . . or sing any more . . . after he had died . . . every one remembered his father's voice . . . it had been a lush voice . . . a promise . . . then that dressing together . . . his mother and himself . . . in the bathroom . . . why was the bathroom always the warmest room in the winter . . . as they had put on their clothes . . . his mother had been telling him what he must do . . . and cried softly . . . and that had made him cry too but you mustn't cry Alex . . . remember you have to be a little man now . . . and that was all . . . didn't other wives and sons cry more for their dead than that . . . anyway people never cried for beautiful sunsets . . . or music . . . and those were the things that hurt . . . the things to sympathize with . . . then out into the snow and dark of the morning . . . first to the undertaker's . . . no first to Uncle Frank's . . . why did Aunt Lula have to act like that . . . to ask again and again . . . but when did he die . . . when did he die . . . I just can't believe it . . . poor Minerva . . . then out into the snow and dark again . . . how had his mother expected him to know where to find the night bell at the undertaker's . . . he was the most sensible of them all tho . . . all he had said was . . . what . . . Harry Francis . . . too bad . . . tell mamma I'll be there first thing in the morning . . . then down the deserted streets again . . . to grandmother's . . . it was growing light now . . . it must be terrible to die in daylight . . . grandpa had been sweeping the snow off the yard . . . he had been glad of that because . . . well he could tell him better than grandma . . . grandpa . . . father's dead . . . and he hadn't acted strange either . . . books lied . . . he had just looked at Alex a moment then continued sweeping . . . all he said was . . . what time did he die . . . she'll want to know . . . then passing thru the lonesome street toward home . . . Mrs. Mamie Grant was closing a window and spied him . . . hallow Alex . . . an' how's your father this morning' . . . dead . . . get out . . . tch tch tch an' I was just around there with a cup a' custard yesterday . . . Alex puffed contentedly on his cigarette . . . he was hungry and comfortable . . . and he had an ivory holder inlaid with red jade and green . . . funny how the smoke seemed to climb up that ray of sunlight . . . went up the slant just like imagination . . . was imagination blue . . . or was it because he had spent his last five cents and couldn't worry . . . anyway it was nice to lay there and wonder . . . and remember . . . why was he so different from other people . . . the only things he remembered of his father's funeral were the crowded church and the ride in the hack . . . so many people there in the church . . . and ladies with tears in their eyes . . . and on their cheeks . . . and some men too . . . why did people cry . . . vanity that was all . . . yet they weren't exactly hypocrites . . . but why . . . it had made him furious . . . all these people crying . . . it wasn't *their* father . . . and he wasn't crying . . . couldn't cry for sorrow altho he had loved his father more than . . . than . . . it had made him so angry that tears had come to his eyes . . . and he had been ashamed of his mother . . . crying into a handkerchief . . . so ashamed that tears had run down his cheeks and he had frowned . . . and some one . . . a woman . . . had said . . . look at that poor little dear . . . Alex is just like his father . . . and the tears had run fast . . . because he *wasn't* like his father . . . he couldn't sing . . . he didn't want to sing . . . he didn't want to sing . . . Alex blew a cloud of smoke . . . blue smoke . . . when they had taken his father from the vault three weeks later . . . he had grown beautiful . . . his nose had become perfect and clear . . . his hair had turned jet black and glossy and silky . . . and his skin was a transparent green . . . like the sea only not so deep . . . and where it was drawn over the cheek bones a pale beautiful red appeared . . . like a blush . . . why hadn't his father looked like that always . . . but no . . . to have sung would have broken the wondrous repose of his lips and maybe that was his beauty . . . maybe it was wrong to think thoughts like these . . . but they were nice and pleasant and comfortable . . . when one was smoking a cigarette thru an ivory holder . . . inlaid with red jade and green . . . .

he wondered why he couldn't find work . . . a job . . . when he had first come to New York he had . . . and he had only been fourteen then was it because he was nineteen now that he felt so idle . . . and contented . . . or because he was an artist . . . but was he an artist . . . was one an artist until one became known . . . of course he was an artist . . . and strangely enough so were all his friends . . . he should be ashamed that he didn't work . . . but . . . was it five years in New York . . . or the fact that he was an artist . . . when his mother said she couldn't understand him . . . why did he vaguely pity her instead of being ashamed . . . he should be . . . his mother and all his relatives said so . . . his brother was three years younger than he and yet he had already been away from home a year . . . on the stage . . . making thirty-five dollars a week . . . had three suits and many clothes and was going to help mother . . . while he . . . Alex . . . was content to lay and smoke and meet friends at night . . . to argue and read Wilde . . . Freud . . . Boccacio and Schnitzler . . . to attend Gurdjieff meetings and know things . . . Why did they scoff at him for knowing such people as Carl . . . Mencken . . . Toomer . . . Hughes . . . Cullen . . . Wood . . . Cabell . . . oh the whole lot of them . . . was it because it seemed incongruous that he . . . who was so little known . . . should call by first names people they would like to know . . . were they jealous . . . no mothers aren't jealous of their sons . . . they are proud of them . . . why then . . . when these friends accepted and liked him . . . no matter how he dressed . . . why did mother ask . . . and you went looking like that . . . Langston was a fine fellow . . . he knew there was something in Alex . . . and so did Rene and Borgia . . . and Zora and Clement and Miguel . . . and . . . and . . . and all of them . . . if he went to see mother she would ask . . . how do you feel Alex with nothing in your pockets . . . I don't see how you can be satisfied . . . Really you're a mystery to me . . . and who you take after . . . I'm sure I don't know . . . none of my brothers were lazy and shiftless . . . I can never remember the time when they weren't sending money home and your father was your age he was supporting a family . . .

where you get your nerve I don't know . . . just because you've tried to write one or two little poems and stories that no one understands . . . you seem to think the world owes you a living . . . you should see by now how much is thought of them . . . you can't sell anything . . . and you won't do anything to make money . . . wake up Alex . . . I don't know what will become of you . . . .

it was hard to believe in one's self after that . . . did Wildes' parents or Shelly's or Goya's talk to them like that . . . but it was depressing to think in that vein . . . Alex stretched and yawned . . . Max had died . . . Margaret had died . . . so had Sonia . . . Cynthia . . . Juan-Jose and Harry . . . all people he had loved . . . loved one by one and together . . . and all had died . . . he never loved a person long before they died . . . in truth he was tragic . . . that was a lovely appellation . . . The Tragic Genius . . . think . . . to go thru life known as The Tragic Genius . . . romantic . . . but it was more or less true . . . Alex turned over and blew another cloud of smoke . . . was all life like that . . . smoke . . . blue smoke from an ivory holder . . . he wished he were in New Bedford . . . New Bedord was a nice place . . . snug little houses set complacently behind protecting lawns . . . half open windows showing prim interiors from behind waving cool curtains . . . inviting . . . like precise courtesans winking from behind lace fans . . . and trees . . . many trees . . . casting lacey patterns of shade on the sun dipped sidewalks . . . small stores . . . naively proud of their pseudo grandeur . . . banks . . . called institutions for saving . . . all naive . . . that was it . . . New Bedford was naive . . . after the sophistication of New York it would fan one like a refreshing breeze . . . and yet he had returned to New York . . . and sophistication . . . was he sophisticated . . . no because he was seldom bored . . . seldom bored by anything . . . and weren't the sophisticated continually suffering from ennui . . . on the contrary . . . he was amused . . . amused by the artificiality of naïveté and sophistication alike . . . but may be that in itself was the essence of sophistication or . . . was it cynicism . . . or were the two identical . . . he blew a cloud of smoke . . . it was growing dark now . . . and the smoke no longer had a ladder to climb . . . but soon the moon would rise and then he would clothe the silver moon in blue smoke garments . . . truly smoke was like imagination . . . .

Alex sat up . . . pulled on his shoes and went out . . . it was a beautiful night . . . and so large . . . the dusky blue hung like a curtain in an immense arched doorway . . . fastened with silver tacks . . . to wander in the night was wonderful . . . myriads of inquisitive lights . . . curiously prying into the dark . . . and fading unsatisfied . . . he passed a woman . . . she was not beautiful . . . and he was sad because she did not weep that she would never be beautiful . . . was it Wilde who had said . . . a cigarette is the most perfect pleasure because it leaves one unsatisfied . . . the breeze gave to him a perfume stolen from some wandering lady of the evening . . . it pleased him . . . why was it that men wouldn't use perfumes . . . they should . . . each and every one of them liked perfumes . . . the man who denied that was a liar . . . or a coward . . . but if ever he were to voice that thought . . . express it . . . he would be misunderstood . . . a fine feeling that . . . to be misunderstood . . . it made him feel tragic and great . . . but may be it would be nicer to be understood . . . but no . . . no great artist is . . . then again neither were fools . . . they were strangely akin these two . . . Alex thought of a sketch he would make . . . a personality sketch of Fania . . . straight classic features tinted proud purple . . . sensuous fine lips . . . gilded for truth . . . eyes . . . half opened and lids colored mysterious green . . . hair black and straight . . . drawn sternly mocking back from the false puritanical forehead . . . maybe he would made Edith too . . . skin a blue . . . infinite like night . . . and eyes . . . slant and grey . . . very complacent like a cat's . . . Mona Lisa lips . . . red and seductive as . . . as pomegranate juice . . . in truth it was fine to be young and hungry and an artist . . . to blow blue smoke from an ivory holder . . . .

here was the cafeteria . . . it was almost as tho it had journeyed to meet him . . . the night was so blue . . . how does blue feel . . . or red or gold or any other color . . . if colors could be heard he could paint most wondrous tunes . . . symphonious . . . think . . . the dulcet clear tone of a blue like night . . . of a red like pomegranate juice . . . like Edith's lips . . . of the fairy tones to be heard in a sunset . . . like rubies shaken in a crystal cup . . . of the symphony of Fania . . . and silver . . . and gold . . . he had heard the sound of gold . . . but they weren't the sounds he wanted to catch . . . no . . . they must be liquid . . . not so staccato but flowing variations of the same caliber . . . there was no one in the cafe as yet . . . he sat and waited . . . that was a clever idea he had had about color music . . . but after all he was a monstrous clever fellow . . . Jurgen had said that . . . funny how characters in books said the things one wanted to say . . . he would like to know Jurgen . . . how does one go about getting an introduction to a fiction character . . . go up to the brown cover of the book and knock gently . . . and say hello . . . then timidly . . . is Duke Jurgen there . . . or . . . no because if entered the book in the beginning Jurgen would only be a pawn broker . . . and one didn't enter a book in the center . . . but what foolishness . . . Alex lit a cigarette . . . but Cabell was a master to have written Jurgen . . . and an artist . . . and a poet . . . Alex blew a cloud of smoke . . . a few lines of one of Langston's poems came to describe Jurgen . . . . .

> Somewhat like Ariel
> Somewhat like Puck
> Somewhat like a gutter boy
> Who loves to play in muck.
> Somewhat like Bacchus
> Somewhat like Pan
> And a way with women
> Like a sailor man . . . .

Langston must have known Jurgen . . . suppose Jurgen had met Tonio Kroeger . . . what a vagrant thought . . . Kroeger . . . Kroeger . . . Kroeger . . . why here was Rene . . . Alex had almost gone to sleep . . . Alex blew a cone of smoke as he took Rene's hand . . . it was nice to have friends like Rene . . . so comfortable . . . Rene was speaking . . . Borgia joined them . . . and de Diego Padro . . . their talk veered to . . . James Branch Cabell . . . beautiful . . . marvelous . . . Rene had an enchanting accent . . . said sank for thank and souse for south . . . but they couldn't know Cabell's greatness . . . Alex searched the smoke for expression . . . he . . . he . . . well he has created a phantasy mire . . . that's it . . . from clear rich imagery . . . life and silver sands . . . that's nice . . . and silver sands . . . imagine lilies growing in such a mire . . . when they close at night their gilded underside would protect . . . but that's not it at all . . . his thoughts just carried and mingled like . . . like odors . . . suggested but never definite . . . Rene was leaving . . . they all were leaving . . . Alex sauntered slowly back . . . the houses all looked sleepy . . . funny . . . made him feel like writing poetry . . . and about death too . . . an elevated crashed by overhead scattering all his thoughts with its noise . . . making them spread . . . in circles . . . then larger circles . . . just like a splash in a calm pool . . . what had he been thinking . . . of . . . a poem about death . . . but he no longer felt that urge . . . just walk and think and wonder . . . think and remember and smoke . . . blow smoke that mixed with his thoughts and the night . . . he would like to live in a large white palace . . . to wear a long black cape . . . very full and lined with vermillion . . . to have many cushions and to lie there among them . . . talking to his friends . . . lie there in a yellow silk shirt and black velvet trousers . . . like music-review artists talking and pouring strange liquors from curiously beautiful bottles . . . bottles with long slender necks . . . he climbed the noisy stair of the odorous tenement . . . smelled of fish . . . of stale fried fish and dirty milk bottles . . . he rather liked it . . . he liked the acrid smell of horse manure too . . . strong . . . thoughts . . . yes to lie back among strangely fashioned cushions and sip eastern wines and talk . . . Alex threw himself on the bed . . . removed his shoes . . . stretched and relaxed . . . yes and have music waft softly into the darkened and incensed room . . . he blew a cloud of smoke . . . oh the joy of being an artist and of blowing blue smoke thru an ivory holder inlaid with red jade and green . . .

the street was so long and narrow . . . so long and narrow . . . and blue . . . in the distance it reached the stars . . . and if he walked long enough . . . far enough . . . he could reach the stars too . . . the narrow blue was so empty . . . quiet . . . Alex walked music . . . it was nice to walk in the blue after a party . . . Zora had shone again . . . her stories . . . she always shone . . . and Monty was glad . . . every one was glad when Zora shone . . . he was glad he had gone to Monty's party . . . Monty had a nice place in the village . . . nice lights . . . and friends and wine . . . mother would be scandalized that he could think of going to a party . . . without a copper to his name . . . but then mother had never been to Monty's . . . and mother had never seen the street seem long and narrow and blue . . . Alex walked music . . . the click of his heels kept time with a tune in his mind . . . he glanced into a lighted cafe window . . . inside were people sipping coffee . . . men . . . why did they sit there in the loud light . . . didn't they know that outside the street . . . the narrow blue street met the stars . . . that if they walked long enough . . . far enough . . . Alex walked and the click of his heels sounded . . . and had an echo . . . sound being tossed back and forth . . . back and forth . . . some one was approaching . . . and their echoes mingled . . . and gave the sound of castenets . . . Alex liked the sound of the approaching man's footsteps . . . he walked music also . . . he knew the beauty of the narrow blue . . . Alex knew that by the way their echoes mingled . . . he wished he would speak . . . but strangers don't speak at four o'clock in the morning . . . at least if they did he couldn't imagine what would be said . . . maybe . . . pardon me but are you walking toward the stars . . . yes, sir, and if you walk long enough . . . then may I walk with you I want to reach the stars too . . . perdone me senor tiene vd. fosforo . . . Alex was glad he had been addressed in Spanish . . . to have been asked for a match in English . . . or to have been addressed in English at all . . . would have been blasphemy just then . . . Alex handed him a match . . . he glanced at his companion apprehensively in the match glow . . . he was afraid that his appearance would shatter the blue thoughts . . . and stars . . . ah . . . his face was a perfect compliment to his voice . . . and the echo of their steps mingled . . . they walked in silence . . . the castanets of their heels clicking accompaniment . . . the stranger inhaled deeply and with a nod of content and a smile . . . blew a cloud of smoke . . . Alex felt like singing . . . the stranger knew the magic of blue smoke also . . . they continued in silence . . . the castanets of their heels clicking rythmically . . . Alex turned in his doorway . . . up the stairs and the stranger waited for him to light the room . . . no need for words . . . they had always known each other . . . . as they undressed by the blue dawn . . . Alex knew he had never seen a more perfect being . . . his body was all symmetry and music . . . and Alex called him Beauty . . . long they lay . . . blowing smoke and exchanging thoughts . . . and Alex swallowed with difficulty . . . he felt a glow of tremor . . . and they talked and . . . slept . . .

Alex wondered more and more why he liked Adrian so . . . he liked many people . . . Wallie . . . Zora . . . Clement . . . Gloria . . . Langston . . . John . . . Gwenny . . . oh many people . . . and they were friends . . . but Beauty . . . it was different . . . once Alex had admired Beauty's strength . . . and Beauty's eyes had grown soft and he had said . . . I like you more than any one Dulce . . . Adrian always called him Dulce . . . and Alex had become confused . . . was it that he was so susceptible to beauty that Alex liked Adrian so much . . . but no . . . he knew other people who were beautiful . . . Fania and Gloria . . . Monty and Bunny . . . but he was never confused before them . . . while Beauty . . . Beauty could make him believe in Buddha . . . or imps . . . and no one else could do that . . . that is no one but Melva . . . but then he was in love with Melva . . . and that explained that . . . he would like Beauty to know Melva . . . they were both so perfect . . . such compliments . . . yes he would like Beauty to know Melva because he loved them both . . . there . . . he had thought it . . . actually dared to think it . . . but Beauty must never know . . . Beauty couldn't understand . . . indeed Alex couldn't understand . . . and it pained him . . . almost physically . . . and tired his mind . . . Beauty . . . Beauty was in the air . . . the smoke . . . Beauty . . . Melva . . . Beauty . . . Melva . . . Alex slept . . . and dreamed . . . . .

he was in a field . . . a field of blue smoke and black poppies and red calla lilies . . . he was searching . . . on his hands and knees . . . searching . . . among black poppies and red calla lilies . . . he was searching pushed aside poppy stems . . . and saw two strong white legs . . . dancer's legs . . . the contours pleased him . . . his eyes wandered . . . on past the muscular hocks to the firm white thighs . . . the rounded buttocks . . . then the lithe narrow waist . . . strong torso and broad deep chest . . . the heavy shoulders . . . the graceful muscled neck . . . squared chin and quizzical lips . . . grecian nose with its temperamental nostrils . . . the brown eyes looking at him . . . like . . . Monty looked at Zora . . . his hair curly and black and all tousled . . . and it was Beauty . . . and Beauty smiled and looked at him and smiled . . . said . . . I'll wait Alex . . . and Alex became confused and continued his search . . . on his hands and knees . . . pushing aside poppy stems and lily stems . . . a poppy . . . a black poppy . . . a lily . . . a red lily . . . and when he looked back he could no longer see Beauty . . . Alex continued his search . . . thru poppies . . . lilies . . . poppies and red calla lilies . . . and suddenly he saw . . . two small feet olive-ivory . . . two well turned legs curving gracefully from slender ankles . . . and the contours soothed him . . . he followed them . . . past the narrow rounded hips to the tiny waist . . . the fragile firm breasts . . . the graceful slender throat . . . the soft rounded chin . . . slightly parting lips and straight little nose with its slightly flaring nostrils . . . the black eyes with lights in them . . . looking at him . . . the forehead and straight cut black hair . . . and it was Melva . . . and she looked at him and smiled and said . . . I'll wait Alex . . . and Alex became confused and kissed her . . . became confused and continued his search . . . on his hands and knees . . . pushed aside a poppy stem . . . a black-poppy stem . . . pushed aside a lily stem . . . a red-lily stem . . . a poppy . . . a poppy . . . a lily . . . and suddenly he stood erect . . . exhultant . . . and in his hand he held . . . an ivory holder . . . inlaid with red jade . . . and green . . . .

and Alex awoke . . . Beauty's hair tickled his nose . . . Beauty was smiling in his sleep . . . half his face stained flush color by the sun . . . the other half in shadow . . . blue shadow . . . his eye lashes casting cobwebby blue shadows on his cheek . . . his lips were so beautiful . . . quizzical . . . Alex wondered why he always thought of that passage from Wilde's Salome . . . when he looked at Beauty's lips . . . I would kiss your lips . . . he *would* like to kiss Beauty's lips . . . Alex flushed warm . . . with shame . . . or was it shame . . . he reached across Beauty for a cigarette . . . Beauty's cheek felt cool to his arm . . . his hair felt soft . . . Alex lay smoking . . . such a dream . . . red calla lilies . . . red calla lilies . . . and . . . what could it all mean . . . did dreams have meanings . . . Fania said . . . and black poppies . . . thousands . . . millions . . . Beauty stirred . . . Alex put out his cigarette . . . closed his eyes . . . he mustn't see Beauty yet . . . speak to him . . . his lips were too hot . . . dry . . . the palms of his hands too cool and moist . . . thru his half closed eyes he could see Beauty . . . propped . . . cheek in hand . . . on one elbow . . . looking at him . . . lips smiling quizzically . . . he wished Beauty wouldn't look so hard . . . Alex was finding it difficult to breathe . . . breathe normally . . . why *must* Beauty look so long . . . and smile *that* way . . . his face seemed nearer . . . it was . . . Alex could feel Beauty's hair on his forehead . . . breathe normally . . . breathe normally . . . could feel Beauty's breath on his nostrils and lips . . . and it was clean and faintly colored with tobacco . . . breathe normally Alex . . . Beauty's lips were nearer . . . Alex closed his eyes . . . how did one act . . . his pulse was hammering . . . from wrists to finger tip . . . wrist to finger tip . . . Beauty's lips touched his . . . his temples throbbed . . . throbbed . . . his pulse hammered from wrist to finger tip . . . Beauty's breath came short now . . . softly staccato . . . breathe normally Alex . . . you are asleep . . . Beauty's lips touched his . . . breathe normally . . . and pressed . . . pressed hard . . . cool . . . his body trembled . . . breathe normally Alex . . . Beauty's lips pressed cool . . . cool and hard . . . how much pressure does it take to waken one . . . Alex sighed . . . moved softly . . . how does one act . . . Beauty's hair barely touched him now . . . his breath was faint on . . . Alex's nostrils . . . and lips . . . Alex stretched and opened his eyes . . . Beauty was looking at him . . . propped on one elbow . . . cheek in his palm . . . Beauty spoke . . . scratch my head please Dulce . . . Alex was breathing normally now . . . propped against the bed head . . . Beauty's head in his lap . . . Beauty spoke . . . I wonder why I like to look at some things Dulce . . . things like smoke and cats . . . and you . . . Alex's pulse no longer hammered from . . . wrist to finger tip . . . wrist to finger tip . . . the rose dusk had become blue night . . . and soon . . . soon they would go out into the blue . . . .

the little church was crowded . . . warm . . . the rows of benches were brown and sticky . . . Harold was there . . . and Constance and Langston and Bruce and John . . . there was Mr. Robeson . . . how are you Paul . . . a young man was singing . . . Caver . . . Caver was a very self assured young man . . . such a dream . . . poppies . . . black poppies . . . they were applauding . . . Constance and John were exchanging notes . . . the benches were sticky . . . a young lady was playing the piano . . . fair . . . and red calla lilies . . . who had ever heard of red calla lilies . . . they were applauding . . . a young man was playing the viola . . . what could it all mean . . . so many poppies . . . and Beauty looking at him like . . . like Monty looked at Zora . . . another young man was playing a violin . . . he was the first real artist'to perform . . . he had a touch of soul . . . or was it only feeling . . . they were hard to differentiate on the violin . . . and Melva standing in the poppies and lilies . . . Mr. Phillips was singing . . . Mr. Phillips was billed as a basso . . . and he had kissed her . . . they were applauding . . . the first young man was singing again . . . Langston's spiritual . . . Fy-ah-fy-ah-Lawd . . . fy-ah's gonna burn ma soul . . . Beauty's hair was so black and curly . . . they were applauding . . . encore . . . Fy-ah Lawd had been a success . . . Langston bowed . . . Langston had written the words . . . Hall bowed . . . Hall had written the music . . . the young man was singing it again . . . Beauty's lips had pressed hard . . . cool . . . cool . . . fy-ah Lawd . . . his breath had trembled . . . fy-ah's gonna burn ma soul . . . they were all leaving . . . first to the roof dance . . . fy-ah Lawd . . . there was Catherine . . . she was beautiful tonight . . . she always was at night . . . Beauty's lips . . . fy-ah Lawd . . . hello Dot . . . why don't you take a boat that sails . . . when are you leaving again . . . and there's Estelle . . . every one was there . . . fy-ah Lawd . . . Beauty's body had pressed close . . . close . . . fy-ah's gonna burn my soul . . . let's leave . . . have to meet some people at the New World . . . then to Augusta's party . . . Harold . . . John . . . Bruce . . . Connie . . . Langston . . . ready . . . down one hundred thirty-fifth street . . . fy-ah . . . meet these people and leave . . . fy-ah Lawd . . . now to Augusta's party . . . fy-ahs gonna burn ma soul . . . they were at Augusta's . . . Alex half lay . . . half sat on the floor . . . sipping a cocktail . . . such a dream . . . red calla lilies . . . Alex left . . . down the narrow streets . . . fy-ah . . . up the long noisy stairs . . . fy-ahs gonna bu'n ma soul . . . his head felt swollen . . . expanding . . . contracting . . . expanding . . . contracting . . . he had never been like this before . . . expanding . . . contracting . . . it was that . . . fy-ah . . . fy-ah Lawd . . . and the cocktails . . . and Beauty . . . he felt two cool strong hands on his shoulders . . . it was Beauty . . . lie down Dulce . . . Alex lay down . . . Beauty . . . Alex stopped . . . no no . . . don't say it . . . Beauty mustn't know . . . Beauty couldn't understand . . . are you going to lie down too Beauty . . . the light went out expanding . . . contracting . . . he felt the bed sink as Beauty lay beside him . . . his lips were dry . . . hot . . . the palms of his hands so moist and cool . . . Alex partly closed his eyes . . . from beneath his lashes he could see Beauty's face over his . . . nearer . . . nearer . . . Beauty's hair touched his forehead now . . . he could feel his breath on his nostrils and lips . . . Beauty's breath came short . . . breathe normally Beauty . . . breathe normally . . . Beauty's lips touched his . . . pressed hard . . . cool . . . opened slightly . . . Alex opened his eyes . . . into Beauty's . . . parted his lips . . . Dulce . . . Beauty's breath was hot and short . . . Alex ran his hand through Beauty's hair . . . Beauty's lips pressed hard against his teeth . . . Alex trembled . . . could feel Beauty's body . . . close against his . . . hot . . . tense . . . white . . . and soft . . . soft . . . soft . . . .

they were at Forno's . . . every one came to Forno's once maybe only once
. . . but they came . . . see that big fat woman Beauty . . . Alex pointed to
an overly stout and bejeweled lady making her way thru the maize of chairs
. . . that's Maria Guerrero . . . Beauty looked to see a lady guiding almost
the whole opera company to an immense table . . . really Dulce . . . for one
who appreciates beauty you do use the most abominable English . . . Alex
lit a cigarette . . . and that florid man with white hair . . . that's Carl . . .
Beauty smiled . . . The Blind bow boy . . . he asked . . . Alex wondered
. . . everything seemed to . . . so just the same . . . here they were laughing and joking about people . . . there's Rene . . . Rene this is my friend
Adrian . . . after that night . . . and he felt so unembarrassed . . . Rene
and Adrian were talking . . . there was Lucricia Bori . . . she was bowing at
their table . . . oh her cousin was with them . . . and Peggy Joyce . . .
every one came to Forno's . . . Alex looked toward the door . . . there was
Melva . . . Alex beckoned . . . Melva this is Adrian . . . Beauty held her
hand . . . they talked . . . smoked . . . Alex loved Melva . . . in Forno's
. . . every one came there sooner or later . . . maybe once . . . but
. . . .

up . . . up . . . slow . . . jerk up . . . up . . . not fast . . . not glorious . . .
but slow . . . up . . . up into the sun . . . slow . . . sure like fate . . . poise
on the brim . . . the brim of life . . . two shining rails straight down . . .
Melva's head was on his shoulder . . . his arm was around her . . . poise
. . . the down . . . gasping . . . straight down . . . straight like sin . . .
down . . . the curving shiny rail rushed up to meet them . . . hit the bottom
then . . . shoot up . . . fast . . . glorious . . . up into the sun . . . Melva
gasped . . . Alex's arm tightened . . . all goes up . . . then down . . .
straight like hell . . . all breath squeezed out of them . . . Melva's head on
his shoulder . . . up . . . up . . . Alex kissed her . . . down . . . they
stepped out of the car . . . walking music . . . now over to the Ferris Wheel
. . . out and up . . . Melva's hand was soft in his . . . out and up . . . over
mortals . . . mortals drinking nectar . . . five cents a glass . . . her cheek
was soft on his . . . up . . . up . . . till the world seemed small . . . tiny
. . . the ocean seemed tiny and blue . . . up . . . up and out . . . over the
sun . . . the tiny red sun . . . Alex kissed her . . . up . . . up . . . their
tongues touched . . . up . . . seventh heaven . . . the sea had swallowed
the sun . . . up and out . . . her breath was perfumed . . . Alex kissed her
. . . drift down . . . soft . . . soft . . . the sun had left the sky flushed . . .
drift down . . . soft down . . . back to earth . . . visit the mortals sipping
nectar at five cents a glass . . . Melva's lips brushed his . . . then out
among the mortals . . . and the sun had left a flush on Melva's cheeks . . .
they walked hand in hand . . . and the moon came out . . . they walked in
silence on the silver strip . . . and the sea sang for them . . . they walked
toward the moon . . . we'll hang our hats on the crook of the moon Melva
. . . softly on the silver strip . . . his hands molded her features and her
cheeks were soft and warm to his touch . . . where is Adrian . . . Alex . . .

Melva trod silver . . . Alex trod sand . . . Alex trod sand . . . the sea *sang* for her . . . Beauty . . . her hand felt cold in his . . . Beauty . . . the sea *dinned* . . . Beauty . . . he led the way to the train . . . and the train dinned . . . Beauty . . . dinned . . . dinned . . . her cheek *had* been soft . . . Beauty . . . Beauty . . . her breath *had* been perfumed . . . Beauty . . . Beauty . . . the sands *had* been silver . . . Beauty . . . Beauty . . . they left the train . . . Melva walked music . . . Melva said . . . don't make me blush again . . . and kissed him . . . Alex stood on the steps after she left him and the night was black . . . down long streets to . . . Alex lit a cigarette . . . and his heels clicked . . . Beauty . . . Melva . . . Beauty . . . Melva . . . and the smoke made the night blue . . .

Melva had said . . . don't make me blush again . . . and kissed him . . . and the street had been blue . . . one *can* love two at the same time . . . Melva had kissed him . . . one *can* . . . and the street had been blue . . . one *can* . . . and the room was clouded with blue smoke . . . drifting vapors of smoke and thoughts . . . Beauty's hair was so black . . . and soft . . . blue smoke from an ivory holder . . . was that why he loved Beauty . . . one *can* . . . or because his body was beautiful . . . and white and warm . . . or because his eyes . . . one *can* love . . . .

BLADES OF STEEL
RUDOLPH FISHER

I.

Negro Harlem's three broad highways form the letter H, Lenox and Seventh Avenues running parallel northward, united a little above their midpoints by east-and-west 135th Street.

Lenox Avenue is for the most part the boulevard of the unperfumed; "rats" they are often termed. Here, during certain hours, there is nothing unusual in the flashing of knives, the quick succession of pistol shots, the scream of a police-whistle or a woman.

But Seventh Avenue is the promenade of high-toned dickties and strivers. It breathes a superior atmosphere, sings superior songs, laughs a superior laugh. Even were there no people, the difference would be clear: the middle of Lenox Avenue is adorned by street-car tracks, the middle of Seventh Avenue by parking [trees and grass, Ed.].

These two highways, frontiers of the opposed extreme of dark-skinned social life, are separated by an intermediate any-man's land, across which they communicate chiefly by way of 135th Street. Accordingly 135th Street is the heart and soul of black Harlem; it is common ground, the natural scene of unusual contacts, a region that disregards class. It neutralizes, equilibrates, binds, rescues union out of diversity.

In a fraction of a mile of 135th Street there occurs every institution necessary to civilization from a Carnegie Library opposite a public school at one point to a police station beside an undertaker's parlor at another. But one institution outnumbers all others, an institution which, like the street itself, represents common ground: the barbershop overwhelmingly predominates.

Naturally on the day of the Barbers' Annual Ball this institution clipped off among other things several working hours. The barbers had their own necks to trim, their own knots to conquer, their own jowls to shave and massage. The inevitable last-minute rush of prospective dancers, eager for eleventh-hour primping, would have kept the hosts themselves from appearing at the dance-hall, in their best, on time. Hence the association had agreed that every member's door be closed and locked today at four.

Shortly before that hour in one of 135th Street's "tonsorial parlors," the head barber, for whom a half dozen men were waiting, dismissed a patron and called "Next!" Already Eight-Ball Eddy Boyd, whose turn it was, had removed coat and collar and started toward the vacated chair.

"Make it boyish, Pop," he grinned to the fat and genial proprietor. "And long as you trimmin' me, lemme have two tickets for the stom-down tonight."

Pop Overton smiled goldenly and assumed the grand manner. "You means to grace our function wid yo' attendance?"

The other's assent was typical Harlemese:

"I don't mean to attend yo' function with my grace."

As Eight-Ball put one foot on the foot-rest of the chair, someone pulled him back ungently.

"My turn, big shorty."

Eight-Ball turned, recognized Dirty Cozzens, an enemy of several days' standing.

"My turn," disagreed he evenly.

"Yo' mistake," Dirty corrected shortly, and moved to brush the smaller man aside.

The move was unsuccessful. The smaller man exhibited something of the stability of a fire-plug which one attempts to boot off the sidewalk. Dirty had bumped him without anticipating such firm footing, and now himself recoiled, careening off toward the mirrored wall with its implement-laden ledge. There was a little giggling jingle of instruments as his elbow struck this ledge. Then there was silence. Of the two barbers, one stopped pushing his clippers, but left them resting against the customer's neck while he gaped; the other halted, his razor poised, his thumb in one corner of his patron's mouth. Those who sat waiting dropped their papers, their conversation, and their lower jaws. Everybody stared. Everybody knew Dirty Cozzens.

Eight-Ball stood pat, as if awaiting an apology for the other's rudeness. Dirty also remained where he had landed, his elbow still amid the paraphernalia on the ledge, his eyes glaring, as if to let everyone see how he had been wronged.

The two made a striking contrast. Dirty Cozzens was a peculiar genetic jest. Heredity had managed to remove his rightful share of pigment even from his hair, which was pale buff. His eyes were gray, their lids rimmed red.

His complexion had won him his nickname, "Dirty Yaller," of which "Dirty," was the familiar abbreviation. In every other particular his African ancestry had been preserved and accentuated. The buff hair was woolly, the nose flat with wide nostrils, the mouth big, bordered by so-called liver-lips, unbelievably thick. Within the shadow of a black skin, even, Dirty would have been a caricature; with the complexion that he actually had he was a cartoon, a malicious cartoon without humor.

So had heredity handed him over to environment, and environment had done its damnedest; had put sly cunning into the eyes, had distorted the lips into a constant sneer, had set the head at a truculent forward thrust on the large, lank body. With its present evil face, his was a head that might well have adorned the scepter of Satan.

His opponent was his antithesis. Eight-Ball had been nicknamed after that pool-ball which is black, and his skin was as dark as it is possible for skin to be, smooth and clean as an infant's. The close-cut hair hugged the scalp evenly, the bright black eyes were alive with quick understanding, the nose was broad but sharp-ridged, with sensitive nostrils, the lips thin and firm above a courageous chin. He was beautifully small, neither heavy nor slight, of proud erect bearing, perfect poise, and a silhouette-like clean-cutness.

In the silence, Dirty's fingers reaching along the marble ledge found and caressed a barber's tool; an instrument which is the subject of many a jest but whose actual use involves no element of humor; a weapon which is as obsolete as a blunderbuss, even among those whose special heritage it is commonly supposed to be—as obsolete and as damaging. Dirty, skilled in the wielding of steel, would have have considered this instrument in a set encounter, but the devil put the thing now in his hand. He decided it would be entertaining to run his enemy out of the shop.

Pop Overton saw the movement, and it lifted him out of his daze. He said: "Aimin' to shave yo'self, Dirty?"

"None yo' dam' business," snapped Dirty, still eyeing Eight-Ball.

"No," said Pop. " 'Tain't none my business. But hit's my razor."

Dirty drew himself together, but not erect,—"You seen what he done?"— moved then with slow menace across the distance between himself and Eight-Ball. "You seen it, didn' y'?"

"Now, listen, big boy. Don't you go startin' nothin' in my shop, you hear?"

"I ain't startin' nothin'. I'm finishin' sump'n. Dis started a week ago. Hot nigger, dis black boy, but I'm goan turn his damper down."

Eight-Ball spoke: "Don't burn yo' fingers."

Dirty advanced another step, knees bent, one hand behind him. Had Eight-Ball retreated a single foot, Dirty would have tossed the razor aside with a contemptuous laugh; would have made a fly crack about fast-black, guaranteed not to run; would have swaggered out, proudly acknowledging that he had picked the quarrel. But Eight-Ball had not retreated. Eight-Ball had stood still and looked at him, had even taunted him: "Don't burn yo' fingers"; had watched him approach to arm's length without budging. Ought to take one swipe at him just to scare him good. Ought to make him jump anyhow—

Whatever might have happened didn't. Instead of the expected swift sweep of an arm Dirty's next movement was a quick furtive bending of his elbow to slip the armed hand into his coat pocket; such a movement as might have greeted the entrance of an officer of the law.

As a flame flares just before it goes out, so the tension heightened, then dropped, when eyes discovered that the figure which had darkened the door was only that of a girl. She was a striking girl, however, who at once took the center of the stage.

"Whew-ee!" she breathed. "Just made it. Hi, Pop. Hello, Eighty. One minute to four! And the head barber waitin' for me! Some service—I scream—some service." Wherewith she clambered into the vacant chair and effervesced directions.

The waiting customers first ogled, then guffawed. It struck them as uproarious that two men should appear to be on the point of bloodshed over a mere turn and neither of them get it. But the girl seemed quite oblivious.

Eight-Ball greeted her: "Hello, Effie,"—grinned, and returned to his seat. Dirty shuffled to the wall opposite the mirrors, got his hat and went toward the door. As he passed the head barber's chair he paused and spoke to the girl:

"It was my turn, Miss Effie—but you kin have it." He smiled so that his thick lips broadened against his teeth, and he touched his hat and went out.

His departure released comment:

"Nice felluh!"

"Doggone! Sposin' he really got mad over sump'n!"

"He wasn't mad. He was jes' playin'."

"He better not play wi' *me* like dat."

"Take 'at thing out'n his hand and he'd run."

"Leave it *in* his hand and *you'd* run."

Then, to everyone's astonishment, before Pop Overton had assembled the proper implements, the girl jumped down from the chair, scattering stealthy glances which had been creeping toward the crimson garters just below her crossed knees.

"Whose turn was it?" she asked Pop.

"Eighty's."

"Thought so. Come on, Eighty. I got mine this morning."

"What's the idea?" wondered Eight-Ball.

"Wasn't it a fight?"

"Pretty near. How'd you know?"

"Anything wrong with these?"

A purely rhetorical question. There was certainly nothing wrong with Effie Wright's eyes—nor with her hair, nor with that rare, almost luminous dark complexion called "sealskin brown." One might complain that she was altogether too capable of taking care of herself, or that she was much too absorbed in Eight-Ball. Beyond that no sane judgment criticized.

Effie ran a beauty-parlor directly across the street, and it was to this that she now referred.

"I was lookin' out the window over there. Saw you drive up in your boss's straight-eight. Your friend was standin' in front of the saloon—he saw you too, so he come in behind you. Pop's window's got too much advertisin' in it to see through, so I come on over. Seem like I spoiled the party.''

"Ain't this sump'n?" Eight-Ball asked the world.

"Angels rush in when fools is almost dead," was Pop's proverb.

"Well, since you won't open a keg o' bay rum, I guess I'll breeze.—Say, Pop, got an extra safety razor blade?—Yes.—Huh?—Oh, a customer gimme a pair o' pumps to wear to the shin-dig tonight, and I got to whittle off here and there till I can get 'em on. Cheatin' the foot-doctor.—A single-edged blade, if you got it, Pop. Double-edged one cuts y' fingers before it cuts anything else.—Thanks. Shall I lock the door on my way out?—Stop by before you haul it, Eighty."

She was gone in a flurry of words.

"Can y' beat that, Pop?" Eight-Ball laughed.

"They ain't but two like her and she's both of 'em," admitted Pop. "But what's that Cozzens boy on you for?"

"We had a little argument in a dark-john game a while back."

"Yea? Well, watch 'im, boy. Bad boogy what knows he's bad. And don't think he won't cut. He will. Thass th' onliest kind o' fightin' he knows, and he sho knows it. They's nineteen niggers 'round Harlem now totin' cuts he gave 'em. They through pullin' knives too, what I mean."

"He's that good, huh?"

"He's that bad. Served time fo' it, but he don't give a damn. Trouble is, ain't nobody never carved *him*. Somebody ought to write shorthand on his face. That'd cure him."

"Yes? Whyn't you shave him sometime, Pop?"

"Mine's accidental. Somebody ought to carve him artistically."

"Well," Eight-Ball considered thoughtfully, "maybe somebody will."

II

The Barbers' Ball does not pretend to be a dickty affair. It is announced, not by engraved cards through the mails, but by large printed placards in barber-shop windows. One is admitted, not by presenting a card of invitation, but by presenting a dollar bill in exchange for a ticket. It is a come-one, come-all occasion, where aspiring local politicians are likely to mount the platform between dances and make announcements and bow while influential bootleggers cheer. It was quite fitting, therefore, that this fête of, for, and in spite of the people should take place on 135th Street—this year in a second-floor dance-hall just east of Lenox Avenue.

"Well, hush my mouth!" exclaimed Eight-Ball as he and Effie entered somewhat before midnight.

"Do tell!" agreed she.

For there were decorations. Nothing subdued and elegant like the So-and-So's dance. Nothing "fly," like the Dirty Dozen's. Just color in dazzling quantity, presented through the inexpensive medium of crêpe paper—

scarlet, orange, brilliant green, embracing the lights, entwining the pillars, concealing the windows, transforming the orchestral platform into a float.

The orchestra also made no pretenses. It was a so-called "low-down" orchestra and it specialized in what are known as shouts. Under the influence of this leisurely rhythm, steady, obsessing, untiring, you gradually forget all else. You can't make a misstep, you can't get uncomfortably warm, you can't grow weary—you simply fall more and more completely into the insistently joyous spirit of the thing until you are laughing and humming aloud like everyone else. You get happy in spite of yourself. This is the inevitable effect of shouts, to which the orchestra tonight largely confined its efforts.

The newcomers joined the gay, noisy dancers, finding their way not too swiftly around the crowded floor. Here someone advised them to "Get off that dime!" and there someone else suggested that they "Shake that thing!"

But the shout to which Eight-Ball and his girl inadvertently kept time had not yet saturated their emotions, and in spite of it they discussed less happy concerns.

"I been so mad I ain't had no dinner," said Eight-Ball.

"'Bout what?"

"Notice I didn't bring the car tonight?"

"Yes. Boss usin' it?"

"No.—Know when I left your place this afternoon, after you showed me that trick?"

"Yes."

"Notice anything wrong with the car when I drove off?"

"Nope. Too busy watchin' the driver."

"I went about half a block and felt somethin' wrong. Pulled up and got out to look. Two flat tires."

"No!"

"Uh-huh. Front and back on the side away from the sidewalk."

"They was O.K. when you parked?"

"Brand new."

"Blow-outs? Slow leaks?"

"No. Cuts."

"What are you ravin' about?"

"Both tires had a six-inch gash in 'em, made with a knife—"

"What!"

"Or a razor."

Effie stopped dancing. "The yellow son-of-a-baboon!"

"Everybody says they ain't nothin' he can't do with a knife. Looks like they ain't nothin' he *won't* do."

The shout, the rhythmically jostling crowd, impelled them back into step.

"Eighty, you ought to half kill 'im. Of all the low, mean, gutter-rat tricks— you ought to lay 'im up f' a year."

"How you know I can?" he grinned.

"Can't y'?"

"I can't prove nothin' on him. Who seen him do it?"

"Nobody didn't have to see him. You know he did it."

"Nope. I can wait. He's sore. He'll keep on messin' around. Thinks he can't be had."

"He can be had all right. All I'm 'fraid of is somebody else'll have 'im first. Everybody that knows that guy hates 'im and most of 'em's scared to boot. Whoever whittles 'im down will be a hero."

As the jazz relented, the object of her anger took form out of the crowd and approached.

"Evenin', Miss Effie," said he, ignoring Eight-Ball. "Been lookin' f' you. I give you my turn in d' barber-shop today. How 'bout givin' me mine now?"

Effie looked through him at the decorations surrounding a post. As if she and Eight-Ball had been discussing the colors, she commented:

"That's one color I'm glad they forgot—I can't stand anything yellow."

Dirty turned garnet; but before his chagrin became active resentment, the music returned with a crash. Eight-Ball and Effie moved on past him, their anger partially appeased by knowing that Effie's tongue had cut like steel.

And now the shout more easily took hold on them, hammering them inexorably into its own mould. The increasing jam of people pressed them more closely into each other's arms. The husky mellowness of soft-throated saxophones against the trumpet's urge, the caress of plaintive blues-melody against the thrill of strange disharmonies, the humor of capricious traps against the solidity of unfailing bass—to these contrasts the pair abandoned themselves. Harsh laughter, queer odors, the impact of the mob became nothing. They closed their eyes and danced.

They might have danced for an hour, only half aware of the jumble of faces about, of their own jests and laughter, of the occasional intervals of rest. Then something woke them, and they suddenly realized that it was at them that people nearby were laughing—that a little space cleared about them wherever they moved and people looked at them and laughed.

At first they were unconvinced and looked around them for something comic. Then Pop Overton appeared, smiling roundly.

"Thought monkey-backs was out o' style, son."

"What—?"

"Did you have yo' coat cut to order?"

Effie switched Eight-Ball around and gasped while onlookers frankly smiled. A triangle of white shirt-back, its apex between Eight-Ball's shoulder-blades, shone through a vertical vent in his coat, a vent twice as long as any designed by a tailor. In the crush and abandonment of the dance a single downward stroke of a keen-edged instrument, light enough not to be noticed, had divided the back of the garment in two as cleanly as if it had been ripped down midseam. The white of the shirt gleamed through like a malicious grin.

As Eight-Ball examined himself unsmilingly, Pop Overton sobered. "I thought it was torn accidental," he said. "Judas Priest—I bet that—! Say,

Eighty, fo' Gawd's sake don't start nothin' here. We ain't never had a row—"
Eight-Ball and Effie, faces set, stood looking at each other in silence.

Dirty Cozzens stood in the shadow of the doorway beside that leading to the Barbers' Ball and in return for a generous drink unburdened himself to a buddy.

"It was in d' back room at Nappy's place. Dis lil spade turns a black-jack and winds d' deal, see? Well, he's a-rifflin' d' cards and talkin' all d' same time, and he says, 'You guys jes' git ready to loosen up, 'cause I'm gonna deal all d' dark-johns home. I promis' my boss I wouldn' gamble no mo', but dis is jes' like pickin' up money in d' street.' Fly line, see? Den he starts dealin'. Well, I figgers dis guy's been so lucky and jes' turned a black-jack for d' deal, it's time fo' his luck to change. So I ups and stops his bank fo' twenty bucks, see? And I be dam' if he don't deal himself another black-jack—makin' two in a row!

"Well, he picks up all d' money befo' we can git our breath, see? Everybody laffs but me. I figgers day's a trick in it. Wouldn' you?"

"Sho I would. Two black-jacks in a row. Huh!"

"So I calls 'im crooked. But he jes' laffs and tells me to talk wid mo' money and less mouf. Natchelly dat makes me mad. A guy pulls a crooked deal and says sump'n like dat. Wouldn' you 'a' got mad?"

"Sho I would. Sho, man."

"So I tells him to pass back my twenty, long as he said he wasn't gamblin'. Den he stops dealin' and asts me is I big enough to take it. Tryin' to start sump'n all d' time, see?"

"Sho he was. Tryin' to staht somp'n."

"So I says I'll either take it out his pile or off his hips, see? But when I starts for him, d' guys won't let me put it on him, see? Fact dey puts me out d' game.—So natchelly I jes' got to get me some o' dis lil spade's meat, dass all. I got to. He can't git away wid nuthin' like dat."

"Tryin' to git away wi' sump'n. Huh!"

"Sho he is. But I'll git 'im."

"What you aim to do?"

"I been primin' 'im fo' a fight."

"Dey claim he's pretty good wif' 'is hands."

"Ain't gonna be no hands. See dis?"

He withdrew from his right-hand coat pocket what appeared to be a quite harmless pocket-knife. He pressed it under his thumb and a steel blade leaped forth, quick as the tongue of a snake, a blade five inches long with a sweeping curve like a tiny scimitar. It was hollow-ground and honed to exquisite sharpness. A little catch fell into place at the junction of blade and handle, preventing the protruding blade from telescoping shut. The steel gleamed like eyes in the dark.

"Whew-ee!" admired the observer.

"He won't be d' fuss one I ever put it on. And here's how I figger. His boss is tight, see. Fired two guys already fo' roughin'. Dis boogy's got two new tires to account fo' now. And when his boss sees he been out, he'll find out it's 'count o' some gamblin' scrape and fire him too. Dass where I laff. See?''

'' 'Deed, boy, it's a shame fo' all dem brains to go to seed in yo' head. You could sell 'em and buy Europe, no stuff.''

Then abruptly both shrank into deeper shadow as Eight-Ball and Effie came out.

III

Diagonally across the street from the dance-hall stands Teddy's place, an establishment which stays open all night and draws all manner of men and women by the common appeal of good food. Oddly, it was once a mere bar-room lunch, and the mahogany bar-counter still serves the majority of Teddy's patrons, those who are content to sit upon stools and rub elbows with anybody. But there is now a back room also, with a side entrance available from the street. Here there are round-top tables beside the walls, and here parties with ladies may be more elegantly served. It is really a "high-class" grill-room, and its relation to the bar-counter lunch-room, the whole situated on democratic 135th Street, marks Teddy a man of considerable business acumen.

In one corner of the grill-room there is an excellent phonograph which plays a record repeatedly without changing. A song ends; you wait a few moments while the instrument is automatically re-wound and adjusted; and the song begins again.

Tonight the long-distance record was Tessie Smith's "Lord Have Mercy Blues," a curious mingling of the secular and the religious, in the tragic refrain of which the unfortunate victim of trouble after trouble resorts to prayer. The record was not playing loudly, but such was the quality of Tessie Smith's voice that you heard its persistent, half-humorous pain through louder, clearer sounds.

Just now there were no such sounds, for the room was almost empty. The theatre crowd had departed; the crowd from the dance-halls had not yet arrived. Three or four couples sat about tête-à-tête, and near the phonograph Eight-Ball and Effie. Eight-Ball's back was turned toward the wall to hide the gape in his coat.

The phonograph wailed:

> My man was comin' to me—said he'd
>   Let me know by mail,
> My man was comin' to me—said he'd let me know by mail—
> The letter come and tole me—
> They'd put my lovin' man in jail.

Grief, affliction, woe, told in a tone of most heartbroken despair; desolation with the merest tincture of humor—yet those who listened heard only the humor, considered only the jest.

Mercy—Lawd, have mercy!
How come I always get bad news?
Mercy—Lawd, have mercy!
How come I always got the blues?

"Them's the blues I ought to be singin'," said Eight-Ball.

"You'll feel better after you eat," soothed the girl.

"I'll feel better after I get one good crack at that half-bleached buzzard."

"You ought to pick your comp'ny, Eighty."

Her tone surprised him. He encounterd her look, mingled tenderness and reproach, and his eyes fell, ashamed.

"All right, kid. I'm off gamblin' for life.—But if that dude keeps messin' around—"

"Don't forget—he cuts."

"He better cut fast, then."

As if willing to oblige, Dirty Cozzens appeared at the door. He stood looking about, head hunched characteristically forward, right hand deep in his right coat pocket; calmly observed the relative desertion of the dining-room; then slowly advanced across the open space in the center of the floor.

Quickly Effie reached into her bag, withdrew something, put it into Eight-Ball's hand. The movement could have been seen, but the object passed was too small for the closest observation to make out. She might merely have been indulging in a heartening handclasp. Eight-Ball looked at her, first with puzzlement, then with understanding and resolution.

This time Dirty ignored Effie. This afternoon he might have had a chance with her; now he knew he had not. Then he had hidden his weapon from her; now he wanted her to see. That, too, had been largely bullying; this was serious challenge. Then he had sought but a momentary satisfaction; the satisfaction pending now would last, arising as it would out of the infliction of physical injury which could cost the victim his job. Let Effie share all of this—by all means let her see.

"Gimme my twenty bucks."

Eight-Ball looked up, allowed his gaze to pause here and there over his enemy's frame; then patted his left trousers' pocket. "It's right here.—You big enough to take it?"

"Listen, lamp-black. You been tryin' to git fly wid me ev'r since las' week, ain't y'? Put d' locks on me wid a crooked deal. Tried to start sump'n in d' barber shop today. Tole yo' woman to freeze me at d' dance tonight. Aw right. I'm warnin' y', see? I done warned you twice. I put my mark on yo' two shoes today and I put it on yo' coat tonight. D' nex' time I'm gonna put it on yo' black hide. See?"

Eight-Ball sat quite still, looking up at the lowering face.

"I tole y' I'd either take it out yo' pile or off yo' hips. Now put up or git up, you—"

Eight-Ball went up as if he'd been on a coil-spring, suddenly released. Dirty staggered backward but did not lose his footing.

Naturally none of Teddy's three waiters was in sight—it is unlikely that they would have interfered if they had been. Indeed, had they seen the initial blow of Eight-Ball—a familiar patron—they would have been satisfied to let him take care of himself. As for the other guests, they were interested but not alarmed. One does not yell or run at such a time unless a pistol is drawn.

Recovering balance, Dirty Cozzens withdrew his right hand from his pocket. It is difficult to believe possible the expression of evil that now contorted his features. That expression, however, was not more evil than the glint of the miniature scimitar, whose handle his right hand grasped.

He held the weapon in what pocket-knife fighters consider best form—three fingers firmly encircling the handle, but the index finger extended along the posterior, dull edge of the blade, tending to direct, brace, and conceal it. A sufficient length of the curved point extended beyond the end of the index finger to permit the infliction of a dangerously deep wound.

Eight-Ball stood ready, leaning a little forward, arms lax, both palms open—and empty.

Dirty's scowl concentrated on Eight-Ball's hands, and that he did not move at once was probably due to his astonishment at seeing no weapon in them. Any such astonishment, however, promptly gave way to quick appreciation of an advantage, and he did what a knifer rarely does. He rushed bringing his blade swiftly across and back in a criss-cross sweep before him.

Eight-Ball neither side-stepped nor attempted to block the motion. Either might have been disastrous. Instead, he ducked by suddenly squatting, and, touching the floor with his left hand for balance, kicked suddenly out with his right foot. The sharp crack of his heel against his antagonist's shin must have almost broken it. Certainly he gained time to jump up and seize Dirty's wrist before it could execute a second descending arc.

One less skilled than Eight-Ball would have found this useless. From such a wrist-hold the knife-hand is effectively liberated by simply inverting the weapon, which the fingers are still free to manipulate. The blade is thus brought back against its own wrist, and any fingers surrounding that wrist usually let go at once. Eighty had forestalled this contingency by a deft slipping of his grip upward over the fingers that held the knife handle. The hold that he now fastened upon those fingers was the same that had yanked two slashed balloon-tires off their rims some hours before, and it held Dirty's fingers, crushed together around their knife, as securely as a pipe-wrench holds a joint.

And now those who had watched this little fellow empty-handed win the advantage over an armed and bigger adversary saw a curious thing occur. Regularly in the ensuing scuffle Eight-Ball's right hand landed open-palmed against Dirty's face—landed again and again with a sounding smack; and for every time that it landed, presently there appeared a short red line, slowly widening into a crimson wheal.

Before long Dirty, rendered helpless now, and losing heart, raised his free hand to his face and as his fingers passed across it, the crimson wheals that they touched all ran together. He looked at the tips of those fingers, saw they were wet and red; his mouth fell open; the hand which Eight-Ball held went limp, the knife fell to the floor; and Dirty Cozzens quailed, as craven now as he'd been evil a moment before.

He began to stammer things, to deprecate, to plead; but Eight-Ball was deaf. The muscles of the latter's left arm seemed about to burst through their sleeve, while the artificial vent in the back of the coat ripped upward to the collar, as with one tremendous twist he brought the other man to his knees.

In that mad moment of triumph no one may say what disproportionate stroke of vengeance might not have brought on real tragedy. But with that strange and terrible open palm raised, a voice halted Eight-Ball's final blow:

> Have mercy—Lawd, have mercy—

Tessie Smith's voice, wailing out of an extremity of despair.

> Letter come and told me—
> They'd put my lovin' man in jail—

The entire engagement had occupied only the few moments during which the phonograph automatically prepared itself to repeat. Now the words came as warning and plea:

> Have mercy—Lawd, have mercy—

Eight-Ball released Dirty Cozzens, stepped back, picked up a crumpled paper napkin from the table where Effie still sat.

"Wipe y' face with this. Go on 'round to the hospital." He urged Dirty, whimpering, out of the side door.

Then he turned back toward Effie, stood over the table a moment, returned her rather proud smile. Two of the men who'd looked on came up. Said one:

"Buddy, show me that trick, will you?"

Eight-Ball extended his right hand, palm downward, and spread the fingers wide open. Freed from its vise-like hiding place between firmly adjacent fingers, something fell upon the porcelain table-top. It fell with a bright flash and a little clinking sound not unlike a quick laugh of surprise— the safety-razor blade which Effie had borrowed that afternoon from Pop Overton.

HARLEM WINE
COUNTEE CULLEN.

This is not water running here,
These thick rebellious streams
That hurtle flesh and bone past fear
Down alleyways of dreams.

This is a wine that must flow on
Not caring how or where,
So it has ways to flow upon
Where song is in the air.

So it can woo an artful flute
With loose, elastic lips,
Its measurement of joy compute
With blithe, ecstatic hips.

HARLEM REVIEWED
NANCY CUNARD

Is it possible to give any kind of visual idea of a place by description? I think
not, least of all of Harlem. When I first saw it, at 7th Avenue, I thought of the
Mile End Road—same long vista, same kind of little low houses with, at first
sight, many indeterminate things out on the pavement in front of them,
same amount of blowing dust, papers, litter. But no; the scale, to begin
with, was different. It was only from one point that the resemblance came to
one. Beginning at the north end of Central Park, edged in on one side by
the rocky hill of Columbia University and on the other by the streets that go
to the East River, widening out more and more north to that peculiarly sinister halt in the town, the curve of the Harlem River, where one walks about
in the dead junk and the refuse-on-a-grand-scale left in the sudden waste
lots that are typical of all parts of New York—this is the area of Harlem.
Manhattan and 8th Avenues, 7th, Lenox, 5th and Madison Avenues, they all
run up here from the zone of the skyscrapers, the gleaming white and blond
towers of down-town that are just visible like a mirage down the Harlem
perspective. These avenues, so grand in New York proper, are in Harlem
very different. They are old, rattled, some of them, by the El on its iron
heights, rattled, some of them, underneath, by the Sub in its thundering
groove.

Why is it called Harlem, and why the so-called capital of the Negro world?
The Dutch made it first, in the 17th century; it was "white" till as recently as
1900. And then, because it was old and they weren't rebuilding it, because
it's a good way from the centre, it was more or less "left" to the coloured
people. Before this they lived in different parts of New York; there was no
Negro "capital." This capital now exists, with its ghetto-like slums around
5th, bourgeois streets, residential areas, a few aristocratic avenues or sections thereof, white-owned stores and cafeterias, small general shops, and
the innumerable "skin-whitening" and "anti-kink" beauty parlors. There is
one large modern hotel, the Dewey Square, where coloured people of
course may stay; and another, far larger, the Teresa, a few paces from it,
where certainly they *may not!* And this is in the centre of Harlem. Such race
barriers are on all sides; it just depends on chance whether you meet them

or no. Some Negro friend maybe will not go into a certain drug-store with you for an ice-cream soda at 108th (where Harlem is supposed to begin, but where it is still largely "white"); "might not get served in there" (and by a coloured server at that—the white boss's orders). Just across the Harlem River some white gentlemen flashing by in a car take it into their heads to bawl, "Can't you get yourself a white man?"—you are walking with a Negro, yet you walk down-town with the same and meet no such hysteria, or again, you do.

In his book, *Black Manhattan*, James Weldon Johnson has made a map of Harlem showing the rapid increase of Negro occupation. This of course cannot be taken otherwise than as percentage, as there are some whites living in all parts of it. The Negro population is always increasing, but the houses do not expand; hence overcrowding in all but the expensive apartments and the middle-class lodgings. These last are pretty similar to our own Bloomsbury kind. And why then do the Negroes continue to flock to Harlem? Because in most other parts of New York they simply "don't let to coloured," at least never *en masse.* More and more of the "white" streets on the fringes of Harlem "go black" and become part of it. It happens this way. A coloured family or two get houses in such or such a street. Prejudiced white neighbours remonstrate with the landlord, who may not care—the more so as he knows that other coloured families will be wanting to move in. The whites have complained of his houses, demanded repairs. He won't make them, and for Negroes he can *double the rent* (this is invariably so), and no repairs need, or will, ever be made. The Negroes come, up go the rents, and the whites abandon that street. One of the reasons why Harlem is so concentrated is that this procedure takes some time; in housing themselves, as in every single other thing, they have to fight and fight; they are penalised for being black or coloured in every imaginable way, and, to the European, in many unthinkable ones.

Some 350,000 Negroes and coloured are living in Harlem and Brooklyn (the second, and quite distinct, area in greater New York where they have congregated). American Negroes, West Indians, Africans, Latin Americans. The latter, Spanish-speaking, have made a centre round 112th St. and Lenox Avenue. Walk round there and you will hear—it is nearly all Spanish. The tempo of the gestures and gait, the atmosphere, are foreign. It is the Porto-Ricans, the Central Americans and the Cubans. Nationalisms exist, more or less fiercely, between them and the American Negro—as indeed does a jealous national spirit between American Negro and black Jamaican. The latter say they are the better at business, that the coloured Americans have no enterprise. (Are we to see here the mantle of the British as a nation of shopkeepers on West Indian shoulders?) The American Negro regards the Jamaican or British West Indian as "less civilised" than himself; jokes about his accent and deportment are constantly made on the Harlem stage. And so they are always at it, falling out about empty "superiorities" and "inferiorities," forgetting the white enemy.

The Jamaican is "a foreigner"—and yet it was Marcus Garvey, from Jamaica, who, more than any living Negro, roused the black people of America just after the war with his "Back to Africa" movement. This sort of Zionism, after a lightning accumulation of millions of dollars, collapsed entirely. "Back to Africa" was held out to all the Negroes in the American continent, a Utopian impossibility at both ends—for how can 12,000,000 transport themselves *en masse,* as Garvey urged them to do, and in what part of Africa would the white imperialists allow such, or even a small part of such, a settlement? Apart from this, the Africans were, not surprisingly, angered by Garvey's self-given title of "Provisional Emperor of Africa." The African country chosen by Garvey was Liberia, which, as is known to everyone, is really an American (Firestone) colony. There is an anomaly now in the position of the Garvey movement. Though he is himself discredited, his followers (and there are several inter-factions too) disavow him but continue to call themselves Garveyites and proclaim his doctrine. Those extraordinary half salvation army, half British military uniforms that you see in the streets occasionally are Garvey's men; you come across them speaking at street corners, holding a large crowd. But it is all hot air. It is not organised in any direction or built on anything solid. Individually they have not the drive of the black Communist orator, for they are not speaking of anything serious; Garvey's theory was "all-black"; he wanted his people to be independent of, to cut away from, the white race entirely. The wrong kind of pride; a race pride which stopped at that, and paid no heed to the very real and concrete misery, oppression and struggles of the Negro toiling millions throughout the States.

If you are "shown" Harlem by day you will inevitably have pointed out to you the new Rockefeller apartments, a huge block towering above a rather sparse and visibly very indigent part of 7th Avenue. These were built by the millionaire of that name, supposedly to better the conditions of Negro workers by providing clean and comfortable lodging for them, but inhabited, however, by those who can afford to pay their rents. The Y.M.C.A. and the newly built Y.W.C.A.—more institutes for "uplift." The Harlem Public Library, with its good collection of books on Negro matters, and just a few pieces of African art, so few that the idea strikes one vexingly: why, in this capital of the Negro world, is there no centre, however small, of Africanology? The American Negroes—this is a generalisation with hardly any exceptions—are utterly uninterested in, callous to what Africa is, and to what it was. Many of them are fiercely "racial," as and when it applies to the States, but concerning their forefathers they have not even curiosity.

At night you will be taken to the Lafayette Theatre, the "cradle of new stars" that will go out on the road all over America and thence come to Europe. It is a sympathetic old hall, where, as they don't bother ever to print any programmes, one supposes that all the audience know all the players; it has that feeling too. Some of the best wit I heard here, and they can get away with a lot of stiff hot stuff. Ralph Cooper's orchestra was playing admirably that night they had "the street" in. This was to give a hearing to anyone who applied. They just went on the stage and did their stuff. And the audience was *merciless* to a whole lot of these new triers, who would have passed with honour anywhere out of America. The dancing of two or three of the street shoe-blacks, box on back, then set down and dancing round it, was so perfect that the crowd gave them a big hand. No-one who has not seen the actual dancing of Harlem in Harlem can have any idea of its superb quality. From year to year it gets richer, more complicated, more exact. And I don't mean the unique Snake-Hips and the marvellous Bo-Jangles, I mean the boys and girls out of the street who later become "chorats" and "chorines" (in the chorus), or who do those exquisite short numbers, as in music the Three Ink Spots (a new trio), adolescents of 16 or 17 perhaps, playing Duke Ellington's *Mood Indigo* so that the tears ran down one's face.

There was a new dance too, one of the sights of the world as done at the Savoy Ballroom, the Lindy-Hop. The fitting third to its predecessors, Charleston and Black Bottom. These were in the days of short skirts, but the Lindy is the more astounding as it is as violent (and as beautiful), with skirts sweeping the floor. Short minuet steps to begin, then suddenly fall back into an air-pocket, recover sideways, and proceed with all the variations of leaves on the wind. For the Lindy is Lindbergh, of course, created by them in honour of his first triumph. These Tuesday nights at the Savoy are very famous, as is the Harlem "Drag Ball" that happens only once a year. To this come the boys dressed as girls—some in magnificent and elaborate costumes made by themselves—and of course many whites from down-town. A word on the celebrated "rent-party" that the American press writes up with such lurid and false suggestions. This is no more nor less than an ordinary evening dance in someone's house. The "rent" part is its reason for being, for the guests give about 50 cents to come in, thereby helping pay the rent, and they buy liquor there which, as everywhere in dry America (and doubtless it will go on even if prohibition is entirely abolished), is made on the premises or by a friend. The music, as like as not, comes from a special kind of electric piano, a nickel a tune, all the best, the latest ones.

But it is the zest that the Negroes put in, and the enjoyment they get out of, things that causes one more envy in the ofay.[1] Notice how many of the whites are unreal in America; they are *dim*. But the Negro is very real; he is *there*. And the ofays know it. That's why they come to Harlem—out of curiosity and jealousy and don't-know-why. This desire to get close to the other race has often nothing honest about it; for where the ofays flock, to nightclubs, for instance, such as Connie's Inn and the Cotton Club and Small's, expensive cabarets, to these two former the coloured clientèle is no longer admitted! To the latter, only just, grudgingly. No, you can't go to Connie's Inn with your coloured friends. The place is *for whites*. "Niggers" to serve, and "coons" to play—and later the same ofay will slip into what he calls "a coloured dive," and there it'll be " 'Evening, Mr. Brown," polite and cordial, because this will be a real coloured place and the ofay is not sure of himself there a-tall. . . .

1. *Ofay:* white.

This applies of course to the mass of whites who treat Harlem in the same way that English toffs used to talk about "going slumming." The class I'm thinking of is "the club-man." They want entertainment. Go to Harlem, it's sharper there. And it doesn't upset their conception of the Negro's social status. From all time the Negro has entertained the whites, but never been thought of by this type as possibly a social equal. There are, however, thousands of artists, writers, musicians, intellectuals, etc., who have good friends in the dark race, and a good knowledge of Harlem life, "the freedom of Harlem," so to speak.

"You must see a revival meeting," they said to me. "It's nothing like what it is in the South, but you shouldn't miss it."

Beforehand I thought I wouldn't be able to stand more than ten minutes of it—ten minutes in any church. . . . When we got into the Rev. Cullen's on 7th Avenue (the Rev. is the father of the poet, Countee Cullen) a very large audience was waiting for the "Dancing Evangelist" (that is Becton's title, because of his terrific physical activity). A group of "sisters" all in white spread itself fan-wise in the balcony. There was a concert stage with deacons and some of Becton's 12 disciples, and the 7 or 8 absolutely first-class musicians who compose the orchestra, of which Lawrence Pierre is a fine organist and a disciple. Nothing like a church, an evening concert.

The music starts, a deep-toned Bach piece, then a short allocution, and then the long spirituals, the robust soloist that a massed chorus, the audience, answers back. They begin to beat time with their feet too. The "spirit" is coming with the volume of sound. At this point Becton enters quietly, stands silent on the stage, will not say a word. They must sing some more first, much more; they must be ripe ground. How do they reconcile Becton's exquisite smartness (pearl-grey suit, top hat, cane, ivory gloves, his youthful look and lovely figure), the whole sparkle about him, with the customary ponderousness of the other drab men of God? A sophisticated audience? No, for they appear to be mainly domestic workers, small shop workers, old and young, an evidently religious public, and one or two whites.

A new spiritual has begun; the singing gets intenser, foot-beating all around now, bodies swaying, and clapping of hands in unison. Now and again a voice, several voices, rise above the rest in a single phrase, the foot-beat becomes a stamp. A forest shoots up—black, brown, ivory, amber hands—spread, stiffened-out fingers, gestures of *mea culpa,* beating of breasts, gestures of stiff arms out, vibrating ecstasy. Far away in the audience a woman gets "seized," leaps up and down on the same spot belabouring her bosom. It comes here, there—who will be the next? At one moment I counted ten women in this same violent trance, not two with the same gestures, yet *all* in rhythm, half-time or double time. A few men too, less spectacular. Then just behind me, so that I see her well, a young girl. She leaps up and down after the first scream, eyes revulsed, arms up-stretched—she is no longer "there." After about a minute those next to her seize her and hold her down.

The apex of the singing has come; it is impossible to convey the scale of these immense sound-waves and rhythmical under-surges. One is transported, completely. It has nothing to do with God, but with life—a collective life for which I know no name. The people are entirely out of themselves—and then, suddenly, the music stops, calm comes immediately.

In this prepared atmosphere Becon now strides about the stage, flaying the people for their sins, leading their ready attention to this or that point of his argument by some adroit word, a wise-crack maybe. He is a poet in speech and very graceful in all his movements. His dramatisation is generous—and how they respond . . . "yeah man . . . tell it, tell it." Sin, he threatens, is "cat-foot," a "double-dare devil." And the sinner? "A double-ankled rascal," thunders this "adagio dancer," as he called himself that night, breaking off sharp into another mood, an admonishment out of "that inexpressible something by which I raise my hand." There are whirlwind gestures when he turns round on himself, one great clap of the palms and a sort of characteristic half-whistle-half-hoot before some point which is going to be emphasised—and the eloquence pours out in richer and richer imagery. Becton is the personification of expressionism, a great dramatic actor. You remember Chaliapine's acting of Boris Godounov; these two are comparable.

Then "when the millenniums are quaking it's time to clap our hands." It is the moment for the "consecrated dime," and the singing begins again, but the trances are over; other preachers may speak later. This ritual goes on from eight till after midnight, about four nights a week, and sometimes both the faithful and the evangelist are so indefatigable that it goes on for 24 hours. These services, really superb concerts, are the gorgeous manifestation of *the emotion* of a race—that part of the Negro people that has been so trammelled with religion that it is still steeped therein. A manifestation of this kind by white people would have been utterly revolting. But with the Negro race it is on another plane, it seems positively another thing, not connected with Christ or bible, the pure outpouring of themselves, a nature-rite. In other words, it is the fervour, intensity, the stupendous rhythm and surge of singing that are so fine—the christianity is only accidental, incidental to these. Not so for the assembly of course, for all of it is deeply, tenaciously religious.

Becton is the most famous evangelist of the coloured race in America. He has a following of more than 200,000, from New York to Florida, from Baltimore to Kansas. Like Christ he has 12 disciples. "The reason I have my party comprised of all men is because Jesus' disciples were all men, and if it was right for him it is right for me." He is one of the most elegantly dressed men in the world. Another comparison: "If Jesus were alive he would dress like me," for "if I came out in a long black coat, a collar turned backwards and looked downcast and forlorn, people would say that if they have got to look like that to be Christians, they don't want to join the church." Some other sayings of Becton's which fetch the religious are: "I work for God on contract and he keeps his bargain." "I told you, Lord, before I started out that I was a high-priced man, but you wanted me." "God ain't broke!" The "consecrated dime" and its fellows of course supply all Becton's needs. His organisation is called "The World's Gospel Feast," which publishes a quarterly called *The Menu,* the motto of which is: "A Square Deal for God"!

I have given all this detail about the revivalist meeting because it is so fantastic, and, *aesthetically* speaking, so moving. But when one considers the appalling waste of this dynamic force of people, and this preying on the prayers and fervours of old-fashioned, misguided, religious Negroes, it is tragic. Some time during this last summer (1933), after a new point in horror had been reached in the Scottsboro case at the Decatur "retrial," a young Negro minister frankly voiced his realisation of the truth; he said that the Communists were the only ones to defend his race, that they had proved it unquestionably throughout the whole history of Scottsboro; he said that for this reason although he was a man of God he was a Communist. Had Becton been honest, had he spoken thus, he would have swept the land. His followers would have had the same faith in these new words as in all his past "heavenly messages." But his was an individual racket.

I went to see Becton. A very handsome and courteous man. During our talk he leant forward earnestly: "In what manner do *you* think will come the freeing of my race?" "Only by organised and militant struggle for their *full* rights, side by side with Communism." He smiled. "And in what way do you think?" I asked him. "I think it will be by prayer," he murmured. I wanted to shout at him "Be honest *now.* Use your great dramatic gift for the right thing; you could be a giant in the freeing of your people." He spoke of the new million-dollar temple he was going to build. "I have not the money, but I shall get it"—and no doubt he would have been able to collect it all by these consecrated dimes. . . . But now, one year after I saw him, Becton is dead. "Bumped off" suddenly and brutally by some gangsters, shot in a car.

Another spectacular man of God is the Rev. Father Devine, who that year was having a hard time with the authorities for what, in Jamaica, used to be called "night noises." The fervent assembled in too great numbers and their exaltation was too loud. Sensational vengeance followed Father Devine's arrest; the judge who condemned him died the next day.

It may seem odd that one's thoughts stay so long with these black priests and their terrific hold over their large following. But religion amonst the Negroes, those that have it (for the younger generation is shaking off its weight, and replacing this by a desire for, an acquisition of, racial and economic facts), their reaction to religion cannot be dissociated in my mind from their past collective reaction to tribal ceremony and custom in Africa. They are *honest* and at home in their belief; that is the whole difference as compared with whites. A white audience in church lifts one's heart in utter disgust; with the Negroes one longs for this collective force to be directed towards the right things, solidarity with those whites who are struggling for their rights too against the super-brutality of American "democracy."

The Negro ministers and churches vary in their attitude to the more and more violent struggle for Negro rights. Since the Scottsboro case and other equally vicious frame-ups, some have helped the International Labor Defence, the organisation which is fighting these cases; some have refused all aid. The same applies to the Negro newspapers. Scandals have occurred, such as misuse of funds collected by *The Amsterdam News,* an important Harlem paper, for the great march on Washington this spring by over 4,000 Harlem Negroes, protesting against the new legal lynch verdict on Heywood Patterson at Decatur.

The Harlem Liberator is the only honest Negro paper in the States, and there are some four or five hundred. . . . Controlled by jacks-in-office at the beck and call of American white money and black philanthropic support, this Negro bourgeoisie sits giving praise to each new president and each party that promises that "new deal to the Negro" that never comes (and will never come from Republican, Democrat or Labour), launching out frantic and crassly ignorant attacks on the Communists (see particularly the so-called "Symposium" of a dozen or so Negro editors in one of the spring 1932 numbers of *The Crisis*). They are worse than the black imperialist lackeys in colonial countries, for they are not without money and some power, neither of which is ever applied to the crying needs of the race. There is not one paper (except *The Harlem Liberator*) that can be called a proper "Race" paper. Although they deal almost entirely with Negro doings, these doings are found to be mainly social events and functions. The coloured stage is much spoken of, which is very much to the good, for the white papers scarcely mention any Negro achievement; yet there is hardly a star who is not at some time or other of his or her career literally pulled to pieces by some scandal of press-invention. As to writing sanely about any inter-racial friendships or associations . . . one might be reading a Southern white rag.

Confusion (and confusing the minds of its readers) is a strong newspaper characteristic. I say confusion, but it is by design. Example: on several pages you will read vulgar, ignorant and abusive articles on Negro "reds"; misrepresentations, and every attempt at discredit. (For instance, the *Pittsburgh Courier* printed a baseless and indescribably vicious attack on Ruby Bates, one of the two white State witnesses in the Scottsboro case, because she admitted having lied in the first trial, thus being part responsible for 9 innocent black boys being in jail under death-sentence for 2½ years, and because now she was speaking all over the country showing up the Southern lynch-terror and race-hate, on the same platform as Communist organisers.) And on another page will be found an honest account of some event in connection with these same Negro comrades. What is the explanation? The editor has been forced into this last by the remonstrances of militant Negroes who are bitterly aware of the sempiternal treacheries of the black bourgeoisie all along the line, but nowhere as vilely so as in their newspapers. The Negro race in America has no worse enemy than its own press.

If treachery and lying are its main attributes so is snobbery flourishing in certain parts of Harlem. "Strivers Row"; that is what 139th Street has been called. An excellent covering-name for "those Astorperious Ethiopians," as one of their own wits put it. There are near-white cliques, mulatto groups, dark-skinned sets who will not invite each other to their houses; some would not let a white cross their thresholds. The Negro "blue-bloods" of Washington are famous for their social exclusivity, there are some in Harlem too. I don't know if a foreign white would get in there, possibly not. The snobbery around skin-colour is terrifying. The light-skins and browns look down on the black; by some, friendships with *ofays* are not tolerated, from an understandable but totally unsatisfactory reaction to the general national attitude of white to coloured on the social equality basis. A number of the younger writers are race-conscious in the wrong way, they make of this a sort of forced, *self*-conscious thing, give the feeling that they are looking for obstacles. All this, indeed, is Society with a vengeance! A bourgeois ideology with no horizon, no philosophical link with life. And out of all this, need it be said, such writers as Van Vechten and Co. have made a revolting and cheap lithograph, so that Harlem, to a large idle-minded public, has come to mean nothing more whatsoever than a round of hooch [1]-filled night-clubs after a round of "snow" [2]-filled boudoirs. Van Vechten, the spirit of vulgarity, has depicted Harlem as a grimace. He would have written the same way about Montparnasse or Limehouse and Soho. Do places exist, or is life itself as described by Paul Morand (another profiteer in coloured "stock")? Claude MacKay has done better. The studies in inter-colour relationships (in *Ginger Town*) are honest. But his people, and himself, have also that wrong kind of race-consciousness; they ring themselves in, they are umbrageous. The "Negro Renaissance" (the literary movement of about 1925, now said to be at a halt, and one wonders on whose authority this is said) produced many books and poems filled with this bitter-sweet of Harlem's glitter and heart-break.

This is not the Harlem one sees. You don't see the Harlem of the romancists; it is romantic in its own right. And it is *hard* and *strong;* its noise, heat, cold, cries and colours are so. And the nostalgia is violent too; the eternal radio seeping through everything day and night, indoors and out, becomes somehow the personification of restlessness, desire, brooding. And then the gorgeous roughness, the gargle of Louis Armstrong's voice breaks through. As everywhere, the real people are in the street. I mean those young men on the corner, and the people all sitting on the steps throughout the breathless, leaden summer. I mean the young men in Pelham Park; the sports groups (and one sees many in their bright sweaters), the strength of a race, its beauty.

For in Harlem one can make an appreciation of a race. Walk down 7th Avenue—the different types are uncountable. Every diversity of bone-structure, of head-shape, of skin colour; mixes between Orientals and pure Negroes, Jews and Negroes, Red Indians and Negroes (a particularly beautiful blend, with the high cheek-bones always, and sometimes straight black

1. Drink.
2. Cocain.

hair), mulattoes of all shades, yellow, "high yaller" girls, and Havana-coloured girls, and, exquisitely fine, the Spanish and Negro blends; the Negro bone, and the Negro fat too, are a joy to the eye. And though there are more and more light-coloured people, there is great satisfaction seeing that the white American features are absorbed in the mulatto, and that the mulatto is not, as so often in England, a coloured man with a white man's features and often expression as well. The white American and the Negro are a good mix physically. The pure black people—there are less of these (more than two-thirds of the race now being mixed with white). These are some of the new race that Embree has written of in his *Brown America;* they are as distinct from the African as they are from the nordic.

The major part of Harlem's inhabitants are of course the Negro workers. Since the depression began the proportion of those that are unemployed is very much higher than that even of the white workers. They have been, they are being sacked, and their wretchedly underpaid jobs given to the whites. Unable to pay the rent, not a week goes by without numerous evictions, they are thrown out into the street. Bailiffs come and move out the few belongings they have. And it is here that the Communists have put up a strong and determined defence. Black and white comrades together go where the evictions are taking place and move the things back. Police and riot squads come with bludgeons and tearbombs, fights and imprisonments, and deaths too, occur. In every form the oppression that the governing class carries out increasingly becomes more brutal as the need of the unemployed makes stronger and stronger demand for food, work and wages.

There is no finer realisation than that of knowing that the black and white proletariat is getting more and more together now on the only real basis that must be established and consolidated for ever: the equal rights of both under the Communist programme. And when this is in practice the full and final abolition of this artificially-bred race-hatred on the part of the whites, bred out of the enslaving of blacks, will be arrived at. In this and in no other way. There is no colour *problem.* The existence of the Negro race is not a problem, it is *a fact.* And in America, as in all other imperialist countries, this use of a wrong word is neither more nor less than a vicious lie on the part of the ruling class in urging the workers of each country into thinking that the Negro, the coloured race, was created by nature as a *menace.* The growing volume of the Communist consciousness among the black workers, and in some of the Negro intellectuals, dates chiefly from five years ago, and has in that time made, and is making, rapid increase. It is something new, *more and more tangible,* as here in England now, in the street as I go by I am immediately aware of a new expression in some of the faces, a look of purpose and responsibility.

One of the first things I was impressed by, the best thing that remains of Harlem, was the magnificent strength and lustiness of the Negro children. As I walked from end to end of it, down the length of 7th Avenue, the schools were just out. The children rushed by in rough leather jackets in the cold wind, some of them playing ball on roller skates, shouting and free.

May these gorgeous children in their leathers be the living symbol of the finally liberated Negro people.

Up with an all-Communist Harlem in an all-Communist United States!

A NEGRO EXTRAVAGANZA
CLAUDE MCKAY

There are shovelfuls of humor and barrels of joy in the Negro Burlesque playing at the Sixty-third Street Music Hall. Despite adverse and pointless criticism, the comedy has survived the summer and should sweep along through this season. A burlesque show is a burlesque with its inevitable commingling of grain and chaff and overdoing of the obvious. And the metropolitan notational critics who have damned *Shuffle Along* for not fulfilling the role of an Italian light opera are as filmy-sighted as the convention-ridden and head-ossified Negro intelligentsia, who censure colored actors for portraying the inimitable comic characteristics of Negro life, because they make white people laugh! Negro artists will be doing a fine service to the world, maybe greater than the combined action of all the white and black radicals yelling revolution together, if by their efforts they can spirit the whites away from lynching and inbred prejudice, to the realm of laughter and syncopated motion. After the ugly post-war riots between white and black in the big English ports, George Lansbury of the *Daily Herald* brought the American Southern Orchestra from the West End of London to sing in Poplar, the very heart of the trouble. And soon all the slums of London, forgetting the riots, were echoing with syncopated songs.

Although so far apart apparently, the ready-to-wear comment of white and black Americans on "Afro-American" artistic endeavor is really very similar. It rises from the same source—colorphobia and antagonism on both sides. The American public is dimly aware of a great storehouse of Negro Art in this country. But with its finer senses blurred by prejudice, it turns to Yankee–Dixie impersonators and Semitic imitators for the presentation of Negro Art. And from these bastard exhibitions the current standards are set. The Negro critics can scarcely perceive and recognize true values through the screen of sneering bigotry put between them and life by the dominant race. So against the worthless standards of the whites, the black intelligentsia, sensitive and pompous, would oppose such solid things as the aristocracy of St. Philip's Church, the compositions of Coleridge-Taylor and Mr. Harry Burleigh, the painting of Mr. Tanner, the prose of Mr. Du Bois, the critiques of Mr. Braithwaite and the poetry of Mr. James Weldon Johnson, as the only expression of Negro Culture. For such a list would earn the solemn approval of the *New York Times.* Negro art, these critics declare, must be dignified and respectable like the Anglo-Saxon's before it can be good. The Negro must get the warmth, color and laughter out of his blood,

Review of *Shuffle Along,* a musical review by Noble Sissle and Eubie Blake.

else the white man will sneer at him and treat him with contumely. Happily the Negro retains his joy of living in the teeth of such criticism; and in Harlem, along Fifth and Lenox avenues, in Marcus Garvey's Hall with its extravagant paraphernalia, in his churches and cabarets, he expresses himself with a zest that is yet to be depicted by a true artist.

Shuffle Along somewhat conflicts with my international intelligence and entices me to become a patriotic barker for my race. It makes me believe that Negroes are not civilized enough to be vulgar, nor will they ever express themselves through the medium of respectability.

"A cheap imitation of Broadway"—this is what some critics say of it. And it is superficially true. Negroes of America, who by an acquired language and suffering, are closer knit together than all the many tribes of Africa, alien to each other by custom and language, cannot satisfy the desire of the hypercritical whites for the Congo wriggle, the tribal war jig, and the jungle whoop. The chastisement of civilization has sobered and robbed them of these unique manifestations. American Negroes have not the means and leisure to tour Africa for ancestral wonders. And those carping whites who are in a like quandary might well visit Coney Island and the circuses to get acquainted with the stunts of Savagedom. Or they might take a look into themselves. The conventions of *Shuffle Along* are those of Broadway, but the voice is nevertheless indubitably Africa expatriate. It is this basic African element which makes all Negro imitations so delightfully humorous and enjoyable. It is this something that always sent me to see the Lafayette Players at 131st Street and Seventh Avenue in white plays after they had been passed up by Broadway. To me the greatest charm is that the erotic movements are different. And besides, "The Negroes make their eyes talk." Such eyes! So luminously alive!

How deliciously appealing is the mimicry of Miss Florence Mills, the sparkling gold star of the show. She can twist her face in imitation of a thousand primitive West African masks, some patterns of which may be seen at the American Museum of Natural History. Her coo-cooing and poohpoohing tintinnabulate all over the hall. She is prettiest in her vivid orange frock. She might have been featured more. She is like one of those Southern rarities that used to bowl one over in the cabarets of Philadelphia and Baltimore during the wonderful wet days. Noble Sissle knows his range and canters over it with the ease and grace of an antelope. The Harmony Kings are in the direct line of the Jubilee Singers, whether they give a plantation melody or syncopate a Tyrolese or Hawaiian song.

The show is built on an excellent framework: the lines and measurements just crazy enough to make everything funny. Black Jimtown is like any other town; the business of governing is graft. Sam Peck and Steve Jenkins are uproariously in the game, and also the perfect "Onion" Jeffrey.

But the ensemble is a little disappointing and lacking in harmony. Instead of making up to achieve a uniform near-white complexion the chorus might have made up to accentuate the diversity of shades among "Afro Americans" and let the white audience in on the secret of the color nomenclature of the Negro world. For, as the whites have their blonde and brunette, so do the blacks have their chocolate, chocolate-to-the-bone, brown, low-brown, teasing-brown, high-brown, yellow, high-yellow and so on. The difference on our side is so much more interesting and funny. It is whispered in some circles that the "Blue-vein" Societies among the Afro-American elite bar the black girls from the stage. But this can hardly be true; for I have rarely seen any social gathering of American Negroes where there were not very dark damsels through whose skin the blue veins could not show! However, there is a dearth of black girls in Negro theatricals whose presence would surely give more distinction and realism to the stage. I believe that the colored actors prefer the lighter-skinned girls. The latter are vivacious, pushing and pretty, but prettiness is always plentiful, while beauty is rare and hard to find. If black men in general favor the lighter women of their race, it is a natural phenomenon beyond criticism. The Negroes of the western world are producing and fostering new types. The deep-rooted animosity of the lily-white and the bombastic mouthings of the "sable-ites" against miscegenation are both but foam on the great, natural, barrier-breaking current of interracial contact. Still, despite this fact, Negro artists ought not to ignore the variety of material at hand.

AFRO-AMERICAN IDENTITY—
WHO AM I?

W. E. B. DuBois, in his Souls of Black Folk (1903), defined the dilemma of Afro-American identity. The Negro's double-consciousness—being black and uncertain of his acceptance as an American—allowed him "no true self-consciousness." So, the question "Who am I?" was a natural one for the Afro-American. The value and the humanity of the individual and the race rested upon the answer.

Like all Americans, except Indians, Afro-Americans had to search beyond their American experience for the roots of self and culture. Africa, necessarily became crucial to their sense of self. For a black American to answer the question of identity, he had to resolve for himself what Africa was, and what Africa meant to him. And that resolution had to contend with a welter of myths, superstitions, and prejudices promulgated by Europeans and Christians about the "Dark Continent." A very important part of the thought and expression of the Harlem Renaissance had to do with the finding of comfortable emotional and intellectual accommodation of Afro-Americans to their African origins. Thus, it is a question of identity which underlies Alain Locke's essay on African art, just as it does much of the poetry of Countee Cullen, Langston Hughes, and Claude McKay. Africa could not be discussed with academic distance. Even DuBois, writing in his diary off the coast of Africa, tells us that his was no mere pleasure trip but a journey to find some part of himself. The question about Africa was asked in many ways; the answers merely fed the enigma. The Harlem Renaissance, however, brought the question to a high level of consciousness among black people.

Identity was also a matter of blood, and the existence of mulattoes, those of mixed blood, posed a peculiar question. To be both black and white—neither black nor white, as some would say—presented an anomaly in a society of sharp and crucial racial distinctions. Americans had never considered mulattoes to have a special status. However white a man might appear, he could be thought of and treated as a black man if he was said to have "Negro blood." A known black forebear invested all of his progeny with the unmitigated burden of race. The possibility—indeed, the certainty—that "whites" had to live as "blacks," and that "blacks" did live as "whites" intrigued the American imagination such that the "tragic mulatto" became a major theme in American literature and drama. Blacks viewed the phenomenon of "passing for white" as very ironic, signaling great temptation and opportunity as well as tragedy. The complexity of the question is merely suggested in the poems by Langston Hughes and Claude McKay, and the story by Jean Toomer that we include here.

To speak of an Afro-American identity is to suggest a special quality of character for black Americans. Langston Hughes's "The Negro Speaks of Rivers," claims such a special quality for "my people." We can also see such assumptions in the poems of Helene Johnson and Gwendolyn Bennett and the excerpt from Claude McKay's novel Banjo.

THE LEGACY OF THE ANCESTRAL ARTS
ALAIN LOCKE

Music and poetry, and to an extent the dance, have been the predominant arts of the American Negro. This is an emphasis quite different from that of the African cultures, where the plastic and craft arts predominate; Africa being one of the great fountain sources of the arts of decoration and design. Except then in his remarkable carry-over of the rhythmic gift, there is little evidence of any direct connection of the American Negro with his ancestral arts. But even with the rude transplanting of slavery, that uprooted the technical elements of his former culture, the American Negro brought over as an emotional inheritance a deep-seated æsthetic endowment. And with a versatility of a very high order, this offshoot of the African spirit blended itself in with entirely different culture elements and blossomed in strange new forms.

There was in this more than a change of art-forms and an exchange of cultural patterns; there was a curious reversal of emotional temper and attitude. The characteristic African art expressions are rigid, controlled, disciplined, abstract, heavily conventionalized; those of the Aframerican,—free, exuberant, emotional, sentimental and human. Only by the misinterpretation of the African spirit, can one claim any emotional kinship between them— for the spirit of African expression, by and large, is disciplined, sophisticated, laconic and fatalistic. The emotional temper of the American Negro is exactly opposite. What we have thought primitive in the American Negro— his naïveté, his sentimentalism, his exuberance and his improvizing spontaneity are then neither characteristically African nor to be explained as an ancestral heritage. They are the result of his peculiar experience in America and the emotional upheaval of its trials and ordeals. True, these are now very characteristic traits, and they have their artistic, and perhaps even their moral compensations; but they represent essentially the working of environmental forces rather than the outcropping of a race psychology; they are really the acquired and not the original artistic temperament.

A further proof of this is the fact that the American Negro, even when he confronts the various forms of African art expression with a sense of its ethnic claims upon him, meets them in as alienated and misunderstanding an attitude as the average European Westerner. Christianity and all the other European conventions operate to make this inevitable. So there would be little hope of an influence of African art upon the western African descendants if there were not at present a growing influence of African art upon European art in general. But led by these tendencies, there is the possibility that the sensitive artistic mind of the American Negro, stimulated by a cultural pride and interest, will receive from African art a profound and galvanizing influence. The legacy is there at least, with prospects of a rich yield. In the first place, there is in the mere knowledge of the skill and unique mastery of the arts of the ancestors the valuable and stimulating realization that the Negro is not a cultural foundling without his own inheritance. Our timid and apologetic imitativeness and overburdening sense of cultural indebtedness have, let us hope, their natural end in such knowledge and realization.

Then possibly from a closer knowledge and proper appreciation of the African arts must come increased effort to develop our artistic talents in the discontinued and lagging channels of sculpture, painting and the decorative arts. If the forefathers could so adroitly master these mediums, why not we? And there may also come to some creative minds among us, hints of a new technique to be taken as the basis of a characteristic expression in the plastic and pictorial arts; incentives to new artistic idioms as well as to a renewed mastery of these older arts. African sculpture has been for contemporary European painting and sculpture just such a mine of fresh *motifs,* just such a lesson in simplicity and originality of expression, and surely, once known and appreciated, this art can scarcely have less influence upon the blood descendants, bound to it by a sense of direct cultural kinship, than upon those who inherit by tradition only, and through the channels of an exotic curiosity and interest.

But what the Negro artist of to-day has most to gain from the arts of the forefathers is perhaps not cultural inspiration or technical innovations, but the lesson of a classic background, the lesson of discipline, of style, of technical control pushed to the limits of technical mastery. A more highly stylized art does not exist than the African. If after absorbing the new content of American life and experience, and after assimilating new patterns of art, the original artistic endowment can be sufficiently augmented to express itself with equal power in more complex patterns and substance, then the Negro may well become what some have predicted, the artist of American life.

As it is, African art has influenced modern art most considerably. It has been the most influential exotic art of our era, Chinese and Japanese art not excepted. The African art object, a half generation ago the most neglected of ethnological curios, is now universally recognized as a "notable instance of plastic representation," a genuine work of art, masterful over its material in a powerful simplicity of conception, design and effect. This artistic discovery of African art came at a time when there was a marked decadence and sterility in certain forms of European plastic art expression, due to generations of the inbreeding of style and idiom. Out of the exhaustion of imitating Greek classicism and the desperate exploitation in graphic art of all the technical possibilities of color by the Impressionists and Post Impressionists, the problem of form and decorative design became emphasized in one of those reactions which in art occur so repeatedly. And suddenly with this new problem and interest, the African representation of form, previously regarded as ridiculously crude and inadequate, appeared cunningly sophisticated and masterful. Once the strong stylistic conventions that had stood between it and a true æsthetic appreciation were thus broken through, Negro art instantly came into marked recognition. Roger Fry in an essay on Negro Sculpture has the following to say: "I have to admit that some of these things are great sculpture—greater, I think, than anything we produced in the Middle Ages. Certainly they have the special qualities of sculpture in a higher degree. They have indeed complete plastic freedom, that is to say, these African artists really can see form in three dimensions. Now this is rare in sculpture. . . . So—far from the clinging to two dimensions, as we tend to do, the African artist actually underlines, as it were, the three-dimensionalness of his forms. It is in some such way that he manages to give to his forms their disconcerting vitality, the suggestion that they make of being not mere echoes of actual figures, but of possessing an inner life of their own. . . . Besides the logical comprehension of plastic from which the Negro shows he has also an exquisite taste in the handling of his material.'' The most authoritative contemporary Continental criticism quite thoroughly agrees with this verdict and estimate.

Indeed there are many attested influences of African art in French and German modernist art. They are to be found in work of Matisse, Picasso, Derain, Modigliani and Utrillo among the French painters, upon Max Pechstein, Elaine Stern, Franz Marc and others of the German Expressionists, and upon Modigliani, Archipenko, Epstein, Lipschitz, Lembruch, and Zadkine and Faggi among sculptors. In Paris, centering around Paul Guillaume, one of its pioneer exponents, there has grown up an art coterie profoundly influenced by an æsthetic developed largely from the idioms of African art. And what has been true of the African sculptures has been in a lesser degree true of the influence of other African art forms—decorative design, musical rhythms, dance forms, verbal imagery and symbolism. Attracted by the appeal of African plastic art to the study of other modes of African expression, poets like Guillaume Appolinaire and Blaisé Cendrars have attempted artistic re-expression of African idioms in poetic symbols and verse forms. So that what is a recognized school of modern French poetry professes the inspiration of African sources,—Appolinaire, Reverdy, Salmon, Fargue and others. The bible of this coterie has been Cendrars' *Anthologie Nègre,* now in its sixth edition.

The starting point of an æsthetic interest in African musical idiom seems to have been H. A. Junod's work,—*Les Chants et les Contes des Barongas* (1897). From the double source of African folk song and the study of American Negro musical rhythms, many of the leading French modernists have derived inspiration. Berard, Satie, Poulenc, Auric, and even Honneger, are all in diverse ways and degrees affected, but the most explicit influence has been upon the work of Darius Milhaud, who is an avowed propagandist of the possibilities of Negro musical idiom. The importance of these absorptions of African and Negro material by all of the major forms of contemporary art, some of them independently of any transfer that might be dismissed as a mere contagion of fad or vogue, is striking, and ought to be considered as a quite unanimous verdict of the modern creative mind upon the values, actual and potential, of this yet unexhausted reservoir of art material.

There is a vital connection between this new artistic respect for African idiom and the natural ambition of Negro artists for a racial idiom in their art expression. To a certain extent contemporary art has pronounced in advance upon this objective of the younger Negro artists, musicians and writers. Only the most reactionary conventions of art, then, stand between the Negro artist and the frank experimental development of these fresh idioms. This movement would, we think, be well under way in more avenues of advance at present but for the timid conventionalism which racial disparagement has forced upon the Negro mind in America. Let us take as a comparative instance, the painting of the Negro subject and notice the retarding effect of social prejudice. The Negro is a far more familiar figure in American life than in European, but American art, barring caricature and *genre,* reflects him scarcely at all. An occasional type sketch of Henri, or local color sketch of Winslow Homer represents all of a generation of painters. Whereas in Europe, with the Negro subject rarely accessible, we have as far back as the French romanticists a strong interest in the theme, an interest that in contemporary French, Belgian, German and even English painting has brought forth work of singular novelty and beauty. This work is almost all above the plane of *genre,* and in many cases represents sustained and lifelong study of the painting of the particularly difficult values of the Negro subject. To mention but a few, there is the work of Julius Hüther, Max Slevogt, Max Pechstein, Elaine Stern, von Reuckterschell among German painters; of Dinet, Lucie Cousturier, Bonnard, Georges Rouault, among the French; Klees van Dongen, the Dutch painter; most notably among the Belgians, Auguste Mambour; and among English painters, Neville Lewis, F. C. Gadell, John A. Wells, and Frank Potter. All these artists have looked upon the African scene and the African countenance, and discovered there a beauty that calls for a distinctive idiom both of color and modelling. The Negro physiognomy must be freshly and objectively conceived on its own patterns if it is ever to be seriously and importantly interpreted. Art must discover and reveal the beauty which prejudice and caricature have overlaid. And all vital art discovers beauty and opens our eyes to that which previously we could not see. While American art, including the work of our own Negro artists, has produced nothing above the level of the *genre* study or more penetrating than a Nordicized transcription, European art has gone on experimenting until the technique of the Negro subject has reached the dignity and skill of virtuoso treatment and a distinctive style. No great art will impose alien canons upon its subject matter. The work of Mambour especially suggests this forceful new stylization; he has brought to the Negro subject a modelling of masses that is truly sculptural and particularly suited to the broad massive features and subtle value shadings of the Negro countenance. After seeing his masterful handling of mass and light and shade in bold solid planes, one has quite the conviction that mere line and contour treatment can never be the classical technique for the portrayal of Negro types.

The work of these European artists should even now be the inspiration and guide-posts of a younger school of American Negro artists. They have too long been the victims of the academy tradition and shared the conventional blindness of the Caucasian eye with respect to the racial material at their immediate disposal. Thus there have been notably successful Negro artists, but no development of a school of Negro art. Our Negro American painter of outstanding success is Henry O. Tanner. His career is a case in point. Though a professed painter of types, he has devoted his art talent mainly to the portrayal of Jewish Biblical types and subjects, and has never maturely touched the portrayal of the Negro subject. Warrantable enough— for to the individual talent in art one must never dictate—who can be certain what field the next Negro artist of note will choose to command, or whether he will not be a landscapist or a master of still life or of purely decorative painting? But from the point of view of our artistic talent in bulk—it is a different matter. We ought and must have a school of Negro art, a local and a racially representative tradition. And that we have not, explains why the generation of Negro artists succeeding Mr. Tanner had only the inspiration of his great success to fire their ambitions, but not the guidance of a distinctive tradition to focus and direct their talents. Consequently they fumbled and fell short of his international stride and reach. The work of Henri Scott, Edwin A. Harleson, Laura Wheeler, in painting, and of Meta Warrick Fuller and May Howard Jackson in sculpture, competent as it has been, has nevertheless felt this handicap and has wavered between abstract expression which was imitative and not highly original, and racial expression which was only experimental. Lacking group leadership and concentration, they were wandering amateurs in the very field that might have given them concerted mastery.

A younger group of Negro artists is beginning to move in the direction of a racial school of art. The strengthened tendency toward representative group expression is shared even by the later work of the artists previously mentioned, as in Meta Warrick Fuller's "Ethiopia Awakening," to mention an outstanding example. But the work of young artists like Archibald Motley, Otto Farrill, Cecil Gaylord, John Urquhart, Samuel Blount, and especially that of Charles Keene and Aaron Douglas shows the promising beginning of an art movement instead of just the cropping out of isolated talent. The work of Winold Reiss, fellow-countryman of Slevogt and von Reuckterschell . . . has been deliberately conceived and executed as a path-breaking guide and encouragement to this new foray of the younger Negro artists. In idiom, technical treatment and objective social angle, it is a bold iconoclastic break with the current traditions that have grown up about the Negro subject in American art. It is not meant to dictate a style to the young Negro artist, but to point the lesson that contemporary European art has already learned—that any vital artistic espression of the Negro theme and subject in art must break through the stereotypes to a new style, a distinctive fresh technique, and some sort of characteristic idiom.

While we are speaking of the resources of racial art, it is well to take into account that the richest vein of it is not that of portraitistic idiom after all, but its almost limitless wealth of decorative and purely symbolic material. It is for the development of this latter aspect of a racial art that the study and example of African art material is so important. The African spirit, as we said at the outset, is at its best in abstract decorative forms. Design, and to a lesser degree, color, are its original *fortes.* It is this aspect of the folk tradition, this slumbering gift of the folk temperament that most needs reachievement and reexpression. And if African art is capable of producing the ferment in modern art that it has, surely this is not too much to expect of its influence upon the culturally awakened Negro artist of the present generation. So that if even the present vogue of African art should pass, and the bronzes of Benin and the fine sculptures of Gabon and Baoulé, and the superb designs of the Bushongo should again become mere items of exotic curiosity, for the Negro artist they ought still to have the import and influence of classics in whatever art expression is consciously and representatively racial.

HERITAGE
COUNTEE CULLEN

What is Africa to me:
Copper sun or scarlet sea,
Jungle star or jungle track,
Strong bronzed men, or regal black
Women from whose loins I sprang
When the birds of Eden sang?
One three centuries removed
From the scenes his fathers loved,
Spicy grove, cinnamon tree,
What is Africa to me?

So I lie, who all day long
Want no sound except the song
Sung by wild barbaric birds
Goading massive jungle herds,
Juggernauts of flesh that pass
Trampling tall defiant grass
Where young forest lovers lie,
Plighting troth beneath the sky.
So I lie, who always hear,
Though I cram against my ear
Both my thumbs, and keep them there,
Great drums throbbing through the air.
So I lie, whose fount of pride,
Dear distress, and joy allied,
Is my somber flesh and skin,
With the dark blood dammed within
Like great pulsing tides of wine

That, I fear, must burst the fine
Channels of the chafing net
Where they surge and foam and fret.

Africa? A book one thumbs
Listlessly, till slumber comes.
Unremembered are her bats
Circling through the night, her cats
Crouching in the river reeds,
Stalking gentle flesh that feeds
By the river brink; no more
Does the bugle-throated roar
Cry that monarch claws have leapt
From the scabbards where they slept.
Silver snakes that once a year
Doff the lovely coats you wear,
Seek no covert in your fear
Lest a mortal eye should see;
What's your nakedness to me?
Here no leprous flowers rear
Fierce corollas in the air;
Here no bodies sleek and wet,
Dripping mingled rain and sweat,
Tread the savage measures of
Jungle boys and girls in love.
What is last year's snow to me,
Last year's anything? The tree
Budding yearly must forget
How its past arose or set—
Bough and blossom, flower, fruit,
Even what shy bird with mute
Wonder at her travail there,
Meekly labored in its hair.
One three centuries removed
From the scenes his fathers loved,
Spicy grove, cinnamon tree,
What is Africa to me?

So I lie, who find no peace
Night or day, no slight release
From the unremittent beat
Made by cruel padded feet
Walking through my body's street.
Up and down they go, and back,
Treading out a jungle track.
So I lie, who never quite

143

Safely sleep from rain at night—
I can never rest at all
When the rain begins to fall;
Like a soul gone mad with pain
I must match its weird refrain;
Ever must I twist and squirm,
Writhing like a baited worm,
While its primal measures drip
Through my body, crying, "Strip!
Doff this new exuberance.
Come and dance the Lover's Dance!"
In an old remembered way
Rain works on me night and day.

Quaint, outlandish heathen gods
Black men fashion out of rods,
Clay, and brittle bits of stone,
In a likeness like their own,
My conversion came high-priced;
I belong to Jesus Christ,
Preacher of humility;
Heathen gods are naught to me.

Father, Son, and Holy Ghost,
So I make an idle boast;
Jesus of the twice-turned cheek,
Lamb of God, although I speak
With my mouth thus, in my heart
Do I play a double part.
Ever at Thy glowing altar
Must my heart grow sick and falter,
Wishing He I served were black,
Thinking then it would not lack
Precedent of pain to guide it,
Let who would or might deride it;
Surely then this flesh would know
Yours had borne a kindred woe.
Lord, I fashion dark gods, too,
Daring even to give You
Dark despairing features where,
Crowned with dark rebellious hair,
Patience wavers just so much as
Mortal grief compels, while touches
Quick and hot, of anger, rise
To smitten cheek and weary eyes.
Lord, forgive me if my need
Sometimes shapes a human creed.

All day long and all night through,
One thing only must I do:
Quench my pride and cool my blood,
Lest I perish in the flood.
Lest a hidden ember set
Timber that I thought was wet
Burning like the dryest flax,
Melting like the merest wax,
Lest the grave restore its dead.
Not yet has my heart or head
In the least way realized
They and I are civilized.

UNCLE JIM
COUNTEE CULLEN

"White folks is white," says Uncle Jim;
"A PLATITUDE," I sneer;
And then I tell him so is milk,
And the froth upon his beer.

His heart walled up with bitterness,
He smokes his pungent pipe,
And nods at me as if to say,
"Young fool, you'll soon be ripe!"

I have a friend who eats his heart
Away with grief of mine,
Who drinks my joy as tipplers drain
Deep goblets filled with wine.

I wonder why here at his side,
Face-in-the-grass with him,
My mind should stray the Grecian urn
To muse on Uncle Jim.

TABLEAU
COUNTEE CULLEN

Locked arm in arm they cross the way,
  The black boy and the white,
The golden splendor of the day,
  The sable pride of night.

From lowered blinds the dark folk stare,
  And here the fair folk talk,

Indignant that these two should dare
   In unison to walk.

Oblivious to look and word
   They pass, and see no wonder
That lightning brilliant as a sword
   Should blaze the path of thunder.

SATURDAY'S CHILD
COUNTEE CULLEN

Some are teethed on a silver spoon,
With the stars strung for a rattle;
I cut my teeth as the black racoon—
For implements of battle.

Some are swaddled in silk and down,
And heralded by a star;
They swathed my limbs in a sackcloth gown
On a night that was black as tar.

For some, godfather and goddame
The opulent fairies be;
Dame Poverty gave me my name,
And Pain godfathered me.

For I was born on Saturday—
"Bad time for planting seed,"
Was all my father had to say,
And, "One mouth more to feed."

Death cut the strings that gave me life,
And handed me to Sorrow,
The only kind of middle wife
My folks could beg or borrow.

AFRO-AMERICAN FRAGMENT
LANGSTON HUGHES

So long,
So far away
Is Africa.
Not even memories alive
Save those that history books create,

Save those that songs
Beat back into the blood—
Beat out of blood with words sad-sung
In strange un-Negro tongue—
So long,
So far away
Is Africa.

Subdued and time-lost
Are the drums—and yet
Through some vast mist of race
There comes this song
I do not understand,
This song of atavistic land,
Of bitter yearnings lost
Without a place—
So long,
So far away
Is Africa's
Dark face.

LUANI OF THE JUNGLES
LANGSTON HUGHES

"Not another shilling," I said. "You must think I'm a millionaire or some-thing. Here I am offering you my best hat, two shirts, and a cigar case, with two shillings besides, and yet you want five shillings more! I wouldn't give five shillings for six monkeys, let alone a mean-looking beast like yours. Come on, let's make a bargain. What do you say?"

But the African, who had come to the wharf on the Niger to sell his monkey remained adamant. "Five shillin' more," he said. "Five shillin'. Him one fine monkey!" However, when he held up the little animal for me to touch, the frightened beast opened his white-toothed mouth viciously and gave a wild scream. "Him no bite," assured the native. "Him good."

"Yes, he's good all right," said Porto Rico sarcastically. "We'll get a mon-key at Burutu cheaper, anyhow. It'd take a year to tame this one."

"I won't buy him," I protested to the native. "You want too much."

"But he is a fine monkey," an unknown voice behind us said, and we turned to see a strange, weak-looking little white man standing there. "He is a good monkey," the man went on in a foreign sort of English. "You ought to buy him here. Not often you get a red monkey of this breed. He is rare."

Then the stranger, who seemed to know whereof he spoke, told us that the animal was worth much more than the native asked, and he advised me softly to pay the other five shillings. "He is like a monkey in a poem," the man said. Meanwhile the slender simian clung tightly to the native's shoulder and snarled shrilly whenever I tried to touch him. But the very wildness of the poor captured beast with the wire cord about his hairy neck fascinated me. Given confidence by the stranger, for one old hat, two blue shirts, a broken cigar case, and seven shillings, I bought the animal. Then for fear of being bitten, I wrapped the wild little thing in my coat, carried him up the gangplank of the "West Illana" and put him into an empty prune box standing near the galley door. Porto Rico and the stranger followed and I saw that Porto Rico carried a large valise, so I surmised that the stranger was a new passenger.

The "West Illana," a freight boat from New York to West Africa, seldom carried passengers other than an occasional trader or a few poor missionaries. But when, as now, we were up one of the tributaries of the Niger, where English passenger steamers seldom came, the captain sometimes consented to take on travellers to the coast. The little white man with the queer accent registered for Lagos, a night's journey away. After he had been shown his stateroom he came out on deck and, in a friendly sort of manner, began to tell me about the various methods of taming wild monkeys. Yet there was a vague far-off air about him as though he were not really interested in what he was saying. He took my little beast in his hands and I noticed that the animal did not bite him nor appear particularly alarmed.

It was late afternoon then and all our cargo for that port,—six Fords from Detroit and some electric motors,—had been unloaded. The seamen closed the hatch, the steamer swung slowly away from the wharf with a blast of the whistle and began to glide lazily down the river. Soon we seemed to be floating through the heart of a dense sullen jungle. A tangled mass of trees and vines walled in the sluggish stream and grew out of the very water itself. None of the soil of the river bank could be seen,—only an impenetrable thickness of trees and vines. Nor were there the brilliant jungle trees one likes to imagine in the tropics. They were rather a monotonous grey-green confusion of trunks and leaves with only an occasional cluster of smoldering scarlet flowers or, very seldom, the flash of some bright-winged bird to vary their hopelessness. Once or twice this well of ashey vegetation was broken by a muddy brook or a little river joining the larger stream and giving, along murkey lengths, a glimpse into the further depths of this colorless and forbidding country. Then the river gradually widened and we could smell the sea, but it was almost dinner time before the ship began to roll slowly on the ocean's green and open waters. When I went into the salon to set the officers' table we were still very near the Nigerian coast and the grey vines and dull trees of the delta region.

After dinner I started aft to join Porto Rico and the seamen, but I saw the little white man seated on one of the hawser posts near the handrail so I stopped. It was dusk and the last glow of sunset was fading on the edge of the sea. I was surprised to find this friend of the afternoon seated there because passengers seldom ventured far from the comfortable deck chairs near the salon.

"Good evening," I said.

"Bon soir," answered the little man.

"Vous êtes francais?" I asked, hearing his greeting.

"Non," he replied slowly. "I am not French but I lived in Paris for a long while." Then he added for seemingly no reason at all, "I am a poet, but I destroy my poems."

The gold streak on the horizon turned to orange.

There was nothing I could logically say except, "Why?"

"I don't know," he said. "I don't know why I destroy my poems. But then there are many things I don't know. . . . I live back in that jungle." He pointed toward the coast. "I don't know why."

The orange in the sunset darkened to blue.

"But why," I asked again stupidly.

"My wife is there," he said. "She is an African."

"Is she?" I could think of nothing other to say.

The blue on the horizon greyed to purple now.

"I'm trying to get away," he went on, paying no attention to my remark. "I'm going down to Lagos now. Maybe I'll forget to come back—back there." And he pointed to the jungles hidden in the distant darkness of the coast. "Maybe I'll forget to come back this time. But I never did before,—not even when I was drunk. I never forgot. I always came back. Yet I hate that woman!"

"What woman?" I asked.

"My wife," he said. "I love her and yet I hate her."

The sea and the sky were uniting in darkness.

"Why?" was again all I could think of saying.

"At Paris," he went on. "I married her at Paris." Then suddenly to me, "Are you a poet, too?"

"Why, yes," I replied.

"Then I can talk to you," he said. "I married her at Paris four years ago when I was a student there in the Sorbonne." As he told his story the night became very black and the stars were warm. "I met her one night at the Bal Bulier,—this woman I love. She was with an African student whom I knew and he told me that she was the daughter of a wealthy native in Nigeria. At once I was fascinated. She seemed to me the most beautiful thing I had ever seen,—dark and wild, exotic and strange,—accustomed as I had been to only pale white women. We sat down at a table and began to talk together in English. She told me she was educated in England but that she lived in Africa. 'With my tribe,' she said. 'When I am home I do not wear clothes like these, nor these things on my fingers.' She touched her evening gown and held out her dark hands sparkling with diamonds. 'Life is simple when I am home,' she said. 'I don't like it here. It is too cold and people wear too many clothes.' She lifted a cigarette holder of platinum and jade to her lips and blew a thin line of smoke into the air. 'Mon dieu!' I thought to myself. 'A child of sophistication and simplicity such as I have never seen!' And suddenly before I knew it, crazy young student that I was, I had leaned across the table and was saying, 'I love you.'

" 'That is what he says, too,' she replied, pointing toward the African student dancing gaily with a blonde girl at the other end of the room. 'You haven't danced with me yet.' We rose. The orchestra played a Spanish waltz full of Gypsy-like nostalgia and the ache of desire. She waltzed as no woman I had ever danced with before could waltz,—her dark body close against my white one, her head on my shoulder, its mass of bushy hair tangled and wild, perfumed with a jungle-scent. I wanted her! I ached for her! She seemed all I had ever dreamed of; all the romance I'd ever found in books; all the lure of the jungle countries; all the passions of the tropic soul.

" 'I need you,' I said. 'I love you.' Her hand pressed mine and our lips met, wedged as we were in the crowd of the Bal Bulier.

" 'I'm sailing from Bordeaux at the end of the month,' she told me as we sat in the Gardens of the Luxemburg at sunset a few days later. 'I'm going back home to the jungle countries and you are coming with me.' "

" 'I know it,' I agreed, as though I had been planning for months to go with her.

" 'You are coming with me back to my people,' she continued. 'You with your whiteness coming to me and my dark land. Maybe I won't love you then. Maybe you won't love me,—but the jungle'll take you and you'll stay there forever.'

" 'It won't be the jungle making me stay,' I protested. 'It'll be you. You'll be the ebony goddest of my heart, the dark princess who saved me from the corrupt tangle of white civilization, who took me away from my books into life, who discovered for me the soul of your dark countries. You'll be the tropic flower of my heart.

"During the following days before our sailing, I made many poems to this black woman I loved and adored. I dropped my courses at the Sorbonne that week and wrote my father in Prague that I would be going on a journey south for my health's sake. I changed my account to a bank in Lagos in West Africa, and paid farewell calls on all my friends in Paris. So much did I love Luani that I had no regrets on taking leave of my classmates nor upon saying adieux to the city of light and joy.

"One night in July we sailed from Bordeaux. We had been married the day before in Paris.

"In August we landed at Lagos and came by river boat to the very wharf where you saw me today. But in the meantime something was lost between us,—something of the first freshness of love that I've never found again. Perhaps it was because of the many days together hour after hour on the boat,—perhaps she saw too much of me. Anyway, when she took off her European clothes at the Liberty Hotel in Lagos to put on the costume of her tribe, and when she sent to the steel safe at the English bank there all of her diamonds and pearls, she seemed to put me away, too, out of her heart, along with the foreign things she had removed from her body. More fascinating than ever in the dress of her people, with the soft cloth of scarlet about her limbs and the little red sandals of buffalo hide on her feet,—more fascinating than ever and yet farther away she seemed, elusive, strange. And she began that day to talk to some of the servants in the language of her land.

"Up to the river town by boat, and then we travelled for days deep into the jungles. After a week we arrived at a high clear space surrounded by bread-fruit, mango, and cocoanut trees. There a hundred or more members of the tribe were waiting to receive her,—beautiful brown-black people whose per-fect bodies glistened in the sunlight, bodies that shamed me and the weakness under my European clothing. That night there was a great festival given in honor of Luani's coming,—much beating of drums and wild fantas-tic dancing beneath the moon,—a festival in which I could take no part for I knew none of their ceremonies, none of their dances. Nor did I understand a word of their language. I could only stand aside and look, or sit in the door of our hut and sip the palm wine they served me. Luani, wilder than any of the others, danced to the drums, laughed and was happy. She seemed to have forgotten me sitting in the doorway of our hut drinking palm wine.

"Weeks passed and months. Luani went hunting and fishing, wandering about for days in the jungles. Sometimes she asked me to go with her, but more often she went with members of the tribe and left me to walk about the village, understanding nobody, able to say almost nothing. No one mo-lested me. I was seemingly respected or at least ignored. Often when Luani was with me she would speak no French or English all day, unless I asked her something. She seemed almost to have forgotten the European lan-guages, to have put them away as she had put away the clothes and cus-toms of the foreigners. Yet she would come when I called and let me kiss her. In a far-off, strange sort of way she still seemed to love me. Even then I was happy because I loved her and could hold her body.

"Then one night, trembling from an ugly dream, I suddenly awoke, sat up in bed and discovered in a daze that she was not beside me. A cold sweat broke out on my body. The room was empty. I leaped to the floor and opened the door of the hut. A great streak of moonlight fell across the threshold. A little breeze was blowing and the leaves of the mango trees rustled dryly. The sky was full of stars. I stepped into the grassy village street,—quiet all around. Filled with worry and fear, I called, 'Luani!' As far as I could see the tiny huts were quiet under the moon and no one an-swered. I was suddenly weak and afraid. The indifference of the silence un-nerved me. I called again, 'Luani!' A voice seemed to reply: 'To the palm forest, to the palm forest. Quick, to the palm forest!' And I began to run toward the edge of the village where a great cocoanut grove lay.

"There beneath the trees it was almost as light as day and I sat down to rest against the base of a tall palm, while the leaves in the wind rustled dryly overhead. No other noise disturbed the night and I rested there wide awake, remembering Paris and my student days at college. An hour must have passed when, through an aisle of the palm trees, I saw two naked figures walking. Very near me they came and then passed on in the moonlight,— two ebony bodies close together in the moonlight. They were Luani and the chief's young son, Awa Unabo.

"I did not move. Hurt and resentment, anger and weakness filled my veins. Unabo, the strongest and greatest hunter of the tribe, possessed the woman I loved. They were walking together in the moonlight, and weakling that I was, I dared not fight him. He'd break my body as though it were a twig. I could only rage in my futile English and no one except Luani would understand. . . . I went back to the hut. Just before dawn she came, taking leave of her lover at my door.

"Like a delicate statue carved in ebony, a dark halo about her head, she stood before me, beautiful and black like the very soul of the tropics, a woman to write poems about, a woman to go mad over. All the jealous anger died in my heart and only a great hurt remained and a feeling of weakness.

" 'I am going away, back to Paris,' I said.

" 'I'm sorry,' she replied with emotion. 'A woman can have two lovers and love them both.' She put her arms around my neck but I pushed her away. She began to cry then and I cursed her in foreign, futile words. That same day, with two guides and four carriers, I set out through the jungles toward the Niger and the boat for Lagos. She made no effort to keep me back. One word from her and I could not have left the village, I knew. I would have been a prisoner,—but she did not utter that word. Only when I left the clearing she waved to me and said, 'You'll come back.'

"Once in Lagos, I engaged passage for Bordeaux, but when the time came to sail I could not leave. I thought of her standing before me naked that last morning like a little ebony statue, and I tore up my ticket! I returned to the hotel and began to drink heavily in an effort to forget, but I could not. I remained drunk for weeks, then after some months had passed I boarded a river boat, went back up the Niger, back through the jungles,—back to her.

"Four times that has happened now. Four times I've left her and four times returned. She has borne a child for Awa Unabo. And she tells me that she loves him. But she says she loves me, too. Only one thing I do know,—she drives me mad. Why I stay with her, I do not know any longer. Why her lover tolerates me, I do not know. Luani humiliates me now,—and fascinates me, tortures me and holds me. I love her. I hate her, too. I write poems about her and destroy them. I leave her and come back. I do not know why. I'm like a mad man and she's like the soul of her jungles, quiet and terrible, beautiful and dangerous, fascinating and death-like. I'm leaving her again, but I know I'll come back. . . . I know I'll come back."

Slowly the moon rose out of the sea and the distant coast of Nigeria was like a shadow on the horizon. The West Illana" rolled languidly through the night. I looked at the little white man, tense and pale, and wondered if he were crazy, or if he were lying.

"We reach Lagos early in the morning, do we not?" he asked. "I must go to sleep. Good night." And the strange passenger went slowly toward the door of the corridor that led to his cabin.

I sat still in the darkness for a few moments, dazed. Then I suddenly came to, heard the chug, chug, of the engines below and the half-audible conversation drifting from the fo'c's'ls, heard the sea lapping at the sides of the ship. Then I got up and went to bed.

DANSE AFRICAINE
LANGSTON HUGHES

The low beating of the tom-toms,
The slow beating of the tom-toms,
   Low . . . slow
Slow . . . low—
Stirs your blood.
     Dance!
A night-veiled girl
   Whirls softly into a
   Circle of light.
   Whirls softly . . . slowly,
Like a wisp of smoke around the fire—
   And the tom-toms beat,
   And the tom-toms beat,
And the low beating of the tom-toms
   Stirs your blood.

NEGRO
LANGSTON HUGHES

I am a Negro:
   Black as the night is black,
   Black like the depths of my Africa.

I've been a slave:
   Caesar told me to keep his door-steps clean.
   I brushed the boots of Washington.

I've been a worker:
   Under my hand the pyramids arose.
   I made mortar for the Woolworth Building.

I've been a singer:
   All the way from Africa to Georgia
   I carried my sorrow songs.
   I made ragtime.

I've been a victim:
   The Belgians cut off my hands in the Congo.
   They lynch me still in Mississippi.

I am a Negro:
   Black as the night is black,
   Black like the depths of my Africa.

CROSS
LANGSTON HUGHES

My old man's a white old man
And my old mother's black.
If ever I cursed my white old man
I take my curses back.

If ever I cursed my black old mother
And wished she were in hell,
I'm sorry for that evil wish
And now I wish her well.

My old man died in a fine big house.
My ma died in a shack.
I wonder where I'm gonna die,
Being neither white nor black?

I TOO SING AMERICA
LANGSTON HUGHES

I, too, sing America

I am the darker brother.
They send me to eat in the kitchen
When company comes,
But I laugh,
And eat well,
And grow strong.

Tomorrow,
I'll be at the table
When company comes.
Nobody'll dare
Say to me,

"Eat in the kitchen,"
Then.

Besides,
They'll see how beautiful I am
And be ashamed—

I, too, am America.

THE NEGRO SPEAKS OF RIVERS
LANGSTON HUGHES

I've known rivers:
I've known rivers ancient as the world and older than the flow of human
   blood in human veins.

My soul has grown deep like the rivers.

I bathed in the Euphrates when dawns were young.
I built my hut near the Congo and it lulled me to sleep.
I looked upon the Nile and raised the pyramids above it.
I heard the singing of the Mississippi when Abe Lincoln
   went down to New Orleans, and I've seen its muddy
   bosom turn all golden in the sunset.

I've known rivers:
Ancient, dusky rivers.

My soul has grown deep like rivers.

FROM
BANJO
CLAUDE MCKAY

V *"Jelly Roll"*

Shake That Thing. The opening of the Café African by a Senegalese had
brought all the joy-lovers of darkest color together to shake that thing.
Never was there such a big black-throated guzzling of red wine, white wine,
and close, indiscriminate jazzing of all the Negroes of Marseilles.

   For the Negro-Negroid population of the town divides sharply into groups.
The Martiniquans and Guadeloupans, regarding themselves as constituting
the dark flower of all Marianne's blacks, make a little aristocracy of themselves. The Madagascans with their cousins from the little dots of islands

around their big island and the North African Negroes, whom the pure Arabs despise, fall somewhere between the Martiniquans and the Senegalese, who are the savages. Senegalese is the geographically inaccurate term generally used to designate all the Negroes from the different parts of French West Africa.

The magic thing had brought all shades and grades of Negroes together. Money. A Senegalese had emigrated to the United States, and after some years had returned with a few thousand dollars. And he had bought a café on the quay. It was a big café, the first that any Negro in the town ever owned.

The tiny group of handsomely-clothed Senegalese were politely proud of the bar, and all the blue overall boys of the docks and the ships were boisterously glad of a spacious place to spread joy in.

All shades of Negroes came together there. Even the mulattoes took a step down from their perch to mix in. For, as in the British West Indies and South Africa, the mulattoes of the French colonies do not usually intermingle with the blacks.

But the magic had brought them all together to shake that thing and drink red wine, white wine, sweet wine. All the British West African blacks, Portuguese blacks, American blacks, all who had drifted into this port that the world goes through.

A great event! And to Banjo it had brought a unique feeling of satisfaction. He did not miss it, as he never missed anything rich that came within his line of living. There was music at the bar and Banjo made much of it. He got a little acquainted with the *patron,* who often chatted with him. The *patron* was proud of his English and liked to display it when there was any distinguished-appearing person at the café.

"Shake That Thing!" That was the version of the "Jelly-Roll Blues" that Banjo loved and always played. And the Senegalese boys loved to shake to it. Banjo was treated to plenty of red wine and white wine when he played that tune. And he would not think of collecting sous. Latnah had gone about once and collected sous in her tiny jade tray. But she never went again. She loved Banjo, but she could not enter into the spirit of that all-Negro-atmosphere of the bar. Banjo was glad she stayed away. He did not want to collect sous from a crowd of fellows just like himself. He preferred to play for them and be treated to wine. Sous! How could he respect sous? He who had burnt up dollars. Why should he care, with a free bed, free love, and wine?

His plan of an orchestra filled his imagination now. Maybe he could use the Café African as a base to get some fellows together. Malty could play the guitar right splendid, but he had no instrument. If that Senegalese *patron* had a little imagination, he might buy Malty a guitar and they would start a little orchestra that would make the bar unique and popular.

Many big things started in just such a little way. Only give him a chance and he would make this dump sit up and take notice—show it how to be sporty and game. How he would love to see a couple of brown chippies from Gawd's own show this Ditch some decent movement—turn themselves jazzing loose in a back-home, brown-skin Harlem way. Oh, Banjo's skin was itching to make some romantic thing.

And one afternoon he walked straight into a dream—a cargo boat with a crew of four music-making colored boys, with banjo, ukelele, mandolin, guitar, and horn. That evening Banjo and Malty, mad with enthusiam, literally carried the little band to the Vieux Port. It was the biggest evening ever at the Senegalese bar. They played several lively popular tunes, but the Senegalese boys yelled for "Shake That Thing." Banjo picked it off and the boys from the boat quickly got it. Then Banjo keyed himself up and began playing in his own wonderful wild way.

> "Old Uncle Jack, the jelly-roll king,
> Just got back from shaking that thing!
>   He can shake that thing, he can shake that thing
>   For he's a jelly-roll king. Oh, shake that thing!"

It roused an Arab-black girl from Algeria into a shaking-mad mood. And she jazzed right out into the center of the floor and shook herself in a low-down African shimmying way. The mandolin player, a stocky, cocky lad of brown-paper complexion, the lightest-skinned of the playing boys, had his eyes glued on her. Her hair was cropped and stood up shiny, crinkly like a curiously-wrought bird's nest. She was big-boned and well-fleshed and her full lips were a savage challenge. Oh, shake that thing!

"Cointreau!" The Negroid girl called when, the music ceasing, the paper-brown boy asked her to take a drink.

"That yaller nigger's sure gone on her," Malty said to Banjo.

"And she knows he's got a roll can reach right up to her figure," said Banjo. "Looka them eyes she shines on him! Oh, Boy! it was the same for you and I when we first landed—every kind of eyes in the chippies' world shining for us!"

"Yes, but you ain't got nothing to kick about. The goodest eyes in this burg ain't shining for anybody else but you."

"Hheh-hheh," Banjo giggled. "I'll be dawggone, Malty, ef I don't think sometimes youse getting soft. Takem as they come, easy and jolly, ole boh."

He poured out a glass of red wine, chinked his glass against Malty's, and toasted, "Oh, you Dixieland, here's praying for you' soul salvation."

"And here is joining you," said Malty.

> "Dry land will nevah be my land,
> Gimme a wet wide-open land for mine."

Handsome, happy brutes. The music is on again. The Senegalese boys crowd the floor, dancing with one another. They dance better male with male or individually, than with the girls, putting more power in their feet, dancing more wildly, more natively, more savagely. Senegalese in blue overalls, Madagascan soldiers in khaki, dancing together. A Martiniquan with his mulatress flashing her gold teeth. A Senegalese sergeant goes round with his fair blonde. A Congo boxer struts it with his Marguerite. And Banjo, grinning, singing, white teeth, great mouth, leads the band. . . . Shake that thing.

The banjo dominates the other instruments; the charming, pretty sound of the ukelele, the filigree notes of the mandolin, the sensuous color of the guitar. And Banjo's face shows that he feels that his instrument is first. The Negroes and Spanish Negroids of the evenly-warm, evergreen and ever-flowering Antilles may love the rich chords of the guitar, but the banjo is preëminently the musical instrument of the American Negro. The sharp, noisy notes of the banjo belong to the American Negro's loud music of life—an affirmation of his hardy existence in the midst of the biggest, the most tumultuous civilization of modern life.

Sing, Banjo! Play, Banjo! Here I is, Big Boss, keeping step, sure step, right long with you in some sort a ways. He-ho, Banjo! Play that thing! Shake that thing!

> "Old Brother Mose is sick in bed.
>   Doctor says he is almost dead
>   From shaking that thing, shaking that thing.
>   He was a jelly-roll king. Oh, shake that thing!"

A little flock of pinks from the Ditch floated into the bar. Seamen from Senegal. Soldiers from Madagascar. Pimps from Martinique. Pimps from everywhere. Pimps from Africa. Seamen fed up with the sea. Young men weary of the work of the docks, scornful of the meager reward—doing that now. Black youth close to the bush and the roots of jungle trees, trying to live the precarious life of the poisonous orchids of civilization.

Shake That Thing! . . .

The slim, slate-colored Martiniquan dances with a gold-brown Arab girl in a purely sensual way. His dog's mouth shows a tiny, protruding bit of pink tongue. Oh, he jazzes like a lizard with his girl. A dark-brown lizard and a gold-brown lizard. . . .

> "Oh, shake that thing,
>   He's a jelly-roll king."

A coffee-black boy from Cameroon and a chocolate-brown from Dakar stand up to each other to dance a native sex-symbol dance. Bending knee and nodding head, they dance up to each other. As they almost touch, the smaller boy spins suddenly round and dances away. Oh, exquisite movement! Like a ram goat and a ram kid. Hands and feet! Shake that thing!

Black skin itching, black flesh warm with the wine of life, the music of life, the love and deep meaning of life. Strong smell of healthy black bodies in a close atmosphere, generating sweat and waves of heat. Oh, shake that thing!

Suddenly in the thick joy of it there was a roar and a rush and sheering apart as a Senegalese leaped like a leopard bounding through the jazzers, and, gripping an antagonist, butted him clean on the forehead once, twice, and again, and turned him loose to fall heavily on the floor like a felled tree.

The *patron* dashed from behind the bar. A babel of different dialects broke forth. Policemen appeared and the musicians slipped outside, followed by most of the Martiniquans.

"Hheh-hheh," Banjo laughed. "The music so good it put them French fellahs in a fighting mood."

"Niggers is niggers all ovah the wul'," said the tall, long-faced chocoate who played the guitar. "Always spoil a good thing. Always the same no matter what color their hide is or what langwidge they talk."

"And I was fixing for that fair brown. I wonder where at she is?" said the mandolin-player.

"Don't worry," said Banjo. "Theah's always some'n' better or as good as what you miss. You should do like me whenevah you hit a new port. Always try to make something as different from what you know as a Leghorn is from a Plymouth Rock."

"Hi-ee! But youse one chicken-knowing fool," said Malty.

Banjo did a little strut-jig. "You got mah number all right, boh. And what wese gwine to do now? The night ain't begin yet at all foh mine. I want to do some moh playing and do some moh wine and what not do?"

A Martinique guide, who had had them under surveillance for a long while, now stepped up and said that he knew of a love shop where they could play music and have some real fun.

"You sure?" asked Banjo. "Don't fool us now, for I lives right down here in this dump and know most a them. And if that joint you know ain't a place that we can lay around in for a while, nothing doing I tell you straight. I'll just take all mah buddies right outa there."

The guide assured the boys that his place was all right. They all went into another bar on the quay and the guitar-player paid for a round of drinks. From there they turned up the Rue de la Mairie and west along the Rue de la Loge to find the Martiniquan's rendezvous.

They went by the Rue de la Reynarde, where a loud jarring cluster of colored lights was shouting its trade. Standing in the slimy litter of a narrow turning, an emaciated, middle-aged, watery-eyed woman was doing a sort of dance and singing in a thin streaky voice. She was advertising the house in whose shadow she danced, and was much like a poorly-feathered hen pecking and clucking on a dunghill.

The boys hesitated a little before the appearance of the drab-fronted building that their escort indicated. Then they entered and were surprised at finding themselves in a showy love shop of methodically assorted things. It was a very international. European, African, Asiatic. Contemporary feminine styles competed with old and forgotten. Rose-petal pajamas, knee-length frocks, silken shifts, the nude, the boyish bob contrasted with shimmering princess gowns, country-girl dresses of striking freshness, severe glove-fitting black setting off a demure lady with Italian-rich, thick, long hair, the piquant semi-nude and Spanish-shawled shoulders.

Banjo saw his first flame of the Ditch between two sailors with batik-like kerchiefs curiously knotted on their heads. They were Malay, perhaps. This time he was not aroused. The Martiniquan talked to a strangely attractive girl. She had almond eyes that were painted in a unique manner to emphasize their exotic effect. Evidently she was not pure Mongolian, but perhaps some casual crossing of Occident and Orient, commerce-spanned, dropped on the shore of the wonderful sea of the world.

There were half a dozen touts. One seemed a person of authority in the place. He was this side of forty, above average height, of meager form, Spanish type, with a face rather disgusting, because, although dark, it was sallow and deep-sunken under the cheek bones. He wore a blue suit, white scarf, heavy gold chain, and patent-leather shoes. The other five were youths. Three sported bright suits and fancy shoes of two and three colors, and two were in ordinary proletarian blue. The proletarian suits among all the striking feminine finery gave a certain elusive tone of distinction to the atmosphere, and one dressed thus was particularly conspicuous, reclining on a red-cushioned seat, under the lavish and intimate caresses of a Negress from the Antilles. Her face was like that of a Pekinese. She wore a bit of orange chiffon and had a green fan, which she opened at intervals against her mouth as she grinned deliciously.

Sitting like a queen in prim fatness, quite high up against a desk near the staircase that led to the regions above, a lady ruled over the scene with smiling business efficiency. When the Martiniquan spoke to her, introducing his evening's catch by a wave of the hand toward where the boys had seated themselves, and explaining that they wanted to play their own music, she smiled a gay acquiescence.

> "Oh, shake, shake, shake that thing!"
> He's a jelly-roll king. . . ."

When Banjo and his fellows entered, many eyes had followed them. And now as they played and hummed and swayed, all eyes were fixed on them, and soon the whole shop was right out on the floor, shaking that thing. Oh, shake that thing!

The little black girl was all in a wild heat of movement as she went rearing up and down with her young Provençal. But he seemed unequal to catch and keep up with her motion, so she exchanged him for the Martiniquan, who went prancing into it. And round and round they went, bounding in and out among the jazzers, rearing and riding together with the speed and freedom of two wild goats. Oh, shake that wonderful thing!

The players paused and some girls tried to order champagne on them, but the Martiniquan intervened and demanded wine and spirits.

"He knows his business," the mandolin-player said to Banjo.

"He's gotta," Banjo replied, "because he's got himself to look out for and me to reckin with."

Suddenly the air was full of a terrible tenseness and gravity as an altercation between the lady at the desk and the meager, sallow-faced man seemed at the point of developing into a fateful affair. The man was leaning against the desk, looking into the woman's face with cold, ghastly earnestness, his hand resting a little in his hip pocket. The woman's face fell flat like paste and all the girls stood tiptoe in silence and trembling excitement. Abruptly, without a word, the man turned and left the room with murder in his stride.

"That must be the boss-man," the mandolin-player said.

"And he looks like a mean mastiff," said the guitar-player.

"Sure seems lak he's just that thing," agreed Banjo.

Tem, tem, ti-tum, tim ti-tim, tum, tem. Banjo and the boys were chording up. Back . . . thing . . . bed . . . black . . . dead. . . . Oh, shake that thing. . . . Jelly-r-o-o-o-o-oll! Again all the shop was out on the floor. No graceful sliding and gliding, but strutting, jigging, shimmying, shuffling, humping, standing-swaying, dogging, doing, shaking that thing. The girls were now tiptoeing to another kind of excitement. Blood had crept back up into the face of the woman at the desk. . . .

The sallow-faced man appeared in the entrance and strode through the midst of it to the desk. Bomb! The fearful report snuffed out the revel and the dame tumbled fatly to the floor. The murderer gloated over the sad mess of flesh for an instant, then with a wild leap he lanced himself like a rat through the paralyzed revelers and disappeared.

The bewildered music-makers halted hesitantly at the foot of the alley.

"Let's all go in here and take a stiff drink." Banjo indicated a little bistro at the corner.

"Better let's leg it a li'l' ways longer," said the ukelele-player, "so the police won't come fooling around us now that wese good and well away outa there. I don't wanta have no truck with the police."

"And they ain't gwineta mess around us, pardner," said Malty. "We don't speak that there lingo a theirn and they ain't studying us. Ise been in on a dozen shooting-ups in this here Ditch, ef Ise been in on one, with the bullets them jest burning pass mah black buttum, and Ise nevah been asked by the police, 'What did you miss?' nor 'What did you see?' "

"Did you say a dozen?" cried the ukelele-player.

"Just that I did, boh, which was what I was pussonally attached to. But that ain't nothing at all, for theah's a shooting-up or a cutting-up—and sometimes moh—every day in this here burg."

"Malty," said Banjo, "youse sure one eggsigirating spade."

"Doughnuts on that there eggsigirating. It's the same crap to me whether there was a dozen or a thousand. They ain't nevah made a hole in me, for Ise got magic in mah skin foh protection, when you done got you souvenir there on you' wrist, Banjo boy."

"Gawd! But it was a bloody affair, all right," said the guitar-player. "I was so frightened I didn't really know what was happening. Bam! Biff! And the big boss-lady was undertaker's business before you could squint."

"Jest spoiled the whole sport," said the ukelele-player. "I kinda liked the nifty dump. It was the goods, all right."

"You said it, boh," the mandolin-player grinned, scratching his person. "It was some moh collection. All the same, I gotta plug."

"With you, buddy," cried Banjo. "Right there with you I sure indeed is."

"Let's go back to the African Bar," suggested the mandolin-player. The picture of the North African girl shaking that jelly-roll thing was still warmly working in his blood.

They found the African Bar closed. Again they left the quay, and Banjo took them up one of the somber, rubbish-strewn alleys of the Ditch. On both sides of the alley were the dingy cubicles whose only lights were the occupants who filled the fronts, gesturing and calling in ludicrous tones: "Viens ici, viens ici," and repeating pridefully the raw expressions of the low love shops that they had learned from English-speaking seamen.

Out of a drinking hole-in-the-wall came the creaky jangling notes of a small, upright and ancient pianola. The place was chock-full of a mixed crowd of girls, seamen, and dockers, with two man-of-war sailors and three soldiers among them.

"What about this here dump?" asked Banjo.

The mandolin-player looked lustfully up and down the alley and into the bistro, where wreaths of smoke settled heavily upon the frowsy air. "Suits me all right," he drawled. "What about you fellows?"

"Well, I hope it won't turn into another bloody mess of a riot this time," said the ukelele-player.

"Here youse just like you would be at home. This is *my* street," said Banjo. A girl came up and, patting him on the shoulder with a familiar phrase, she pushed him into the bistro.

As they entered a Senegalese who had been dancing to their voluptuous playing at the African Bar, exclaimed:"Here they are! Now we're going to hear some real music—something ravishing." And he begged Banjo to play the "Jelly-Roll."

One of the soldiers was evidently "slumming." There was a neat elegance about his uniform and shoes that set him apart from the ambiguous dandies of military service, the *habituées* of shady places. His features and his manner betrayed class distinction. He offered Banjo and his companions a round of drinks, saying in slow English: "Please play. You American? I like much *les Negres* play the jazz American. I hear them in Paris. *Epatant!*"

Banjo grinned and tossed off his Cap Corse. "All right, fellows. Let's play them that thing first."

"And then the once-over," said the mandolin-player.

Shake That Thing! That jelly-roll Thing!

Shake to the loud music of life playing to the primeval round of life. Rough rhythm of darkly-carnal life. Strong surging flux of profound currents forced into shallow channels. Play that thing! One movement of the thousand movements of the eternal life-flow. Shake that thing! In the face of the shadow of Death. Treacherous hand of murderous Death, lurking in sinister alleys, where the shadows of life dance, nevertheless, to their music of life. Death over there! Life over here! Shake down Death and forget his commerce, his purpose, his haunting presence in a great shaking orgy. Dance down the Death of these days, the Death of these ways in shaking that thing.

Jungle jazzing, Orient wriggling, civilized stepping. Shake that thing! Sweet dancing thing of primitive joy, perverse pleasure, prostitute ways, many-colored variations of the rhythm, savage, barbaric, refined—eternal rhythm of the mysterious, magical, magnificent—the dance divine of life. . . . Oh, Shake That Thing!

.   .   .

XI Everybody Doing It

Ray had put on his carefully-tended suit for special occasions to go to an agency on the Canebière, the great Main Street of Marseilles. The broad short stretch of thoroughfare was in gala dress, just as crazy as could be.

A Dollar Line boat, and a British ship from the Far East, had come into port that morning and their passengers had swelled the human stream of the ever-overflowing Canebière. Conspicuous on the pavement before a tourist agency of international fame, a bloated, livid-skinned Egyptian solicited all the male tourists that passed by.

"Gu-ide, gentlemen? Will you have a gu-ide?" he insinuated in a tone of the color of mustard and the smell of Camembert. "Show you all the sights of Marseilles. Hot stuff in the quarter. Tableaux vivants and blue cinema."

Other guides were working the crowd, Spanish, French, Italian, Greek—an international gang of them, but none so outstanding as this oleaginous mass out of Egypt with his heavy, eunuch-like face with its drooping fish eyes that seemed unable to look up straight at anything.

There were a number of touring cars filled with sightseers. Cocottes, gigolos, touts, sailors, soldiers everywhere. The cocottes passed in pairs and singly, attractive in their striking frocks and fancy shoes. The Arab-black girl in orange went by arm in arm with a white girl wearing rose. They smiled at Ray, standing on the corner.

Brazenly the gigolos made their signs for the delectation of the tourists. Such signs as monkeys in the zoo delight in when women, fascinated, are watching them.

Two gentlemen in golf clothes, very English-looking and smoking cigarettes, were spending a long time before a shop window, apparently absorbed in a plaster-of-Paris advertisement of a little dog with its nozzle to a funnel. It was a reproduction of the popular American painting that assails the eye in all the shopping centers of the world; under it was the legend: *La voix de son Maître.* The gentlemen were intent on it. A short distance from them were two sailors with large crimson pommels on their jauntily fixed caps, extra-fine blue capes, and their hands thrust deep in their pockets. Glancing furtively at the gentlemen, who were tongue-licking their lips in a curious, gentlemanly way, one of the sailors approached with a convenient cigarette butt. As they were exchanging lights, two passing cocottes bounced purposely into them and kept going, hip-shimmying and smirking, looking behind. . . . Nothing doing.

A small party of English shouldered Ray against the corner, talking animatedly in that overdone accent they call the Oxford. Ray remarked again, as he often had before, how the pronunciation of some of the words, like "there" "here" and "where," was similar to that of the Southern Negro.

Two policemen were standing near and as the party passed one of them spat and said, "Les sale Anglais." Ray started and, looking from the policeman who had spewed out his salival declaration of contempt to the English group crossing the street, he grinned. Just the evening before (he had read in the morning newspaper) an Englishwoman and her escort were nearly lynched by a theater crowd. Police intervened to save them. The woman had tried to push her way too hastily through the crowd *while talking English.* Commenting on it, the local paper had said such incidents would not happen if the post-war policy of the Anglo-Saxons were not to treat France as if she were a colony.

In Paris and elsewhere tourists were having a hot time of it. The franc was tobogganing and the Anglo-Saxon nations, according to the French press, were responsible for that as well. The panic in the air had reached even Marseilles, the most international place in the country. Up till yesterday these very journals had been doping the unthinking literate mob with pages of peace talk. Today they were feeding the same hordes with war. And to judge from the excitement in the air the mob was as ready for it as the two white apes of policemen standing on the corner.

Ray grinned again, showing all his teeth, and a girl across the street, thinking it was for her, smiled at him. But he was grinning at the civilized world of nations, all keeping their tiger's claws sharp and strong under the thin cloak of international amity and awaiting the first favorable opportunity to spring. During his passage through Europe it had been an illuminating experience for him to come in contact with the mind of the average white man. A few words would usually take him to the center of a guarded, ancient treasure of national hates.

In conversation he sometimes posed as British, sometimes as American, depending upon his audience. There was no posing necessary with the average Frenchman because he takes it without question that a black man under French civilization is better off than he would be under any other social order in the world. Sometimes, on meeting a French West Indian, Ray would say he was American, and the other, like his white compatriot, could not resist the temptation to be patronizing.

"We will treat you right over here! It's not like America."

Yet often when he was in public with one of these black *élites* who could speak a little English, Ray would be asked to speak English instead of French. Upon demanding why, the answer would invariably be, "Because they will treat us better and not as if we were Senegalese."

Ray had undergone a decided change since he had left America. He enjoyed his rôle of a wandering black without patriotic or family ties. He loved to pose as this or that without really being any definite thing at all. It was amusing. Sometimes the experience of being patronized provided food for thoughtful digestion. Sometimes it was very embarrassing and deprived an emotion of its significance.

Nevertheless, he was not unaware that his position as a black boy looking on the civilized scene was a unique one. He was having a good grinning time of it. Italians against French, French against Anglo-Saxons, English against Germans, the great *Daily Mail* shrieking like a mad virago that there were still Germans left who were able to swill champagne in Italy when deserving English gentlemen could not afford to replenish their cellars. . . . Oh it was a great civilization indeed, too entertaining for any savage ever to have the feeling of boredom.

The evening before, an American acquaintance had remarked to Ray that when he had come to Europe he had cut loose from all the back-home strings and had come wanting to *love* it. But Europe had taught him to be *patriotic;* it had taught him that he was an American.

He was a jolly nice fellow with French blood from his mother's line, and after two years of amusing himself in the European scene he was returning to America to settle down to the business of marriage. Ray could see what he was trying to express, but he could not feel it. First, because he had never yet indulged in any illusions about any species of the civilized mammal, and second, because his was not a nature that would let his appetite for the fruit of life be spoiled by the finding of a worm at the core of one apple or more.

The sentiment of patriotism was not one of Ray's possessions, perhaps because he was a child of deracinated ancestry. To him it was a poisonous seed that had, of course, been planted in his child's mind, but happily, not having any traditional soil to nourish it, it had died out with other weeds of the curricula of education in the light of mature thought.

It seemed a most unnatural thing to him for a man to love a nation—a swarming hive of human beings bartering, competing, exploiting, lying, cheating, battling, suppressing, and killing among themselves; possessing, too, the faculty to organize their villainous rivalries into a monstrous system for plundering weaker peoples.

Man loves individuals. Man loves things. Man loves places. And the vagabond lover of life finds individuals and things to love in many places and not in any one nation. Man loves places and no one place, for the earth, like a beautiful wanton, puts on a new dress to fascinate him wherever he may go. A patriot loves not his nation, but the spiritual meannesses of his life of which he has created a frontier wall to hide the beauty of other horizons.

So . . . Ray had fallen into one of his frequent fits of contemplation there on the corner, alone with his mind and the traffic of life surging around him, when he was tapped on the shoulder and addressed by the smaller Britisher of Taloufa's shirt-tail night.

Ray had learned more about the two friends since that entertaining night. The colonial was a careless, roving sort of fellow, ever ready for anything with a touch of novelty that was suggested to him. Yet he seemed to be devoid of any capacity for real enjoyment or deep distaste. He apparently existed for mere unexciting drifting, a purposeless, live-for-the-moment, negative person.

The initiative of planning for both of them rested with his friend, who was

English-born. Both had been in the war. The Englishman had a small face with a tight expression. His lips were remarkably thin and compressed, and they twitched, but so imperceptibly that a casual observer would not notice it. He had not been wounded, but had been a prisoner and the experience had left him a little neurotic, and probably more interesting. He liked jazz music, and he liked to hear Negroes play it.

The pair had told Ray that they were just bums. He would not believe it, thinking that they were well-to-do poseurs plumbing low-down bohemian life. But they soon convinced him that it was true. Quite young, they had been called for service during the last year of the war, and, now that it was over, they either could not find a permanent interest in life or could not bring themselves to settle down. Whatever it was, they were gentlemen panhandlers. They had bummed all over continental Europe—Naples, Genoa, Barcelona, Bordeaux, Antwerp, Hamburg, Berlin and Paris.

Since the night when Banjo had played for them they had gone over to Toulon to meet a ship coming from Australia, and had cleaned up twenty pounds panhandling and showing passengers through the bordel quarter of that interesting town of matelots.

Strangely, they preferred the great commercial ports and cities to the popular tourist resorts. They were not interested in crooked games. Like the beach boys, they were honest bums.

Ray admired the Britisher's well-fitting clothes.

"It's the only way to get the jack," he said. "Wear good clothes and speak like a gentleman. They'll give you either a real raise or nothing at all, but they won't treat you like a beggar. The Americans are pretty good. And you can tap an Englishman abroad, if you take him the right way, when you couldn't at home."

At that moment a big beefy Englishman went by and Ray's friend said: "Just a minute. I'm going to get him."

He caught up with the man on the opposite corner. The tourist was visibly embarrassed as his compatriot solicited him, and, rather avoiding looking in his face, he handed out a five-franc note. The proffered money hung suspended in air, the gentleman panhandler, not deigning to take it, coldly pressing his need of a more substantial amount. Something he said made the big man turn all puffy red in the face, and glancing hastily at the younger man from head to foot, he took from his pocketbook a pound note and handed it to him. The young man took it and thanked him in a politely reserved manner.

Rejoining Ray, he vented his scorn: "The big bastard. Tried to give *me* five francs." His funny slit of a lip twitched nervously. "Come and have a drink with me," he said.

They turned down the Canebière. An old tune was ringing in Ray's head.

"Everybody's Doing It. . . ."

It was the song-and-dance that had tickled him so wonderfully that first year he had landed in America. Talk about "Charleston" and "Black Bottom!'' They're all right for exercise, but for a jazzing jig, when a black boy and a gal can get right up together and do that rowdy thing, ''Charlestons'' and ''Black Bottoms'' are a long way behind the ''Turkey Trot.'' . . .

Great big dancing-hall over the grocery store in the barracks town. Day laborers, porters, black students, black soldiers, brown sporting-girls swaying and reeling so close together, turkey-trotting, bunny-hugging, bear-and-dog walking ''That Thing'' and the delirious black boys singing and playing:

> ''Everybody's doing it. . . .
> Everybody's doing it now. . . .''

Ray and the Britisher took a table on a café terrace at the corner of the Rue de la République and the Quai du Port. Down the Canebiére the traffic bore like a flooded river to pile up against the bar of the immense horse-shoe (on which rested the weight of the city) and flow out on either side of it.

The scene was a gay confusion—peddlers with gaudy bagatelles; Greek and Armenian venders of cacahuettes and buns; fishermen crying shell-fish; idling boys in proletarian blue wearing vivid cache-col and caps; long-armed Senegalese soldiers in khaki, some wearing the red fez; zouaves in striking Arab costumes; surreptitious sou gamblers with their dice stands; a strong mutilated man in tights stunting; excursion boats with tinted signs and pennants rocking thick against each other at the moorings—everything massed pell-mell together in a great gorgeous bowl.

A waiter brought them two large cool glasses of orangeade. While they were enjoying it one of the many sidewalk-feature girls stopped by their table with a little word for the Englishman.

''Fiche-moi la paix!'' he shot at her.

The girl shrugged and went off, working her hips.

''Bloody wench! Because I was with her last night she tries to get familiar now. She wouldn't dare do it in London.''

''Don't say!'' said Ray. ''Why, back home in America we lift our hats to such as exist.''

''That's one reason why I don't like democracies.''

''Is that how you feel about them?'' Ray chuckled. ''I can't go with you. Ordinarily I would like to treat those girls like anybody else, but they won't let you. They are too class-conscious.''

After the cocotte came Banjo.

''Hello!'' said Ray. ''How's the plugging?''

''Fine and dandy, pardner. I got the whole wul' going my way. Look at me!''

''Perfection, kid.''

Banjo was in wonderful form in his coca-colored Provençal suit, the steel-gray Australian felt hat he had bought in Sydney, the yellow scarf hanging down his front, and full-square up-at-the-heel. Banjo had struck it right again.

The blues had bitten Taloufa badly after his praiseworthy little affair of race conservation had turned out so disastrously and he had left soon after for England. But before he went Banjo had persuaded him to redeem his suit from the Mont de Piété and had "borrowed" a little cash from him until they should meet again—an eventuality that was taken as a matter of course in the beach boys' and seamen's life.

"Sit down and have a drink," said the white.

"Time is in a hurry with me now, chief," replied Banjo. "I'm going down to the Dollar Line pier. Theah's a boat in. What about you, pardner? Going? I been looking foh you. The fellahs am waiting foh me down at Joliette."

"Sure thing I'll go," said Ray. "Want to come?" he asked his white friend.

"No. It's too far. It's the farthest dock down. Have a drink with us, Banjo, before you go. Let's go to the little café in that side street up there. They'll serve us quicker at the bar."

The three of them entered the café hurriedly, talking. They had three glasses of *vin blanc.* The Englishman paid with a five-franc note. When he received his change he told the barwoman that it was not right.

"Comment?" she asked.

"Comment? Because day before yesterday here I paid five sous less for a glass of *vin blanc.* And I know the price hasn't gone up since."

"The pound and the dollar have, though," Ray grinned.

"Maybe, but I'm not going to pay for banditry in high places."

"It's always we who pay heaviest for that," said Ray.

"We?"

"Yes, we the poor, the vagabonds, the bums of life. You said you were one; that's why I say we."

The woman made the change right, saying that she had been mistaken, and the boys left the bar.

"Them's all sou-crazy, these folkses," said Banjo.

"It's a cheap trick," said the Briton. "I didn't care about the few sous, but it was the principle of the thing."

"You English certainly love to play with that word 'principle,' " said Ray.

The white laughed slightly, reddening around the ears. "These people make you pay à *l'Anglaise* every time they hear you talk English," he said. "I don't like to be always paying for that. It's irritating. And I irritate them, too, in revenge, letting them know they are cheating. Maybe one cause of it is that these little businesses are always changing hands. About a year ago I was in a little bar behind the Bourse. Six months later I saw the proprietor at Toulon, where he had bought another bar, and the other day I saw him at Nice, where he had just taken over a third after selling out at Toulon. I prefer going to an honest bourgeois brasserie. And even then you've got to look out for the waiters if they think you're a greenhorn. Just yesterday one of them brought my friend change for a fifty after he had given him a hundred-franc note. My friend doesn't speak French, and when I called the bluff he had it all ready for me right on the tip of his tongue like that Bistro woman: 'Pardon. I've made a mistake!' "

Curiously, the song kept singing in Ray's head:

"Everybody's doing it,
   Everybody's doing it. . . ."

"I get along with the little bistros, all right," said Ray. "They take me for Senegalese and treat me right. But whenever I'm with fellows speaking English they've got to pay for it just like you. I never make any trouble when the others pay, especially American fellows. They don't know, the price is ridiculously cheap to *them,* coming from a dry country. But when *I've* got to pay for it, I kick like hell. I'll be damned if I'm going to be a sucker for these hoggish *petits commerçants.* I know it's the dollar complex these people have that makes them like that, but I'm no dollar baby. I don't ever see enough francs, much less dollars. And they can get bloody insulting sometimes when you call their hand. For instance, I found out the woman who did my laundry was overcharging Banjo and the boys whenever they could afford to have their clothes done. The next time they were getting their laundry I went with them to straighten it out, and she got mad and shouted, 'Dollah, dollah,' and refused to do any more for us. What the hell do we boys know about dollars?"

"The only time they'll lose anything is when they do it to insult you," said the white. "They lose more than they gain by such pettiness. Some months ago we picked up a couple of toffs and they took us for a spree down the coast. We stayed a little time in Antibes. One night my friend telephoned me from a café in the square and the proprietor himself told the waiter to charge him two francs. He happened to mention it and I knew the cost was half a franc. The next morning I went and asked the fat old thing why he had overcharged my friend. He tried to make out that it was a double call, which wasn't true, of course, and would only have amounted to a franc in any case. I left it like that. It was enough for me to see the proprietor in an embarrassing position. I get a devilish lot of fun out of them and their sous. And that's why I am always correcting their subtraction and addition. But of course we never went back to *that* café while we stayed in Antibes."

"I wish they wouldn't figure against us poor black boys when *we* speak English," said Ray. "The trouble is you Europeans make no color distinction—when it is a matter of the color of our money."

"You mean the French," said the young man, his Anglo-Saxon pride suddenly bursting forth. "You don't find anybody in England playing such penny tricks."

"Oh, well, you've got a different method, that's all," said Ray. "I've got a very definite opinion about it all. When I was in England I always felt myself in an atmosphere of grim, long-headed honesty—honesty because it was the best business policy in the long run. You felt it was a little hard on the English soul. It made it as bleak as a London fog and you felt it was an atmosphere that could chill to the bone anybody who didn't have a secure living. I wouldn't want to be broke and be on the bum there for a day, and you wouldn't, either, I guess."

"You bet I wouldn't," the young man laughed, "judging by where I am now."

"In America it's different," Ray continued. "I didn't sense any soul-destroying honesty there. What I felt was an awful big efficiency sweeping all over me. You felt that business in its mad race didn't have time to worry about honesty, and if you thought about honesty at all it was only as a technical thing, like advertising, to help efficiency forward. If you were to go to New York and shop in the popular districts, then do Delancey Street and the Bowery afterward, you'd get what I mean. Down in those tedious-bargain streets, you feel that you are in Europe on the shores of the Mediterranean again, and that their business has nothing to do with the great steam-rolling efficiency of America.

"But in Germany I felt something quite different from anything that impressed me in other white countries. I felt a real terrible honesty that you might call moral or religious or national. It seemed like something highly organized, patriotic, rooted in the soul—not a simple, natural, instinctive thing. And with it I felt a confident blind bluntness in the people's character that was as hard and obvious as a stone wall. I was there when the mark had busted like a bomb in the sky and you could pick up worthless paper marks thrown away in the street. There were exchange booths all over Berlin— some of them newly set up in the street. I saw Americans as heedless as a brass band, lined up to change their dollars in face of misery that was naked to the eye at every step. Yet I never felt any overt hostility to strangers there as I do here.

"When I was going there the French black troops were in the Ruhr. A big campaign of propaganda was on against them, backed by German-Americans, Negro-breaking Southerners, and your English liberals and Socialists. The odd thing about that propaganda was that it said nothing about the exploitation of primitive and ignorant black conscripts to do the dirty work of one victorious civilization over another, but it was all about the sexuality of Negroes—that strange, big bug forever buzzing in the imagination of white people. Friendly whites tried to dissuade me from going to Germany at that time, but I was determined to go.

"And I must tell you frankly I never met any white people so courteous in all my life. I traveled all over Prussia, from Hamburg to Berlin, Potsdam, Stettin, Dresden, Leipzig, and I never met with any discourtesy, not to mention hostility. Maybe it was there underneath the surface, but I never felt it. I went to the big cafés and cabarets in the Friederickstrasse, Potsdammer Platz, and Charlottenburg, and I had a perfectly good time. I went everywhere. I've never felt so safe in the low quarters of any city as I have in those of Berlin and Hamburg. One day I went to buy some shirts after noting the prices marked in the shop window. When the clerk gave me the check it was more than the price marked, so I protested. He called the manager and he was so apologetic I felt confused. 'It's not my fault,' he said, 'but the law. All strangers must pay ten per cent more.' And he turned red as if he were ashamed of the law. Yet I never liked Germany. It was a country too highly organized for my temperament. I felt something American about it, but without the dynamic confusion of America.''

They had reached Joliette, where the Britisher said he must turn back.

"Come on, let's have a look at the Dollar boat," said Ray.

"No. I have an important engagement with my friend."

.   .   .

XVI   The "Blue Cinema"

Ray had met a Negro student from Martinique, to whom the greatest glory of the island was that the Empress Josephine was born there. That event placed Martinique above all the other islands of the Antilles in importance.

"I don't see anything in that for you to be so proud about," said Ray. "She was not colored."

"Oh no, but she was Créole, and in Martinique we are rather Créole than Negro. We are proud of the Empress in Martinique. Down there the best people are very distinguished and speak a pure French, not anything like this vulgar Marseilles French."

Ray asked him if he had ever heard of René Maran's *Batouala*. He replied that the sale of *Batouala* had been banned in the colony and sniggered approvingly. Ray wondered about the truth of that; he had never heard any mention of it.

"It was a naughty book, very strong, very strong," said the student, defending the act.

They were in a café on the Canebière. That evening Ray had a rendezvous at the African Bar with another student, an African from the Ivory Coast, and asked the Martiniquan to go with him to be introduced. He refused, saying that he did not want to mix with the Senegalese and that the African Bar was in the *bas-fonds*. He warned Ray about mixing with the Senegalese.

"They are not like us," he said. "The whites would treat Negroes better in this town if it were not for the Senegalese. Before the war and the coming of the Senegalese it was splendid in France for Negroes. We were liked, we were respected, but now——"

"It's just about the same with the white Americans," said Ray. "You must judge civilization by its general attitude toward primitive peoples, and not by the exceptional cases. You can't get away from the Senegalese and other black Africans any more than you can from the fact that our forefathers were slaves. We have the same thing in the States. The Northern Negroes are stand-offish toward the Southern Negroes and toward the West Indians, who are not as advanced as they in civilized superficialities. We educated Negroes are talking a lot about a racial renaissance. And I wonder how we're going to get it. On one side we're up against the world's arrogance—a mighty cold hard white stone thing. On the other the great sweating army— our race. It's the common people, you know, who furnish the bone and sinew and salt of any race or nation. In the modern race of life we're merely beginners. If this renaissance we're talking about is going to be more than a sporadic and scabby thing, we'll have to get down to our racial roots to create it."

"I believe in a racial renaissance," said the student, "but not in going back to savagery."

"Getting down to our native roots and building up from our own people," said Ray, "is not savagery. It is culture."

"I can't see that," said the student.

"You are like many Negro intellectuals who are bellyaching about race," said Ray. "What's wrong with you-all is your education. You get a white man's education and learn to despise your own people. You read biased history of the whites conquering the colored and primitive peoples, and it thrills you just as it does a white boy belonging to a great white nation.

"Then when you come to maturity you realize with a shock that you don't and can't belong to the white race. All your education and achievements cannot put you in the intimate circles of the whites and give you a white man's full opportunity. However advanced, clever, and cultivated you are, you will have the distinguishing adjective of 'colored' before your name. And instead of accepting it proudly and manfully, most of you are soured and bitter about it—especially you mixed-bloods.

"You're a lost crowd, you educated Negroes, and you will only find yourself in the roots of your own mind. You can't choose as your models the haughty-minded educated white youths of a society living solid on its imperial conquests. Such pampered youths can afford to despise the sweating white brutes of the lower orders.

"If you were sincere in your feelings about racial advancement, you would turn for example to whites of a different type. You would study the Irish cultural and social movement. You would turn your back on all these tiresome clever European novels and read about the Russian peasants, the story and struggle of their lowly, patient, hard-driven life, and the great Russian novelists who described it up to the time of the Russian Revolution. You would learn all you can about Ghandi and what he is doing for the common hordes of India. You would be interested in the native African dialects and, though you don't understand, be humble before their simple beauty instead of despising them."

The mulatto student was not moved in his determination not to go to the African Bar, and so Ray went alone. He loved to hear the African dialects sounding around him. The dialects were so rich and round and ripe like soft tropical fruit, as if they were fashioned to eliminate all things bitter and harsh to express. They tasted like brown unrefined cane sugar—Sousou, Bambara, Woloff, Fula, Dindie. . . .

The *patron* of the African Bar pointed out men of the different tribes to Ray. It was easy to differentiate the types of the interior from those of the port towns, for they bore tribal marks on their faces. Among civilized people they were ashamed, most of them, of this mutilation of which their brothers of the towns under direct European administration were free; but, because tattooing was the fashion among seamen, they were not ashamed to have their bodies pricked and figured all over with the souvenirs of the brothels of civilization.

172

It was so superior condescension, no feeling of race solidarity or Back-to-Africa demonstration—no patriotic effort whatsoever—that made Ray love the environment of the common black drifters. He loved it with the poetical enthusiasm of the vagabond black that he himself was. After all, he had himself lived the rough-and-tumble laboring life, and the most precious souvenirs of it were the joyful friendships that he had made among his pals. There was no intellectual friendship to be compared with them.

It was always interesting to compare the African with the West Indian and American Negroes. Indeed, he found the Africans of the same class as the New World Negroes less "savage" and more "primitive." The Senegalese drunk was a much finer and more tractable animal than the American Negro drunk. And although the Senegalese were always loudly quarreling and fighting among themselves, they always made use of hands, feet, and head (butting was a great art among them) and rarely of a steel weapon as did the American and West Indian Negroes. The colored touts that were reputed to be dangerous gunmen were all from the French West Indies. The few Senegalese who belonged to the sweet brotherhood were disquietingly simple, as if they had not the slightest comprehension of the social stigma attaching to them.

At the African Bar the conversation turned on the hostile feeling that existed between the French West Indians and the native Africans. The *patron* said that the West Indians felt superior because many of them were appointed as petty officials in the African colonies and were often harder on the natives than the whites.

"Fils d'esclaves! Fils d'esclaves!" cried a Senegalese sergeant. "Because they have a chance to be better instructed than we, they think we are the savages and that they are 'white' Negroes. Why, they are only the descendants of the slaves that our forefathers sold."

"They got more advantages than we and they think they're the finest and most important Negroes in the world," said the student from the Ivory Coast.

"They're crazy," said the *patron*. "The most important Negroes in the world and the best off are American Negroes."

"That's not true! That can't be true!" said a chorus of voices.

"I think Negroes are treated worse in America than in any other country," said the student. "They lynch Negroes in America."

"They do," said the *patron,* "but it's not what you imagine it. It's not an everyday affair and the lynchings are pulled off in the Southern parts of the country, which are very backward."

"The Southern States are a powerful unit of the United States," said Ray, "and you mustn't forget that nine-tenths of American Negroes live in them."

"More people are murdered in one year in Marseilles than they lynch in ten years in America," said the *patron.*

"But all that comes under the law in spite of the comedy of extenuating circumstances," said Ray, "while lynch law is its own tribunal."

"And they Jim Crow all the Negroes in America," said the student.

"What is Jim Crow?" asked the Senegalese sergeant.

"Negroes can't ride first class in the trains nor in the same tramcars with white people, no matter how educated and rich they are. They can't room in the same hotels or eat in the same restaurants or sit together in the same theaters. Even the parks are closed to them——"

"That's only in the Southern States and not in the North," the *patron* cut in.

"But Ray has just told us that ninety per cent of the Negroes live in those states," said the student, "and that there are about fifteen millions in America. Well then, the big majority don't have any privileges at all. There is no democracy for them. Because you went to New York and happened to make plenty of money to come back here and open a business, you are over-proud of America and try to make the country out finer than it is, although the Negroes there are living in a prison."

"You don't understand," said the *patron.* "I wasn't in the North alone. I was in the old slave states also. I have traveled all over America and I tell you the American Negro is more go-getting than Negroes anywhere else in the world—the Antilles or any part of Africa. Just as the average white American is a long way better off than the European. Look at all these fellows here. What can they do if they don't go to sea as firemen? Nothing but stay here and become *maquereaux.* The Italians hog all the jobs on the docks, and the Frenchman will take Armenians and Greeks in the factories because they are white, and leave us. The French won't come straight out and tell us that they treat us differently because we are black, but we know it. I prefer the American white man. He is boss and he tells you straight where he can use you. He is a brute, but he isn't a hypocrite."

The student, perplexed, realizing that from the earnestness of the café proprietor's tone there was truth in what he said, appealed to Ray in face of the contradictory facts.

"You are both right," Ray said to the student. "All the things you say about the Negro in the States are facts and what he says about the Negro's progress is true. You see race prejudice over there drives the Negroes together to develop their own group life. American Negroes have their own schools, churches, newspapers, theaters, cabarets, restaurants, hotels. They work for the whites, but they have their own social group life, an intense, throbbing, vital thing in the midst of the army of whites milling around them. There is nothing like it in the West Indies nor in Africa, because there you don't have a hundred-million-strong white pressure that just carries the Negro group along with it. Here in Europe you have more social liberties than Negroes have in America, but you have no warm group life. You need colored women for that. Women that can understand us as human beings and not as wild over-sexed savages. And you haven't any. The successful Negro in Europe always marries a white woman, and I have noticed in almost every case that it is a white woman inferior to himself in brains and physique. The energy of such a Negro is lost to his race and goes to build up some decaying white family."

"But look at all the mulattoes you have in America," said the student. "White men are continually going with colored women."

"Because the colored women like it as much as the white men," replied Ray.

"Ray!" exclaimed Goosey who had entered the café, "you are scandalous and beneath contempt."

"That's all right, Goosey. I know that the American Negro press says that American colored women have no protection from the lust and passion of white men on account of the Southern state laws prohibiting marriage between colored and white and I know that you believe that. But that is newspaper truth and no more real than the crackers shouting that white women live in fear and trembling of black rapists. The days of chivalry are stone dead, and the world today is too enlightened about sex to be fooled by white or black propaganda.

"In the West Indies, where there are no prohibitory laws, the Europeans have all the black and mulatto concubines they need. In Africa, too. Woman is woman all over the world, no matter what her color is. She is cast in a passive rôle and she worships the active success of man and rewards it with her body. The colored woman is no different from the white in this. If she is not inhibited by race feeling she'll give herself to the white man because he stands for power and property. Property controls sex.

"When you understand that, Goosey, you'll understand the meaning of the struggle between class and class, nation and nation, race and race. You'll understand that society chases after power just as woman chases after property, because society is feminine. And you'll see that the white races today are ahead of the colored because their women are emancipated, and that there is greater material advancement among those white nations whose women have the most freedom.

"Understand this and you will understand why the white race tries so hard to suppress the colored races. You'll understand the root of the relation between colored women and white man and why white men will make love to colored women but will not marry them."

"But white women marry colored men, all the same," said Goosey. "White women feel better toward colored people than white men."

"You're a fool," replied Ray. "White men are what their women make them. That's plain enough to see in the South. White women hate Negroes because the colored women steal their men and so many of them are society wives in name only. You know what class of white women marry colored men."

"There are Negroes in America who had their fortunes made by white women," said Goosey.

"There *are* exceptions—white women with money who are fed up. But the majority are what I said a while ago. . . . Show me a white woman or man who can marry a Negro and belong to respectable society in London or New York or any place. I can understand these ignorant black men marrying broken-down white women because they are under the delusion that there is some superiority in the white skin that has suppressed and bossed it over them all their lives. But I can't understand an intelligent race-conscious man doing it. Especially a man who is bellyaching about race rights. He is the one who should exercise a certain control and self-denial of his desires. Take Senghor and his comrades in propaganda for example. They are the bitterest and most humorless of propagandists and they are all married to white women. It is as if the experience has oversoured them. As if they thought it would bring them closer to the white race, only to realize too late that it couldn't.

"Why marry, I ask? There are so many other ways of doing it. Europe can afford some of its excess women to successful Negroes and that may help to keep them loyal to conventional ideals. America 'keeps us in our place' and in our race. Which may be better for the race in the long run.

"The Jews have kept intact, although they were scattered all over the world, and it was easier for them than for Negroes to lose themselves.

"To me the most precious thing about human life is difference. Like flowers in a garden, different kinds for different people to love. I am not against miscegenation. It produces splendid and interesting types. But I should not crusade for it because I should hate to think of a future in which the identity of the black race in the Western World should be lost in miscegenation."

Six distinguished whites entered the café, putting an end to the conversation. They were the two gentlemen bums, three other men and one woman. The woman saw Ray and greeted him effusively with surprise.

"Oh, Ray, this is where you ran away to hide yourself, leaving all the artists to mourn for their fine model."

"But she is American," the Ivory Coast student, pop-eyed at the woman's friendly manner, whispered to the *patron*.

"Sure," he answered, in malicious triumph. "Did you think there were no human relations between white and black in America, that they were just like two armies fighting against each other all the time?"

Ray did not know who the woman was, whether she was American or European. She spoke French and German as readily as she spoke English. He had met her at the studio of a Swiss painter in Paris (a man who carried a title on his card) when he was posing there, and she had made polite and agreeable conversation with him while he posed. Later, he saw her twice at cabarets in Montmartre, where he had been taken by bohemian artists, and she had not snubbed him.

The gentlemen bums were as surprised as the Ivory Coast student (but differently) when woman greeted Ray. They had met the group and were going through the town with them. The leading spirit of the party had desired to stop in the bar when he was told that it was a rendezvous for Negroes.

He was a stout, audacious-looking man, a tireless international traveler, who liked to visit every country in the world except the unpleasantly revolutionary ones. The accidental meeting was a piquant thing for Ray, because he had heard strange talk of the man before. Of celebrations of occult rites and barbaric saturnalia with the tempo of nocturnal festivities regulated by the crack of whips. A bonfire made of a bungalow to show the beauties of the landscape when the night was dark. And a splendid stalwart, like one of the Sultan of Morocco's guards, brought from Africa, as a result of which he had been involved in trouble with governmental authorities in Europe.

Certainly, Ray had long been desirous of seeing this personage who had been gossiped about so much, for he had a penchant for exotic sins. Indeed, a fine Jewish soul with a strong Jeremiah flame in him had warned Ray in Paris about what he chose to call his cultivation of the heathenish atavistic propensities of the subterranean personality. The Jewish idealist thought that Ray had a talent and a personality so healthily austere at times that they should be fostered for the uplift of his race to the rigorous exclusion of the dark and perhaps damnable artistic urge. But . . .

Well, here was this bold, bad, unregenerate man of whom he had heard so much, and who did not make any deeper impression than a picturesque woman of Ray's acquaintance, who carried her excessive maternal feelings under a cloak of aggressive masculinity.

The two other men were Americans. The party was bound for any place in the Mediterranean basin that the leader could work up any interest for. They were spending the night in Marseilles and wanted to see the town. The gentlemen bums had taken them through Boody Lane where they had had their hats snatched and had paid to get them back. The hectic setting of Boody Lane with the girls and painted boys in pyjamas posing in their wide-open holes in the wall, the soldiers and sailors and blue-overalled youths loitering through, had given the party the impression that there were many stranger, weirder and unmentionable things to see in the quarter.

"I tell them there is nothing else to show," said the Britisher, speaking generally and to Ray in particular. "Paris is a show city. This is just a rough town like any other port town, where you'll see rough stuff if you stick round long enough. I can take you to the *boîtes de nuit,* but they're less interesting than they are in Paris."

"Oh no, not the cabarets. They bore me so," said the woman. "We're just running away from them."

She was tall and of a very pale whiteness. She seated herself on a chair in a posture of fatigue. Ray remembered that strange tired attitudes of hers each time he had seen her. Yet her eyes were brimful of life and she was always in an energetic flutter about something.

"There's nothing else here," the Britisher apologized to the leader of the party, "but the *maisons fermées* and the 'Blue Cinema,' and they are all better in Paris."

"The 'Blue Cinema,' " the leader repeated casually. "I've never seen the thing. We might as well see it."

He ordered some drinks, cognac and port wine, which they all had standing at the bar. A white tout drifted into the bar. Three girls from Boody Lane followed. Another tout, this time a mulatto from the Antilles, and after him two black ones from Dakar. More girls of the Ditch. The news had spread round that there were distinguished people at the café.

"We'll go and have dinner and see the 'Blue Cinema' afterward," said the leader.

Sitting on the terrace, a Senegalese in a baboon attitude was flicking his tongue at everything and everybody that passed by. He reclined, lazily contented, in a chair tilted against the wall. One of the girls, following the party as they came out, called him by name and, leaning against the chair, fondled him. He smiled lasciviously, his tongue strangely visible in his pure ebony face.

Ray, turning his head, saw in the face of the woman the same disgust he felt. Those monkey tricks were the special trade-marks of the great fraternity of civilized touts and gigolos, born and trained to prey on the carnal passions of humanity.

A primitive person could not play the game as neatly as they. During a winter spent at Nice, he had found the cocottes and gigolos monkeying on the promenade more interesting to watch than the society people. The white monkeys were essential to the great passion play of life to understudy the parts of those who were holding the stage by power of wealth, place, name, title, and class—everything but the real thing.

And as there were civilized white monkeys, so were there black monkeys, created by the conquests of civilization, learning to imitate the white and even beating them at their game. He recalled the colored sweetmen and touts and girls with whom he had been familiar in America, some who lived in the great obscure region of the boundary between white and black. Following as they did their own shady paths, he had never been strongly repelled by their way of living, because it was a rôle that they played admirably, scavengers feeding on the backwash of the broad streaming traffic of American life. They were not very different from the monkeys of the French Antilles who carried on their antics side by side with the Provençals and Corsicans and others of the Mediterranean breed. They had acquired enough of civilized tricks to play their parts fittingly.

But not so the Africans, who were closer to the bush, the jungle, where their primitive sex life had been controlled by ancient tribal taboos. Within those taboos they had courted their women, married and made families. And so it was not natural for them, so close to the tradition of paying in cash or kind or hard labor for the joy of a woman, to live the life of the excrescences attaching like mushrooms to the sexual life of civilization. Released from their taboos, turned loose in an atmosphere of prostitution and perversion and trying to imitate the white monkeys, it was no wonder they were very ugly.

After the dinner the younger American created a problem. He was of middle build, wearing a fine New York suit, reddish-brown stuff. He was the clean-shaven, clean-cut type that might have been either a graduate student looking at the world with the confident air of one who is able to go anywhere, or a successful salesman of high-class goods. He wore no horn-rimmed glasses to hide his clear-seeing eyes, and his jaw was developing into the kind common to the men who are earnest, big, and prosperous in the ideals of Americanism.

"But this 'Blue Cinema,' what is it, really?" he demanded.

"I suppose it is a cinematic version of the picture cards the guides try to sell you in the street," the leader answered. "You don't have to go, you know."

"Oh, I'd like to see the thing, all right," replied the young man, "but—are there colored or white persons in the picture?"

"White, I suppose. The colored people are not as advanced and inventive as we in such matters. Excepting what we teach them," the leader added, facetiously; "they often beat us at our game when they learn."

"But she isn't going, is she?" The American indicated the young woman. "They won't let her in a *maison de rendezvous.*"

"Most certainly I am. Am I not one of the party? There isn't anything I am not old enough to see, if I want to. Do you want to discriminate against me because I am a woman?"

"They'll let her in in any place if we pay the price," said the Britisher.

"But she can't go if he is going." The young man looked at Ray.

"Oh, Ray!" The young woman laughed. "That's what it's all about. You needn't worry about him. He has posed In the nude for my friends and he was a perfectly-behaved *sauvage.*" She stressed the word broadly.

"That's all right," said Ray to the young man. "I am not going if you go. I am full of prejudices myself."

"Well, good night," the young man said. Abruptly he left the party.

"My friend has done his bit for the honor of the Great Nordic race," the remaining American remarked.

Nobody thought that the "Blue Cinema" would be really entertaining. The leader was blasé and desired anything that was merely different. But they were all curious, except the gentlemen bums, who had seen the show several times as guides and were indifferent. It was very high-priced, costing fifty francs for each person.

The fee of admission was paid. In the large dim hall they were the only audience. . . .

Before the first reel had finished the leader asked the young woman if she preferred to go.

"No, I'd rather see it out," she said.

There was no brutal, beastly, orgiastic rite that could rouse terror or wild-animal feeling. It was a calculating, cold, naked abortion.

The "Blue Cinema" struck them with the full force of a cudgel, beating them down into the depths of disgust. Ray wondered if the men who made it had a moral purpose in mind: to terrify and frighten away all who saw it from that phase of life. Or was it possible that there were human beings whose instincts were so brutalized and blunted in the unsparing struggle of modern living that they needed that special stimulating scourge of ugliness. Perhaps. The "Blue Cinema," he had heard, was a very flourishing business.

He was sitting against a heavy red velvet curtain. Toward the end of the show the curtain was slightly agitated, as if some one on the other side had stirred it. He caught the curtain aside and saw some half a dozen Chinese, conspicuous by their discolored teeth and unlovely bland smiles, standing among a group of girls in a kind of alcove-room which the curtain divided from the cinema hall. The woman of the party saw them, too, before Ray could pull the curtain back, and gave a little scream. The Chinese there did not surprise Ray. He knew that they were hired to perform like monkeys. There were other houses that specialized in Arabs, Corsicans, and Negroes when they were in demand.

As they were leaving the lady president of affairs appeared and suggested their seeing also the tableaux vivants.

"Oh no, the dead ones were enough," replied the leader.

"Why did you scream?" the leader asked, roughly, when the party was in the street again.

"It was my fault," said Ray. "I pulled the curtain back and she suddenly saw a roomful of people behind it."

"That was nothing. I saw them, too, as you did, but I didn't scream." He turned on her again. "You say you want to go to any place a man goes and stand anything a man can stand, and yet you scream over a few filthy Chinese."

"I'm sorry," she said. "It was out before I could check myself."

"I suggested leaving in the beginning, but you insisted on staying it out; I didn't expect you to scream. Did you enjoy it?"

"It was *so* ugly," she said, adding: "I think I'll go to the hotel. You men can stay, but I'm finished for tonight."

The leader laughed and asked the American to take her home.

"Oh, I don't need an escort. I'll just take a taxi," she said.

"You'd better not go alone. The taxis are not safe this time of night," said Ray.

"I don't care whether you need an escort or not. I am taking you to the hotel," said the American.

They walked to the main street and Ray hailed a green Mattei taxicab. "They are run by a big company and are safe," he said. "The unsafe ones here hang around the shady places—just as in New York and Chicago. Some of the private drivers are touts, and as you never know which is which, I always recommend my friends to ride with the Trust."

"Where shall I find you fellows afterward?" the American asked.

"Where now?" said the leader. "After this 'blue' refinement I should like to go to the roughest and dirties place we can find."

"I think Banjo's hangout down Bum Square way is just the place we are looking for," said Ray.

"That's the place," the Britisher agreed.

They told the American how to find it.

"Whether it is blue or any other color of the rainbow, the cinema is for the mob," said the leader. "It will never be an art."

"I don't agree," said Ray. "Pictorial pantomime can be just as fine an art as any. What about Charlie Chaplin?"

"He's an exception. A conscientious artist with a popular appeal."

"All real art is an exception," said Ray. "You can't condemn an art whole-sale because inartistic people make a bad business of it. The same condition exists in the other arts. Everybody is in a wild business race and the conscientious workers are few. It's a crazy circle of blue-cinema people, poor conscientious artists, cynical professionals and an indifferent public."

"You know I like the cinema for exactly the reverse of its object," said the leader. "Because it's about the easiest way to see what people really are under the acting."

Ray laughed and said: "The 'Blue Cinema' was just that," and he added: "Some of us don't need the cinema, though, to show us up. We are so obvious."

In the Bum Square they ran into Banjo with his instrument.

"Where you coming from?" Ray asked.

"Just finish performing and said *bonne nuit* to a kelt."

The leader was curious to know what "kelt" meant.

Banjo and Ray exchanged glances and grinned.

"That's a word in black freemasonry," explained Ray, "but I don't object to initiating you if Banjo doesn't."

"Shoot," said Banjo.

"In the States," said Ray, "we Negroes have humorous little words of our own with which we replace unpleasant stock words. And we often use them when we are among white people and don't want them to know just what we are referring to, especially when it is anything delicate or taboo between the races. For example, we have words like ofay, pink, fade, spade, Mr. Charlie, cracker, peckawood, hoojah, and so on—nice words and bitter. The stock is always increasing because as the whites get on to the old words we invent new ones. 'Kelt' I picked up in Marseilles. I think Banjo brought it here and made it popular among the boys. I don't know if it has anything to do with 'keltic.' "

"Oh no," said the leader. "Kelt is a real word of Scottish origin, I think."

"That might explain how Banjo got it, then. He used to live in Canada."

The party went to Banjo's hangout and the whole gang was there drinking and dancing.

The American joined them very late, worried about his younger friend. A panhandling Swede had accosted him in the Bum Square and told him that he had seen his friend in Joliette, helplessly drunk and getting into a taxicab with a couple of mean-looking touts. The American had gone at once to his friend's hotel, to Joliette, and then had searched in all the bars of the quarter, but could not obtain any information about him.

The next day he was found in a box car on a lonely quay beyond Joliette, stripped of everything and wearing a dirty rag of a loin-cloth for his only clothing. The sudden and forced reversal to a savage state had shocked him temporarily daft.

AFRICA
CLAUDE MCKAY

The sun sought thy dim bed and brought forth light,
The sciences were sucklings at thy breast;
When all the world was young in pregnant night
Thy slaves toiled at thy monumental best.
Thou ancient treasure-land, thou modern prize.

New peoples marvel at thy pyramids!
The years roll on, thy sphinx of riddle eyes
Watches the mad world with immobile lids.
The Hebrews humbled them at Pharaoh's name.
Cradle of Power! Yet all things were in vain!
Honor and Glory, Arrogance and Fame!
They went. The darkness swallowed thee again.
Thou art the harlot, now thy time is done,
Of all the mighty nations of the sun.

MULATTO
CLAUDE MCKAY

Because I am the white man's son—his own,
Bearing his bastard birth-mark on my face,
I will dispute his title to his throne,
Forever fighting him for my rightful place.
There is a searing hate within my soul,
A hate that only kin can feel for kin,
A hate that makes me vigorous and whole,
And spurs me on increasingly to win.
Because I am my cruel father's child,
My love of justice stirs me up to hate,
A warring Ishmaelite, unreconciled,
When falls the hour I shall not hesitate
Into my father's heart to plunge the knife
To gain the utmost freedom that is life.

SONNET TO A NEGRO IN HARLEM
HELENE JOHNSON

You are disdainful and magnificent—
Your perfect body and your pompous gait,

182

Your dark eyes flashing solemnly with hate,
Small wonder that you are incompetent
To imitate those whom you so despise—
Your shoulders towering high above the throng,
Your head thrown back in rich, barbaric song,
Palm trees and mangoes stretched before your eyes.
Let others toil and sweat for labor's sake
And wring from grasping hands their meed of gold.
Why urge ahead your supercilious feet?
Scorn will efface each footprint that you make.
I love your laughter arrogant and bold.
You are too splendid for this city street.

POEM
HELENE JOHNSON

Little brown boy,
Slim, dark, big-eyed,
Crooning love songs to your banjo
Down at the Lafayette—
Gee, boy, I love the way you hold your head,
High sort of and a bit to one side,
Like a prince, a jazz prince. And I love
Your eyes flashing, and your hands,
And your patent-leathered feet,
And your shoulders jerking the jig-wa.
And I love your teeth flashing,
And the way your hair shines in the spotlight
Like it was the real stuff.
Gee, brown boy, I loves you all over.
I'm glad I'm a jig. I'm glad I can
understand your dancin' and your
Singin', and feel all the happiness
And joy and don't-care in you.
Gee, boy, when you sing, I can close my ears
And hear tomtoms just as plain.
Listen to me, will you, what do I know
About tomtoms? But I like the word, sort of,
Don't you? It belongs to us.
Gee, boy, I love the way you hold your head,
And the way you sing and dance,
And everything.
Say, I think you're wonderful. You're
All right with me,
You are.

FROM
CANE
JEAN TOOMER

Bona and Paul

1

On the school gymnasium floor, young men and women are drilling. They are going to be teachers, and go out into the world . . thud, thud . . and give precision to the movements of sick people who all their lives have been drilling. One man is out of step. In step. The teacher glares at him. A girl in bloomers, seated on a mat in the corner because she has told the director that she is sick, sees that the footfalls of the men are rhythmical and syncopated. The dance of his blue-trousered limbs thrills her.

Bona: He is a candle that dances in a grove swung with pale balloons.

Columns of the drillers thud towards her. He is in the front row. He is in no row at all. Bona can look close at him. His red-brown face—

Bona: He is a harvest moon. He is an autumn leaf. He is a nigger. Bona! But dont all the dorm girls say so? And dont you, when you are sane, say so? Thats why I love— Oh, nonsense. You have never loved a man who didnt first love you. Besides—

Columns thud away from her. Come to a halt in line formation. Rigid. The period bell rings, and the teacher dismisses them.

A group collects around Paul. They are choosing sides for basket-ball. Girls against boys. Paul has his. He is limbering up beneath the basket. Bona runs to the girl captain and asks to be chosen. The girls fuss. The director comes to quiet them. He hears what Bona wants.

"But, Miss Hale, you were excused—"

"So I was, Mr. Boynton, but—"

"—you can play basket-ball, but you are too sick to drill."

"If you wish to put it that way."

She swings away from him to the girl captain.

"Helen, I want to play, and you must let me. This is the first time I've asked and I dont see why—"

"Thats just it, Bona. We have our team."

"Well, team or no team, I want to play and thats all there is to it."

She snatches the ball from Helen's hands, and charges down the floor.

Helen shrugs. One of the weaker girls says that she'll drop out. Helen accepts this. The team is formed. The whistle blows. The game starts. Bona, in center, is jumping against Paul. He plays with her. Out-jumps her, makes a quick pass, gets a quick return, and shoots a goal from the middle of the floor. Bona burns crimson. She fights, and tries to guard him. One of her team-mates advises her not to play so hard. Paul shoots his second goal.

Bona begins to feel a little dizzy and all in. She drives on. Almost hugs Paul to guard him. Near the basket, he attempts to shoot, and Bona lunges into his body and tries to beat his arms. His elbow, going up, gives her a sharp crack on the jaw. She whirls. He catches her. Her body stiffens. Then becomes strangely vibrant, and bursts to a swift life within her anger. He is about to give way before her hatred when a new passion flares at him and makes his stomach fall. Bona squeezes him. He suddenly feels stifled, and wonders why in hell the ring of silly gaping faces that's caked about him doesnt make way and give him air. He has a swift illusion that it is himself who has been struck. He looks at Bona. Whir. Whir. They seem to be human distortions spinning tensely in a fog. Spinning . . dizzy . . spinning. . . Bona jerks herself free, flushes a startling crimson, breaks through the bewildered teams, and rushes from the hall.

2

Paul is in his room of two windows.
    Outside, the South-Side L track cuts them in two.
    Bona is one window. One window, Paul.
    Hurtling Loop-jammed L trains throw them in swift shadow.
    Paul goes to his. Gray slanting roofs of houses are tinted lavender in the setting sun. Paul follows the sun, over the stock-yards where a fresh stench is just arising, across wheat lands that are still waving above their stubble, into the sun. Paul follows the sun to a pine-matted hillock in Georgia. He sees the slanting roofs of gray unpainted cabins tinted lavender. A Negress chants a lullaby beneath the mate-eyes of a southern planter. Her breasts are ample for the suckling of a song. She weans it, and sends it, curiously weaving, among lush melodies of cane and corn. Paul follows the sun into himself in Chicago.
    He is at Bona's window.
    With his own glow he looks through a dark pane.

Paul's room-mate comes in.
    "Say, Paul, I've got a date for you. Come on. Shake a leg, will you?"
    His blonde hair is combed slick. His vest is snug about him.
    He is like the electric light which he snaps on.
    "Whatdoysay, Paul? Get a wiggle on. Come on. We havent got much time by the time we eat and dress and everything."
    His bustling concentrates on the brushing of his hair.
    Art: What in hell's getting into Paul of late, anyway? Christ, but he's getting moony. Its his blood. Dark blood: moony. Doesnt get anywhere unless you boost it. You've got to keep it going—
    "Say, Paul!"
    —or it'll go to sleep on you. Dark blood; nigger? Thats what those jealous she-hens say. Not Bona though, or she . . from the South . . wouldnt want me to fix a date for him and her. Hell of a thing, that Paul's dark: you've got to always be answering questions.
    "Say, Paul, for Christ's sake leave that window, cant you?"

"Whats it, Art?"

"Hell, I've told you about fifty times. Got a date for you. Come on."

"With who?"

Art: He didnt use to ask; now he does. Getting up in the air. Getting funny.

"Heres your hat. Want a smoke? Paul! Here. I've got a match. Now come on and I'll tell you all about it on the way to supper."

Paul: He's going to Life this time. No doubt of that. Quit your kidding. Some day, dear Art, I'm going to kick the living slats out of you, and you wont know what I've done it for. And your slats will bring forth Life . . beautiful woman. . .

Pure Food Restaurant.

"Bring me some soup with a lot of crackers, understand? And then a roast-beef dinner. Same for you, eh, Paul? Now as I was saying, you've got a swell chance with her. And she's game. Best proof: she dont give a damn what the dorm girls say about you and her in the gym, or about the funny looks that Boynton gives her, or about what they say about, well, hell, you know, Paul. And say, Paul, she's a sweetheart. Tall, not puffy and pretty, more serious and deep—the kind you like these days. And they say she's got a car. And say, she's on fire. But you know all about that. She got Helen to fix it up with me. The four of us—remember the last party? Crimson Gardens! Boy!"

Paul's eyes take on a light that Art can settle in.

3

Art has on his patent-leather pumps and fancy vest. A loose fall coat is swung across his arm. His face has been massaged, and over a close shave, powdered. It is a healthy pink the blue of evening tints a purple pallor. Art is happy and confident in the good looks that his mirror gave him. Bubbling over with a joy he must spend now if the night is to contain it all. His bubbles, too, are curiously tinted purple as Paul watches them. Paul, contrary to what he had thought he would be like, is cool like the dusk, and like the dusk, detached. His dark face is a floating shade in evening's shadow. He sees Art, curiously. Art is a purple fluid, carbon-charged, that effervesces besides him. He loves Art. But is it not queer, this pale purple facsimile of a red-blooded Norwegian friend of his? Perhaps for some reason, white skins are not supposed to live at night. Surely, enough nights would transform them fantastically, or kill them. And their red passion? Night paled that too, and made it moony. Moony. Thats what Art thought of him. Bona didnt, even in the daytime. Bona, would she be pale? Impossible. Not that red glow. But the conviction did not set his emotion flowing.

"Come right in, wont you? The young ladies will be right down. Oh, Mr. Carlstrom, do play something for us while you are waiting. We just love to listen to your music. You play so well."

Houses, and dorm sitting-rooms are places where white faces seclude themselves at night. There is a reason. . .

Art sat on the piano and simply tore it down. Jazz. The picture of Our Poets hung perilously.

Paul: I've got to get the kid to play that stuff for me in the daytime. Might be different. More himself. More nigger. Different? There is. Curious, though.

The girls come in. Art stops playing, and almost immediately takes up a petty quarrel, where he had last left it, with Helen.

Bona, black-hair curled staccato, sharply contrasting with Helen's puffy yellow, holds Paul's hand. She squeezes it. Her own emotion supplements the return pressure. And then, for no tangible reason, her spirits drop. Without them, she is nervous, and slightly afraid. She resents this. Paul's eyes are critical. She resents Paul. She flares at him. She flares to poise and security.

"Shall we be on our way?"

"Yes, Bona, certainly."

The Boulevard is sleek in asphalt, and, with arc-lights and limousines, aglow. Dry leaves scamper behind the whir of cars. The scent of exploded gasoline that mingles with them is faintly sweet. Mellow stone mansions overshadow clapboard homes which now resemble Negro shanties in some southern alley. Bona and Paul, and Art and Helen, move along an island-like, far-stretching strip of leaf-soft ground. Above them, worlds of shadow-planes and solids, silently moving. As if on one of these, Paul looks down on Bona. No doubt of it: her face is pale. She is talking. Her words have no feel to them. One sees them. They are pink petals that fall upon velvet cloth. Bona is soft, and pale, and beautiful.

"Paul, tell me something about yourself—or would you rather wait?"

"I'll tell you anything you'd like to know."

"Not what I want to know, Paul; what you want to tell me."

"You have the beauty of a gem fathoms under sea."

"I feel that, but I dont want to be. I want to be near you. Perhaps I will be if I tell you something. Paul, I love you."

The sea casts up its jewel into his hands, and burns them furiously. To tuck her arm under his and hold her hand will ease the burn.

"What can I say to you, brave dear woman—I cant talk love. Love is a dry grain in my mouth unless it is wet with kisses."

"You would dare? right here on the Boulevard? before Arthur and Helen?"

"Before myself? I dare."

"Here then."

Bona, in the slim shadow of a tree trunk, pulls Paul to her. Suddenly she stiffens. Stops.

"But you have not said you love me."

"I cant—yet—Bona."

187

"Ach, you never will. Youre cold. Cold."
Bona: Colored; cold. Wrong somewhere.
She hurries and catches up with Art and Helen.

4

Crimson Gardens. Hurrah! So one feels. People . . . University of Chicago
students, members of the stock exchange, a large Negro in crimson uniform
who guards the door . . had watched them enter. Had leaned towards each
other over ash-smeared tablecloths and highballs and whispered: What is
he, a Spaniard, an Indian, an Italian, a Mexican, a Hindu, or a Japanese? Art
had at first fidgeted under their stares . . what are *you* looking at, you
godam pack of owl-eyed hyenas? . . but soon settled into his fuss with
Helen, and forgot them. A strange thing happened to Paul. Suddenly he
knew that he was apart from the people around him. Apart from the pain
which they had unconsciously caused. Suddenly he knew that people saw,
not attractiveness in his dark skin, but difference. Their stares, giving him to
himself, filled something long empty within him, and were like green blades
sprouting in his consciousness. There was fullness, and strength and peace
about it all. He saw himself, cloudy, but real. He saw the faces of the people
at the tables round him. White lights, or as now, the pink lights of the Crimson Gardens gave a glow and immediacy to white faces. The pleasure of it,
equal to that of love or dream, of seeing this. Art and Bona and Helen? He'd
look. They were wonderfully flushed and beautiful. Not for himself; because
they were. Distantly. Who were they, anyway? God, if he knew them. He'd
come in with them. Of that he was sure. Come where? Into life? Yes. No.
Into the Crimson Gardens. A part of life. A carbon bubble. Would it look
purple if he went out into the night and looked at it? His sudden starting to
rise almost upset the table.

"What in hell—pardon—whats the matter, Paul?"
"I forgot my cigarettes—"
"Youre smoking one."
"So I am. Pardon me."
The waiter straightens them out. Takes their order.
Art: What in hell's eating Paul? Moony aint the word for it. From bad to
worse. And those godam people staring so. Paul's a queer fish. Doesnt
seem to mind. . . He's my pal, let me tell you, you horn-rimmed owl-eyed
hyena at that table, and a lot better than you whoever you are. . . Queer
about him. I could stick up for him if he'd only come out, one way or the
other, and tell a feller. Besides, a room-mate has a right to know. Thinks I
wont understand. Said so. He's got a swell head when it comes to brains, all
right. God, he's a good straight feller, though. Only, moony. Nut. Nuttish.
Nuttery. Nutmeg. . . "What'd you say, Helen?"
"I was talking to Bona, thank you."
"Well, its nothing to get spiffy about."

188

"What? Oh, of course not. Please lets dont start some silly argument all over again."

"Well."

"Well."

"Now thats enough. Say, waiter, whats the matter with our order? Make it snappy, will you?"

Crimson Gardens. Hurrah! So one feels. The drinks come. Four highballs. Art passes cigarettes. A girl dressed like a bare-back rider in flaming pink, makes her way through tables to the dance floor. All lights are dimmed till they seem a lush afterglow of crimson. Spotlights the girl. She sings. "Liza, Little Liza Jane."

Paul is rosy before his window.

He moves, slightly, towards Bona.

With his own glow, he seeks to penetrate a dark pane.

Paul: From the South. What does that mean, precisely, except that you'll love or hate a nigger? Thats a lot. What does it mean except that in Chicago you'll have the courage to neither love or hate. A priori. But it would seem that you have. Queer words, arent these, for a man who wears blue pants on a gym floor in the daytime. Well, never matter. You matter. I'd like to know you whom I look at. Know, not love. Not that knowing is a greater pleasure; but that I have just found the joy of it. You came just a month too late. Even this afternoon I dreamed. To night, along the Boulevard, you found me cold. Paul Johnson, cold! Thats a good one, eh, Art, you fine old stupid fellow, you! But I feel good! The color and the music and the song. . . A Negress chants a lullaby beneath the mate-eyes of a southern planter. O song! . . And those flushed faces. Eager brilliant eyes. Hard to imagine them as unawakened. Your own. Oh, they're awake all right. "And you know it too, dont you Bona?"

"What, Paul?"

"The truth of what I was thinking."

"I'd like to know I know—something of you."

"You will—before the evening's over. I promise it."

Crimson Gardens. Hurrah! So one feels. The bare-back rider balances agilely on the applause which is the tail of her song. Orchestral instruments warm up for jazz. The flute is a cat that ripples its fur against the deep-purring saxophone. The drum throws sticks. The cat jumps on the piano keyboard. Hi diddle, hi diddle, the cat and the fiddle. Crimson Gardens . . hurrah! . . jumps over the moon. Crimson Gardens! Helen . . O Eliza . . rabbit-eyes sparkling, plays up to, and tries to placate what she considers to be Paul's contempt. She always does that . . Little Liza Jane. . . Once home, she burns with the thought of what she's done. She says all manner of snidy things about him, and swears that she'll never go out again when he is along. She tries to get Art to break with him, saying, that if Paul, whom the whole dormitory calls a nigger, is more to him than she is, well, she's through. She does not break with Art. She goes out as often as she can with Art and Paul. She explains this to herself by a piece of information which a friend of hers had given her: men like him (Paul) can fascinate. One is not responsible for fascination. Not one girl had really loved Paul; he fascinated them. Bona didnt; only thought she did. Time would tell. And of course, *she* didnt. Liza. . . She plays up to, and tries to placate, Paul.

"Paul is so deep these days, and I'm so glad he's found some one to interest him."

"I dont believe I do."

The thought escapes from Bona just a moment before her anger at having said it.

Bona: You little puffy cat, I do. I do!

Dont I, Paul? her eyes ask.

Her answer is a crash of jazz from the palm-hidden orchestra. Crimson Gardens is a body whose blood flows to a clot upon the dance floor. Art and Helen clot. Soon, Bona and Paul. Paul finds her a little stiff, and his mind, wandering to Helen (silly little kid who wants every highball spoon her hands touch, for a souvenir), supple, perfect little dancer, wishes for the next dance when he and Art will exchange.

Bona knows that she must win him to herself.

"Since when have men like you grown cold?"

"The first philosopher."

"I thought you were a poet—or a gym director."

"Hence, your failure to make love."

Bona's eyes flare. Water. Grow red about the rims. She would like to tear away from him and dash across the clotted floor.

"What do you mean?"

"Mental concepts rule you. If they were flush with mine—good. I dont believe they are."

"How do you know, Mr. Philosopher?"

"Mostly a priori."

"You talk well for a gym director."

"And you—"

"I hate you. Ou!"

She presses away. Paul, conscious of the convention in it, pulls her to him. Her body close. Her head still strains away. He nearly crushes her. She tries to pinch him. Then sees people staring, and lets her arms fall. Their eyes meet. Both, contemptuous. The dance takes blood from their minds and packs it, tingling, in the torsos of their swaying bodies. Passionate blood leaps back into their eyes. They are a dizzy blood clot on a gyrating floor. They know that the pink-faced people have no part in what they feel. Their instinct leads them away from Art and Helen, and towards the big uniformed black man who opens and closes the gilded exit door. The cloak-room girl is tolerant of their impatience over such trivial things as wraps. And slightly superior. As the black man swings the door for them, his eyes are knowing. Too many couples have passed out, flushed and fidgety, for him not to know. The chill air is a shock to Paul. A strange thing happens. He sees the Gardens purple, as if he were way off. And a spot is in the purple. The spot comes furiously towards him. Face of the black man. It leers. It smiles sweetly like a child's. Paul leaves Bona and darts back so quickly that he doesnt give the door-man a chance to open. He swings in. Stops. Before the huge bulk of the Negro.

"Youre wrong."

"Yassur."

"Brother, youre wrong.

"I came back to tell you, to shake your hand, and tell you that you are wrong. That something beautiful is going to happen. That the Gardens are purple like a bed of roses would be at dusk. That I came into the Gardens, into life in the Gardens with one whom I did not know. That I danced with her, and did not know her. That I felt passion, contempt and passion for her whom I did not know. That I thought of her. That my thoughts were matches thrown into a dark window. And all the while the Gardens were purple like a bed of roses would be at dusk. I came back to tell you, brother, that white faces are petals of roses. That dark faces are petals of dusk. That I am going out and gather petals. That I am going out and know her whom I brought here with me to these Gardens which are purple like a bed of roses would be at dusk."

Paul and the black man shook hands.

When he reached the spot where they had been standing, Bona was gone.

TO A DARK GIRL
GWENDOLYN BENNETT

I love you for your brownness
And the rounded darkness of your breast.
I love you for the breaking sadness in your voice
And shadows where your wayward eye-lids rest.

Something of old forgotten queens
Lurks in the lithe abandon of your walk,
And something of the shackled slave
Sobs in the rhythm of your talk.

Oh, little brown girl, born for sorrow's mate,
Keep all you have of queenliness,
Forgetting that you once were slave,
And let your full lips laugh at Fate!

WEDDING DAY
GWENDOLYN BENNETT

His name was Paul Watson and as he shambled down rue Pigalle he might have been any other Negro of enormous height and size. But as I have said, his name was Paul Watson. Passing him on the street, you might not have known or cared who he was, but any one of the residents about the great Montmartre district of Paris could have told you who he was as well as many interesting bits of his personal history.

He had come to Paris in the days before colored jazz bands were the style. Back home he had been a Prize fighter. In the days when Joe Gans was in his glory Paul was following the ring, too. He didn't have that fine way about him that Gans had and for that reason luck seemed to go against him. When he was in the ring he was like a mad bull, especially if his opponent was a white man. In those days there wasn't any sympathy or nicety about the ring and so pretty soon all the ringmasters got down on Paul and he found it pretty hard to get a bout with anyone. Then it was that he worked his way across the Atlantic Ocean on a big liner—in the days before colored jazz bands were the style in Paris.

Things flowed along smoothly for the first few years with Paul's working here and there in the unfrequented places of Paris. On the side he used to give boxing lessons to aspiring youths or gymnastic young women. At that time he was working so steadily that he had little chance to find out what was going on around Paris. Pretty soon, however, he grew to be known among the trainers and managers began to fix up bouts for him. After one or two successful bouts a little fame began to come into being for him. So it was that after one of the prize-fights, a colored fellow came to his dressing room to congratulate him on his success as well as invite him to go to Montmartre to meet "the boys."

Paul had a way about him and seemed to get on with the colored fellows who lived in Montmartre and when the first Negro jazz band played in a tiny Parisian cafe Paul was among them playing the banjo. Those first years were without event so far as Paul was concerned. The members of that first band often say now that they wonder how it was that nothing happened during those first seven years, for it was generally known how great was Paul's hatred for American white people. I suppose the tranquility in the light of what happened afterwards was due to the fact that the cafe in which they worked was one in which mostly French people drank and danced and then too, that was before there were so many Americans visiting Paris. However, everyone had heard Paul speak of his intense hatred of American white folks. It only took two Benedictines to make him start talking about what he would do to the first "Yank" that called him "nigger." But the seven years came to an end and Paul Watson went to work in a larger cafe with a larger band, patronized almost solely by Americans.

I've heard almost every Negro in Montmartre tell about the night that a drunken Kentuckian came into the cafe where Paul was playing and said:

"Look heah, Bruther, what you all doin' ovah heah?"

"None ya bizness. And looka here, I ain't your brother, see?"

"Jack, do you heah that nigger talkin' lak that tah me?"

As he said this, he turned to speak to his companion. I have often wished that I had been there to have seen the thing happen myself. Every tale I have heard about it was different and yet there was something of truth in each of them. Perhaps the nearest one can come to the truth is by saying that Paul beat up about four full-sized white men that night besides doing a great deal of damage to the furniture about the cafe. I couldn't tell you just what did happen. Some of the fellows say that Paul seized the nearest table and mowed down men right and left, others say he took a bottle, then again the story runs that a chair was the instrument of his fury. At any rate, that started Paul Watson on his seige against the American white person who brings his native prejudices into the life of Paris.

It is a verity that Paul was the "black terror." The last syllable of the word, nigger, never passed the lips of a white man without the quick reflex action of Paul's arm and fist to the speaker's jaw. He paid for more glassware and cafe furnishings in the course of the next few years than is easily imaginable. And yet, there was something likable about Paul. Perhaps that's the reason that he stood in so well with the policemen of the neighborhood. Always some divine power seemed to intervene in his behalf and he was excused after the payment of a small fine with advice about his future conduct. Finally, there came the night when in a frenzy he shot the two American sailors.

They had not died from the wounds he had given them hence his sentence had not been one of death but rather a long term of imprisonment. It was a piliable sight to see Paul sitting in the corner of his cell with his great body hunched almost double. He seldom talked and when he did his words were interspersed with oaths about the lowness of "crackers." Then the World War came.

It seems strange that anything so horrible as that wholesale slaughter could bring about any good and yet there was something of a smoothing quality about even its baseness. There has never been such equality before or since such as that which the World War brought. Rich men fought by the side of paupers; poets swapped yarns with dry-goods salesmen, while Jews and Christians ate corned beef out of the same tin. Along with the general leveling influence came France's pardon of her prisoners in order that they might enter the army. Paul Watson became free and a French soldier. Because he was strong and had innate daring in his heart he was placed in the aerial squad and cited many times for bravery. The close of the war gave him his place in French society as a hero. With only a memory of the war and an ugly scar on his left cheek he took up his old life.

His firm resolutions about American white people still remained intact and many chance encounters that followed the war are told from lip to lip proving that the war and his previous imprisonment had changed him little. He was the same Paul Watson to Montmartre as he shambled up rue Pigalle.

Rue Pigalle in the early evening has a sombre beauty—gray as are most Paris streets and other-worldish. To those who know the district it is the Harlem of Paris and rue Pigalle is its dusky Seventh Avenue. Most of the colored musicians that furnish Parisians and their visitors with entertainment live somewhere in the neighborhood of rue Pigalle. Some time during every day each of these musicians makes a point of passing through rue Pigalle. Little wonder that almost any day will find Paul Watson going his shuffling way up the same street.

He reached the corner of rue de la Bruyere and with sure instinct his feet stopped. Without half thinking he turned into "the Pit." Its full name is The Flea Pit. If you should ask one of the musicians why it was so called, he would answer you to the effect that it was called "the pit" because all the "fleas" hang out there. If you did not get the full import of this explanation, he would go further and say that there were always "spades" in the pit and they were as thick as fleas. Unless you could understand this latter attempt at clarity you could not fully grasp what the Flea-Pit means to the Negro musicians in Montmartre. It is a tiny cafe of the genus that is called *bistro* in France. Here the fiddle players, saxophone blowers, drumbeaters and ivory ticklers gather at four in the afternoon for a porto or a game of billiards. Here the cabaret entertainers and supper musicians meet at one o'clock at night or thereafter for a whiskey and soda, or more billiards. Occasional sandwiches and a "quiet game" also play their parts in the popularity of the place. After a season or two it becomes a settled fact just what time you may catch so-and-so at the famous "Pit."

The musicians were very fond of Paul and took particular delight in teasing him. He was one of the chosen few that all of the musicians conceded as being "regular." It was the pet joke of the habitues of the cafe that Paul never bothered with girls. They always said that he could beat up ten men but was scared to death of one woman.

"Say fellow, when ya goin' a get hooked up?"

"Can't say, Bo. Ain't so much on skirts."

"Man alive, ya don't know what you're missin'—somebody little and cute telling ya sweet things in your ear. Paris is full of women folks."

"I ain't much on 'em all the same. Then too, they're all white."

"What's it to ya? This ain't America."

"Can't help that. Get this—I'm collud, see? I ain't got nothing for no white meat to do. If a woman eva called me nigger I'd have to kill her, that's all!"

"You for it, son. I can't give you a thing on this Mr. Jefferson Lawd way of lookin' at women.

"Oh, tain't that. I guess they're all right for those that wants 'em. Not me!"

"Oh you ain't so forty. You'll fall like all the other spades I've ever seen. Your kind falls hardest."

And so Paul went his way—alone. He smoked and drank with the fellows and sat for hours in the Montmartre cafes and never knew the companionship of a woman. Then one night after his work he was walking along the street in his queer shuffling way when a woman stepped up to his side.

"Voulez vous."

"Naw, gowan away from here."

"Oh, you speak English, don't you?"

"You an 'merican woman?"

"Used to be 'fore I went on the stage and got stranded over here."

"Well, get away from here. I don't like your kind!"

"Aw, Buddy, don't say that. I ain't prejudiced like some fool women."

"You don't know who I am, do you? I'm Paul Watson and I hate American white folks, see?"

He pushed her aside and went on walking alone. He hadn't gone far when she caught up to him and said with sobs in her voice:—

"Oh, Lordy, please don't hate me 'cause I was born white and an American. I ain't got a sou to my name and all the men pass me by cause I ain't spruced up. Now you come along and won't look at me cause I'm white."

Paul strode along with her clinging to his arm. He tried to shake her off several times but there was no use. She clung all the more desperately to him. He looked down at her frail body shaken with sobs, and something caught at his heart. Before he knew what he was doing he had said:—

"Naw, I ain't that mean. I'll get you some grub. Quit your cryin'. Don't like seein' women folks cry."

It was the talk of Montmartre. Paul Watson takes a woman to Gavarnni's every night for dinner. He comes to the Flea Pit less frequently, thus giving the other musicians plenty of opportunity to discuss him.

"How times do change. Paul, the woman-hater, has a Jane now."

"You ain't said nothing, fella. That ain't all. She's white and an 'merican, too."

"That's the way with these spades. They beat up all the white men they can lay their hands on but as soon as a gang of golden hair with blue eyes rubs up close to them they forget all they ever said about hatin' white folks."

"Guess he thinks that skirt's gone on him. Dumb fool!"

"Don' be no chineeman. That old gag don' fit for Paul. He cain't understand it no more'n we can. Says he jess can't help himself, everytime she looks up into his eyes and asks him does he love her. They sure are happy together. Paul's goin' to marry her, too. At first she kept saying that she didn't want to get married cause she wasn't the marrying kind and all that talk. Paul jus' laid down the law to her and told her he never would live with no woman without being married to her. Then she began to tell him all about her past life. He told her he didn't care nothing about what she used to be jus' so long as they loved each other now. Guess they'll make it."

"Yeah, Paul told me the same tale last night. He's sure gone on her all right."

"They're gettin' tied up next Sunday. So glad it's not me. Don't trust these American dames. Me for the Frenchies."

"She ain't so worse for looks, Bud. Now that he's been furnishing the green for the rags."

"Yeah, but I don't see no reason for the wedding bells. She was right— she ain't the marrying kind."

. . . and so Montmartre talked. In every cafe where the Negro musicians congregated Paul Watson was the topic for conversation. He had suddenly fallen from his place as bronze God to almost less than the dust.

The morning sun made queer patterns on Paul's sleeping face. He grimaced several times in his slumber, then finally half-opened his eyes. After a succession of dream-laden blinks he gave a great yawn, and rubbing his eyes, looked at the open window through which the sun shone brightly. His first conscious thought was that this was the bride's day and that bright sunshine prophesied happiness for the bride throughout her married life. His first impulse was to settle back into the covers and think drowsily about Mary and the queer twists life brings about, as is the wont of most bride-grooms on their last morning of bachelorhood. He put this impulse aside in favor of dressing quickly and rushing downstairs to telephone to Mary to say "happy wedding day" to her.

One huge foot slipped into a worn bedroom slipper and then the other dragged painfully out of the warm bed were the courageous beginnings of his bridal toilette. With a look of triumph he put on his new grey suit that he had ordered from an English tailor. He carefully pulled a taffeta tie into place beneath his chin, noting as he looked at his face in the mirror that the scar he had received in the army was very ugly—funny, marrying an ugly man like him.

French telephones are such human faults. After trying for about fifteen minutes to get Central 32.01 he decided that he might as well walk around to Mary's hotel to give his greeting as to stand there in the lobby of his own, wasting his time. He debated this in his mind a great deal. They were to be married at four o'clock. It was eleven now and it did seem a shame not to let her have a minute or two by herself. As he went walking down the street towards her hotel he laughed to think of how one always cogitates over doing something and finally does the thing he wanted to in the beginning anyway.

Mud on his nice gray suit that the English tailor had made for him. Damn—gray suit—what did he have a gray suit on for, anyway. Folks with black faces shouldn't wear gray suits. Gawd, but it was funny that time when he beat up that cracker at the Periquet. Fool couldn't shut his mouth he was so surprised. Crackers—damn 'em—he was one nigger that wasn't 'fraid of 'em. Wouldn't he have a hell of a time if he went back to America where black was black. Wasn't white nowhere, black wasn't. What was that thought he was trying to get ahold of—bumping around in his head—something he started to think about but couldn't remember it somehow.

The shrill whistle that is typical of the French subway pierced its way into his thoughts. Subway—why was he in the subway—he didn't want to go any place. He heard doors slamming and saw the blue uniforms of the conduc-tors swinging on to the cars as the trains began to pull out of the station. With one or two strides he reached the last coach as it began to move up the platform. A bit out of breath he stood inside the train and looking down at what he had in his hand he saw that it was a tiny pink ticket. A first class ticket in a second class coach. The idea set him to laughing. Everyone in the car turned and eyed him, but that did not bother him. Wonder what stop he'd get off—funny how these French said descend when they meant get off—funny he couldn't pick up French—been here so long. First class ticket in a second class coach!—that was one on him. Wedding day today, and that damn letter from Mary. How'd she say it now, "just couldn't go through with it," white women just don't marry colored men, and she was a street woman, too. Why couldn't she have told him flat that she was just getting back on her feet at his expense. Funny that first class ticket he bought, wish he could see Mary—him a-going there to wish her "happy wedding day," too. Wonder what that French woman was looking at him so hard for? Guess it was the mud.

ODYSSEY OF BIG BOY
STERLING BROWN

Lemme be wid Casey Jones,
   Lemme be wid Stagolee,
Lemme be wid such like men
   When Death takes hol' on me,
     When Death takes hol' on me. . . .

Done skinned as a boy in Kentucky hills,
   Druv steel dere as a man,
Done stripped tobacco in Virginia fiel's
   Alongst de River Dan,
     Alongst de River Dan;

Done mined de coal in West Virginia
   Liked dat job jes' fine
Till a load o' slate curved roun' my head
   Won't work in no mo' mine,
     Won't work in no mo' mine;

Done shocked de corn in Marylan',
   In Georgia done cut cane,
Done planted rice in South Caline,
   But won't do dat again
     Do dat no mo' again.

Been roustabout in Memphis,
   Dockhand in Baltimore,
Done smashed up freight on Norfolk wharves
   A fust class stevedore,
     A fust class stevedore. . . .

Done slung hash yonder in de North
   On de ole Fall River Line

Done busted suds in li'l New Yawk
 Which ain't no work o'mine—
  Lawd, ain't no work o' mine.

Done worked and loafed on such like jobs
 Seen what dey is to see
Done had my time with a pint on my hip
 An' a sweet gal on my knee
  Sweet mommer on my knee:

Had stovepipe blonde in Macon
 Yaller gal in Marylan'
In Richmond had a choklit brown
 Called me huh monkey man—
  Huh big fool monkey man.

Had two fair browns in Arkansaw
 And three in Tennessee
Had Creole gal in New Orleans
 Sho Gawd did two time me—
  Lawd two time, fo' time me—

But best gal what I evah had
 Done put it over dem
A gal in Southwest Washington
 At Four'n half and M—
  Four'n half and M. . . .

Done took my livin' as it came
 Done grabbed my joy, done risked my life
Train done caught me on de trestle
 Man done caught me wid his wife
  His doggone purty wife. . . .

I done had my women,
 I done had my fun
Cain't do much complainin'
 When my jag is done,
  Lawd, Lawd, my jag is done.

An' all dat Big Boy axes
 When time comes fo' to go
Lemme be wid John Henry, steel drivin' man
 Lemme be wid ole Jazzbo;
  Lemme be wid ole Jazzbo. . . .

SWEAT
ZORA NEALE HURSTON

It was eleven o'clock of a Spring night in Florida. It was Sunday. Any other night, Delia Jones would have been in bed for two hours by this time. But she was a washwoman, and Monday morning meant a great deal to her. So she collected the soiled clothes on Saturday when she returned the clean things. Sunday night after church, she sorted them and put the white things to soak. It saved her almost a half day's start. A great hamper in the bedroom held the clothes that she brought home. It was so much neater than a number of bundles lying around.

She squatted in the kitchen floor beside the great pile of clothes, sorting them into small heaps according to color, and humming a song in a mournful key, but wondering through it all where Sykes, her husband, had gone with her horse and buckboard.

Just then something long, round, limp and black fell upon her shoulders and slithered to the floor beside her. A great terror took hold of her. It softened her knees and dried her mouth so that it was a full minute before she could cry out or move. Then she saw that it was the big bull whip her husband liked to carry when he drove.

She lifted her eyes to the door and saw him standing there bent over with laughter at her fright. She screamed at him.

"Sykes, what you throw dat whip on me like dat? You know it would skeer me—looks just like a snake, an' you knows how skeered Ah is of snakes."

"Course Ah knowed it! That's how come Ah done it." He slapped his leg with his hand and almost rolled on the ground in his mirth. "If you such a big fool dat you got to have a fit over a earth worm or a string, Ah don't keer how bad Ah skeer you."

"You aint got no business doing it. Gawd knows it's a sin. Some day Ah'm gointuh drop dead from some of yo' foolishness. 'Nother thing, where you been wid mah rig? Ah feeds dat pony. He aint fuh you to be drivin' wid no bull whip."

"You sho is one aggravatin' nigger woman!" he declared and stepped into the room. She resumed her work and did not answer him at once. "Ah done tole you time and again to keep them white folks' clothes outa dis house."

He picked up the whip and glared down at her. Delia went on with her work. She went out into the yard and returned with a galvanized tub and sit it on the washbench. She saw that Sykes had kicked all of the clothes together again, and now stood in her way truculently, his whole manner hoping, *praying,* for an argument. But she walked calmly around him and commenced to re-sort the things.

"Next time, Ah'm gointer kick 'em outdoors," he threatened as he struck a match along the leg of his corduroy breeches.

Delia never looked up from her work, and her thin, stooped shoulders sagged further.

"Ah aint for no fuss t'night Sykes. Ah just come from taking sacrament at the church house."

He snorted scornfully. "Yeah, you just come from de church house on a Sunday night, but heah you is gone to work on them clothes. You ain't nothing but a hypocrite. One of them amen-corner Christians—sing, whoop, and shout, then come home and wash white folks clothes on the Sabbath."

He stepped roughly upon the whitest pile of things, kicking them helter-skelter as he crossed the room. His wife gave a little scream of dismay and quickly gathered them together again.

"Sykes, you quit grindin' dirt into these clothes! How can Ah git through by Sat'day if Ah don't start on Sunday?"

"Ah don't keer if you never git through. Anyhow, Ah done promised Gawd and a couple of other men, Ah aint gointer have it in mah house. Don't gimme no lip neither, else Ah'll throw 'em out and put mah fist up side yo' head to boot."

Delia's habitual meekness seemed to slip from her shoulders like a blown scarf. She was on her feet; her poor little body, her bare knuckly hands bravely defying the strapping hulk before her.

"Looka heah, Sykes, you done gone too fur. Ah been married to you fur fifteen years, and Ah been takin' in washin' fur fifteen years. Sweat, sweat, sweat! Work and sweat, cry and sweat, pray and sweat!"

"What's that got to do with me?" he asked brutally.

"What's it got to do with you, Sykes? Mah tub of suds is filled yo' belly with vittles more times than yo' hands is filled it. Mah sweat is done paid for this house and Ah reckon Ah kin keep on sweatin' in it."

She seized the iron skillet from the stove and struck a defensive pose, which act surprised him greatly, coming from her. It cowed him and he did not strike her as he usually did.

"Naw you won't," she panted, "that ole snaggle-toothed black woman you runnin' with aint comin' heah to pile up on *mah* sweat and blood. You aint paid for nothin' on this place, and Ah'm gointer stay right heah till Ah'm toted out foot foremost."

"Well, you better quit gittin' me riled up, else they'll be totin' you out sooner than you expect. Ah'm so tired of you Ah don't know whut to do. Gawd! how Ah hates skinny wimmen!"

A little awed by this new Delia, he sidled out of the door and slammed the back gate after him. He did not say where he had gone, but she knew too well. She knew very well that he would not return until nearly daybreak also. Her work over, she went on to bed but not to sleep at once. Things had come to a pretty pass!

She lay awake, gazing upon the debris that cluttered their matrimonial trail. Not an image left standing along the way. Anything like flowers had long ago been drowned in the salty stream that had been pressed from her heart. Her tears, her sweat, her blood. She had brought love to the union and he had brought a longing after the flesh. Two months after the wedding, he had given her the first brutal beating. She had the memory of his numerous trips to Orlando with all of his wages when he had returned to her penniless, even before the first year had passed. She was young and soft then, but now she thought of her knotty, muscled limbs, her harsh knuckly hands, and drew herself up into an unhappy little ball in the middle of the big feather bed. Too late now to hope for love, even if it were not Bertha it would be someone else. This case differed from the others only in that she was bolder than the others. Too late for everything except her little home. She had built it for her old days, and planted one by one the trees and flowers there. It was lovely to her, lovely.

Somehow, before sleep came, she found herself saying aloud: "Oh well, whatever goes over the Devil's back, is got to come under his belly. Sometime or ruther, Sykes, like everybody else, is gointer reap his sowing." After that she was able to build a spiritual earthworks against her husband. His shells could no longer reach her. *Amen.* She went to sleep and slept until he announced his presence in bed by kicking her feet and rudely snatching the cover away.

"Gimme some kivah heah, an' git yo' damn foots over on yo' own side! Ah oughter mash you in yo' mouf fuh drawing dat skillet on me."

Delia went clear to the rail without answering him. A triumphant indifference to all that he was or did.

The week was as full of work for Delia as all other weeks, and Saturday found her behind her little pony, collecting and delivering clothes.

It was a hot, hot day near the end of July. The village men on Joe Clarke's porch even chewed cane listlessly. They did not hurl the cane-knots as usual. They let them dribble over the edge of the porch. Even conversation had collapsed under the heat.

"Heah come Delia Jones," Jim Merchant said, as the shaggy pony came 'round the bend of the road toward them. The rusty buckboard was heaped with baskets of crisp, clean laundry.

"Yep," Joe Lindsay agreed. "Hot or col', rain or shine, jes ez reg'lar ez de weeks roll roun' Delia carries 'em an' fetches 'em on Sat'day."

"She better if she wanter eat," said Moss. "Syke Jones aint wuth de shot an' powder hit would tek tuh kill 'em. Not to *huh* he aint."

"He sho' aint," Walter Thomas chimed in. "It's too bad, too, cause she wuz a right pritty lil trick when he got huh. Ah'd uh mah'ied huh mahseff if he hadnter beat me to it."

Delia nodded briefly at the men as she drove past.

"Too much knockin' will ruin *any* 'oman. He done beat huh 'nough tuh kill three women, let 'lone change they looks," said Elijah Mosely. "How Syke kin stommuck dat big black greasy Mogul he's layin' roun' wid, gits me. Ah swear dat eight-rock couldn't kiss a sardine can Ah done thowed out de back do' 'way las' yeah."

"Aw, she's fat, thass how come. He's allus been crazy 'bout fat women," put in Merchant. "He'd a' been tied up wid one long time ago if he could a' found one tuh have him. Did Ah tell yuh 'bout him come sidlin' roun' *mah* wife—bringin' her a basket uh pee-cans outa his yard fuh a present? Yessir, mah wife! She tol' him tuh take 'em right straight back home, cause Delia works so hard ovah dat washtub she reckon everything on de place taste lak sweat an' soapsuds. Ah jus' wisht Ah'd a' caught 'im 'roun' dere! Ah'd a' made his hips ketch on fiah down dat shell road."

"Ah know he done it, too. Ah sees 'im grinnin' at every 'oman dat passes," Walter Thomas said. "But even so, he useter eat some mighty big hunks uh humble pie tuh git dat lil' 'oman he got. She wuz ez pritty ez a speckled pup! Dat wuz fifteen yeahs ago. He useter be so skeered uh losin' huh, she could make him do some parts of a husband's duty. Dey never wuz de same in de mind."

"There oughter be a law about him," said Lindsay. He aint fit tuh carry guts tuh a bear."

Clarke spoke for the first time. "Taint no law on earth dat kin make a man be decent if it aint in 'im. There's plenty men dat takes a wife lak dey do a joint uh sugar-cane. It's round, juicy an' sweet when dey gits it. But dey squeeze an' grind, squeeze an' grind an' wring tell dey wring every drop uh pleasure dat's in 'em out. When dey's satisfied dat dey is wrung dry, dey treats 'em jes lak dey do a cane-chew. Dey thows 'em away. Dey knows whut dey is doin' while dey is at it, an' hates theirselves fuh it but they keeps on hangin' after huh tell she's empty. Den dey hates huh fuh bein' a cane-chew an' in de way."

"We oughter take Syke an' dat stray 'oman uh his'n down in Lake Howell swamp an' lay on de rawhide till they cain't say 'Lawd a' mussy.' He allus wuz uh ovahbearin' niggah, but since dat white 'oman from up north done teached 'im how to run a automobile, he done got too biggety to live—an' we oughter kill 'im." Ole Man Anderson advised.

A grunt of approval went around the porch. But the heat was melting their civic virtue and Elijah Moseley began to bait Joe Clarke.

"Come on, Joe, git a melon outa dere an' slice it up for yo' customers. We'se all sufferin' wid de heat. De bear's done got *me!*"

"Thass right, Joe, a watermelon is jes' whut Ah needs tuh cure de eppizudicks," Walter Thomas joined forces with Moseley. "Come on dere, Joe. We all is steady customers an' you aint set us up in a long time. Ah chooses dat long, bowlegged Floridy favorite."

"A god, an' be dough. You all gimme twenty cents and slice away," Clarke retorted. "Ah needs a col' slice m'self. Heah, everybody chip in. Ah'll lend y'll mah meat knife."

The money was quickly subscribed and the huge melon brought forth. At that moment, Sykes and Bertha arrived. A determined silence fell on the porch and the melon was put away again.

Merchant snapped down the blade of his jackknife and moved toward the store door.

"Come on in, Joe, an' gimme a slab uh sow belly an' uh pound uh coffee—almost fuhgot 'twas Sat'day. Got to git on home." Most of the men left also.

Just then Delia drove past on her way home, as Sykes was ordering magnificently for Bertha. It pleased him for Delia to see.

"Git whutsoever yo' heart desires, Honey. Wait a minute, Joe. Give huh two botles uh strawberry soda-water, uh quart uh parched ground-peas, an' a block uh chewin' gum."

With all this they left the store, with Sykes reminding Bertha that this was his town and she could have it if she wanted it.

The men returned soon after they left, and held their watermelon feast.

"Where did Syke Jones git dat 'oman from nohow?" Lindsay asked.

"Ovah Apopka. Guess dey musta been cleanin' out de town when she lef'. She don't look lak a thing but a hunk uh liver wid hair on it."

"Well, she sho' kin squall," Dave Carter contributed. "When she gits ready tuh laff, she jes' opens huh mouf an' latches it back tuh de las' notch. No ole grandpa alligator down in Lake Bell ain't got nothin' on huh."

Bertha had been in town three months now. Sykes was still paying her room rent at Della Lewis'—the only house in town that would have taken her in. Sykes took her frequently to Winter Park to "stomps." He still assured her that he was the swellest man in the state.

"Sho' you kin have dat lil' ole house soon's Ah kin git dat 'oman outa dere. Everything b'longs tuh me an' you sho' kin have it. Ah sho' 'bominates uh skinny 'oman. Lawdy, you sho' is got one portly shape on you! You kin git *anything* you wants. Dis is *mah* town an' you sho' kin have it."

Delia's work-worn knees crawled over the earth in Gethsemane and up the rocks of Calvary many, many times during these months. She avoided the villagers and meeting places in her efforts to be blind and deaf. But Bertha nullified this to a degree, by coming to Delia's house to call Sykes out to her at the gate.

Delia and Sykes fought all the time now with no peaceful interludes. They slept and ate in silence. Two or three times Delia had attempted a timid friendliness, but she was repulsed each time. It was plain that the breaches must remain agape.

The sun had burned July to August. The heat streamed down like a million hot arrows, smiting all things living upon the earth. Grass withered, leaves browned, snakes went blind in shedding and men and dogs went mad. Dog days!

Delia came home one day and found Sykes there before her. She wondered, but started to go on into the house without speaking, even though he was standing in the kitchen door and she must either stoop under his arm or ask him to move. He made no room for her. She noticed a soap box beside the steps, but paid no particular attention to it, knowing that he must have brought it here. As she was stooping to pass under his outstretched arm, he suddenly pushed her backward, laughingly.

"Look in de box dere Delia, Ah done brung yuh somethin'!"

She nearly fell upon the box in her stumbling, and when she saw what it held, she all but fainted outright.

"Syke! Syke, mah Gawd! You take dat rattlesnake 'way from heah! You *gottuh.* Oh, Jesus, have mussy!"

"Ah aint gut tuh do nuthin' uh de kin'—fact is Ah aint got tuh do nothin' but die. Taint no use uh you puttin' on airs makin' out lak you skeered uh dat snake—he's gointer stay right heah tell he die. He wouldn't bite me cause Ah knows how tuh handle 'im. Nohow he wouldn't risk breakin' out his fangs 'gin *yo'* skinny laigs."

"Naw, now Syke, don't keep dat thing 'roun' heah tuh skeer me tuh death. You knows Ah'm even feared uh earth worms. Thass de biggest snake Ah evah did see. Kill 'im Syke, please."

"Doan ast me tuh do nothin' fuh yuh. Goin' 'round' tryin' tuh be so damn asterperious. Naw, Ah aint gonna kill it. Ah tink uh damn sight mo' uh him dan you! Dat's a nice snake an' anybody doan lak 'im kin jes' hit de grit."

The village soon heard that Sykes had the snake, and came to see and ask questions.

"How de hen-fire did you ketch dat six-foot rattler, Syke?" Thomas asked.

"He's full uh frogs so he caint hardly move, thass how Ah eased up on 'm. But Ah'm a snake charmer an' knows how tuh handle 'em. Shux, dat aint nothin'. Ah could ketch one eve'y day if Ah so wanted tuh."

"Whut he needs is a heavy hick'ry club leaned real heavy on his head. Dat's de bes 'way tuh charm a rattlesnake."

"Naw, Walt, y'll jes' don't understand dese diamon' backs lak Ah do," said Sykes in a superior tone of voice.

The village agreed with Walter, but the snake stayed on. His box remained by the kitchen door with its screen wire covering. Two or three days later it had digested its meal of frogs and literally came to life. It rattled at every movement in the kitchen or the yard. One day as Delia came down the kitchen steps she saw his chalky-white fangs curved like scimitars hung in the wire meshes. This time she did not run away with averted eyes as usual. She stood for a long time in the doorway in a red fury that grew bloodier for every second that she regarded the creature that was her torment.

That night she broached the subject as soon as Sykes sat down to the table.

"Syke, Ah wants you tuh take dat snake 'way fum heah. You done starved me an' Ah put up widcher, you done beat me an Ah took dat, but you done kilt all mah insides bringin' dat varmint heah."

Sykes poured out a saucer full of coffee and drank it deliberately before he answered her.

"A whole lot Ah keer 'bout how you feels inside uh out. Dat snake aint goin' no damn wheah till Ah gits ready fuh 'im tuh go. So fur as beatin' is concerned, yuh aint took near all dat you gointer take ef yuh stay 'roun' *me.*"

Delia pushed back her plate and got up from the table. "Ah hates you,

Sykes,'' she said calmly. ''Ah hates you tuh de same degree dat Ah useter love yuh. Ah done took an' took till mah belly is full up tuh mah neck. Dat's de reason Ah got mah letter fum de church an' moved mah membership tuh Woodbridge—so Ah don't haftuh take no sacrament wid yuh. Ah don't wantuh see yuh 'roun' me atall. Lay 'roun' wid dat 'oman all yuh wants tuh, but gwan 'way furm me an' mah house. Ah hates yuh lak uh suck-egg dog.''

Sykes almost let the huge wad of corn bread and collard greens he was chewing fall out of his mouth in amazement. He had a hard time whipping himself up to the proper fury to try to answer Delia.

''Well, Ah'm glad you does hate me. Ah'm sho' tiahed uh you hangin' ontuh me. Ah don't want yuh. Look at yuh stringey ole neck! Yo' rawbony laigs an' arms is enough tuh cut uh man tuh death. You looks jes' lak de devvul's doll-baby tuh *me.* You cain't hate me no worse dan Ah hates you. Ah been hatin' *you* fuh years.''

''Yo' ole black hide don't look lak nothin' tuh me, but uh passle uh wrinkled up rubber, wid yo' big ole yeahs flappin' on each side lak up paih uh buzzard wings. Don't think Ah'm gointuh be run 'way fum mah house neither. Ah'm goin' tuh de white folks bout *you,* mah young man, de very nex' time you lay yo' han's on me. Mah cup is done run ovah.'' Delia said this with no signs of fear and Sykes departed from the house, threatening her, but made not the slightest move to carry out any of them.

That night he did not return at all, and the next day being Sunday, Delia was glad that she did not have to quarrel before she hitched up her pony and drove the four miles to Woodbridge.

She stayed to the night service—''love feast''—which was very warm and full of spirit. In the emotional winds her domestic trials were borne far and wide so that she sang as she drove homeward,

> ''Jurden water, black an' col'
> Chills de body, not de soul
> An' Ah wantah cross Jurden in uh calm time.''

She came from the barn to the kitchen door and stopped.

''Whut's de mattah, ol' satan, you aint kickin' up yo' racket?'' She addressed the snake's box. Complete silence. She went on into the house with a new hope in its birth struggles. Perhaps her threat to go to the white folks had frightened Sykes! Perhaps he was sorry! Fifteen years of misery and suppression had brought Delia to the place where she would hope *anything* that looked towards a way over or through her wall of inhibitions.

She felt in the match safe behind the stove at once for a match. There was only one there.

''Dat niggah wouldn't fetch nothin' heah tuh save his rotten neck, but he kin run thew whut Ah brings quick enough. Now he done toted off nigh on tuh haff uh box uh matches. He done had dat 'oman heah in mah house, too.''

Nobody but a woman could tell how she knew this even before she struck the match. But she did and it put her into a new fury.

Presently she brought in the tubs to put the white things to soak. This time she decided she need not bring the hamper out of the bedroom; she would go in there and do the sorting. She picked up the pot-bellied lamp and went in. The room was small and the hamper stood hard by the foot of the white iron bed. She could sit and reach through the bedposts—resting as she worked.

"Ah wantah cross Jurden in uh calm time." She was singing again. The mood of the "love feast" had returned. She threw back the lid of the basket almost gaily. Then, moved by both horror and terror, she lept back, toward the door. *There lay the snake in the basket!* He moved sluggishly at first, but even as she turned round and round, jumped up and down in an insanity of fear, he began to stir vigorously. She saw him pouring his awful beauty from the basket upon the bed, then she seized the lamp and ran as fast as she could to the kitchen. The wind from the open door blew out the light and the darkness added to her terror. She sped to the darkness of the yard, slamming the door after her before she thought to set down the lamp. She did not feel safe even on the ground, so she climbed up in the hay barn.

There for an hour or more she lay sprawled upon the hay a gibbering wreck.

Finally she grew quiet, and after that, coherent thought. With this, stalked through her a cold, bloody rage. Hours of this. A period of introspection, a space of retrospection, then a mixture of both. Out of this an awful calm.

"Well, Ah done de bes' Ah could. If things aint right, Gawd knows taint mah fault."

She went to sleep—a twitchy sleep—and woke up to a faint gray sky. There was a loud hollow sound below. She peered out. Sykes was at the wood-pile, demolishing a wire-covered box.

He hurried to the kitchen door, but hung outside there some minutes before he entered, and stood some minutes more inside before he closed it after him.

The gray in the sky was spreading. Delia descended without fear now, and crouched beneath the low bedroom window. The drawn shade shut out the dawn, shut in the night. But the thin walls held back no sound.

"Dat ol' scratch is woke up now!" She mused at the tremendous whirr inside, which every woodsman knows, is one of the sound illusions. The rattler is a ventriloquist. His whirr sounds to the right, to the left, straight ahead, behind, close under foot—everywhere but where it is. Woe to him who guesses wrong unless he is prepared to hold up his end of the argument! Sometimes he strikes without rattling at all.

Inside, Sykes heard nothing until he knocked a pot lid off the stove while trying to reach the match safe in the dark. He had emptied his pockets at Bertha's.

The snake seemed to wake up under the stove and Sykes made a quick leap into the bedroom. In spite of the gin he had had, his head was clearing now.

"Mah Gawd!" he chattered, "ef Ah could on'y strack uh light!"

The rattling ceased for a moment as he stood paralyzed. He waited. It seemed that the snake waited also.

"Oh, fuh de light! Ah thought he'd be too sick"—Sykes was muttering to himself when the whirr began again, closer, right underfoot this time. Long before this, Sykes' ability to think had been flattened down to primitive instinct and he leaped—onto the bed.

Outside Delia heard a cry that might have come from a maddened chimpanzee, a stricken gorilla. All the terror, all the horror, all the rage that man possibly could express, without a recognizable human sound.

A tremendous stir inside there, another series of animal screams, the intermittent whirr of the reptile. The shade torn violently down from the window, letting in the red dawn, a huge brown hand seizing the window stick, great dull blows upon the wooden floor punctuating the gibberish of sound long after the rattle of the snake had abruptly subsided. All this Delia could see and hear from her place beneath the window, and it made her ill. She crept over to the four-o'clocks and stretched herself on the cool earth to recover.

She lay there, "Delia, Delia!" She could hear Sykes calling in a most despairing tone as one who expected no answer. The sun crept on up, and he called. Delia could not move—her legs were gone flabby. She never moved, he called, and the sun kept rising.

"Mah Gawd!" She heard him moan, "Mah Gawd fum Heben!" She heard him stumbling about and got up from her flower-bed. The sun was growing warm. As she approached the door she heard him call out hopefully, "Delia, is dat you Ah heah?"

She saw him on his hands and knees as soon as she reached the door. He crept an inch or two toward her—all that he was able, and she saw his horribly swollen neck and his one open eye shining with hope. A surge of pity too strong to support bore her away from the eye that must, could not, fail to see the tubs. He would see the lamp. Orlando with its doctors was too far. She could scarcely reach the Chinaberry tree, where she waited in the growing heat while inside she knew the cold river was creeping up and up to extinguish that eye which must know by now that she knew.

AFRICAN DIARY
W. E. B. DUBOIS

I have just come back from a journey in the world of nearly five months. I have travelled 15,000 miles. I set foot on three continents. I have visited five countries, four African islands and five African colonies. I have sailed under five flags. I have seen a black president inaugurated. I have walked in the African big bush and heard the night cry of leopards. I have traded in African markets, talked with African chiefs and been the guest of white governors. I have seen the Alhambra and the great mosque at Cordova and lunched with H. G. Wells; and I am full, very full with things that must be said.

December 16, 1923

Today I sailed from Tenerife for Africa. The night was done in broad black masses across the blue and the sun burned a great livid coal in the sky. Above rose the Peak of Tenerife, round like a woman's breast, pale with snow patches, immovable, grand.

On the boat—the *Henner* from Bremen—I am in Germany and opposite is a young man who fought four and a half years in the German army on all fronts—bitter, bitter. War is not done yet, he says. He's going to Angola.

We are six Germans in this little floating Germany: a captain, fifty or fifty-five, world roamer—San Francisco, Klondike, all Africa, *gemüthlich,* jovial; a bull-headed, red-necked first officer, stupid, good, funny; a doctor, well bred, kindly; a soldier and business man, bitter, keen, hopeful; others dumber and more uncertain. We drink Bremer beer, smoke, tell tales and the cabin rings.

December 17

On the sea—slipping lazily south, in cloud and sun and languorous air. The food is good and German. The beer is such as I have not tasted for a quarter century—golden as wine, light with almost no feel of alcohol. And I sense rather than hear a broken, beaten, but unconquered land, a spirit bruised, burned, but immortal. There is defense eager, but not apology; there is always the pointing out of the sin of all Europe.

My cabin is a dream. It is white and clean, with windows—not portholes—and pretty curtains at berth, door and window; electric light.

December 19

The languorous days are creeping lazily away. We have passed Cape Bojador of historic memory; we have passed the Tropic of Cancer, we are in the Tropics! There is a moon and by day an almost cloudless sky. I rise at eight and breakfast at eight thirty. Then I write and read until lunch at 12:30. About 1:30 I take a nap and coffee at four. Then read until 6:30 and supper. We linger at the table until nearly 9. Then reading, walking and bed by 10.

December 20

It is Thursday. Day after tomorrow I shall put my feet on the soil of Africa. As yet I have seen no land, but last night I wired to Monrovia by way of Dakar—"President King—Monrovia—Arrive Saturday, *Henner*—Du Bois." I wonder what it all will be like? Meantime it's getting hot—*hot,* and I've put on all the summer things I've got.

December 20

Tonight the sun, a dull gold ball, strange shaped and rayless sank before a purple sky into a bright green and sinking turned the sky to violet blue and gray and the sea turned dark. But the sun itself blushed from gold to shadowed burning crimson, then to red. The sky above, blue-green; the waters blackened and then the sun did not set—it died and was not. And behind gleamed the pale silver of the moon across the pink effulgence of the clouds.

December 21

Tomorrow—Africa! Inconceivable! As yet no sight of land, but it was warm and we rigged deck chairs and lay at ease. I have been reading that old novel of mine—it has points. Twice we've wired Liberia. I'm all impatience.

December 22

Waiting for the first gleam of Africa. This morning I photographed the officers and wrote an article on Germany. Then I packed my trunk and big bag. The step for descending to the boat had been made ready. Now I read and write and the little boat runs sedately on.

3:33 p.m.—I see Africa—Cape Mount in two low, pale semicircles, so pale it looks a cloud. So my great great grandfather saw it two centuries ago. Clearer and clearer it rises and now land in a long low line runs to the right and melts into the mist and sea and Cape Mount begins. Liberia—what a citadel for the capital of Negrodom!

When shall I forget the night I first set foot on African soil—I, the sixth generation in descent from my stolen forefathers. The moon was at the full and the waters of the Atlantic lay like a lake. All the long slow afternoon as the sun robed itself in its western scarlet with veils of misty cloud, I had seen Africa afar. Cape Mount—that mighty headland with its twin curves, northern sentinel of the vast realm of Liberia gathered itself out of the cloud at half past three and then darkened and grew clear. On beyond flowed the dark low undulating land quaint with palm and breaking sea. The world darkened. Africa faded away, the stars stood forth curiously twisted—Orion in the zenith—the Little Bear asleep and the Southern Cross rising behind the horizon. Then afar, ahead, a lone light, straight at the ship's fore. Twinkling lights appeared below, around and rising shadows.

"Monrovia," said the Captain. Suddenly we swerved to our left. The long arms of the bay enveloped us and then to the right rose the twinkling hill of Monrovia, with its crowning star. Lights flashed on the shore—here, there. Then we sensed a darker shadow in the shadows; it lay very still. "It's a boat," one said. "It's two boats." Then the shadow drifted in pieces and as the anchor roared into the deep five boats outlined themselves on the waters—great ten-oared barges black with men swung into line and glided toward us. I watched them fascinated.

Nine at Night

It was nine at night—above, the shadows, there the town, here the sweeping boats. One forged ahead with the stripes and lone star flaming behind, the ensign of the customs floating wide and bending to the long oars, the white caps of ten black sailors. Up the stairway clambered a soldier in khaki, aide-de-camp of the President of the Republic, a custom house official, the clerk of the American legation—and after them sixty-five lithe, lean black steve-dores with whom the steamer would work down to Portuguese Angola and back.

A few moments of formalities, greetings and good-byes and I was in the great long boat with the President's Aide—a brown major in brown khaki. On the other side the young clerk and at the back the black, barelegged pilot. Before us on the high thwarts were the rowers: men, boys, black, thin, trained in muscle and sinew, little larger than the oars in thickness, they bent their strength to them and swung upon them.

One in the centre gave curious little cackling cries to keep the rhythm, and for the spurts, the stroke, a bit thicker and sturdier, gave a low guttural command now and then and the boat, alive, quivering, danced beneath the moon, swept a great curve to the bar to breast its narrow teeth of foam— *t'chick-a-tickity, t'chick-a-tickity* sang the boys and we glided and raced, now between boats, now near the landing—now oars aloft at the dock. And lo! I was in Africa!

December 25

Christmas eve and Africa is singing in Monrovia. They are Krus and Fanti—men, women and children and all the night they march and sing. The music was once the music of revival hymns. But it is that music now transformed and the words hidden in an unknown tongue—liquid and sonorous. It is tricked and expounded with cadence and turn. And this is that same trick I heard first in Tennessee thirty-eight years ago: The air is raised and carried by men's strong voices, while floating above in obligato, come the high mellow voices of women—it is the ancient African art of part singing so curiously and insistently different.

And so they come, gay apparelled, lit by a transparency. They enter the gate and flow over the high steps and sing and sing and sing. They saunter round the house, pick flowers, drink water and sing and sing and sing. The warm dark heat of the night steams up to meet the moon. And the night is song.

Christmas day, 1923. We walk down to the narrow, crooked wharves of Monrovia, by houses old and gray and steps like streets of stone. Before is the wide St. Paul river, double-mouthed, and beyond, the sea, white, curling on the sand. Before is the isle—the tiny isle, hut-covered and guarded by a cotton tree, where the pioneers lived in 1821. We circle round, then up the river.

Great bowing trees, festoons of flowers, golden blossoms, star-faced palms and thatched huts; tall spreading trees lifting themselves like vast umbrellas, low shrubbery with gray and laced and knotted roots—the broad, black, murmuring river. Here a tree holds wide fingers out and stretches them over the water in vast incantation; bananas throw their wide green fingers to the sun. Iron villages, scarred clearings with gray, sheet-iron homes staring grim and bare at the ancient tropical flood of green.

The river sweeps wide and the shrubs bow low. Behind, Monrovia rises in clear, calm beauty. Gone are the wharves, the low and clustered houses of the port, the tight-throated business village, and up sweep the villas and the low wall, brown and cream and white, with great mango and cotton tree, with light house and spire, with porch and pillar and the green and color of shrubbery and blossom.

We climbed the upright shore to a senator's home and received his kindly hospitality—curious blend of feudal lord and modern farmer—sandwiches, cake and champagne.

Again we glided up the drowsy river—five, ten, twenty miles and came to our hostess. A mansion of five generations with a compound of endless native servants and cows under the palm thatches. The daughters of the family wore, on the beautiful black skin of their necks, the exquisite pale gold chains of the Liberian artisan and the slim, black little granddaughter of the house had a wide pink ribbon on the thick curls of her dark hair, that lay like sudden sunlight on the shadows. Double porches, one above the other, welcomed us to ease. A native man, gay with Christmas and a dash of gin, danced and sang and danced in the road. Children ran and played in the blazing sun. We sat at a long broad table and ate duck, chicken, beef, rice, plantain and collards, cake, tea, water and Madeira wine. Then we went and looked at the heavens, the uptwisted sky—Orion and Cassiopeia at zenith; the Little Bear beneath the horizon, new unfamiliar sights in the Milky Way—all awry, a-living—sun for snow at Christmas, and happiness and cheer.

ON BEING BLACK
W. E. B. DUBOIS

My friend, who is pale and positive, said to me yesterday, as the tired sun was nodding: "You are too sensitive."

I admit, I am—senstive, I am artificial. I cringe or am bumptious or immobile. I am intellectually dishonest, art-blind, and I lack humor.

"Why don't you stop all this," she retorts triumphantly.

You will not let us.

"There you go, again. You know that I—"

Wait! I answer. Wait!

I arise at seven. The milkman has neglected me. He pays little attention to colored districts. My white neighbor glares elaborately. I walk softly, lest I disturb him. The children jeer as I pass to work. The women in the streetcar withdraw their skirts or prefer to stand. The policeman is truculent. The elevator man hates to serve Negroes. My job is insecure because the white union wants it and does not want me. I try to lunch, but no place near will serve me. I go forty blocks to Marshall's, but the Committee of Fourteen closes Marshall's; they say that white women frequent it.

"Do all eating places discriminate?"

No, but how shall I know which do not—except—

I hurry home through crowds. They mutter or get angry. I go to a mass meeting. They stare. I go to a church. "We don't admit niggers!"

Or perhaps I leave the beaten track. I seek new work. "Our employees would not work with you; our customers would object."

I ask to help in social uplift.

"Why—er—we will write you."

I enter the free field of science. Every laboratory door is closed and no endowments are available.

I seek the universal mistress, Art; the studio door is locked.

I write literature. "We cannot publish stories of colored folk of that type." It's the only type I know.

This is my life. It makes me idiotic. It gives me artificial problems. I hesitate, I rush, I waver. In fine—I am sensitive!

My pale friend looks at me with disbelief and curling tongue.

"Do you mean to sit there and tell me that this is what happens to you each day?"

Certainly not, I answer low.

"Then you only fear it will happen?"

I fear!

"Well, haven't you the courage to rise above a—almost a craven fear?"

Quite—quite craven is my fear, I admit; but the terrible thing is—these things do happen!

"But you just said—"

They do happen. Not all each day—surely not. But now and then—now seldom; now, sudden; now after a week, now in a chain of awful minutes; not everywhere, but anywhere—in Boston, in Atlanta. That's the hell of it. Imagine spending your life looking for insults or for hiding places from them—shrinking (instinctively and despite desperate bolsterings of courage) from blows that are not always, but ever; not each day, but each week, each month, each year. Just, perhaps, as you have choked back the craven fear and cried, "I am and will be the master of my—"

"No more tickets downstairs; here's one to the smoking gallery."

You hesitate. You beat back your suspicions. After all, a cigarette with Charlie Chaplin—then a white man pushes by—

"Three in the orchestra."

"Yes, sir." And in he goes.

Suddenly your heart chills. You turn yourself away toward the golden twinkle of the purple night and hesitate again. What's the use? Why not always yield—always take what's offered—always bow to force, whether of cannons or dislike? Then the great fear surges in your soul, the real fear—the fear beside which other fears are vain imaginings; the fear lest right there and then you are losing your own soul; that you are losing your own soul and the soul of a people; that millions of unborn children, black and gold and mauve, are being there and then despoiled by you because you are a coward and dare not fight!

Suddenly that silly orchestra seat and the cavorting of a comedian with funny feet become matters of life, death, and immortality; you grasp the pillars of the universe and strain as you sway back to that befrilled ticket girl. You grip your soul for riot and murder. You choke and sputter, and she, seeing that you are about to make a "fuss," obeys her orders and throws the tickets at you in contempt. Then you slink to your seat and crouch in the darkness before the film, with every tissue burning! The miserable wave of reaction engulfs you. To think of compelling puppies to take your hard-earned money; fattening hogs to hate you and yours; forcing your way among cheap and tawdry idiots—God! What a night of pleasure!

Why do not those who are scarred in the world's battle and hurt by its hardness, travel to these places of beauty and drown themselves in the utter joy of life? I asked this once sitting in a southern home. Outside, the spring of a Georgia February was luring gold to the bushes and languor to the soft air. Around me sat color in human flesh—brown that crimsoned readily; dim soft-yellow that escaped description; cream-like duskiness that shadowed to rich tints of autumn leaves. And yet a suggested journey in the world brought no response.

"I should think you would like to travel," said the white one.

But no, the thought of a journey seemed to depress them.

Did you ever see a "Jim-Crow" waiting-room? There are always exceptions, as at Greensboro—but usually there is no heat in winter and no air in summer; with undisturbed loafers and train hands and broken, disreputable settees; to buy a ticket is torture; you stand and stand and wait and wait until every white person at the "other window" is waited on. Then the tired agent yells across, because all the tickets and money are over there—

"What d'y'e want? What? Where?"

The agent browbeats and contradicts you, hurries and confuses the ignorant, gives many persons the wrong change, compels some to purchase their tickets on the train at a higher price, and sends you and me out on the platform, burning with indignation and hatred!

The "Jim-Crow" car is up next the baggage car and engine. It stops out beyond the covering in the rain or sun or dust. Usually there is no step to help you climb on, and often the car is a smoker cut in two, and you must pass through the white smokers or else they pass through your part, with swagger and noise and stares. Your compartment is a half or a quarter or an eighth of the oldest car in service on the road. Unless it happens to be a through express, the plush is caked with dirt, the floor is grimy, and the windows dirty. An impertinent white newsboy occupies two seats at the end of the car and importunes you to the point of rage to buy cheap candy, Coca-Cola, and worthless, if not vulgar, books. He yells and swaggers, while a continued stream of white men saunters back and forth from the smoker, to buy and hear. The white train crew from the baggage car uses the "Jim-Crow" to lounge in and perform their toilet. The conductor appropriates two seats for himself and his papers and yells gruffly for your tickets almost before the train has started. It is best not to ask him for information even in the gentlest tones. His information is for white persons chiefly. It is difficult to get lunch or clean water. Lunchrooms either don't serve niggers or serve them at some dirty and ill-attended hole in the wall. As for toilet rooms—don't! If you have to change cars, be wary of junctions which are usually without accommodation and filled with quarrelsome white persons who hate a "darky dressed up." You are apt to have the company of a sheriff and a couple of meek or sullen black prisoners on part of your way and dirty colored section hands will pour in toward night and drive you to the smallest corner.

"No," said the little lady in the corner (she looked like an ivory cameo and her dress flowed on her like a caress) "We don't travel much."

Pessimism is cowardice. The man who cannot frankly acknowledge the "Jim-Crow" car as a fact and yet live and hope, is simply afraid either of himself or of the world. There is not in the world a more disgraceful denial of human brotherhood than the "Jim-Crow" car of the southern United States; but, too, just as true, there is nothing more beautiful in the universe than sunset and moonlight on Montego Bay in far Jamaica. And both things are true and both belong to this, our world, and neither can be denied.

High in the tower, where I sit above the loud complaining of the human sea, I know many souls that toss and whirl and pass, but none there are that intrigue me more than the Souls of White Folk.

Of them I am singularly clairvoyant. I see in and through them. I view them from unusual points of vantage. Not as a foreigner do I come, for I am native, not foreign, bone of their thought and flesh of their language. Mine is not the knowledge of the traveler of the colonial composite of dear memories, words and wonder. Nor yet is my knowledge that which servants have of masters, or mass of class, or capitalist of artisan. Rather I see the working of their entrails. I know their thoughts and they know that I know. This knowledge makes them now embarrassed, now furious! They deny my right to live and be and call me misbirth! My word is to them mere bitterness and my soul, pessimism. And yet as they preach and strut and shout and threaten, crouching as they clutch at rags of facts and fancies to hide their nakedness, they go twisting, flying by my tired eyes and I see them ever stripped—ugly, human.

The discovery of personal whiteness among the world's peoples is a very modern thing—a nineteenth and twentieth century matter, indeed. The ancient world would have laughed at such a distinction. The Middle-Age regarded skin color with mild curiosity; and even up into the eighteenth century we were hammering our national manikins into one, great, Universal Man, with fine frenzy which ignored color and race even more than birth.

Today we have changed all that, and the world in a sudden, emotional conversion has discovered that it is white and by that token, wonderful!

As we saw the dead dimly through rifts of battlesmoke and heard faintly the cursings and accusations of blood brothers, we darker men said: This is not Europe gone mad; this is not aberration nor insanity; this is Europe; this seeming Terrible is the real soul of white culture—back of all culture—stripped and visible today. This is where the world has arrived—these dark and awful depths, and not the shining and ineffable heights of which it boasted. Here is wither the might and energy of modern humanity has really gone.

But may not the world cry back at us and ask: "What better thing have you to show? What have you done or would do better than this if you had today the world rule? Paint with all riot of hateful colors the thin skin of European culture—is it not better than any culture that arose in Africa or Asia?"

It is. Of this there is no doubt and never has been; but why is it better? Is it better because Europeans are better, nobler, greater, and more gifted than other folk? It is not. Europe has never produced and never will in our day bring forth a single human soul who cannot be matched and overmatched in every line of human endeavor by Asia and Africa. Run the gamut, if you will, and let us have the Europeans who in sober truth overmatch Nefertari, Mohammed, Rameses, and Askea, Confucius, Buddha, and Jesus Christ. If we could scan the calendar of thousands of lesser men, in like comparison, the result would be the same; but we cannot do this because of the deliberately educated ignorance of white schools by which they remember Napoleon and forget Sonni Ali.

Why, then, is Europe great? Because of the foundations which the mighty past have furnished her to build upon: the iron trade of ancient, black Africa, the religion and empire-building of yellow Asia, the art and science of the "dago" Mediterranean shore, east, south, and west, as well as north. And where she has builded securely upon this great past and learned from it, she has gone forward to greater and more splendid human triumph; but where she has ignored this past and forgotten and sneered at it, she has shown the cloven hoof of poor, crucified humanity—she has played, like other empires gone, the world fool!

AFRO-AMERICAN PAST—
HISTORY AND FOLK TRADITION

It was assumed that if Afro-Americans were to have an art and literature of distinctiveness and character, and if blacks were to achieve the self-respect that would be essential to winning equality in America, they would have to reconstruct and use their history and folk tradition. It would be no easy task. The most striking thing about the Afro-American's past was that he had been a slave in "the land of the free." It would seem that little pride could be drawn from that. Furthermore, the schools and universities of the United States—where national and ethnic histories and myths were spawned and nurtured—found little interest in the story of black Americans. From the colonial period, there had been sporadic efforts on the part of blacks to tell their story to one another and to the world. In 1915, with the founding of the Association for the Study of Negro Life and History by Carter G. Woodson, and with the publication of that association's Journal of Negro History, *this long-lived wish acquired an institutional means for fulfillment. Like Woodson, Arthur A. Schomburg, one of whose essays appears here, was a major figure in the establishment of a basis and resource for the study of Afro-American history. Schomburg, a bibliophile and collector of books, managed in his life to gather one of the great collections of books and materials on African and Afro-American subjects. The Schomburg Collection is now a part of the New York Public Library.*

Like history, a folk tradition also gives one a sense of place and value. But for a people struggling to demonstrate their urbanity and sophistication, a peasant and folk tradition could be seen with ambivalence. Thus, Harlemites were not always comfortable with spirituals, the blues, and other such products of a country-folk's imagination. Zora Neale Hurston, a student of anthropology at Columbia University, had an exceptional "feel" for the Afro-American folk idiom. If one were to search for a distinctive Afro-American culture, one would have to begin as Zora Neale Hurston did, by defining what is characteristic in "Negro Expression."

THE NEGRO DIGS UP HIS PAST
ARTHUR A. SCHOMBURG

The American Negro must remake his past in order to make his future. Though it is orthodox to think of America as the one country where it is unnecessary to have a past, what is a luxury for the nation as a whole becomes a prime social necessity for the Negro. For him, a group tradition must supply compensation for persecution, and pride of race the antidote for prejudice. History must restore what slavery took away, for it is the social damage of slavery that the present generations must repair and offset. So among the rising democratic millions we find the Negro thinking more collectively, more retrospectively than the rest, and apt, out of the very pressure of the present, to become the most enthusiastic antiquarian of them all.

Vindicating evidences of individual achievement have as a matter of fact been gathered and treasured for over a century: Abbé Grégoire's liberal-minded book on Negro notables in 1808 was the pioneer effort; it has been followed at intervals by less-known and often less-discriminating compendiums of exceptional men and women of African stock. But this sort of thing was on the whole pathetically over-corrective, ridiculously over-laudatory; it was apologetics turned into biography. A true historical sense develops slowly and with difficulty under such circumstances. But to-day, even if for the ultimate purpose of group justification, history has become less a matter of argument and more a matter of record. There is the definite desire and determination to have a history, well-documented, widely known at least within race circles, and administered as a stimulating and inspiring tradition for the coming generations.

Gradually, as the study of the Negro's past has come out of the vagaries of rhetoric and propaganda and become systematic and scientific, three outstanding conclusions have been established:

First, that the Negro has been, throughout the centuries of controversy, an active collaborator, and often a pioneer, in the struggle for his own freedom and advancement. This is true to a degree which makes it the more surprising that it has not been recognized earlier.

Second, that by virtue of their being regarded as something "exceptional," even by friends and well-wishers, Negroes of attainment and genius have been unfairly disassociated from the group, and group credit lost accordingly.

Third, that the remote racial origins of the Negro, far from being what the race and the world have been given to understand, offer a record of credible group achievement, when scientifically viewed, and more important still, that they are of vital general interest because of their bearing upon the beginnings and early development of culture.

With such crucial truths to document and establish, an ounce of fact is worth a pound of controversy. So the Negro historian to-day digs under the spot where his predecessor stood and argued. Not long ago, the Public

Library of Harlem housed a special exhibition of books, pamphlets, prints and old engravings, that simply said, to skeptic and believer alike, to scholar and school-child, to proud black and astonished white, "Here is the evidence." Assembled from the rapidly growing collections of the leading Negro book-collectors and research societies, there were in these cases, materials not only for the first true writing of Negro history, but for the rewriting of many important paragraphs of our common American history. Slow though it be, historical truth is no exception to the proverb.

Here among the rarities of early Negro Americana was Jupiter Hammon's "Address to the Negroes of the State of New York," edition of 1787, with the first American Negro poet's famous: "If we should ever get to Heaven, we shall find nobody to reproach us for being black, or for being slaves." Here was Phyllis Wheatley's MSS. poem of 1767, addressed to the students of Harvard, her spirited encomiums upon George Washington and the Revolutionary Cause, and John Marrant's St. John's Day eulogy to the "Brothers of African Lodge, No. 459," delivered at Boston in 1784. Here, too, were Lemuel Haynes' Vermont commentaries on the American Revolution and his learned sermons to his white congregation in Rutland, Vermont, and the sermons of the year 1808 by the Rev. Absalom Jones of St. Thomas Church, Philadelphia, and Peter Williams of St. Philip's, New York, pioneer Episcopal rectors who spoke out in daring and influential ways on the Abolition of the Slave Trade. Such things and many others are more than mere items of curiosity: they educate any receptive mind.

Reinforcing these were still rarer items of Africana and foreign Negro interest, the volumes of Juan Latino, the best Latinist of Spain in the reign of Philip V, incumbent of the chair of Poetry at the University of Granada, and author of Poems printed in Granada, 1573, and a book on the Escurial, published 1576; the Latin and Dutch treatises of Jacobus Eliza Capitein, a native of West Coast Africa and graduate of the University of Leyden; Gustavus Vassa's celebrated autobiography that supplied so much of the evidence in 1796 for Granville Sharpe's attack on slavery in the British colonies, Julien Raymond's Paris exposé of the disabilities of the free people of color in the then (1791) French colony of Hayti, and Baron de Vastey's *Cry of the Fatherland,* the famous polemic by the secretary of Christophe that precipitated the Haytian struggle for independence. The cumulative effect of such evidences of scholarship and moral prowess is too weighty to be dismissed as exceptional.

But weightier surely than any evidence of individual talent and scholarship could ever be, is the evidence of important collaboration and significant pioneer initiative in social service and reform, in the efforts toward race emancipation, colonization, and race betterment. From neglected and rust-spotted pages comes testimony to the black men and women who stood shoulder to shoulder in courage and zeal, and often on a parity of intelligence and talent, with their notable white benefactors. There was the already cited work of Vassa that aided so materially the efforts of Granville Sharpe, the record of Paul Cuffee, the Negro colonization pioneer, associated so importantly with the establishment of Sierra Leone as a British colony for the occupancy of free people of color in West Africa; the dramatic and history-making exposé of John Baptist Phillips, African graduate of Edinburgh, who compelled, through Lord Bathhurst, in 1824, the enforcement of the articles of capitulation guaranteeing freedom to the blacks of Trinidad. There is the record of the pioneer colonization project of Rev. Daniel Coker in conducting a voyage of ninety expatriates to West Africa in 1820, of the missionary efforts of Samuel Crowther in Sierra Leone, first Anglican bishop of his diocese, and that of the work of John Russwurm, a leader in the work and foundation of the American Colonization Society.

When we consider the facts, certain chapters of American history will have to be reopened. Just as black men were influential factors in the campaign against the slave trade, so they were among the earliest instigators of the abolition movement. Indeed, there was a dangerous calm between the agitation for the suppression of the slave trade and the beginning of the campaign for emancipation. During that interval colored men were very influential in arousing the attention of public men who in turn aroused the conscience of the country. Continuously between 1808 and 1845, men like Prince Saunders, Peter Williams, Absalom Jones, Nathaniel Paul, and Bishops Varick and Richard Allen, the founders of the two wings of African Methodism, spoke out with force and initiative and men like Denmark Vesey (1822), David Walker (1828), and Nat Turner (1831) advocated and organized schemes for direct action. This culminated in the generally ignored but important conventions of Free People of Color in New York, Philadelphia, and other centers, whose platforms and efforts are to the Negro of as great significance as the nationally cherished memories of Faneuil and Independence Halls. Then with Abolition comes the better-documented and more recognized collaboration of Samuel R. Ward, William Wells Brown, Henry Highland Garnett, Martin Delaney, Harriet Tubman, Sojourner Truth, and Frederick Douglass, with their great colleagues, Tappan, Phillips, Sumner, Mott, Stowe and Garrison.

But even this latter group who came within the limelight of national and international notice, and thus into open comparison with the best minds of their generation, the public too often regards as a group of inspired illiterates, eloquent echoes of their abolitionist sponsors. For a true estimate of their ability and scholarship, however, one must go with the antiquarian to the files of the *Anglo-African Magazine*, where page by page comparisons may be made. Their writings show Douglass, McCune Smith, Wells Brown, Delaney, Wilmot Blyden, and Alexander Crummell to have been as scholarly and versatile as any of the noted publicists with whom they were associated. All of them labored internationally in the cause of their fellows; to Scotland, England, France, Germany, and Africa, they carried their brilliant offensive of debate and propaganda, and with this came instance upon instance of signal foreign recognition, from academic, scientific, public and official sources. Delaney's *Principia of Ethnology* won public reception from learned societies, Penington's discourses an honorary doctorate from Heidelberg, Wells Brown's three-year mission the entrée to the salons of London and Paris, and Douglass' tours, receptions second only to Henry Ward Beecher's.

After this great era of public interest and discussion, it was Alexander Crummell, who, with the reaction already setting in, first organized Negro brains defensively through the founding of the American Negro Academy in 1874 at Washington. A New York boy whose zeal for education had suffered a rude shock when refused admission to the Episcopal Seminary by Bishop Onderdonk, he had been befriended by John Jay and sent to Cambridge University, England, for his education and ordination. On his return, he was beset with the idea of promoting race scholarship, and the Academy was the final result. It has continued ever since to be one of the bulwarks of our intellectual life, though unfortunately its members have had to spend too much of their energy and effort answering detractors and disproving popular fallacies. Only gradually have the men of this group been able to work toward pure scholarship. Taking a slightly different start, the Negro Society for Historical Research was later organized in New York, and has succeeded in stimulating the collection from all parts of the world of books and documents dealing with the Negro. It has also brought together for the first time cooperatively in a single society African, West Indian, and Afro-American scholars. Direct offshoots of this same effort are the extensive private collections of Henry P. Slaughter of Washington, the Rev. Charles D. Martin of Harlem, of Arthur Schomburg of Brooklyn, and of the late John E. Bruce, who was the enthusiastic and far-seeing pioneer of this movement. Finally, and more recently, the Association for the Study of Negro Life and History has extended these efforts into a scientific research project of great achievement and promise. Under the direction of Dr. Carter G. Woodson, it has continuously maintained, for nine years, the publication of the learned quarterly, *The Journal of Negro History,* and with the assistance and recognition of two large educational foundations has maintained research and published valuable monographs in Negro history. Almost keeping pace with the work of scholarship has been the effort to popularize the results, and to place before Negro youth in the schools the true story of race vicissitude, struggle and accomplishment. So that quite largely now the ambition of Negro youth can be nourished on its own milk.

Such work is a far cry from the puerile controversy and petty braggadocio with which the effort for race history first started. But a general, as well as a racial, lesson has been learned. We seem lately to have come at last to realize what the truly scientific attitude requires, and to see that the race issue has been a plague on both our historical houses, and that history cannot be properly written with either bias or counterbias. The blatant Caucasian racialist with his theories and assumptions of race superiority and dominance has in turn bred his Ethiopian counterpart—the rash and rabid amateur who has glibly tried to prove half of the world's geniuses to have been Negroes and to trace the pedigree of nineteenth-century Americans from the Queen of Sheba. But fortunately to-day there is on both sides of a really common cause less of the sand of controversy and more of the dust of digging.

Of course, a racial motive remains—legitimately compatible with scientific method and aim. The work our race students now regard as important, they undertake very naturally to overcome in part certain handicaps of disparagement and omission too well known to particularize. But they do so not merely that we may not wrongfully be deprived of the spiritual nourishment of our cultural past, but also that the full story of human collaboration and interdependence may be told and realized. Especially is this likely to be the effect of the latest and most fascinating of all of the attempts to open up the closed Negro past, namely, the important study of African cultural origins and sources. The bigotry of civilization, which is the taproot of intellectual prejudice, begins far back and must be corrected at its source. Fundamentally, it has come about from that depreciation of Africa which has sprung up from ignorance of her true rôle and position in human history and the early development of culture. The Negro has been a man without a history because he has been considered a man without a worthy culture. But a new notion of the cultural attainment and potentialities of the African stocks has recently come about, partly through the corrective influence of the more scientific study of African institutions and early cultural history, partly through growing appreciation of the skill and beauty, and in many cases, the historical priority of the African native crafts, and finally, through the signal recognition which first in France and Germany but now very generally, the astonishing art of the African sculptures has received. Into these fascinating new vistas, with limited horizons lifting in all directions, the mind of the Negro has leapt forward faster than the slow clearings of scholarship will yet safely permit. But there is no doubt that here is a field full of the most intriguing and inspiring possibilities. Already the Negro sees himself against a reclaimed background, in a perspective that will give pride and self-respect ample scope, and make history yield for him the same values that the treasured past of any people affords.

SONG OF THE SON
JEAN TOOMER

Pour O pour that parting soul in song
O pour it in the sawdust glow of night,
Into the velvet pine-smoke air to-night,
And let the valley carry it along.
And let the valley carry it along.

O land and soil, red soil and sweet-gum tree,
So scant of grass, so profligate of pines,
Now just before an epoch's sun declines

Thy son, in time, I have returned to thee,
Thy son, I have in time returned to thee.

In time, for though the sun is setting on
A song-lit race of slaves, it has not set;
Though late, O soil, it is not too late yet
To catch thy plaintive soul, leaving, soon gone,
Leaving, to catch thy plaintive soul soon gone.

O Negro slaves, dark purple ripened plums,
Squeezed, and bursting in the pine-wood air,
Passing, before they stripped the old tree bare
One plum was saved for me, one seed becomes
an everlasting song, a singing tree,
Caroling softly souls of slavery,
What they were, and what they are to me,
Caroling softly souls of slavery.

FIFTY YEARS (1863–1913)
JAMES WELDON JOHNSON

*On the Fiftieth Anniversary of the Signing
of the Emancipation Proclamation*

O brothers mine, today we stand
   Where half a century sweeps our ken,
Since God, through Lincoln's ready hand,
   Struck off our bonds and made us men.

Just fifty years—a winter's day—
   As runs the history of a race;
Yet, as we look back o'er the way,
   How distant seems our starting place!

Look farther back! Three centuries!
   To where a naked, shivering score,
Snatched from their haunts across the seas,
   Stood, wild-eyed, on Virginia's shore.
      .   .   .   .   .

For never let the thought arise
   That we are here on sufferance bare;
Outcasts, asylumed 'neath these skies,
   And aliens without part or share.

222

This land is ours by right of birth,
   This land is ours by right of toil;
We helped to turn its virgin earth,
   Our sweat is in its fruitful soil.

Where once the tangled forest stood—
   Where flourished once rank weed and thorn—
Behold the path-traced, peaceful wood,
   The cotton white, the yellow corn.

To gain these fruits that have been earned,
   To hold these fields that have been won,
Our arms have strained, our backs have burned
   Bent bare beneath a ruthless sun.

That Banner which is now the type
   Of victory on field and flood—
Remember, its first crimson stripe
   Was dyed by Attucks' willing blood.

And never yet has come the cry—
   When that fair flag has been assailed—
For men to do, for men to die,
   That we have faltered or have failed.

We've helped to bear it, rent and torn,
   Through many a hot-breath'd battle breeze
Held in our hands, it has been borne
   And planted far across the seas.

And never yet—O haughty Land
   Let us, at least, for this be praised—
Has one black, treason-guided hand
   Ever against that flag been raised.

Then should we speak but servile words,
   Or shall we hang our heads in shame?
Stand back of new-come foreign hordes,
   And fear our heritage to claim?

No! stand erect and without fear,
   And for our foes let this suffice—
We've bought a rightful sonship here,
   And we have more than paid the price.

And yet, my brothers, well I know
  The tethered feet, the pinioned wings,
The spirit bowed beneath the blow,
  The heart grown faint from wounds and stings;

The staggering force of brutish might,
  That strikes and leaves us stunned and dazed;
The long, vain waiting through the night
  To hear some voice for justice raised.

Full well I know the hour when hope
  Sinks dead, and round us everywhere
Hangs stifling darkness, and we grope
  With hands uplifted in despair.

Courage! Look out, beyond, and see
  The far horizon's beckoning span!
Faith in your God-known destiny!
  We are a part of some great plan.

Because the tongues of Garrison
  And Phillips now are cold in death,
Think you their work can be undone?
  Or quenched the fires lit by their breath?

Think you that John Brown's spirit stops?
  That Lovejoy was but idly slain?
Or do you think those precious drops
  From Lincoln's heart were shed in vain?

That for which millions prayed and sighed,
  That for which tens of thousands fought,
For which so many freely died,
  God cannot let it come to naught.

CHARACTERISTICS OF NEGRO EXPRESSION
ZORA NEALE HURSTON

Drama

The Negro's universal mimicry is not so much a thing in itself as an evidence of something that permeates his entire self. And that thing is drama.

His very words are action words. His interpretation of the English language is in terms of pictures. One act described in terms of another. Hence the rich metaphor and simile.

The metaphor is of course very primitive. It is easier to illustrate than it is to explain because action came before speech. Let us make a parallel. Language is like money. In primitive communities actual goods, however bulky, are bartered for what one wants. This finally evolves into coin, the coin being not real wealth but a symbol of wealth. Still later even coin is abandoned for legal tender, and still later for cheques in certain usages.

Every phase of Negro life is highly dramatised. No matter how joyful or how sad the case there is sufficient poise for drama. Everything is acted out. Unconsciously for the most part of course. There is an impromptu ceremony always ready for every hour of life. No little moment passes unadorned.

Now the people with highly developed languages have words for detached ideas. That is legal tender. "That-which-we-squat-on" has become "chair." "Groan-causer" has evolved into "spear" and so on. Some individuals even conceive of the equivalent of cheque words, like "ideation" and "pleonastic." Perhaps we might say that *Paradise Lost* and *Sartor Resartus* are written in cheque words.

The primitive man exchanges descriptive words. His terms are all close fitting. Frequently the Negro, even with detached words in his vocabulary—not evolved in him but transplanted on his tongue by contact—must add action to it to make it do. So we have "chop-axe," "sitting-chair," "cook-pot" and the like because the speaker has in his mind the picture of the object in use. Action. Everything illustrated. So we can say the white man thinks in a written language and the Negro thinks in hieroglyphics.

A bit of Negro drama familiar to all is the frequent meeting of two opponents who threaten to do atrocious murder one upon the other.

Who has not observed a robust young Negro chap posing upon a street corner, possessed of nothing but his clothing, his strength and his youth? Does he bear himself like a pauper? No, Louis XIV could be no more insolent in his assurance. His eyes say plainly "Female, halt!" His posture exults "Ah, female, I am the eternal male, the giver of life. Behold in my hot flesh all the delights of this world. Salute me, I am strength." All this with a languid posture, there is no mistaking his meaning.

A Negro girl strolls past the corner lounger. Her whole body panging [1] and posing. A slight shoulder movement that calls attention to her bust, that is all of a dare. A hippy undulation below the waist that is a sheaf of promises tied with conscious power. She is acting out "I'm a darned sweet woman and you know it."

These little plays by strolling players are acted out daily in a dozen streets in a thousand cities, and no one ever mistakes the meaning.

Will To Adorn

The will to adorn is the second most notable characteristic in Negro expression. Perhaps his idea of ornament does not attempt to meet conventional standards, but it satisfies the soul of its creator.

1. From "pang."

In this respect the American Negro has done wonders to the English language. It has often been stated by etymologists that the Negro has introduced no African words to the language. This is true, but it is equally true that he has made over a great part of the tongue to his liking and has his revision accepted by the ruling class. No one listening to a Southern white man talk could deny this. Not only has he softened and toned down strongly consonanted words like "aren't" to "aint" and the like, he has made new force words out of old feeble elements. Examples of this are "ham-shanked," "battle-hammed," "double-teen," "bodaciously," "muffle-jawed."

But the Negro's greatest contribution to the language is: (1) the use of metaphor and simile; (2) the use of the double descriptive; (3) the use of verbal nouns.

1. Metaphor and Simile

One at a time, like lawyers going to heaven.
That's a rope.
You sho is propaganda.
Cloakers—deceivers.
Sobbing hearted.
Regular as pig-tracks.
I'll beat you till: (a) rope like okra, (b) slack like lime, (c) smell like onions.
Mule blood—black molasses.
Fatal for naked.
Syndicating—gossiping.
Kyting along.
Flambeaux—cheap café (lighted by flambeaux).
That's a lynch.
To put yo'self on de ladder.

2. The Double Descriptive

High-tall.
Hot-boiling.
Little-tee-ninchy (tiny).
Chop-axe.
Low-down.
Sitting-chairs.
Top-superior.
De watch wall.
Sham-polish.
Speedy-hurry.
Lady-people.
More great and more better.
Kill-dead.

3. Verbal Nouns

She features somebody I know.
Jooking—playing piano or guitar as it is done in Jook-houses (houses of ill-fame).
Funeralize.
Sense me into it.
Puts the shamery on him.
Uglying away.
'Taint everybody you kin confidence.
I wouldn't scorn my name all up on you.
I wouldn't friend with her.
Bookooing (beaucoup) around—showing off.

Nouns from Verbs

Won't stand a broke.
That is such a compliment.
She won't take a listen.
That's a lynch.
He won't stand straightening.

The stark, trimmed phrases of the Occident seem too bare for the voluptuous child of the sun, hence the adornment. It arises out of the same impulse as the wearing of jewelry and the making of sculpture—the urge to adorn.

On the walls of the homes of the average Negro one always finds a glut of gaudy calendars, wall pockets and advertising lithographs. The sophisticated white man or Negro would tolerate none of these, even if they bore a likeness to the Mona Lisa. No commercial art for decoration. Nor the calendar nor the advertisement spoils the picture for this lowly man. He sees the beauty in spite of the declaration of the Portland Cement Works or the butcher's announcement. I saw in Mobile a room in which there was an over-stuffed mohair living-room suite, an imitation mahogany bed and chifferobe, a console victrola. The walls were gaily papered with Sunday supplements of the *Mobile Register*. There were seven calendars and three wall pockets. One of them was decorated with a lace doily. The mantel-shelf was covered with a scarf of deep home-made lace, looped up with a huge bow of pink crêpe paper. Over the door was a huge lithograph showing the Treaty of Versailles being signed with a Waterman fountain pen.

It was grotesque, yes. But it indicated the desire for beauty. And decorating a decoration, as in the case of the doily on the gaudy wall pocket, did not seem out of place to the hostess. The feeling back of such an act is that there can never be enough of beauty, let alone too much. Perhaps she is right. We each have our standards of art, and thus are we all interested parties and so unfit to pass judgment upon the art concepts of others.

Whatever the Negro does of his own volition he embellishes. His religious service is for the greater part excellent prose poetry. Both prayers and sermons are tooled and polished until they are true works of art. The supplication is forgotten in the frenzy of creation. The prayer of the white man is considered humorous in its bleakness. The beauty of the Old Testament does not exceed that of a Negro prayer.

Angularity

After adornment the next most striking manifestation of the Negro is Angularity. Everything that he touches becomes angular. In all African sculpture and doctrine of any sort we find the same thing.

Anyone watching Negro dancers will be struck by the same phenomenon. Every posture is another angle. Pleasing, yes. But an effect achieved by the very means which an European strives to avoid.

The pictures on the walls are hung at deep angles. Furniture is always set at an angle. I have instances of a piece of furniture in the *middle* of a wall being set with one end nearer the wall than the other to avoid the simple straight line.

Asymmetry

Asymmetry is a definite feature of Negro art. I have no samples of true Negro painting unless we count the African shields, but the sculpture and carvings are full of this beauty and lack of symmetry.

It is present in the literature, both prose and verse. I offer an example of this quality in verse from Langston Hughes:

> I aint gonna mistreat ma good gal any more,
> I'm just gonna kill her next time she makes me sore.
>
> I treats her kind but she don't do me right,
> She fights and quarrels most ever' night.
>
> I can't have no woman's got such low-down ways
> Cause de blue gum woman aint de style now'days.
>
> I brought her from the South and she's goin on back,
> Else I'll use her head for a carpet track.

It is the lack of symmetry which makes Negro dancing so difficult for white dancers to learn. The abrupt and unexpected changes. The frequent change of key and time are evidences of this quality in music (Note the St. Louis Blues.)

The dancing of the justly famous Bo-Jangles and Snake Hips are excellent examples.

The presence of rhythm and lack of symmetry are paradoxical, but there they are. Both are present to a marked degree. There is always rhythm, but it is the rhythm of segments. Each unit has a rhythm of its own, but when the whole is assembled it is lacking in symmetry. But easily workable to a Negro who is accustomed to the break in going from one part to another, so that he adjusts himself to the new tempo.

Dancing

Negro dancing is dynamic suggestion. No matter how violent it may appear to the beholder, every posture gives the impression that the dancer will do much more. For example, the performer flexes one knee sharply, assumes a ferocious face mask, thrusts the upper part of the body forward with clenched fists, elbows taut as in hard running or grasping a thrusting blade. That is all. But the spectator himself adds the picture of ferocious assault, hears the drums and finds himself keeping time with the music and tensing himself for the struggle. It is compelling insinuation. That is the very reason the spectator is held so rapt. He is participating in the performance himself—carrying out the suggestions of the performer.

The difference in the two arts is: the white dancer attempts to express fully; the Negro is restrained, but succeeds in gripping the beholder by forcing him to finish the action the performer suggests. Since no art ever can express all the variations conceivable, the Negro must be considered the greater artist, his dancing is realistic suggestion, and that is about all a great artist can do.

Negro Folklore

Negro folklore is not a thing of the past. It is still in the making. Its great variety shows the adaptability of the black man: nothing is too old or too new, domestic or foreign, high or low, for his use. God and the Devil are paired, and are treated no more reverently than Rockefeller and Ford. Both of these men are prominent in folklore, Ford being particularly strong, and they talk and act like good-natured stevedores or mill-hands. Ole Massa is sometimes a smart man and often a fool. The automobile is ranged alongside of the ox-cart. The angels and the apostles walk and talk like section hands. And through it all walks Jack, the greatest culture hero of the South; Jack beats them all—even the Devil, who is often smarter than God.

Culture Heroes

The Devil is next after Jack as a culture hero. He can out-smart everyone but Jack. God is absolutely no match for him. He is good-natured and full of humour. The sort of person one may count on to help out in any difficulty.

Peter the Apostle is the third in importance. One need not look far for the explanation. The Negro is not a Christian really. The primitive gods are not deities of too subtle inner reflection; they are hard-working bodies who serve their devotees just as laboriously as the suppliant serves them. Gods of physical violence, stopping at nothing to serve their followers. Now of all the apostles Peter is the most active. When the other ten fell back trembling in the garden, Peter wielded the blade on the posse. Peter first and foremost in all action. The gods of no peoples have been philosophic until the people themselves have approached that state.

The rabbit, the bear, the lion, the buzzard, the fox are culture heroes from the animal world. The rabbit is far in the lead of all the others and is blood brother to Jack. In short, the trickster-hero of West Africa has been transplanted to America.

John Henry is a culture hero in song, but no more so than Stacker Lee, Smokey Joe or Bad Lazarus. There are many, many Negroes who have never heard of any of the song heroes, but none who do not know John (Jack) and the rabbit.

Examples of Folklore and the Modern Culture Hero
Why de Porpoise's Tail is on Crosswise

Now, I want to tell you 'bout de porpoise. God had done made de world and everything. He set de moon and de stars in de sky. He got de fishes of de sea, and de fowls of de air completed.

He made de sun and hung it up. Then He made a nice gold track for it to run on. Then He said, "Now, Sun, I got everything made but Time. That's up to you. I want you to start out and go round de world on dis track just as fast as you kin make it. And de time it takes you to go and come, I'm going to call day and night." De Sun went zoonin' on cross de elements. Now, de porpoise was hanging round there and heard

God what he told de Sun, so he decided he'd take dat trip round de world hisself. He looked up and saw de Sun kytin' along, so he lit out too, him and dat Sun!

So de porpoise beat de Sun round de world by one hour and three minutes. So God said, "Aw naw, this aint gointer do! I didn't mean for nothin' to be faster than de Sun!" So God run dat porpoise for three days before he run him down and caught him, and took his tail off and put it on crossways to slow him up. Still he's de fastest thing in de water.

And dat's why de porpoise got his tail on crossways.

Rockefeller and Ford

Once John D. Rockefeller and Henry Ford was woofing at each other. Rockefeller told Henry Ford he could build a solid gold road round the world. Henry Ford told him if he would he would look at it and see if he liked it, and if he did he would buy it and put one of his tin lizzies on it.

Originality

It has been said so often that the Negro is lacking in originality that it has almost become a gospel. Outward signs seem to bear this out. But if one looks closely its falsity is immediately evident.

It is obvious that to get back to original sources is much too difficult for any group to claim very much as a certainty. What we really mean by originality is the modification of ideas. The most ardent admirer of the great Shakespeare cannot claim first source even for him. It is his treatment of the borrowed material.

So if we look at it squarely, the Negro is a very original being. While he lives and moves in the midst of a white civilisation, everything that he touches is re-interpreted for his own use. He has modified the language, mode of food preparation, practice of medicine, and most certainly the religion of his new country, just as he adapted to suit himself the Sheik haircut made famous by Rudolph Valentino.

Everyone is familiar with the Negro's modification of the whites' musical instruments, so that his interpretation has been adopted by the white man himself and then re-interpreted. In so many words, Paul Whiteman is giving an imitation of a Negro orchestra making use of white-invented musical instruments in a Negro way. Thus has arisen a new art in the civilised world, and thus has our so-called civilisation come. The exchange and re-exchange of ideas between groups.

Imitation

The Negro, the world over, is famous as a mimic. But this in no way damages his standing as an original. Mimicry is an art in itself. If it is not, then all art must fall by the same blow that strikes it down. When sculpture, painting, dancing, literature neither reflect nor suggest anything in nature or human experience we turn away with a dull wonder in our hearts at why the thing was done. Moreover, the contention that the Negro imitates from a feeling of inferiority is incorrect. He mimics for the love of it. The group of Negroes who slavishly imitate is small. The average Negro glories in his ways. The highly educated Negro the same. The self-despisement lies in a middle class who scorns to do or be anything Negro. "That's just like a Nigger" is the most terrible rebuke one can lay upon this kind. He wears drab clothing, sits through a boresome church service, pretends to have no interest in the community, holds beauty contests, and otherwise apes all the mediocrities of the white brother. The truly cultured Negro scorns him, and the Negro "farthest down" is too busy "spreading his junk" in his own way to see or care. He likes his own things best. Even the group who are not Negroes but belong to the "sixth race," buy such records as "Shake dat thing" and "Tight lak dat." They really enjoy hearing a good bible-beater preach, but wild horses could drag no such admission from them. Their ready-made expression is: "We done got away from all that now." Some refuse to countenance Negro music on the grounds that it is niggerism, and for that reason should be done away with. Roland Hayes was thoroughly denounced for singing spirituals until he was accepted by white audiences. Langston Hughes is not considered a poet by this group because he writes of the man in the ditch, who is more numerous and real among us than any other.

But, this group aside, let us say that the art of mimicry is better developed in the Negro than in other racial groups. He does it as the mocking-bird does it, for the love of it, and not because he wishes to be like the one imitated. I saw a group of small Negro boys imitating a cat defecating and the subsequent toilet of the cat. It was very realistic, and they enjoyed it as much as if they had been imitating a coronation ceremony. The dances are full of imitations of various animals. The buzzard lope, walking the dog, the pig's hind legs, holding the mule, elephant squat, pigeon's wing, falling off the log, seabord (imitation of an engine starting), and the like.

Absence of the Concept of Privacy

It is said that Negroes keep nothing secret, that they have no reserve. This ought not to seem strange when one considers that we are an outdoor people accustomed to communal life. Add this to all-permeating drama and you have the explanation.

There is no privacy in an African village. Loves, fights, possessions are, to misquote Woodrow Wilson, "Open disagreements openly arrived at." The community is given the benefit of a good fight as well as a good wedding. An audience is a necessary part of any drama. We merely go with nature rather than against it.

Discord is more natural than accord. If we accept the doctrine of the survival of the fittest there are more fighting honors than there are honors for other achievements. Humanity places premiums on all things necessary to its well-being, and a valiant and good fighter is valuable in any community. So why hide the light under a bushel? Moreover, intimidation is a recognised part of warfare the world over, and threats certainly must be listed under that head. So that a great threatener must certainly be considered an aid to the fighting machine. So then if a man or woman is a facile hurler of threats, why should he or she not show their wares to the community? Hence the holding of all quarrels and fights in the open. One relieves one's pent-up anger and at the same time earns laurels in intimidation. Besides, one does the community a service. There is nothing so exhilarating as watching well-matched opponents go into action. The entire world likes action, for that matter. Hence prize-fighters become millionaires.

Likewise love-making is a biological necessity the world over and an art among Negroes. So that a man or woman who is proficient sees no reason why the fact should not be moot. He swaggers. She struts hippily about. Songs are built on the power to charm beneath the bed-clothes. Here again we have individuals striving to excel in what the community considers an art. Then if all of his world is seeking a great lover, why should he not speak right out loud?

It is all in a view-point. Love-making and fighting in all their branches are high arts, other things are arts among other groups where they brag about their proficiency just as brazenly as we do about these things that others consider matters for conversation behind closed doors. At any rate, the white man is despised by Negroes as a very poor fighter individually, and a very poor lover. One Negro, speaking of white men, said, "White folks is alright when dey gits in de bank and on de law bench, but dey sho' kin lie about wimmen folks."

I pressed him to explain. "Well you see, white mens makes out they marries wimmen to look at they eyes, and they know they gits em for just what us gits em for. 'Nother thing, white mens say they goes clear round de world and wins all de wimmen folks way from they men folks. Dat's a lie too. They don't win nothin, they buys em. Now de way I figgers it, if a woman don't want me enough to be wid me, 'thout I got to pay her, she kin rock right on, but these here white men don't know what do wid a woman when they gits her—dat's how come they gives they wimmen so much. They got to. Us wimmen works jus as hard as us does an come home an sleep wid us every night. They own wouldn't do it and its de mens fault. Dese white men done fooled theyself bout dese wimmen.

"Now me, I keeps me some wimmens all de time. Dat's whut dey wuz put here for—us mens to use. Dat's right now, Miss. Y'll wuz put here so us mens could have some pleasure. Course I don't run round like heap uh men folks. But if my ole lady go way from me and stay more'n two weeks, I got to git me somebody, aint I?"

The Jook

Jook is the word for a Negro pleasure house. It may mean a bawdy house. It may mean the house set apart on public works where the men and women dance, drink and gamble. Often it is a combination of all these.

In past generations the music was furnished by "boxes," another word for guitars. One guitar was enough for a dance; to have two was considered excellent. Where two were playing one man played the lead and the other seconded him. The first player was "picking" and the second was "framming," that is, playing chords while the lead carried the melody by dexterous finger work. Sometimes a third player was added, and he played a tom-tom effect on the low strings. Believe it or not, this is excellent dance music.

Pianos soon came to take the place of the boxes, and now player-pianos and victrolas are in all of the Jooks.

Musically speaking, the Jook is the most important place in America. For in its smelly, shoddy confines has been born the secular music known as blues, and on blues has been founded jazz. The singing and playing in the true Negro style is called "jooking."

The songs grow by incremental repetition as they travel from mouth to mouth and from Jook to Jook for years before they reach outside ears. Hence the great variety of subject-matter in each song.

The Negro dances circulated over the world were also conceived inside the Jooks. They too make the round of Jooks and public works before going into the outside world.

In this respect it is interesting to mention the Black Bottom. I have read several false accounts of its origin and name. One writer claimed that it got its name from the black sticky mud on the bottom of the Mississippi river. Other equally absurd statements gummed the press. Now the dance really originated in the Jook section of Nashville, Tennessee, around Fourth Avenue. This is a tough neighbourhood known as Black Bottom—hence the name.

The Charleston is perhaps forty years old, and was danced up and down the Atlantic seaboard from North Carolina to Key West, Florida.

The Negro social dance is slow and sensuous. The idea in the Jook is to gain sensation, and not so much exercise. So that just enough foot movement is added to keep the dancers on the floor. A tremendous sex stimulation is gained from this. But who is trying to avoid it? The man, the woman, the time and the place have met. Rather, little intimate names are indulged in to heap fire on fire.

These too have spread to all the world.

The Negro theatre, as built up by the Negro, is based on Jook situations, with women, gambling, fighting, drinking. Shows like "Dixie to Broadway" are only Negro in cast, and could just as well have come from pre-Soviet Russia.

Another interesting thing—Negro shows before being tampered with did not specialise in octoroon chorus girls. The girl who could hoist a Jook song from her belly and lam it against the front door of the theatre was the lead, even if she were as black as the hinges of hell. The question was "Can she jook?" She must also have a good belly wobble, and her hips must, to quote a popular work song, "Shake like jelly all over and be so broad, Lawd, Lawd, and be so broad." So that the bleached chorus is the result of a white demand and not the Negro's.

The woman in the Jook may be nappy headed and black, but if she is a good lover she gets there just the same. A favorite Jook song of the past has this to say:

> *Singer:* It aint good looks dat takes you through dis world.
> *Audience:* What is it, good mama?
> *Singer:* Elgin [1] movements in your hips
> Twenty years guarantee.

And it always brought down the house too.

> Oh de white gal rides in a Cadillac,
> De yaller gal rides de same,
> Black gal rides in a rusty Ford
> But she gits dere just de same.

The sort of woman her men idealise is the type that is put forth in the theatre. The art-creating Negro prefers a not too thin woman who can shake like jelly all over as she dances and sings, and that is the type he put forth on the stage. She has been banished by the white producer and the Negro who takes his cue from the white.

Of course a black woman is never the wife of the upper class Negro in the North. This state of affairs does not obtain in the South, however. I have noted numerous cases where the wife was considerably darker than the husband. People of some substance, too.

This scornful attitude towards black women receives mouth sanction by the mud-sills.

Even on the works and in the Jooks the black man sings disparagingly of black women. They say that she is evil. That she sleeps with her fists doubled up and ready for action. All over they are making a little drama of waking up a yaller [2] wife and a black one.

A man is lying beside his yaller wife and wakes her up. She says to him, "Darling, do you know what I was dreaming when you woke me up?" He says, "No honey, what was you dreaming?" She says, "I dreamt I had done cooked you a big, fine dinner and we was setting down to eat out de same plate and I was setting on yo' lap jus huggin you and kissin you and you was so sweet."

Wake up a black woman, and before you kin git any sense into her she be done up and lammed you over the head four or five times. When you git her quiet she'll say, "Nigger, know whut I was dreamin when you woke me up?"

You say, "No honey, what was you dreamin?" She says, "I dreamt you shook yo' rusty fist under my nose and I split yo' head open wid a axe."

But in spite of disparaging fictitious drama, in real life the black girl is drawing on his account at the commissary. Down in the Cypress Swamp as he swings his axe he chants:

> Dat ole black gal, she keep on grumblin,
> New pair shoes, new pair shoes,

1. Elegant (?). [from the Elgin Watch, Ed.]
2. Yaller (yellow), light mulatto.

234

> I'm goint to buy her shoes and stockings
> Slippers too, slippers too.

Then adds aside: "Blacker de berry, sweeter de juice."

To be sure the black gal is still in power, men are still cutting and shooting their way to her pillow. To the queen of the Jook!

Speaking of the influence of the Jook, I noted that Mae West in "Sex" had much more flavor of the turpentine quarters than she did of the white bawd. I know that the piece she played on the piano is a very old Jook composition. "Honey let yo' drawers hang low" had been played and sung in every Jook in the South for at least thirty-five years. It has always puzzled me why she thought it likely to be played in a Canadian bawdy house.

Speaking of the use of Negro material by white performers, it is astonishing that so many are trying it, and I have never seen one yet entirely realistic. They often have all the elements of the song, dance, or expression, but they are misplaced or distorted by the accent falling on the wrong element. Every one seems to think that the Negro is easily imitated when nothing is further from the truth. Without exception I wonder why the black-face comedians *are* black-face; it is a puzzle—good comedians, but darn poor niggers. Gershw and the other "Negro" rhapsodists come under this same axe. Just about as Negro as caviar or Ann Pennington's athletic Black Bottom. When the Negroes who knew the Black Bottom in its cradle saw the Broadway version they asked each other, "Is you learnt dat *new* Black Bottom yet?" Proof that it was not *their* dance.

And God only knows what the world has suffered from the white damsels who try to sing Blues.

The Negroes themselves have sinned also in this respect. In spite of the goings up and down on the earth, from the original Fisk Jubilee Singers down to the present, there has been no genuine presentation of Negro songs to white audiences. The spirituals that have been sung around the world are Negroid to be sure, but so full of musicians' tricks that Negro congregations are highly entertained when they hear their old songs so changed. They never use the new style songs, and these are never heard unless perchance some daughter or son has been off to college and returns with one of the old songs with its face lifted, so to speak.

I am of the opinion that this trick style of delivery was originated by the Fisk Singers; Tuskeegee and Hampton followed suit and have helped spread this misconception of Negro spirituals. This Glee Club style has gone on so long and become so fixed among concert singers that it is considered quite authentic. But I say again, that not one concert signer in the world is singing the songs as the Negro song-makers sing them.

If anyone wishes to prove the truth of this let him step into some unfashionable Negro church and hear for himself.

To those who want to institute the Negro theatre, let me say it is already established. It is lacking in wealth, so it is not seen in the high places. A creature with a white head and Negro feet struts the Metropolitan boards. The real Negro theatre is in the Jooks and the cabarets. Self-conscious individuals may turn away the eye and say, "Let us search elsewhere for our dramatic art." Let 'em search. They certainly won't find it. Butter Beans and Susie, Bo-Jangles and Snake Hips are the only performers of the real Negro school it has ever been my pleasure to behold in New York.

Dialect

If we are to believe the majority of writers of Negro dialect and the burnt-cork artists, Negro speech is a weird thing, full of "ams" and "Ises." Fortunately we don't have to believe them. We may go directly to the Negro and let him speak for himself.

I know that I run the risk of being damned as an infidel for declaring that nowhere can be found the Negro who asks "am it?" nor yet his brother who announces "Ise uh gwinter." He exists only for a certain type of writers and performers.

Very few Negroes, educated or not, use a clear clipped "I." It verges more or less upon "Ah." I think the lip form is responsible for this to a great extent. By experiment the reader will find that a sharp "I" is very much easier with a thin taut lip than with a full soft lip. Like tightening violin strings.

If one listens closely one will note too that a word is slurred in one position in the sentence but clearly pronounced in another. This is particularly true of the pronouns. A pronoun as a subject is likely to be clearly enunciated, but slurred as an object. For example: "You better not let me ketch yuh."

There is a tendency in some localities to add the "h" to "it" and pronounce it "hit." Probably a vestige of old English. In some localities "if" is "ef."

In story telling "so" is universally the connective. It is used even as an introductory word, at the very beginning of a story. In religious expression "and" is used. The trend in stories is to state conclusions; in religion, to enumerate.

I am mentioning only the most general rules in dialect because there are so many quirks that belong only to certain localities that nothing less than a volume would be adequate.

Now He told me, He said: "You got the three witnesses. One is water, one is spirit, and one is blood. And these three correspond with the three in heben—Father, Son and Holy Ghost."
Now I ast Him about this lyin in sin and He give me a handful of seeds and He tole me to sow 'em in a bed and He tole me: "I want you to watch them seeds." The seeds come up about in places and He said: "Those seeds that come up, they died in the heart of the earth and quickened and come up and brought forth fruit. But those seeds that didn't come up, they died in the heart of the earth and rottened.
"And a soul that dies and quickens through my spirit they will live forever, but those that dont never pray, they are lost forever."　　　　　(Rev. JESSIE JEFFERSON.)

SHOUTING
ZORA NEALE HURSTON

There can be little doubt that shouting is a survival of the African "possession" by the gods. In Africa it is sacred to the priesthood or acolytes, in America it has become generalised. The implication is the same, however. It is a sign of special favor from the spirit that it chooses to drive out the individual consciousness temporarily and use the body for its expression.

In every case the person claims ignorance of his actions during the possession.

Broadly speaking, shouting is an emotional explosion, responsive to rhythm. It is called forth by (1) sung rhythm; (2) spoken rhythm; (3) humming rhythm; (4) the foot-patting or hand-clapping that imitates very closely the tom-tom.

The more familiar the expression, the more likely to evoke response. For instance, "I am a soldier of the cross, a follower of the meek and lowly lamb. I want you all to know I am fighting under the blood-stained banner of King Jesus" is more likely to be amen-ed than any flourish a speaker might get off. Perhaps the reason for this is that the hearers can follow the flow of syllables without stirring the brain to grasp the sense. Perhaps it is the same urge that makes a child beg for the same story even though he knows it so well that he can correct his parents if a word is left out.

Shouting is a community thing. It thrives in concert. It is the first shout that is difficult for the preacher to arouse. After that one they are likely to sweep like fire over the church. This is easily understood, for the rhythm is increasing with each shouter who communicated his fervor to someone else.

It is absolutely individualistic. While there are general types of shouting, the shouter may mix the different styles to his liking, or he may express himself in some fashion never seen before.

Women shout more frequently than men. This is not surprising since it is generally conceded that women are more emotional than men.

The shouter always receives attention from the church. Members rush to the shouter and force him into a seat or support him as the case might be. Sometimes it is necessary to restrain him to prevent injury to either the shouter or the persons sitting nearest, or both. Sometimes the arms are swung with such violence that others are knocked down. Sometimes in the ecstasy the shouter climbs upon the pew and kicks violently away at all; sometimes in catalepsis he falls heavily upon the floor and might injure himself if not supported, or fall upon others and wound. Often the person injured takes offense, believing that the shouter was paying off a grudge. Unfortunately this is the case at times, but it is not usual.

There are two main types of shouters: (1) Silent; (2) Vocal. There is a sort of intermediary type where one stage is silent and the other vocal.

The silent type take with violent retching and twitching motions. Sometimes they remain seated, sometimes they jump up and down and fling the body about with great violence. Lips tightly pursed, eyes closed. The seizure ends by collapse.

The vocal type is the more frequent. There are all gradations from quiet weeping while seated, to the unrestrained screaming while leaping pews and running up and down the aisle. Some, unless restrained, run up into the pulpit and embrace the preacher. Some are taken with hysterical laughing spells.

The cases will illustrate the variations.

(1) During sermon. Cried "well, well," six times. Violent action for forty seconds. Collapsed and restored to her seat by members

(2) During chant, Cried "Holy, holy! Great God A'mighty!" Arose and fell in cataleptic fit backwards over pew. Flinging of arms with clenched fists, gradually subsiding to quiet collapse. Total time: two minutes.

(3) During pre-prayer humming chant. Short screams. Violent throwing of arms. Incoherent speech. Total time: one minute thirty seconds.

(4) During sermon. One violent shout as she stood erect: two seconds. Voiceless gestures for twenty-nine seconds. She suddenly resumed her seat and her attention to the words of the preacher.

(5) During sermon. One single loud scream: one and one-half seconds.

(6) During singing. Violent jumping up and down without voice. Pocket book cast away. Time: one minute forty seconds.

(7) During prayer. Screaming: one second. Violent shoulder-shaking, hat discarded: nineteen seconds.

(8) During sermon. Cataleptic. Stiffly back over the pew. Violent but voiceless for twenty seconds. Then arms stiff and outstretched, palms open stark and up. Collapse. Time: three minutes.

(9) During sermon. Young girl. Running up and down the aisle: thirty seconds. Then silence and rush to the pulpit: fourteen seconds; prevented at the altar rail by deacon. Collapse in the deacon's arms and returned to seat. Total time: one minute fifteen seconds.

(10) During chant after prayer. Violent screams: twelve seconds. Scrambles upon pew and steps upon the back of pew still screaming: five seconds. Voiceless struggle with set teeth as three men attempt to restore her to seat. She is lifted horizontal but continues struggle: one minute forty-eight seconds. Decreasing violence, making ferocious faces: two minutes. Calm with heavy breathing: twenty-one seconds.

(11) During sermon. Man quietly weeping: nineteen seconds. Cried "Lawd! My soul is burning with hallow-ed fire!" Rises and turns round and round six times. Carried outside by the deacons.

(12) During sermon. Man jumping wildly up and down flat-footed crying "Hallelujah!": twenty-two seconds. Pulled back into his seat. Muscular twitching: one minute thirty-five seconds. Quiet weeping: one minute. Perfect calm.

THE SERMON
AS HEARD BY ZORA NEALE HURSTON
FROM C. C. LOVELACE,
AT EAU GALLIE IN FLORIDA, MAY 3, 1929

Introduction (spoken)

"Our theme this morning is the wounds of Jesus. When the father shall ast, 'What are these wounds in thine hand?' He shall answer, 'Those are they with which I was wounded in the house of my friends.' (Zach, xiii, 6.)

"We read in the 53rd Chapter of Isaiah where He was wounded for our transgressions and bruised for our iniquities; and the apostle Peter affirms that His blood was spilt from before the foundation of the world.

"I have seen gamblers wounded. I have seen desperadoes wounded; thieves and robbers and every other kind of characters, law-breakers, and each one had a reason for his wounds. Some of them was unthoughtful, and some for being overbearing, some by the doctor's knife. But all wounds disfigures a person.

"Jesus was not unthoughtful. He was not overbearing. He was never a bully. He was never sick. He was never a criminal before the law and yet He was wounded. Now a man usually gets wounded in the midst of his enemies; but this man was wounded, says the text, in the house of His friends. It is not your enemies that harm you all the time. Watch that close friend. Every believer in Christ is considered His friend, and every sin we commit is a wound to Jesus. The blues we play in our homes is a club to beat up Jesus; and these social card parties . . ."

The Sermon

Jesus have always loved us from the foundation of the world.
When God
Stood out on the apex of His power
Before the hammers of creation
Fell upon the anvils of Time and hammered out the ribs of the earth
Before He made ropes
By the breath of fire
And set the boundaries of the ocean by gravity of His power
When God said, ha!
Let us make man
And the elders upon the altar cried, ha!
If you make man, ha!
He will sin.
God my master, ha!
Christ, yo' friend said
Father!! Ha-aa!

I am the teeth of Time
That comprehended de dust of de earth
And weighed de hills in scales
Painted de rainbow dat marks de end of de departing storm
Measured de seas in de holler of my hand
Held de elements in a unbroken chain of controllment.
Make man, ha!
If he sin, I will redeem him
I'll break de chasm of hell
Where de fire's never quenched
I'll go into de grave
Where de worm never dies, Ah!
So God A'mighty, ha!
Got His stuff together
He dipped some water out of de mighty deep
He got Him a handful of dirt, ha!
From de foundation sills of de earth
He seized a thimble full of breath, ha!
From de drums of de wind, ha!
God my master!
Now I'm ready to make man
Aa-aah!
Who shall I make him after? Ha!
Worlds within worlds begin to wheel and roll
De Sun, Ah!
Gethered up de fiery skirts of her garments
And wheeled around de throne, Ah!
Saying, Ah, make man after me, Ah!
God gazed upon the sun
And sent her back to her blood-red socket
And shook His head, ha!
De Moon, Ha!
Grabbed up de reins of de tides
And dragged a thousand seas behind her
As she walked around de throne—
Ah-h, please make man after me
But God said, No.
De stars bust out from their diamond sockets
And circled de glitterin throne cryin
A-aah! Make man after me
God said, No!
I'll make man in my own image, ha!
I'll put him in de garden
And Jesus said, ha!
And if he sin,
I'll go his bond before yo mighty throne

Ah, He was yo friend
He made us all, ha!
Delegates to de judgement convention
Ah!
Faith hasnt got no eyes, but she's long-legged
But take de spy-glass of Faith
And look into dat upper room
When you are alone to yourself
When yo' heart is burnt with fire, ha!
When de blood is lopin thru yo veins
Like de iron monasters (monsters) on de rail
Look into dat upper chamber, ha!
We notice at de supper table
As He gazed upon His friends, ha!
His eyes flowin wid tears, ha!
"My soul is exceedingly sorrowful unto death, ha!
For this night, ha!
One of you shall betray me, ha!
It were not a Roman officer, ha!
It were not a centurion soldier
But one of you
Who I have choosen my bosom friend
That sops in the dish with me shall betray me."
I want to draw a parable.
I see Jesus
Leaving heben with all of His grandeur
Disrobin Hisself of His matchless honor
Yieldin up de sceptre of revolvin worlds
Clothing Hisself in de garment of humanity
Coming into de world to rescue His friends.
Two thousand years have went by on their rusty ankles
But with the eye of faith I can see Him
Look down from His high towers of elevation
I can hear Him when He walks about the golden streets
I can hear 'em ring under his footsteps
Sol me-e-e, Sol do
Sol me-e-e, Sol do
I can see Him step out upon the rim bones of nothing
Crying I am de way
De truth and de light
Ah!
God A'mighty!
I see Him grab de throttle
Of de well ordered train of mercy
I see kingdoms crush and crumble
Whilst de arc angels held de winds in de corner chambers

I see Him arrive on dis earth
And walk de streets thirty and three years
Oh-h-hhh!
I see Him walking beside de sea of Galilee wid His disciples
This declaration gendered on His lips
"Let us go on the other side"
God A'mighty!
Dey entered de boat
Wid their oarus (oars) stuck in de back
Sails unfurled to de evenin breeze
And de ship was now sailin
As she reached de center of de lake
Jesus was 'sleep on a pillow in de rear of de boat
And de dynamic powers of nature become disturbed
And de mad winds broke de heads of de western drums
And fell down on de Lake of Galilee
And buried themselves behind de gallopin waves
And de white-caps marbilized themselves like an army
And walked out like soldiers goin to battle
And de ziz-zag lightning
Licked out her fiery tongue
And de flying clouds
Threw their wings in the channels of the deep
And bedded de waters like a road-plow
And faced de current of de chargin billows
And de terrific bolts of thunder—they bust in de clouds
And de ship begin to reel and rock
God A'mighty!
And one of de disciples called Jesus
"Master!! Carest thou not that we perish?"
And He arose
And de storm was in its pitch
And de lightnin played on His raiments as He stood on the prow of the boat
And placed His foot upon the neck of the storm
And spoke to the howlin winds
And de sea fell at His feet like a marble floor
And de thunders went back in their vault
Then He set down on de rim of de ship
And took de hooks of his power
And lifted de billows in His lap
And rocked de winds to sleep on His arm
And said, "Peace be still."
And de Bible says there was a calm.
I can see Him wid de eye of faith
When He went from Pilate's house
Wid the crown of 72 wounds upon His head

I can see Him as He mounted Calvary and hung upon de cross for our sins.
I can see-eee-ee
De mountains fall to their rocky knees when He cried
"My God, my God! Why hast thou forsaken me?"
The mountains fell to their rocky knees and trembled like a beast
From the stroke of the master's axe
One angel took the flinches of God's eternal power
And bled the veins of the earth
One angel that stood at the gate with a flaming sword
Was so well pleased with his power
Until he pierced the moon with his sword
And she ran down in blood
And de sun
Batted her fiery eyes and put on her judgement robe
And laid down in de cradle of eternity
And rocked herself into sleep and slumber.
He died until the great belt in the wheel of time
And de geological strata fell aloose
And a thousand angels rushed to de canopy of heben
With flamin swords in their hands
And placed their feet upon blue ether's bosom and looked back
    at de dazzlin throne
And de arc angels had veiled their faces
And de throne was draped in mournin
And de orchestra had struck silence for the space of half an hour
Angels had lifted their harps to de weepin willows
And God had looked off to-wards immensity
And blazin worlds fell off His teeth
And about that time Jesus groaned on de cross and said, "It is finished"
And then de chambers of hell explode
And de damnable spirits
Come up from de Sodomistic world and rushed into de smoky
    camps of eternal night
And cried "Woe! Woe! Woe!"
And then de Centurion cried out
"Surely this is the Son of God."
And about dat time
De angel of Justice unsheathed his flamin sword and ripped
    de veil of de temple
And de High Priest vacated his office
And then de sacrificial energy penetrated de mighty strata
And quickened de bones of de prophets
And they arose from their graves and walked about in
    de streets of Jerusalem.
I heard de whistle of de damnation train
Dat pulled out from Garden of Eden loaded wid cargo goin to hell

243

Ran at break-neck speed all de way thru de law
All de way thru de prophetic age
All de way thru de reign of kings and judges—
Plowed her way thru de Jurdan
And on her way to Calvary when she blew for de switch
Jesus stood out on her track like a rough-backed mountain
And she threw her cow-catcher in His side and His blood ditched de train,
He died for our sins.
Wounded in the house of His friends.
Thats where I got off de damnation train
And dats where you must get off, ha!
For in dat mor-ornin', ha!
When we shall all be delegates, ha!
To dat judgement convention, ha!
When de two trains of Time shall meet on de trestle
And wreck de burning axels of de unformed ether
And de mountains shall skip like lambs
When Jesus shall place one foot on de neck of de sea, ha!
One foot on dry land
When His chariot wheels shall be running hub-deep in fire
He shall take His friends thru the open bosom of a unclouded sky
And place in their hands de hosanna fan
And they shall stand round and round His beatific throne
And praise His name forever.
Amen.

UNCLE MONDAY
ZORA NEALE HURSTON

People talk a whole lot about Uncle Monday, but they take good pains not to let him near none of it. Uncle Monday is an out-and-out conjure doctor. That in itself is enough to make the people handle him carefully, but there is something about him that goes past hoodoo. Nobody knows anything about him, and that's a serious matter in a village of less than three hundred souls, especially when a person has lived there for forty years and more.

Nobody knows where he came from nor who his folks might be. Nobody knows for certain just when he did come to town. He was just there one morning when the town awoke. Joe Lindsay was the first to see him. He had some turtle lines set down on Lake Belle. It is a hard lake to fish because it is entirely surrounded by a sooky marsh that is full of leeches and moccasins. There is plenty of deep water once you pole a boat out beyond the line of cypress pines, but there are so many alligators out there that most people don't think the trout are worth the risk. But Joe had baited some turtle lines and thrown them as far as he could without wading into the marsh. So next morning he went as early as he could see light to look after his lines. There was a turtle head on every line, and he pulled them up cursing the 'gators for robbing his hooks. He says he started on back home, but when he was a few yards from where his lines had been set something made him look back, and he nearly fell dead. For there was an old man walking out of the lake between two cypress knees. The water there was too deep for any wading, and besides, he says the man was not wading, he was walking vigorously as if he were on dry land.

Lindsay says he was too scared to stand there and let the man catch up with him, and he was too scared to move his feet; so he just stood there and saw the man cross the marshy strip and come down the path behind him. He says he felt the hair rise on his head as the man got closer to him, and somehow he thought about an alligator slipping up on him. But he says that alligators were in the front of his mind that morning because first, he had heard bull 'gators fighting and bellowing all night long down in this lake, and then his turtle lines had been robbed. Besides, everybody knows that the father of all 'gators lives in Belle Lake.

The old man was coming straight on, taking short quick steps as if his legs were not long enough for his body, and working his arms in unison. Lindsay says it was all he could do to stand his ground and not let the man see how scared he was, but managed to stand still anyway. The man came up to him and passed him without looking at him seemingly. After he had passed, Lindsay noticed that his clothes were perfectly dry, so he decided that his own eyes had fooled him. The old man must have come up to the cypress knees in a boat and then crossed the marsh by stepping from root to root. But when he went to look, he found no convenient roots for anybody to step on. Moreover, there was no boat on the lake either.

The old man looked queer to everybody, but still no one would believe Lindsay's story. They said that he had seen no more than several others— that is, that the old man had been seen coming from the direction of the lake. That was the first that the village saw of him, way back in the late 'eighties, and so far, nobody knows any more about his past than that. And that worries the town.

Another thing that struck everybody unpleasantly was the fact that he never asked a name nor a direction. Just seemed to know who everybody was, and called each and every one by their right name. Knew where everybody lived too. Didn't earn a living by any of the village methods. He didn't garden, hunt, fish, nor work for the white folks. Stayed so close in the little shack that he had built for himself that sometimes three weeks would pass before the town saw him from one appearance to another.

Joe Clarke was the one who found out his name was Monday. No other name. So the town soon was calling him Uncle Monday. Nobody can say exactly how it came to be known that he was a hoodoo man. But it turned out that that was what he was. People said he was a good one too. As much as they feared him, he had plenty of trade. Didn't take him long to take all the important cases away from Ant Judy, who had had a monopoly for years.

He looked very old when he came to the town. Very old, but firm and strong. Never complained of illness.

But once, Emma Lou Pittman went over to his shack early in the morning to see him on business, and ran back with a fearsome tale. She said that she noticed a heavy trail up to his door and across the steps, as if a heavy, bloody body had been dragged inside. The door was cracked a little and she could hear a great growling and snapping of mighty jaws. It wasn't exactly a growling either, it was more a subdued howl in a bass tone. She shoved the door a little and peeped inside to see if some varmint was in there attacking Uncle Monday. She figured he might have gone to sleep with the door ajar and a catamount, or a panther, or a bob-cat might have gotten in. He lived near enough to Blue Sink Lake for a 'gator to have come in the house, but she didn't remember ever hearing of them tracking anything but dogs.

But no; no varmint was inside there. The voice she heard was being made by Uncle Monday. He was lying on a pallet of pine-straw in such agony that his eyes were glazed over. His right arm was horribly mangled. In fact, it was all but torn away from right below the elbow. The side of his face was terribly torn too. She called him, but he didn't seem to hear her. So she hurried back for some men to come and do something for him. The men came as fast as their legs would bring them, but the house was locked from the outside and there was no answer to their knocking. Mrs. Pittman would have been made out an awful liar if it were not for the trail of blood. So they concluded that Uncle Monday had gotten hurt somehow and had dragged himself home, or had been dragged by a friend. But who could the friend have been?

Nobody saw Uncle Monday for a month after that. Every day or so, someone would drop by to see if hide or hair could be found of him. A full month passed before there was any news. The town had about decided that he had gone away as mysteriously as he had come.

But one evening around dusk-dark Sam Merchant and Jim Gooden were on their way home from a squirrel hunt around Lake Belle. They swore that, as they rounded the lake and approached the footpath that leads towards the village, they saw what they thought was the great 'gator that lives in the lake crawl out of the marsh. Merchant wanted to take a shot at him for his hide and teeth, but Gooden reminded him that they were loaded with bird shot, which would not even penetrate a 'gator's hide, let alone kill it. They say the thing they took for the 'gator then struggled awhile, pulling off something that looked like a long black glove. Then he scraped a hole in the soft ground with his paws and carefully buried the glove which had come from his right paw. Then without looking either right or left, he stood upright and walked on towards the village. Everybody saw Uncle Monday come thru the town, but still Merchant's tale was hard to swallow. But, by degrees, people came to believe that Uncle Monday would shed any injured member of his body and grow a new one in its place. At any rate, when he reappeared his right hand and arm bore no scars.

The village is even sceptical about his dying. Once Joe Clarke said to Uncle Monday, "I'god, Uncle Monday, ain't you skeered to stay way off by yo'self, old as you is?"

Uncle Monday asked, "Why would I be skeered?"

"Well, you liable to take sick in de night sometime, and you'd be dead befo' anybody would know you was even sick."

Uncle Monday got up off the nail keg and said in a voice so low that only the men right close to him could hear what he said, "I have been dead for many a year. I have come back from where you are going." Then he walked away with his quick short steps, and his arms bent at the elbow, keeping time with his feet.

It is believed that he has the singing stone, which is the greatest charm, the most powerful "hand" in the world. It is a diamond and comes from the mouth of a serpent (which is thought of as something different from an ordinary snake) and is the diamond of diamonds. It not only lights your home without the help of any other light, but it also warns its owner of approach.

The serpents who produce these stones live in the deep waters of Lake Maitland. There is a small island in this lake and a rare plant grows there, which is the only food of this serpent. She only comes to nourish herself in the height of a violent thunderstorm, when she is fairly certain that no human will be present.

It is impossible to kill or capture her unless nine healthy people have gone before to prepare the way with THE OLD ONES, and then more will die in the attempt to conquer her. But it is not necessary to kill or take her to get the stone. She has two. One is embedded in her head, and the other she carries in her mouth. The first one cannot be had without killing the serpent, but the second one may be won from her by trickery.

Since she carries this stone in her mouth, she cannot eat until she has put it down. It is her pilot, that warns her of danger. So when she comes upon the island to feed, she always vomits the stone and covers it with earth before she goes to the other side of the island to dine.

To get this diamond, dress yourself all over in black velvet. Your assistant must be dressed in the same way. Have a velvet-covered bowl along. Be on the island before the storm reaches its height, but leave your helper in the boat and warn him to be ready to pick you up and flee at a moment's notice.

Climb a tall tree and wait for the coming of the snake. When she comes out of the water, she will look all about her on the ground to see if anyone is about. When she is satisfied that she is alone, she will vomit the stone, cover it with dirt and proceed to her feeding ground. Then, as soon as you feel certain that she is busy eating, climb down the tree as swiftly as possible, cover the mound hiding the stone with the velvet-lined bowl and flee for your life to the boat. The boatman must fly from the island with all possible speed. For as soon as you approach the stone it will ring like chiming bells, and the serpent will hear it. Then she will run to defend it. She will return to the spot, but the velvet-lined bowl will make it invisible to her. In her wrath she will knock down grown trees and lash the island like a hurricane. Wait till a calm fair day to return for the stone. She never comes up from the bottom of the lake in fair weather. Furthermore, a serpent who has lost her mouth-stone cannot come to feed alone after that. She must bring her mate.

The mouth-stone is their guardian, and when they lose it they remain in constant danger unless accompanied by one who has the singing stone.

They say that Uncle Monday has a singing stone, and that is why he knows everything without being told.

Whether he has the stone or not, nobody thinks of doubting his power as a hoodoo man. He is feared, but sought when life becomes too powerful for the powerless. Mary Ella Shaw backed out on Joe-Nathan Moss the day before the wedding was to have come off. Joe-Nathan had even furnished the house and bought rations. His people, her people, everybody tried to make her marry the boy. He loved her so, and besides he had put out so much of his little cash to fix for the marriage. But Mary Ella just wouldn't. She had seen Caddie Brewton, and she was one of the kind who couldn't keep her heart still after her eye had wandered.

So Joe-Nathan's mama went to see Uncle Monday. He said, "Since she is the kind of woman that lets her mind follow her eye, we'll have to let the snake-bite cure itself. You go on home. Never no man will keep her. She kin grab the world full of men, but she'll never keep one any longer than from one full moon to the other."

Fifteen years have passed. Mary Ella has been married four times. She was a very pretty girl, and men just kept coming, but not one man has ever stayed with her longer than the twenty-eight days. Besides her four husbands, no telling how many men she has shacked up with for a few weeks at a time. She has eight children by as many different men, but still no husband.

John Wesley Hogan was another driver of sharp bargains in love. By his own testimony and experience, all women from eight to eighty were his meat, but the woman who was sharp enough to make him marry her wasn't born and her mama was dead. They couldn't frame him and they couldn't scare him.

Mrs. Bradley came to him nevertheless about her Dinkie. She called him out from his work-place and said, "John Wesley, you know I'm a widder-woman and I aint got no husband to go to de front for me, so I reckon I got to do de talkin' for me and my chile. I come in de humblest way I know how to ast you to go 'head and marry my chile befo' her name is painted on de signposts of scorn."

If it had not made John Wesley so mad, it would have been funny to him. So he asked her scornfully, " 'Oman, whut you take me for? You better git outa my face wid dat mess! How you reckon *I* know who Dinkie been foolin roun wid? Don't try to come dat mess over *me*. I been all over de North. I aint none of yo' fool. You must think I'm Big Boy. They kilt Big Boy shootin after Fat Sam so there aint no mo' fools in de world. Ha ha! All de wimmen *I* done seen! I'll tell you like de monkey tole de elephant—don't bull me, big boy! If you want Dinkie to git married off so bad, go grab one of dese country clowns. I aint yo' man. Taint no use you goin runnin to de high-sheriff neither. I got witness to prove Dinkie knowed more'n I do."

Mrs. Bradley didn't bother with the sheriff. All he could do was to make

John Wesley marry Dinkie; but by the time the interview was over that wasn't what the stricken mother wanted. So she waited till dark, and went on over to Uncle Monday.

Everybody says you don't have to explain things to Uncle Monday. Just go there, and you will find that he is ready for you when you arrive. So he set Mrs. Bradley down at a table, facing a huge mirror hung against the wall. She says he had a loaded pistol and a huge dirk lying on the table before her. She looked at both of the weapons, but she could not decide which one she wanted to use. Without a word, he handed her a gourd full of water and she took a swallow. As soon as the water passed over her tongue she seized the gun. He pointed towards the looking-glass. Slowly the form of John Wesley formed in the glass and finally stood as vivid as life before her. She took careful aim and fired. She was amazed that the mirror did not shatter. But there was a loud report, a cloud of bluish smoke and the figure vanished.

On the way home, Brazzle told her that John Wesley had dropped dead, and Mr. Watson had promised to drive over to Orlando in the morning to get a coffin for him.

Ant Judy Bickerstaff

Uncle Monday wasn't the only hoodoo doctor around there. There was Ant Judy Bickerstaff. She was there before the coming of Uncle Monday. Of course it didn't take long for professional jealousy to arise. Uncle Monday didn't seem to mind Ant Judy, but she resented him, and she couldn't hide her feelings.

This was natural when you consider that before his coming she used to make all the "hands" around there, but he soon drew off the greater part of the trade.

Year after year this feeling kept up. Every now and then some little incident would accentuate the rivalry. Monday was sitting on top of the heap, but Judy was not without her triumphs.

Finally she began to say that she could reverse anything that he put down. She said she could not only reverse it, she could throw it back on *him,* let alone his client. Nobody talked to him about her boasts. People never talked to him except on business anyway. Perhaps Judy felt safe in her boasting for this reason.

Then one day she took it in her head to go fishing. Her children and grandchildren tried to discourage her. They argued with her about her great age and her stiff joints. But she had her grandson to fix her a trout pole and a bait pole and set out for Blue Sink, a lake said to be bottomless by the villagers. Furthermore, she didn't set out till near sundown. She didn't want any company. It was no use talking, she felt that she just must go fishing in Blue Sink.

She didn't come home when dark came, and her family worried a little. But they reasoned she had probably stopped at one of her friend's houses to rest and gossip, so they didn't go to hunt her right away. But when the night wore on and she didn't return, the children were sent out to locate her.

She was not in the village. A party was organised to search Blue Sink for her. It was after nine o'clock at night when the party found her. She was in the lake. Lying in shallow water and keeping her old head above the water by supporting it on her elbow. Her son Ned said that he saw a huge alligator dive away as he shined the torch upon his mother's head.

They bore Ant Judy home and did everything they could for her. Her legs were limp and useless and she never spoke a word, not a coherent word, for three days. It was more than a week before she could tell how she came to be in the lake.

She said that she hadn't really wanted to go fishing. The family and the village could witness that she never had fooled round the lakes. But that afternoon she *had* to go. She couldn't say why, but she knew she must go. She baited her hooks and stood waiting for a bite. She was afraid to sit down on the damp ground on account for her rheumatism. She got no bites. When she saw the sun setting she wanted to come home, but somehow she just couldn't leave the spot. She was afraid, terribly afraid down there on the lake, but she couldn't leave.

When the sun was finally gone and it got dark, she says she felt a threatening, powerful evil all around her. She was fixed to the spot. A small but powerful whirlwind arose right under her feet. Something terrific struck her and she fell into the water. She tried to climb out, but found that she could not use her legs. She thought of 'gators and otters, and leeches and garfish, and began to scream, thinking maybe somebody would hear her and come to her aid.

Suddenly a bar of red light fell across the lake from one side to the other. It looked like a fiery sword. Then she saw Uncle Monday walking across the lake to her along this flaming path. On either side of the red road swam thousands of alligators, like an army behind its general.

The light itself was awful. It was red, but she never had seen any red like it before. It jumped and moved all the time, but always it pointed straight across the lake to where she lay helpless in the water. The lake is nearly a mile wide, but Ant Judy says Uncle Monday crossed it in less than a minute and stood over her. She closed her eyes from fright, but she saw him right on thru her lids.

After a brief second she screamed again. Then he growled and leaped at her. "Shut up!" he snarled. "Part your lips just one more time and it will be your last breath! Your bragging tongue has brought you here and you are going to stay here until you acknowledge my power. So you can throw back my work, eh? I put you in this lake; show your power and get out. You will not die, and you will not leave this spot until you give consent in your heart that I am your master. Help will come the minute you knuckle under."

She fought against him. She felt that once she was before her own altar she could show him something. He glowered down upon her for a spell and then turned and went back across the lake the way he had come. The light vanished behind his feet. Then a huge alligator slid up beside her where she lay trembling and all her strength went out of her. She lost all confidence in her powers. She began to feel if only she might either die or escape from the horror, she would never touch another charm again. If only she could escape the maw of the monster beside her! Any other death but that. She wished that Uncle Monday would come back so that she might plead with him for deliverance. She opened her mouth to call, but found that speech had left her. But she saw a light approaching by land. It was the rescue party.

Ant Judy never did regain the full use of her legs, but she got to the place where she could hobble about the house and yard. After relating her adventure on Lake Blue Sink she never called the name of Uncle Monday again.

The rest of the village, always careful in that respect, grew almost as careful as she. But sometimes when they would hear the great bull 'gator, that everybody knows lives in Lake Belle, bellowing on cloudy nights, some will point the thumb in the general direction of Uncle Monday's house and whisper, "The Old Boy is visiting the home folks tonight."

STERLING BROWN:
THE NEW NEGRO FOLK-POET
ALAIN LOCKE

Many critics, writing in praise of Sterling Brown's first volume of verse, have seen fit to hail him as a significant new Negro poet. The discriminating few go further; they hail a new era in Negro poetry, for such is the deeper significance of this volume (*The Southern Road,* Sterling Brown, Harcourt Brace, New York, 1932). Gauging the main objective of Negro poetry as the poetic portrayal of Negro folk-life true in both letter and spirit to the idiom of the folk's own way of feeling and thinking, we may say that here for the first time is that much-desired and long-awaited acme attained or brought within actual reach.

Almost since the advent of the Negro poet public opinion has expected and demanded folk-poetry of him. And Negro poets have tried hard and voluminously to cater to this popular demand. But on the whole, for very understandable reasons, folk-poetry by Negroes, with notable flash exceptions, has been very unsatisfactory and weak, and despite the intimacy of the race poet's attachments, has been representative in only a limited, superficial sense. First of all, the demand has been too insistent. "They required of us a song in a strange land." "How could we sing of thee, O Zion?" There was the canker of theatricality and exhibitionism planted at the very heart of Negro poetry, unwittingly no doubt, but just as fatally. Other captive nations have suffered the same ordeal. But with the Negro another spiritual handicap was imposed. Robbed of his own tradition, there was no internal compensation to counter the external pressure. Consequently the Negro spirit had a triple plague on its heart and mind—morbid self-consciousness, self-pity and forced exhibitionism. Small wonder that so much poetry by Negroes exhibits in one degree or another the blights of bombast, bathos and artificiality. Much genuine poetic talent has thus been blighted either by these spiritual faults or their equally vicious over-compensations. And so it is epoch-making to have developed a poet whose work, to quote a recent criticism, "has no taint of music-hall convention, is neither arrogant nor servile"—and plays up to neither side of the racial dilemma. For it is as fatal to true poetry to cater to the self-pity or racial vanity of a persecuted group as to pander to the amusement complex of the overlords and masters.

I do not mean to imply that Sterling Brown's art is perfect, or even completely mature. It is all the more promising that this volume represents the work of a young man just in his early thirties. But a Negro poet with almost complete detachment, yet with a tone of persuasive sincerity, whose muse neither clowns nor shouts, is indeed a promising and a grateful phenomenon.

By some deft touch, independent of dialect, Mr. Brown is able to compose with the freshness and naturalness of folk balladry—*Maumee Ruth, Dark O'the Moon, Sam Smiley, Slim Green, Johnny Thomas,* and *Memphis Blues* will convince the most sceptical that modern Negro life can yield real balladry and a Negro poet achieve in authentic folk-touch.

Or this from *Sam Smiley:*

> The mob was in fine fettle, yet
> The dogs were stupid-nosed, and day
> Was far spent when the men drew round
> The scrawny wood where Smiley lay.
>
> The oaken leaves drowsed prettily,
> The moon shone benignly there;
> And big Sam Smiley, King Buckdancer,
> Buckdanced on the midnight air.

This is even more dramatic and graphic than that fine but more melodramatic lyric of Langston Hughes:

> Way down South in Dixie
> (Break the heart of me!)
> They hung my black young lover
> To a cross-road's tree.

With Mr. Brown the racial touch is quite independent of dialect; it is because in his ballads and lyrics he has caught the deeper idiom of feeling or the peculiar paradox of the racial situation. That gives the genuine earthy folk-touch, and justifies a statement I ventured some years back: "the soul of the Negro will be discovered in a characteristic way of thinking and in a homely philosophy rather than in a jingling and juggling of broken English."

As a matter of fact, Negro dialect is extremely local—it changes from place to place, as do white dialects. And what is more, the dialect of Dunbar and the other early Negro poets never was on land or sea as a living peasant speech; but it has had such wide currency, especially on the stage, as to have successfully deceived half the world, including the many Negroes who for one reason or another imitate it.

Sterling Brown's dialect is also local, and frankly an adaptation, but he has localised it carefully, after close observation and study, and varies it according to the brogue of the locality of the characteristic jargon of the *milieu* of which he is writing. But his racial effects, as I have said, are not dependent on dialect. Consider *Maumee Ruth:*

> Might as well bury her
> And bury her deep,
> Might as well put her
> Where she can sleep. . . .
>
> Boy that she suckled
> How should he know,
> Hiding in city holes
> Sniffing the "snow"? *
>
> And how should the news
> Pierce Harlem's din,
> To reach her baby gal
> Sodden with gin?
>
> Might as well drop her
> Deep in the ground,
> Might as well pray for her,
> That she sleep sound.

That is as uniquely racial as the straight dialect of *Southern Road:*

> White man tells me—hunh—
> Damn yo' soul;
> White man tells me—hunh—
> Damn yo' soul;
> Got no need, bebby,
> To be tole.

If we stop to inquire—as unfortunately the critic must—into the magic of these effects, we find the secret, I think, in this fact more than in any other: Sterling Brown has listened long and carefully to the folk in their intimate hours, when they were talking to themselves, not, so to speak, as in Dunbar, but actually as they do when the masks of protective mimicry fall. Not only has he dared to give quiet but bold expression to this private thought and

* Cocaine.

253

speech, but he has dared to give the Negro peasant credit for thinking. In this way he has recaptured the shrewd Aesopian quality of the Negro folk-thought, which is more profoundly characteristic than their types of metaphors or their mannerisms of speech. They are, as he himself says,

> Illiterate, and somehow very wise,

and it is this wisdom, bitter fruit of their suffering, combined with their characteristic fatalism and irony, which in this book gives a truer soul picture of the Negro than has ever yet been given poetically. The traditional Negro is a clown, a buffoon, an easy laugher, a shallow sobber and a credulous christian; the real Negro underneath is more often an all but cynical fatalist, a shrewd pretender, and a boldly whimsical pagan; or when not, a lusty, realistic religionist who tastes its nectars here and now.

> Mammy
> With deep religion defeating the grief
> Life piled so closely about her

is the key picture to the Negro as christian; Mr. Brown's *When the Saints Come Marching Home* is worth half a dozen essays on the Negro's religion. But to return to the question of bold exposure of the intimacies of Negro thinking—read that priceless apologia of kitchen stealing in the *Ruminations of Luke Johnson,* reflective husband of Mandy Jane, tromping early to work with a great big basket, and tromping wearily back with it at night laden with the petty spoils of the day's picking:

> Well, taint my business noway,
> An' I ain' near fo'gotten
> De lady what she wuks fo',
> An' how she got her jack;
> De money dat she live on
> Come from niggers pickin' cotton,
> Ebbery dollar dat she squander
> Nearly bust a nigger's back.
>
> So I'm glad dat in de evenins
> Mandy Jane seems extra happy,
> An' de lady at de big house
> Got no kick at all I say—
> Cause what huh "dear grandfawthaw"
> Took from Mandy Jane's grandpappy—
> Ain' no basket in de worl'
> What kin tote all dat away. . . .

Or again in that delicious epic of *Sporting Beasley* entering heaven:

> Lord help us, give a look at him,
> Don't make him dress up in no nightgown, Lord.

> Don't put no fuss and feathers on his shoulders, Lord.
>   Let him know it's heaven,
> Let him keep his hat, his vest, his elkstooth, and everything.
> Let him have his spats and cane.

It is not enough to sprinkle "dis's and dat's" to be a Negro folk-poet, or to jingle rhymes and juggle popularised clichés traditional to sentimental minor poetry for generations. One must study the intimate thought of the people who can only state it in an ejaculation, or a metaphor, or at best a proverb, and translate that into an articulate attitude, or a folk philosophy or a daring fable, with Aesopian clarity and simplicity—and above all, with Aesopian candor.

The last is most important; other Negro poets in many ways have been too tender with their own, even though they have learned with the increasing boldness of new Negro thought not to be too gingerly and conciliatory to and about the white man. The Negro muse weaned itself of that in McKay, Fenton Johnson, Toomer, Countee Cullen and Langston Hughes. But in Sterling Brown it has learned to laugh at itself and to chide itself with the same broomstick. I have space for only two examples: *Children's Children:*

> When they hear
> These songs, born of the travail of their sires,
> Diamonds of song, deep buried beneath the weight
> Of dark and heavy years;
> They laugh.
>
> They have forgotten, they have never known
> Long days beneath the torrid Dixie sun,
> In miasma'd rice swamps;
> The chopping of dried grass, on the third go round
> In strangling cotton;
> Wintry nights in mud-daubed makeshift huts,
> With these songs, sole comfort.
>
> They have forgotten
> What had to be endured—
> That they, babbling young ones,
> With their paled faces, coppered lips,
> And sleek hair cajoled to Caucasian straightness,
> Might drown the quiet voice of beauty
> With sensuous stridency;
>
> And might, on hearing these memories of their sires,
> Giggle,
> And nudge each other's satin-clad
> Sleek sides.

Anent the same broomstick, it is refreshing to read *Mr. Samuel and Sam,* from which we can only quote in part:

> Mister Samuel, he belong to Rotary,
> Sam, to de Sons of Rest;
> Both wear red hats like monkey men,
> An' you cain't say which is de best. . . .
>
> Mister Samuel die, an' de folks all know,
> Sam die widout no noise;
> De worl' go by in de same ol' way,
> And dey's both of 'em po' los' boys.

There is a world of psychological distance between this and the rhetorical defiance and the plaintive, furtive sarcasms of even some of our other contemporary poets—even as theirs, it must be said in all justice, was miles better and more representative than the sycophancies and platitudes of the older writers.

In closing it might be well to trace briefly the steps by which Negro poetry has scrambled up the sides of Parnassus from the ditches of minstrelsy and the trenches of race propaganda. In complaining against the narrow compass of dialect poetry (dialect is an organ with only two stops—pathos and humor), Weldon Johnson tried to break the Dunbar mould and shake free of the traditional stereotypes. But significant as it was, this was more a threat than an accomplishment; his own dialect poetry has all of the clichés of Dunbar without Dunbar's lilting lyric charm. Later in the *Negro Sermons* Weldon Johnson discovered a way out—in a rhapsodic form free from the verse shackles of classical minor poetry, and in the attempt to substitute an idiom of racial thought and imagery for a mere dialect of peasant speech. Claude McKay then broke with all the moods conventional in his day in Negro poetry, and presented a Negro who could challenge and hate, who knew resentment, brooded intellectual sarcasm, and felt contemplative irony. In this, so to speak, he pulled the psychological cloak off the Negro and revealed, even to the Negro himself, those facts disguised till then by his shrewd protective mimicry or pressed down under the dramatic mask of living up to what was expected of him. But though McKay sensed a truer Negro, he was at times too indignant at the older sham, and, too, lacked the requisite native touch—as of West Indian birth and training—with the local color of the American Negro. Jean Toomer went deeper still—I should say higher—and saw for the first time the glaring paradoxes and the deeper ironies of the situation, as they affected not only the Negro but the white man. He realised, too, that Negro idiom was anything but trite and derivative, and also that it was in emotional substance pagan—all of which he convincingly demonstrated, alas, all too fugitively, in *Cane*. But Toomer was not enough of a realist, or patient enough as an observer, to reproduce extensively a folk idiom.

Then Langston Hughes came with his revelation of the emotional color of Negro life, and his brilliant discovery of the flow and rhythm of the modern and especially the city Negro, substituting this jazz figure and personality for the older plantation stereotype. But it was essentially a jazz version of

Negro life, and that is to say as much American, or more, as Negro; and though fascinating and true to an epoch this version was surface quality after all.

Sterling Brown, more reflective, a closer student of the folk-life, and above all a bolder and more detached observer, has gone deeper still, and has found certain basic, more sober and more persistent qualities of Negro thought and feeling; and so has reached a sort of common denominator between the old and the new Negro. Underneath the particularities of one generation are hidden universalities which only deeply penetrating genius can fathom and bring to the surface. Too many of the articulate intellects of the Negro group—including sadly enough the younger poets—themselves children of opportunity, have been unaware of these deep resources of the past. But here, if anywhere, in the ancient common wisdom of the folk, is the real treasure trove of the Negro poet; and Sterling Brown's poetic divining-rod has dipped significantly over this position. It is in this sense that I believe *Southern Road* ushers in a new era in Negro folk-expression and brings a new dimension in Negro folk-portraiture.

VISUAL ARTS:
TO CELEBRATE BLACKNESS

Just as the decades of the 1920s and 1930s witnessed an aggressively new Afro-American writer and musician, they also saw the coming of a new breed of painters and sculptors. Many of the themes that we have seen articulated in the literature of the New Negro were reflected in the visual arts as well. The search for identity, a distinctive self in history or in African culture, the celebration of the beauty of black people, and the illumination of the history and folk context of the Afro-American experience were essential elements of the art of black men and women of the period.

Africa was inspiration to the style and thought of Afro-American artists. Just as African art had influenced European artists to break from tradition at the turn of the century, it encouraged black Americans to search for new methods, new idioms, and new standards of beauty. The African craftsmen's emphasis on design rather than on representation had much to do with Aaron Douglas' choice of flat colors and his stylized, two-dimensional illustrations and paintings. Douglas' designs illuminated many of the works that we associate with the Harlem Renaissance: the magazines, *Fire* and *Harlem,* Alain Locke's *The New Negro,* and James Weldon Johnson's *God's Trombones.* Douglas completed a mural, comprising five panels, for the W.P.A. in 1934. It was called "Aspects of Negro Life," and interpreted the Afro-American experience from its backgrounds in Africa to twentieth-century urban America. His reporting of history was quite specific in the second panel which has as a central focus the reading of the Emancipation Proclamation as blacks move from slavery to freedom with the specter of the Ku Klux Klan hovering above their future. In "Idyll of the Deep South," Douglas represents the wide range of black life in the South: work, play, worship, and mourning for the lynched victim.

It was also through Africa that the black artist could find the means of defining and celebrating the physical and spiritual beauty of black people. Sargent Johnson, whose work was mainly in terracotta and porcelain, developed the form of the African mask into idealized representations of the black face and head. The Afro-American mother is celebrated for her strength and beauty in Johnson's "Forever Free." She is a powerful, unflinching figure with her children in bas-relief against her skirts. In his panel "White and Black," Johnson also experimented with cubism, itself derivative of African sources.

The beauty of the African and the Afro-American was idealized and romanticised in the work of Sargent Johnson. The same can be said for the sculpture of Richmond Barthé which treats African or black American subjects. For Barthé, the beauty of the African was in balance, rhythm, and grace as represented in dance. As one sees in Barthé's "African Dancer" and "Feral Benga," the effort to synthesize these qualities could result in idealized form.

History and Africa were also the subject of Hale Woodruff's murals depicting the drama of the Amistad mutiny. The first panel celebrates the courage and determination of Africans rebelling to gain their liberty, overcoming the crew of their slave ship and taking it captive. This narrative mural ends in its final panel, as did the true history, with the return of Cinqué and the other Amistad rebels to their native Africa. Significantly, however, Woodruff shows them returning as Africans no longer, but as Afro-Americans. Their dress and manner tell us that the experience has transformed them. One man kneels as a Christian in prayer; Western tools and books are part of their baggage. Perhaps these men, who can bridge two cultures, suggest the special calling of Afro-Americans.

Certainty of the essential beauty and strength in the Afro-American could free the black artist to distort form, to analyze rather than to describe, and to risk the grotesque in order to illustrate the underlying character of his subject. Thus, William H. Johnson's "Minnie" departs from the idealized expressions of Sargent Johnson and Richmond Barthé. In this departure, however, the artist achieved a powerful and moving portrait of a personality rather than a type. William H. Johnson was a pioneer modernist among the black artists of the period. His self-portraits illustrate the strong shift in his own approach to art, from the chiaroscura of the one (suggesting the realism of Thomas Eakin or, perhaps, a self-portrait of Rembrandt) to the post-impressionistic color dominance of the other (reminding us of Vincent Van Gogh). In his later work, such as "Jacobia Hotel" and "Sun Setting, Denmark," we see Johnson to be firmly a part of the school of such European painters as Van Gogh, Soutine, and Rouault.

Augusta Savage's "Gamin" is as far removed from Africa as is the Harlem River from the Congo. Hers is a city boy, as if from the streets of Harlem. Savage, like William H. Johnson, felt no need to idealize or romanticize. Afro-American life in the city created tough realists, even among children. It is in the toughness and the realism of her "Gamin" that one finds its beauty.

Archibald Motley's early work also leaned toward realism, avoiding the idealized form and statement. His "Portrait of My Grandmother" asserts a beauty and strength of an inner character because of the realistic treatment of surface features. On the other hand, the tone and mood of the entire composition provide an emotional texture to "Brown Girl after the Bath," suggesting the substance of beauty to be an inward quality rather than the pretty subject herself. As these paintings bring to mind poems out of the Harlem Renaissance by Countee Cullen and Langston Hughes, Motley's "Blues" evokes the spirit of the cabaret scenes of Harlem. In "Blues," Motley has moved from his earlier realism to the one-color key, social genre scenes that were to characterise much of his later work.

Palmer Hayden found Afro-American city life to be a source of vitality and amusement. His "Midsummer Night in Harlem" is a social document of Harlem life as much as would be stories of Rudolph Fisher or Eric Walrond.

And, like some of the writing of the period, Hayden's painting employs race-types to achieve the tone of satire.

Like Aaron Douglas, Sargent Johnson, and Richmond Barthé, Palmer Hayden commented on the Afro-American as a type rather than as an individual personality. All of these artists, however, captured visually some aspect of what black intellectuals had been calling the New Negro.

1.
Aaron Douglas: *Aspects of Negro Life.* Panel #1: *The Negro in an African Setting*, W.P.A., 1934 (Schomburg Center for Research in Black Culture, Art & Artifacts Division, The New York Public Library, Astor, Lenox and Tilden Foundations).

2.
Aaron Douglas: *Aspects of Negro Life.* Panel #2: *From Slavery through Reconstruction,* W.P.A., 1934 (Schomburg Center for Research in Black Culture, Art & Artifacts Division, The New York Public Library, Astor, Lenox and Tilden Foundations).

3.
Aaron Douglas: *Aspects of Negro Life.* Panel #3: *The Idyll of the Deep South,* W.P.A., 1934 (Schomburg Center for Research in Black Culture, Art & Artifacts Division, The New York Public Library, Astor, Lenox and Tilden Foundations).

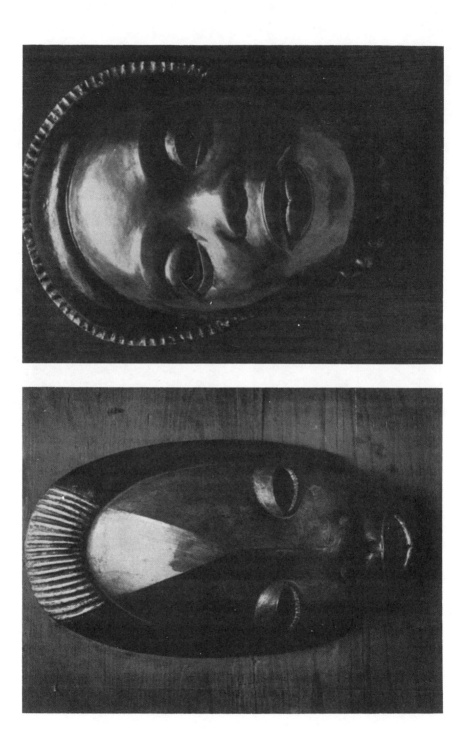

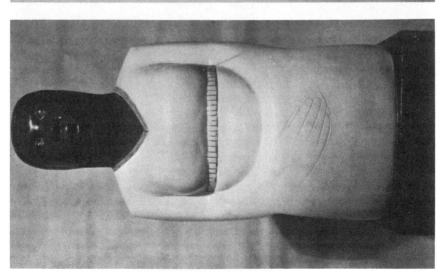

4. (above, left)
Sargent Johnson: *Mask*, n.d.
(San Francisco Museum of Art,
Albert M. Bender Collection).

5. (above, right)
Sargent Johnson: *Mask* (Negro
Mother), 1935 (San Francisco
Museum of Art, Albert M.
Bender Collection).

6. (far left)
Sargent Johnsor: *Negro
Woman*, n.d. (San Francisco
Museum of Art, Albert M.
Bender Collection).

7. (near left)
Sargent Johnson: Forever Free,
1933 (San Francisco
Museum of Modern Art, Gift of
Mrs. E. D. Lederman).

8.
Sargent Johnson:
Negro Woman, 1933
(San Francisco Mu-
seum of Art, Albert
M. Bender
Collection).

9.
Sargent Johnson:
*Head of a Negro
Woman,* 1935 (San
Francisco Museum
of Art, Albert M.
Bender Collection).

10.
Sargent Johnson:
White and Black, n.d.
(San Francisco Museum of Art, Albert
M. Bender Collection).

11.
Richmond Barthé: *Feral Benga,*
1935 (Collection of The Newark
Museum, Purchase by
exchange, Gift of Mr. and Mrs.
Charles W. Engelhard 1989).

12.
Richmond Barthé: *African Dan-
cer,* 1933 (Collection of Whitney
Museum of American Art,
Purchase)

13.
Augusta Savage: *Gamin,* 1930
(Schomburg Center for
Research in Black Culture, Art
& Artifacts Division, The New
York Public Library, Astor, Lenox
and Tilden Foundations).

14.
Hale Woodruff: *Mutiny on the Amistad* from *The Amistad Murals*, 1939 (Savery Library, Talladega College).

15.
Hale Woodruff: *The Trial of the Captive Slaves* from *The Amistad Murals*, 1939 (Savery Library, Talladega College).

16.
Hale Woodruff: *Return of the Natives* from *The Amistad Murals*, 1939 (Savery Library, Talladega College).

17. *(above left)*
William H. Johnson: *Self-Portrait,* 1921–26 (National Museum of American Art, Smithsonian Institution, Gift of the Harmon Foundation).

18. *(above right)*
William H. Johnson: *Minnie,* 1930 (National Museum of American Art, Smithsonian Institution, Gift of the Harmon Foundation).

19. *(left)*
William H. Johnson: *Self-Portrait,* 1929 (National Museum of American Art, Smithsonian Institution, Gift of the Harmon Foundation).

20.
William H. Johnson: *Sun Setting, Denmark, c.* 1930–32
(National Museum of American Art, Smithsonian Institution, Gift of the Harmon Foundation).

21.
William H. Johnson: *Jacobia Hotel*, 1930 (National Museum of American Art, Smithsonian Institution, Gift of the Harmon Foundation).

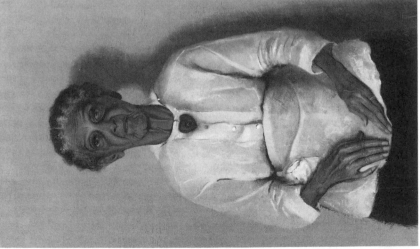

22. *(above left)*
Archibald J. Motley:
*Portrait of My
Grandmother*, 1922
(Chicago Historical
Society, Collection
of Archie Motley
and Valerie Gerrard
Browne).

23. *(above right)*
Archibald J. Motley:
*Brown Girl after the
Bath*, 1931
(Chicago Historical
Society, Collection
of Archie Motley
and Valerie Gerrard
Browne).

24. *(left)*
Archibald J. Motley:
Blues, 1929
(Chicago Historical
Society, Collection
of Archie Motley
and Valerie Gerrard
Browne).

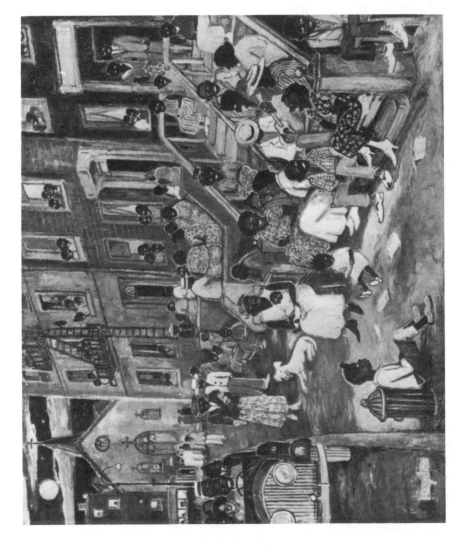

25.
Palmer Hayden: *Midsummer Night in Harlem*, 1936 (Courtesy of Mrs. Miriam C. Hayden, photograph by Eeva-Inkeri Photographers).

AFRO-AMERICAN ART:
ART OR PROPAGANDA?
HIGH OR LOW CULTURE?

Some black intellectuals of the 1920s claimed that art and literature could signal the achievement or the "arrival" of a people, the existence of the works of art themselves being the basis of a racial self-respect, that there could be, there ought to be, an Afro-American art, and that art could become a means to social respect in American life for the Afro-American. The argument rested on the assumption that much of the racial problem in the United States was due to the ignorance of whites of the true character of blacks, and ignorance of blacks of their own true qualities as a people. The production of art and literature would serve to lift this cloud of ignorance by demonstrating to the white world that blacks could achieve on the highest level, measured by Euro-American standards. Black Americans, then, should put their experience and sensibilities into the form of poems, stories, and pictures—the highest achievement of Western civilization.

The attitudes, however, were paradoxical. If there was a distinctive Afro-American sensibility and expression, would conventional Euro-American forms be the ideal vehicle for his art? If the primary purpose of Afro-American art was racial acceptance in the eyes of whites, was not the effort simply, as DuBois had said it, measuring oneself by the tape of others, who look on with contempt or pity? These contradictions were voiced by the questions that were raised. Was there really an Afro-American art, or was the black artist just another American? Langston Hughes and George S. Schuyler argued the two sides of that question. James Weldon Johnson made a strong case for a major black achievement in poetry. But his "Preface" assumes a "high culture" as measured by Euro-American standards. It is worth noting that the second edition of Johnson's Book of American Negro Poetry, *which appeared in 1931, included the works of Langston Hughes, Countee Cullen, Gwendolyn Bennett, Sterling Brown, Arna Bontemps, and Helene Johnson, poets whose work had not been ready for his first edition which had appeared in 1922. This difference is suggestive of the achievement of the Harlem Renaissance. But the expectation of being judged by a white cultural and intellectual elite, implied by Johnson, goes far toward explaining why much of the poetry of the period was strangely raceless and conventional, not reflecting the stylistic and aesthetic innovations of contemporary white American poets such as T. S. Eliot, Ezra Pound, e. e. cummings, and others. Consider, for instance the poems of Jessie*

Fauset and Countee Cullen. The paradox of Afro-American art gives special meaning to Cullen's "Yet Do I Marvel."

Assumptions about the nature of art also brought into question the proper subject of Afro-American poetry and prose. If art had to do with beauty and universal values, could it be used, directly and intentionally, as an instrument for social change or for political and social pleading? Those, like Alain Locke, who would answer no, would call all such efforts propaganda and not art. But such an analysis placed an unusual burden on the Afro-American artist, for the human realities that touched him most were enmeshed in social and political realities of racism. Perhaps Locke posed the wrong question. It was not either art or propaganda but how the Afro-American—victimized by a social and political system which was often brutal and ugly—might effectively express his experience in art. Another question, implied by both Hughes and Locke, queried whether an Afro-American should (or could) produce an art that was raceless. Few today would question that art can be a weapon in social conflict, and many, joining Hughes, would be contemptuous of a black man who claimed to be a poet rather than a Negro poet. It is characteristic of the 1920s that these questions were raised in the way that they were by these writers.

The Harlem Renaissance reflected an extraordinary self-consciousness about art and the nature of Afro-American art. It is this self-consciousness, and the pretensions of it, that Wallace Thurman satirized in his novel Infants of the Spring. Ironically, jazz—the music which was to define the age—was being created and performed without a similar debate about the nature of art. Since they were innovators and creators of a new idiom, black musicians, unlike black artists and writers, were able to be their own judges of what was good jazz. They did not have to depend on outside critics or a learned and alien tradition to give them validity. The problems raised by Locke, Hughes, and Johnson seemed unimportant to J. P. Johnson (one of the most celebrated jazz pianists of all time) or Eubie Blake (rag-time composer who wrote for the musical stage, notably the music for Shuffle Along).

FROM THE BOOK OF AMERICAN NEGRO POETRY
JAMES WELDON JOHNSON

Preface to the First Edition

There is, perhaps, a better excuse for giving an Anthology of American Negro Poetry to the public than can be offered for many of the anthologies that have recently been issued. The public, generally speaking, does not know that there are American Negro poets—to supply this lack of information is, alone, a work worthy of somebody's effort.

Moreover, the matter of Negro poets and the production of literature by the colored people in this country involves more than supplying information that is lacking. It is a matter which has a direct bearing on the most vital of American problems.

A people may become great through many means, but there is only one measure by which its greatness is recognized and acknowledged. The final measure of the greatness of all peoples is the amount and standard of the literature and art they have produced. The world does not know that a people is great until that people produces great literature and art. No people that has produced great literature and art has ever been looked upon by the world as distinctly inferior.

The status of the Negro in the United States is more a question of national mental attitude toward the race than of actual conditions. And nothing will do more to change that mental attitude and raise his status than a demonstration of intellectual parity of the Negro through the production of literature and art.

Is there likelihood that the American Negro will be able to do this? There is, for the good reason that he possesses the innate powers. He has the emotional endowment, the originality and artistic conception, and, what is more important, the power of creating that which has universal appeal and influence.

I make here what may appear to be a more startling statement by saying that the Negro has already proved the possession of these powers by being the creator of the only things artistic that have yet sprung from American soil and been universally acknowledged as distinctive American products.[1]

These creations by the American Negro may be summed up under four heads. The first two are the Uncle Remus stories, which were collected by Joel Chandler Harris, and the "spirituals" or slave songs, to which the Fisk Jubilee Singers made the public and the musicians of both the United States and Europe listen. The Uncle Remus stories constitute the greatest body of folk lore that America has produced, and the "spirituals" the greatest body of folk song. I shall speak of the "spirituals" later because they are

---

1. This statement should probably be modified by the inclusion of American skyscraper architecture. (*Editor, 1931.*)

more than folk songs, for in them the Negro sounded the depths, if he did not scale the heights, of music.

The other two creations are the cakewalk and ragtime. We do not need to go very far back to remember when cakewalking was the rage in the United States, Europe and South America. Society in this country and royalty abroad spent time in practicing the intricate steps. Paris pronounced it the "poetry of motion." The popularity of the cakewalk passed away but its influence remained. The influence can be seen today on any American stage where there is dancing.

The influence which the Negro has exercised on the art of dancing in this country has been almost absolute. For generations the "buck and wing" and the "stop-time" dances, which are strictly Negro, have been familiar to American theater audiences. A few years ago the public discovered the "turkey trot," the "eagle rock," "ballin' the jack," and several other varieties that started the modern dance craze. These dances were quickly followed by the "tango," a dance originated by the Negroes of Cuba and later transplanted to South America. (This fact is attested by no less authority than Vicente Blasco Ibañez in his *Four Horsemen of the Apocalypse.*) Half the floor space in the country was then turned over to dancing, and highly paid exponents sprang up everywhere. The most noted, Mr. Vernon Castle, and, by the way, an Englishman, never danced except to the music of a colored band, and he never failed to state to his audiences that most of his dances had long been done by "your colored people," as he put it.

Any one who witnesses a musical production in which there is dancing cannot fail to notice the Negro stamp on all the movements; a stamp which even the great vogue of Russian dances that swept the country about the time of the popular dance craze could not affect. That peculiar swaying of the shoulders which you see done everywhere by the blond girls of the chorus is nothing more than a movement from the Negro dance referred to above, the "eagle rock." Occasionally the movements takes on a suggestion of the now outlawed "shimmy."

As for Ragtime, I go straight to the statement that it is the one artistic production by which America is known the world over. It has been all-conquering. Everywhere it is hailed as "American music."

For a dozen years or so there has been a steady tendency to divorce Ragtime from the Negro; in fact, to take from him the credit of having originated it. Probably the younger people of the present generation do not know that Ragtime is of Negro origin. The change wrought in Ragtime and the way in which it is accepted by the country have been brought about chiefly through the change which has gradually been made in the words and stories accompanying the music. Once the text of all Ragtime songs was written in Negro dialect, and was about Negroes in the cabin or in the cotton field or on the levee or at a jubilee or on Sixth Avenue or at a ball, and about their love affairs. Today, only a small proportion of Ragtime songs relate at all to the Negro. The truth is, Ragtime is now national rather than racial. But that does not abolish in any way the claim of the American Negro as its originator.

Ragtime music was originated by colored piano players in the questionable resorts of St. Louis, Memphis, and other Mississippi River towns. These men did not know any more about the theory of music than they did about the theory of the universe. They were guided by their natural musical instinct and talent, but above all by the Negro's extraordinary sense of rhythm. Any one who is familiar with Ragtime may note that its chief charm is not in melody, but in rhythms. These players often improvised crude and, at times, vulgar words to fit the music. This was the beginning of the Ragtime song.

Ragtime music got its first popular hearing at Chicago during the World's Fair in that city. From Chicago it made its way to New York, and then started on its universal triumph.

The earliest Ragtime songs, like Topsy, "jes' grew." Some of these earliest songs were taken down by white men, the words slightly altered or changed, and published under the names of the arrangers. They sprang into immediate popularity and earned small fortunes. The first to become widely known as "The Bully," a levee song which had been long used by roustabouts along the Mississippi. It was introduced in New York by Miss May Irwin, and gained instant popularity. Another one of these "jes' grew" songs was one which for a while disputed for place with Yankee Doodle; perhaps, disputes it even today. That song was "A Hot Time in the Old Town Tonight"; introduced and made popular by the colored regimental bands during the Spanish-American War.

Later there came along a number of colored men who were able to transcribe the old songs and write original ones. I was, about that time, writing words to music for the music show stage in New York. I was collaborating with my brother, J. Rosamond Johnson, and the late Bob Cole. I remember that we appropriated about the last one of the old "jes' grew" songs. It was a song which had been sung for years all through the South. The words were unprintable, but the tune was irresistible, and belonged to nobody. We took it, re-wrote the verses, telling an entirely different story from the original, left the chorus as it was, and published the song, at first under the name of "Will Handy." It became very popular with college boys, especially at football games, and perhaps still is. The song was "Oh, Didn't He Ramble!"

In the beginning, and for quite a while, almost all of the Ragtime songs that were deliberately composed were the work of colored writers. Now, the colored composers, even in this particular field, are greatly outnumbered by the white.

The reader might be curious to know if the "jes' grew" songs have ceased to grow. No, they have not; they are growing all the time. The country has lately been flooded with several varieties of "The Blues." These "Blues," too, had their origin in Memphis, and the towns along the Mississippi. They are a sort of lament of a lover who is feeling "blue" over the loss of his sweetheart. The "Blues" of Memphis have been adulterated so much on Broadway that they have lost their pristine hue. But whenever you hear a piece of music which has a strain like this in it:

you will know you are listening to something which belonged originally to Beale Avenue, Memphis, Tennessee. The original "Memphis Blues," so far as it can be credited to a composer, must be credited to Mr. W. C. Handy, a colored musician of Memphis.

As illustrations of the genuine Ragtime song in the making, I quote the words of two that were popular with the Southern colored soldiers in France. Here is the first:

> Mah mammy's lyin' in her grave,
>   Mah daddy done run away,
> Mah sister's married a gamblin' man,
>   An' I've done gone astray.
> Yes, I've done gone astray, po' boy,
>   An' I've done gone astray,
> Mah sister's married a gamblin' man,
>   An' I've done gone astray, po' boy.

These lines are crude, but they contain something of real poetry, of that elusive thing which nobody can define and that you can only tell is there when you feel it. You cannot read these lines without becoming reflective and feeling sorry for "Po' Boy."

Now, take in this word picture of utter dejection:

> I'm jes' as misabul as I can be,
> I'm unhappy even if I am free,
> I'm feelin' down, I'm feelin' blue;
> I wander 'round, don't know what to do.
> I'm go'n lay mah haid on de railroad line,
> Let de B. & O. come and pacify mah min'.

These lines are, no doubt, one of the many versions of the famous "Blues." They are also crude, but they go straight to the mark. The last two lines move with the swiftness of all great tragedy.

In spite of the bans which musicians and music teachers have placed on it, the people still demand and enjoy Ragtime. In fact, there is not a corner of the civilized world in which it is not known and liked. And this proves its originality, for if it were an imitation, the people of Europe, at least, would not have found it a novelty. And it is proof of a more important thing, it is proof that Ragtime possesses the vital spark, the power to appeal universally, without which any artistic production, no matter how approved its form may be, is dead.

Of course, there are those who will deny that Ragtime is an artistic production. American musicians, especially, instead of investigating Ragtime, dismiss it with a contemptuous word. But this has been the course of scholasticism in every branch of art. Whatever new thing the people like is poohpoohed; whatever is popular is regarded as not worth while. The fact is, nothing great or enduring in music has ever sprung full-fledged from the brain of any master; the best he gives the world he gathers from the hearts of the people, and runs it through the alembic of his genius.

Ragtime deserves serious attention. There is a lot of colorless and vicious imitation, but there is enough that is genuine. In one composition alone, "The Memphis Blues," the musician will find not only great melodic beauty, but a polyphonic structure that is amazing.

It is obvious that Ragtime has influenced and, in a large measure, become our popular music; but not many would know that it has influenced even our religious music. Those who are familiar with gospel hymns can at once see this influence if they will compare the songs of thirty years ago, such as "In the Sweet Bye and Bye," "The Ninety and Nine," etc., with the up-to-date, syncopated tunes that are sung in Sunday Schools, Christian Endeavor Societies, Y.M.C.A.'s and like gatherings today.

Ragtime has not only influenced American music, it has influenced American life; indeed, it has saturated American life. It has become the popular medium for our national expression musically. And who can say that it does not express the blare and jangle and the surge, too, of our national spirit?

Any one who doubts that there is a peculiar heel-tickling, smile-provoking, joy-awakening, response-compelling charm in Ragimte needs only to hear a skillful performer play the genuine article, needs only to listen to its bizarre harmonies, its audacious resolutions often consisting of an abrupt jump from one key to another, its intricate rhythms in which the accents fall in the most unexpected places but in which the fundamental beat is never lost, in order to be convinced. I believe it has its place as well as the music which draws from us sighs and tears.

Now, these dances which I have referred to and Ragtime music may be lower forms of art, but they are evidence of a power that will some day be applied to the higher forms. And even now we need not stop at the Negro's accomplishment through these lower forms. In the "spirituals," or slave songs, the Negro has given America not only its only folk songs, but a mass of noble music. I never think of this music but that I am struck by the wonder, the miracle of its production. How did the men who originated these songs manage to do it? The sentiments are easily accounted for; they are, for the most part, taken from the Bible. But the melodies, where did they come from? Some of them so weirdly sweet, and others so wonderfully strong. Take, for instance, "Go Down, Moses"; I doubt that there is a stronger theme in the whole musical literature of the world.

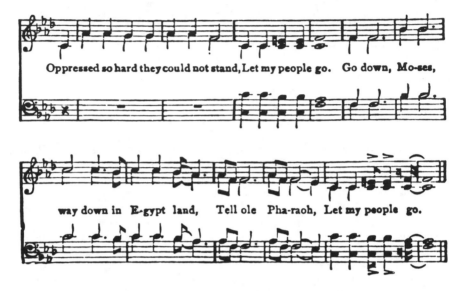

Oppressed so hard they could not stand, Let my people go. Go down, Mo-ses, way down in E-gypt land, Tell ole Pha-raoh, Let my people go.

It is to be noted that whereas the chief characteristic of Ragtime is rhythm, the chief characteristic of the "spirituals" is melody. The melodies of "Steal Away to Jesus," "Swing Low Sweet Chariot," "Nobody Knows de Trouble I See," "I Couldn't Hear Nobody Pray," "Deep River," "O, Freedom Over Me," and many others of these songs possess a beauty that is—what shall I say? poignant. In the riotous rhythms of Ragtime the Negro expressed his irrepressible buoyancy, his keen response to the sheer joy of living; in the "spirituals" he voiced his sense of beauty and his deep religious feeling.

Naturally, not as much can be said for the words of these songs as for the music. Most of the songs are religious. Some of them are songs expressing faith and endurance and a longing for freedom. In the religious songs, the sentiments and often the entire lines are taken bodily from the Bible. However, there is no doubt that some of these religious songs have a meaning apart from the Biblical text. It is evident that the opening lines of "Go Down, Moses,"

> Go down, Moses,
> 'Way down in Egypt land;

> Tell old Pharaoh,
>> Let my people go.

have a significance beyond the bondage of Israel in Egypt.

The bulk of the lines to these songs, as is the case in all communal music, is made up of choral iteration and incremental repetition of the leader's lines. If the words are read, this constant iteration and repetition are found to be tiresome; and it must be admitted that the lines themselves are often very trite. And, yet, there is frequently revealed a flash of real primitive poetry. I give the following examples:

> Sometimes I feel like an eagle in de air.

> You may bury me in de East,
> You may bury me in de West,
> But I'll hear de trumpet sound
>> In-a dat mornin'.

> I know de moonlight, I know de starlight;
>> I lay dis body down.
> I walk in de moonlight, I walk in de starlight;
>> I lay dis body down.
> I know de graveyard, I know de graveyard,
>> When I lay dis body down.
> I walk in de graveyard, I walk troo de graveyard
>> To lay dis body down.

> I lay in de grave an' stretch out my arms;
>> I lay dis body down.
> I go to de judgment in de evenin' of de day
>> When I lay dis body down.
> An' my soul an' yo soul will meet in de day
>> When I lay dis body down.

Regarding the line, "I lay in de grave an' stretch out my arms," Col. Thomas Wentworth Higginson of Boston, one of the first to give these slave songs serious study, said: "Never, it seems to me, since man first lived and suffered, was his infinite longing for peace uttered more plaintively than in that line."

These Negro folk songs constitute a vast mine of material that has been neglected almost absolutely. The only white writers who have in recent years given adequate attention and study to this music, that I know of, are Mr. H. E. Krehbiel and Mrs. Natalie Curtis Burlin. We have our native composers denying the worth and importance of this music, and trying to manufacture grand opera out of so-called Indian themes.

But there is a great hope for the development of this music, and that hope is the Negro himself. A worthy beginning has already been made by Burleigh, Cook, Johnson, and Dett. And there will yet come great Negro composers who will take this music and voice through it not only the soul of their race, but the soul of America.

And does it not seem odd that this greatest gift of the Negro has been the most neglected of all he possesses? Money and effort have been expended upon his development in every direction except this. This gift has been regarded as a kind of side show, something for occasional exhibition; wherein it is the touchstone, it is the magic thing, it is that by which the Negro can bridge all chasms. No persons, however hostile, can listen to Negroes singing this wonderful music without having their hostility melted down.

This power of the Negro to suck up the national spirit from the soil and create something artistic and original, which, at the same time, possesses the note of universal appeal, is due to a remarkable racial gift of adaptability; it is more than adaptability, it is a transfusive quality. And the Negro has exercised this transfusive quality not only here in America, where the race lives in large numbers, but in European countries, where the number has been almost infinitesimal.

Is it not curious to know that the greatest poet of Russia is Alexander Pushkin, a man of African descent; that the greatest romancer of France is Alexandre Dumas, a man of African descent; and that one of the greatest musicians of England is Coleridge-Taylor, a man of African descent?

The fact is fairly well known that the father of Dumas was a Negro of the French West Indies, and that the father of Coleridge-Taylor was a native-born African; but the facts concerning Pushkin's African ancestry are not so familiar.

When Peter the Great was Czar of Russia, some potentate presented him with a full-blooded Negro of gigantic size. Peter, the most eccentric ruler of modern times, dressed this Negro up in soldier clothes, christened him Hannibal, and made him a special body-guard.

But Hannibal had more than size, he had brain and ability. He not only looked picturesque and imposing in soldier clothes, he showed that he had in him the making of a real soldier. Peter recognized this, and eventually made him a general. He afterwards ennobled him, and Hannibal, later, married one of the ladies of the Russian court. This same Hannibal was great-grandfather of Pushkin, the national poet of Russia, the man who bears the same relation to Russian literature that Shakespeare bears to English literature.

I know the question naturally arises: If out of the few Negroes who have lived in France there came a Dumas; and out of the few Negroes who have lived in England there came a Coleridge-Taylor; and if from the man who was at the time, probably, the only Negro in Russia there sprang that country's national poet, why have not the millions of Negroes in the United States with all the emotional and artistic endowment claimed for them produced a Dumas, or a Coleridge-Taylor, or a Pushkin?

The question seems difficult, but there is an answer. The Negro in the United States is consuming all of his intellectual energy in this grueling race-struggle. And the same statement may be made in a general way about the white South. Why does not the white South produce literature and art? The white South, too, is consuming all of its intellectual energy in this lamentable conflict. Nearly all of the mental efforts of the white South run through one narrow channel. The life of every Southern white man and all of his activities are impassably limited by the ever present Negro problem. And that is why, as Mr. H. L. Mencken puts it, in all that vast region, with its thirty or forty million people and its territory as large as a half dozen Frances or Germanys, there is not a single poet, not a serious historian, not a creditable composer, not a critic good or bad, not a dramatist dead or alive.[1]

But, even so, the American Negro has accomplished something in pure literature. The list of those who have done so would be surprising both by its length and the excellence of the achievements. One of the great books written in this country since the Civil War is the work of a colored man, *The Souls of Black Folk,* by W. E. B. Du Bois.

Such a list begins with Phillis Wheatley. In 1761 a slave ship landed a cargo of slaves in Boston. Among them was a little girl seven or eight years of age. She attracted the attention of John Wheatley, a wealthy gentleman of Boston, who purchased her as a servant for his wife. Mrs. Wheatley was a benevolent woman. She noticed the girl's quick mind and determined to give her opportunity for its development. Twelve years later Phillis published a volume of poems. The book was brought out in London, where Phillis was for several months an object of great curiosity and attention.

Phillis Wheatley has never been given her rightful place in American literature. By some sort of conspiracy she is kept out of most of the books, especially the text-books on literature used in the schools. Of course, she is not a *great* American poet—and in her day there were no great American poets—but she is an important American poet. Her importance, if for no other reason, rests on the fact that, save one, she is the first in order of time of all the women poets of America. And she is among the first of all American poets to issue a volume.

It seems strange that the books generally give space to a mention of Urian Oakes, President of Harvard College, and to quotations from the crude and lengthy elegy which he published in 1667; and print examples from the execrable versified version of the Psalms made by the New England divines, and yet deny a place to Phillis Wheatley.

Here are the opening lines from the elegy by Oakes, which is quoted from in most of the books on American literature:

1. This statement was quoted in 1921. The reader may consider for himself the changes wrought in the decade. (*Editor, 1931.*)

> Reader, I am no poet, but I grieve.
> Behold here what that passion can do,
> That forced a verse without Apollo's leave,
> And whether the learned sisters would or no.

There was no need for Urian to admit what his handiwork declared. But this from the versified Psalms is still worse, yet it is found in the books:

> The Lord's song sing can we? being
> in stranger's land, then let
> lose her skill my right hand if I
> Jerusalem forget.

Anne Bradstreet preceded Phillis Wheatley by a little over one hundred and twenty years. She published her volume of poems, *The Tenth Muse,* in 1650. Let us strike a comparison between the two. Anne Bradstreet was a wealthy, cultivated Puritan girl, the daughter of Thomas Dudley, Governor of Bay Colony. Phillis, as we know, was a Negro slave girl born in Africa. Let us take them both at their best and in the same vein. The following stanza is from Anne's poem entitled "Contemplation":

> While musing thus with contemplation fed,
> And thousand fancies buzzing in my brain,
> The sweet tongued Philomel percht o'er my head,
> And chanted forth a most melodious strain,
> Which rapt me so with wonder and delight,
> I judged my hearing better than my sight,
> And wisht me wings with her awhile to take my flight.

And the following is from Phillis' poem entitled "Imagination":

> Imagination! who can sing thy force?
> Or who describe the swiftness of thy course?
> Soaring through air to find the bright abode,
> Th' empyreal palace of the thundering God,
> We on thy pinions can surpass the wind,
> And leave the rolling universe behind.
> From star to star the mental optics rove,
> Measure the skies, and range the realms above;
> There in one view we grasp the mighty whole,
> Or with new worlds amaze th' unbounded soul.

We do not think the black woman suffers much by comparison with the white. Thomas Jefferson said of Phillis: "Religion has produced a Phillis Wheatley, but it could not produce a poet; her poems are beneath contempt." It is quite likely that Jefferson's criticism was directed more against religion than against Phillis' poetry. On the other hand, General George Washington wrote her with his own hand a letter in which he thanked her for a poem which she had dedicated to him. He later received her with marked courtesy at his camp at Cambridge.

It appears certain that Phillis was the first person to apply to George Washington the phrase, "First in peace." The phrase occurs in her poem addressed to "His Excellency, General George Washington," written in 1775. The encomium, "First in war, first in peace, first in the hearts of his countrymen," was originally used in the resolutions presented to Congress on the death of Washington, December, 1799.

Phillis Wheatley's poetry is the poetry of the Eighteenth Century. She wrote when Pope and Gray were supreme; it is easy to see that Pope was her model. Had she come under the influence of Wordsworth, Byron or Keats or Shelley, she would have done greater work. As it is, her work must not be judged by the work and standards of a later day, but by the work and standards of her own day and her own contemporaries. By this method of criticism she stands out as one of the important characters in the making of American literature, without any allowances for her sex or her antecedents.

According to A Bibliographical Checklist of American Negro Poetry, compiled by Mr. Arthur A. Schomburg, more than one hundred Negroes in the United States have published volumes of poetry ranging in size from pamphlets to books of from one hundred to three hundred pages. About thirty of these writers fill in the gap between Phillis Wheatley and Paul Laurence Dunbar. Just here it is of interest to note that a Negro wrote and published a poem before Phillis Wheatley arrived in this country from Africa. He was Jupiter Hammon, a slave belonging to a Mr. Lloyd of Queens-Village, Long Island. In 1760 Hammon published a poem, eighty-eight lines in length, entitled "An Evening Thought, Salvation by Christ, with Penettential Cries." In 1788 he published "An Address to Miss Phillis Wheatley, Ethiopian Poetess in Boston, who came from Africa at eight years of age, and soon became acquainted with the Gospel of Jesus Christ." These two poems do not include all that Hammon wrote.

The poets between Phillis Wheatley and Dunbar must be considered more in the light of what they attempted than of what they accomplished. Many of them showed marked talent, but barely a half dozen of them demonstrated even mediocre mastery of technique in the use of poetic material and forms. And yet there are several names that deserve mention. George M. Horton, Frances E. Harper, James M. Bell and Alberry A. Whitman, all merit consideration when due allowances are made for their limitations in education, training and general culture. The limitations of Horton were greater than those of either of the others; he was born a slave in North Carolina in 1797, and as a young man began to compose poetry without being able to write it down. Later he received some instruction from professors of the University of North Carolina, at which institution he was employed as a janitor. He published a volume of poems, The Hope of Liberty, in 1829.

Mrs. Harper, Bell, and Whitman would stand out if only for the reason that each of them attempted sustained work. Mrs. Harper published her first volume of poems in 1854, but later she published "Moses, a Story of the Nile," a poem which ran to 52 closely printed pages. Bell in 1864 published a poem of 28 pages in celebration of President Lincoln's Emancipation Proclamation. In 1870 he published a poem of 32 pages in celebration of the ratification of the Fifteenth Amendment to the Constitution. Whitman published his first volume of poems, a book of 253 pages, in 1877; but in 1884 he published "The Rape of Florida," an epic poem written in four cantos and done in the Spenserian stanza, and which ran to 97 closely printed pages. The poetry of both Mrs. Harper and of Whitman had a large degree of popularity; one of Mrs. Harper's book went through more than twenty editions.

Of these four poets, it is Whitman who reveals not only the greatest imagination but also the more skillful workmanship. His lyric power at its best may be judged from the following stanza from the "Rape of Florida":

"Come now, my love, the moon is on the lake;
Upon the waters is my light canoe;
Come with me, love, and gladsome oars shall make
A music on the parting wave for you.
Come o'er the waters deep and dark and blue;
Come where the lilies in the marge have sprung,
Come with me, love, for Oh, my love is true!"
This is the song that on the lake was sung,
The boatman sang it when his heart was young.

Some idea of Whitman's capacity for dramatic narration may be gained from the following lines taken from "Not a Man, and Yet a Man," a poem of even greater length than "The Rape of Florida."

A flash of steely lightning from his hand,
Strikes down the groaning leader of the band;
Divides his startled comrades, and again
Descending, leaves fair Dora's captors slain.
Her, seizing then within a strong embrace,
Out in the dark he wheels his flying pace;

.   .   .   .   .

He speaks not, but with stalwart tenderness
Her swelling bosom firm to his doth press;
Springs like a stag that flees the eager hound,
And like a whirlwind rustles o'er the ground.
Her locks swim in disheveled wildness o'er
His shoulders, streaming to his waist and more;
While on and on, strong as a rolling flood,
His sweeping footsteps part the silent wood.

It is curious and interesting to trace the growth of individuality and race consciousness in this group of poets. Jupiter Hammon's verses were almost entirely religious exhortations. Only very seldom does Phillis Wheatley sound a native note. Four times in single lines she refers to herself as "Afric's muse." In a poem of admonition addressed to the students at the "University of Cambridge in New England" she refers to herself as follows:

> Ye blooming plants of human race divine,
> An Ethiop tells you 'tis your greatest foe.

But one looks in vain for some outburst or even complaint against the bondage of her people, for some agonizing cry about her native land. In two poems she refers definitely to Africa as her home, but in each instance there seems to be under the sentiment of the lines a feeling of almost smug contentment at her own escape therefrom. In the poem, "On Being Brought from Africa to America," she says:

> 'Twas mercy brought me from my pagan land,
> Taught my benighted soul to understand
> That there's a God and there's a Saviour too;
> Once I redemption neither sought nor knew.
> Some view our sable race with scornful eye—
> "Their color is a diabolic dye."
> Remember, Christians, Negroes black as Cain,
> May be refined, and join th' angelic train.

In the poem addressed to the Earl of Dartmouth, she speaks of freedom and makes a reference to the parents from whom she was taken as a child, a reference which cannot but strike the reader as rather unimpassioned:

> Should you, my lord, while you peruse my song,
> Wonder from whence my love of Freedom sprung,
> Whence flow these wishes for the common good,
> By feeling hearts alone best understood;
> I, young in life, by seeming cruel fate
> Was snatch'd from Afric's fancy'd happy seat;
> What pangs excruciating must molest,
> What sorrows labor in my parents' breast?
> Steel'd was that soul and by no misery mov'd
> That from a father seiz'd his babe belov'd;
> Such, such my case. And can I then but pray
> Others may never feel tyrannic sway?

The bulk of Phillis Wheatley's work consists of poems addressed to people of prominence. Her book was dedicated to the Countess of Huntington, at whose house she spent the greater part of her time while in England. On his repeal of the Stamp Act, she wrote a poem to King George III, whom she saw later; another poem she wrote to the Earl of Dartmouth, whom she knew. A number of her verses were addressed to other persons of distinction. Indeed, it is apparent that Phillis was far from being a democrat. She was far from being a democrat not only in her social ideas but also in her political ideas; unless a religious meaning is given to the closing lines of her ode to General Washington, she was a decided royalist:

> A crown, a mansion, and a throne that shine
> With gold unfading, Washington! be thine.

Nevertheless, she was an ardent patriot. Her ode to General Washington (1775), her spirited poem, "On Major General Lee" (1776), and her poem, "Liberty and Peace," written in celebration of the close of the war, reveal not only strong patriotic feeling but an understanding of the issues at stake. In her poem, "On Major General Lee," she makes her hero reply thus to the taunts of the British commander into whose hands he has been delivered through treachery:

> O arrogance of tongue!
> And wild ambition, ever prone to wrong!
> Believ'st thou, chief, that armies such as thine
> Can stretch in dust that heaven-defended line?
> In vain allies may swarm from distant lands,
> And demons aid in formidable bands.
> Great as thou art, thou shun'st the field of fame,
> Disgrace to Britain and the British name!
> When offer'd combat by the noble foe
> (Foe to misrule) why did the sword forego
> The easy conquest of the rebel-land?
> Perhaps too easy for they martial hand.
> What various causes to the field invite!
> For plunder you, and we for freedom fight;
> Her cause divine with generous ardor fires,
> And every bosom glows as she inspires!
> Already thousands of your troops have fled
> To the drear mansions of the silent dead:
> Columbia, too, beholds with streaming eyes
> Her heroes fall—'tis freedom's sacrifice!
> So wills the power who with convulsive storms
> Shakes impious realms, and nature's face deforms;
> Yet those brave troops, innum'rous as the sands,
> One soul inspires, one General Chief commands;
> Find in your train of boasted heroes, one
> To match the praise of Godlike Washington.
> Thrice happy Chief in whom the virtues join,
> And heaven taught prudence speaks the man divine.

What Phillis Wheatley failed to achieve is due in no small degree to her education and environment. Her mind was steeped in the classics; her verses are filled with classical and mythological allusions. She knew Ovid thoroughly and was familiar with other Latin authors. She must have known Alexander Pope by heart. And, too, she was reared and sheltered in a wealthy and cultured family,—a wealthy and cultured Boston family; she never had the opportunity to learn life; she never found out her own true relation to life and to her surroundings. And it should not be forgotten that she was only about thirty years old when she died. The impulsion or the compulsion that might have driven her genius off the worn paths, out on a journey of exploration, Phillis Wheatley never received. But, whatever her limitations, she merits more than America has accorded her.

Horton, who was born three years after Phillis Wheatley's death, expressed in all of his poetry strong complaint at his condition of slavery and a deep longing for freedom. The following verses are typical of his style and his ability:

> Alas! and am I born for this,
>   To wear this slavish chain?
> Deprived of all created bliss,
>   Through hardship, toil, and pain?
>
> Come, Liberty! thou cheerful sound,
>   Roll through my ravished ears;
> Come, let my grief in joys be drowned,
>   And drive away my fears.

In Mrs. Harper we find something more than the complaint and the longing of Horton. We find an expression of a sense of wrong and injustice. The following stanzas are from a poem addressed to the white women of America:

> You can sigh o'er the sad-eyed Armenian
>   Who weeps in her desolate home.
> You can mourn o'er the exile of Russia
>   From kindred and friends doomed to roam.
>
> But hark! from our Southland are floating
>   Sobs of anguish, murmurs of pain;
> And women heart-stricken are weeping
>   O'er their tortured and slain.
>
> Have ye not, oh, my favored sisters,
>   Just a plea, a prayer or a tear
> For mothers who dwell 'neath the shadows
>   Of agony, hatred and fear?
>
> Weep not, oh, my well sheltered sisters,
>   Weep not for the Negro alone,
> But weep for your sons who must gather
>   The crops which their fathers have sown.

Whitman, in the midst of "The Rape of Florida," a poem in which he related the taking of the State of Florida from the Seminoles, stops and discusses the race question. He discusses it in many other poems; and he dis-

cusses it from many different angles. In Whitman we find not only an expression of a sense of wrong and injustice, but we hear a note of faith and a
note also of defiance. For example, in the opening to Canto II of "The Rape
of Florida":

> Greatness by nature cannot be entailed;
> It is an office ending with the man,—
> Sage, hero, Saviour, tho' the Sire be hailed,
> The son may reach obscurity in the van:
> Sublime achievements know no patent plan,
> Man's immortality's a book with seals,
> And none but God shall open—none else can—
> But opened, it the mystery reveals,—
> Manhood's conquest of man to heaven's respect appeals.
>
> Is manhood less because man's face is black?
> Let thunders of the loosened seals reply!
> Who shall the rider's restive steed turn back?
> Or who withstand the arrows he lets fly
> Between the mountains of eternity?
> Genius ride forth! Thou gift and torch of heav'n!
> The mastery is kindled in thine eye;
> To conquest ride! thy bow of strength is giv'n—
> The trampled hordes of caste before thee shall be driv'n!
>
> 'Tis hard to judge if hatred of one's race,
> By those who deem themselves superior-born,
> Be worse than that quiescence in disgrace,
> Which only merits—and should only—scorn.
> Oh, let me see the Negro night and morn,
> Pressing and fighting in, for place and power!
> All earth is place—all time th' auspicious hour,
> While heaven leans forth to look, oh, will he quail or cower?
>
> Ah! I abhor his protest and complaint!
> His pious looks and patience I despise!
> He can't evade the test, disguised as saint;
> The manly voice of freedom bids him rise,
> And shake himself before Philistine eyes!
> And, like a lion roused, no sooner than
> A foe dare come, play all his energies,
> And court the fray with fury if he can;
> For hell itself respects a fearless, manly man.

It may be said that none of these poets strike a deep native strain or sound a
distinctly original note, either in matter or form. That is true; but the same
thing may be said of all the American poets down to the writers of the
present generation, with the exception of Poe and Walt Whitman. The thing

in which these black poets are mostly excelled by their contemporaries is mere technique.

Paul Laurence Dunbar stands out as the first poet from the Negro race in the United States to show a combined mastery over poetic material and poetic technique, to reveal innate literary distiction in what he wrote, and to maintain a high level of performance. He was the first to rise to a height from which he could take a perspective view of his own race. He was the first to see objectively its humor, its superstitions, its shortcomings; the first to feel sympathetically its heart-wounds, its yearnings, its aspirations, and to voice them all in a purely literary form.

Dunbar's fame rests chiefly on his poems in Negro dialect. This appraisal of him is, no doubt, fair; for in these dialect poems he not only carried his art to the highest point of perfection, but he made a contribution to American literature unlike what any one else had made, a contribution which, perhaps, no one else could have made. Of course, Negro dialect poetry was written before Dunbar wrote, most of it by white writers; but the fact stands out that Dunbar was the first to use it as a medium for the true interpretation of Negro character and psychology. And yet, dialect poetry does not constitute the whole or even the bulk of Dunbar's work. In addition to a large number of poems of a very high order done in literary English, he was the author of four novels and several volumes of short stories.

Indeed, Dunbar did not begin his career as a writer of dialect. I may be pardoned for introducing here a bit of reminiscence. My personal friendship with Paul Dunbar began before he had achieved recognition, and continued to be close until his death. When I first met him he had published a thin volume, *Oak and Ivy,* which was being sold chiefly through his own efforts. *Oak and Ivy* showed no distinctive Negro influence, but rather the influence of James Whitcomb Riley. At this time Paul and I were together every day for several months. He talked to me a great deal about his hopes and ambitions. In these talks he revealed that he had reached a realization of the possibilities of poetry in the dialect, together with a recognition of the fact that it offered the surest way by which he could get a hearing. Often he said to me: "I've got to write dialect poetry; it's the only way I can get them to listen to me." I was with Dunbar at the beginning of what proved to be his last illness. He said to me then: "I have not grown. I am writing the same things I wrote ten years ago, and am writing them no better." His self-accusation was not fully true; he had grown, and he had gained a surer control of his art, but he had not accomplished the greater things of which he was constantly dreaming; the public had held him to the things for which it had accorded him recognition. If Dunbar had lived he would have achieved some of those dreams, but even while he talked so dejectedly to me he seemed to feel that he was not to live. He died when he was only thirty-three.

It has a bearing on this entire subject to note that Dunbar was of unmixed Negro blood; so, as the greatest figure in literature which the colored race in the United States has produced, he stands as an example at once refuting and confounding those who wish to believe that whatever extraordinary ability an Aframerican shows is due to an admixture of white blood.

As a man, Dunbar was kind and tender. In conversation he was brilliant and polished. His voice was his chief charm, and was a great element in his success as a reader of his own works. In his actions he was impulsive as a child, sometimes even erratic; indeed, his intimate friends almost looked upon him as a spoiled boy. He was always delicate in health. Temperamentally, he belonged to that class of poets who Taine says are vessels too weak to contain the spirit of poetry, the poets whom poetry kills, the Byrons, the Burnses, the De Mussets, the Poes.

To whom may he be compared, this boy who scribbled his early verses while he ran an elevator, whose youth was a battle against poverty, and who, in spite of almost insurmountable obstacles, rose to success? A comparison between him and Burns is not unfitting. The similarity between many phases of their lives is remarkable, and their works are not incommensurable. Burns took the strong dialect of his people and made it classic; Dunbar took the humble speech of his people and in it wrought music.

Mention of Dunbar brings up for consideration the fact that, although he is the most outstanding figure in literature among the Aframericans of the United States, he does not stand alone among the Aframericans of the whole Western world. There are Plácido and Manzano in Cuba; Vieux and Durand in Haiti; Machado de Assis in Brazil, and others still that might be mentioned, who stand on a plane with or even above Dunbar. Plácido and Machado de Assis rank as great in the literatures of their respective countries without any qualifications whatever. They are world figures in the literature of the Latin languages. Machado de Assis is somewhat handicapped in this respect by having as his tongue and medium the lesser known Portuguese, but Plácido, writing in the language of Spain, Mexico, Cuba and of almost the whole of South America, is universally known. His works have been republished in the original in Spain, Mexico and in most of the Latin-American countries; several editions have been published in the United States; translations of his works have been made into French and German.

Plácido is in some respects the greatest of all the Cuban poets. In sheer genius and the fire of inspiration he surpasses his famous compatriot, Heredia. Then, too, his birth, his life and his death ideally contained the tragic elements that go into the making of a halo about a poet's head. Plácido was born in Habana in 1809. The first months of his life were passed in a foundling asylum; indeed, his real name, Gabriel de la Concepcion Valdés, was in honor of its founder. His father took him out of the asylum, but shortly afterwards went to Mexico and died there. His early life was a struggle against poverty; his youth and manhood was a struggle for Cuban independence. His death placed him in the list of Cuban martyrs. On the twenty-seventh of June, 1844, he was lined up against a wall with ten others and shot by order of the Spanish authorities on a charge of conspiracy. In his short but eventful life he turned out work which bulks more than six hundred pages. During the few hours preceding his execution he wrote three of his best-known poems, among them his famous sonnet, "Mother, Farewell!"

Plácido's sonnet to his mother has been translated into every important language; William Cullen Bryant did it in English; but in spite of its wide popularity, it is, perhaps, outside of Cuba the least understood of all Plácido's poems. It is curious to note how Bryant's translation totally misses the intimate sense of the delicate subtility of the poem. The American poet makes it a tender and loving farewell of a son who is about to die to a heart-broken mother; but that is not the kind of a farewell that Plácido intended to write or did write.

The key to the poem is in the first word, and the first word is the Spanish conjunction *Si* (if). The central idea, then, of the sonnet, is, "If the sad fate which now overwhelms me should bring a pang to your heart, do not weep, for I die a glorious death and sound the last note of my lyre to you." Bryant either failed to understand or ignored the opening word, "If," because he was not familiar with the poet's history.

While Plácido's father was a Negro, his mother was a Spanish white woman, a dancer in one of the Habana theaters. At his birth she abandoned him to a foundling asylum, and perhaps never saw him again, although it is known that she outlived her son. When the poet came down to his last hours he remembered that somewhere there lived a woman who was his mother; that although she had heartlessly abandoned him; that although he owed her no filial duty, still she might, perhaps, on hearing of his sad end feel some pang of grief or sadness; so he tells her in his last words that he dies happy and bids her not to weep. This he does with nobility and dignity, but absolutely without affection. Taking into account these facts, and especially their humiliating and embittering effect upon a soul so sensitive as Plácido's, this sonnet, in spite of the obvious weakness of the sestet as compared with the octave, is a remarkable piece of work.

In considering the Aframerican poets of the Latin languages I am impelled to think that, as up to this time the colored poets of greater universality have come out of the Latin-American countries rather than out of the United States, they will continue to do so for a good many years. The reason for this I hinted at in the first part of this preface. The colored poet in the United States labors within limitations which he cannot easily pass over. He is always on the defensive or the offensive. The pressure upon him to be propagandic is well nigh irresistible. These conditions are suffocating to breadth and to real art in poetry. In addition he labors under the handicap of finding culture not entirely colorless in the United States. On the other hand, the colored poet of Latin America can voice the national spirit without any reservations. And he will be rewarded without any reservations, whether it be to place him among the great or declare him the greatest.

So I think it probable that the first world-acknowledged Aframerican poet will come out of Latin America. Over against this probability, of course, is the great advantage possessed by the colored poet in the United States of writing in the world-conquering English language.

299

This preface has gone far beyond what I had in mind when I started. It was my intention to gather together the best verses I could find by Negro poets and present them with a bare word of introduction. It was not my plan to make this collection inclusive nor to make the book in any sense a book of criticism. I planned to present only verses by contemporary writers; but, perhaps, because this is the first collection of its kind, I realized the absence of a starting-point and was led to provide one and to fill in with historical data what I felt to be a gap.

It may be surprising to many to see how little of the poetry being written by Negro poets today is being written in Negro dialect. The newer Negro poets show a tendency to discard dialect; much of the subject-matter which went into the making of traditional dialect poetry, 'possums, watermelons, etc., they have discarded altogether, at least, as poetic material. This tendency will, no doubt, be regretted by the majority of white readers; and, indeed, it would be a distinct loss if the American Negro poets threw away this quaint and musical folk speech as a medium of expression. And yet, after all, these poets are working through a problem not realized by the reader, and, perhaps, by many of these poets themselves not realized consciously. They are trying to break away from, not Negro dialect itself, but the limitations on Negro dialect imposed by the fixing effects of long convention.

The Negro in the United States has achieved or been placed in a certain artistic niche. When he is thought of artistically, it is as a happy-go-lucky, singing, shuffling, banjo-picking being or as a more or less pathetic figure. The picture of him is in a log cabin amid fields of cotton or along the levees. Negro dialect is naturally and by long association the exact instrument for voicing this phase of Negro life; and by that very exactness it is an instrument with but two full stops, humor and pathos. So even when he confines himself to purely racial themes, the Aframerican poet realizes that there are phases of Negro life in the United States which cannot be treated in the dialect either adequately or artistically. Take, for example, the phases rising out of life in Harlem, that most wonderful Negro city in the world. I do not deny that a Negro in a log cabin is more picturesque than a Negro in a Harlem flat, but the Negro in the Harlem flat is here, and he is but part of a group growing everywhere in the country, a group whose ideals are becoming increasingly more vital than those of the traditionally artistic group, even if its members are less picturesque.

What the colored poet in the United States needs to do is something like what Synge did for the Irish; he needs to find a form that will express the racial spirit by symbols from within rather than by symbols from without, such as the mere mutilation of English spelling and pronunciation. He needs a form that is freer and larger than dialect, but which will still hold the racial flavor; a form expressing the imagery, the idioms, the peculiar turns of thought, and the distinctive humor and pathos, too, of the Negro, but which will also be capable of voicing the deepest and highest emotions and aspirations, and allow of the widest range of subjects and the widest scope of treatment.

Negro dialect is at present a medium that is not capable of giving expression to the varied conditions of Negro life in America, and much less is it capable of giving the fullest interpretation of Negro character and psychology. This is no indictment against the dialect as dialect, but against the mold of convention in which Negro dialect in the United States has been set. In time these conventions may become lost, and the colored poet in the United States may sit down to write in dialect without feeling that his first line will put the general reader in a frame of mind which demands that the poem be humorous or pathetic. In the meantime, there is no reason why these poets should not continue to do the beautiful things that can be done, and done best, in the dialect.

In stating the need for Aframerican poets in the United States to work out a new and distinctive form of expression I do not wish to be understood to hold any theory that they should limit themselves to Negro poetry, to racial themes; the sooner they are able to write *American* poetry spontaneously, the better. Nevertheless, I believe that the richest contribution the Negro poet can make to the American literature of the future will be the fusion into it of his own individual artistic gifts.

Not many of the writers here included, except Dunbar, are known at all to the general reading public; and there is only one of these who has a widely recognized position in the American literary world, William Stanley Braithwaite. Mr. Braithwaite is not only unique in this respect, but he stands unique among all the Aframerican writers the United States has yet produced. He has gained his place, taking as the standard and measure for his work the identical standard and measure applied to American writers and American literature. He has asked for no allowances or rewards, either directly or indirectly, on account of his race.

Mr. Braithwaite is the author of two volumes of verses, lyrics of delicate and tenuous beauty. In his more recent and uncollected poems he shows himself more and more decidedly the mystic. But his place in American literature is due more to his work as a critic and anthologist than to his work as a poet. There is still another rôle he has played, that of friend of poetry and poets. It is a recognized fact that in the work which preceded the present revival of poetry in the United States, no one rendered more unremitting and valuable service than Mr. Braithwaite. And it can be said that no future study of American poetry of this age can be made without reference to Braithwaite.

Two authors included in the book are better known for their work in prose than in poetry: W. E. B. Du Bois whose well-known prose at its best is, however, impassioned and rhythmical; and Benjamin Brawley who is the author, among other works, of one of the best handbooks on the English drama that has yet appeared in America.

But the group of the new Negro poets, whose work makes up the bulk of this anthology, contains names destined to be known. Claude McKay, although still quite a young man, has already demonstrated his power, breadth and skill as a poet. Mr. McKay's breadth is as essential a part of his equipment as his power and skill. He demonstrates mastery of the three when as a Negro poet he pours out the bitterness and rebellion in his heart in those two sonnet-tragedies, "If We Must Die" and "To the White Fiends," in a manner that strikes terror; and when as a cosmic poet he creates the atmosphere and mood of poetic beauty in the absolute, as he does in "Spring in New Hampshire" and "The Harlem Dancer." Mr. McKay gives evidence that he has passed beyond the danger which threatens many of the new Negro poets—the danger of allowing the purely polemical phases of the race problem to choke their sense of artistry.

Mr. McKay's earliest work is unknown in this country. It consists of poems written and published in his native Jamaica. I was fortunate enough to run across this first volume, and I could not refrain from reproducing here one of the poems written in the West Indian Negro dialect. I have done this not only to illustrate the widest range of the poet's talent and to offer a comparison between the American and the West Indian dialects, but on account of the intrinsic worth of the poem itself. I was much tempted to introduce several more, in spite of the fact that they might require a glossary, because however greater work Mr. McKay may do he can never do anything more touching and charming than these poems in the Jamaica dialect.

Fenton Johnson is a young poet of the ultra-modern school who gives promise of greater work than he has yet done. Jessie Fauset shows that she possesses the lyric gift, and she works with care and finish. Miss Fauset is especially adept in her translations from the French. Georgia Douglas Johnson is a poet neither afraid nor ashamed of her emotions. She limits herself to the purely conventional forms, rhythms and rhymes, but through them she achieves striking effects. The principal theme of Mrs. Johnson's poems is the secret dread down in every woman's heart, the dread of the passing of youth and beauty, and with them love. An old theme, one which poets themselves have often wearied of, but which, like death, remains one of the imperishable themes on which is made the poetry that has moved men's hearts through all ages. In her ingenuously wrought verses, through sheer simplicity and spontaneity, Mrs. Johnson often sounds a note of pathos or passion that will not fail to waken a response, except in those too sophisticated or cynical to respond to natural impulses. Of the half dozen or so colored women writing creditable verse, Anne Spencer is the most modern and least obvious in her methods. Her lines are at times involved and turgid and almost cryptic, but she shows an originality which does not depend upon eccentricities. In her "Before the Feast of Shushan" she displays an opulence, the love of which has long been charged against the Negro as one of his naïve and childish traits, but which in art may infuse a much needed color, warmth and spirit of abandon into American poetry.

John W. Holloway, more than any Negro poet writing in the dialect today, summons to his work the lilt, the spontaneity and charm of which Dunbar was the supreme master whenever he employed that medium. It is well to say a word here about the dialect poems of James Edwin Campbell. In dialect, Campbell was a precursor of Dunbar. A comparison of his idioms and phonetics with those of Dunbar reveals great differences. Dunbar is a shade or two more sophisticated and his phonetics approach nearer to a mean standard of the dialects spoken in the different sections. Campbell's is more primitive and his phonetics are those of the dialect as spoken by the Negroes of the sea islands off the coasts of South Carolina and Georgia, which to this day remains comparatively close to its African roots, and is strikingly similar to the speech of the uneducated Negroes of the West Indies. An error that confuses many persons in reading or understanding Negro dialect is the idea that it is uniform. An ignorant Negro of the uplands of Georgia would have almost as much difficulty in understanding an ignorant sea island Negro as an Englishman would have. Not even in the dialect of any particular section is a given word always pronounced in precisely the same way. Its pronunciation depends upon the preceding and following sounds. Sometimes the combination permits of a liaison so close that to the uninitiated the sound of the word is almost completely lost.

The constant effort in Negro dialect is to elide all troublesome consonants and sounds. This negative effort may be after all only positive laziness of the vocal organs, but the result is a softening and smoothing which makes Negro dialect so delightfully easy for singers.

Daniel Webster Davis wrote dialect poetry at the time when Dunbar was writing. He gained great popularity, but it did not spread beyond his own race. Davis had unctuous humor, but he was crude. For illustration, note the vast stretch between his "Hog Meat" and Dunbar's "When de Co'n Pone's Hot," both of them poems on the traditional ecstasy of the Negro in contemplation of "good things" to eat.

It is regrettable that two of the most gifted writers included were cut off so early in life. R. C. Jamison and Joseph S. Cotter, Jr., died several years ago, both of them in their youth. Jamison was barely thirty at the time of his death, but among his poems there is one, at least, which stamps him as a poet of superior talent and lofty inspiration. "The Negro Soldiers" is a poem with the race problem as its theme, yet it transcends the limits of race and rises to a spiritual height that makes it one of the noblest poems of the Great War. Cotter died a mere boy of twenty, and the latter part of that brief period he passed in an invalid state. Some months before his death he published a thin volume of verses which were for the most part written on a sick bed. In this little volume Cotter showed fine poetic sense and a free and bold mastery over his material. A reading of Cotter's poems is certain to induce that mood in which one will regretfully speculate on what the young poet might have accomplished had he not been cut off so soon.

As intimated above, my original idea for this book underwent a change in the writing of the introduction. I first planned to select twenty-five to thirty poems which I judged to be up to a certain standard, and offer them with a few words of introduction and without comment. In the collection, as it grew to be, that "certain standard" has been broadened if not lowered; but I believe that this is offset by the advantage of the wider range given the reader and the student of the subject.

I offer this collection without making apology or asking allowance. I feel confident that the reader will find not only an earnest for the future, but actual achievement. The reader cannot but be impressed by the distance already covered. It is a long way from the plaints of George Horton to the invectives of Claude McKay, from the obviousness of Frances Harper to the complexness of Anne Spencer. Much ground has been covered, but more will yet be covered. It is this side of prophecy to declare that the undeniable creative genius of the Negro is destined to make a distinctive and valuable contribution to American poetry.

O BLACK AND UNKNOWN BARDS
JAMES WELDON JOHNSON

O black and unknown bards of long ago,
How came your lips to touch the sacred fire?
How, in your darkness, did you come to know
The power and beauty of the minstrel's lyre?
Who first from midst his bonds lifted his eyes?
Who first from out the still watch, lone and long,
Feeling the ancient faith of prophets rise
Within his dark-kept soul, burst into song?

Heart of what slave poured out such melody
As "Steal away to Jesus"? On its strains
His spirit must have nightly floated free,
Though still about his hands he felt his chains.
Who heard great "Jordan roll"? Whose starward eye
Saw chariot "swing low"? And who was he
That breathed that comforting, melodic sigh,
"Nobody knows de trouble I see"?

What merely living clod, what captive thing,
Could up toward God through all its darkness grope,
And find within its deadened heart to sing
These songs of sorrow, love and faith, and hope?
How did it catch that subtle undertone,
That note in music heard not with the ears?
How sound the elusive reed so seldom blown,
Which stirs the soul or melts the heart to tears.

Not that great German master in his dream
Of harmonies that thundered amongst the stars

At the creation, ever heard a theme
Nobler than "Go down, Moses." Mark its bars
How like a mighty trumpet-call they stir
The blood. Such are the notes that men have sung
Going to valorous deeds; such tones there were
That helped make history when Time was young.

There is a wide, wide wonder in it all,
That from degraded rest and servile toil
The fiery spirit of the seer should call
These simple children of the sun and soil.
O black slave singers, gone, forgot, unfamed,
You—you alone, of all the long, long line
Of those who've sung untaught, unknown, unnamed,
Have stretched out upward, seeking the divine.

You sang not deeds of heroes or of kings;
No chant of bloody war, no exulting pean
Of arms-won triumphs; but your humble strings
You touched in chord with music empyrean.
You sang far better than you knew; the songs
That for your listeners' hungry hearts sufficed
Still live,—but more than this to you belongs:
You sang a race from wood and stone to Christ.

THE NEGRO ARTIST AND
THE RACIAL MOUNTAIN
LANGSTON HUGHES

One of the most promising of the young Negro poets said to me once, "I want to be a poet—not a Negro poet," meaning, I believe, "I want to write like a white poet"; meaning subconsciously, "I would like to be a white poet"; meaning behind that, "I would like to be white." And I was sorry the young man said that, for no great poet has ever been afraid of being himself. And I doubted then that, with his desire to run away spiritually from his race, this boy would ever be a great poet. But this is the mountain standing in the way of any true Negro art in America—this urge within the race toward whiteness, the desire to pour racial individuality into the mold of American standardization, and to be as little Negro and as much American as possible.

But let us look at the immediate background of this young poet. His family is of what I suppose one would call the Negro middle class: people who are by no means rich yet never uncomfortable nor hungry—smug, contented, respectable folk, members of the Baptist church. The father goes to work every morning. He is a chief steward at a large white club. The mother sometimes does fancy sewing or supervises parties for the rich families of the town. The children go to a mixed school. In the home they read white papers and magazines. And the mother often says "Don't be like niggers" when the children are bad. A frequent phrase from the father is, "Look how well a white man does things." And so the word white comes to be unconsciously a symbol of all virtues. It holds for the children beauty, morality, and money. The whisper of "I want to be white" runs silently through their minds. This young poet's home is, I believe, a fairly typical home of the colored middle class. One sees immediately how difficult it would be for an artist born in such a home to interest himself in interpreting the beauty of his own people. He is never taught to see that beauty. He is taught rather not to see it, or if he does, to be ashamed of it when it is not according to Caucasian patterns.

For racial culture the home of a self-styled "high-class" Negro has nothing better to offer. Instead there will perhaps be more aping of things white than in a less cultured or less wealthy home. The father is perhaps a doctor, lawyer, landowner, or policitican. The mother may be a social worker, or a teacher, or she may do nothing and have a maid. Father is often dark but he has usually married the lightest woman he could find. The family attend a fashionable church where few really colored faces are to be found. And they themselves draw a color line. In the North they go to white theatres and white movies. And in the South they have at least two cars and house "like white folks." Nordic manners, Nordic faces, Nordic hair, Nordic art (if any), and an Episcopal heaven. A very high mountain indeed for the would-be racial artist to climb in order to discover himself and his people.

But then there are the low-down folks, the so-called common element, and they are the majority—may the Lord be praised! The people who have their hip of gin on Saturday nights and are not too important to themselves or the community, or too well fed, or too learned to watch the lazy world go round. They live on Seventh Street in Washington or State Street in Chicago and they do not particularly care whether they are like white folks or anybody else. Their joy runs, bang! into ecstasy. Their religion soars to a shout. Work maybe a little today, rest a little tomorrow. Play awhile. Sing awhile. O, let's dance! These common people are not afraid of spirituals, as for a long time their more intellectual brethren were, and jazz is their child. They furnish a wealth of colorful, distinctive material for any artist because they still hold their own individuality in the face of American standardizations. And perhaps these common people will give to the world its truly great Negro artist, the one who is not afraid to be himself. Whereas the better-class Negro would tell the artist what to do, the people at least let him alone when he does appear. And they are not ashamed of him—if they know he exists at all. And they accept what beauty is their own without question.

Certainly there is, for the American Negro artist who can escape the restrictions the more advanced among his own group would put upon him, a great field of unused material ready for his art. Without going outside his race, and even among the better classes with their "white" culture and conscious American manners, but still Negro enough to be different, there is sufficient matter to furnish a black artist with a lifetime of creative work. And when he chooses to touch on the relations between Negroes and whites in this country with their innumerable overtones and undertones surely, and especially for literature and the drama, there is an inexhaustible supply of themes at hand. To these the Negro artist can give his racial individuality, his heritage of rhythm and warmth, and his incongruous humor that so often, as in the Blues, becomes ironic laughter mixed with tears. But let us look again at the mountain.

A prominent Negro clubwoman in Philadelphia paid eleven dollars to hear Raquel Meller sing Andalusian popular songs. But she told me a few weeks before she would not think of going to hear "that woman," Clara Smith, a great black artist, sing Negro folksongs. And many an upper-class Negro church, even now, would not dream of employing a spiritual in its services. The drab melodies in white folks' hymnbooks are much to be preferred. "We want to worship the Lord correctly and quietly. We don't believe in 'shouting.' Let's be dull like the Nordics," they say, in effect.

The road for the serious black artist, then, who would produce a racial art is most certainly rocky and the mountain is high. Until recently he received almost no encouragement for his work from either white or colored people. The fine novels of Chesnutt go out of print with neither race noticing their passing. The quaint charm and humor of Dunbar's dialect verse brought to him, in his day, largely the same kind of encouragement one would give a sideshow freak (A colored man writing poetry! How odd!) or a clown (How amusing!).

The present vogue in things Negro, although it may do as much harm as good for the budding colored artist, has at least done this: it has brought him forcibly to the attention of his own people among whom for so long, unless the other race had noticed him beforehand, he was a prophet with little honor. I understand that Charles Gilpin acted for years in Negro theatres without any special acclaim from his own, but when Broadway gave him eight curtain calls, Negroes, too, began to beat a tin pan in his honor. I know a young colored writer, a manual worker by day, who had been writing well for the colored magazines for some years, but it was not until he recently broke into the white publications and his first book was accepted by a prominent New York publisher that the "best" Negroes in his city took the trouble to discover that he lived there. Then almost immediately they decided to give a grand dinner for him. But the society ladies were careful to whisper to his mother that perhaps she'd better not come. They were not sure she would have an evening gown.

The Negro artist works against an undertow of sharp criticism and misunderstanding from his own group and unintentional bribes from the whites. "Oh, be respectable, write about nice people, show how good we are," say the Negroes. "Be stereotyped, don't go too far, don't shatter our illusions about you, don't amuse us too seriously. We will pay you," say the whites. Both would have told Jean Toomer not to write *Cane.* The colored people did not praise it. The white people did not buy it. Most of the colored people who did read *Cane* hate it. They are afraid of it. Although the critics gave it good reviews the public remained indifferent. Yet (excepting the work of Du Bois) *Cane* contains the finest prose written by a Negro in America. And like the singing of Robeson, it is truly racial.

But in spite of the Nordicized Negro intelligentsia and the desires of some white editors we have an honest American Negro literature already with us. Now I await the rise of the Negro theatre. Our folk music, having achieved world-wide fame, offers itself to the genius of the great individual American composer who is to come. And within the next decade I expect to see the work of a growing school of colored artists who paint and model the beauty of dark faces and create with new technique the expressions of their own soul-world. And the Negro dancers who will dance like flame and the singers who will continue to carry our songs to all who listen—they will be with us in even greater numbers tomorrow.

Most of my own poems are racial in theme and treatment, derived from the life I know. In many of them I try to grasp and hold some of the meanings and rhythms of jazz. I am as sincere as I know how to be in these poems and yet after every reading I answer questions like these from my own people: Do you think Negroes should always write about Negroes? I wish you wouldn't read some of your poems to white folks. How do you find anything interesting in a place like a cabaret? Why do you write about black people? You aren't black. What makes you do so many jazz poems?

But jazz to me is one of the inherent expressions of Negro life in America; the eternal tom-tom beating in the Negro soul—the tom-tom of revolt against weariness in a white world, a world of subway trains, and work, work, work; the tom-tom of joy and laughter, and pain swallowed in a smile. Yet the Philadelphia clubwoman is ashamed to say that her race created it and she does not like me to write about it. The old subconscious "white is best" runs through her mind. Years of study under white teachers, a lifetime of white books, pictures, and papers, and white manners, morals, and Puritan standards made her dislike the spirituals. And now she turns up her nose at jazz and all its manifestations—likewise almost everything else distinctly racial. She doesn't care for the Winold Reiss portraits of Negroes because they are "too Negro." She does not want a true picture of herself from anybody. She wants the artist to flatter her, to make the white world believe that all Negroes are as smug and as near white in soul as she wants to be. But, to my mind, it is the duty of the younger Negro artist, if he accepts any duties at all from outsiders, to change through the force of his art that old whispering "I want to be white," hidden in the aspirations of his people, to "Why should I want to be white? I am a Negro—and beautiful?

So I am ashamed for the black poet who says, "I want to be a poet, not a Negro poet," as though his own racial world were not as interesting as any other world. I am ashamed, too, for the colored artist who runs from the painting of Negro faces to the painting of sunsets after the manner of the academicians because he fears the strange un-whiteness of his own features. An artist must be free to choose what he does, certainly, but he must also never be afraid to do what he might choose.

Let the blare of Negro jazz bands and the bellowing voice of Bessie Smith singing Blues penetrate the closed ears of the colored near-intellectuals until they listen and perhaps understand. Let Paul Robeson singing "Water Boy," and Rudolph Fisher writing about the streets of Harlem, and Jean Toomer holding the heart of Georgia in his hands, and Aaron Douglas drawing strange black fantasies cause the smug Negro middle class to turn from their white, respectable, ordinary books and papers to catch a glimmer of their own beauty. We younger Negro artists who create now intend to express our individual dark-skinned selves without fear or shame. If white people are pleased we are glad. If they are not, it doesn't matter. We know we are beautiful. And ugly too. The tom-tom cries and the tom-tom laughs. If colored people are pleased we are glad. If they are not, their displeasure doesn't matter either. We build our temples for tomorrow, strong as we know how, and we stand on top of the mountain, free within ourselves.

HURT
LANGSTON HUGHES

Who cares
About the hurt in your heart?

> Make a song like this
> For a jazz band to play:

> > Nobody cares.
> > Nobody cares.

Make a song like that
From your lips.

> Nobody cares.

THE NEGRO-ART HOKUM
GEORGE S. SCHUYLER

Negro art "made in America" is as non-existent as the widely advertised profundity of Cal Coolidge, the "seven years of progress" of Mayor Hylan, or the reported sophistication of New Yorkers. Negro art there has been, is, and will be among the numerous black nations of Africa; but to suggest the possibility of any such development among the ten million colored people in this republic is self-evident foolishness. Eager apostles from Greenwich Village, Harlem, and environs proclaimed a great renaissance of Negro art just around the corner waiting to be ushered on the scene by those whose hobby is taking races, nations, peoples, and movements under their wing. New art forms expressing the "peculiar" psychology of the Negro were about to flood the market. In short, the art of Homo Africanus was about to electrify the waiting world. Skeptics patiently waited. They still wait.

True, from dark-skinned sources have come those slave songs based on Protestant hymns and Biblical texts known as the spirituals, work songs and secular songs of sorrow and tough luck known as the blues, that outgrowth of rag-time known as jazz (in the development of which whites have assisted), and the Charleston, an eccentric dance invented by the gamins around the public market-place in Charleston, S.C. No one can or does deny this. But these are contributions of a caste in a certain section of the country. They are foreign to Northern Negroes, West Indian Negroes, and African Negroes. They are no more expressive or characteristic of the Negro race than the music and dancing of the Appalachian highlanders or the Dalmatian peasantry are expressive or characteristic of the Caucasian race. If one wishes to speak of the musical contributions of the peasantry of the South, very well. Any group under similar circumstances would have produced something similar. It is merely a coincidence that this peasant class happens to be of a darker hue than the other inhabitants of the land. One recalls the remarkable likeness of the minor strains of the Russian mujiks to those of the Southern Negro.

As for the literature, painting, and sculpture of Aframericans—such as there is—it is identical in kind with the literature, painting, and sculpture of white Americans: that is, it shows more or less evidence of European influence. In the field of drama little of any merit has been written by and about Negroes that could not have been written by whites. The dean of the Aframerican literati is W. E. B. Du Bois, a product of Harvard and German universities; the foremost Aframerican sculptor is Meta Warwick Fuller, a graduate of leading American art schools and former student of Rodin; while the most noted Aframerican painter, Henry Ossawa Tanner, is dean of American painters in Paris and has been decorated by the French Government. Now the work of these artists is no more "expressive of the Negro soul"—as the gushers put it—than are the scribblings of Octavus Cohen or Hugh Wiley.

This, of course, is easily understood if one stops to realize that the Aframerican is merely a lampblacked Anglo-Saxon. If the European immigrant after two or three generations of exposure to our schools, politics, advertising, moral crusades, and restaurants becomes indistinguishable from the mass of Americans of the older stock (despite the influence of the foreign-language press), how much truer must it be of the sons of Ham who have been subjected to what the uplifters call Americanism for the last three hundred years. Aside from his color, which ranges from very dark brown to pink, your American Negro is just plain American. Negroes and whites from the same localities in this country talk, think, and act about the same. Because a few writers with a paucity of themes have seized upon imbecilities of the Negro rustics and clowns and palmed them off as authentic and characteristic Aframerican behavior, the common notion that the black American is so "different" from his white neighbor has gained wide currency. The mere mention of the word "Negro" conjures up in the average white American's mind a composite stereotype of Bert Williams, Aunt Jemima, Uncle Tom, Jack Johnson, Florian Slappey, and the various monstrosities scrawled by the cartoonists. Your average Aframerican no more resembles this stereotype than the average American resembles a composite of Andy Gump, Jim Jeffries, and a cartoon by Rube Goldberg.

Again, the Africamerican is subject to the same economic and social forces that mold the actions and thoughts of the white Americans. He is not living in a different world as some whites and a few Negroes would have us believe. When the jangling of his Connecticut alarm clock gets him out of his Grand Rapids bed to a breakfast similar to that eaten by his white brother across the street; when he toils at the same or similar work in mills, mines, factories, and commerce alongside the descendants of Spartacus, Robin Hood, and Eric the Red; when he wears similar clothing and speaks the same language with the same degree of perfection; when he reads the same Bible and belongs to the Baptist, Methodist, Episcopal, or Catholic church; when his fraternal affiliations also include the Elks, Masons, and Knights of Pythias; when he gets the same or similar schooling, lives in the same kind of houses, owns the same makes of cars (or rides in them), and nightly sees the same Hollywood version of life on the screen; when he smokes the same brands of tobacco, and avidly peruses the same puerile periodicals; in short, when he responds to the same political, social, moral, and economic stimuli in precisely the same manner as his white neighbor, it is sheer nonsense to talk about "racial differences" as between the American black man and the American white man. Glance over a Negro newspaper (it is printed in good Americanese) and you will find the usual quota of crime news, scandal, personals, and uplift to be found in the average white newspaper—which, by the way, is more widely read by the Negroes than is the Negro press. In order to satisfy the cravings of an inferiority complex engendered by the colorphobia of the mob, the readers of the Negro newspapers are given a slight dash of racialistic seasoning. In the homes of the black and white Americans of the same cultural and economic level one finds similar furniture, literature, and conversation. How, then, can the black American be expected to produce art and literature dissimilar to that of the white American?

Consider Coleridge-Taylor, Edward Wilmot Blyden, and Claude McKay, the Englishmen; Pushkin, the Russian; Bridgewater, the Pole; Antar, the Arabian; Latino, the Spaniard; Dumas, *père* and *fils,* the Frenchmen; and Paul Laurence Dunbar, Charles W. Chestnutt, and James Weldon Johnson, the Americans. All Negroes; yet their work shows the impress of nationality rather than race. They all reveal the psychology and culture of their environment—their color is incidental. Why should Negro artists of America vary from the national artistic norm when Negro artists in other countries have not done so? If we can foresee what kind of white citizens will inhabit this neck of the woods in the next generation by studying the sort of education and environment the children are exposed to now, it should not be difficult to reason that the adults of today are what they are because of the education and environment they were exposed to a generation ago. And that education and environment were about the same for blacks and whites. One contemplates the popularity of the Negro-art hokum and murmurs, "How come?"

This nonsense is probably the last stand of the old myth palmed off by Negrophobists for all these many years, and recently rehashed by the sainted Harding, that there are "fundamental, eternal, and inescapable differences" between white and black Americans. That there are Negroes who will lend this myth a helping hand need occasion no surprise. It has been broadcast all over the world by the vociferous scions of slaveholders, "scientists" like Madison Grant and Lothrop Stoddard, and the patriots who flood the treasury of the Ku Klux Klan; and is believed, even today, by the majority of free, white citizens. On this baseless premise, so flattering to the white mob, that the blackamoor is inferior and fundamentally different, is erected the postulate that he must needs be peculiar; and when he attempts to portray life through the medium of art, it must of necessity be a peculiar art. While such reasoning may seem conclusive to the majority of Americans, it must be rejected with a loud guffaw by intelligent people.

ART OR PROPAGANDA?
ALAIN LOCKE

Artistically it is the one fundamental question for us today,—Art or Propaganda. Which? Is this more the generation of the prophet or that of the poet; shall our intellectual and cultural leadership preach and exhort or sing? I believe we are at that interesting moment when the prophet becomes the poet and when prophecy becomes the expressive song, the chant of fulfillment. We have had too many Jeremiahs, major and minor;— and too much of the drab wilderness. My chief objection to propaganda, apart from its besetting sin of monotony and disproportion, is that it perpetuates the position of group inferiority even in crying out against it. For it leaves and speaks under the shadow of a dominant majority whom it harangues, cajoles, threatens or supplicates. It is too extroverted for balance or poise or inner dignity and self-respect. Art in the best sense is rooted in self-expression and whether naive or sophisticated is self-contained. In our spiritual growth genius and talent must more and more choose the role of group expression, or even at times the role of free individualistic expression,—in a word must choose art and put aside propaganda.

The literature and art of the younger generation already reflects this shift of psychology, this regeneration of spirit. David should be its patron saint: it should confront the Phillistines with its five smooth pebbles fearlessly. There is more strength in a confident camp than in a threatened enemy. The sense of inferiority must be innerly compensated, self-conviction must supplant self-justification and in the dignity of this attitude a convinced minority must confront a condescending majority. Art cannot completely accomplish this, but I believe it can lead the way.

Our espousal of art thus becomes no mere idle acceptance of "art for art's sake," or cultivation of the last decadences of the over-civilized, but rather a deep realization of the fundamental purpose of art and of its function as a tap root of vigorous, flourishing living. Not all of our younger writers are deep enough in the sub-soil of their native materials,—too many are pot-plants seeking a forced growth according to the exotic tastes of a pampered and decadent public. It is the art of the people that needs to be cultivated, not the art of the coteries. Propaganda itself is preferable to shallow, truckling imitation. Negro things may reasonably be a fad for others; for us they must be a religion. Beauty, however, is its best priest and psalms will be more effective than sermons.

To date we have had little sustained art unsubsidized by propaganda; we must admit this debt to these foster agencies. The three journals which have been vehicles of most of our artistic expressions have been the avowed organs of social movements and organized social programs. All our purely artistic publications have been sporadic. There is all the greater need then for a sustained vehicle of free and purely artistic expression. If HARLEM should happily fill this need, it will perform an honorable and constructive service. I hope it may, but should it not, the need remains and the path toward it will at least be advanced a little.

We need, I suppose in addition to art some substitute for propaganda. What shall that be? Surely we must take some cognizance of the fact that we live at the centre of a social problem. Propaganda at least nurtured some form of serious social discussion, and social discussion was necessary, is still necessary. On this side; the difficulty and shortcoming of propaganda is its partisanship. It is one-sided and often pre-judging. Should we not then have a journal of free discussion, open to all sides of the problem and to all camps of belief? Difficult, that,—but intriguing. Even if it has to begin on the note of dissent and criticism and assume Menckenian scepticism to escape the common-places of conformity. Yet, I hope we shall not remain at this negative pole. Can we not cultivate truly free and tolerant discussion, almost Socratically minded for the sake of truth? After Beauty, let Truth come into the Renaissance picture,—a later cue, but a welcome one. This may be premature, but one hopes not,—for eventually it must come and if we can accomplish that, instead of having to hang our prophets, we can silence them or change their lamentations to song with a Great Fulfillment.

DEAD FIRES
JESSIE REDMOND FAUSET

If this is peace, this dead and leaden thing,
    Then better far the hateful fret, the sting,

Better the wound forever seeking balm
   Than this gray calm!

Is this pain's surcease? Better far the ache,
   The long-drawn dreary day, the night's white wake,
Better the choking sigh, the sobbing breath
   Than passion's death!

TO JOHN KEATS, POET, AT SPRINGTIME
COUNTEE CULLEN

I cannot hold my peace, John Keats;
There never was a spring like this;
It is an echo, that repeats
My last year's song and next year's bliss.
I know, in spite of all men say
Of Beauty, you have felt her most.
Yea, even in your grave her way
Is laid. Poor, troubled, lyric ghost,
Spring never was so fair and dear
As Beauty makes her seem this year.

I cannot hold my peace, John Keats,
I am as helpless in the toil
Of Spring as any lamb that bleats
To feel the solid earth recoil
Beneath his puny legs. Spring beats
Her tocsin call to those who love her,
And lo! the dogwood petals cover
Her breast with drifts of snow, and sleek
White gulls fly screaming to her, and hover
About her shoulders, and kiss her cheek,
While white and purple lilacs muster
A strength that bears them to a cluster
Of color and odor; for her sake
All things that slept are now awake.

And you and I, shall we lie still,
John Keats, while Beauty summons us?
Somehow I feel your sensitive will
Is pulsing up some tremulous
Sap road of a maple tree, whose leaves
Grow music as they grow, since your
Wild voice is in them, a harp that grieves
For life that opens death's dark door.

Though dust, your fingers still can push
The Vision Splendid to a birth,
Though now they work as grass in the hush
Of the night on the broad sweet page of the earth.

"John Keats is dead," they say, but I
Who hear your full insistent cry
In bud and blossom, leaf and tree,
Know John Keats still writes poetry.
And while my head is earthward bowed
To read new life sprung from your shroud,
Folks seeing me must think it strange
That merely spring should so derange
My mind. They do not know that you,
John Keats, keep revel with me, too.

FOR A POET
COUNTEE CULLEN

I have wrapped my dreams in a silken cloth,
And laid them away in a box of gold;
Where long will cling the lips of the moth,
I have wrapped my dreams in a silken cloth;
I hide no hate, I am not even wroth
Who found earth's breath so keen and cold;
I have wrapped my dreams in a silken cloth,
And laid them away in a box of gold.

YET DO I MARVEL
COUNTEE CULLEN

I doubt not God is good, well-meaning, kind,
And did He stoop to quibble could tell why
The little buried mole continues blind,
Why flesh that mirrors Him must some day die,
Make plain the reason tortured Tantalus
Is baited by the fickle fruit, declare
If merely brute caprice dooms Sisyphus
To struggle up a never-ending stair.
Inscrutable His ways are, and immune
To catechism by a mind too strewn
With petty cares to slightly understand
What awful brain compels His awful hand.
Yet do I marvel at this curious thing:
To make a poet black, and bid him sing!

FROM
INFANTS OF THE SPRING
WALLACE THURMAN

XXI

After Stephen's unexpected visit and their long conversation together, Raymond seemed to have developed a new store of energy. For three days and nights, he had secluded himself in his room, and devoted all his time to the continuance of his novel. For three years it had remained a project. Now he was making rapid progress. The ease with which he could work once he set himself to it amazed him, and at the same time he was suspicious of this unexpected facility. Nevertheless, his novel was progressing, and he intended to let nothing check him.

In line with this resolution, he insisted that Paul and Eustace hold their nightly gin parties without his presence, and they were also abjured to steer all company clear of his studio.

Stephen had gone upstate on a tutoring job. Lucille had not been in evidence since the donation party, and Raymond had made no attempt to get in touch with her. There was no one else in whom he had any interest. Aline and Janet he had dismissed from his mind, although Eustace and Paul had spent an entire dinner hour telling him of their latest adventures. Both had now left Aline's mother's house and were being supported by some white man, whom Aline had met at a downtown motion picture theater. They had an apartment in which they entertained groups of young colored boys on the nights their white protector was not in evidence.

Having withdrawn from every activity connected with Niggeratti Manor, Raymond had also forgotten that Dr. Parkes had promised to communicate with him, concerning some mysterious idea, and he was taken by surprise when Eustace came into the room one morning, bearing a letter from Dr. Parkes.

"Well, I'm plucked," Raymond exclaimed.

"What's the matter?" Eustace queried.

"Will you listen to this?" He read the letter aloud.

"My dear Raymond:

I will be in New York on Thursday night. I want you to do me a favor. It seems to me that with the ever increasing number of younger Negro artists and intellectuals gathering in Harlem, some effort should be made to establish what well might become a distinguished salon. All of you engaged in creative work, should, I believe, welcome the chance to meet together once every fortnight, for the purpose of exchanging ideas and expressing and criticizing individual theories. This might prove to be both stimulating and profitable. And it might also bring into active being a concerted movement which would establish the younger Negro talent once and for all as a vital artistic force. With this in mind, I would appreciate your inviting as many of your colleagues as possible to your studio on Thursday evening. I will be there to preside. I hope you are intrigued by the idea and willing to coöperate. Please wire me your answer. Collect, of course.

Very sincerely yours,
Dr. A. L. Parkes."

"Are you any more good?" Raymond asked as he finished reading.

"Sounds like a great idea," Eustace replied enthusiastically.

"It *is* great. Too great to miss," Raymond acquiesced mischievously. "Come on, let's get busy on the telephone."

Thursday night came and so did the young hopefuls. The first to arrive was Sweetie May Carr. Sweetie May was a short story writer, more noted for her ribald wit and personal effervescence than for any actual literary work. She was a great favorite among those whites who went in for Negro prodigies. Mainly because she lived up to their conception of what a typical Negro should be. It seldom occurred to any of her patrons that she did this with tongue in cheek. Given a paleface audience, Sweetie May would launch forth into a saga of the little all-colored Mississippi town where she claimed to have been born. Her repertoire of tales was earthy, vulgar and funny. Her darkies always smiled through their tears, sang spirituals on the slightest provocation, and performed buck dances when they should have been working. Sweetie May was a master of southern dialect, and an able raconteur, but she was too indifferent to literary creation to transfer to paper that which she told so well. The intricacies of writing bored her, and her written work was for the most part turgid and unpolished. But Sweetie May knew her white folks.

"It's like this," she had told Raymond. "I have to eat. I also wish to finish my education. Being a Negro writer these days is a racket and I'm going to make the most of it while it lasts. Sure I cut the fool. But I enjoy it, too. I don't know a tinker's damn about art. I care less about it. My ultimate ambition, as you know, is to become a gynecologist. And the only way I can live easily until I have the requisite training is to pose as a writer of potential ability. *Voila!* I get my tuition paid at Columbia. I rent an apartment and have all the furniture contributed by kind hearted o'fays. I receive bundles of groceries from various sources several times a week . . . all accomplished by dropping a discreet hint during an evening's festivities. I find queer places for whites to go in Harlem . . . out of the way primitive churches, sidestreet speakeasies. They fall for it. About twice a year I manage to sell a story. It is acclaimed. I am a genius in the making. Thank God for this Negro literary renaissance! Long may it flourish!"

Sweetie May was accompanied by two young girls, recently emigrated from Boston. They were the latest to be hailed as incipient immortals. Their names were Doris Westmore and Hazel Jamison. Doris wrote short stories. Hazel wrote poetry. Both had become known through a literary contest fostered by one of the leading Negro magazines. Raymond liked them more than he did most of the younger recruits to the movement. For one thing, they were characterized by a freshness and naïveté which he and his cronies had lost. And, surprisingly enough for Negro prodigies, they actually gave promise of possessing literary talent. He was most pleased to see them. He was also amused by their interest and excitement. A salon! A literary gathering! It was one of the civilized institutions they had dreamed of finding in New York, one of the things they had longed and hoped for.

As time passed, others came in. Tony Crews, smiling and self-effacing, a mischievous boy, grateful for the chance to slip away from the backwoods college he attended. Raymond had never been able to analyze this young poet. His work was interesting and unusual. It was also spotty. Spasmodically he gave promise of developing into a first rate poet. Already he had published two volumes, prematurely, Raymond thought. Both had been excessively praised by whites and universally damned by Negroes. Considering the nature of his work this was to be expected. The only unknown quantity was the poet himself. Would he or would he not fulfill the promise exemplified in some of his work? Raymond had no way of knowing and even an intimate friendship with Tony himself had failed to enlighten him. For Tony was the most close-mouthed and cagey individual Raymond had ever known when it came to personal matters. He fended off every attempt to probe into his inner self and did this with such an unconscious and naïve air that the prober soon came to one of two conclusions: Either Tony had no depth whatsoever, or else he was too deep for plumbing by ordinary mortals.

DeWitt Clinton, the Negro poet laureate, was there, too, accompanied, as ususal, by his *fideles achates,* David Holloway. David had been acclaimed the most handsome Negro in Harlem by a certain group of whites. He was in great demand by artists who wished to paint him. He had become a much touted romantic figure. In reality he was a fairly intelligent school teacher, quite circumspect in his habits, a rather timid beau, who imagined himself to be bored with life.

Dr. Parkes finally arrived, accompanied by Carl Denny, the artist, and Carl's wife, Annette. Next to arrive was Cedric Williams, a West Indian, whose first book, a collection of short stories with a Caribbean background, in Raymond's opinion, marked him as one of the three Negroes writing who actually had something to say, and also some concrete idea of style. Cedric was followed by Austin Brown, a portrait painter whom Raymond personally despised, a Dr. Manfred Trout, who practiced medicine and also wrote exceptionally good short stories, Glenn Madison, who was a Communist, and a long, lean professorial person, Allen Fenderson, who taught school and had ambitions to become a crusader modeled after W. E. B. Du Bois.

The roster was now complete. There was an hour of small talk and drinking of mild cocktails in order to induce ease and allow the various guests to become acquainted and voluble. Finally, Dr. Parkes ensconced himself in Raymond's favorite chair, where he could get a good view of all in the room, and clucked for order.

Raymond observed the professor closely. Paul's description never seemed more apt. He was a mother hen clucking at her chicks. Small, dapper, with sensitive features, graying hair, a dominating head, and restless hands and feet, he smiled benevolently at his brood. Then, in his best continental manner, which he had acquired during four years at European Universities, he began to speak.

"You are," he perorated, "the outstanding personalities in a new generation. On you depends the future of your race. You are not, as were your predecessors, concerned with donning armor, and clashing swords with the enemy in the public square. You are finding both an escape and a weapon in beauty, which beauty when created by you will cause the American white man to reëstimate the Negro's value to his civilization, cause him to realize that the American black man is too valuable, too potential of utilitarian accomplishment, to be kept downtrodden and segregated.

"Because of your concerted storming up Parnassus, new vistas will be spread open to the entire race. The Negro in the south will no more know peonage, Jim Crowism, or loss of the ballot, and the Negro everywhere in America will know complete freedom and equality.

"But," and here his voice took on a more serious tone, "to accomplish this, your pursuit of beauty must be vital and lasting. I am somewhat fearful of the decadent strain which seems to have filtered into most of your work. Oh, yes, I know you are children of the age and all that, but you must not, like your paleface contemporaries, wallow in the mire of post-Victorian license. You have too much at stake. You must have ideals. You should become . . . well, let me suggest your going back to your racial roots, and cultivating a healthy paganism based on African traditions.

"For the moment that is all I wish to say. I now want you all to give expression to your own ideas. Perhaps we can reach a happy mean for guidance."

He cleared his throat and leaned contentedly back in his chair. No one said a word. Raymond was full of contradictions, which threatened to ooze forth despite his efforts to remain silent. But he knew that once the ooze began there would be no stopping the flood, and he was anxious to hear what some of the others might have to say.

However, a glance at the rest of the people in the room assured him that most of them had not the slightest understanding of what had been said, nor any ideas on the subject, whatsoever. Once more Dr. Parkes clucked for discussion. No one ventured a word. Raymond could see that Cedric, like himself, was full of argument, and also like him, did not wish to appear contentious at such an early stage in the discussion. Tony winked at Raymond when he caught his eye, but the expression on his face was as inscrutable as ever. Sweetie May giggled behind her handkerchief. Paul amused himself by sketching the various people in the room. The rest were blank.

"Come, come, now," Dr. Parkes urged somewhat impatiently, "I'm not to do all the talking. What have you to say, DeWitt?"

All eyes sought out the so-called Negro poet laureate. For a moment he stirred uncomfortably in his chair, then in a high pitched, nasal voice proceeded to speak.

"I think, Dr. Parkes, that you have said all there is to say. I agree with you. The young Negro artist must go back to his pagan heritage for inspiration and to the old masters for form."

Raymond could not suppress a snort. For DeWitt's few words had given him a vivid mental picture of that poet's creative hours—eyes on a page of Keats, fingers on typewriter, mind frantically conjuring African scenes. And there would of course be a Bible nearby.

Paul had ceased being intent on his drawing long enough to hear "pagan heritage," and when DeWitt finished he inquired inelegantly:

"What old black pagan heritage?"

DeWitt gasped, surprised and incredulous.

"Why, from your ancestors."

"Which ones?" Paul pursued dumbly.

"Your African ones, of course." DeWitt's voice was full of disdain.

"What about the rest?"

"What rest?" He was irritated now.

"My German, English and Indian ancestors," Paul answered willing. "How can I go back to African ancestors when their blood is so diluted and their country and times so far away? I have no conscious affinity for them at all."

Dr. Parkes intervened: "I think you've missed the point, Paul."

"And I," Raymond was surprised at the suddenness with which he joined in the argument, "think he has hit the nail right on the head. Is there really any reason why *all* Negro artists should consciously and deliberately dig into African soil for inspiration and material unless they actually wish to do so?"

"I don't mean that. I mean you should develop your inherited spirit."

DeWitt beamed. The doctor had expressed his own hazy theory. Raymond was about to speak again, when Paul once more took the bit between his own teeth.

"I ain't got no African spirit."

Sweetie May giggled openly at this, as did Carl Denny's wife, Annette. The rest looked appropriately sober, save for Tony, whose eyes continued to telegraph mischievously to Raymond. Dr. Parkes tried to squelch Paul with a frown. He should have known better.

"I'm not an African," the culprit continued. "I'm an American and a perfect product of the melting pot."

"That's nothing to brag about." Cedric spoke for the first time.

"And I think you're all on the wrong track." All eyes were turned toward this new speaker, Allen Fenderson. "Dr. Du Bois has shown us the way. We must be militant fighters. We must not hide away in ivory towers and prate of beauty. We must fashion cudgels and bludgeons rather than sensitive plants. We must excoriate the white man, and make him grant us justice. We must fight for complete social and political and economic equality."

"What we ought to do," Glenn Madison growled intensely, "is to join hands with the workers of the world and overthrow the present capitalistic régime. We are all the proletariat and must fight our battles allied with them, rather than singly and selfishly."

"All of us?" Raymond inquired quietly.

"All of us who have a trace of manhood and are more interested in the rights of human beings than in gin parties and neurotic capitalists."

"I hope you're squelched," Paul stage whispered to Raymond.

"And how!" Raymond laughed. Several joined in. Dr. Parkes spoke quickly to Fenderson, ignoring the remarks of the Communist.

"But, Fenderson . . . this is a new generation and must make use of new weapons. Some of us will continue to fight in the old way, but there are other things to be considered, too. Remember, a beautiful sonnet can be as effectual, nay even more effectual, than a rigorous hymn of hate."

"The man who would understand and be moved by a hymn of hate would not bother to read your sonnet and, even if he did, he would not know what it was all about."

"I don't agree. Your progress must be a boring in from the top, not a battle from the bottom. Convert the higher beings and the lower orders will automatically follow."

"Spoken like a true capitalistic minion," Glenn Madison muttered angrily.

Fenderson prepared to continue his argument, but be was forestalled by Cedric.

"What does it matter," he inquired diffidently, "what any of you do so long as you remain true to yourselves? There is no necessity for this movement becoming standardized. There is ample room for everyone to follow his own individual track. Dr. Parkes wants us all to go back to Africa and resurrect our pagan heritage, become atavistic. In this he is supported by Mr. Clinton. Fenderson here wants us all to be propagandists and yell at the top of our lungs at every conceivable injustice. Madison wants us all to take a cue from Leninism and fight the capitalistic bogey. Well . . . why not let each young hopeful choose his own path? Only in that way will anything at all be achieved."

"Which is just what I say," Raymond smiled gratefully at Cedric. "One cannot make movements nor can one plot their course. When the work of a given number of individuals during a given period is looked at in retrospect, then one can identify a movement and evaluate its distinguishing characteristics. Individuality is what we should strive for. Let each seek his own salvation. To me, a wholesale flight back to Africa or a wholesale allegiance to Communism or a wholesale adherence to an antiquated and for the most part ridiculous propagandistic program are all equally futile and unintelligent."

Dr. Parkes gasped and sought for an answer. Cedric forestalled him.

"To talk of an African heritage among American Negroes *is* unintelligent. It is only in the West Indies that you can find direct descendants from African ancestors. Your primitive instincts among all but the extreme proletariat have been ironed out. You're standardized Americans."

"Oh, no," Carl Denny interrupted suddenly. "You're wrong. It's in our blood. It's . . ." he fumbled for a word, "fixed. Why . . ." he stammered again, "remember Cullen's poem, *Heritage:*

" 'So I lie who find no peace
Night or day, no slight release
From the unremittant beat
Made by cruel padded feet
Walking through my body's street.
Up and down they go, and back,
Treading out a jungle track.'

"We're all like that. Negroes are the only people in America not standard-ized. The feel of the African jungle is in their blood. Its rhythms surge through their bodies. Look how Negroes laugh and dance and sing, all spontaneous and individual."

"Exactly," Dr. Parkes and DeWitt nodded assent.

"I have yet to see an intelligent or middle class American Negro laugh and sing and dance spontaneously. That's an illusion, a pretty sentimental fic-tion. Moreover your songs and dances are not individual. Your spirituals are mediocre folk songs, ignorantly culled from Methodist hymn books. There are white men who can sing them just as well as Negroes, if not better, should they happen to be untrained vocalists like Robeson, rather than highly trained technicians like Hayes. And as for dancing spontaneously and feeling the rhythms of the jungle . . . humph!"

Sweetie May jumped into the breach.

"I can do the Charleston better than any white person."

"I particularly stressed . . . intelligent people. The lower orders of any race have more vim and vitality than the illuminated tenth."

Sweetie May leaped to her feet.

"Why, you West Indian . . ."

"Sweetie, Sweetie," Dr. Parkes was shocked by her polysyllabic expletive.

Pandemonium reigned. The master of ceremonies could not cope with the situation. Cedric called Sweetie an illiterate southern hussy. She called him all types of profane West Indian monkey chasers. DeWitt and David were shocked and showed it. The literary doctor, the Communist and Fen-derson moved uneasily around the room. Annette and Paul giggled. The two child prodigies from Boston looked on wide-eyed, utterly bewildered and dismayed. Raymond leaned back in his chair, puffing on a cigarette, de-tached and amused. Austin, the portrait painter, audibly repeated over and over to himself: "Just like niggers . . . just like niggers." Carl Denny inter-posed himself between Cedric and Sweetie May. Dr. Parkes clucked for civilized behavior, which came only when Cedric stalked angrily out of the room.

After the alien had been routed and peace restored, Raymond passed a soothing cocktail. Meanwhile Austin and Carl had begun arguing about painting. Carl did not possess a facile tongue. He always had difficulty formulating in words the multitude of ideas which seethed in his mind. Austin, to quote Raymond, was an illiterate cad. Having examined one of Carl's pictures on Raymond's wall, he had disparaged it. Raymond listened attentively to their argument. He despised Austin mainly because he spent most of his time imploring noted white people to give him a break by posing for a portrait. Having the gift of making himself pitiable, and having a glib tongue when it came to expiating on the trials and tribulations of being a Negro, he found many sitters, all of whom thought they were encouraging a handicapped Negro genius. After one glimpse at the completed portrait, they invariably changed their minds.

"I tell you," he shouted, "your pictures are distorted and grotesque. Art is art, I say. And art holds a mirror up to nature. No mirror would reflect a man composed of angles. God did not make man that way. Look at Sargent's portraits. He was an artist."

"But he wasn't," Carl expostulated. "We . . . we of this age . . . we must look at Matisse, Gauguin, Picasso and Renoir for guidance. They get the feel of the age. . . . They . . ."

"Are all crazy and so are you," Austin countered before Carl could proceed.

Paul rushed to Carl's rescue. He quoted Wilde in rebuttal: Nature imitates art, then went on to blaspheme Sargent. Carl, having found some words to express a new idea fermenting in his brain, forgot the argument at hand, went off on a tangent and began telling the dazed Dr. Parkes about the Negroid quality in his drawings. DeWitt yawned and consulted his watch. Raymond mused that he probably resented having missed the prayer meeting which he attended every Thursday night. In another corner of the room the Communist and Fenderson had locked horns over the ultimate solution of the Negro problem. In loud voices each contended for his own particular solution. Karl Marx and Lenin were pitted against Du Bois and his disciples. The writing doctor, bored to death, slipped quietly from the room without announcing his departure or even saying good night. Being more intelligent than most of the others, he had wisely kept silent. Tony and Sweetie May had taken adjoining chairs, and were soon engaged in comparing their versions of original verses to the St. James Infirmary, which Tony contended was soon to become as epical as the St. Louis Blues. Annette and Howard began gossiping about various outside personalities. The child prodigies looked from one to the other, silent, perplexed, uncomfortable, not knowing what to do or say. Dr. Parkes visibly recoiled from Carl's incoherent expository barrage, and wilted in his chair, willing but unable to effect a courteous exit. Raymond sauntered around the room, dispensing cocktails, chuckling to himself.

Such was the first and last salon.

THE BANJO PLAYER
FENTON JOHNSON

There is music in me, the music of a peasant people.
I wander through the levee, picking my banjo and singing my songs of the
cabin and the field. At the Last Chance Saloon I am as welcome as the
violets in March; there is always food and drink for me there, and the dimes
of those who love honest music. Behind the railroad tracks the little children clap their hands and love me as they love Kris Kringle.
But I fear that I am a failure. Last night a woman called me a troubadour.
What is a troubadour?

CONVERSATION WITH JAMES P. JOHNSON
TOM DAVIN

In the early 1930's the late Tom Davin worked as publicity man for several
Harlem night clubs. He later became an editor of magazines and books, but
never lost his love for jazz and particularly the Harlem "stride" school. He
did his interviewing of James P. Johnson on successive Saturdays at the latter's Jamaica, Long Island, home.
   Pianist Dick Wellstood wrote in a record review:

*One of the most famous quotes of 1957 was the remark made by Thelonious Monk
while he was listening to the playback of one of his solos: "That sounds like James P.
Johnson." Strangely enough, Monk does sound like James P. from time to time, and
so do Fats, Basie, Tatum, and Duke (as well as Willie Gant and Q. Roscoe Snowden).
Since James P. has had such a strong influence on so many well-known pianists, it is
amazing that . . . the average fan confuses him with Pete Johnson ("Do you really
like boogie woogie?") and the average musician thinks of him affectionately, if dimly,
as an early teacher of Fats Waller.*

*James P. was not Pete Johnson, nor a mere "teacher" of Fats Waller. He was a
much more interesting musician than Waller. His bass lines are better constructed,
his right hand is freer and less repetitive, his rhythm is more accurate, and his playing
is not so relentlessly two-beat as that of Fats. Although he lacked the smooth technique of Tatum (and of Fats) and the striking harmonic imagination of Ellington, he
nonetheless carved out a style which was rich enough in general musical resources
to have re-created at least fragments of itself in the playing of such unlike musicians
as Monk and John Lewis.*

*Unfortunately, James P.'s recording career was a bit too long. He was playing his
best in the thirties, but he is currently represented on record either by recordings of
his old piano rolls, which sound exactly like piano rolls, or by records from the forties, which were made after his health had begun to fail.*

Davin's own introduction to the series of conversations went this way:

324

His show music includes: Plantation Days, Runnin' Wild, Keep Shufflin, Sugar Hill, Meet Miss Jones *and* De Organizer, *a one-act opera with libretto by Langston Hughes.*

In the symphonic field, his orchestral compositions embrace the Harlem Symphony, Symphony in Brown, Suite in Sonata Form on the St. Louis Blues for Piano and Orchestra, Drums *(African themes and rhythms arranged for orchestra),* Carolina Balmoral *arranged for symphony orchestra, as well as many others.*

This is quite a range of achievement for an informally taught, honky-tonk piano player. Who has topped it?

In The Story of Jazz, *Marshall Stearns writes: "In the early fifties, James P. Johnson, old and sick, often wondered what could have happened to his beloved ragtime. For a brief moment, it seemed that the large compositions on which he had been working were about to be accepted and played, along with the time-honored classics of Mozart and Beethoven. Johnson's concertos were quite as complex and, in a sense, twice as difficult to play as Mozart's. Perhaps his Afro-American folk origins betrayed him, for the average classical musician is utterly incapable of the rhythmic sensitivity that is necessary to play Johnson's pieces. Only an orchestra composed of Smiths (Willie the Lion), Wallers, and Johnsons could have done it."*

Two years before he died, in 1955, I was fortunate to be able to interview him extensively about the early New York jazz scene, the people and music which influenced his style. From the notes on his career, these conversations emerge.

We have included here excerpts from two of the conversations which we published—the two which caused most comment, as a matter of fact. The entire series plus Davin's other manuscripts will form the basis of a posthumous book, now in progress, on Harlem jazz and James P. Johnson's career.

Q. James P., how did you get launched as a professional pianist?

A. I told you before how I was impressed by my older brothers' friends. They were real ticklers—cabaret and sporting-house players. They were my heroes and led what I felt was a glamorous life—welcome everywhere because of their talent.

In the years before World War I, there was a piano in almost every home, colored or white. The piano makers had a slogan: "What Is Home Without A Piano?" It was like having a radio or a TV today. Phonographs were feeble and scratchy.

Most people who had pianos couldn't play them, so a piano player was important socially. There were so many of them visiting and socializing that some people would have their pianos going day and night all week long.

If you could play piano good, you went from one party to another and everybody made a fuss about you and fed you ice cream, cake, food and drinks. In fact, some of the biggest men in the profession were known as the biggest eaters we had. At an all-night party, you started at 1:00 A.M., had another meal at 4:00 A.M. and sat down again at 6:00 A.M. Many of us suffered later because of eating and drinking habits started in our younger socializing days.

But that was the life for me when I was seventeen.

In the summer of 1912, during high-school vacation, I went out to Far Rockaway, a beach resort near Coney Island, and got a chance to play at a place run by a fellow named Charlie Ett. It was just a couple of rooms knocked together to make a cabaret. They had beer and liquor, and out in the back yard there was a crib house for fast turnover.

It was a rough place, but I got nine dollars and tips, or about eighteen dollars a week over-all. That was so much money that I didn't want to go back to high school. I never got but quarters when I played before.

Q. Oh, you *did* play professionally before?

A. Yes, but it didn't count. When I was about eight in Jersey City, I was walking down the block, and a woman came out of a doorway and asked me if I wanted to make a quarter. She knew I could play a little, from neighbors, so she took me into her parlor where there were about three or four couples drinking beer, set me down on the piano stool and said: "Go ahead and play and don't turn your head."

I played my *Little Brown Jug* tune and a couple of other hymns and nursery-rhyme arrangements for a couple of hours. I never looked around.

She gave me a quarter, and I went on my way. I guess she was running some kind of sporting house. They were all around the neighborhood.

Q. Excuse my interruption. Tell me more about Far Rockaway.

A. There was another place there called "The Cool Off," located down near the station. Some Clef Club members played there, and they used to come over after hours to hear me play dirty. Kid Sneeze was among them, and Dude Finley, a pianist who played a rag in D minor that had the same trio that was later used in *Shake It, Break It, Throw It Out The Window; Catch It Before It Falls.*

That fall, instead of going back to school, I went to Jersey City and got a job in a cabaret run by Freddie Doyle. He gave me a two-dollar raise.

In a couple of months, Doyle's folded up, and I came back to Manhattan and played in a sporting house on 27th Street between 8th and 9th Avenues, which was the Tenderloin then. I was run by a fellow named Dan Williams, and he had two girl entertainers that I used to accompany.

Q. What type of music were you playing in 1912?

A. Oh, generally popular stuff. I played *That Barbershop Chord* . . . *Lazy Moon* . . . Berlin's *Alexander's Ragtime Band.* Some rags, too, my own and others . . . Joplin's *Maple Leaf Rag* (everybody knew that by then) . . . his *Sunflower Slow Drag* . . . *Maori,* by Will Thiers . . . *The Peculiar Rag* and *The Dream,* by Jack the Bear.

Then there were "instrumentals"; piano arrangements of medleys of Herbert and Friml, popular novelties and music-hall hits—many by Negro composers.

Indian songs were popular then, and the girls at Dan Williams' used to sing *Hiawatha . . . Red Wing . . . Big Chief Battleaxe . . . Come With Me To My Big Teepee . . . Pony Boy*—all popular in the music halls then.

Blues had not come into popularity at that time—they weren't known or sung by New York entertainers.

Q. Had you done any composing by that time?

A. No, but I was working out a number of rags of my own that they wanted to publish at Gotham & Attucks, a Negro music publishing firm whose offices were at 37th Street, off Broadway. I couldn't write them down and I didn't know anybody who would do them for me.

Cecil Mack was president of Gotham & Attucks. All the great colored musicians had gathered around the firm—Bert Williams, George Walker, Scott Joplin, Will Marion Cook, Joe Jordan, Tim Brymm.

They had a lot of hit songs . . . *Just a Word Of Consolation . . . Red, Red Rose . . . Down Among the Sugar Cane . . . Good Morning, Carrie.* Gussie L. Davis, who wrote white-style ballads for them, was the composer of *The Baggage Coach Ahead,* the greatest tear-jerker of the time.

Q. Were you long at Dan Williams' place?

A. No, only a couple of months. I had a number of jobs in the winter of 1912–13. One was playing movie piano at the Nickelette at 8th Avenue and 37th Street. They had movies and short acts for short money. Many vaudeville acts broke in there. Florence Mills first sang there I recall.

In the spring of 1913, I really got started up in The Jungles. This was the Negro section of Hell's Kitchen and ran from 60th to 63rd Street, west of 9th Avenue. It was the toughest part of New York. There were two to three killings a night. Fights broke out over love affairs, gambling, or arguments in general. There were race fights with the white gangs on 66th and 67th Street. It was just as tough in the white section of Hell's Kitchen.

Q. Where did you play there?

A. In 1910 and 1911, I used to drop in at Jim Allan's place at 61st Street and 10th Avenue, where I'd wear my knickers long so they wouldn't notice that I was a short-pants punk. After they heard me play, they would let me come when I wanted.

So, in the spring of 1913, I went uptown and got a job playing at Jim Allan's. It was a remodeled cellar, and since it operated after hours, it had an iron-plated door—like the speak-easies had later. There was a bar upstairs, but downstairs there was a rathskeller, and in the back of the cellar there was a gambling joint.

When the cops raided us now and then, they always had to go back to the station house for axes and sledge hammers, so we usually made a clean getaway.

My NEW YORK JAZZ album [on Asch] tried to show some types of music played in The Jungles at that time . . . Joplin's *Euphonic Sounds* . . . *The Dream* . . . Handy's *Hesitation Blues*.

One night a week, I played piano for Drake's Dancing Class on 62nd Street, which we called "The Jungles Casino." It was officially a dancing school, since it was very hard for Negroes to get a dance-hall license. But you could get a license to open a dancing school very cheap.

The Jungles Casino was just a cellar, too, without fixings. The furnace, coal, and ashes were still there behind a partition. The coal bin was handy for guests to stash their liquor in case the cops dropped in.

There were dancing classes all right, but there were no teachers. The "pupils" danced sets, two-steps, waltzes, schottisches, and "The Metropolitan Glide," a new step.

I played for these regulation dances, but instead of playing straight, I'd break into a rag in certain places. The older ones didn't care too much for this, but the younger ones would scream when I got good to them with a bit of rag in the dance music now and then.

The floor of the dancing class was plain cement like any cellar, and it was hard on the dancers' shoes. I saw many actually wear right through a pair of shoes in one night. They danced hard.

When it rained, the water would run down the walls from the street so we all had to stop and mop up the floor.

The people who came to The Jungles Casino were mostly from around Charleston, South Carolina, and other places in the South. Most of them worked for the Ward Line as longshoremen or on ships that called at southern coast ports. There were even some Gullahs among them.

They picked their partners with care to show off their best steps and put sets, cotillions and cakewalks that would give them a chance to get off.

The Charleston, which became a popular dance step on its own, was just a regulation cotillion step without a name. It had many variations—all danced to the rhythm that everybody knows now. One regular at the Casino, named Dan White, was the best dancer in the crowd and he introduced the Charleston step as we know it. But there were dozens of other steps used, too.

It was while playing for these southern dancers that I composed a number of Charlestons—eight in all—all with the same rhythm. One of these later became my famous *Charleston* when it hit Broadway.

My *Carolina Shout* was another type of ragtime arrangement of a set dance of this period. In fact, a lot of famous jazz compositions grew out of cotillion music—such as *The Wildcat Blues*. Jelly Roll Morton told me that his *King Porter Stomp* and *High Society* were taken from cotillion music.

The dances they did at The Jungles Casino were wild and comical—the more pose and the more breaks, the better. These Charleston people and the other Southerners had just come to New York. They were country people and they felt homesick. When they got tired of two-steps and schottisches (which they danced with a lot of spieling), they'd yell: "Let's go back home!" . . . "Let's do a set!" . . . or, "Now, put us in the alley!" I did my *Mule Walk* or *Gut Stomp* for these country dances.

Breakdown music was the best for such sets, the more solid and groovy the better. They'd dance, hollering and screaming until they were cooked. The dances ran from fifteen to thirty minutes, but they kept up all night long or until their shoes wore out—most of them after a heavy day's work on the docks.

Q. Who were some of the other ticklers in The Jungles at that time?

A. Well, there was Bob Gordon, the March King, who played at Allan's before me, He wrote *Oh, You Drummer!* which was popular because it had a lot of breaks for drums.

Then there was Freddie Singleton who used to relieve me at The Jungles Casino now and then. When I would lay off at Allan's, I would play at Georgie Lee's near by, which was laid out the same as Allan's, except that it had a cabaret in the back room, instead of gambling.

About this time, I played my first "Pigfoot Hop" at Phil Watkin's place on 61st Street. He was a very clever entertainer and he paid me $1.50 for a night's playing with all the gin and chitterlings that I could get down.

This was my first "Chitterlin' Strut" or parlor social, but later in the depression I became famous at "Gumbo Suppers," "Fish Fries," "Egg Nog Parties," and "Rent Parties." I loved them all. You met people.

When I was at Allan's, I met Luckey Roberts at a party.

Q. What was Luckey like in those days of his prime?

A. Luckey Roberts was the outstanding pianist in New York in 1913—and for years before and after. He had composed *The Elks March* . . . *Spanish Venus* . . . *Palm Beach Rag* . . . *The Junkman's Rag.*

Luckey had massive hands that could stretch a fourteenth on the keyboard, and he played tenths as easy as others played octaves. His tremolo was terrific, and he could drum on one note with two or three fingers in either hand. His style in making breaks was like a drummer's: he'd flail his hands in and out, lifting them high. A very spectacular pianist.

He was playing at Barron Wilkins' place in Harlem then, and when I could get away I went uptown and studied him (I was working at Allan's from 9:00 P.M. to 7:00 A.M.). Later we became good friends, and he invited me to his home. Afterwards, I played at Barron Wilkins', too, as did my friend Ernest Green, who first introduced me to Luckey. Ernest was a good classical pianist. Luckey used to ask him to play the *William Tell Overture* and the *White Cavalry Overture.* These were considered tops in "classical" music amongst us.

Ernest Green's mother was studying then with a piano and singing teacher named Bruto Gianinni. She did house cleaning in return for lessons—several Negro singers got their training that way. Mrs. Green told me: "James, you have too much talent to remain ignorant of musical principles." She inspired me to study seriously. So I began to take lessons from

Gianinni, but I got tired of the dull exercises. However, he taught me a lot of concert effects.

I was starting to develop a good technique. I was born with absolute pitch and could catch a key that a player was using and copy it, even Luckey's. I played rags very accurately and brilliantly—running chromatic octaves and glissandos up and down with both hands. It made a terrific effect.

I did double glissandos straight and backhand, glissandos in sixths and double tremolos. These would run other ticklers out of the place at cutting sessions. They wouldn't play after me. I would put these tricks in on the breaks and I could think of a trick a minute. I was playing a lot of piano then, traveling around and listening to every good player I could. I'd steal their breaks and style and practice them until I had them perfect.

From listening to classical piano records and concerts, from friends of Ernest Green such as Mme. Garret, who was a fine classical pianist, I would learn concert effects and build them into blues and rags.

Sometimes I would play basses a little lighter than the melody and change harmonies. When playing a heavy stomp, I'd soften it right down—then, I'd make an abrupt change like I heard Beethoven do in a sonata.

Some people thought it was cheap, but it was effective and dramatic. With a solid bass like a metronome, I'd use chords with half and quarter changes. Once I used Liszt's *Rigoletto Concert Paraphrase* as an introduction to a stomp. Another time, I'd use pianissimo effects in the groove and let the dancers' feet be heard scraping on the floor. It was used by dance bands later.

In practicing technique, I would play in the dark to get completely familiar with the keyboard. To develop clear touch and the feel of the piano, I'd put a bed sheet over the keyboard and play difficult pieces through it.

I had gotten power and was building a serious orchestral piano. I did rag variations on the *William Tell Overture,* Grieg's *Peer Gynt Suite* and even a *Russian Rag* based on Rachmaninoff's *Prelude in C. Shart Minor,* which was just getting popular then.

In my *Imitators' Rag* the last strain had *Dixie* in the right hand and *The Star Spangled Banner* in the left. (It wasn't the national anthem then.) Another version had *Home, Sweet Home* in the left hand and *Dixie* in the right.

When President Wilson's "Preparedness" campaign came on, I wrote a march fantasia called *Liberty.*

From 1914 to 1916, I played at Allan's, Lee's, The Jungles Casino, occasionally uptown at Barron Wilkins', Leroy's and Wood's (run then by Edmund Johnson). I went around copping piano prize contests and I was considered one of the best in New York—if not the best. I was slim and dapper, and they called me "Jimmie" then.

Q. Had you done any composing yet?

A. I had started to compose my first rag about this time (1914), but nothing was done with it, and I threw it away. I also wrote and threw away a number of songs, although some people seemed to like them.

Entertainers used to sing blues to me, homemade blues, and I'd arrange them for piano, either to accompany them or play as solos. One of these homemade blues, *All Night Long,* was made into a song by Shelton Brooks who also wrote *The Darktown Strutters' Ball.*

Then I met Will Farrell, a Negro song writer, and he showed me how to set down my pieces down in writing. He also wrote lyrics for them. With him, I set down my first composition to be published, *Mamma's and Pappa's Blues.*

There had been a piece around at the time called *Left Her On The Railroad Track* or *Baby, Get That Towel Wet.* All pianists knew it and could play variations on it. It was a sporting-house favorite. I took one opening strain and did a paraphrase from this and used it in *Mamma's and Pappa's Blues.* It was also developed later into *Crazy Blues,* by Perry Bradford.

I had composed *Carolina Shout* before that. It wasn't written down, but was picked up by other pianists. My *Steeplechase Rag* and *Daintiness Rag* had spread all over the country, too, although they hadn't been published.

With Farrell, I also wrote *Stop It, Joe!* at this time. I sold it, along with *Mamma's and Pappa's Blues* for twenty-five dollars apiece to get enough money for a deposit on a grand piano.

In the summer of 1914, I went for a visit to Atlantic City and heard Eubie Blake (who composed *Shuffle Along* later), one of the foremost pianists of all time. He was playing at The Belmont, and Charles Johnson was playing at The Boat House, both all-night joints.

Eubie was a marvelous song player. He also had a couple of rags. One, *Troublesome Ivories,* was very good. I caught it.

I saw how Eubie, like Willie Smith and Luckey Roberts, could play songs in all keys, so as to be ready for any singer—or if one of them started on a wrong note. So I practiced that, too. I also prepared symphonic vamps— gutty, but not very full.

While in New Jersey that summer, I won a piano contest in Egg Harbor, playing my *Twilight Rag* (which had a chimes effect in syncopation), *Stee-plechase Rag,* and *Nighttime in Dixieland.*

There was a pianist there who played quadrilles, sets, rags, etc. From him, I first heard the walking Texas or boogie-woogie bass. The boogie woogie was a cotillion step for which a lot of music was composed. I never got his name, but he played the *Kitchen Tom Rag* which was the signal for a "Jazz" dance.

When I came back to New York, I met the famous Abba Labba in the Chelsea district. To this day, I can't remember his right name, either. He was a friend and pupil of Luckey Roberts'.

Abba Labba was the working girls' Jelly Roll. His specialty was to play a lot of piano for girls who were laundresses and cooks. They would supply him with stylish clothes from their customers' laundry and make him elaborate rosettes for his sleeve guards. The cooks furnished him with wonderful meals, since they had fine cold kina (keena) then. Cold kina was leftover food from a white family's dinner that the cook was entitled to. This was an old southern cooks' custom: they fed their own family with these leftovers and they were sure to see that there was plenty of good food left. That's why old southern home cooking was so famous—the cook shared it.

Most of the full-time hustlers used to cultivate a working girl like that, so they could have good meals and fancy laundry.

Abba Labba had a beautiful left hand and did wonderful bass work. He played with half-tone and quarter-tone changes that were new ideas then. He would run octaves in chords, and one of his tricks was to play *Good Night, Beloved, Good Night* in schottische, waltz and ragtime.

I fell on his style and copied a lot of it.

Q. Were there other pianists you learned tricks from at this time?

A. Oh, yes. I was getting around town and hearing everybody. If they had anything I didn't have, I listened and stole it.

Sam Gordon played at The Elks Café at 137th and 138th Streets and Lenox Avenue. He was a great technician who played an arabesque style that Art Tatum made famous later. He played swift runs in sixths and thirds, broken chords, one-note tremolandos and had a good left hand. He had been a classical pianist and had studied in Germany. He picked up syncopation here.

Fred Bryant from Brooklyn was a good all-around pianist. He played classical music and had a velvet touch. The piano keys seemed to be extensions of his fingers. Incidentally, as far as I know, he invented the backward tenth. I used it and passed it on to Fats Waller later. It was the keynote of our style.

Down in Chelsea, there was a player named Fats Harris, who looked like Waller did later. He had a rag in D called *Fats Harris's Rag,* a great stomp tune.

Then in the fall of 1914, I went over to Newark, New Jersey, and first met Willie (The Lion) Smith and Dickie Huff who were playing on "The Coast," a tough section around Arlington and Augusta Streets. I played at Kinney Hall and Lewis', which was located in an old church.

Both were great players. I don't have to tell you about Willie, he's still playing great. He's the last of the real old-time ticklers—along with Luckey.

Q. What was Willie (The Lion) Smith like in his young days?

A. Willie Smith was one of the sharpest ticklers I ever met—and I met most of them. When we first met in Newark, he wasn't called Willie The Lion—he got that nickname after his terrific fighting record overseas during World War I. He was a fine dresser, very careful about the cut of his clothes and a fine dancer, too, in addition to his great playing. All of us used to be proud of our dancing—Louis Armstrong, for instance, was considered the finest dancer among the musicians. It made for attitude and stance when you walked into a place, and made you strong with the gals. When Willie Smith walked into a place, his every move was a picture.

Q. You mean he would make a studied entrance, like a theatrical star?

A. Yes, every move we made was studied, practiced, and developed just like it was a complicated piano piece.

Q. What would such an entrance be like?

A. When a real smart tickler would enter a place, say in winter, he'd leave his overcoat on and keep his hat on, too. We used to wear military overcoats or what was called a Peddock Coat, like a coachman's; a blue double-breasted, fitted to the waist and with long skirts. We'd wear a light pearl-gray Fulton or Homburg hat with three buttons or eyelets on the side, set at a rakish angle over on the side of the head. Then a white silk muffler and a white silk handkerchief in the overcoat's breast pocket. Some carried a gold-headed cane, or if they were wearing a cutaway, a silver-headed cane. A couple of fellows used to wear Inverness capes, which were in style in white society then.

Many fellows had their overcoats lined with the same material as the out-side—they even had their suits made that way. Pawnbrokers, special ones, would give you twenty or twenty-five dollars on such a suit or overcoat. They knew what it was made of. A fellow belittling another would be able to say: "G'wan, the inside of my coat would make you a suit."

But to go back . . . when you came into a place you had a three-way play. You never took your overcoat or hat off until you were at the piano. First you laid your cane on the music rack. Then you took off your overcoat, folded it and put it on the piano, with the lining showing.

You then took off your hat before the audience. Each tickler had his own gesture for removing his hat with a little flourish; that was part of his atti-tude, too. You took out your silk handkerchief, shook it out and dusted off the piano stool.

Now, with your coat off, the audience could admire your full-back or box-back suit, cut with very square shoulders. The pants had about fourteen-inch cuffs and broidered clocks.

Full-back coats were always single-breasted, to show your gold watch fob and chain. Some ticklers wore a horseshoe tiepin in a strong single-colored tie and a gray shirt with black pencil stripes.

We all wore French, Shriner & Urner or Hanan straight or French last shoes with very pointed toes, or patent-leather turnup toes, in very narrow sizes. For instance, if you had a size 7 foot, you'd wear an 8½ shoe on a very narrow last. They cost from twelve to eighteen dollars a pair.

If you had an expensive suit made, you'd have the tailor take a piece of cloth and give it to you, so that you could have either spats or button cloth-tops for your shoes to match the suit.

Some sharp men would have a suit and overcoat made of the same bolt of cloth. Then they'd take another piece of the same goods and have a three-button Homburg made out of it. This was only done with solid-color cloth—tweeds or plaids were not in good taste for formal hats.

There was a tailor named Bromberger down on Carmine Street, near Sheridan Square in the old 15th Ward, who made all the hustlers' clothes. That was a Negro section around 1912. He charged twenty-five to forty dollars a suit.

Another tailoring firm, Clemens & Ostreicher, at 40th Street and 6th Avenue, would make you a sharp custom suit for $11.75—with broadlap seams (¾ in.), a finger-tip coat, shirred in at the waist with flared skirts, patch pockets, five-button cuffs and broad lapels.

Up on 153rd Street there was a former barber named Hart who had invented a hair preparation named Kink-No-More, called "Conk" for short. His preparation was used by all musicians—the whole Clef Club used him. You'd get your hair washed, dyed and straightened; then trimmed. It would last about a month.

Of course each tickler had his own style of appearance. I used to study them carefully and copy those attitudes that appealed to me.

There was a fellow named Fred Tunstall, whom I mentioned before. He was a real dandy. I remember he had a Norfolk coat with eighty-two pleats in the back. When he sat down to the piano, he'd slump a little in a half hunch, and those pleats would fan out real pretty. That coat was long and flared at the waist. It had a very short belt sewn on the back. His pants were very tight.

He had a long neck, so he wore a high, stiff collar that came up under his chin with a purple tie. A silk handkerchief was always draped very carefully in his breast pocket. His side view was very striking.

Tunstall was very careful about his hair, which was ordinary, but he used lots of pomade. His favorite shoes were patent-leather turnups.

His playing was fair, but he had the reputation of being one of our most elegant dressers. He had thirty-five suits of clothes—blacks, grays, brown pin stripes, oxfords, pepper and salts.

Some men would wear a big diamond ring on their pinky, the right-hand one, which would flash in the treble passages. Gold teeth were in style, and a real sharp effect was to have a diamond set on one tooth. One fellow went further and had diamonds set in the teeth of his toy Boston bulldog. There was a gal named Diamond Floss, a big sporting-house woman, a hot clipper and a high-powered broad, who had diamonds in all her front teeth. She had a place in Chelsea, the West 30's, in the Tenderloin days.

Q. Where did these styles come from, the South?

A. No, we saw them right here in New York City. They were all copied from the styles of the rich whites. Most of the society folks had colored valets and some of them would give their old clothes to their valets and household help.

Then we'd see rich people at society gigs in the big hotels where they had Clef Club bands for their dances. So we wanted to dress good, copied them and made improvements.

Q. Please tell me more about the great ticklers' styles.

A. As I was saying, when I was a young fellow, I was very much impressed with such manners. I didn't know much about style, but I wanted to learn. I didn't want to be a punk all my life.

In the sporting world of gamblers, hustlers and ticklers, the lowest rank is called a punk. He's nothing. He doesn't have any sense; he doesn't know anything about life or the school of the smart world. He doesn't even know how to act in public. You had to have an attitude, a style of behaving that was your personal, professional trade-mark.

The older Clef Club musicians were artists at this kind of acting. The club was a place to go to study these glamorous characters. I got a lot of my style from ticklers like Floyd Keppard, who I knew in Jersey City, Dan Avery, Bob Hawkins, Lester Wilson, Freddie Tunstall, Kid Sneeze, Abba Labba, Willie Smith and many others.

I've seen Jelly Roll Morton, who had a great attitude, approach a piano. He would take his overcoat off. It had a special lining that would catch everybody's eye. So he would turn it inside out and, instead of folding it, he would lay it lengthwise along the top of the upright piano. He would do this very slowly, very carefully and very solemnly as if the coat was worth a fortune and had to be handled very tenderly.

Then he'd take a big silk handkerchief, shake it out to show it off properly, and dust off the stool. He'd sit down then, hit his special chord (every tickler had his special trade-mark chord, like a signal) and he'd be gone! The first rag he'd play was always a spirited one to astound the audience.

Other players would start off by sitting down, wait for the audience to quiet down and then strike their chord, holding it with the pedal to make it ring.

Then they'd do a run up and down the piano—a scale or arpeggios—or if they were real good they might play a set of modulations, very offhand, as if there was nothing to it. They'd look around idly to see if they knew any chicks near the piano. If they saw somebody, they'd start a light conversation about the theater, the races or social doings—light chat. At this time, they'd drift into a rag, any kind of pretty stuff, but without tempo, particularly without tempo. Some ticklers would sit sideways to the piano, cross their legs and go on chatting with friends near by. It took a lot of practice to play this way, while talking and with your head and body turned.

Then, without stopping the smart talk or turning back to the piano, he'd *attack* without any warning, smashing right into the regular beat of the piece. That would knock them dead.

A big-timer would, of course, have a diamond ring he would want to show off to some gal near by that he wanted to make. So he would adjust his hand so that the diamond would catch her eye and blind her. She'd know he was a big shot right off.

A lot of this was taught to me by old-timers, when they would be sitting around when I was a kid and only playing social dance music. I wasn't a very good-looking fellow, but I dressed nice and natty. I learned all their stuff and practiced it carefully.

In the old days, these effects were studied to attract the young gals who hung around such places. Ed Avery, whose style I copied, was a great actor and a hell of a ladies' man. He used to run big harems of all kinds of women.

After your opening piece to astound the audience, it would depend on the gal you were playing for or the mood of the place for what you would play next. It might be sentimental, moody, stompy or funky. The good player had to know just what the mood of the audience was.

At the end of his set, he'd always finish up with a hot rag and then stand up quickly, so that everybody in the place would be able to see who knocked it out.

Every tickler kept these attitudes even when he was socializing at parties or just visiting. They were his professional personality and prepared the audience for the artistic performance to come. I've watched high-powered actors today, and they all have that professional approach. In the old days they really worked at it. It was designed to show a personality that women would admire. With the music he played, the tickler's manners would put the question in the ladies' minds: "Can he do it like he can play it?"

Q. The high-style clothes you described seem to have disappeared in recent years. How did it happen?

A. Well, full-back clothes became almost a trade-mark for pimps and sharps. Church socials and dancing classes discriminated against all who wore full-back clothes. They would have a man at the door to keep them out. So, in self-defense, the hustlers had to change to English drape styles, which were rumored to be worn only by pansies and punks.

Q. Don't tell me that those sharp hustlers frequented church socials?

A. Oh, yes. Some of the toughest guys would even attend Sunday school classes regularly, just to get next to the younger and better-class gals there. They wore the square style of pinch-back coats and peg-top pants and would even learn hymns to impress a chick they had their eye on. They were very versatile cats.

INTERVIEW WITH EUBIE BLAKE, OCTOBER 16, 1973
NATHAN IRVIN HUGGINS

N.H. Regarding the practice of stealing music in the early years of the century.

E.B. Sissle and Blake made some records for Emerson, that was about 1921 or 1922 [Sissle and Blake recorded for Emerson, 1920–1922]. The engineer, who was working the machine said, after we had finished, "hey Eubie, play a rag," cause I hadn't played a rag during the session. So, I played a rag for him. It was my *Charleston Rag.* Then, we left, cause we had finished. Ten, fifteen years after that, when I was in Chicago, one of the old timers who knew me for years said, "well, you must be making money now. I hear your *Charleston Rag* all the time." Now, the song that he heard wasn't called that. I never named that tune. Will Marion Cook named it. I told him that I had never published that song. So, this guy said, "hey Jim, come here and tell him about *Sounds of Africa* (that's what Will Marion Cook named it). So, I said, "yeh, I wrote that song, I composed it." He said, "well, it's all over the radio out here." They had never played it in New York, so this was the first time that I had heard about the record. The engineer just took it and sold it to the bootlegger, bootlegging music.

N.H. You had to be careful in those days. You had a piece of music and somebody would steal it right out from under you.

E.B. People don't know what we went through in those days. Well, that's what happened. You used to go into the publishing houses, up and down Broadway, what we called hustling songs. You'd play a tune for the publisher—the guy would be sitting right there and tell you he didn't want your song. Then, after a while, about two months after that, we would hear the song. They didn't do it to us because we were colored. They did it to everybody who wasn't big.

N.H. Regarding vaudeville and black performers.

E.B. We went into vaudeville—Sissle and Blake. Now, I'm not bragging, but I'm telling what actually would happen. We were a sensation in vaudeville. Not only us, but other black performers. We were top acts on the Keith circuit. Any time you saw a colored act on Keith circuit, they were better than anybody else on there. See, that's the only way that you could get on. They put us on in the number 2 spot. You know why they did that? Because the newspapers didn't come in until the number 3 act; see, that kept us from getting a good write-up. We were "also-ran." You know, like at the racetrack. So, the colored acts' names were on the bill, that's about all. But the third act down got write ups. We know why they did that. But this is what happened. There were nine acts on the bill. The money starts at the third act—the real money. Sissle and Blake never got—we got $400 a week, not much more.

But I'll tell you how we changed shows. Ziegfeld, George White, the Shuberts. . . . They all had reviews with girls—beautiful girls. They walked around in beautiful clothes. The people who danced in these shows were specialties. These shows didn't have a real chorus. These girls in beautiful costumes would just walk and kick a little. So, we came in with our show. Our girls were beautiful, and they *danced!!!* They *danced!!!* And they *sang!!!* Those others didn't do nothing but [sings] "A Pretty Girl is Like a Melody . . ." and all were beautiful. But after you had seen them once, well, that's it. But our girls were—white people have a name they call dancers—hoofers—these girls *DANCED!!!* There had never been anything like it. You could see a little dancing in burlesque, but better people didn't go to burlesque, especially ladies.

N.H. So, *Shuffle Along* brought the dancing chorus to the shows.

E.B. They danced. You see, I wrote rhythmic tunes so that they could dance. You know rhythm is the most—rhythm and laughing is the most contagious thing in the whole world. I'm not a scientist, but I'm saying that on my own. But rhythm [claps hands to rhythm] See? This is the way white people do it, see, watch my foot. [Claps hands and pats foot on the beat]. See that? See, we don't clap like that—with the music. See, we come down after the beat. See, you don't have to have music. You can use a tom tom, anything. Just watch the audience. See, that's how contagious rhythm is . . . and laughing.

N.H. So the real contribution of *Shuffle Along* was in the music and dancing. *Shuffle Along* was really bringing the spirit of black folks to the New York theater world where it had not been before.

E.B. The people had heard it all along, of course. But the real elite people had heard it, maybe on the radio. But they had not *experienced* it.

N.H. So, when they had to pat their foot too, that was something that captured them.

E.B. Yes! It captured them.

N.H.. You referred to yourself as a composer, not a songwriter. Now, in *Shuffle Along*—the music that you were writing at the time—did you see yourself as doing something new and different, musically?

E.B. No. I wasn't doing anything different. I'm 90 years old, and I heard that music when I was 5 or 6 years old: the bands coming up and down the streets in Baltimore, the colored bands. They would go to a funeral. Now, New Orleans claims that the music originated there. There's only one man in New Orleans (Kid Ory, just died) who is older than I. And I heard ever since I was 5 or 6 years old in Baltimore [hums Chopin's Funeral March at normal tempo and beat]. They would come back from the funerals [hums and claps hands in a syncopation of the Chopin march]. Same thing! Whatever they played going out, they played the same thing coming back , but to ragtime. All the Negro bands did that. I heard that in my time.

But, you see, my mother hated it. You see, ragtime wasn't nothing—wasn't supposed to be nothing. It came from the small-time bars and backrooms and houses of ill repute.

N.H.. Your mother hated it? And a lot of other "respectable" people hated it. How did you feel about that? About their hating it?

E.B. I always liked it. But I'm of that group. I'm a part of that group.

N.H. But how did you feel about how the others were dealing with your music?

E.B. Well, I didn't have a say in it. Because the powers that be—the white people—they said it was nothing, it was terrible. We follow the white people—you follow the people who are on top, you can't help it. So the Negroes did. But, when you go to the church [Sings and claps in syncopation] "Jesus knows all about my struggles . . ." In the church!!! There was rhythm in the church! Now white people would sing [sings in straight rhythm] "Jesus knows all about my struggles . . ." See the difference? But, it is born in us. That don't mean that white people can't do it. I don't mean that they can't play it, like they said that we couldn't sing opera. Black Patti could sing opera even when she couldn't go to an opera.

N.H. At the same time that *Shuffle Along* was a hit, what they talked about as the spirit of the times—other people talked about—had to do with writers and artists and others who were in Harlem writing novels, painting pictures, people like Aaron Douglas, Langston Hughes, people like that. Now, the musical people, the people in the musical theater, like yourself, did you have any relationship with them?

E.B. Yes. I had. Not with Douglas. I had relationships with Langston Hughes, I wrote one of the funniest songs with him—we never published it. I only wrote one song with him. I knew Langston Hughes, Weldon Johnson. I knew these fellows. Cecil Mack, Bob Cole, Rosamund Johnson—that's Weldon's brother.

Joe Jordon wrote "Lovie Joe" for Fanny Brice. And they had that girl, the girl now—Barbra Streisand—doing a show about Fanny Brice [*Funny Girl*] and Jordan and his song were never mentioned. She didn't sing "Lovie Joe" even though it was one of Fanny Brice's big songs.

So they did the GREAT ZIEGFELD, and they never had Bert Williams in it. Of course, Bert Williams was dead when they made the movie, but I mean they didn't represent him. And he was one of Ziegfeld's biggest stars. The only thing they did, the girls came down the spiral stairs, backstage—this is the movie I'm talking about—the chorus girls chattering and the stage manager said "you girls shut up, Mr. Bert Williams is on"—no—"Bert Williams is on." That's the only time they mentioned him. That's the only time—I saw the show—that's the only time. But they had all the rest of the guys—the big shots who were dead—they had them represented there. Well, it's their show. They're the ones that are putting up the money. And when Walter White went out there [to Hollywood] to see about the discrimination of Negroes in pictures. Well, he was a white man to them. He didn't look colored. He didn't act colored. He'd been around white people so much, he had absorbed their attitudes. They respected him while he was there. And when he left, they still had Negroes playing maids and porters . . .

N.H. Now you were talking about the Harlem Renaissance and the people in it. Did you, yourself, have any impressions of what was going on in the Harlem Renaissance?

E.B. My impression of Harlem was, what we in show business call a "heat wave." The white people were coming up to Harlem to hear this music. And when we would go downtown and play for millionaires. . . .

N.H. You are saying that white people were coming uptown, following the music. And it was that sense of the music that was at the center of the Harlem Renaissance?

E.B. The music and the entertainment. There was this guy, Oscar Hammerstein (that was not his real name. He was a black man who could pass for white). He did the same thing uptown as—what's the guy who jumped off the bridge?—Steve Brody did in the Bowery. Millionaires used to go down to the Bowery to see how derelicts lived. [Oscar Hammerstein] had a good education. He used to guide them around Harlem. They had their jewels. But nobody would bother them with Oscar Hammerstein around. They would not dare. He knew all the crooks and hustlers.

N.H. Some of the clubs uptown, like the Cotton Club, would not allow black people in them. Is that right?

E.B. No! No! Paul Whiteman, he took Ethel Waters and me into hear Duke Ellington's band. We got in because we were with Paul Whiteman—he was the Lord of Music.

N.H. Yes. He was called the father of Jazz.

E.B. That's what *they* said. Jim Europe was the original . . . But they've got the newspapers, so they made him the King of Jazz. Anyway, that's how Ethel Waters and Eubie Blake got into the Cotton Club.

N.H. Of course there were clubs that blacks could get into.

E.B. Connie's Inn, Broadway Jones's Place—white and colored went in. But the Cotton Club, you couldn't get into. After the theater, white people would come uptown.

N.H. All of these clubs specialized in black entertainers?

E.B. Yes. Sissle and Blake and Andy Razaf put on so many colored shows—floor shows, they called them—that Gene Buck, President of ASCAP, and David Stamper wrote a song: "Broadway's Gettin' Darker Every Nite." Meaning, that we were pushing the whites out. It was something new to them. It wasn't new. They had just never seen it. Then it moved to Chicago and the other cities. It wasn't just New York.

CHRISTIANITY: ALIEN GOSPEL OR SOURCE OF INSPIRATION?

To the Afro-American in the 1920s, Christianity had a variety of faces. Institutionalized, it was a church and one of the few institutional forms through which blacks could work, and yet it was a means of exploiting poor blacks to its own profit and to that of its preachers. Ideologically, it was a doctrine and a set of values, shared by the dominant society, against which America and whites could be held to account, and yet it counselled forbearance and seemed a moral obligation only to the weak. Spiritually, it had provided the conduit for the voiced hopes and feelings of blacks from their first arrival in America, and yet it was the way to escape to other-wordly preoccupations. The dilemmas, therefore, were torturous and troubling. To find a racial self-respect meant for Afro-Americans to honor the religious expression and imagination of their people. But to be modern—to be a New Negro—would necessitate a new and critical look at Christianity.

Thus, James Weldon Johnson and Zora Neale Hurston are able to celebrate the power of Christianity in the folk idiom. But Countee Cullen (whose adoptive father was a Methodist minister) often used Christian themes only to show his deep, personal ambivalence. For others, like Waring Cuney, Georgia Douglas Johnson, and Helene Johnson, Christianity was a target of satire.

GO DOWN DEATH
JAMES WELDON JOHNSON

A Funeral Sermon

Weep not, weep not,
She is not dead;
She's resting in the bosom of Jesus.
Heart-broken husband—weep no more;
Grief-stricken son—weep no more;
Left-lonesome daughter—weep no more;
She's only just gone home.

Day before yesterday morning,
God was looking down from his great, high heaven,
Looking down on all his children,
And his eye fell on Sister Caroline,
Tossing on her bed of pain.
And God's big heart was touched with pity,
With the everlasting pity.

And God sat back on his throne,
And he commanded that tall, bright angel standing at his right hand:
Call me Death!
And that tall, bright angel cried in a voice
That broke like a clap of thunder:
Call Death!—Call Death!
And the echo sounded down the streets of heaven
Till it reached away back to that shadowy place,
Where Death waits with his pale, white horses.

And Death heard the summons,
And he leaped on his fastest horse,
Pale as a sheet in the moonlight.
Up the golden street Death galloped,
And the hoofs of his horse struck fire from the gold,
But they didn't make no sound.
Up Death rode to the Great White Throne,
And waited for God's command.

And God said: Go down, Death, go down,
Go down to Savannah, Georgia,
Down in Yamacraw,
And find Sister Caroline.
She's borne the burden and heat of the day,
She's labored long in my vineyard,

And she's tired—
She's weary—
Go down, Death, and bring her to me.

And Death didn't say a word,
But he loosed the reins on his pale, white horse,
And he clamped the spurs to his bloodless sides,
And out and down he rode,
Through heaven's pearly gates,
Past suns and moons and stars;
On Death rode,
And the foam from his horse was like a comet in the sky;
On Death rode,
Leaving the lightning's flash behind;
Straight on down he came.

While we were watching round her bed,
She turned her eyes and looked away,
She saw what we couldn't see;
She saw Old Death. She saw Old Death
Coming like a falling star.
But Death didn't frighten Sister Caroline;
He looked to her like a welcome friend.
And she whispered to us: I'm going home,
And she smiled and closed her eyes.

And Death took her up like a baby,
And she lay in his icy arms,
But she didn't feel no chill.
And Death began to ride again—
Up beyond the evening star,
Out beyond the morning star,
Into the glittering light of glory,
On to the Great White Throne.
And there he laid Sister Caroline
On the loving breast of Jesus.

And Jesus took his own hand and wiped away her tears,
And he smoothed the furrows from her face,
And the angels sang a little song,
And Jesus rocked her in his arms,
And kept a-saying: Take your rest,
Take your rest, take your rest.

Weep not—weep not,
She is not dead;
She's resting in the bosom of Jesus.

SPIRITUALS AND NEO-SPIRITUALS
ZORA NEALE HURSTON

The real spirituals are not really just songs. They are unceasing variations around a theme.

Contrary to popular belief their creation is not confined to the slavery period. Like the folk-tales, the spirituals are being made and forgotten everyday. There is this difference: the makers of the songs of the present go about from town to town and church to church singing their songs. Some are printed and called ballads, and offered for sale after the services at ten and fifteen cents each. Others just go about singing them in competition with other religious minstrels. The lifting of the collection is the time for the song battles. Quite a bit of rivalry develops.

These songs, even the printed ones, do not remain long in their original form. Every congregation that takes it up alters it considerably. For instance, *The Dying Bed Maker,* which is easily the most popular of the recent compositions, has been changed to *He's a Mind Regulator* by a Baptist church in New Orleans.

The idea that the whole body of spirituals are "sorrow songs" is ridiculous. They cover a wide range of subjects from a peeve at gossipers to Death and Judgment.

The nearest thing to a description one can reach is that they are Negro religious songs, sung by a group, and a group bent on expression of feelings and not on sound effects.

There never has been a presentation of genuine Negro spirituals to any audience anywhere. What is being sung by the concert artists and glee clubs are the works of Negro composers or adaptors *based* on the spirituals. Under this head come the works of Harry T. Burleigh, Rosamond Johnson, Lawrence Brown, Nathaniel Dett, Hall Johnson and Work. All good work and beautiful, but *not* the spirituals. These neo-spirituals are the outgrowth of the glee clubs. Fisk University boasts perhaps the oldest and certainly the most famous of these. They have spread their interpretation over America and Europe. Hampton and Tuskegee have not been unheard. But with all the glee clubs and soloists, there has not been one genuine spiritual presented.

To begin with, Negro spirituals are not solo or quartette material. The jagged harmony is what makes it, and it ceases to be what it was when this is absent. Neither can any group be trained to reproduce it. Its truth dies under training like flowers under hot water. The harmony of the true spiritual is not regular. The dissonances are important and not to be ironed out by the trained musician. The various parts break in at any old time. Falsetto often takes the place of regular voices for short periods. Keys change. Moreover, each singing of the piece is a new creation. The congregation is bound by no rules. No two times singing is alike, so that we must consider the rendition of a song not as a final thing, but as a mood. It won't be the same thing next Sunday.

Negro songs to be heard truly must be sung by a group, and a group bent on expression of feelings and not on sound effects.

Glee clubs and concert singers put on their tuxedoes, bow prettily to the audience, get the pitch and burst into magnificent song—but not *Negro* song. The real Negro singer cares nothing about pitch. The first notes just burst out and the rest of the church join in—fired by the same inner urge. Every man trying to express himself through song. Every man for himself. Hence the harmony and disharmony, the shifting keys and broken time that make up the spiritual.

I have noticed that whenever an untampered-with congregation attempts the renovated spirituals, the people grow self-conscious. They sing sheepishly in unison. None of the glorious individualistic flights that make up their own songs. Perhaps they feel on strange ground. Like the unlettered parent before his child just home from college. At any rate they are not very popular.

This is no condemnation of the neo-spirituals. They are a valuable contribution to the music and literature of the world. But let no one imagine that they are the songs of the people, as sung by them.

The lack of dialect in the religious expression—particularly in the prayers—will seem irregular.

The truth is, that the religious service is a conscious art expression. The artist is consciously creating—carefully choosing every syllable and every breath. The dialect breaks through only when the speaker has reached the emotional pitch where he loses self-consciousness.

In the mouth of the Negro the English language loses its stiffness, yet conveys its meaning accurately. "The booming bounderries of this whirling world" conveys just as accurate a picture as mere "boundaries," and a little music is gained besides. "The rim bones of nothing" is just as truthful as "limitless space."

Negro singing and formal speech are breathy. The audible breathing is part of the performance and various devices are resorted to to adorn the breath taking. Even the lack of breath is embellished with syllables. This is, of course, the very antithesis of white vocal art. European singing is considered good when each syllable floats out on a column of air, seeming not to have any mechanics at all. Breathing must be hidden. Negro song ornaments both the song and the mechanics. It is said of a popular preacher, "He's got a good straining voice." I will make a parable to illustrate the difference between Negro and European.

A white man built a house. So he got it built and he told the man: "Plaster it good so that nobody can see the beams and uprights." So he did. Then he had it papered with beautiful paper, and painted the outside. And a Negro built him a house. So when he got the beams and all in, he carved beautiful grotesques over all the sills and stanchions, and beams and rafters. So both went to live in their houses and were happy.

The well-known "ha!" of the Negro preacher is a breathing device. It is the tail end of the expulsion just before inhalation. Instead of permitting the breath to drain out, when the wind gets too low for words, the remnant is expelled violently. Example: (inhalation) "And oh!"; (full breath) "my Father and my wonder-working God"; (explosive exhalation) "ha!"

Chants and hums are not used indiscriminately as it would appear to a casual listener. They have a definite place and time. They are used to "bear up" the speaker. As Mama Jane of Second Zion Baptist Church, New Orleans, explained to me: "What point they come out on, you bear 'em up."

For instance, if the preacher should say: "Jesus will lead us," the congregation would bear him up with: "I'm got my ha-hands in my Jesus' hands." If in prayer or sermon, the mention is made of nailing Christ to the cross: "Didn't Calvary tremble when they nailed Him down."

There is no definite post-prayer chant. One may follow, however, because of intense emotion. A song immediately follows prayer. There is a pre-prayer hum which depends for its material upon the song just sung. It is usually a pianissimo continuation of the song without words. If some of the people use the words it is done so indistinctly that they would be hard to catch by a person unfamiliar with the song.

As indefinite as hums sound, they also are formal and can be found unchanged all over the South. The Negroised white hymns are not exactly sung. They are converted into a barbaric chant that is not a chant. It is a sort of liquefying of words. These songs are always used at funerals and on any solemn occasion. The Negro has created no songs for death and burials, in spite of the sombre subject matter contained in some of the spirituals. Negro songs are one and all based on a dance-possible rhythm. The heavy interpretations have been added by the more cultured singers. So for funerals fitting white hymns are used.

Beneath the seeming informality of religious worship there is a set formality. Sermons, prayers, moans and testimonies have their definite forms. The individual may hang as many new ornaments upon the traditional form as he likes, but the audience would be disagreeably surprised if the form were abandoned. Any new and original elaboration is welcomed, however, and this brings out the fact that all religious expression among Negroes is regarded as art, and ability is recognised as definitely as in any other art. The beautiful prayer receives the accolade as well as the beautiful song. It is merely a form of expression which people generally are not accustomed to think of as art. Nothing outside of the Old Testament is as rich in figure as a Negro prayer. Some instances are unsurpassed anywhere in literature.

There is a lively rivalry in the technical artistry of all of these fields. It is a special honor to be called upon to pray over the covered communion table, for the greatest prayer-artist present is chosen by the pastor for this, a lively something spreads over the church as he kneels, and the "bearing up" hum precedes him. It continues sometimes through the introduction, but ceases as he makes the complimentary salutation to the deity. This consists in giving to God all the titles that form allows.

The introduction to the prayer usually consists of one or two verses of some well-known hymn. "O, that I knew a secret place" seems to be the favorite. There is a definite pause after this, then follows an elaboration of all or parts of the Lord's Prayer. Follows after that what I call the setting, that is, the artist calling attention to the physical situation of himself and the church. After the dramatic setting, the action begins.

There are certain rhythmic breaks throughout the prayer, and the church "bears him up" at every one of these. There is in the body of the prayer an accelerando passage where the audience takes no part. It would be like applauding in the middle of a solo at the Metropolitan. It is here that the artist comes forth. He adorns the prayer with every sparkle of earth, water and sky, and nobody wants to miss a syllable. He comes down from this height to a slower tempo and is borne up again. The last few sentences are unaccompanied, for here again one listens to the individual's closing peroration. Several may join in the final amen. The best figure that I can think of is that the prayer is an obligato over and above the harmony of the assembly.

BLACK MAGDALENS
COUNTEE CULLEN

These have no Christ to spit and stoop
　　To write upon the sand,
Inviting him that has not sinned
　　To raise the first rude hand.

And if he came they could not buy
　　Rich ointment for his feet,
The body's sale scarce yields enough
　　To let the body eat.

The chaste clean ladies pass them by
　　And draw their skirts aside,
But Magdalens have a ready laugh;
　　They wrap their wounds in pride.

They fare full ill since Christ forsook
　　The cross to mount a throne,
And Virtue still is stooping down
　　To cast the first hard stone.

SIMON THE CYRENIAN SPEAKS
COUNTEE CULLEN

He never spoke a word to me,
And yet He called my name;

He never gave a sign to me,
And yet I knew and came.

At first I said, "I will not bear
His cross upon my back;
He only seeks to place it there
Because my skin is black."

But He was dying for a dream,
And He was very meek,
And in His eyes there shone a gleam
Men journey far to seek.

It was Himself my pity bought;
I did for Christ alone
What all of Rome could not have wrought
With bruise of lash or stone.

FRUIT OF THE FLOWER
COUNTEE CULLEN

My father is a quiet man
With sober, steady ways;
For simile, a folded fan;
His nights are like his days.

My mother's life is puritan,
No hint of cavalier,
A pool so calm you're sure it can
Have little depth to fear.

And yet my father's eyes can boast
How full his life has been;
There haunts them yet the languid ghost
Of some still sacred sin.

And though my mother chants of God,
And of the mystic river,
I've seen a bit of checkered sod
Set all her flesh aquiver.

Why should he deem it pure mischance
A son of his is fain

To do a naked tribal dance
Each time he hears the rain?

Why should she think it devil's art
That all my songs should be
Of love and lovers, broken heart,
And wild sweet agony?

Who plants a seed begets a bud,
Extract of that same root;
Why marvel at the hectic blood
That flushes this wild fruit?

SHE OF THE DANCING FEET SINGS
COUNTEE CULLEN

And what would I do in heaven, pray,
Me with my dancing feet,
And limbs like apple boughs that sway
When the gusty rain winds beat?

And how would I thrive in a perfect place
Where dancing would be sin,
With not a man to love my face,
Nor an arm to hold me in?

The seraphs and the cherubim
Would be too proud to bend
To sing the faery tunes that brim
My heart from end to end.

The wistful angels down in hell
Will smile to see my face,
And understand, because they fell
From that all-perfect place.

CONCEPTION
WARING CUNEY

Jesus' mother never had no man.
God came to her one day an' said,
"Mary, chile, kiss ma han'."

THE SUPPLIANT
GEORGIA DOUGLAS JOHNSON

Long have I beat with timid hands upon life's leaden door,
Praying the patient, futile prayer my fathers prayed before,
Yet I remain without the close, unheeded and unheard,
And never to my listening ear is borne the waited word.

Soft o'er the threshold of the years there comes this counsel cool:
The strong demand, contend, prevail; the beggar is a fool!

A MISSIONARY BRINGS
A YOUNG NATIVE TO AMERICA
HELENE JOHNSON

All day she heard the mad stampede of feet
Push by her in a thick unbroken haste.
A thousand unknown terrors of the street
Caught at her timid heart, and she could taste
The city grit upon her tongue. She felt
A steel-spiked wave of brick and light submerge
Her mind in cold immensity. A belt
Of alien tenets choked the songs that surged
Within her when alone each night she knelt
At prayer. And as the moon grew large and white
Above the roof, afraid that she would scream
Aloud her young abandon to the night,
She mumbled Latin litanies and dreamed
Unholy dreams while waiting for the light.

ALIENATION, ANGER, RAGE

It is hardly surprising that most of the writing to come from the Harlem Renaissance would reflect the sense of alienation, anger, or rage of black people in general. Indeed, one could justify placing practically all of the work in this volume under this heading. The selection here is intended to draw the reader's attention to certain particular manifestations. In his poem, "Brothers," while treating the emotionally charged issue of lynching, James Weldon Johnson assumes a distance which allows him to accept the possible guilt of the black victim in order to link him in brotherhood with his white murderers. Claude McKay's famous poem, "If We Must Die," is grouped with other of his sonnets, illuminating the persona which characterized his protest poetry. Few of the women poets of the Harlem Renaissance went on to achieve successful careers or celebrity as poets. Yet, some of the most forceful and effective poetry of the period was written by such women as Georgia Douglas Johnson, Gwendolyn Bennett, and Helene Johnson. If the spirit of the New Negro was to be articulated in McKay's "If We Must Die," Sterling Brown reminds us that the New Negro's spirit is at least as old as Nat Turner. Alienation and anger had a soft voice as well as a strident one. So that while the poems of Langston Hughes and Countee Cullen are gentle and modulated, they nevertheless resonate chords of black protest. And George S. Schuyler, who in another place in this volume, directs his sarcasm against the concept of Negro Art, in this essay makes the United States and its peculiar racial customs target of his satire.

BROTHERS

JAMES WELDON JOHNSON

See! There he stands; not brave, but with an air
Of sullen stupor. Mark him well! Is he
Not more like brute than man? Look in his eye!

No light is there; none, save the glint that shines
In the now glaring, and now shifting orbs
Cf some wild animal caught in the hunter's trap.

   How came this beast in human shape and form?
Speak, man!—We call you man because you wear
His shape—How are you thus? Are you not from
That docile, child-like, tender-hearted race
Which we have known three centuries? Not from
That more than faithful race which through three wars
Fed our dear wives and nursed our helpless babes
Without a single breach of trust? Speak out!

   I am, and am not.

      Then who, why are you?

   I am a thing not new, I am as old
As human nature. I am that which lurks,
Ready to spring whenever a bar is loosed;
The ancient trait which fights incessantly
Against restraint, balks at the upward climb;
The weight forever seeking to obey
The law of downward pull—and I am more:
The bitter fruit am I of planted seed;
The resultant, the inevitable end
Of evil forces and the powers of wrong.

   Lessons in degradation, taught and learned,
The memories of cruel sights and deeds,
The pent-up bitterness, the unspent hate
Filtered through fifteen generations have
Sprung up and found in me sporadic life.
In me the muttered curse of dying men,
On me the stain of conquered women, and
Consuming me the fearful fires of lust,
Lit long ago, by other hands than mine.
In me the down-crushed spirit, the hurled-back prayers
Of wretches now long dead—their dire bequests—

In me the echo of the stifled cry
Of children for their bartered mothers' breasts.

  I claim no race, no race claims me; I am
No more than human dregs; degenerate;
The monstrous offspring of the monster, Sin;
I am—just what I am. . . . The race that fed
Your wives and nursed your babes would do the same
Today, but I—
          Enough, the brute must die!
Quick! Chain him to that oak! It will resist
The fire much longer than this slender pine.
Now bring the fuel! Pile it 'round him! Wait!
Pile not so fast or high! or we shall lose
The agony and terror in his face.

And now the torch! Good fuel that! the flames
Already leap head-high. Ha! hear that shriek!
And there's another! Wilder than the first.
Fetch water! Water! Pour a little on
The fire, lest it should burn too fast. Hold so!
Now let it slowly blaze again. See there!
He squirms! He groans! His eyes bulge wildly out,
Searching around in vain appeal for help!
Another shriek, the last! Watch how the flesh
Grows crisp and hangs till, turned to ash, it sifts
Down through the coils of chain that hold erect
The ghastly frame against the bark-scorched tree.

  Stop! to each man no more than one man's share.
You take that bone, and you this tooth; the chain—
Let us divide its links; this skull, of course,
In fair division, to the leader comes.

  And now his fiendish crime has been avenged;
Let us back to our wives and children.—Say,
What did he mean by those last muttered words,
"Brothers in spirit, brothers in deed are we"?

IF WE MUST DIE
CLAUDE MCKAY

If we must die, let it not be like hogs
Hunted and penned in an inglorious spot,
While round us bark the mad and hungry dogs,

Making their mock at our accursed lot.
If we must die, O let us nobly die,
So that our precious blood may not be shed
In vain; then even the monsters we defy
Shall be constrained to honor us though dead!
O kinsmen! we must meet the common foe!
Though far outnumbered let us show us brave,
And for their thousand blows deal one deathblow!
What though before us lies the open grave?
Like men we'll face the murderous, cowardly pack,
Pressed to the wall, dying but fighting back!

THE WHITE HOUSE
CLAUDE MCKAY

Your door is shut against my tightened face,
And I am sharp as steel with discontent;
But I possess the courage and the grace
To bear my anger proudly and unbent.
The pavement slabs burn loose beneath my feet,
A chafing savage, down the decent street;
And passion rends my vitals as I pass,
Where boldly shines your shuttered door of glass.
Oh, I must search for wisdom every hour,
Deep in my wrathful bosom sore and raw,
And find in it the superhuman power
To hold me to the letter of your law!
Oh, I must keep the heart inviolate
Against the potent poison of your hate.

THE LYNCHING
CLAUDE MCKAY

His Spirit in smoke ascended to high heaven.
His father, by the cruelest way of pain,
Had bidden him to his bosom once again;
The awful sin remained still unforgiven.
All night a bright and solitary star
(Perchance the one that ever guided him,
Yet gave him up at last to Fate's wild whim)
Hung pitifully o'er the swinging char.
Day dawned, and soon the mixed crowds came to view

The ghastly body swaying in the sun.
The women thronged to look, but never a one
Showed sorrow in her eyes of steely blue.

And little lads, lynchers that were to be,
Danced round the dreadful thing in fiendish glee.

AMERICA
CLAUDE MCKAY

Although she feeds me bread of bitterness,
And sinks into my throat her tiger's tooth,
Stealing my breath of life, I will confess
I love this cultured hell that tests my youth!
Her vigor flows like tides into my blood,
Giving me strength erect against her hate.
Her bigness sweeps my being like a flood.
Yet as a rebel fronts a king in state,
I stand within her walls with not a shred
Of terror, malice, not a word of jeer.
Darkly I gaze into the days ahead,
And see her might and granite wonders there,
Beneath the touch of Time's unerring hand,
Like priceless treasures sinking in the sand.

A BLACK MAN TALKS OF REAPING
ARNA BONTEMPS

I have sown beside all waters in my day.
I planted deep within my heart the fear
That wind or fowl would take the grain away.
I planted safe against this stark, lean year.

I scattered seed enough to plant the land
In rows from Canada to Mexico.
But for my reaping only what the hand
Can hold at once is all that I can show.

Yet what I sowed and what the orchard yields
My brother's sons are gathering stalk and root,
Small wonder then my children glean in fields
They have not sown, and feed on bitter fruit.

OLD BLACK MEN
GEORGIA DOUGLAS JOHNSON

They have dreamed as young men dream
Of glory, love and power;
They have hoped as youth will hope
Of life's sun-minted hour.

They have seen as others saw
Their bubbles burst in air,
They have learned to live it down
As though they did not care.

HATRED
GWENDOLYN BENNETT

I shall hate you
Like a dart of singing steel
Shot through still air
At even-tide.
Or solemnly
As pines are sober
When they stand etched
Against the sky.
Hating you shall be a game
Played with cool hands
And slim fingers.
Your heart will yearn
For the lonely splendor
Of the pine tree;
While rekindled fires
In my eyes
Shall wound you like swift arrows.
Memory will lay its hands
Upon your breast
And you will understand
My hatred.

REMEMBERING NAT TURNER
STERLING A. BROWN

We saw a bloody sunset over Courtland, once Jerusalem,
As we followed the trail that old Nat took

When he came out of Cross Keys down upon Jerusalem,
In his angry stab for freedom a hundred years ago.
The land was quiet, and the mist was rising,
Out of the woods and the Nottaway swamp,
Over Southampton the still night fell,
As we rode down to Cross Keys where the march began.

When we got to Cross Keys, they could tell us little of him,
The Negroes had only the faintest recollections:
   "I ain't been here so long, I come from up roun' Newsome;
    Yassah, a town a few miles up de road,
    The old folks who coulda told you is all dead an' gone.
    I heard something, sometime; I doan jis remember what.
    'Pears lak I heard that name somewheres or other.
    So he fought to be free. Well. You doan say."

And old white woman recalled exactly
How Nat crept down the steps, axe in his hand,
After murdering a woman and child in bed,
"Right in this house at the head of these stairs."
(In a house built long after Nat was dead.)
She pointed to a brick store where Nat was captured,
(Nat was taken in a swamp, three miles away)
With his men around him, shooting from the windows
(She was thinking of Harper's Ferry and old John Brown.)
She cackled as she told how they riddled Nat with bullets
(Nat was tried and hanged at Courtland, ten miles away)
She wanted to know why folks would come miles
Just to ask about an old nigger fool.
   "Ain't no slavery no more, things is going all right,
    Pervided thar's a good goober market this year.
    We had a sign post here with printing on it,
    But it rotted in the hole and thar it lays;
    And the nigger tenants split the marker for kindling.
    Things is all right, naow, ain't no trouble with the niggers.
    Why they make this big to-do over Nat?"

As we drove from Cross Keys back to Courtland,
Along the way that Nat came down from Jerusalem,
A watery moon was high in the cloud-filled heavens,
The same moon he dreaded a hundred years ago.
The tree they hanged Nat on is long gone to ashes,
The trees he dodged behind have rotted in the swamps.

The bus for Miami and the trucks boomed by,
And touring cars, their heavy tires snarling on the pavement.

Frogs piped in the marshes, and a hound bayed long,
And yellow lights glowed from the cabin windows.

As we came back the way that Nat led his army,
Down from Cross Keys, down to Jerusalem,
We wondered if his troubled spirit still roamed the Nottaway,
Or if it fled with the cock-crow at daylight,
Or lay at peace with the bones in Jerusalem,
Its restlessness stifled by Southampton clay.

We remembered the poster rotted through and falling,
The marker split for kindling a kitchen fire.

DREAM VARIATION
LANGSTON HUGHES

To fling my arms wide
In some place of the sun,
To whirl and to dance
Till the white day is done.
Then rest at cool evening
Beneath a tall tree
While night comes on gently,
   Dark like me—
That is my dream!

To fling my arms wide
In the face of the sun,
Dance! whirl! whirl!
Till the quick day is done.
Rest at pale evening. . . .
A tall, slim tree. . . .
Night coming tenderly
   Black like me.

SONG FOR A DARK GIRL
LANGSTON HUGHES

Way Down South in Dixie
   (Break the heart of me)
They hung my dark young lover
   To a cross roads tree.

Way Down South in Dixie
  (Bruised body high in air)
I asked the white Lord Jesus
  What was the use of prayer.

Way Down South in Dixie
  (Break the heart of me)
Love is a naked shadow
  On a gnarled and naked tree.

MOTHER TO SON
LANGSTON HUGHES

Well, son, I'll tell you:
Life for me ain't been no crystal stair.
It's had tacks in it,
And splinters,
And boards torn up,
And places with no carpet on the floor—
Bare.
But all the time
I'se been a-climbin' on,
And reachin' landin's,
And turnin' corners,
And sometimes goin' in the dark
Where there ain't been no light.
So, boy, don't you turn back.
Don't you set down on the steps
'Cause you finds it's kinder hard.
Don't you fall now—
For I'se still goin', honey,
I'se still climbin',
And life for me ain't been no crystal stair.

INCIDENT
COUNTEE CULLEN

Once riding in old Baltimore,
Heart-filled, head-filled with glee,
I saw a Baltimorean
Keep looking straight at me.

Now I was eight and very small,
And he was no whit bigger,

And so I smiled, but he poked out
His tongue, and called me, "Nigger."

I saw the whole of Baltimore
From May until December;
Of all the things that happened there
That's all that I remember.

FROM THE DARK TOWER
COUNTEE CULLEN

We shall not always plant while other reap
The golden increment of bursting fruit,
Not always countenance, abject and mute,
That lesser men should hold their brothers cheap;
Not everlastingly while others sleep
Shall we beguile their limbs with mellow flute,
Not always bend to some more subtle brute;
We were not made eternally to weep.

The night whose sable breast relieves the stark,
White stars is no less lovely being dark,
And there are buds that cannot bloom at all
In light, but crumple, piteous, and fall;
So in the dark we hide the heart that bleeds,
And wait, and tend our agonizing seeds.

A SOUTHERN ROAD
HELENE JOHNSON

Yolk-colored tongue
Parched beneath a burning sky,
A lazy little tune
Hummed up the crest of some
Soft sloping hill.
One streaming line of beauty
Flowing by a forest
Pregnant with tears.
A hidden nest for beauty
Idly flung by God
In one lonely lingering hour
Before the Sabbath.
A blue-fruited black gum,
Like a tall predella,

Bears a dangling figure,—
Sacrificial dower to the raff,
Swinging alone,
A solemn, tortured shadow in the air.

OUR GREATEST GIFT TO AMERICA
GEORGE S. SCHUYLER

On divers occasions some eloquent Ethiop arises to tell this enlightened nation about the marvelous contributions of his people to our incomparable civilization. With glib tongue or trenchant pen, he starts from the arrival of the nineteen unfortunate dinges at Jamestown in 1619, or perhaps with the coming of the celebrated Columbus to these sacred shores with his Negro mate in 1492, and traces the multiple gifts of the black brethren to the present day. He will tell us of the vast amount of cotton picked by the Negro, of the hundreds of roads and levees the black laborers have constructed, of the miles of floors Negro women have scrubbed, and the acres of clothes they have washed, of the numerous wars in which, for some unknown reason, the Sambo participated, of the dances and cookery he invented, or of the spirituals and work songs composed by the sons of Ham and given to a none too grateful nation. The more erudite of these self-appointed spokesmen of the race will even go back to the Garden of Eden, the walls of Babylon, the pyramids of Egypt and the palaces of Ethiopia by way of introduction, and during their prefatory remarks they will not fail, often, to claim for the Negro race every person of importance that has ever resided on the face of the earth. Ending with a forceful and fervent plea for justice, equality, righteousness, humanitarianism, and other such things conspicuous in the world by their absence, they close amid a storm of applause from their sable auditors—and watch the collection plate.

This sort of thing has been going on regularly for the last century. No Negro meeting is a success without one or more such encouraging addresses, and no Negro publication that fails to carry one such article in almost every issue is considered worthy of purchase. So general has the practice become that even white audiences and magazines are no longer immune. It has become not unusual in the past few years for the Tired Society Women's Club of Keokuk, Iowa, or the Delicatessen Proprietors' Chamber of Commerce or the Hot Dog Venders' Social Club to have literary afternoons devoted exclusively to the subject of the lowly smoke. On such occasions there will be some notable Aframerican speakers as Prof. Hambone of Moronia Institute or Dr. Lampblack of the Federal Society for the Exploitation of Lynching, who will eloquently hold forth for the better part of an hour on the blackamoor's gifts to the Great Republic and why, therefore, he should not be kept down. Following him there will usually be a soulful rendition by the Charcoal Singers of their selected repertoire of genuine spirituals, and then, mayhap one of the younger Negro poets will recite one of his inspiring verses anent a ragged black prostitute gnawing out her soul in the dismal shadows of Hog Maw Alley.

It was not so many years ago that Negro writers used to chew their finger-nails and tear as much of their hair as they could get hold of, because the adamantine editors of white magazines and journals invariably returned unread their impassioned manuscripts in which they sought to tell how valuable the Aframerican had always been to his country and what a dirty shame it was to incinerate a spade without benefit of jury. Not so today, my friends. The swarms of Negro hacks and their more learned associates have at last come into their own. They have ridden into popular demand on the waves of jazz music, the Charleston, Mammy Songs and the ubiquitous, if intricate, Black Bottom. Pick up almost any of the better class periodicals of national note nowadays and you are almost sure to find a lengthy paper by some sable literatus on the Negro's gifts to America, on his amazing progress in becoming just like other Americans in habit and thought, or on the horrible injustice of Jim Crow cars. The cracker editors are paying gen-erously for the stuff (which is more than the Negro editors did in the old days), and as a result, the black scribblers, along with the race orators, are now wallowing in the luxury of four-room apartments, expensive radios, Chickering pianos, Bond Street habiliments, canvas-back duck, pre-war Scotch and high yellow mistresses.

All of which is very well and good. It is only natural that the peckerwoods, having become bored to death with their uninteresting lives, should turn to the crows for inspiration and entertainment. It is probably part of their wide-spread rationalization of the urge they possess to mix with the virile blacks. One marvels, however, that the principal contribution of our zigaboos to the nation has been entirely overlooked by our dusky literati and peripatetic platform prancers. None of them, apparently, has ever thought of it. While they have been ransacking their brains and the shelves of the public li-braries for new Negro gifts of which to inform their eager listeners at so much per word or per engagement, they have ignored the principal gift sprawling everywhere about them. They had but to lift their eyes from the pages of their musty tome and glance around. But they didn't.

"And what," I can hear these propagandists feverishly inquiring with poised fountain pens and notebooks, "is this unchronicled contribution to the worth of our nation?" Well, I am not unwilling to divulge this "secret" that has been all too apparent to the observing. And though the brownish intelligentsia are now able to pay for the information—and probably willing to do so—I modestly ask nothing, save perhaps a quart of decent rye or pos-sibly one of the numerous medals shoveled out every year to deserving coons. Hence, like all of the others, I now arise, flick a speck off my dinner jacket, adjust my horn-rimmed nose glasses, and, striking an attitude, de-claim the magic word: Flattery!

Yes folks, the greatest gift we have made to America is flattery. Flattery, if you please, of the buckra majority; inflation of the racial ego of the domi-nant group by our mere proximity, by our actions and by our aspirations.

"How come?" I am belligerently and skeptically quizzed, and very in-dulgently I elucidate. Imitation, some one has said, is the sincerest flattery. It is quite human to be pleased and feel very important when we are aped and imitated. Consider how we Negroes shove out our chests when an article appears in an enterprising darky newspaper from the pen of some promi-nent African chief saying that his dingy colleagues on the Dark Continent look to their American brethren, with their amazing progress, for inspira-tion. How sweet is flattery, the mother of pride. And pride, we have been told, is absolutely essential to progress and achievement. If all of this be true of the dark American, how much truer must it be of the pink American? By constant exposure to his energetic propagandists in press, on platform and in pulpit, the colored brother has forged ahead—to borrow an expres-sion from the *Uplift*—until he can now eat with Rogers silver off Haviland china, sprawl on overstuffed couches and read spicy literature under the glow of ornate floor lamps, while the strains of "Beer Bucket Blues" are wafted over the radio. This is generally known as progress. Now if the down-trodden Negro, under the influence of his flattering propagandists, has been able to attain such heights of material well-being, is it any wonder that the noble rednecks have leaped so much farther up the scale of living when sur-rounded by millions of black flatterers, both mute and vocal? Most certainly not.

Look, for example, at Isadore Shankersoff. By hook or by crook (probably the latter) he grabbed off enough coin of his native land to pay his passage to America. In Russia he was a nobody—hoofed by everybody—the mudsill of society. Quite naturally his inferiority complex was Brobdingnagian. Ar-riving under the shadow of the Statue of Liberty, he is still Isadore Shanker-soff, the prey of sharpers and cheap grafters, but now he has moved consid-erably higher in the social scale. Though remaining mentally adolescent, he is no longer at the bottom; he is a white man! Over night he has become a member of the superior race. Ellis Island marked his metamorphosis. For the first time in his life he is better than somebody. Without the presence of the blackamoor in these wonderfully United States, he would still know him-self for the thick-pated underling that he is, but how can he go on believing that when America is screaming to him on every hand that he is a white man, and as such entitled to certain rights and privileges forbidden to Negro scientists, artists, clergymen, journalists, and merchants. One can un-derstand why Isadore walks with firmer tread.

Or glance at Cyrus Leviticus Dumbell. He is of Anglo-Saxon stock that is so old that it has very largely gone to seed. In the fastnesses of the Blue Ridge Mountains his racial strain has been safely preserved from pollution by black and red men, for over two hundred years. Thus he is a stalwart fellow untouched by thrift or education. Cy finally tires of the bushes and descends to one of the nearby towns. There he finds employment in a mill on a twelve-hour shift. The company paternalistically furnishes him every-thing he needs and thoughtfully deducts the cost regularly from his slender pay envelope, leaving him about two dollars for corn liquor and moving pictures. Cy has never had cause to think himself of any particular importance in the scheme of things, but his fellow workers tell him differently. He is a white man, they say, and therefore divinely appointed to "keep the nigger down." He must, they insist, protect white womanhood and preserve white supremacy. This country, he learns, is a white man's country, and although he owns none of it, the information strikes him not unpleasantly. Shortly he scrapes together ten dollars, buys Klan regalia, and is soon engaged in attending midnight meetings, burning crosses, repeating ritual from the Kloran, flogging erring white womanhood for the greater purity of Anglo-Saxondom, and keeping vigilantly on the lookout for uppish and offensive zigaboos to lynch. Like the ancient Greeks and Romans, he now believes himself superior to everybody different from him. Nor does the presence of Jim Crow institutions on every hand contribute anything toward lessening that belief. Whatever his troubles may be, he has learned from his colleagues and the politicians, to blame it all on the dark folks, who are, he is now positive, without exception his inferiors.

Think, also, of demure little Dorothy Dunce. For twelve years she attended the palatial public school. Now, at eighteen, having graduated, she is about to apply her Latin, Greek, English literature, ancient history, geometry and botany to her everyday work as packer in a spaghetti factory. When she was very young, before she entered the kindergarten, her indulgent parents used to scare her by issuing a solemn warning that a big, black nigger would kidnap her if she wasn't a good little girl. Now that she has had American popular education turned loose upon her, she naturally believes differently: *i.e.,* that every big, burly, black nigger she meets on a dark street is ready to relieve her by force of what remains of her virtue. A value is placed upon her that she would not have in Roumania, Scotland, Denmark, or Montenegro. She is now a member of that exalted aggregation known as pure, white womanhood. She is also confident of her general superiority because education has taught her that Negroes are inferior, immoral, diseased, lazy, unprogressive, ugly, odoriferous, and should be firmly kept in their place at the bottom of the social and industrial scale. Quite naturally she swells with race pride, for no matter how low she falls, she will always be a white woman.

But enough of such examples. It is fairly well established, I think, that our presence in the Great Republic has been of incalculable psychological value to the masses of white citizens. Descendants of convicts, serfs and half-wits, with the rest have been buoyed up and greatly exalted by being constantly assured of their superiority to all other races and their equality with each other. On the stages of a thousand music halls, they have had their vanity tickled by blackface performers parading the idiocies of mythical black roustabouts and rustics. Between belly-cracking guffaws they have secretly congratulated themselves on the fact that they are not like these buffoons. Their books and magazines have told them, or insinuated, that morality, beauty, refinement and culture are restricted to Caucasians. On every hand they have seen smokes endeavoring to change from black to white, and from kinky hair to straight, by means of deleterious chemicals, and constantly they hear the Negroes urging each other to do this and that "like white folks." Nor do the crackers fail to observe, either, that pink epidermis is as highly treasured among blacks as in Nordic America, and that the most devastating charge that one Negro can make against another is that "he acts just like a nigger." Anything excellent they hear labeled by the race conscious Negroes as "like white folks," nor is it unusual for them, while loitering in the Negro ghetto, to hear black women compared to Fords, mulatto women to Cadillacs and white women to Packards. With so much flattery it is no wonder that the Caucasians have a very high opinion of themselves and attempt to live up to the lofty niche in which the Negroes have placed them. We should not marvel that every white elevator operator, school teacher and bricklayer identifies himself with Shakespeare, Julius Cæsar, Napoleon, Newton, Edison, Wagner, Tennyson, and Rembrandt as creators of this great civilization. As a result we have our American society, where everybody who sports a pink color believes himself to be the equal of all other whites by virtue of his lack of skin pigmentation, and his classic Caucasian features.

It is not surprising, then, that democracy has worked better in this country than elsewhere. This belief in the equality of all white folks—making skin color the gauge of worth and the measure of citizenship rights—has caused the lowest to strive to become among the highest. Because of this great ferment, America has become the Utopia of the material world; the land of hope and opportunity. Without the transplanted African in their midst to bolster up the illusion, America would have unquestionably been a very different place; but instead the shine has served as a mudsill upon which all white people alike can stand and reach toward the stars. I submit that here is the gift par excellence of the Negro to America. To spur ten times our number on to great heights of achievement; to spare the nation the enervating presence of a destructive social caste system, such as exists elsewhere, by substituting a color caste system that roused the hope and pride of teeming millions of ofays—this indeed is a gift of which we can well be proud.

REFLECTIONS ON
THE RENAISSANCE AND
ART FOR A NEW DAY

3

The Depression shattered the optimism of the Harlem Renaissance. The innocent faith in easy art fell victim to breadlines. From the perspective of the 1930s, the artists of the Renaissance looked strangely foolish and irrelevant, even to themselves. Poverty, which had always been obvious in Harlem, suddenly seemed more to characterize the area than did art and jazz. What was more, Harlem was shaken by riots in 1935. By the mid-thirties, even those who had taken part in the movement had little good to say about it.

Langston Hughes, James Weldon Johnson, and Carl Van Vechten found it all to have been a bit naïve. Challenge, a new magazine edited by Dorothy West, was to be the vehicle for a new art that was more realistic. Violence in Harlem was on all minds. Claude McKay and Alain Locke wrote essays about the riots (though Locke's essay is too long for inclusion here).

Thus, there was a new spirit of social realism in art. Locke's critique of McKay's autobiography reflects this new concern for art with a social purpose. There were echoes of the political radicalism of the war years in the new artistic temper which can be discerned in Richard Wright's "Blueprint for Negro Writing." Black American writing had outgrown its innocence. As Richard Wright's stories in Uncle Tom's Children indicate, the writing of the thirties, forties, and after was much more tough and self-confident than could have been possible in the twenties.

THE BIG SEA
LANGSTON HUGHES

When the Negro Was in Vogue

The 1920's were the years of Manhattan's black Renaissance. It began with *Shuffle Along, Running Wild,* and the Charleston. Perhaps some people would say even with *The Emperor Jones,* Charles Gilpin, and the tom-toms at the Provincetown. But certainly it was the musical revue, *Shuffle Along,* that gave a scintillating send-off to that Negro vogue in Manhattan, which reached its peak just before the crash of 1929, the crash that sent Negroes, white folks, and all rolling down the hill toward the Works Progress Administration.

Shuffle Along was a honey of a show. Swift, bright, funny, rollicking, and gay, with a dozen danceable, singable tunes. Besides, look who were in it: The now famous choir director, Hall Johnson, and the composer, William Grant Still, were a part of the orchestra. Eubie Blake and Noble Sissle wrote the music and played and acted in the show. Miller and Lyles were the comics. Florence Mills skyrocketed to fame in the second act. Trixie Smith sang "He May Be Your Man But He Comes to See Me Sometimes." And Caterina Jarboro, now a European prima donna, and the internationally celebrated Josephine Baker were merely in the chorus. Everybody was in the audience—including me. People came back to see it innumerable times. It was always packed.

To see *Shuffle Along* was the main reason I wanted to go to Columbia. When I saw it, I was thrilled and delighted. From then on I was in the gallery of the Cort Theatre every time I got a chance. That year, too, I saw Katharine Cornell in *A Bill of Divorcement,* Margaret Wycherly in *The Verge,* Maugham's *The Circle* with Mrs. Leslie Carter, and the Theatre Guild production of Kaiser's *From Morn Till Midnight.* But I remember *Shuffle Along* best of all. It gave just the proper push—a pre-Charleston kick—to that Negro vogue of the 20's, that spread to books, African sculpture, music, and dancing.

Put down the 1920's for the rise of Roland Hayes, who packed Carnegie Hall, the rise of Paul Robeson in New York and London, of Florence Mills over two continents, of Rose McClendon in Broadway parts that never measured up to her, the booming voice of Bessie Smith and the low moan of Clara on thousands of records, and the rise of that grand comedienne of song, Ethel Waters, singing: "Charlie's elected now! He's in right for sure!" Put down the 1920's for Louis Armstrong and Gladys Bentley and Josephine Baker.

White people began to come to Harlem in droves. For several years they packed the expensive Cotton Club on Lenox Avenue. But I was never there, because the Cotton Club was a Jim Crow club for gangsters and monied whites. They were not cordial to Negro patronage, unless you were a celebrity like Bojangles. So Harlem Negroes did not like the Cotton Club and never appreciated its Jim Crow policy in the very heart of their dark community. Nor did ordinary Negroes like the growing influx of whites toward Harlem after sundown, flooding the little cabarets and bars where formerly only colored people laughed and sang, and where now the strangers were given the best ringside tables to sit and stare at the Negro customers—like amusing animals in a zoo.

The Negroes said: "We can't go downtown and sit and stare at you in your clubs. You won't even let us in your clubs." But they didn't say it out loud—for Negroes are practically never rude to white people. So thousands of whites came to Harlem night after night, thinking the Negroes loved to have them there, and firmly believing that all Harlemites left their houses at sundown to sing and dance in cabarets, because most of the whites saw nothing but the cabarets, not the houses.

Some of the owners of Harlem clubs, delighted at the flood of white patronage, made the grievous error of barring their own race, after the manner of the famous Cotton Club. But most of these quickly lost business and folded up, because they failed to realize that a large part of the Harlem attraction for downtown New Yorkers lay in simply watching the colored customers amuse themselves. And the smaller clubs, of course, had no big floor shows or a name band like the Cotton Club, where Duke Ellington usually held forth, so, without black patronage, they were not amusing at all.

Some of the small clubs, however, had people like Gladys Bentley, who was something worth discovering in those days, before she got famous, acquired an accompanist, specially written material, and conscious vulgarity. But for two or three amazing years, Miss Bentley sat, and played a big piano all night long, literally all night, without stopping—singing songs like "The St. James Infirmary," from ten in the evening until dawn, with scarcely a break between the notes, sliding from one song to another, with a powerful and continuous underbeat of jungle rhythm. Miss Bentley was an amazing exhibition of musical energy—a large, dark, masculine lady, whose feet pounded the floor while her fingers pounded the keyboard—a perfect piece of African sculpture, animated by her own rhythm.

But when the place where she played became too well known, she began to sing with an accompanist, became a star, moved to a larger place, then downtown, and is now in Hollywood. The old magic of the woman and the piano and the night and the rhythm being one is gone. But everything goes, one way or another. The '20's are gone and lots of fine things in Harlem night life have disappeared like snow in the sun—since it became utterly commercial, planned for the downtown tourist trade, and therefore dull.

The lindy-hoppers at the Savoy even began to practise acrobatic routines, and to do absurd things for the entertainment of the whites, that probably never would have entered their heads to attempt merely for their own effortless amusement. Some of the lindy-hoppers had cards printed with their names on them and became dance professors teaching the tourists. Then Harlem nights became show nights for the Nordics.

Some critics say that that is what happened to certain Negro writers, too—that they ceased to write to amuse themselves and began to write to amuse and entertain white people, and in so doing distorted and over-colored their material, and left out a great many things they thought would offend their American brothers of a lighter complexion. Maybe—since Negroes have writer-racketeers, as has any other race. But I have known almost all of them, and most of the good ones have tried to be honest, write honestly, and express their world as they saw it.

All of us know that the gay and sparkling life of the so-called Negro Renaissance of the '20's was not so gay and sparkling beneath the surface as it looked. Carl Van Vechten, in the character of Byron in *Nigger Heaven,* captured some of the bitterness and frustration of literary Harlem that Wallace Thurman later so effectively poured into his *Infants of the Spring*—the only novel by a Negro about that fantastic period when Harlem was in vogue.

It was a period when, at almost every Harlem upper-crust dance or party, one would be introduced to various distinguished white celebrities there as guests. It was a period when almost any Harlem Negro of any social importance at all would be likely to say casually: "As I was remarking the other day to Heywood—," meaning Heywood Broun. Or: "As I said to George—," referring to George Gershwin. It was a period when local and visiting royalty were not at all uncommon in Harlem. And when the parties of A'Lelia Walker, the Negro heiress, were filled with guests whose names would turn any Nordic social climber green with envy. It was a period when Harold Jackman, a handsome young Harlem school teacher of modest means, calmly announced one day that he was sailing for the Riviera for a fortnight, to attend Princess Murat's yachting party. It was a period when Charleston preachers opened up shouting churches as sideshows for white tourists. It was a period when at least one charming colored chorus girl, amber enough to pass for a Latin American, was living in a pent house, with all her bills paid by a gentleman whose name was banker's magic on Wall Street. It was a period when every season there was at least one hit play on Broadway acted by a Negro cast. And when books by Negro authors were being published with much greater frequency and much more publicity than ever before or since in history. It was a period when white writers wrote about Negroes more successfully (commercially speaking) than Negroes did about themselves. It was the period (God help us!) when Ethel Barrymore appeared in blackface in *Scarlet Sister Mary!* It was the period when the Negro was in vogue.

I was there. I had a swell time while it lasted. But I thought it wouldn't last long. (I remember the vogue for things Russian, the season the Chauve-Souris first came to town.) For how could a large and enthusiastic number of people be crazy about Negroes forever? But some Harlemites thought the millennium had come. They thought the race problem had at last been solved through Art plus Glady's Bentley. They were sure the New Negro would lead a new life from then on in green pastures of tolerance created by

Countee Cullen, Ethel Waters, Claude McKay, Duke Ellington, Bojangles, and Alain Locke.

I don't know what made any Negroes think that—except that they were mostly intellectuals doing the thinking. The ordinary Negroes hadn't heard of the Negro Renaissance. And if they had, it hadn't raised their wages any. As for all those white folks in the speakeasies and night clubs of Harlem— well, maybe a colored man could find *some* place to have a drink that the tourists hadn't yet discovered.

Then it was that house-rent parties began to flourish—and not always to raise the rent either. But, as often as not, to have a get-together of one's own, where you could do the black-bottom with no stranger behind you trying to do it, too. Non-theatrical, non-intellectual Harlem was an unwilling victim of its own vogue. It didn't like to be stared at by white folks. But perhaps the downtowners never knew this—for the cabaret owners, the entertainers, and the speakeasy proprietors treated them fine—as long as they paid.

The Saturday night rent parties that I attended were often more amusing than any night club, in small apartments where God knows who lived— because the guests seldom did—but where the piano would often be augmented by a guitar, or an odd cornet, or somebody with a pair of drums walking in off the street. And where awful bootleg whiskey and good fried fish or steaming chitterling were sold at very low prices. And the dancing and singing and impromptu entertaining went on until dawn came in the windows.

These parties, often termed whist parties or dances, were usually announced by brightly colored cards stuck in the grille of apartment house elevators. Some of the cards were highly entertaining in themselves:

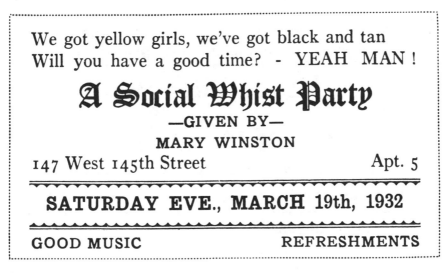

We got yellow girls, we've got black and tan
Will you have a good time? - YEAH MAN !

A Social Whist Party

—GIVEN BY—

MARY WINSTON

147 West 145th Street   Apt. 5

SATURDAY EVE., MARCH 19th, 1932

GOOD MUSIC   REFRESHMENTS

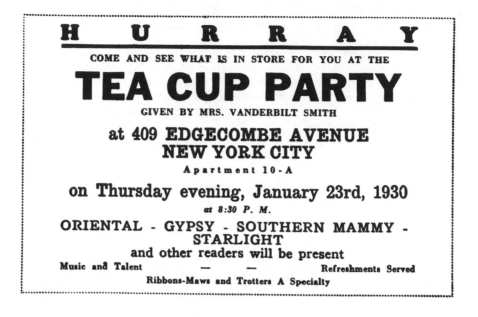

H U R R A Y

COME AND SEE WHAT IS IN STORE FOR YOU AT THE

TEA CUP PARTY

GIVEN BY MRS. VANDERBILT SMITH

at 409 EDGECOMBE AVENUE
NEW YORK CITY

Apartment 10-A

on Thursday evening, January 23rd, 1930

at 8:30 P. M.

ORIENTAL - GYPSY - SOUTHERN MAMMY -
STARLIGHT
and other readers will be present

Music and Talent   —   —   Refreshments Served

Ribbons-Maws and Trotters A Specialty

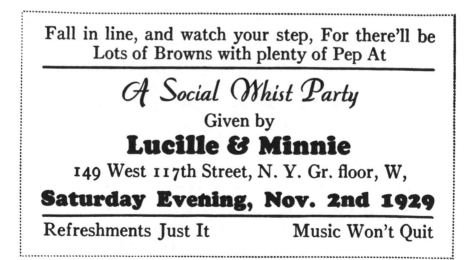

Fall in line, and watch your step, For there'll be
Lots of Browns with plenty of Pep At

A Social Whist Party

Given by

Lucille & Minnie

149 West 117th Street, N. Y. Gr. floor, W,

Saturday Evening, Nov. 2nd 1929

Refreshments Just It   Music Won't Quit

Railroad Men's Ball

AT CANDY'S PLACE

FRIDAY, SATURDAY & SUNDAY,

April 29-30, May 1, 1927

Black Wax, says change your mind and say they
do and he will give you a hearing, while MEAT
HOUSE SLIM, laying in the bin
killing all good men.

L. A. VAUGH, *President*

If Sweet Mamma is running wild, and you are looking
for a Do-right child, just come around and
linger awhile at a

SOCIAL WHIST PARTY

GIVEN BY

PINKNEY & EPPS

260 West 129th Street   Apartment 10

SATURDAY EVENING, JUNE 9, 1928

GOOD MUSIC   REFRESHMENTS

OH BOY   OH JOY

The Eleven Brown Skins

of the

Evening Shadow Social Club

are giving their

Second Annual St. Valentine Dance

Saturday evening, Feb. 18th, 1928

At 129 West 136th Street, New York City

Good Music   Refreshments Served

Subscription   **25 Cents**

---

*Some wear pajamas, some wear pants, what does it matter
just so you can dance, at*

A Social Whist Party

GIVEN BY

MR. & MRS. BROWN

AT 258 W. 115TH STREET, APT. 9

SATURDAY EVE., SEPT. 14, 1929

The music is sweet and everything good to eat!

Almost every Saturday night when I was in Harlem I went to a house-rent party. I wrote lots of poems about house-rent parties, and ate thereat many a fried fish and pig's foot—with liquid refreshments on the side. I met ladies' maids and truck drivers, laundry workers and shoe shine boys, seamstresses and porters. I can still hear their laughter in my ears, hear the soft slow music, and feel the floor shaking as the dancers danced.

Harlem Literati

The summer of 1926, I lived in a rooming house on 137th Street, where Wallace Thurman and Harcourt Tynes also lived. Thurman was then managing editor of the *Messenger,* a Negro magazine that had a curious career. It began by being very radical, racial, and socialistic, just after the war. I believe it received a grant from the Garland Fund in its early days. Then it later became a kind of Negro society magazine and a plugger for Negro business, with photographs of prominent colored ladies and their nice homes in it. A. Phillip Randolph, now President of the Brotherhood of Sleeping Car Porters, Chandler Owen, and George S. Schuyler were connected with it. Schuyler's editorials, à la Mencken, were the most interesting things in the magazine, verbal brickbats that said sometimes one thing, sometimes another, but always vigorously. I asked Thurman what kind of magazine the *Messenger* was, and he said it reflected the policy of whoever paid off best at the time.

Anyway, the *Messenger* bought my first short stories. They paid me ten dollars a story. Wallace Thurman wrote me that they were very bad stories, but better than any others they could find, so he published them.

Thurman had recently come from California to New York. He was a strangely brilliant black boy, who had read everything, and whose critical mind could find something wrong with everything he read. I have no critical mind, so I usually either like a book or don't. But I am not capable of liking a book and then finding a million things wrong with it, too—as Thurman was capable of doing.

Thurman had read so many books because he could read eleven lines at a time. He would get from the library a great pile of volumes that would have taken me a year to read. But he would go through them in less than a week, and be able to discuss each one at great length with anybody. That was why, I suppose, he was later given a job as a reader at Macaulay's—the only Negro reader, so far as I know, to be employed by any of the larger publishing firms.

Later Thurman became a ghost writer for *True Story,* and other publications, writing under all sorts of fantastic names, like Ethel Belle Mandrake or Patrick Casey. He did Irish and Jewish and Catholic "true confessions." He collaborated with William Jordan Rapp on plays and novels. Later he ghosted books. In fact, this quite dark young Negro is said to have written *Men, Women, and Checks.*

Wallace Thurman wanted to be a great writer, but none of his own work ever made him happy. *The Blacker the Berry,* his first book, was an important novel on a subject little dwelt upon in Negro fiction—the plight of the very dark Negro woman, who encounters in some communities a double wall of color prejudice within and without the race. His play, *Harlem,* considerably distorted for box office purposes, was, nevertheless, a compelling study—and the only one in the theater—of the impact of Harlem on a Negro family fresh from the South. And his *Infants of the Spring,* a superb and bitter study of the bohemian fringe of Harlem's literary and artistic life, is a compelling book.

But none of these things pleased Wallace Thurman. He wanted to be a *very* great writer, like Gorki or Thomas Mann, and he felt that he was merely a journalistic writer. His critical mind, comparing his pages to the thousands of other pages he had read, by Proust, Melville, Tolstoy, Galsworthy, Dostoyevski, Henry James, Sainte-Beauve, Taine, Anatole France, found his own pages vastly wanting. So he contented himself by writing a great deal for money, laughing bitterly at his fabulously concocted "true stories," creating two bad motion pictures of the "Adults Only" type for Hollywood, drinking more and more gin, and then threatening to jump out of windows at people's parties and kill himself.

During the summer of 1926, Wallace Thurman, Zora Neale Hurston, Aaron Douglas, John P. Davis, Bruce Nugent, Gwendolyn Bennett, and I decided to publish 'a Negro quarterly of the arts" to be called *Fire*—the idea being that it would burn up a lot of the old, dead conventional Negro-white ideas of the past, *épater le bourgeois* into a realization of the existence of the younger Negro writers and artists, and provide us with an outlet for publication not available in the limited pages of the small Negro magazines then existing, the *Crisis, Opportunity,* and the *Messenger*—the first two being house organs of inter-racial organizations, and the latter being God knows what.

Sweltering summer evenings we met to plan *Fire.* Each of the seven of us agreed to give fifty dollars to finance the first issue. Thurman was to edit it, John P. Davis to handle the business end, and Bruce Nugent to take charge of distribution. The rest of us were to serve as an editorial board to collect material, contribute our own work, and act in any useful way that we could. For artists and writers, we got along fine and there were no quarrels. But October came before we were ready to go to press. I had to return to Lincoln, John Davis to Law School at Harvard, Zora Hurston to her studies at Barnard, from whence she went about Harlem with an anthropologist's ruler, measuring heads for Franz Boas.

Only three of the seven had contributed their fifty dollars, but the others faithfully promised to send theirs out of tuition checks, wages, or begging. Thurman went on with the work of preparing the magazine. He got a printer. He planned the layout. It had to be on good paper, he said, worthy of the drawings of Aaron Douglas. It had to have beautiful type, worthy of the first Negro art quarterly. It had to be what we seven young Negroes dreamed our magazine would be—so in the end it cost almost a thousand dollars, and nobody could pay the bills.

I don't know how Thurman persuaded the printer to let us have all the copies to distribute, but he did. I think Alain Locke, among others, signed notes guaranteeing payments. But since Thurman was the only one of the seven of us with a regular job, for the next three or four years his checks were constantly being attached and his income seized to pay for *Fire.* And whenever I sold a poem, mine went there, too—to *Fire.*

None of the older Negro intellectuals would have anything to do with *Fire.* Dr. DuBois in the *Crisis* roasted it. The Negro press called it all sorts of bad names, largely because of a green and purple story by Bruce Nugent, in the Oscar Wilde tradition, which we had included. Rean Graves, the critic for the *Baltimore Afro-American,* began his review by saying: "I have just tossed the first issue of *Fire* into the fire." Commenting upon various of our contributors, he said: "Aaron Douglas who, in spite of himself and the meaningless grotesqueness of his creations, has gained a reputation as an artist, is permitted to spoil three perfectly good pages and a cover with his pen and ink hudge pudge. Countee Cullen has written a beautiful poem in his 'From a Dark Tower,' but tries his best to obscure the thought in super-fluous sentences. Langston Hughes displays his usual ability to say nothing in many words."

So *Fire* had plenty of cold water thrown on it by the colored critics. The white critics (except for an excellent editorial in the *Bookman* for November, 1926) scarcely noticed it at all. We had no way of getting it distributed to bookstands or news stands. Bruce Nugent took it around New York on foot and some of the Greenwich Village bookshops put it on display, and sold it for us. But then Bruce, who had no job, would collect the money and, on account of salary, eat it up before he got back to Harlem.

Finally, irony of ironies, several hundred copies of *Fire* were stored in the basement of an apartment where an actual fire occurred and the bulk of the whole issue was burned up. Even after that Thurman had to go on paying the printer.

Now *Fire* is a collector's item, and very difficult to get, being mostly ashes.

That taught me a lesson about little magazines. But since white folks had them, we Negroes thought we could have one, too. But we didn't have the money.

Wallace Thurman laughed a long bitter laugh. He was a strange kind of fellow, who liked to drink gin, but *didn't* like to drink gin; who liked being a Negro, but felt it a great handicap; who adored bohemianism, but thought it wrong to be a bohemian. He liked to waste a lot of time, but he always felt guilty wasting time. He loathed crowds, yet he hated to be alone. He almost always felt bad, yet he didn't write poetry.

Once I told him if I could feel as bad as he did *all* the time, I would surely produce wonderful books. But he said you had to know how to *write,* as well as how to feel bad. I said I didn't have to know how to feel bad, be-cause, every so often, the blues just naturally overtook me, like a blind beggar with an old guitar:

> You don't know,
> You don't know my mind—

> When you see me laughin',
> I'm laughin' to keep from cryin'.

About the future of Negro literature Thurman was very pessimistic. He thought the Negro vogue had made us all too conscious of ourselves, had flattered and spoiled us, and had provided too many easy opportunities for some of us to drink gin and more gin, on which he thought we would always be drunk. With his bitter sense of humor, he called the Harlem literati, the "niggerati."

Of this "niggerati," Zora Neale Hurston was certainly the most amusing. Only to reach a wider audience, need she ever write books—because she is a perfect book of entertainment in herself. In her youth she was always getting scholarships and things from wealthy white people, some of whom simply paid her just to sit around and represent the Negro race for them, she did it in such a racy fashion. She was full of side-splitting anecdotes, humorous tales, and tragicomic stories, remembered out of her life in the South as a daughter of a travelling minister of God. She could make you laugh one minute and cry the next. To many of her white friends, no doubt, she was a perfect "darkie," in the nice meaning they give the term—that is a naïve, childlike, sweet, humorous, and highly colored Negro.

But Miss Hurston was clever, too—a student who didn't let college give her a broad *a* and who had great scorn for all pretensions, academic or otherwise. That is why she was such a fine folk-lore collector, able to go among the people and never act as if she had been to school at all. Almost nobody else could stop the average Harlemite on Lenox Avenue and measure his head with a strange-looking, anthropological device and not get bawled out for the attempt, except Zora, who used to stop anyone whose head looked interesting, and measure it.

When Miss Hurston graduated from Barnard she took an apartment in West 66th Street near the park, in that row of Negro houses there. She moved in with no furniture at all and no money, but in a few days friends had given her everything, from decorative silver birds, perched atop the linen cabinet, down to a footstool. And on Saturday night, to christen the place, she had a *hand*-chicken dinner, since she had forgotten to say she needed forks.

She seemed to know almost everybody in New York. She had been a secretary to Fannie Hurst, and had met dozens of celebrities whose friendship she retained. Yet she was always having terrific ups-and-downs about money. She tells this story on herself, about needing a nickel to go downtown one day and wondering where on earth she would get it. As she approached the subway, she was stopped by a blind beggar holding out his cup.

"Please help the blind! Help the blind! A nickel for the blind!"

"I need money worse than you today," said Miss Hurston, taking five cents out of his cup. "Lend me this! Next time, I'll give it back." And she went on downtown.

Harlem was like a great magnet for the Negro intellectual, pulling him from everywhere. Or perhaps the magnet was New York—but once in New York, he had to live in Harlem, for rooms were hardly to be found elsewhere unless one could pass for white or Mexican or Eurasian and perhaps live in the Village—which always seemed to me a very arty locale, in spite of the many real artists and writers who lived there. Only a few of the New Negroes lived in the Village, Harlem being their real stamping ground.

The wittiest of these New Negroes of Harlem, whose tongue was flavored with the sharpest and saltiest humor, was Rudolph Fisher, whose stories appeared in the *Atlantic Monthly.* His novel, *Walls of Jericho,* captures but slightly the raciness of his own conversation. He was a young medical doctor and X-ray specialist, who always frightened me a little, because he could think of the most incisively clever things to say—and I could never think of anything to answer. He and Alain Locke together were great for intellectual wise-cracking. The two would fling big and witty words about with such swift and punning innuendo that an ordinary mortal just sat and looked wary for fear of being caught in a net of witticisms beyond his cultural ken. I used to wish I could talk like Rudolph Fisher. Besides being a good writer, he was an excellent singer, and had sung with Paul Robeson during their college days. But I guess Fisher was too brilliant and too talented to stay long on this earth. During the same week, in December, 1934, he and Wallace Thurman both died.

Thurman died of tuberculosis in the charity ward at Bellevue Hospital, having just flown back to New York from Hollywood.

HARLEM RUNS WILD
CLAUDE MCKAY

Docile Harlem went on a rampage last week, smashing stores and looting them and piling up destruction of thousands of dollars worth of goods. But the mass riot in Harlem was not a race riot. A few whites were jostled by colored people in the melee, but there was no manifest hostility between colored and white as such. All night until dawn on the Tuesday of the outbreak white persons, singly and in groups, walked the streets of Harlem without being molested. The action of the police was commendable in the highest degree. The looting was brazen and daring, but the police were restrained. In extreme cases, when they fired, it was into the air. Their restraint saved Harlem from becoming a shambles.

The outbreak was spontaneous. It was directed against the stores exclusively. One Hundred and Twenty-fifth Street is Harlem's main street and the theatrical and shopping center of the colored thousands. Anything that starts there will flash through Harlem as quick as lightning. The alleged beating of a kid caught stealing a trifle in one of the stores merely served to

From *Nation,* vol. 140 (April 3, 1935), pp. 382–83.

explode the smoldering discontent of the colored people against the Harlem merchants.

It would be too sweeping to assert that radicals incited the Harlem mass to riot and pillage. The *Young Liberators* seized an opportune moment, but the explosion on Tuesday was not the result of Communist propaganda. There were, indeed, months of propaganda in it. But the propagandists are eager to dissociate themselves from Communists. Proudly they declare that they have agitated only in the American constitutional way for fair play for colored Harlem.

Colored people all over the world are notoriously the most exploitable material, and colored Harlem is no exception. The population is gullible to an extreme. And apparently the people are exploited so flagrantly because they invite and take it. It is their gullibility that gives to Harlem so much of its charm, its air of insouciance and gaiety. But the façade of the Harlem masses' happy-go-lucky and hand-to-mouth existence has been badly broken by the Depression. A considerable part of the population can no longer cling even to the hand-to-mouth margin.

Wherever an ethnologically related group of people is exploited by others, the exploiters often operate on the principle of granting certain concessions as sops. In Harlem the exploiting group is overwhelmingly white. And it gives no sops. And so for the past two years colored agitators have exhorted the colored consumers to organize and demand of the white merchants a new deal: that they should employ Negroes as clerks in the colored community. These agitators are crude men, theoretically. They have little understanding of and little interest in the American labor movement, even from the most conservative trade-union angle. They address their audience mainly on the streets. Their following is not so big as that of the cultists and occultists. But it is far larger than that of the Communists.

One of the agitators is outstanding and picturesque. He dresses in turban and gorgeous robe. He has a bigger following than his rivals. He calls himself Sufi Abdul Hamid. His organization is the Negro Industrial and Clerical Alliance. It was the first to start picketing the stores of Harlem demanding clerical employment for colored persons. Sufi Hamid achieved a little success. A few of the smaller Harlem stores engaged colored clerks. But on 125th Street the merchants steadfastly refused to employ colored clerical help. The time came when the Negro Industrial and Clerical Alliance felt strong enough to picket the big stores on 125th Street. At first the movement got scant sympathy from influential Negroes and the Harlem intelligentsia as a whole. Physically and mentally, Sufi Hamid is a different type. He does not belong. And moreover he used to excoriate the colored newspapers, pointing out that they would not support his demands on the bigger Harlem stores because they were carrying the stores' little ads.

Harlem was excited by the continued picketing and the resultant "incidents." Sufi Hamid won his first big support last spring when one of the most popular young men in Harlem, the Reverend Adam Clayton Powell, Jr. assistant pastor of the Abyssinian Church—the largest in Harlem—went on the picket line on 125th Street. This gesture set all Harlem talking and thinking and made the headlines of the local newspapers. It prompted the formation of a Citizens' League for Fair Play. The league was endorsed and supported by sixty-two organizations, among which were eighteen of the leading churches of Harlem. And at last the local press conceded some support.

One of the big stores capitulated and took on a number of colored clerks. The picketing of other stores was continued. And soon business was not so good as it used to be on 125th Street

In the midst of the campaign Sufi Hamid was arrested. Sometime before his arrest a committee of Jewish Minute Men had visited the Mayor and complained about an anti-Semitic movement among the colored people and the activities of a black Hitler in Harlem. The *Day* and the *Bulletin,* Jewish newspapers, devoted columns to the Harlem Hitler and anti-Semitism among Negroes. The articles were translated and printed in the Harlem newspapers under big headlines denouncing the black Hitler and his work.

On October 13 of last year Sufi Hamid was brought before the courts charged with disorderly conduct and using invective against the Jews. The witnesses against him were the chairman of the Minute Men and other persons more or less connected with the merchants. After hearing the evidence and defense, the judge decided that the evidence was biased and discharged Sufi Hamid. Meanwhile Sufi Hamid had withdrawn from the Citizens' League for Fair Play. He had to move from his headquarters and his immediate following was greatly diminished. An all-white Harlem Merchants' Association came into existence. Dissension divided the Citizens' League; the prominent members denounced Sufi Hamid and his organization.

In an interview last October Sufi Hamid told me that he had never styled himself the black Hitler. He said that once when he visited a store to ask for the employment of colored clerks, the proprietor remarked, "We are fighting Hitler in Germany." Sufi said that he replied, "We are fighting Hitler in Harlem." He went on to say that although he was a Moslem he had never entertained any prejudices against Jews as Jews. He was an Egyptian * and in Egypt the relations between Moslem and Jew were happier than in any other country. He was opposed to Hitlerism, for he had read Hitler's book, *Mein Kampf,* and knew Hitler's attitude and ideas about all colored peoples. Sufi Hamid said that the merchants of Harlem spread the rumor of anti-Semitism among the colored people because they did not want to face the issue of giving them a square deal.

The Citizens' League continued picketing, and some stores capitulated. But the Leaguers began quarreling among themselves as to whether the clerks employed should be light-skinned or dark-skinned. Meanwhile the united white Harlem Merchants' Association was fighting back. In November the picketing committee was enjoined from picketing by Supreme Court

* Sufi Hamid was actually Afro-American.

Justice Samuel Rosenman. The court ruled that the Citizen's League was not a labor organization. It was the first time that such a case had come before the courts of New York. The chairman of the picketing committee remarked that "the decision would make trouble in Harlem."

One by one the colored clerks who had been employed in 125th Street stores lost their places. When inquiries were made as to the cause, the managements gave the excuse of slack business. The clerks had no organization behind them. Of the grapevine intrigue and treachery that contributed to the debacle of the movement, who can give the facts? They are as obscure and inscrutable as the composite mind of the Negro race itself. So the masses of Harlem remain disunited and helpless, while their would-be leaders wrangle and scheme and denounce one another to the whites. Each one is ambitious to wear the piebald mantle of Marcus Garvey.

On Tuesday the crowds went crazy like the remnants of a defeated, abandoned, and hungry army. Their rioting was the gesture of despair of a bewildered, baffled, and disillusioned people.

A NEGRO NATION WITHIN THE NATION
W. E. B. DUBOIS

No more critical situation ever faced the Negroes of American than that of today—not in 1830, nor in 1861, nor in 1867. More than ever the appeal of the Negro for elementary justice falls on deaf ears.

Three-fourths of us are disfranchised; yet no writer on democratic reform, no third-party movement says a word about Negroes. The Bull Moose crusade in 1912 refused to notice them; the La Follette uprising in 1924 was hardly aware of them; the Socialists still keep them in the background. Negro children are systematically denied education; when the National Educational Association asks for federal aid to education it permits discrimination to be perpetuated by the present local authorities. Once or twice a month Negroes convicted of no crime are openly and publicly lynched, and even burned; yet a National Crime Convention is brought to perfunctory and unwilling notice of this only by mass picketing and all but illegal agitation. When a man with every qualification is refused a position simply because his great-grandfather was black there is not a ripple of comment or protest.

Long before the depression Negroes in the South were losing "Negro" jobs, those assigned them by common custom—poorly paid and largely undesirable toil, but nevertheless life-supporting. New techniques, new enterprises, mass production, impersonal ownership and control have been largely displacing the skilled white and Negro worker in tobacco manufacturing, in iron and steel, in lumbering and mining, and in transportation. Negroes are now restricted more and more to common labor and domestic service of the lowest paid and worst kind. In textile, chemical and other manufactures Negroes were from the first nearly excluded, and just as slavery kept the poor white out of profitable agriculture, so freedom prevents the poor Negro from finding a place in manufacturing. The world-wide decline in agriculture has moreover carried the mass of black farmers, despite heroic endeavor among the few, down to the level of landless tenants and peons.

The World War and its wild aftermath seemed for a moment to open a new door; two million black workers rushed North to work in iron and steel, make automobiles and pack meat, build houses and do the heavy toil in factories. They met first the closed trade union which excluded them from the best-paid jobs and pushed them into the low-wage gutter, denied them homes and mobbed them. Then they met the depression.

Since 1929 Negro workers, like white workers, have lost their jobs, have had mortgages foreclosed on their farms and homes, have used up their small savings. But, in the case of the Negro worker, everything has been worse in larger or smaller degree; the loss has been greater and more permanent. Technological displacement, which began before the depression, has been accelerated, while unemployment and falling wages struck black men sooner, went to lower levels and will last longer.

Negro public schools in the rural South have often disappeared, while southern city schools are crowded to suffocation. The Booker Washington High School in Atlanta, built for 1,000 pupils, has 3,000 attending in double daily sessions. Above all, federal and state relief holds out little promise for the Negro. It is but human that the unemployed white man and the starving white child should be relieved first by local authorities who regard them as fellowmen, but often regard Negroes as subhuman. While the white worker has sometimes been given more than relief and been helped to his feet, the black worker has often been pauperized by being just kept from starvation. There are some plans for national rehabilitation and the rebuilding of the whole industrial system. Such plans should provide for the Negro's future relations to American industry and culture, but those provisions the country is not only unprepared to make but refuses to consider.

In the Tennessee Valley beneath the Norris Dam, where do Negroes come in? And what shall be their industrial place? In the attempt to rebuild agriculture the southern landholder will in all probability be put on his feet, but the black tenant has been pushed to the edge of despair. In the matter of housing, no comprehensive scheme for Negro homes has been thought out and only two or three local projects planned. Nor can broad plans be made until the nation or the community decides where it wants or will permit Negroes to live. Negroes are largely excluded from subsistence homesteads because Negroes protested against segregation, and whites, anxious for cheap local labor, also protested.

The colored people of America are coming to face the fact quite calmly that most white Americans do not like them, and are planning neither for their survival, nor for their definite future if it involves free, self-assertive modern manhood. This does not mean all Americans. A saving few are worried about the Negro problem; a still larger group are not ill-disposed, but they fear prevailing public opinion. The great mass of Americans are, however, merely representatives of average humanity. They muddle along with their own affairs and scarcely can be expected to take seriously the affairs of strangers or people whom they partly fear and partly despise.

For many years it was the theory of most Negro leaders that this attitude was the insensibility of ignorance and inexperience, that white America did not know of or realize the continuing plight of the Negro. Accordingly, for the last two decades, we have striven by book and periodical, by speech and appeal, by various dramatic methods of agitation, to put the essential facts before the American people. Today there can be no doubt that Americans know the facts; and yet they remain for the most part indifferent and unmoved.

The main weakness of the Negro's position is that since emancipation he has never had an adequate economic foundation. Thaddeus Stevens recognized this and sought to transform the emancipated freedmen into peasant proprietors. If he had succeeded, he would have changed the economic history of the United States and perhaps saved the American farmer from his present plight. But to furnish 50,000,000 acres of good land to the Negroes would have cost more money than the North was willing to pay, and was regarded by the South as highway robbery.

The whole attempt to furnish land and capital for the freedmen fell through, and no comprehensive economic plan was advanced until the advent of Booker T. Washington. He had a vision of building a new economic foundation for Negroes by incorporating them into white industry. He wanted to make them skilled workers by industrial education and expected small capitalists to rise out of their ranks. Unfortunately, he assumed that the economic development of America in the twentieth century would resemble that of the nineteenth century, with free industrial opportunity, cheap land and unlimited resources under the control of small competitive capitalists. He lived to see industry more and more concentrated, land monopoly extended and industrial technique changed by wide introduction of machinery.

As a result, technology advanced more rapidly than Hampton or Tuskegee could adjust their curricula. The chance of an artisan's becoming a capitalist grew slimmer, even for white Americans, while the whole relation of labor to capital became less a matter of technical skill than of basic organization and aim.

Those of us who in that day opposed Booker Washington's plans did not foresee exactly the kind of change that was coming, but we were convinced that the Negro could succeed in industry and in life only if he had intelligent leadership and far-reaching ideals. The object of education, we declared, was not "to make men artisans but to make artisans men." The Negroes in America needed leadership so that, when change and crisis came, they could guide themselves to safety.

The educated American Negroes is still small, but it is large enough to begin planning for preservation through economic advancement. The first definite movement of this younger group was toward direct alliance of the

Negro with the labor movement. But white labor today as in the past refuses to respond to these overtures.

For a hundred years, beginning in the thirties and forties of the nineteenth century, the white laborers of Ohio, Pennsylvania and New York beat, murdered and drove away fellow workers because they were black and had to work for what they could get. Seventy years ago in New York, the center of the new American labor movement, white laborers hanged black ones to lamp posts instead of helping to free them from the worst of modern slavery. In Chicago and St. Louis, New Orleans and San Francisco, black men still carry the scars of the bitter hatred of white laborers for them. Today it is white labor that keeps Negroes out of decent low-cost housing, that confines the protection of the best unions to "white" men, that often will not sit in the same hall with black folk who already have joined the labor movement. White labor has to hate scabs; but it hates black scabs not because they are scabs but because they are black. It mobs white scabs to force them into labor fellowship. It mobs black scabs to starve and kill them. In the present fight of the American Federation of Labor against company unions it is attacking the only unions that Negroes can join.

Thus the Negro's fight to enter organized industry has made little headway. No Negro, no matter what his ability, can be a member of any of the railway unions. He cannot be an engineer, fireman, conductor, switchman, brakeman or yardman. If he organizes separately, he may, as in the case of the Negro Firemen's Union, be assaulted and even killed by white firemen. As in the case of the Pullman Porters' Union, he may receive empty recognition without any voice or collective help. The older group of Negro leaders recognize this and simply say it is a matter of continued striving to break down these barriers.

Such facts are, however, slowly forcing Negro thought into new channels. The interests of labor are considered rather than those of capital. No greater welcome is expected from the labor monopolist who mans armies and navies to keep Chinese, Japanese and Negroes in their places than from the captains of industry who spend large sums of money to make laborers think that the most worthless white man is better than any colored man. The Negro must prove his necessity to the labor movement and that it is a disastrous error to leave him out of the foundation of the new industrial state. He must settle beyond cavil the question of his economic efficiency as a worker, a manager and controller of capital.

The dilemma of these younger thinkers gives men like James Weldon Johnson a chance to insist that the older methods are still the best; that we can survive only by being integrated into the nation, and that we must consequently fight segregation now and always and force our way by appeal, agitation and law. This group, however, does not seem to recognize the fundamental economic bases of social growth and the changes that face American industry. Greater democratic control of production and distribution is bound to replace existing autocratic and monopolistic methods.

In this broader and more intelligent democracy we can hope for progressive softening of the asperities and anomalies of race prejudice, but we cannot hope for its early and complete disappearance. Above all, the doubt, deep-planted in the American mind, as to the Negro's ability and efficiency as worker, artisan and administrator will fade but slowly. Thus, with increased democratic control of industry and capital, the place of the Negro will be increasingly a matter of human choice, of willingness to recognize ability across the barriers of race, of putting fit Negroes in places of power and authority by public opinion. At present, on the railroads, in manufacturing, in the telephone, telegraph and radio business, and in the larger divisions of trade, it is only under exceptional circumstances that any Negro no matter what his ability, gets an opportunity for position and power. Only in those lines where individual enterprise still counts, as in some of the professions, in a few of the trades, in a few branches of retail business and in artistic careers, can the Negro expect a narrow opening.

Negroes and other colored folk nevertheless, exist in larger and growing numbers. Slavery, prostitution to white men, theft of their labor and goods have not killed them and cannot kill them. They are growing in intelligence and dissatisfaction. They occupy strategic positions, within nations and beside nations, amid valuable raw material and on the highways of future expansion. They will survive, but on what terms and conditions? On this point a new school of Negro thought is arising. It believes in the ultimate uniting of mankind and in a unified American nation, with economic classes and racial barriers leveled, but it believes this is an ideal and is to be realized only by such intensified class and race consciousness as will bring irresistible force rather than mere humanitarian appeals to bear on the motives and actions of men.

The peculiar position of Negroes in America offers an opportunity. Negroes today cast probably 2,000,000 votes in a total of 40,000,000, and their vote will increase. This gives them, particularly in northern cities, and at critical times, a chance to hold a very considerable balance of power, and the mere threat of this being used intelligently and with determination may often mean much. The consuming power of 2,800,000 Negro families has recently been estimated at $166,000,000 a month—a tremendous power when intelligently directed. Their manpower as laborers probably equals that of Mexico or Yugoslavia. Their illiteracy is much lower than that of Spain or Italy. Their estimated per capita wealth about equals that of Japan.

For a nation with this start in culture and efficiency to sit down and await the salvation of a white God is idiotic. With the use of their political power, their power as consumers, and their brainpower, added to that chance of personal appeal which proximity and neighborhood always give to human beings, Negroes can develop in the United States an economic nation within a nation, able to work through inner cooperation, to found its own institutions, to educate its genius, and at the same time, without mob violence or extremes of race hatred, to keep in helpful touch and cooperate with the mass of the nation. This has happened more often than most people realize, in the case of groups not so obviously separated from the mass of people as are American Negroes. It must happen in our case, or there is no hope for the Negro in America.

Any movement toward such a program is today hindered by the absurd Negro philosophy of Scatter, Suppress, Wait, Escape. There are even many of our educated young leaders who think that because the Negro problem is not in evidence where there are few or no Negroes, this indicates a way out! They think that the problem of race can be settled by ignoring it and suppressing all reference to it. They think that we have only to wait in silence for the white people to settle the problem for us; and finally and predominantly, they think that the problem of twelve million Negro people, mostly poor, ignorant workers, is going to be settled by having their more educated and wealthy classes gradually and continually escape from their race into the mass of the American people, leaving the rest to sink, suffer and die.

Proponents of this program claim, with much reason, that the plight of the masses is not the fault of the emerging classes. For the slavery and exploitation that reduced Negroes to their present level or at any rate hindered them from rising, the white world is to blame. Since the age-long process of raising a group is through the escape of its upper class into welcome fellowship with risen peoples, the Negro intelligentsia would submerge itself if it bent its back to the task of lifting the mass of people. There is logic in this answer, but futile logic.

If the leading Negro classes cannot assume and bear the uplift of their own proletariat, they are doomed for all time. It is not a case of ethics; it is a plain case of necessity. The method by which this may be done is, first, for the American Negro to achieve a new economic solidarity.

There exists today a chance for the Negroes to organize a cooperative state within their own group. By letting Negro farmers feed Negro artisans, and Negro technicians guide Negro home industries, and Negro thinkers plan this integration of cooperation, while Negro artists dramatize and beautify the struggle, economic independence can be achieved. To doubt that this is possible is to doubt the essential humanity and the quality of brains of the American Negro.

No sooner is this proposed than a great fear sweeps over older Negroes. They cry "No segregation"—no further yielding to prejudice and race separation. Yet any planning for the benefit of American Negroes on the part of a Negro intelligentsia is going to involve organized and deliberate self-segregation. There are plenty of people in the United States who would be only too willing to use such a plan as a way to increase existing legal and customary segregation between the races. This threat which many Negroes see is no mere mirage. What of it? It must be faced.

If the economic and cultural salvation of the American Negro calls for an increase in segregation and prejudice, then that must come. American Negroes must plan for their economic future and the social survival of their fellows in the firm belief that this means in a real sense the survival of colored folk in the world and the building of a full humanity instead of a petty white tyranny. Control of their own education, which is the logical and inevitable end of separate schools, would not be an unmixed ill; it might prove a supreme good. Negro schools once meant poor schools. They need not today; they must not tomorrow. Separate Negro sections will increase race antagonism, but they will also increase economic cooperation, organized self-defense and necessary self-confidence.

The immediate reaction of most white and colored people to this suggestion will be that the thing cannot be done without extreme results. Negro thinkers have from time to time emphasized the fact that no nation within a nation can be built because of the attitude of the dominant majority, and because all legal and police power is out of Negro hands, and because large-scale industries, like steel and utilities, are organized on a national basis. White folk, on the other hand, simply say that, granting certain obvious exceptions, the American Negro has not the ability to engineer so delicate a social operation calling for such self-restraint, careful organization and sagacious leadership.

In reply, it may be said that this matter of a nation within a nation has already been partially accomplished in the organization of the Negro church, the Negro school and the Negro retail business, and, despite all the justly due criticism, the result has been astonishing. The great majority of American Negroes are divided not only for religious but for a large number of social purposes into self-supporting economic units, self-governed, self-directed. The greatest difficulty is that these organizations have no logical and reasonable standards and do not attract the finest, most vigorous and best educated Negroes. When all these things are taken into consideration it becomes clearer to more and more American Negroes that, through voluntary and increased segregation, by careful autonomy and planned economic organization, they may build so strong and efficient a unit that twelve million men can no longer be refused fellowship and equality in the United States.

FOREWORD TO *CHALLENGE,* VOL. I (MARCH, 1934)
JAMES WELDON JOHNSON

It is a good thing that Dorothy West is doing in instituting a magazine through which the voices of younger Negro writers may be heard. The term "younger Negro writers" connotes a degree of disillusionment and disappointment for those who a decade ago hailed with loud huzzas the dawn of the Negro literary millennium. We expected much; perhaps, too much. I now judge that we ought to be thankful for the half-dozen younger writers who did emerge and make a place for themselves. But we ought not to be satisfied; many newer voices should be constantly striving to make themselves heard. But these younger writers must not be mere dilettantes; they have serious work to do. They can bring to bear a tremendous force for breaking down and wearing away the stereotyped ideas about the Negro, and for creating a higher and more enlightened opinion about the race. To do this, they need not be propagandists; they need only be sincere artists, disdaining all cheap applause and remaining always true to themselves.

It seems to me that the greatest lack of our younger writers is not talent or ability, but persistent and intelligent industry. That, I think, explains why the work of so many of them was but a flash in the pan. It is one thing just to dabble in writing and another thing to be a writer. To those who really desire to become writers let me say: Writing is not only an art, it is also a trade, a trade that demands long, arduous and dogged effort for mastery.

FROM *CHALLENGE*
DOROTHY WEST

Dear Reader

It gives us considerable pleasure to print excerpts from these letters to the Editor, because they were written for our eye alone and are from the heart. If subsequent letters are self-consciously written, we shall be sorry.

We received many communications, from China even, where Pearl S. Buck writes that she will send us an editorial by the next boat, and Edward J. O'Brien sends a similar promise from Oxford. There were other letters, and for all of them we are grateful.

Countee Cullen writes in part, "I hope you are getting in touch with Langston (Hughes); he has been doing some very good prose recently. . . . I wish I had his objectivity. . . . Lord knows I wish we could recapture the spirit of '26; I hope the bird hasn't flown forever. And there must be ever so many new recruits who would flock to the sort of banner you are raising! I rather look to them instead of to us who have grown old before our time."

Carl Van Vechten closes with, "silver spoons to you and five blue and green dolphins!"

From Charles S. Johnson at Fisk comes, "The current here, as generally, seems to be more in the direction of prose than poetry. This may seem significant for literary people. . . . I happen to be in the midst of a very consuming task at the moment of analysing and interpreting the results of my study of Negro college graduates. There will be something that I shall want to say on this when I have gotten farther along."

We like Arna Bontemps' letter, ". . . . with the chickens to be fed and the fall garden to be tended I'm a busy man. Then there is the Scottsboro thing at our door, and the production of 'St. Louis Woman' in Cleveland (for my fancy), and the new book (only begun) which, of course, is my daily meat and drink, and withal I am a busy man and a lazy one. . . . I have just one poem of recent date that has not been published. I am holding it as one sometimes holds a good-luck penny, lest he should go completely broke.

Vol. I (March, 1934).

But I had a short story that might do, and if you will give me time to find it and make a copy, I'll gladly send it along for your brave new project."

This magazine is primarily an organ for the new voice. It is our plan to bring out the prose and poetry of the newer Negroes. We who were the New Negroes challenge them to better our achievements. For we did not altogether live up to our fine promise.

CARL VAN VECHTEN COMMENTS
DOROTHY WEST

Occasionally, some one is heard to croak hoarsely that the Negro "Renaissance" that was launched so bravely in 1926–27 has not continued its voyage on the seas of art as triumphantly as might have been wished. Personally I feel no sympathy with these complaints, no disappointment in the results. On the contrary, I believe the Negro of today to be on a much more solid basis as an artist and as a social individual than he was then. Certainly James Weldon Johnson's *Along This Way* is an autobiography to rank with the very best books in that department and presently will appear two other volumes, each of which, fine in its particular way, should do a great deal to lift the excellent average of Negro fiction to a higher level: Langston Hughes's *The Ways of White Folks* (Knopf) and Zora Neale Hurston's *Jonah's Gourd Vine* (Lippincott's).

Miss Ethel Waters, who is very probably the greatest living singer of popular ballads, has paved the way for future Negro stars (if they are good enough) to climb into white revues, while the production of *Four Saints in Three Acts,* the Gertrude Stein-Virgil Thomson opera, utilizes Negroes in a new field, as singing actors in alien Spanish roles. Miss Caterina Jarboro, too, has exhibited her talent in the congenial character of *Aida.*

These are all symbols of better days. If standards are higher, the talent of genius expressed is greater too. In fact, nowadays, there is no inclination on the part of the great public to say, "Pretty good for a Negro." If it cannot say, "Extraordinary from any point of view," it is not likely to show much interest.

DEAR READER
DOROTHY WEST

We continue to feel that the interesting excerpts from the letters of our contributors and friends (Our enemies don't write us. We wish they would) fill the editor's page much better than any piece we might write ourselves.

From *Challenge* September, 1934.
From *Challenge* September 1934.

Only one word. We were disappointed in the contributions that came in from the new voices. There was little that we wanted to print. Bad writing is unbelievably bad. We felt somewhat crazily that the authors must be spoofing and that they didn't really mean us to take their stuff for prose and poetry.

That largely explains why we are become a quarterly. We were just not ready to go to press at the end of a month. And we had to fall back on the tried and true voices. And we are that embarrassed.

Here is a fine excerpt from the letter of Arna Bontemps which might well be, "I told you so." He writes, "I am not convinced about the 'younger writers.' We're not washed up, not by a jugful. It is a pretty pose, this attitude about, 'old before our time.' I will not have it. We left Egypt in the late twenties and presently crossed the Red Sea. Naturally the wandering in the wilderness followed. The promised land is ahead. Why, Langston (Hughes) has just recently been spying it out for us, and the grapes are promising. Furthermore we are well able to go over and possess it. Now if the 'younger writers' can take our crowns, here is their chance and here is our challenge. But they will have to take them. We have just achieved our growth. Nobody knows our strength."

We are afraid we are always going to quote Bontemps, whose letters should be preserved. His prose is a joy forever.

EDITORIAL
BY THE EDITORS OF THE NEW CHALLANGE

We envisage *New Challenge* as an organ designed to meet the needs of writers and people interested in literature which cannot be met by those Negro magazines which are sponsored by organizations and which, therefore, cannot be purely literary. Through it we hope to break down much of the isolation which exists between Negro writers themselves, and between the Negro writer and the rest of the writing world. We hope that through our pages we may be able to point social directives and provide a basis for the clear recognition of and solution to the problems which face the contemporary writer.

We are not attempting to re-stage the "revolt" and "renaissance" which grew unsteadily and upon false foundations ten years ago. A literary movement among Negroes, we feel, should, first of all, be built upon the writer's placing his material in the proper perspective with regard to the life of the Negro masses. For that reason we want to indicate, through examples in our pages, the great fertility of folk material as a source of creative material.

We want *New Challenge* to be a medium of literary expression for all writers who realize the present need for the realistic depiction of life through the sharp focus of social consciousness. Negro writers themselves and the audience which they reach must be reminded, and in many instances taught, that writing should not be *in vacuo* but placed within a definite social context.

The reorganization of the magazine has been carried through, not only with the idea of a change in policy, but also in terms of the best way to fulfill our plans for relating it to communities beyond New York City. We want to see *New Challenge* as the organ of regional groups composed of writers opposed to fascism, war and general reactionary policies. There is already one such group functioning in Chicago, and we are eager to see other groups in other cities follow this example. Contributing editors from several large cities have been selected in the hope that the organizational activity of groups in those areas will be facilitated.

The success of this magazine depends upon the avoidance of any petty restrictions with regard to policy. We want it to be an organ for young writers who are seriously concerned with the problems facing them in their defense of existing culture and in their sincere creation of higher cultural values.

While our emphasis is upon Negro writers and the particular difficulties which they must meet, we are not limiting our contributors to Negroes alone. Any writer dealing with materials which reflect a sincere interest in the ultimate understanding of the interdependence of cultures will be welcomed. The magazine is one of progressive writers, and adheres to the prescriptions of no one dogma. We do ask, however, that the bigot and potential fascist keep away from our door.

The magazine, being non-political, is not subsidized by any political party, nor does it receive huge contributions from any such group (or from individuals). We are dependent upon subscriptions, support of benefit affairs, and outright donations. We are, in this respect, responsible only to ourselves, a fact which is contrary to the belief of the skeptics and agonizing to our enemies. But we recognize our obligations to our friends and advisers and to our sincere critics; and we hope that we shall prove our multiple sense of responsibility.

BLUEPRINT FOR NEGRO WRITING
RICHARD WRIGHT

1) *The Role of Negro Writing: Two Definitions*

Generally speaking, Negro writing in the past has been confined to humble novels, poems, and plays, prim and decorous ambassadors who went a-begging to white America. They entered the Court of American Public Opinion dressed in the knee-pants of servility, curtsying to show that the Negro was not inferior, that he was human, and that he had a life comparable to that of other people. For the most part these artistic ambassadors were received as though they were French poodles who do clever tricks.

Vol. II (Fall, 1937).

White America never offered these Negro writers any serious criticism. The mere fact that a Negro could write was astonishing. Nor was there any deep concern on the part of white America with the role Negro writing should play in American culture; and the role it did play grew out of accident rather than intent or design. Either it crept in through the kitchen in the form of jokes; or it was the fruits of that foul foil which was the result of a liaison between inferiority-complexed Negro "geniuses" and burnt-out white Bohemians with money.

On the other hand, these often technically brilliant performances by Negro writers were looked upon by the majority of literate Negroes as something to be proud of. At best, Negro writing has been something external to the lives of educated Negroes themselves. That the productions of their writers should have been something of a guide in their daily living is a matter which seems never to have been raised seriously.

Under these conditions Negro writing assumed two general aspects: 1) It became a sort of conspicuous ornamentation, the hallmark of "achievement." 2) It became the voice of the educated Negro pleading with white America for justice.

Rarely was the best of this writing addressed to the Negro himself, his needs, his sufferings, his aspirations. Through misdirection, Negro writers have been far better to others than they have been to themselves. And the mere recognition of this places the whole question of Negro writing in a new light and raises a doubt as to the validity of its present direction.

2) *The Minority Outlook*

Somewhere in his writings Lenin makes the observation that oppressed minorities often reflect the techniques of the bourgeoisie more brilliantly than some sections of the bourgeoisie themselves. The psychological importance of this becomes meaningful when it is recalled that oppressed minorities, and especially the petty bourgeois sections of oppressed minorities, strive to assimilate the virtues of the bourgeoisie in the assumption that by doing so they can lift themselves into a higher social sphere. But not only among the oppressed petty bourgeoisie does this occur. The workers of a minority people, chafing under exploitation, forge organizational forms of struggle to better their lot. Lacking the handicaps of false ambition and property, they have access to a wide social vision and a deep social consciousness. They display a greater freedom and initiative in pushing their claims upon a civilization than even do the petty bourgeoisie. Their organizations show greater strength, adaptability, and efficiency than any other group or class in society.

That Negro workers, propelled by the harsh conditions of their lives, have demonstrated this consciousness and mobility for economic and political action there can be no doubt. But has this consciousness been reflected in the work of Negro writers to the same degree as it has in the Negro workers' struggle to free Herndon and the Scottsboro Boys, in the drive toward unionism, in the fight against lynching? Have they as creative writers taken advantage of their unique minority position?

The answer decidedly is *no*. Negro writers have lagged sadly, and as time passes the gap widens between them and their people.

How can this hiatus be bridged? How can the enervating effects of this standing split be eliminated?

In presenting questions of this sort an attitude of self-consciousness and self-criticism is far more likely to be a fruitful point of departure than a mere recounting of past achievements. An emphasis upon tendency and experiment, a view of society as something becoming rather than as something fixed and admired is the one which points the way for Negro writers to stand shoulder to shoulder with Negro workers in mood and outlook.

3) *A Whole Culture*

There is, however, a culture of the Negro which is his and has been addressed to him; a culture which has, for good or ill, helped to clarify his consciousness and create emotional attitudes which are conducive to action. This culture has stemmed mainly from two sources: 1) the Negro church; 2) and the folklore of the Negro people.

It was through the portals of the church that the American Negro first entered the shrine of western culture. Living under slave conditions of life, bereft of his African heritage, the Negroes' struggle for religion on the plantations between 1820–60 assumed the form of a struggle for human rights. It remained a relatively revolutionary struggle until religion began to serve as an antidote for suffering and denial. But even today there are millions of American Negroes whose only sense of a whole universe, whose only relation to society and man, and whose only guide to personal dignity comes through the archaic morphology of Christian salvation.

It was, however, in a folklore moulded out of rigorous and inhuman conditions of life that the Negro achieved his most indigeous and complete expression. Blues, spirituals, and folk tales recounted from mouth to mouth; the whispered words of a black mother to her black daughter on the ways of men; the confidential wisdom of a black father to his black son; the swapping of sex experiences on street corners from boy to boy in the deepest vernacular; work songs sung under blazing suns—all these formed the channels through which the racial wisdom flowed.

One would have thought that Negro writers of the last century in striving at expression would have continued and deepened this folk tradition, would have tried to create a more intimate and yet a more profoundly social system of artistic communication between them and their people. But the illusion that they could escape through individual achievement the harsh lot of their race swung Negro writers away from any such path. Two separate cultures sprang up: one for the Negro masses, unwritten and unrecognized; and the other for the sons and daughters of a rising Negro bourgeoisie, parasitic and mannered.

Today the question is: Shall Negro writing be for the Negro masses, moulding the lives and consciousness of those masses toward new goals, or shall it continue begging the question of the Negroes' humanity?

4) The Problem of Nationalism in Negro Writing

In stressing the difference between the role Negro writing failed to play in the lives of the Negro people, and the role it should play in the future if it is to serve its historic function; in pointing out the fact that Negro writing has been addressed in the main to a small white audience rather than to a Negro one, it should be stated that no attempt is being made here to propagate a specious and blatant nationalism. Yet the nationalist character of the Negro people is unmistakable. Psychologically this nationalism is reflected in the whole of Negro culture, and especially in folklore.

In the absence of fixed and nourishing forms of culture, the Negro has a folklore which embodies the memories and hopes of and struggle for freedom. Not yet caught in paint or stone, and as yet but feebly depicted in the poem and novel, the Negroes' most powerful images of hope and despair still remain in the fluid state of daily speech. How many John Henrys have lived and died on the lips of these black people? How many mythical heroes in embryo have been allowed to perish for lack of husbanding by alert intelligence?

Negro folklore contains, in a measure that puts to shame more deliberate forms of Negro expression, the collective sense of Negro life in America. Let those who shy at the nationalist implications of Negro life look at this body of folklore, living and powerful, which rose out of a unified sense of a common life and a common fate. Here are those vital beginnings of a recognition of value in life as it is *lived,* a recognition that marks the emergence of a new culture in the shell of the old. And at the moment this process starts, at the moment when a people begin to realize a *meaning* in their suffering, the civilization that engenders that suffering is doomed.

The nationalist aspects of Negro life are as sharply manifest in the social institutions of Negro people as in folklore. There is a Negro church, a Negro press, a Negro social world, a Negro sporting world, a Negro business world, a Negro school system, Negro professions; in short, a Negro way of life in America. The Negro people did not ask for this, and deep down, though they express themselves through their institutions and adhere to this special way of life, they do not want it now. This special existence was forced upon them from without by lynch rope, bayonet and mob rule. They accepted these negative conditions with the inevitability of a tree which must live or perish in whatever soil it finds itself.

The few crumbs of American civilization which the Negro has got from the tables of capitalism have been through these segregated channels. Many Negro institutions are cowardly and incompetent; but they are all that the Negro has. And, in the main, any move, whether for progress or reaction, must come through these institutions for the simple reason that all other channels are closed. Negro writers who seek to mould or influence the consciousness of the Negro people must address their messages to them through the ideologies and attitudes fostered in this warping way of life.

5) *The Basis and Meaning of Nationalism in Negro Writing*

The social institutions of the Negro are imprisoned in the Jim Crow political system of the South, and this Jim Crow political system is in turn built upon a plantation-feudal economy. Hence, it can be seen that the emotional expression of group-feeling which puzzles so many whites and leads them to deplore what they call "black chauvinism" is not a morbidly inherent trait of the Negro, but rather the reflex expression of a life whose roots are imbedded deeply in Southern soil.

Negro writers must accept the nationalist implications of their lives, not in order to encourage them, but in order to change and transcend them. They must accept the concept of nationalism because, in order to transcend it, they must *possess* and *understand* it. And a nationalist spirit in Negro writing means a nationalism carrying the highest possible pitch of social consciousness. It means a nationalism that knows its origins, its limitations; that is aware of the dangers of its position; that knows its ultimate aims are unrealizable within the framework of capitalist America; a nationalism whose reason for being lies in the simple fact of self-possession and in the consciousness of the interdependence of people in modern society.

For purposes of creative expression it means that the Negro writer must realize within the area of his own personal experience those impulses which, when prefigured in terms of broad social movements, constitute the stuff of nationalism.

For Negro writers even more so than for Negro politicians, nationalism is a bewildering and vexing question, the full ramifications of which cannot be dealt with here. But among Negro workers and the Negro middle class the spirit of nationalism is rife in a hundred devious forms; and a simple literary realism which seeks to depict the lives of these people devoid of wider social connotations, devoid of the revolutionary significance of these nationalist tendencies, must of necessity do a rank injustice to the Negro people and alienate their possible allies in the struggle for freedom.

6) *Social Consciousness and Responsibility*

The Negro writer who seeks to function within his race as a purposeful agent has a serious responsibility. In order to do justice to his subject matter, in order to depict Negro life in all of its manifold and intricate relationships, a deep, informed, and complex consciousness is necessary; a consciousness which draws for its strength upon the fluid lore of a great people, and moulds this lore with the concepts that move and direct the forces of history today.

With the gradual decline of the moral authority of the Negro church, and with the increasing irresolution which is paralyzing Negro middle class leadership, a new role is devolving upon the Negro writer. He is being called upon to do no less than create values by which his race is to struggle, live and die.

By his ability to fuse and make articulate the experiences of men, because his writing possesses the potential cunning to steal into the inmost recesses of the human heart, because he can create the myths and symbols that inspire a faith in life, he may expect either to be consigned to oblivion, or to be recognized for the valued agent he is.

This raises the question of the personality of the writer. It means that in the lives of Negro writers must be found those materials and experiences which will create a meaningful picture of the world today. Many young writers have grown to believe that a Marxist analysis of society presents such a picture. It creates a picture which, when placed before the eyes of the writer, should unify his personality, organize his emotions, buttress him with a tense and obdurate will to change the world.

And, in turn, this changed world will dialectically change the writer. Hence, it is through a Marxist conception of reality and society that the maximum degree of freedom in thought and feeling can be gained for the Negro writer. Further, this dramatic Marxist vision, when consciously grasped, endows the writer with a sense of dignity which no other vision can give. Ultimately, it restores to the writer his lost heritage, that is, his role as a creator of the world in which he lives, and as a creator of himself.

Yet, for the Negro writer, Marxism is but the starting point. No theory of life can take the place of life. After Marxism has laid bare the skeleton of society, there remains the task of the writer to plant flesh upon those bones out of his will to live. He may, with disgust and revulsion, say *no* and depict the horrors of capitalism encroaching upon the human being. Or he may, with hope and passion, say *yes* and depict the faint stirrings of a new and emerging life. But in whatever social voice he chooses to speak, whether positive or negative, there should always be heard or *over*-heard his faith, his necessity, his judgement.

His vision need not be simple or rendered in primer-like terms; for the life of the Negro people is not simple. The presentation of their lives should be simple, yes; but all the complexity, the strangeness, the magic wonder of life that plays like a bright sheen over the most sordid existence, should be there. To borrow a phrase from the Russians, it should have a *complex simplicity.* Eliot, Stein, Joyce, Proust, Hemingway, and Anderson; Gorky, Barbusse, Nexo, and Jack London no less than the folklore of the Negro himself should form the heritage of the Negro writer. Every iota of gain in human thought and sensibility should be ready grist for his mill, no matter how far-fetched they may seem in their immediate implications.

7) *The Problem of Perspective*

What vision must Negro writers have before their eyes in order to feel the impelling necessity for an about face? What angle of vision can show them all the forces of modern society in process, all the lines of economic development converging toward a distant point of hope? Must they believe in some "ism"?

They may feel that only dupes believe in "isms"; they feel with some measure of justification that another commitment means only another disillusionment. But anyone destitute of a theory about the meaning, structure and direction of modern society is a lost victim in a world he cannot understand or control.

But even if Negro writers found themselves through some "ism," how would that influence their writing? Are they being called upon to "preach"? To be "salesmen"? To "prostitute" their writing? Must they "sully" themselves? Must they write "propaganda"?

No; it is a question of awareness, of consciousness; it is, above all, a question of perspective.

Perspective is that part of a poem, novel, or play which a writer never puts directly upon paper. It is that fixed point in intellectual space where a writer stands to view the struggles, hopes, and sufferings of his people. There are times when he may stand too close and the result is a blurred vision. Or he may stand too far away and the result is a neglect of important things.

Of all the problems faced by writers who as a whole have never allied themselves with world movements, perspective is the most difficult of achievement. At its best, perspective is a pre-conscious assumption, something which a writer takes for granted, something which he wins through his living.

A Spanish writer recently spoke of living in the heights of one's time. Surely, perspective means just *that*.

It means that a Negro writer must learn to view the life of a Negro living in New York's Harlem or Chicago's South Side with the consciousness that one-sixth of the earth surface belongs to the working class. It means that a Negro writer must create in his readers' minds a relationship between a Negro woman hoeing cotton in the South and the men who loll in swivel chairs in Wall Street and take the fruits of her toil.

Perspective for Negro writers will come when they have looked and brooded so hard and long upon the harsh lot of their race and compared it with the hopes and struggles of minority peoples everywhere that the cold facts have begun to tell them something.

8) *The Problem of Theme*

This does not mean that a Negro writer's sole concern must be with rendering the social scene; but if his conception of the life of his people is broad and deep enough, if the sense of the *whole* life he is seeking is vivid and strong in him, then his writing will embrace all those social, political, and economic forms under which the life of his people is manifest.

In speaking of theme one must necessarily be general and abstract; the temperament of each writer moulds and colors the world he sees. Negro life may be approached from a thousand angles, with no limit to technical and stylistic freedom.

Negro writers spring from a family, a clan, a class, and a nation; and the social units in which they are bound have a story, a record. Sense of theme will emerge in Negro writing when Negro writers try to fix this story about some pole of meaning, remembering as they do so that in the creative process meaning proceeds *equally* as much from the contemplation of the subject matter as from the hopes and apprehensions that rage in the heart of the writer.

Reduced to its simplest and most general terms, theme for Negro writers will rise from understanding the meaning of their being transplanted from a "savage" to a "civilized" culture in all of its social, political, economic, and emotional implications. It means that Negro writers must have in their consciousness the foreshortened picture of the *whole,* nourishing culture from which they were torn in Africa, and of the long, complex (and for the most part, unconscious) struggle to regain in some form and under alien conditions of life a *whole* culture again.

It is not only this picture they must have, but also a knowledge of the social and emotional milieu that gives it tone and solidity of detail. Theme for Negro writers will emerge when they have begun to feel the meaning of the history of their race as though they in one life time had lived it themselves throughout all the long centuries.

9) *Autonomy of Craft*

For the Negro writer to depict this new reality requires a greater discipline and consciousness than was necessary for the so-called Harlem school of expression. Not only is the subject matter dealt with far more meaningful and complex, but the new role of the writer is qualitatively different. The Negro writers' new position demands a sharper definition of the status of his craft, and a sharper emphasis upon its functional autonomy.

Negro writers should seek through the medium of their craft to play as meaningful a role in the affairs of men as do other professionals. But if their writing is demanded to perform the social office of other professions, then the autonomy of craft is lost and writing detrimentally fused with other interests. The limitations of the craft constitute some of its greatest virtues. If the sensory vehicle of imaginative writing is required to carry too great a load of didactic material, the artistic sense is submerged.

The relationship between reality and the artistic image is not always direct and simple. The imaginative conception of a historical period will not be a carbon copy of reality. Image and emotion possess a logic of their own. A vulgarized simplicity constitutes the greatest danger in tracing the reciprocal interplay between the writer and his environment.

Writing has its professional autonomy; it should complement other professions, but it should not supplant them or be swamped by them.

10) *The Necessity for Collective Work*

It goes without saying that these things cannot be gained by Negro writers if their present mode of isolated writing and living continues. This isolation exists *among* Negro writers as well as *between* Negro and white writers. The Negro writers' lack of thorough integration with the American scene, their lack of a clear realization among themselves of their possible role, have bred generation after generation of embittered and defeated literati.

Barred for decades from the theater and publishing houses, Negro writers have been *made* to feel a sense of difference. So deep has this white-hot iron of exclusion been burnt into their hearts that thousands have all but lost the desire to become identified with American civilization. The Negro writers' acceptance of this enforced isolation and their attempt to justify it is but a defense-reflex of the whole special way of life which has been rammed down their throats.

This problem, by its very nature, is one which must be approached contemporaneously from two points of view. The ideological unity of Negro writers and the alliance of that unity with all the progressive ideas of our day is the primary prerequisite for collective work. On the shoulders of white writers and Negro writers alike rest the responsibility of ending this mistrust and isolation.

By placing cultural health above narrow sectional prejudices, liberal writers of all races can help to break the stony soil of aggrandizement out of which the stunted plants of Negro nationalism grow. And, simultaneously, Negro writers can help to weed out these choking growths of reactionary nationalism and replace them with hardier and sturdier types.

These tasks are imperative in light of the fact that we live in a time when the majority of the most basic assumptions of life can no longer be taken for granted. Tradition is no longer a guide. The world has grown huge and cold. Surely this is the moment to ask questions, to theorize, to speculate, to wonder out of what materials can a human world be built.

Each step along this unknown path should be taken with thought, care, self-consciousness, and deliberation. When Negro writers think they have arrived at something which smacks of truth, humanity, they should want to test it with others, feel it with a degree of passion and strength that will enable them to communicate it to millions who are groping like themselves.

Writers faced with such tasks can have no possible time for malice or jealousy. The conditions for the growth of each writer depend too much upon the good work of other writers. Every first rate novel, poem, or play lifts the level of consciousness higher.

FOR A NEGRO MAGAZINE *
CLAUDE MCKAY

Ten years ago all the literary circles of America were enlivened by talk of a Negro Renaissance. Appreciative and interpretative articles in newspaper and magazines were duly followed by a fat little crop of Negro books by white and colored authors. The vogue for Negro music attained its peak. Af-

* A circular, 1934. [Ed.].

rican Negro sculpture found a place in modern art circles beside the art of other peoples.

Looking back to that period today the Negro Renaissance seems to have been no more than a mushroom growth that could send no roots down in the soil of Negro life.

About this apparent setback there are many opinions. Some think that the field was over unscrupulously exploited. Others that the national interest in the artistic expression of the Negro was only a passing fad.

But we believe that any genuine artistic expression can transcend a fad; that the Negro's contribution to literature and art should have a permanent place in American life; that American life will be richer by such contribution; and that it should find an outlet and a receptive audience.

Therefore, our aim is to found a magazine to give expression to the literary and artistic aspirations of the Negro; to make such a magazine of national significance as an esthetic interpretation of Negro life, exploiting the Negro's racial background and his racial gifts and accomplishments.

We want to encourage Negroes to create artistically as an ethnological group irrespective of class and creed. We want to help the Negro as writer and artist to free his mind of the shackles imposed upon it from outside as well as within his own racial group.

We mean to go forward in the vanguard of ideas, trends, thoughts and movements. But we are not demanding that the creative Negro should falsely accept nostrums and faiths that he does not understand. We realize that there are creative persons whose reaction to life is instinctive and emotional like actors who say their lines grandly without knowing what they really are about. We are not demanding that writers and artists should be more intellectual and social-minded in their work than they are constitutionally capable of being.

Nevertheless we have standards to which we will hold our contributors, such as:

SINCERITY OF PURPOSE
FRESHNESS AND KEENNESS OF PERCEPTION
ADEQUATE FORM OF EXPRESSION

The magazine is to be established under the editorship of CLAUDE McKAY, who has often been referred to as a pioneer of the so-called Negro Renaissance.

Mr. McKay has returned to this country after over 11 years' residence abroad, during which time he has traveled extensively and written a number of novels. He has not only kept in close touch with the social and artistic trends of American Negro life in their purely racial as well as radical phases, but he has also an international outlook on the Negro besides a store of experience from his long residence in different countries of Europe and [Africa].

From his mature experiences and broad outlook we believe that he will forge an adequate and keen instrument for the expression of genuine Negro talent.

SPIRITUAL TRUANCY
ALAIN LOCKE

When in 1928, from self-imposed exile, Claude McKay wrote *Home to Harlem,* many of us hoped that a prose and verse writer of stellar talent would himself come home, physically and psychologically, to take a warranted and helpful place in the group of "New Negro" writers. But although now back on the American scene and obviously attached to Harlem by literary adoption, this undoubted talent is still spiritually unmoored, and by the testimony of this latest book, is a longer way from home than ever. A critical reader would know this without his own confession; but Mr. McKay, exposing others, succeeds by chronic habit in exposing himself and paints an apt spiritual portrait in two sentences when he says: "I had wandered far and away until I had grown into a truant by nature and undomesticated in the blood"—and later,—"I am so intensely subjective as a poet, that I was not aware, at the moment of writing, that I was transformed into a medium to express a mass sentiment." All of which amounts to self-characterization as the unabashed "playboy of the Negro Renaissance."

Real spokesmanship and representative character in the "Negro Renaissance,"—or for that matter any movement, social or cultural,—may depend, of course, on many factors according to time and circumstance, but basic and essential, at least, are the acceptance of some group loyalty and the intent, as well as the ability, to express mass sentiment. Certainly and peculiarly in this case: otherwise the caption of race is a misnomer and the racial significance so irrelevant as to be silly. We knew before 1925 that Negroes could be poets; what we forecast and expected were Negro writers expressing a folk in expressing themselves. Artists have a right to be individuals, of course, but if their work assumes racial expression and interpretation, they must abide by it. On this issue, then, instead of repudiating racialism and its implied loyalties, Mr. McKay blows hot and cold with the same breath; erratically accepting and rejecting racial representatives, like a bad boy who admits he ought to go to school and then plays truant. It is this spiritual truancy which is the blight of his otherwise splendid talent.

Lest this seem condemnation out of court, let us examine the record. If out of a half dozen movements to which there could have been some deep loyalty of attachment, none has claimed McKay's whole-hearted support, then surely this career is not one of cosmopolitan experiment or even of innocent vagabondage, but, as I have already implied, one of chronic and perverse truancy. It is with the record of these picaresque wanderings that McKay crowds the pages of *A Long Way from Home.* First, there was a possible brilliant spokesmanship of the Jamaican peasant-folk, for it was as their balladist that McKay first attracted attention and help from his West Indian patrons. But that was soon discarded for a style and philosophy of aesthetic individualism in the then current mode of pagan impressionism. As the author of this personalism,—so unrecognizable after the tangy dialect of the Clarendon hill-folk,—

Your voice is the colour of a robin's breast
And there's a sweet sob in it like rain,
Still rain in the night among the leaves of the trumpet tree

McKay emigrated to our shores and shortly adopted the social realism and racial Negro notes of *Harlem Shadows* and *The Harlem Dancer.* These were among the first firmly competent accents of New Negro poetry, and though an adopted son, McKay was hailed as the day-star of that bright dawn. However, by his own admission playing off Max Eastman against Frank Harris and James Oppenheimer, he rapidly moved out toward the humanitarian socialism of *The Liberator* with the celebrated radical protest of *If We Must Die;* and followed that adventuresome flourish, still with his tongue in his cheek, to Moscow and the lavish hospitality and hero-worship of the Third Comintern. Then by a sudden repudiation there was a prolonged flight into expatriate cosmopolitanism and its irresponsible exoticisms. Even McKay admits the need for some apologia at this point. Granting, for the sake of argument, that the "adventure in Russia" and the association with *The Liberator* were not commitments to some variety of socialism (of this, the author says:—"I had no radical party affiliations, and there was no reason why I should consider myself under any special obligations to the Communists . . . I had not committed myself to anything. I had remained a free agent . . .") what, we may reasonably ask, about the other possible loyalty, on the basis of which the Russian ovation had been earned, viz,—the spokesmanship for the proletarian Negro? In the next breath, literally the next paragraph, McKay repudiates that also in the sentence we have already quoted:—"I was not aware, at the moment of writing, that I was transformed into a medium to express a mass sentiment." Yet the whole adventuresome career between 1918 and 1922, alike in Bohemian New York, literary Harlem and revolutionary Moscow, was predicated upon this assumed representativeness, cleverly exploited. One does not know whether to recall Peter before the triple cock-crow or Paul's dubious admonition about being "all things to all men." Finally, in the face of the obvious Bohemianism of the wanderings on the Riviera and in Morocco, we find McKay disowning common cause with the exotic cosmopolitans,—"my white fellow-expatriates," and claiming that "color-consciousness was the fundamental of my restlessness." Yet from this escapist escapade, we find our prodigal racialist returning expecting the fatted calf instead of the birch-rod, with a curtain lecture on "race salvation" from within and the necessity for a "Negro Messiah," whose glory he would like to celebrate "in a monument of verse."

Even a fascinating style and the naivest egotism cannot cloak such inconsistency or condone such lack of common loyalty. One may not dictate a man's loyalties, but must, at all events, expect him to have some. For a genius maturing in a decade of racial self-expression and enjoying the fruits of it all and living into a decade of social issues and conflict and aware of all that, to have repudiated all possible loyalties amounts to self-imposed apostasy. McKay is after all the dark-skinned psychological twin of that same

Frank Harris, whom he so cleverly portrays and caricatures; a versatile genius caught in the ego-centric predicament of aesthetic vanity and exhibitionism. And so, he stands to date, the *enfant terrible* of the Negro Renaissance, where with a little loyalty and consistency he might have been at least its Villon and perhaps its Voltaire.

If this were merely an individual fate, it could charitably go unnoticed. But in some vital sense these aberrations of spirit, this lack of purposeful and steady loyalty of which McKay is the supreme example have to a lesser extent vitiated much of the talent of the first generation of "New Negro" writers and artists. They inherited, it is true, a morbid amount of decadent aestheticism, which they too uncritically imitated. They also had to reckon with "shroud of color." To quote Countee Cullen, they can be somewhat forgiven for "sailing the doubtful seas" and for being tardily, and in some cases only half-heartedly led "to live persuaded by their own." But, with all due allowances, there was an unpardonable remainder of spiritual truancy and social irresponsibility. The folk have rarely been treated by these artists with unalloyed reverence and unselfish loyalty. The commitment to racial materials and "race expression" should be neither that of a fashionable and profitable fad nor of a condescending and missionary duty. The one great flaw of the first decade of the Negro Renaissance was its exhibitionist flair. It should have addressed itself more to the people themselves and less to the gallery of faddist Negrophiles. The task confronting the present younger generation of Negro writers and artists is to approach the home scene and the folk with high seriousness, deep loyalty, racial reverence of the unspectacular, unmelodramatic sort, and when necessary, sacrificial social devotion. They must purge this flippant exhibitionism, this posy but not too sincere racialism, this care-free and irresponsible individualism.

The program of the Negro Renaissance was to interpret the folk to itself, to vitalize it from within; it was a wholesome, vigorous, assertive racialism, even if not explicitly proletarian in conception and justification. McKay himself yearns for some such thing, no doubt, when he speaks in his last chapter of the Negro's need to discover his "group soul." A main aim of the New Negro movement will be unrealized so long as that remains undiscovered and dormant; and it is still the task of the Negro writer to be a main agent in evoking it, even if the added formula of proletarian art be necessary to cure this literary anaemia and make our art the nourishing life blood of the people rather than the caviar and cake of the artists themselves. Negro writers must become truer sons of the people, more loyal providers of spiritual bread and less aesthetic wastrels and truants of the streets.

BARREL STAVES
ARNA BONTEMPS

Skeeter Gordon was an exile. His friends in Harlem had turned on him. His young chocolate-colored wife had bristled like a porcupine and evicted him with sudden dispatch and finality. When the door banged behind him, Skeeter was sprawled face downward on a small landing a dozen steps below. He was convinced that Harlem was no longer safe for him. He had been cast from his last stronghold.

The explanation is simple: Skeeter was dishonest. He had double-crossed his young friends, the black boys who had stood by him; and he had deceived the girl who had taken up with him when he was ragged as a picked sparrow. He was a no-'count, ungrateful nigger, and he deserved the worst thing that could happen to him.

During his exile the lean spidery black boy took refuge in the upper Bronx. There, in the vicinity of East 225th Street, he found many other black faces sprinkled like pepper over the Jewish and Italian neighborhood. Here in this far end of the Bronx, however, he was a total stranger; and if he had no friends, neither had he enemies. Life, miserably tangled in Harlem, seemed to him very simple here; and best of all, it was safe.

He shuffled serenely down White Plains Avenue, his hands in his hip pockets, a tune on his lips.

> Walked de streets from sun to sun,
> Lawd, Lawd!
> Walked de streets from sun to sun—
> Ain't got no money an' don't want none.

He was coatless, with a frayed shirt and a pair of purplish blue pants that hit him six inches above the ankles; but as he walked he flapped his long comical feet proudly, swaying from one side of the pavement to the other, as if he owned the street.

"Heah's where I gits a fresh start," he told himself. "I gonna 'gin all over 'gin. I gonna git me a lil odd job an' a steady hard-workin' gal whut ain't so hot-haided an' settle down. Tha's whut I gonna do. I ain't gonna be no mo' devilish tramp. Hm!"

He turned into 223rd Street and lazied eastward in the bright afternoon sunlight. His slick round head glistened like ebony. After a month of stuffy Harlem pigeon-holes, this fresh air was a blessing. The Skeeter was feeling good and he didn't care who knew it. He was as happy as a colt in a new pasture.

"If it wa'n't so hot, I'd jus break and run," he said. "I feels lak another nigger. I done almost forgit ma name's bad-luck Skeeter."

There were two or three small apartment houses at long intervals in the block between the rows of private dwellings. On the sidewalk, in front of one of the smallest of these tenements, Skeeter saw black youngsters playing. That indicated the sort of place he had been seeking. He flopped on the step, stretched his incredible legs, produced from his pockets a mashed-up-palm-leaf fan and leaned back to refresh himself.

"Ah!" he grunted. "Hm!"

The children frisked wildly about his feet. Since he had decided to remain in this part of the city, his interest kept running out to those features of the neighborhood that might effect his living. He wondered about the sources of food, about a place to sleep. Given a chance, he could at that very moment have punished a stiff bait of victuals. And as for sleeping, that was never out of the question. He could always sleep. He could sleep standing up. The fact that he felt drowsy there in the sunshine, on the warm concrete steps, was neither odd or significant.

Presently an old rheumatic Negro came up from the basement and eyed Skeeter pleasantly. The old fellow wore a pair of striped overalls and a battered cap that had once, perhaps, belonged to some steamboat man. His face was matted with frizzly whiskers, and Skeeter noticed that he was not more than five feet tall.

"He-o, fas' company," the old fellow offered.

"He-o, Cap'n," Skeeter grinned.

"Is you a Harlem boy?"

"Hm. I was, I ain't no mo'. I done leave town."

"Dis heah is a slow-time place for city niggers."

"You reckon I can find me a lil odd job an' a place to sleep round heah, Cap'n?"

The old sawed-off black looked the long indolent boy up and down.

"Is you any 'count?"

"Me? I's one mo' hard workin' nigger, Cap'n. I's de workingest nigger you mos' ever set eyes on."

"Yo' look is kind o' deceivin'. Reckon you could tote a ash can up these heah steps by yo'self?"

Skeeter tried to show scorn. "Shucks! I could come up them there steps wid a ash can under both arms an' one on ma back."

"Lemme study a minute. If you's worth a dime, you might could stay heah an' sleep in de boiler room an' help me wid de garbage an' wid de ash cans."

They descended the steps to the basement and Skeeter followed the Cap'n down a dark hallway. The old fellow pointed out the boiler room, the little hot-water furnace, the coal bins, and the dumb waiter shafts. Half a dozen large cans were arranged against the wall.

"Heah they is," the Cap'n said.

But Skeeter was no longer interested. His head was raised; his eyes were turned skyward; he had caught a glimpse of something two floors above that deflected his attention. A glossy velvet-skinned young woman was standing at the window, her face split with a huge smile.

The black girl was evidently in the midst of her cooking. In one hand she held a dish rag, in the other a long-handled spoon. And there was an odor of food pouring from her window, an odor so strong and compelling it made Skeeter's jaws hang apart like a pair of tongs.

Suddenly the young woman turned away from the window and burst into song:

> "Ma daddy is a business man, a business man,
> Keys in his pocket an' a diamond on his han."

"I done decide, Cap'n." Skeeter said.

"It's your'n if it suits you."

"It suits me good, Cap'n. Look out o' ma way now whilst I shows you how to tote three ash cans at a time."

Skeeter's little gesture in the areaway did not go unnoticed. Adina, the velvety gal at the kitchen window, saw him juggling the heavy cans and she was deeply impressed.

"Hush ma mouth wide open," she exclaimed. "Wonder where de Super' found dat old good-lookin' devil."

She forgot her pots. Resting her elbows on the window sill, leaning as far out as she dared, she became engrossed in the performance below. Suddenly she shouted:

"Hey Super! Look lak you gonna have some help?"

"Yeah, Miss Dina, I done got me a 'sistant."

"Reckon he any 'count?"

"Don't know yet, but I gonna put him through de mill directly."

"Whyn't you send him up heah an' start him on dis sink o' mine, whut I been tryin' to git you to fix ever since las' month?"

"Das a notion, Miss Dina." The Cap'n dropped his eyes. Skeeter was returning empty-handed. The old fellow pointed to the gal in the window. "Dat lady yonder is havin' trouble wid her sink. You mind lookin' at it for me?"

Skeeter threw another glance upwards.

"Open de door, Miss Sheba, I's comin' up fas' an' I is apt to bus' it down."

He made a break for the tools. When Adina reached the door he was already there. He arched his neck and entered the little kitchen. The room was bursting with the odors of frying meat and onions, boiling vegetables and ham hocks. Skeeter stood in the center of the floor, dazed by his surroundings.

"M-m-m!" He shook his head expressively, "I ain't been this close to a bait o' good old home cookin' in mo' days'n I can count."

"You's right pitiful."

"Sho is. De womens in Harlem was fixin' to let me die. Tha's how come me out heah."

"Dis heah is a mo' betta place to die," she said compassionately. "Was you to pass out in one o' dem cellars in Harlem, de rats'd eat you."

He shuddered. "Dat dey would. But I gonna die out heah on y'all's hands."

"Whyn't you try me on a lil smell o' dem victuals you's cookin'? You'll see what a big diff'ence it'll make in papa Skeeter."

Adina was a short, big-hipped girl. She wore a checkered house dress without sleeves, and as she carried on with Skeeter she leaned against the ice box with obvious coquetry.

"Maby I will an' maby I won't," she said. "I gonna wait an' see how good you fixes ma sink."

Skeeter banged the tool box on the floor.

"You ole big eyed sumpin o' nuther."

He quickly disconnected the drain, fitted a new washer, then reattached the pipe. It was like sleight-of-hand. Skeeter was a case. He was one of the most handiest boys Adina had ever set eyes on.

"How dat suit you, Miss?"

"Ah, so-so," she said. "I 'spect you'll do."

Adina took a large plate from the shelf, heaped it to capacity and placed it at a tiny rickety table. Skeeter adjusted a chair, stretched his legs and went to work.

That one mighty meal did not satisfy Skeeter for long, however, and the next day he was out job-hunting. The sun had come up strong and the streets were dry and dusty. Dust had settled on the leaves of the trees like powder. A string of empty milk wagons lined the curb near 219th Street. The proprietors of countless fruit stands were busy arranging their displays. These impressed Skeeter. He planted himself in front of one, drew his fan and stood calmly inspecting the pyramids of red apples, ripe oranges and yellow pears.

"Dog if dat ain't a sight," he mused. "Tha's jest nachal-born putty."

Around the heaps of bright fruit were designs of fresh mustard greens, lettuce, spinach, cabbages and collards, green onions, carrots, beets, asparagus—all looking fresh and moist as if they had never been harvested, as if the natural dew was still on them. From the ceiling suspended great bunches of bananas, ripe and yellow and fine. And elsewhere strings of crimson peppers hung against the walls, strings of dried figs and mushrooms. Mountains of earth-colored potatoes rose in the background, and cocoanuts were scattered among the green things as if literally dropped there from the trees. Watermelons lay about the floor, between the sacks and baskets.

Skeeter was too absorbed to move. He stood in the middle of the sidewalk, the palm leaf fan in his hand, mouth open. His little glossy head suggested a billiard ball.

The fruit man's small motor truck, parked at the curb, was still partly loaded with crates and boxes of vegetables from the wholesale market. Angelo had neglected it for the moment and was passing over his display with a water sprinkler to protect the greens from the wilting heat of the sun. A few morning customers, too, had begun to require his attention. He was a short, thickly built Italian with loose curly hair, a white apron, and a tiny cap on the back of his head. At the moment his face was red with the hurry and excitement of setting his stand in order.

"M-m!" Skeeter ejaculated. "Dat gits it. Tha's howdy-do, I thank you."

"Yeah? You like um?"

"I'm tellin' you."

"You wanna buy some nice sweet oranges? bananas? apples?"

"You done mistook me, Mistah. I couldn't buy a pair o' slippers for a muskeeter. Money an' me ain't speakin'. I's jes studyin' 'bout you in dis great big fruit sto' by yo'self. You oughta have a black boy to keep it all sweep up nice an' clean an' unload de truck an' one thing an' another."

Angelo inspected the long boy carefully. Then he looked at his floor and his half-loaded truck. That was an idea, especially since Skeeter appeared to be such inexpensive help. A boy as ragged as this bare-headed stranger surely wouldn't have a large salary in mind.

"You t'ink so, hunh? You like-a job?"

"Yes suh, me like-a'," Skeeter grinned. "Me 'like-a plenty."

"Al'ight. Sweep um up." He thrust a broom into Skeeter's hands. "You good boy, maybe I keep you."

"Yes suh!"

Skeeter commenced working with a flourish that won the Italian's eye immediately. His broom danced over the floor with a grace and skill like magic. Not a straw or leaf was missed. That finished he turned to the truck, unloaded the remainder of the vegetables, quickly transported them through the store out into the shady back yard, and covered them with wet sacks.

Angelo sat on a box watching the performance. He became limber with amusement and good humor. When Skeeter finished, the fruit man gave him a handful of over-ripe bananas and sent him into the back yard to eat. Skeeter grinned as he disappeared. He felt sure that he had at last landed on his feet.

"I knows when I's well off," he told himself." "I done got lucky again. I done got dat fresh start, an' I ain't fixin' to muff it neither. No suh."

He sat down beneath the horse-chestnut tree that leaned across the fence and began skinning and devouring the ripe fruit.

Later in the afternoon Skeeter discovered a little two-wheeled delivery cart upturned behind a stack of old boxes, out of use. That gave him another thought. He could now become delivery man for Angelo. And that would given him an opportunity to go about the neighborhood and seek amusement during the midday lull. He visualized himself majestically piloting the empty cart over the rugged side streets, bumping and rattling it with an air of great importance. He could imagine the womenfolks of the neighborhood high-balling him from the kitchen windows, beseeching him to hurry back with a soup bunch or a mess of new potatoes.

"Heah where I puts some git-up in these lil ole sleepy streets," he thought. "When papa Skeeter gits on de road, folks gonna sit up an' take notice. To heah me comin', they gonna think I's drivin' de fire wagon, cause I aims to travel wid horns and drums."

He adjusted a small flat strip of wood on the body of the cart in such a manner as to clap against each spoke when the wheel turned. He hung a tin can to the axle by a string just long enough to let the bottom of the can reach the ground. In the can he put nails and bits of iron, such things as he thought would make a first rate noise to help remind folks that papa Skeeter was on the road.

Angelo was satisfied. If this overgrown black idiot wanted to rattle around the neighborhood with that old discarded cart, he was welcome to do so.

Angelo frequently had need of a delivery boy; had in fact, on several occasions hired school boys for this purpose, but he saw no reason why the cart would be needed. In that, however, he let Skeeter have his wish.

Angelo was so well pleased with the comical boy he had hired that on the third day he made the mistake of leaving Skeeter alone in the fruit store. Skeeter began immediately to explore the spaces beneath the counter, the backs of the shelves, and the dark corners of the back room. Within a few moment he had found and substantially damaged a jug of Angelo's private wine.

Meanwhile Skeeter's interest in Adina had stood still. Once or twice since his meal in her kitchen, she had yelled at him pleasantly in the areaway. But he was no better acquainted than he had been the first day he saw her. He wasn't even sure that she would be eligible for his attentions; not knowing her well, he couldn't guess what she would require of a gentleman who came to court her regularly. Now that he was settled, with a job in the fruit store and a cot in the furnace room, she got on his mind again.

"Wonder whut ole good-lookin' Dina's doin'," he worried. "Guess she think I done plum forget her. She right, too; I been had me mind on work, an' I been eatin' and drinkin' so much on de side I wa'nt fittin' for nuthin' but sleep when I knocked off in de evenin'."

Skeeter was returning to the fruit store with his empty cart, down a quiet tree-shaded street. The sun was low, the yellow light flashing directly in the black boy's eyes. He had walked rapidly and was dripping with sweat, but he felt good. He felt like chewing the rag with some such big-eyed gal as Adina.

He brought his cart booming into the back alley and wheeled it into the yard behind the fruit store. Then he went inside to tell Angelo he was ready to go home. The fat Italian was nodding on his box. He grunted when Skeeter spoke but paid him no attention. Skeeter's eyes rolled in their deep sockets. As Angelo sank back into slumber the boy quickly grabbed up a small bunch of bananas, perhaps a dozen, and three large cocoanuts. With these under his arms he flashed through the back door.

Skeeter went directly to Adina's apartment and rang the bell. She came to the door, mopping the perspiration from her face with the corner of her · apron.

"Look lak I's too late." Skeeter said.

"Too late for what?"

"For supper. Ain't you done boarded?"

"Is you hungry? Adina settled back on her heels and seemed exasperated.

"I ain't huntin' grub, sweetness," Skeeter smiled. "I's bringin' you sumpin'. Reckon you could make 'way wid these?"

"Could I! I done et a lil bit," she admitted, "but I ain't half full."

"Well pitch in, baby. Gimme sumpin' to crack these heah cocoanuts wid."

Skeeter went to work on the hard shells with the aid of a flat iron.

Adina was a matter-of-fact young woman, and one who was not ashamed to eat in the presence of masculine company. Neither was she embarrassed by her weight and the surplus flesh under her chin. She smacked her lips with pleasure as she masticated the cocoanut meat.

Skeeter enjoyed watching her. Tilted backwards and rocking on two legs of his chair, it occurred to him that he and Adina had a great deal in common. Each of them had ravenous appetites and they seemed to like the same foods. That had not been true of the thin hot-tempered girl in Harlem with whom he had failed to live in harmony and from whom he had fled. She liked cold meats, pickles, delicatessen foods; and that sort of thing had irked the Skeeter. Adina was more like his kind, a gal with a taste for tropical fruits, green vegetables, and pork meat. It was time, he figured, they become better acquainted.

"Is you a single gal, 'Dina?"

"Well yes 'n no. I's a widder woman."

"Oh."

"Ma ole man got hisself a job on de railroad an' I ain't seen head or tail o' him since."

"He done disert you?"

"Um hunh! Tha's it."

"Devilish scoundrel! A nigger lak dat ain't fit to have a good steady woman."

"Sho ain't. But y'all menfolks is putty much all de same."

"Don't say dat, sweetness." Skeeter was deeply serious. "I ain't one o' dem jack rabbit mens. I's a true-love boy."

"Yo' looks is kinda deceivin', papa Skeeter."

"Eve'ybody tell me dat," he said. "That de firs' thing de Cap'n met me wid. I don't know whut cause it neither."

"Maybe it's a birthmark."

"Mus' be is."

"You ain't never run off an' lef' a lovin' woman whut was good to you?"

"Not lessen she sent me 'way," he vowed. "I been married wid a old hot-haided gal once—signed up at de cou't house an' got a receipt an' ev'ything—but it ain't 'mounted to a hill o' beans. Dat gal kicked me out head foremost an' tore up the permit an' th'owed it at me."

"So you's a widder, too?"

"I mean."

"An' you ain't goin' back?"

"How can I go back when she done tore up de permit. I's free as a jay bird."

"Tha's a notion," she said. "I b'lieve I'll tear up mine, too."

Skeeter rolled his eyes at Adina. "Hmp! Tha's whut you gonna have to do," he said. "I gonna see to dat."

"Why you so worried up?"

"I feels ma love comin' down. Tha's how come I's worried. You an' me's gonna be sweet if I's got anything to say 'bout it."

"Hm. You ain't got nuthin' to say 'bout it though, long boy. I'm gonna wait an' make up ma own mind 'bout dat."

413

"You betta make it up in a hurry," he commanded, " 'cause if yo' don't I'm apt to make it up for you."

They understood each other. Skeeter reared back, open his mouth wide enough to swallow a cocoanut and emitted a gale of laughter that could be heard half a mile. Adina chirped and giggled so hard tears came to her eyes, and the fat on her shoulders shook like jelly.

The next day Skeeter brought Adina a half dozen of Angelo's biggest and finest yams. He hid them in his shirt and slipped away with them while the Italian fruit store man nodded in the entrance of his shop. Adina was delighted and, in return, invited the long boy to stay for dinner. While the two were bending over the steaming plates, she mentioned something to him that was on her mind.

"Is you goin' to de New Covenant bus ride?"

"Whut ole New Covenant bus ride?" Skeeter corrugated his brow. "I ain't heared 'bout no sich come-off."

"No? It's gonna be next week. It's sumpin'."

"Good time, hunh?"

"I mean. Righteous."

"How come you ain't invited me to come an' be yo' company?"

"Cause you ain't give me time. I's jes fixin' to say would you like to 'tend?"

"I like to go anywheres you gonna be, honey. All I wants to do is to be wid you. Tha's all I studies 'bout now."

"Well now, 'bout goin' wid me, I er . . . . I gotta 'splain dat. Brother Sam Chalmers, de 'sistant shepherd at New Covenant, got his head set on bein' ma company, too."

Skeeter's mouth fell open. It closed and opened again, but no words came. His eye blinked. He swallowed a lump in his throat. Still he was unable to talk. Adina, seeing that he was paralyzed, hurried to his rescue.

"Course I ain't give him ma word yet," she said. "I jes waitin' to see how you'd take it."

Skeeter regained his strength with a long sigh.

"Honey," he said, "I gonna be so close to you dat day de Brother Sam Chalmers ain't gonna be able to see you for me. An' dat ain't all. I'm gonna bring you an' me mo' good stuff from de fruit sto' 'n you can shake a stick at."

"Dat suits me, son. I'll jes fix up some fried chicken an' sandwiches an' things like that. An' if you makes a good showin' wid de fruits we'll be set for de day."

" 'Pend on me, baby."

"You'll have to be on de spot early, too. De bus gonna pull out at eight o'clock sharp."

Skeeter smiled broadly. "I'm gonna be sittin' on de church house steps at ha'-past seben."

During the days that intervened, Skeeter walked on air. Time after time he unfolded the prospects of that bus ride and picnic in his mind as he expected them to materialize. He would work late the preceding night, however, and while the boss was busy with the last of the customers he would sneak the fruit he wanted into the back room, put it in a basket and cover it. Then he would be careful to unlock the back window. This would enable him to come in by way of the alley, get the fruit and carry it away while Angelo was off with the truck doing the regular wholesale marketing. On the bus and at the picnic, there would be nothing but bliss. Skeeter could see himself lolling on a green spot, legs crossed, a chicken bone in his hand and Adina smiling affectionately at his side, while Brother Sam Chalmers shot malicious glances at them and wrung his hands.

He planned and selected the basket of fruit with an eye toward impressing Adina. The gift should be the last necessary ounce. He had started well, he would be sure to finish strong. To be Adina's company on that bus ride, in the presence of all the church folks would be like a banner in his hand. That was what he wanted. He wanted the world to know he was papa Skeeter from Harlem, the shiniest black boy in that end of town and a devil with the gals.

With these notions stirring in his head, he began the pleasant chore of selecting the fruit. He hid a basket under a pile of sacks in the back room. Then, throughout the day, at such times as he found Angelo's back turned, he slipped oranges, apples, pears, bananas, cocoanuts and canteloupes into it. Skeeter was deft on this business. It was not new to him. And when the day preceding the bus ride came, he had a lunch basket assortment worthy of any picnic. It was so "worthy," in fact, Skeeter wondered how he could get the thing away. He lifted it at a time to make sure he could handle it conveniently. Yes, he could manage. Then Skeeter put his shoulders back, smiled from ear to ear, and poked out his chest.

The next morning he was out at the crack of day. And when the time came for Angelo to be away with the truck, Skeeter slipped quietly into the yard behind the fruit store.

The window, through which it was necessary to get the basket, had no weight or pulleys. It was a heavy window, and Skeeter could not hold it up while lifting the fruit. So he found a stick of suitable length and with it propped the pane. He then put his head and shoulders through the waist-high window and reached for his treasure.

But as he leaned forward in this position a surprising thing happened. The window came down suddenly with a bang that left Skeeter pinned as tightly as a mouse in a trap, his head and shoulders inside, his body and legs outside.

Angelo, suspecting his store-boy's dishonesty for some days, had discerned Skeeter's plans and set himself accordingly. When Skeeter got his head well through the window, the Italian had quickly slipped from behind the boxes where he was crouched and withdrawn the stick supporting the heavy pane.

So the Skeeter was helpless. Inside, his little head was all mouth and eyes, bellowing like forty bulls and blazing fire. Outside, his lean frog-like hindparts wriggled and twisted and beat the air. Angelo went calmly to the corner of the yard, selected a barrel, crushed it, returned with an arm full of staves, took a firm position with heels braced, and began studiously breaking the staves one at a time across the protruding legs and body.

In the meantime a crowd gathered in front of the New Covenant Church. The bus was filled. The driver insisted on getting away on schedule. The motor rumbled and the heavy vehicle pulled out.

Skeeter came around the corner limping like a man with rheumatism, bruised, crestfallen, and empty-handed. He stood with stooped shoulders, nursing his bruises and watching the diminishing picture of his own dreams plowing down the yellow road, obscured by a cloud of dust.

One thing was very distinct. In the back seat was old big-eyed Adina, and beside her the Brother Sam Chalmers. The glossy black deacon was wearing a new milk-white straw hat. His face was split by a smile that rippled like an ocean wave. He was swollen worse than a pouter pigeon, and as he leaned back caressing Adina's broad shoulders with affection and triumph, he shot mean and spiteful glances over his shoulder.

Skeeter blinked, rubbed his tiny slick head and turned his face in the opposite direction. He drew the palm-leaf fan from his pocket, refreshed himself and started walking.

"I'm going back to Harlem," he decided. "This heah place is bad luck."

WIDOW WITH A MORAL OBLIGATION
HELENE JOHNSON

Won't you come again, my friend?
I'll not be so shy.
I shall have a candle lit
To light you by.
I shall have my hair unbound,
My gown undone,
And we shall have a night of love
And death in one.
I was very foolish
To have run away before,
But you see I thought I heard
Him knocking at the door,
But you see I thought I saw
Him smiling in your smile,
And I saw his lips call
Me something very vile.
It must have been my conscience
Or a quirk in my head,
For I knew he'd been
A long time dead.

We buried him one morning
In the sweet cool rain.
But when you come tonight,
We must bury him again.
You must come and rid me
Of my dear leal wraith.
We can bury him so easy
When he's lost his faith.
Stab with little poniards—
Every kiss will be a knife.
And we will be cruel,
For life is life.
Ah come again, my friend,
I'll not be so shy.
I shall have a candle lit
To light you by.
I shall have my hair unbound,
My gown undone,
And we shall have a night of love
And death in one.

POEM
LANGSTON HUGHES

Wandering in the dusk,
Sometimes
You get lost in the dusk—
And sometimes not.

Beating your fists against the wall,
Sometimes
You break your bones
Against the wall—
But sometimes not.

Walls have been known
To fall,
Dusk
Turn to dawn,
Chains
To be gone!

Keep on!

417

ALWAYS THE SAME
LANGSTON HUGHES

It is the same everywhere for me:
On the docks at Sierra Leone,
In the cotton fields of Alabama,
In the diamond mines of Kimberley,
On the coffee hills of Hayti,
The banana lands of Central America,
The streets of Harlem,
And the cities of Morocco and Tripoli.

Black:
Exploited, beaten and robbed,
Shot and killed.
Blood running into
  Dollars
  Pounds
  Francs
  Pesetas
  Lire
For the wealth of the exploiters—
Blood that never comes back to me again.
Better that my blood
Runs into the deep channels of Revolution,
Runs into the strong hands of Revolution,
Stains all flags red,
Drives me away from
  Sierra Leone
  Kimberley
  Alabama
  Hayti
  Central America
  Harlem
  Morocco
  Tripoli
And all the black lands everywhere.
The force that kills,
The power that robs,
And the greed that does not care.

Better that my blood makes one with the blood
Of all the struggling workers in the world—
Till every land is free of
  Dollar robbers
  Pound robbers

Franc robbers
Peseta robbers
Lire robbers
Life robbers—
Until the Red Armies of the International Proletariat
Their faces, black, white, olive, yellow, brown,
Unite to raise the blood-red flag that
Never will come down!

GOODBYE, CHRIST
LANGSTON HUGHES

Listen, Christ,
You did alright in your day, I reckon—
But that day's gone now.
They ghosted you up a swell story, too,
Called it Bible—
But it's dead now.
The popes and the preachers've
Made too much money from it.
They've sold you to too many

Kings, generals, robbers, and killers—
Even to the Tzar and the Cossacks,
Even to Rockefeller's Church,
Even to THE SATURDAY EVENING POST.
You ain't no good no more.
They've pawned you
Till you've done wore out.

Goodbye,
Christ Jesus Lord God Jehova,
Beat it on away from here now.
Make way for a new guy with no religion at all—
A real guy named
Marx Communist Lenin Peasant Stalin Worker ME—

I said, ME!

Go ahead on now,
You're getting in the way of things, Lord.
And please take Saint Ghandi with you when you go,
And Saint Pope Pius,
And Saint Aimee McPherson,
And big black Saint Becton

Of the Consecrated Dime.
Move!

Don't be so slow about movin'!
The world is mine from now on—
And nobody's gonna sell ME
To a king, or a general,
Or a millionaire.

LONG BLACK SONG
RICHARD WRIGHT

I

Go t sleep, baby
Papas gone t town
Go t sleep, baby
The suns goin down
Go t sleep, baby
Yo candys in the sack
Go t sleep, baby
Papas comin back . . .

Over and over she crooned, and at each lull of her voice she rocked the wooden cradle with a bare black foot. But the baby squalled louder, its wail drowning out the song. She stopped and stood over the cradle, wondering what was bothering it, if its stomach hurt. She felt the diaper; it was dry. She lifted it up and patted its back. Still it cried, longer and louder. She put it back into the cradle and dangled a string of red beads before its eyes. The little black fingers clawed them away. She bent over, frowning, murmuring: "Whuts the mattah, chile? Yuh wan some watah?" she held a dripping gourd to the black lips, but the baby turned its head and kicked its legs. She stood a moment, perplexed. Whuts wrong wid that chile? She ain never carried on like this this tima day. She picked it up and went to the open door. "See the sun, baby?" she asked, pointing to a big ball of red dying between the branches of trees. The baby pulled back and strained its round black arms and legs against her stomach and shoulders. She knew it was tired; she could tell by the halting way it opened its mouth to draw in air. She sat on a wooden stool, unbuttoned the front of her dress, brought the baby closer and offered it a black teat. "Don baby wan suppah?" It pulled away and went limp, crying softly, piteously, as though it would never stop. Then it pushed its fingers against her breasts and wailed. Lawd, chile, what yuh wan? Yo ma cant help yuh less she knows whut yuh wan. Tears gushed; four white teeth flashed in red gums; the little chest heaved up and down and round black fingers stretched floorward. Lawd, child, whuts wrong wid yuh? She stooped slowly, allowing her body to be guided by the downward tug. As soon as the little fingers touched the floor the wail quieted into a broken sniffle. She turned the baby loose and watched it crawl toward a corner. She followed and saw the little fingers reach for the tail-end of an old eight-day clock. "Yuh wan tha ol clock?" She dragged the clock into the center of the floor. The baby crawled after it, calling, "Ahh!" Then it raised its hands and beat on the top of the clock Bink! Bink! Bink! "Naw, yuhll hurt yo hans!" She held the baby and looked around. It cried and struggled. "Wait, baby!" She fetched a small stick from the top of a rickety dresser. "Here," she said, closing the little fingers about it. "Beat wid this, see?" She heard each blow landing squarely on top of the clock Bang! Bang! Bang! And with each bang the baby smiled and said, "Ahh!" Mabbe thall keep yuh quiet erwhile. Maybe Ah kin git some res now. She stood in the doorway. Lawd, tha chiles a pain! She mus be teethin. Er something . . .

She wiped sweat from her forehead with the bottom of her dress and looked out over the green fields rolling up the hillsides. She sighed, fighting a feeling of loneliness. Lawd, its sho hard t pass the days wid Silas gone. Been mos a week now since he took the wagon outta here. Hope ain nothin wrong. He must be buyin a heapa stuff there in Colwatah t be stayin all this time. Yes; maybe Silas would remember and bring that five-yard piece of red calico she wanted. Oh, Lawd! Ah _hope_ he don fergit it!

She saw green fields wrapped in the thickening gloom. It was as if they had left the earth, those fields, and were floating slowly skyward. The afterglow lingered, red, dying, somehow tenderly sad. And far away, in front of her, earth and sky met in a soft swoon of shadow. A cricket chirped, sharp and lonely; and it seemed she could hear it chirping long after it had stopped. Silas oughta c mon soon. Ahm tireda staying here by mahsef.

Loneliness ached in her. She swallowed, hearing Bang! Bang! Bang! Tom been gone t war mos a year now. N tha ol wars over n we ain heard nothing yit. Lawd, don let Tom be dead! She frowned into the gloom and wondered about that awful war so far away. They said it was over now. Yeah, Gawd had t stop em fo they killed everybody. She felt that merely to go so far away from home was a kind of death in itself. Just to go that far away was to be killed. Nothing good could come from men going miles across the sea to fight. N how come they wanna kill each other? How come they wanna make blood? Killing was not what men ought to do. Shucks! she thought.

She sighed, thinking of Tom, hearing Bang! Bang! Bang! She saw Tom, saw his big black smiling face; her eyes went dreamily blank, drinking in the red afterglow. Yes, God; it could have been Tom instead of Silas who was having her now. Yes; it could have been Tom she was loving. She smiled and asked herself, Lawd, Ah wondah how would it been wid Tom? Against the plush sky she saw a white bright day and a green cornfield and she saw Tom walking in his overalls and she was with Tom and he had his arm about her waist. She remembered how weak she had felt feeling his fingers sinking into the flesh of her hips. Her knees had trembled and she had had a hard time trying to stand up and not just sink right there to the ground. Yes;

that was what Tom had wanted her to do. But she had held Tom up and he had held her up; they had held each other up to keep from slipping to the ground there in the green cornfield. Lawd! Her breath went and she passed her tongue over her lips. But that was not as exciting as that winter evening when the grey skies were sleeping and she and Tom were coming home from church down dark Lover's Lane. She felt the tips of her teats tingling and touching the front of her dress as she remembered how he had crushed her against him and hurt her. She had closed her eyes and was smelling the acrid scent of dry October leaves and had gone weak in his arms and had felt she could not breathe any more and had torn away and run, run home. And the sweet ache which had frightened her then was stealing back to her loins now with the silence and the cricket calls and the red afterglow and Bang! Bang! Bang! Lawd, Ah wondah how would it been wid Tom?

She stepped out on the porch and leaned against the wall of the house. Sky sang a red song. Fields whispered a green prayer. And song and prayer were dying in silence and shadow. Never in all her life had she been so much alone as she was now. Days were never so long as these days; and nights were never so empty as these nights. She jerked her head impatiently, hearing Bang! Bang! Bang! Shucks! she thought. When Silas had gone something had ebbed so slowly that at first she had not noticed it. Now she felt all of it as though the feeling had no bottom. She tried to think just how it had happened. Yes; there had been all her life the long hope of white bright days and the deep desire of dark black nights and then Silas had gone. Bang! Bang! Bang! There had been laughter and eating and singing and the long gladness of green cornfields in summer. There had been cooking and sewing and sweeping and the deep dream of sleeping grey skies in winter. Always it had been like that and she had been happy. But no more. The happiness of those days and nights, of those green cornfields and grey skies had started to go from her when Tom had gone to war. His leaving had left an empty black hole in her heart, a black hole that Silas had come in and filled. But not quite. Silas had not quite filled that hole. No; days and nights were not as they were before.

She lifted her chin, listening. She had heard something, a dull throb like she had heard that day Silas had called her outdoors to look at the airplane. Her eyes swept the sky. But there was no plane. Mabbe its behin the house? She stepped into the yard and looked upward through paling light. There were only a few big wet stars trembling in the east. Then she heard the throb again. She turned, looking up and down the road. The throb grew louder, droning; and she heard Bang! Bang! Bang! There! A car! Wondah whuts a car doin coming out here? A black car was winding over a dusty road, coming toward her. Mabbe some white mans bringing Silas home wida loada goods? But, Lawd, Ah *hope* its no trouble! The car stopped in front of the house and a white man got out. Wondah whut he wans? She looked at the car, but could not see Silas. The white man was young; he wore a straw hat and had no coat. He walked toward her with a huge black package under his arm.

422

"Well, howre yuh today, Aunty?"

"Ahm well. How yuh?"

"Oh, so-so. Its sure hot today, hunh?"

She brushed her hand across her forehead and sighed.

"Yeah; it is kinda warm."

"You busy?"

"Naw, Ah ain doin nothin."

"Ive got something to show you. Can I sit here, on your porch?"

"Ah reckon so. But, Mistah, Ah ain got no money."

"Haven't you sold your cotton yet?"

"Silas gone t town wid it now."

"Whens he coming back?"

"Ah don know. Ahm waitin fer im."

She saw the white man take out a handkerchief and mop his face. Bang! Bang! Bang! He turned his head and looked through the open doorway, into the front room.

"Whats all that going on in there?"

She laughed.

"Aw, thas jus Ruth."

"Whats she doing?"

"She beatin tha ol clock."

"Beating a *clock?*"

She laughed again.

"She wouldn't go t sleep so Ah give her tha ol clock t play wid."

The white man got up and went to the front door; he stood a moment looking at the black baby hammering on the clock. Bang! Bang! Bang!

"But why let her tear your clock up?"

"It ain no good."

"You could have it fixed."

"We ain got no money t be fixin' no clocks."

"Haven't you got a clock?"

"Naw."

"But how do you keep time?"

"We git erlong widout time."

"But how do you know when to get up in the morning?"

"We jus git up, thas all."

"But how do you know what time it is when you get up?"

"We git up wid the sun."

"And at night, how do you tell when its night?"

"It gits dark when the sun goes down."

"Haven't you ever had a clock?"

She laughed and turned her face toward the silent fields. "Mistah, we don need no clock."

"Well, this beats everything! I don't see how in the world anybody can live without time."

"We just don need no time, Mistah."

The white man laughed and shook his head; she laughed and looked at him. The white man was funny. Jus like lil boy. Astin how do Ah know when t git up in the mawnin! She laughed again and mused on the baby, hearing Bang! Bang! Bang! She could hear the white man breathing at her side; she felt his eyes on her face. She looked at him; she saw he was looking at her breasts. Hes jus lika lil boy. Acks like he cant understand *nothin!*

"But you need a clock," the white man insisted. "Thats what Im out here for. I'm selling clocks and graphophones. The clocks are made right into the graphophones, a nice sort of combination, hunh? You can have music and time all at once. Ill show you . . ."

"Mistah, we don need no clock!"

"You dont have to buy it. It wont cost you anything just to look."

He unpacked the big black box. She saw the strands of his auburn hair glinting in the afterglow. His back bulged against his white shirt as he stooped. He pulled out a square brown graphophone. She bent forward, looking. Lawd, but its pretty! She saw the face of a clock under the horn of the graphophone. The gilt on the corners sparkled. The color in the wood glowed softly. It reminded her of the light she saw sometimes in the baby's eyes. Slowly she slid a finger over a beveled edge; she wanted to take the box into her arms and kiss it.

"Its eight o'clock," he said.

"Yeah?"

"It only costs fifty dollars. And you dont have to pay for it all at once. Just five dollars down and five dollars a month."

She smiled. The white man was just like a little boy. Jus like a chile. She saw him grinding the handle of the box.

There was a sharp, scratching noise; then she moved nervously, her body caught in the ringing coils of music.

When the trumpet of the Lord shall sound . . .

She rose on circling waves of white bright days and dark black nights.

. . . and tume shall be no more . . .

Higher and higher she mounted.

And the morning breaks . . .

Earth fell far behind, forgotten.

. . . eternal, bright and fair . .

Echo after echo sounded.

When the saved of the earth shall gather . . .

Her blood surged like the long gladness of summer.

. . . over the other shore . . .

Her blood ebbed like the deep dream of sleep in winter.

And when the roll is called up yonder . . .

She gave up, holding her breath.

I'll be there . . .

A lump filled her throat. She leaned her back against a post, trembling, feeling the rise and fall of days and nights, of summer and winter; surging, ebbing, leaping about her, beyond her, far out over the fields to where earth and sky lay folded in darkness. She wanted to lie down and sleep, or else leap up and shout. When the music stopped she felt herself coming back, being let down slowly. She sighed. It was dark now. She looked into the doorway. The baby was sleeping on the floor. Ah gotta git up n put tha chile t bed, she thought.

"Wasn't that pretty?"

"It wuz pretty, awright."

"When do you think your husbands coming back?"

"Ah don know, Mistah."

She went into the room and put the baby into the cradle. She stood again in the doorway and looked at the shadowy box that had lifted her up and carried her away. Crickets called. The dark sky had swallowed up the earth, and more stars were hanging, clustered, burning. She heard the white man sigh. His face was lost in shadow. She saw him rub his palms over his forehead. Hes jus lika lil boy.

"Id like to see your husband tonight," he said. "Ive got to be in Lilydale at six o'clock in the morning and I wont be back through here soon. I got to pick up my buddy over there and we're heading North."

She smiled into the darkness. He was just like a little boy. A little boy selling clocks.

"Yuh sell them things alla time?" she asked.

"Just for the summer," he said. "I go to school in winter. If I can make enough money out of this Ill go to Chicago to school this fall . . ."

"Whut yuh gonna be?"

"*Be?* What do you mean?"

"Whut yuh goin to school fer?"

"Im studying science."

"Whuts tha?"

"Oh, er . . ." He looked at her. "Its about why things are as they are."

"Why things is as they *is?*"

"Well, its something like that."

"How come yuh wanna study tha?"

"Oh, you wouldnt understand."

She sighed.

"Naw, Ah guess Ah wouldnt."

"Well, I reckon Ill be getting along," said the white man. "Can I have a drink of water?"

"Sho. But we ain got nothin but well-watah, n yuhll have t come n git."

"Thats all right."

She slid off the porch and walked over the ground with bare feet. She heard the shoes of the white man behind her, falling to the earth in soft whispers. It was dark now. She led him to the well, groped her way, caught the bucket and let it down with a rope; she heard a splash and the bucket grew heavy. She drew it up, pulling against its weight, throwing one hand over the other, feeling the cool wet of the rope on her palms.

"Ah don git watah outa here much," she said, a little out of breath. "Silas gits the watah mos of the time. This buckets too heavy fer me."

"Oh, wait! Ill help!"

His shoulder touched hers. In the darkness she felt his warm hands fumbling for the rope.

"Where is it?"

"Here."

She extended the rope through the darkness. His fingers touched her breasts.

"Oh!"

She said it in spite of herself. He would think she was thinking about that. And he was a white man. She was sorry she had said that.

"Wheres the gourd?" he asked. "Gee, its dark!"

She stepped back and tried to see him.

"Here."

"I cant see!" he said, laughing.

Again she felt his fingers on the tips of her breasts. She backed away, saying nothing this time. She thrust the gourd out from her. Warm fingers met her cold hands. He had the gourd. She heard him drink; it was the faint, soft music of water going down a dry throat, the music of water in a silent night. He sighed and drank again.

"I was thirsty," he said. "I hadnt had any water since noon."

She knew he was standing in front of her; she could not see him, but she felt him. She heard the gourd rest against the wall of the well. She turned, then felt his hands full on her breasts. She struggled back.

"Naw, Mistah!"

"Im not going to hurt you!"

White arms were about her, tightly. She was still. But hes a *white* man. A *white* man. She felt his breath coming hot on her neck and where his hands held her breasts the flesh seemed to knot. She was rigid, poised; she swayed backward, then forward. She caught his shoulders and pushed.

"Naw, naw . . . Mistah, Ah cant do that!"

She jerked away. He caught her hand.

"Please . . ."

"Lemme go!"

She tried to pull her hand out of his and felt his fingers tighten. She pulled harder, and for a moment they were balanced, one against the other. Then he was at her side again, his arms about her.

"I wont hurt you! I wont hurt you . . ."

She leaned backward and tried to dodge his face. Her breasts were full against him; she gasped, feeling the full length of his body. She held her head far to one side; she knew he was seeking her mouth. His hands were on her breasts again. A wave of warm blood swept into her stomach and loins. She felt his lips touching her throat and where he kissed it burned.

"Naw, naw . . ."

Her eyes were full of the wet stars and they blurred, silver and blue. Her knees were loose and she heard her own breathing; she was trying to keep from falling. But hes a *white* man! A *white* man! Naw! Naw! And still she would not let him have her lips; she kept her face away. Her breasts hurt where they were crushed against him and each time she caught her breath she held it and while she held it it seemed that if she would let it go it would kill her. Her knees were pressed hard against his and she clutched the upper parts of his arms, trying to hold on. Her loins ached. She felt her body sliding.

"Gawd . . ."

He helped her up. She could not see the stars now; her eyes were full of the feeling that surged over her body each time she caught her breath. He held her close, breathing into her ear; she straightened, rigidly, feeling that she had to straighten or die. And then her lips felt his and she held her breath and dreaded ever to breathe again for fear of the feeling that would sweep down over her limbs. She held tightly, hearing a mountain tide of blood beating against her throat and temples. Then she gripped him, tore her face away, emptied her lungs in one long despairing gasp and went limp. She felt his hand; she was still, taut, feeling his hand, then his fingers. The muscles in her legs flexed and she bit her lips and pushed her toes deep into the wet dust by the side of the well and tried to wait and tried to wait until she could wait no longer. She whirled away from him and a streak of silver and blue swept across her blood. The wet ground cooled her palms and knee-caps. She stumbled up and ran, blindly, her toes flicking warm, dry dust. Her numbed fingers grabbed at a rusty nail in the post at the porch and she pushed ahead of hands that held her breasts. Her fingers found the door-facing; she moved into the darkened room, her hands before her. She touched the cradle and turned till her knees hit the bed. She went over, face down, her fingers trembling in the crumpled folds of his shirt. She moved and moved again and again, trying to keep ahead of the warm flood of blood that sought to catch her. A liquid metal covered her and she rode on the curve of white bright days and dark black nights and the surge of the long gladness of summer and the ebb of the deep dream of sleep in winter till a high red wave of hotness drowned her in a deluge of silver and blue and boiled her blood and blistered her flesh *bangbangbang* . . .

II

"Yuh bettah go," she said.

She felt him standing by the side of the bed, in the dark. She heard him clear his throat. His belt-buckle tinkled.

"Im leaving that clock and graphophone," he said.

She said nothing. In her mind she saw the box glowing softly, like the light in the baby's eyes. She stretched out her legs and relaxed.

"You can have it for forty instead of fifty. Ill be by early in the morning to see if your husbands in."

She said nothing. She felt the hot skin of her body growing steadily cooler.

"Do you think hell pay ten on it? Hell only owe thirty then."

She pushed her toes deep into the quilt, feeling a night wind blowing through the door. Her palms rested lightly on top of her breasts.

"Do you think hell pay ten on it?"

"Hunh?"

"Hell pay ten, wont he?"

"Ah don know," she whispered.

She heard his shoe hit against a wall; footsteps echoed on the wooden porch. She started nervously when she heard the roar of his car; she followed the throb of the motor till she heard it when she could hear it no more, followed it till she heard it roaring faintly in her ears in the dark and silent room. Her hands moved on her breasts and she was conscious of herself, all over; she felt the weight of her body resting heavily on shucks. She felt the presence of fields lying out there covered with night. She turned over slowly and lay on her stomach, her hands tucked under her. From somewhere came a creaking noise. She sat upright, feeling fear. The wind sighed. Crickets called. She lay down again, hearing shucks rustle. Her eyes looked straight up in the darkness and her blood sogged. She had lain a long time, full of a vast peace, when a far away tinkle made her feel the bed again. The tinkle came through the night; she listened, knowing that soon she would hear the rattle of Silas' wagon. Even then she tried to fight off the sound of Silas' coming, even then she wanted to feel the peace of night filling her again; but the tinkle grew louder and she heard the jangle of a wagon and the quick trot of horses. Thas Silas! She gave up and waited. She heard horses neighing. Out of the window bare feet whispered in the dust, then crossed the porch, echoing in soft booms. She closed her eyes and saw Silas come into the room in his dirty overalls as she had seen him come in a thousand times before.

"Yuh sleep. Sarah?"

She did not answer. Feet walked across the floor and a match scratched. She opened her eyes and saw Silas standing over her with a lighted lamp. His hat was pushed far back on his head and he was laughing.

"Ah reckon yuh thought Ah waznt never comin back, hunh? Cant yuh wake up? See, Ah got that red cloth yuh wanted . . ." He laughed again and threw the red cloth on the mantel.

"Yuh hongry?" she asked.

"Naw, Ah kin make out till mawnin." Shucks rustled as he sat on the edge of the bed. "Ah got two hundred n fifty fer mah cotton."

"Two hundred n fifty?"

"Nothin different! N guess whut Ah dond?"

"Whut?"

"Ah bought ten mo acres o lan. Got em from ol man Burgess. Paid im a hundred n fifty dollahs down. Ahll pay the rest next year ef things go erlong awright. Ahma have t git a man t hep me nex spring . . ."

"Yuh mean hire somebody?"

"Sho, hire somebody! Whut yuh think? Ain tha the way the white folks do? Ef yuhs gonna git anywheres yuhs gotta do just like they do." He paused. "Whut yuh been doin since Ah been gone?"

"Nothin. Cookin, clean, n . . ."

"How Ruth?"

"She awright." She lifted her head. "Silas, yuh git any lettahs?"

"Naw. But Ah heard Tom wuz in town."

"In *town?*"

She sat straight up.

"Yeah, thas whut the folks wuz sayin at the sto."

"Back from the war?"

"Ah ast erroun t see ef Ah could fin im. But Ah couldnt."

"Lawd, Ah wish hed c mon home."

"Them white folks shos glad the wars over. But things wuz kinda bad there in town. Everywhere Ah looked wuznt nothin but black n white soljers. N them white folks beat up a black soljer yestiddy. He was jus in from France. Wuz still wearin his soljers suit. They claimed he sassed a white woman . . ."

"Who wuz he?"

"Ah don know. Never saw im befo."

"Yuh see An Peel?"

"Naw."

"Silas!" she said reprovingly.

"Aw, Sarah, Ah just couldn't git out there."

"Whut else yuh bring sides the cloth?"

"Ah got yuh some high-top shoes." He turned and looked at her in the dim light of the lamp. "Woman, ain yuh glad Ah bought yuh some shoes n cloth?" He laughed and lifted his feet to the bed. "Lawd, Sarah, yuhs sho sleepy, ain yuh?"

"Bettah put tha lamp out, Silas . . ."

"Aw . . ." He swung out of the bed and stood still for a moment. She watched him, then turned her face to the wall.

"Whuts that by the windah?" he asked.

She saw him bending over and touching the graphophone with his fingers.

"Thasa graphophone."

"Where yuh git it from?"

"A man lef it here."

"When he bring it?"

"Today."

"But how come he t leave it?"

"He says hell be out here in the mawnin t see ef yuh wans t buy it."

He was on his knees, feeling the wood and looking at the gilt on the edges of the box. He stood up and looked at her.

"Yuh ain never said yuh wanted one of these things."

She said nothing.

"Where wuz the man from?"

"Ah don know."

"He white?"

"Yeah."

He put the lamp back on the mantel. As he lifted the globe to blow out the flame, his hand paused.

"Whos hats this?"

She raised herself and looked. A straw hat lay bottom upwards on the edge of the mantel. Silas picked it up and looked back to the bed, to Sarah.

"Ah guess its the white mans. He must a lef it . . ."

"Whut he doin *in our room?*"

"He wuz talkin t me bout that graphophone."

She watched him go to the window and stoop again to the box. He picked it up, fumbled with the price-tag and took the box to the light.

"Whut this thing cos?"

"Forty dollahs."

"But its marked fifty here."

"Oh, Ah means he said fifty . . ."

He took a step toward the bed.

"Yuh lyin t me!"

"Silas!"

He heaved the box out of the front door; there was a smashing, tinkling noise as it bounded off the front porch and hit the ground. "Whut in hell yuh lie t me fer?"

"Yuh broke the box!"

"Ahma break yo Gawddam neck ef yuh don stop lyin t me!"

"Silas, Ah ain lied t yuh!"

"Shut up, Gawddammit! Yuh did!"

He was standing by the bed with the lamp trembling in his hand. She stood on the other side, between the bed and the wall.

"How come yuh tell me that thing cos *forty* dollahs when it cos *fifty?*"

"Thas whut he tol me."

"How come he tak *ten* dollars off fer yuh?"

"He ain took nothin off fer me, Silas!"

"Yuh lyin t me! N yuh lied t me bout Tom, too!"

She stood with her back to the wall, her lips parted, looking at him silently, steadily. Their eyes held for a moment. Silas looked down, as though he were about to believe her. Then he stiffened.

"Whos this?" he asked, picking up a short yellow pencil from the crumpled quilt.

She said nothing. He started toward her.

"Yuh wan me t take mah raw-hide whip n make yuh talk?"

"Naw, naw, Silas! Yuh wrong! He wuz figgerin wid tha pencil!"

He was silent a moment, his eyes searching her face.

"Gawddam yo black soul t hell, don yuh try lyin t me! Ef yuh start layin wid white men Ahll hosswhip yuh t a incha yo life. Shos theres a Gawd in Heaven Ah will! From sunup t sundown Ah works mah guts out t pay them white trash bastards whut Ah owe em, n then Ah comes n fins they been in mah house! Ah cant go into their houses, n yuh know Gawddam well Ah cant! They don have no mercy on no black folks; wes jus like dirt under their feet! Fer ten years Ah slaves lika dog t git mah farm free, givin ever penny Ah kin t em, n then Ah comes n fins they been in mah house . . ." He was speechless with outrage. "If yuh wans t eat at mah table yuhs gonna keep them white trash bastards out, yuh hear? Tha white ape kin come n git tha damn box n Ah ain gonna pay im a cent! He had no bisness leavin it here, n yuh had no bisness lettin im! Ahma tell tha sonofabitch something when he comes out here in the mawnin, so hep me Gawd! Now git back in tha bed!"

She slipped beneath the quilt and lay still, her face turned to the wall. Her heart thumped slowly and heavily. She heard him walk across the floor in his bare feet. She heard the bottom of the lamp as it rested on the mantel. She stiffened when the room darkened. Feet whispered across the floor again. The shucks rustled from Silas' weight as he sat on the edge of the bed. She was still, breathing softly. Silas was mumbling. She felt sorry for him. In the darkness it seemed that she could see the hurt look on his black face. The crow of a rooster came from far away, came so faintly that it seemed she had not heard it. The bed sank and the shucks cried out in dry whispers; she knew Silas had stretched out. She heard him sigh. Then she jumped because he jumped. She could feel the tenseness of his body; she knew he was sitting bolt upright. She felt his hands fumbling jerkily under the quilt. Then the bed heaved amid a wild shout of shucks and Silas' feet hit the floor with a loud boom. She snatched herself to her elbows, straining her eyes in the dark, wondering what was wrong now. Silas was moving about, cursing under his breath.

"Don wake Ruth up!" she whispered.

"Eh yuh say one mo word t me Ahma slap yuh inter a black spasm!"

She grabbed her dress, got up and stood by the bed, the tips of her fingers touching the wall behind her. A match flared in yellow flame; Silas' face was caught in a circle of light. He was looking downward, staring intently at a white wad of cloth balled in his hand. His black cheeks were hard, set; his lips were tightly pursed. She looked closer; she saw that the white cloth was a man's handkerchief. Silas' fingers loosened; she heard the handkerchief hit the floor softly, damply. The match went out.

"Yuh little bitch!"

Her knees gave. Fear oozed from her throat to her stomach. She moved in the dark toward the door, struggling with the dress, jamming it over her head. She heard the thick skin of Silas' feet swish across the wooden planks.

"Ah got mah raw-hide whip n Ahm takin yuh t the barn!"

She ran on tiptoe to the porch and paused, thinking of the baby. She shrank as something whined through the air. A red streak of pain cut across the small of her back and burned its way into her body, deeply.

"Silas!" she screamed.

She grabbed for the post and fell in dust. She screamed again and crawled out of reach.

"Git t the barn, Gawddammit!"

She scrambled up and ran through the dark, hearing the baby cry. Behind her leather thongs hummed and feet whispered swiftly over the dusty ground.

"C mere, yuh bitch! C mere, Ah say!"

She ran to the road and stopped. She wanted to go back and get the baby, but she dared not. Not as long as Silas had that whip. She stiffened, feeling that he was near.

"Yuh jus as well c mon back n git yo beatin!"

She ran again, slowing now and then to listen. If she only knew where he was she would slip back into the house and get the baby and walk all the way to Aunt Peel's.

"Yuh ain comin back in mah house till Ah beat yuh!"

She was sorry for the anger she knew he had out there in the field. She had a bewildering impulse to go to him and ask him not to be angry; she wanted to tell him that there was nothing to be angry about; that what she had done did not matter; that she was sorry; that after all she was his wife and still loved him. But there was no way she could do that now; if she went to him he would whip her as she had seen him whip a horse.

"Sarah! Sarah!"

His voice came from far away. Ahm goin git Ruth. Back through dust she sped, going on her toes, holding her breath.

"Saaaarah!"

From far off his voice floated over the fields. She ran into the house and caught the baby in her arms. Again she sped through dust on her toes. She did not stop till she was so far away that his voice sounded like a faint echo falling from the sky. She looked up; the stars were paling a little. Mus be gittin near mawnin. She walked now, letting her feet sink softly into the cool dust. The baby was sleeping; she could feel the little chest swelling against her arm. She looked up again; the sky was solid black. Its gittin near mawnin. Ahma take Ruth t An Peels. N mabbe Ahll fin Tom . . . But she could not walk all that distance in the dark. Not now. Her legs were tired. For a moment a memory of surge and ebb rose in her blood; she felt her legs straining, upward. She sighed. Yes, she would go to the sloping hillside back of the garden and wait until morning. Then she would slip away. She stopped, listened. She heard a faint, rattling noise. She imagined Silas' kicking or throwing the smashed graphophone. Hes mad! Hes sho mad! Aw, Lawd! . . . She stopped stock still, squeezing the baby till it whimpered. What would happen when that white man came out in the morning? She had forgotten him. She would have to head him off and tell him. Yeah, cause Silas jus mad ernuff t kill! Lawd, hes mad ernuff t kill!

432

III

She circled the house widely, climbing a slope, groping her way, holding the baby high in her arms. After awhile she stopped and wondered where on the slope she was. She remembered there was an elm tree near the edge; if she could find it she would know. She groped farther, feeling with her feet. Ahm gittin los! And she did not want to fall with the baby. Ahma stop here, she thought. When morning came she would see the car of the white man from this hill and she would run down the road and tell him to go back; and then there would be no killing. Dimly she saw in her mind a picture of men killing and being killed. White men killed the black and black men killed the white. White men killed the black men because they could, and the black men killed the white men to keep from being killed. And killing was blood. Lawd, Ah wish Tom wuz here. She shuddered, sat on the ground and watched the sky for signs of morning. Mabbe Ah oughta walk on down the road? Naw . . . Her legs were tired. Again she felt her body straining. Then she saw Silas holding the white man's handkerchief. She heard it hit the floor, softly, damply. She was sorry for what she had done. Silas was as good to her as any black man could be to a black woman. Most of the black women worked in the fields as croppers. But Silas had given her her own home, and that was more than many others had done for their women. Yes, she knew how Silas felt. Always he had said he was as good as any white man. He had worked hard and saved his money and bought a farm so he could grow his own crops like white men. Silas hates white folks! Lawd, he sho hates em!

The baby whimpered. She unbuttoned her dress and nursed her in the dark. She looked toward the east. There! A tinge of grey hovered. It wont be long now. She could see ghostly outlines of trees. Soon she would see the elm, and by the elm she would sit till it was light enough to see the road.

The baby slept. Far off a rooster crowed. Sky deepened. She rose and walked slowly down a narrow, curving path and came to the elm tree. Standing on the edge of a slope, she saw a dark smudge in a sea of shifting shadows. That was her home. Wondah how come Silas didnt light the lamp? She shifted the baby from her right hip to her left, sighed, struggled against sleep. She sat on the ground again, caught the baby close and leaned against the trunk of a tree. Her eye-lids drooped and it seemed that a hard cold hand caught hold of her right leg or was it her left leg? she did not know which—and began to drag her over a rough litter of shucks and when she strained to see who it was that was pulling her no one was in sight but far ahead was darkness and it seemed that out of the darkness some force came and pulled her like a magnet and she went sliding along over a rough bed of screeching shucks and it seemed that a wild fear made her want to scream but when she opened her mouth to scream she could not scream and she felt she was coming to a wide black hole and again she made ready to scream and then it was too late for she was already over the wide black hole falling falling falling . . .

She awakened with a start and blinked her eyes in the sunshine. She found she was clutching the baby so hard that it had begun to cry. She got to her feet, trembling from fright of the dream, remembering Silas and the white man and Silas' running her out of the house and the white man's coming. Silas was standing in the front yard; she caught her breath. Yes, she had to go and head that white man off! Naw! She could not do that, not with Silas standing there with that whip in his hand. If she tried to climb any of those slopes he would see her surely. And Silas would never forgive her for something like that. If it were anybody but a white man it would be different.

Then, while standing there on the edge of the slope looking wonderingly at Silas striking the whip against his overall-leg—and then, while standing there looking—she froze. There came from the hills a distant throb. Lawd! The baby whimpered. She loosened her arms. The throb grew louder, droning. Hes comin fas! She wanted to run to Silas and beg him not to bother the white man. But he had that whip in his hand. She should not have done what she had done last night. This was all her fault. Lawd, ef anything happens t im its mah blame . . . Her eyes watched a black car speed over the crest of a hill. She should have been out there on the road instead of sleeping here by the tree. But it was too late now. Silas was standing in the yard; she saw him turn with a nervous jerk and sit on the edge of the porch. He was holding the whip stiffly. The car came to a stop. A door swung open. A white man got out. Thas im! She saw another white man in the front seat of the car. N that his buddy . . . The white man who had gotten out walked over the ground, going to Silas. They faced each other, the white man standing up and Silas sitting down; like two toy men they faced each other. She saw Silas point the whip to the smashed graphophone. The white man looked down and took a quick step backward. The white man's shoulders were bent and he shook his head from left to right. Then Silas got up and they faced each other again; like two dolls, a white doll and a black doll, they faced each other in the valley below. The white man pointed his finger into Silas' face. Then Silas' right arm went up; the whip flashed. The white man turned, bending, flinging his hands to shield his head. Silas' arm rose and fell, rose and fell. She saw the white man crawling in dust, trying to get out of reach. She screamed when she saw the other white man get out of the car and run to Silas. Then all three were on the ground, rolling in dust, grappling for the whip. She clutched the baby and ran. Lawd! Then she stopped, her mouth hanging open. Silas had broken loose and was running toward the house. She knew he was going for his gun.

"Silas!"

Running, she stumbled and fell. The baby rolled in the dust and bawled. She grabbed it up and ran again. The white men were scrambling for their car. She reached level ground, running. Hell be killed! Then again she stopped. Silas was on the front porch, aiming a rifle. One of the white men was climbing into the car. The other was standing, waving his arms, shouting at Silas. She tried to scream, but choked; and she could not scream till she heard a shot ring out.

"Silas!"

One of the white men was on the ground. The other was in the car. Silas was aiming again. The car started, running in a cloud of dust. She fell to her knees and hugged the baby close. She heard another shot, but the car was roaring over the top of the southern hill. Fear was gone now. Down the slopes she ran. Silas was standing on the porch, holding his gun and looking at the fleeing car. Then she saw him go to the white man lying in dust and stoop over him. He caught one of the man's legs and dragged the body into the middle of the road. Then he turned and came slowly back to the house. She ran, holding the baby, and fell at his feet.

"Silas!"

IV

"Git up, Sarah!"

His voice was hard and cold. She lifted her eyes and saw blurred black feet. She wiped tears away with dusty fingers and pulled up. Something took speech from her and she stood with bowed shoulders. Silas was standing still, mute; the look on his face condemned her. It was as though he had gone far off and had stayed a long time and had come back changed even while she was standing there in the sunshine before him. She wanted to say something, to give herself. She cried.

"Git the chile up, Sarah!"

She lifted the baby and stood waiting for him to speak, to tell her something to change all this. But he said nothing. He walked toward the house. She followed. As she attempted to go in, he blocked the way. She jumped to one side as he threw the red cloth outdoors to the ground. The new shoes came next. Then Silas heaved the baby's cradle. It hit the porch and a rocker splintered; the cradle swayed for a second, then fell to the ground, lifting a cloud of brown dust against the sun. All of her clothes and the baby's clothes were thrown out.

"Silas!"

She cried, seeing blurred objects sailing through the air and hearing them hit softly in the dust.

"Git yo things n go!"

"Silas!"

"Ain no use yuh sayin *nothin* now!"

"But theyll kill yuh!"

"There ain nothin Ah kin do. N there ain nothin yuh kin do. Yuh done done too Gawddam much awready. Git yo things n go!"

"Theyll kill yuh, Silas!"

He pushed her off the porch.

"GIT YO THINGS N GO T AN PEELS!"

"Les *both* go, Silas!"

"Ahm stayin here till they come back!"

She grabbed his arm and he slapped her hand away. She dropped to the edge of the porch and sat looking at the ground.

"Go way," she said quietly. "Go way fo they comes. Ah didnt mean no harm . . ."

"Go way fer whut?"

"Theyll *kill* yuh . . ."

"It don make no difference." He looked out over the sunfilled fields. "Fer ten years Ah slaved mah life out t git mah farm free . . ." His voice broke off. His lips moved as though a thousand words were spilling silently out of his mouth, as though he did not have breath enough to give them sound. He looked to the sky, and then back to the dust. "Now, its all gone. *Gone . . .* Ef Ah run erway, Ah ain got nothin. Ef Ah stay n fight, Ah ain got nothin. It dont make no difference which way Ah go. Gawd! Gawd, Ah wish all them white folks wuz dead! *Dead,* Ah tell yuh! Ah wish Gawd would kill em *all!*"

She watched him run a few steps and stop. His throat swelled. He lifted his hands to his face; his fingers trembled. Then he bent to the ground and cried. She touched his shoulders.

"Silas!"

He stood up. She saw he was staring at the white man's body lying in the dust in the middle of the road. She watched him walk over to it. He began to talk to no one in particular; he simply stood over the dead white man and talked out of his life, out of a deep and final sense that now it was all over and nothing could make any difference.

"The white folks ain never gimme a chance! They ain never give no black man a chance! There ain nothin in yo whole life yuh kin keep from em! They take yo lan! They take yo freedom! They take yo women! N then they take yo life!" He turned to her, screaming. "N then Ah gits stabbed in the back by mah own blood! When mah eyes is on the white folks to keep em from killin me, mah own blood trips me up!" He knelt in the dust again and sobbed; after a bit he looked to the sky, his face wet with tears. "Ahm gonna be hard like they is! So hep me, Gawd, Ah'm gonna be *hard!* When they come fer me Ahm gonna *be here!* N when they git me outta here theys gonna *know* Ahm gone! Ef Gawd lets me live Ahm gonna make me *feel* it!" He stopped and tried to get his breath. "But, Lawd, Ah don wanna be this way! I don mean nothin! Yuh die ef yuh fight! Yuh die ef yuh don fight! Either way yuh die n it don mean nothin . . ."

He was lying flat on the ground, the side of his face deep in dust. Sarah stood nursing the baby with eyes black and stony. Silas pulled up slowly and stood again on the porch.

"Git on t An Peels, Sarah!"

A dull roar came from the south. They both turned. A long streak of brown dust was weaving down the hillside.

"Silas!"

"Go on cross the fiels, Sarah!"

"We kin *both* go! Git the hosses!"

He pushed her off the porch, grabbed her hand, and led her to the rear of the house, past the well, to where a path led up a slope to the elm tree.

"Silas!"

"Yuh git on fo they ketch yuh too!"

Blind from tears, she went across the swaying fields, stumbling over blurred grass. It ain no use! She knew it was now too late to make him change his mind. The calves of her legs knotted. Suddenly her throat tightened, aching. She stopped, closed her eyes and tried to stem a flood of sorrow that drenched her. Yes, killing of white men by black men and killing of black men by white men went on in spite of the hope of white bright days and the desire of dark black nights and the long gladness of green cornfields in summer and the deep dream of sleepy grey skies in winter. And when killing started it went on, like a river flowing. Oh, she felt sorry for Silas! Silas. . . . He was following that long river of blood. Lawd, how come he wans t stay there like tha? And he did not want to die; she knew he hated dying by the way he talked of it. Yet he followed the old river of blood, knowing that it meant nothing. He followed it, cursing and whimpering. But he followed it. She stared before her at the dry, dusty grass. Somehow, men, black men and white men, land and houses, green cornfields and grey skies, gladness and dreams, were all a part of that which made life good. Yes, somehow, they were linked, like the spokes in a spinning wheel. She felt they were. She knew they were. She felt it when she breathed and knew it when she looked. But she could not say how; she could not put her finger on it and when she thought hard about it it became all mixed up, like milk spilling suddenly. Or else it knotted in her throat and chest in a hard aching lump, like the one she felt now. She touched her face to the baby's face and cried again.

There was a loud blare of auto horns. The growing roar made her turn round. Silas was standing, seemingly unafraid, leaning against a post of the porch. The long line of cars came speeding in clouds of dust. Silas moved toward the door and went in. Sarah ran down the slope a piece, coming again to the elm tree. Her breath was slow and hard. The cars stopped in front of the house. There was a steady drone of motors and drifting clouds of dust. For a moment she could not see what was happening. Then on all sides white men with pistols and rifles swarmed over the fields. She dropped to her knees, unable to take her eyes away, unable it seemed to breathe. A shot rang out. A white man fell, rolling over, face downward.

"Hes gotta gun!"

"Git back!"

"Lay down!"

The white men ran back and crouched behind cars. Three more shots came from the house. She looked, her head and eyes aching. She rested the baby in her lap and shut her eyes. Her knees sank into the dust. More shots came, but it was no use looking now. She knew it all by heart. She could feel it happening even before it happened. There were men killing and being killed. Then she jerked up, being compelled to look.

"Burn the bastard out!"

"Set the sonofabitch on fire!"

"Cook the coon!"

"Smoke im out!"

She saw two white men on all fours creeping past the well. One carried a gun and the other a red tin can. When they reached the back steps the one with the tin can crept under the house and crept out again. Then both rose and ran. Shots. One fell. A yell went up. A yellow tongue of fire licked out from under the back steps.

"Burn the nigger!"

"C mon out, nigger, n git yos!"

She watched from the hill-slope; the back steps blazed. The white men fired a steady stream of bullets. Black smoke spiraled upward in the sun-shine. Shots came from the house. The white men crouched out of sight, behind their cars.

"Make up your mind, nigger!"

"C mon out er burn, yuh black bastard!"

"Yuh think yuhre white now, nigger?"

The shack blazed, flanked on all sides by whirling smoke filled with flying sparks. She heard the distant hiss of flames. White men were crawling on their stomachs. Now and then they stopped, aimed, and fired into the bulg-ing smoke. She looked with a tense numbness; she looked, waiting for Silas to scream, or run out. But the house cracked and blazed, spouting yellow plumes to the blue sky. The white men shot again, sending a hail of bullets into the furious pillars of smoke. And still she could not see Silas running out, or hear his voice calling. Then she jumped, standing. There was a loud crash; the roof caved in. A black chimney loomed amid crumbling wood. Flames roared and black smoke billowed, hiding the house. The white men stood up, no longer afraid. Again she waited for Silas, waited to see him fight his way out, waited to hear his call. Then she breathed a long, slow breath, emptying her lungs. She knew now. Silas had killed as many as he could and stayed on to burn, had stayed without a murmur. She filled her lungs with a quick gasp as the walls fell in; the house was hidden by eager plumes of red. She turned and ran with the baby in her arms, ran blindly across the fields, crying "Naw, Gawd!"